Spatial-Economic Metamorphosis of a Nebula City

T0295665

This book analyses the long term spatial-economic metamorphosis of Schiphol and the Schiphol region as archetypal for a wider international phenomenon of urban development of metropolises across the world. It studies the origins and course of urban development process by identifying and explaining which (collective) arrangements, including their ambient factors and the visual representations of the city and urbanity, have influenced this metamorphosis in a decisive manner.

Although the book focuses on Schiphol airport and its relationship to the surrounding urban areas, the entangling of airport and urban development is an emerging issue in metropolises across the world; and Schiphol and Amsterdam are one of the leading and most characteristic examples of this.

This book is cutting-edge and innovative. First, it focuses on an emergent, topical phenomenon in the development of cities and regions. Second, it takes a multidisciplinary approach in studying a complex spatial phenomenon and shedding light on the multiple dimensions and social-spatial entanglements of urban development. In both respects the book is quite unique. In addition, it offers a rich and varied empirical base, providing a uniquely articulated view into the subject.

This book will be of great interest to urban geographers, urban planners, urban historians, and urban economists. It is a 'must read' for those students and academics with a particular interest in the airport and the region.

A. El Makhloufi is Researcher/Lecturer at Fontys University of Applied Sciences at Eindhoven, the Netherlands.

Routledge Studies in Human Geography

This series provides a forum for innovative, vibrant, and critical debate within Human Geography. Titles will reflect the wealth of research which is taking place in this diverse and ever-expanding field.

Contributions will be drawn from the main sub-disciplines and from innovative areas of work which have no particular sub-disciplinary allegiances.

Published:

Spatial-Economic Metamorphosis of a Nebula City

Schiphol and the Schiphol region during the 20th Century

Abderrahman El Makhloufi

Routledge
Taylor & Francis Group

LONDON AND NEW YORK

First published 2013
by Routledge
2 Park Square, Milton Park, Abingdon, Oxfordshire OX14 4RN

Simultaneously published in the USA and Canada
by Routledge
711 Third Avenue, New York, NY 10017

First issued in paperback 2014

Routledge is an imprint of the Taylor and Francis Group, an informa business

British Library Cataloguing in Publication Data
A catalogue record for this book is available from the British Library

Library of Congress Cataloging in Publication Data
A catalog record for this book has been requested.

ISBN 978-0-415-62711-5 (hbk)
ISBN 978-1-138-90757-7 (pbk)

Typeset in Times New Roman
by Cenveo Publisher Services

Contents

Figures

Maps

Tables

Acknowledgements

When I started working on this book, I noticed that its accomplishment would not be an easy task because of the complexity and the multiple facets of the research topic. From the first moment, I realised that this would not be the kind of research that could be completed by hunkering down in my office studying archives and analysing data gathered from various sources, and then writing this book as a solitary endeavour. However, working in a multidisciplinary research group of specialists from different scientific disciplines has the advantage of offering many opportunities to review one's own ideas and to approach the complexity of the research questions from different perspectives. Through knowledge sharing and regular discussions with my colleagues from the VU University of Amsterdam, many new questions were raised and, at the same time, many other problems were solved.

During meetings with the members of the Schiphol research group and, sometimes, the intense discussions which took place at various moments during the realisation of this work, it became clear to me that this book should be written in a way that combines rigorous and deep analysis with comprehensible theoretical arguments and uncontested and verifiable historical facts. I hope that I have succeeded, at least partly, in realising these objectives.

This book would not have been possible without the intensive and close cooperation of my colleagues of the 'Schiphol group', and the direct and indirect external assistance of various individuals and institutions. I would like to express my gratitude to Professor C. A. Davids, whose expertise, understanding and patience added considerably to my experience and research interest in the field of economic and social history. Very special thanks go out to Professor Koos Bosma, Dr Heidi de Mare, Iris Burger, Michel Geertse, Jan Willem De Wijn and Tim de Groot, all from the Department of the History of Architecture and Planning, without whose critical discussions and encouragement I would not have considered writing this book. They contributed to my research mainly by forcing me to rethink my theoretical framework and hypotheses. Sometimes their questions and sceptical assessments from the economist's point of view were frustrating, but in the end our discussions improved my work very much. Without them the book would definitely be different.

I appreciate the support of National Bureau of Statistics (CBS) for the provision of the statistical and historical materials evaluated in this study, the Schiphol Group for facilitating the examination of annual reports, policy documents and archives at Schiphol as well as at the Aviodrom in Lelystad. Special thanks go to the director and the supporting staff of the Amsterdam City Archives who gave us the opportunity to examine the Schiphol archives. I thank also everyone at the Haarlemmermeer archives, the North Holland archives in Haarlem, and the National Archives in providing the needed documents and data used in our research work.

My appreciation goes to the Dutch historian Dr Marc Dierikx, a great 'connoisseur' of the history of Dutch aviation, Schiphol, KLM and Fokker, for his willingness to share with us the historical data of the Schiphol airport company.

I am also thankful to J. Fokkema for his technical assistance throughout the years in scanning and digitalising various historical maps of Schiphol and the Amsterdam region, and providing valuable GIS data and the historical cadaster maps used in our study.

This research would not have been possible without the financial support of the Netherlands Organisation for Scientific Research (NWO). Also, I would like to express my gratitude to the countless people who contributed to this book with formal and informal comments, suggestions and fixes (among them, Professor Nick Bullock, Professor E. Taverne, Professor A. M. J. Kreukels, Professor Dr L. A. de Klerk and all the participants at the NWO International Conference (2009) at the Hague.

Finally, very special thanks go to my wife and our two lovely daughters Sanae and Nisrin, who, for many years, got to hear that dad is very busy and still working on the book. Thanks for your unconditional support, understanding, patience and love. You're my perfect counterbalance.

Part I

Theory

Theoretical foundations of
spatial-economic transformation
of urban spaces: an institutionalist
approach

1 Spatial-economic transformation of the Schiphol region

1900–present

1.1 Introduction

During the nineteenth and twentieth centuries the socio-demographic, political and economic processes have jerkily transformed big cities from compact and dense urban areas, with relatively sharp borders between their city centres and urban fringe, into 'urban nebulae', in which town and countryside have become interwoven in complex urban systems. The interdependency of changes in the urban landscape since the Second World War is to be found in the major advances in terms of technological development and forms of economic production in agriculture and industry, which have had considerable impacts on land use patterns and the economic functions of cities and the countryside. Other important factors of change are the rapid urbanisation of cities (which is intimately connected with technological developments in infrastructure and communications and population growth, economic development and growth, the increase in wealth (i.e. more leisure time, higher incomes)) and the change in economic structure of cities and regions.

Historically, spatial and economic changes have been the result of long processes of accumulation of incremental small changes, i.e. spatial, technological, political, economic, social and cultural, that have resulted in the emergence of a new economic production system and a complex array of polycentric urban constellations (Sieverts, 2003; Ascher, 1995) reflected in the emergence of the post-industrial urban form such as the 'city-region'. Others have referred to it as the 'urban field' or 'urban ecological field', the urban nebula, the metropolis, the network city, etc.

The next step in the development of the city-region is the rise of the metropolitan structure composed of several big cities or when one regional city becomes so extensive and complex that a single concentrated core that animates the whole region is no longer clearly identifiable (Gottman, 1961).

In this study, the term 'urban nebula' refers to 'multi-urban centres' in a polynuclear urban system characterised by the stretching and dispersing of parts of the city-region. We define the nebula city as a 'functionally integrated area consisting of both a core and central city [...] and, contiguous with it, a region that serves the multiple collective needs of this city and provides a space for its future expansion' (Friedman, 2001: 123).

4 *Spatial-economic metamorphosis of a nebula city*

The most striking characteristic of the current processes of urban transformation which result in the emergence of urban nebulae are the rescaling dimension
of current urban systems (Brenner, 1998; Brenner *et al.*, 2003; Taylor, 2003) and
the emergence of the 'space of flow', e.g. relational/network geography, with its
focus on 'flows of social and economic interactions' and the 'scope of activities
in functional networks'. This in addition to the more traditional notions of 'space
of places' (e.g. bounded spaces) and 'nested territorial jurisdictions', which still
characterise most urban forms all over the world. However, the emerging urban
nebula, as the result of changes in urban society, reflects the physical, social and
economic fragmentation of 'splintering' economic space. This in turn creates
unbalanced political, environmental and spatial systems (Graham and Marvin,
2001). At a lower scale of the urban nebula, different nodes of (new) economic
development show strong relations through the integrating forces of infrastructure, economic structure (i.e. agglomeration economies) and their interlinked
position with the increasing scale of the urban labour market and housing market
in particular (ibid.). For example, many urban functions are now located outside
the cities and this tendency has been very pronounced in the metropolitan region.
Various new internationally oriented economic focal points are developing
around the economic magnet of 'cityports' like Schiphol, for example. In this
region, flower export is concentrated around the international auction in Aalsmeer
and the media industry is no longer confined to its traditional home in the city of
Hilversum but has recently spread to the city of Almere and to the centre of
Amsterdam. The financial sector has regrouped along Amsterdam's South Axis,
which has recently developed into one of the main business and financial centres
in Europe. The various urban residential areas too are now highly scattered
throughout the metropolitan region (the new town of Almere for example).

However, based on the Dutch experience, one may note that complementary
and sometimes substitute functions have been developing between the cityport
region of Schiphol and the core city Amsterdam. This may be explained by the
specific nature and function of the airport Schiphol: first as an important network
node in a city-region, and second as a strategic development location fulfilling the
function of a port, place and a hub in international networks at the same time. In
this sense, the Schiphol region has established strong links between economic
activities and infrastructure, and it is a concentration spot for activities which
generate their own agglomeration economies (through the opportunities for
localisation and concentration, spatial quality and mixed land use) and participate
independently in the economic development of the whole metropolitan region. At
the regional level, however, no functional integration is developing between the
core cities of the city-region through which the collection of urban cores could
form a strong metropolitan region. Instead, cities compete for the same functions,
and together they show very little specialisation except in some limited areas
(Musterd and Salet, 2003: 22). This may be interpreted as the result of economic
and spatial structural changes occurring at local and regional levels which have
far reaching consequences in various fields, e.g. land use and the demand from
firms for new locations, town planning, the labour and housing markets, public

amenities, infrastructure, and urban governance and management of urban space by different administrative tiers (local, regional, national).

In a climate of increasing globalisation and the rise of the knowledge economy, firms are theoretically not bound to a specific national location but, as many recent studies show, to spatially bounded locational advantages such as the quality of life, housing quality, public amenities, the safety and livability of cities, cultural industries, the knowledge stock, the availability of a qualified workforce, the quality of infrastructure, etc. Yet, the traditional big cities possess many unique selling points, in terms of locational advantages, in international competition. In addition, the implications of globalisation for regions and nations and the emergence of the knowledge society in a growing globalising economy have opened and enlarged the non-location bound variety of 'glocal' urban spaces, making 'connectedness' and 'accessibility' of urban interactions the most important conditions of localisation rather than the traditional focus on 'proximity' and 'physical density'. In this sense, the traditional perception of territorial space and its bounded institutions have to be reconsidered in light of these developments. Note, however, that these local institutional specificities still play a key strategic role in enhancing the regional competitiveness of cities and regions. Established norms and the cultural identity of urbanism partly depend on developed culture and identity but also on political and administrative relationships that have arisen in the cities.

Today, the creation of the right conditions and institutional arrangements, among other things, through 'metropolitan governance' is essential for sustaining the spatial and economic growth of the rising urban nebula. This requires a fresh new vision on the part of the city and regional authorities where the key decision-making process is no longer serving purely local interests but collective interests at the level of the city-region. Therefore, the framing of new strategic decision-making processes regarding urban regions has to become more responsive to this multiplication of urban spaces, and must transcend the frames of actions to encompass multi-level networks (Scott, 2001; Salet *et al.*, 2003). This means that existing institutional and collective arrangements have to be reconsidered, i.e. old arrangements have to be changed and new ones have to be developed, in order to face the new challenges posed by new spatial and economic realities and facilitate the application of new strategic decision-making processes at the level of the metropolitan region. From the urban spatial planning perspective, and as Salet *et al.* (2003) rightly put it, the key to strategic planning in a context of multi-level governance is in the quality of interconnectivity between different spheres of actions, i.e. private sector domains of action, and regional, interregional and international spheres of action. However, an important issue that has been raised recently in relation to spatial urban planning in the Netherlands is the institutional condition of developing new collective arrangements that may facilitate the creation of a new 'intermediate region' whose main task is to communicate and coordinate various tasks and policies among the different layers of governance (Advies Commissie Versterking Randstad, 2007). At the moment, this solution seems difficult to implement because of the resistance from existing intermediate regional bodies such as the provinces to delegate parts of their decision-making power to the rising and powerful urban agglomerations.

In this study, we consider the 'urban nebula' to be a spatial-economic configuration with a complex structure formed by various heterogeneous aspects, substances, actors and factors. The most important characteristics of the urban nebula are the economic, spatial, socio-politic, cultural and cognitive aspects. This last aspect is reflected in different mental horizons or representations, e.g. a mental world, concerning the precise meaning of urban nebula.

Note that the urban field or urban nebula shows the characteristics of a post-industrial city which is dominated by the diversity of activities and the complementarity of specialised functions (Moulaert and Djellal, 1995), e.g. increased mobility, better communication technologies, wider leisure possibilities and greater external returns and knowledge externalities, etc., have accompanied the shift of the employment structure from manufacturing activities toward services and high-tech activities. Furthermore, the urban nebula structure derives its coherence from collective interventions, agreements and regulations. These interventions, whether (un)intentionally planned (e.g. actions) or unplanned (e.g. reaction to unexpected external shocks), are reflected in policy plans, designs, investments, conventions about spatial planning, perceptions and the everyday rituals in using public space. In short, the configuration of the urban nebula is constructed by the institutional and collective arrangements that are specific in space and time.

The nebula city has adopted the organic centralised shape of the historical city and covers a much larger urban area that can be understood as the 'urban field' (Brand, 2002). The main characteristics of the urban nebula are:

1. Highly diversified movements of people, goods and information which are largely oriented to the built-up city core, to its downtown as well as to the industrial, shopping and educational and cultural activities nodes. At the same time, a complex pattern of criss-cross-directional movement occurs oriented to the activities nodes, both small and large, within the dispersed parts of the regional city.
2. Existence of overlapping life spaces involved in different life functions. The work space is separated from the living space, and the shopping and social spaces are separated in yet other directions from the home or 'shelter space'.
3. The networks in the regional city and between cities depend on their accessibility and the proximity to resources, factors of production and information and communication means. The density of the links in a network of cities gives a great advantage to the urban field because it is there where such dense links are available.

More generally, the nebula city is primarily structured by aboveground, underground and decentralised communication networks, and therefore may be understood morphologically as infrastructure and topologically as network structure. In this sense, the urban nebula is heterogeneous and exists mainly in fragmented, often contradictory, agreements/covenants between various parties/actors and stakeholders. When we interpret the network city as a scientific equivalent of the nebula city or urban nebula, then the nebula city can be considered as a multi-layered urban structure with morphological, economic, social-politic and cultural aspects, from which the structure takes shape through the flows of people, goods, money, knowledge and information with accompanying social-economic and spatial interventions, arrangements and regulations.

In this book, the absorption of the historical city into an urban nebula and the emergence of a nebula city will be studied in terms of spatial and economic trans-formations over the long term and the role and significance of collective arrange-ments for this transformation process. Our proposition is that specific urban characteristics of the nebula city are created by purposive interventions that can be described as collective arrangements. In other words, the nebula city may be seen as a spatial-economic configuration that is formed and maintained by:

1. collective arrangements embodied into institutional arrangements and institutions;
2. a community of actors, e.g. lobby groups, professional advisers, architects, planners, policy-makers, research institutes, universities, etc.;
3. corpora, e.g. architecture, design, infrastructural plans and concepts, visual images/material, photos, marketing campaigns, etc.; and
4. the electorate community that, in an active or passive way, maintains arrangements and, hence, the nebula city in the long term.

Collective arrangements are considered here as sets of ideas, actors and products. They result from the interactions between various actors/parties influencing the spatial and economic configuration of localities and determining their develop-ment trajectories. More specifically, collective arrangements can be understood as a powerful combination of policy, ideas, actors and products that aim at the amelioration, adaptation and/or transformation of urban space. Such arrange-ments – in terms of their spatial manifestations, imagination and the use of public space – are usually steered by economic, financial, political, cultural and moral principles. A classic example of a collective arrangement is the Housing Act of 1901 in the Netherlands. The introduction of the Housing Law constitutes the political-juridical framework of housing planning and the dwelling quarter is the spatial manifestation of this arrangement.

In this study, the development and spatial-economic transformation of Schiphol and the Schiphol-Amsterdam region during the twentieth century into a nebula city is used as the prototype of the spatial and economic transformation of a metropolitan region that can be extended to similar metropolitan regions in the world. It demonstrates how different forms and types of collective arrangements, and behind them the most relevant factors and actors, have changed the spatial and economic landscape of this region during different historical episodes of its development. We approach the phenomenon of collective arrangements synchron-ically by identifying its different components and important elements of change, continuity and sustainability, by examining and analysing the path dependence trajectories, and by linking these elements to the rise, development and spatial-economic transformation of the Schiphol region into a nebula city within the city-region. In addition, the different constitutive layers and elements of artifacts are judged on their own merits, by taking into account their own substances, traditions, values, weights and meanings.

It is important to note that collective arrangements are conceived as a specific type of convention that are given substance in bounding agreements – which may or may not have a financial character – connecting different actors, e.g. informal and formal agreements fixed by legislation (law and rules). They represent a structural formation that covers the particularity of the long-term development and growth of the urban nebula, including the analytical and methodological instruments describing the inherent arrangements and spatial-economic transformation of the region.

In the case of Schiphol and the Schiphol region, collective arrangements concern mainly the relationships that Schiphol airport has established and maintained through different historical episodes with local, regional and national (political and economic) actors/parties, such as governmental bodies (ministries, public organisations, etc.), the Dutch airline company (KLM) and other airline companies (Air France), and various local and regional actors, i.e. municipalities, the province, firms in the transport and logistics sector, project development companies, retail companies, financial and service firms, etc.

1.2 Research questions and scientific interests

As we have mentioned above, this book analyses the long-term spatial-economic metamorphosis of Schiphol and the Schiphol region as archetypal for a wider international phenomenon of urban development of metropolises across the world. It studies the origins and course of the metamorphosis of urban landscape and the urban development process by identifying and explaining which (collective) arrangements – including their ambient factors and the visual representations of the city and urban life – have influenced this metamorphosis in a decisive manner.

We address the following two central questions concerning the spatial and economic metamorphosis of Schiphol and the Schiphol region during the twentieth century. First, how could this nebulous urban structure arise? Second, what forces, factors and actors caused the emergence and the development of this typical urban structure into a fully integrated urban nebula?

More specifically, concerning our particular case study, we ask the following questions:

1. To what extent can the transformation of the Schiphol region from a countryside area into a fully integrated urban nebula be explained through the interplay between the spatial-economic and socio-cultural factors, and (the corresponding) collective arrangements from 1900 to the present?

2.   What are the type, nature and form of collective arrangements that created and sustained (and/or constrained) the spatial and economic development of Schiphol and the Schiphol region? To what extent were they path-dependent (or inherited historical structures)? How did they create opportunities/obstacles to further development of Schiphol and the region?

3.   To what extent did Schiphol airport contribute to the economic development of the surrounding suburbs and the city-region?

The answers to these questions are sought in the relationships between the collective arrangements and four ambient factors: the physical patterns and economic structures, the planning concepts and planning policies for the region, and the development of infrastructural networks (see Figure 1.1).

Our main argument is that the rise and development of Schiphol airport into a nebula city can be understood by looking at the interplay between various actors and factors that have contributed to the articulation of collective arrangements that (were) are necessary to deal with the dynamic aspects of the spatial economic transformation of this urban area.

Although the book focuses on a single case study, i.e. Schiphol airport and its relationships with the surrounding Amsterdam urban area (Amsterdam metropolitan

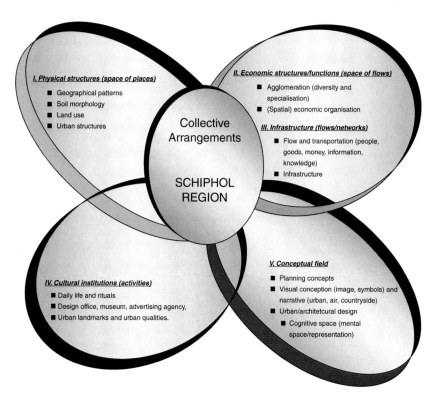

Figure 1.1 Conceptualisation of collective arrangements. (Only dimensions (i), (ii), (iii) and partly (v) are analysed in this study)

region), the entangling of (city) airport and urban development is an emerging issue in metropolises across the world and the Schiphol and Amsterdam region is one of the leading and most characteristic examples of this.

One may argue that infrastructure, infrastructural networks and the development of industry have been the main triggers of the growth of cities since the Industrial Revolution. Indeed, many studies on urban development show that the major characteristic in the development of cities during the late nineteenth and twentieth centuries is their dependency on infrastructural networks, and the multiplication, the growing variety and the intensity, power, speed and range of these connections (Graham and Marvin, 2001). However, infrastructural networks do not come about autonomously: they are themselves related to other factors. For example, entrepreneurs, householders, developers, politicians, administrators and other interest groups make great spatial claims. Their visions contribute to the articulation of collective arrangements that are necessary to deal with the legal, administrative, sanitary and socio-economic problems in urban areas. This is the reason why we focus attention in this study on the institutional aspects of the dynamic process of spatial-economic transformation of urban areas in general and Schiphol and the Schiphol region in particular. This implies, on the one hand, that the study of the relationships between the city and the countryside is viewed as a complex urban system, comprising various dimensions: geographical, economic, institutional, political and socio-cultural. Each dimension involves many different components of the total environment system. The same components may have different values associated with them. For example, land contains economic, social and natural environment values, which play an important role in shaping the quality of life in cities and regions. On the other hand, the spatial and temporal aspects of (economic) factors and actors, and the different coalitions of decision-making frames must also be considered within the geographical, economic and institutional dimensions, e.g. economic actors and public agencies are important elements of analysis in understanding the urban-economic transformation of cities and their countryside.

The potential role of actors in the construction of new urban space is even more important with regard to the integration of economic, socio-cultural and spatial purposes. Therefore it is necessary to frame the configuration of decision-making in the urban space, the different roles and coalitions of actors and the changes in them over time. This can be realised by focusing on the concept of collective arrangements as one of the main explanatory factors of the rising urban nebula. More specifically, our focus will be oriented towards the investigation of different dimensions of the processes of spatial and economic urban transformation and urban and regional development, the economic dimension (including meso/macro-economic changes and socio-demographic and cultural tendencies), the spatial dimension (including the focus on change and sustainability of new urban space) and the institutional dimension (as the integrating element of the three dimensions). The processes of the second and third dimensions (e.g. the physical adaptation of urban space and the evolution of institutions) have to match the dynamics of the first dimension of economic tendency.

In addition to these three dimensions, the urban planning dimension must be added as an integrating part of this dynamic view. The main argument for this is that spatial planning and urban design are thought to be indispensable to framing urbanisation processes. More specifically, the conceptualisation of collective arrangements can be understood as physical, economic, political and cultural activity that is aiming at the transformation of the historical patterns and visualisation of the (elements of the) city (see Figure 1.1). Consequently, infrastructural networks, planning concepts and cultural images of the city will, vice versa, depend on the physical structure within which urbanisation processes take place.

It is worth mentioning, in this respect, that research into the significance of steering the urbanisation processes, their streamlining by economic, social and institutional-spatial layout and infrastructural reshuffling of the relation between central cities and their countryside, all organised by design concepts that propagate an 'urban form' and hence an 'urban imagination', is an area that hitherto has been hardly studied from the point of view of its rich and varied empirical base that provides a uniquely articulated and thick view into the subject. We hope through this study to produce a refreshing contribution on this topic through the focus on an emergent, topical phenomenon in the development of cities and regions, the rise of the airport city complex and its development into a nebula city, and the use of a mixed disciplines and methods approach that sheds light on the multiple dimensions and social-spatial entanglements of urban development. In both respects the book is quite unique in its attempt to relate the transformation and continuity in physical patterns (land use patterns) and economic structures, planning concepts and collective arrangements of urban space and the rise of the nebula city to the analysis of the way different actors (central government, local/ regional government bodies, economic and political actors, social groups, etc.) deal with the opportunities of the spatial and economic dynamics within local and regional institutional dynamic contexts.

Because governments are not the sole actors coordinating market economies, questions about the nature, mechanisms and factors influencing the evolution of urban space (and thus its transformation), by focusing on the nature, cause and effects of the interactions between different actors at the level of the city and the city-region, become relevant. It is believed that, in more liberal economies, the institutional setting (through coordinated market economies such as in the Netherlands) enhances both the possibilities for revolutionary development and innovations suited to specific economic sectors. However, the variety of institutional arrangements leads to institutional complementarities as well as to competition which may result in a variety of institutional models and spatial scales.

> ... in order to understand the variety of models, institutional differences (e.g. institutional arrangements), similarities and complementarities need to be examined. (Hall and Soskice, 2001)

Accordingly, globalisation, differentiation (of actors), (semi-)governmental acting and an increasing variety of spatial scales, as well as the increased importance of private actors in policy-making, are the dominant tendencies that ignite institutional change (Salet *et al.*, 2003). Note in this perspective that a systematic analysis of intuitional change requires the identification, categorisation and time-space analysis of institutional arrangements making the rules of the game governing the interactions between actors within a specific urban governance structure (socio-cultural institutions, financial and economic institutions, institutional governance and legal institutions). In this sense – and as we will show in this study – Schiphol and the Schiphol region have developed intermittently and therefore in phases. The more we move forward in time, the more footloose these phases become, meaning that there exists a fuzzy relationship between the features of the morphological space and the use of it. For example, at the end of the nineteenth century there was a clear separation between towns and their fringes, a number of commuter villages and an extended agricultural area.

This neatly arranged urban region was broken adrift by the spread of trade and industrialisation, the increasing use of physical space, the relatively fast-growing spatial movements of persons and households, the growing size of the market, the diversity of products and the growing facilities in private houses and industrial and commercial parks. As a result, increased suburbanisation and urban sprawl took on unprecedented forms after the Second World War. Regions and suburban areas became intertwined and functionally integrated in wide intra- and inter-regional networks that extended beyond the regional and national boundaries.

Network cities and nebula cities, especially the airport-city-regions, became more and more interconnected in massive and extensive multi-nodal networks (of flow) taking place at higher spatial scales (national and international). In his study on cityports in the city-regions, Wijk correctly argues that 'At [the] intersection of economics, infrastructure and urban development, new [cityports] develop. [...] It is a topology of urban concentration in the city-region that shows rapid economic development and is internationally connected by infrastructure. They fulfil the role of port to the city-region, a place to stay and a traffic node' (2007: 16).

Competitiveness and economic performance are considered as the main driving force in determining the position and the importance of these nebula cities, while maintaining and strengthening internal linkages and internal geographical structure at the local and regional level as a counterpart of globalisation (Hall, 2001). The combination of an economic dynamic (e.g. economic growth) and the development of infrastructure and urbanisation creates new spatial structures (differentiation and specialisation) and concentrations of activities and households.

1.3 Periodisation and chronology of changes

The main aim of any periodisation or chronology of historical events and changes is to interpret historical classified events and/or processes in terms of their internal affinities and external differences in order to identify successive periods of relative invariance and the transitions between them. Consequently, the basic assumption of our periodisation of historical events is to identify the simultaneity of continuity and discontinuity in the flow of historical time events concerning changes in spatial patterns and economic structure of urban regions during the twentieth century. Because change is not random, periodisation always refers to particular problems and units of analysis. This means that there can be no specific periodisation that captures the essence of a period for all purposes.

What matters for the purposes of this study is not the content of this sequential ordering of historical events, but the fact that it is grounded in the alternation of relative continuity and discontinuity of collective arrangements as explanatory elements of the spatial-economic transformation of Schiphol and the Schiphol region. Hence, the scope of our periodisation depends on the nature, scope, scale and direction of the development paths taken on the one hand by the urbanisation and industrialisation processes of the greater Amsterdam region during the twentieth century, and on the other hand, by the spatial-economic development of the Schiphol airport in particular and the Schiphol region in general. Figure 1.2 shows a spatial-temporal model based on the historical periodisation of the development path of these two urban areas.

The idea that we want to stress here is that collective arrangements have a temporal structure that is deeply rooted in space and time, e.g. in different historical periods of time. In this sense, the collective arrangement involves an ever-changing balance between historical cycles, continuous transformation and different phases of profound transformations. Very often, these transformations are closely linked to patterns emerging from time-space relations and to the shifts in the dominant spatial-temporal horizons. In turn, these spatial and temporal aspects offer solid grounds in the periodisation of economic and urbanisation processes and the transformation of urban space in the long run.

Methodologically, applying a periodisation approach to study the spatial and economic transformation of the Schiphol region is more relevant to our study than the chronology approach applied in historical analysis (Jessop, 1990, 2002). The reasons for this are as follows.

First, a periodisation approach attempts to relate one or more series of historical events to other significant events or interests in order to explain them in

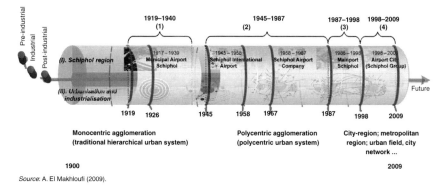

Source: A. El Makhloufi (2009).

Figure 1.2 Spatial-temporal model of transformation and continuity of Schiphol and Schiphol region.

a non-narrative manner while a chronology offers a simple narrative account of the succession of historical events, i.e. the emphasis falls on the simple temporal succession or coincidence of a single series of actions and events. In this sense, a chronology is essentially one-dimensional in its timescale, ordering actions and events in non-linear time according to clock time or some other relevant marker (such as business cycles or intervals between specific spatial policies for example).

Second, a periodisation orders actions and events in terms of multiple time horizons (e.g. the event, tendencies, the *longue durée*, the time frame of economic calculation vs. the time frame of political cycles, or past futures, present pasts and future presents) and focuses on conjunctures. It classifies actions and events into stages according to their conjectural implications (as specific combinations of constraints and opportunities) for different social, economic and political forces over different time horizons and/or for different sites of social and economic actions. This is very important in our study because we focus our attention on different orders of actions and events in different dimensions and time horizons (e.g. Schiphol vs. Greater Amsterdam, local vs. regional and national, etc.) (Jessop, 2002).

Third, a periodisation presupposes an explanatory framework aiming to explain historical outcomes generated by more than one series of events. In other words, consideration must be given to how diverse actions and events are generated as the result of multiple individual and collective actions.

Taking into consideration what has been said above, a typical periodisation of these changes concerning the spatial-economic transformations of cities and urban spaces can be briefly sketched as follows:

1.3.1 Period 1880–1940

Initially, cities are characterised by a concentration of living, working and trading on a relatively small area. Migration flows to larger cities and, to a lesser extent to small municipalities, increased substantially during this historical period because of growth and prosperity in cities, and the improvements of transport technology, which has enlarged substantially the radius of action of individuals. Immigration leads to a growing heterogeneity in citizenship. The first suburbs could be reached by rail. The planning instruments that were used in the Netherlands to steer urban growth during the first half of the twentieth century were the local zoning plan (since 1901) and the regional plan (since ca. 1920). Perhaps the most influential collective arrangement introduced in this period was the Road Tax Law (1926). Various taxes on (motor) bikes and cars were collected in a Road Fund from which the provinces received a percentage of the total collected taxes to finance their provincial road plans. The physical result of this new arrangement resulted in the creation of a clear hierarchy of state, provincial and local roads/highways.

1.3.2 Period 1940–65

More extensive urban land use and increases in geographical scale have resulted in a more differentiated spatial structure between cities and regions. The growing numbers in urban populations during the postwar period resulted in successive and large spatial expansions of cities. Changes in the behaviour of individuals, the radius of action and the formation of households have created a completely different spatial order in terms of the use of urban space. The old historical city can no longer cope with the scale and size of the new (auto)mobility of the urban population. Rural areas between urban centres are not only used for overflow (caravan areas, wrecker's yards, etc.), but are also cut across by highways, railways, recreational resorts and suburban living areas. In addition, the applied policies of industrialisation aimed at spreading employment to the countryside and the periphery regions has exerted a strong spatial impact on rural areas, more particularly by generating new commuting flows. As a result, new urban systems, based on one or more urban centres and their surrounding satellites (i.e. sub-centres and a number of suburban villages), began to emerge and to dominate the urban landscape.

1.3.3 Period 1965–90

The number of people living in and around the old historical cities decreased significantly, due to the increased decentralisation of households to emerging suburban areas (for instance, the case of the Zaanstad area to the north of Amsterdam), which was partly steered by the policy of 'growth cities' laid down in the second spatial planning scheme of 1965. The suburbanisation process was followed by the delocalisation of activities, especially by the service sector, to suburban areas around the city. In the Amsterdam region, for example, this tendency was clearly the case when some major service firms began to delocalise their activities from the city centre to the north (in the direction of Purmerend-Hoorn and Zaanstad-Alkmaar), and to the southern parts of the city of Amsterdam, more particularly in the direction of the suburban centre of Amstelveen. During the 1980s, a new business district (World Trade Center) was built in the southeast of the city to accommodate these service firms, especially those from the banking, finance and insurance sectors.

Another important development during this period was the increased immigration flows to the Netherlands. As a result of immigration flows from the former Dutch colonies, the southern European countries and North Africa, the Dutch urban population increased significantly, and big cities become more and more diversified. Meanwhile the historical city was no longer the only important urban centre, but became increasingly challenged by several emerging specialised suburban centres. Consequently, the existing urban system based on a hierarchy of urban centres started to fade out.

In the case of Amsterdam, for example, and because of a great shortage of suitable land on which to build new houses in the city, completely new cities were constructed in the new province of Flevoland. These were, respectively, the cities of Almere and Lelystad (being the capital city of the new province). The city of Almere has become the fifth city of the Netherlands. However, due to the lack of employment opportunities in these two emerging cities, which were intended in the first instance to accommodate the urban population of the Amsterdam region, most of the residents in work were forced into commuting daily to their work places in the cities of Amsterdam, Haarlemmermeer and/or their surrounding areas. Note that during this period, the number of commuters between cities in the Schiphol-Amsterdam region increased significantly, due to the democratisation of the private car and hence the increase of auto-mobility. Therefore the radius of action by people increased further to reach higher levels than before. Accordingly, alongside the existing point-to-point commuting flows between cities and regions, a new commuting pattern emerged that was based on crisscross commuting flows between cities and regions.

Finally, it is worth mentioning that the rise and development of Schiphol airport fits well within the patterns sketched above, not only as a multimodal infrastructural place and an important hub in international air networks, but also as a powerful landowner and real estate development company that is gradually acquiring a growing slice of the relatively empty Haarlemmermeer polder.

1.3.4 From 1990 to the present

This period may be considered as one of urban splintering and the rise of the nebula city in a city-network urban system. Urban expansion now took place mainly at the fringes of existing urban centres, more particularly in the suburban growth centres surrounding big cities. Two typical examples illustrate this tendency in urban expansion during this period. First, a new large and mixed retail and leisure suburban centre in the Amsterdam South East district, where the new Ajax football stadium – 'Amsterdam Arena' – was built in the vicinity of several leisure facilities like the new Movies Theater and the Heineken concert building, etc. These developments followed closely the application of the national spatial planning of 'compact cities'. In the context of this national planning policy, Schiphol grew into a fully dynamic nebula city.

Second, the inner city of Amsterdam lost its position as the main economic centre, especially in favour of business services (i.e. banking, finance and insurance activities), and transport and communication services. Although the inner city is still of great importance as a centre for culture, shopping, leisure and small-scale business activities like graphic design and multimedia, the large-scale business services are now located alongside the Amsterdam ring road in the southwest boundary of Amsterdam (the so-called 'South Axis') and around the Schiphol national airport. Note, however, that the outlined noise contours around the Schiphol airport have had tremendous spatial effects not only on the surrounding suburban areas but also at the level of the city-region and even the whole province of North Holland (e.g. a ban on building houses and the location of economic activities in the areas surrounding Schiphol airport).

Today, the Amsterdam South Axis (in Dutch *Zuidas*) is the prime office location in the Netherlands with the most prestigious office buildings. Situated on the southern ring of Amsterdam, directly connected by rail and highway to the airport and still near to the city centre, the location takes advantage of the region's full economic and social network opportunities. The strategic position of this growth centre was improved by the opening of the high-speed train in 2007, and even more significantly by the realisation of the North–South subway trajectory, which is currently in full construction.

One striking feature of urban expansion during this period is the further blurring of the hierarchy of urban centres and the increasing overlap in their sphere of influence. The disappearance of the familiar dichotomous urban–rural image can be illustrated for the case of the Netherlands at the regional level by the growing tendency to conceive the protected green space at the centre of the Randstad-Holland (the so-called 'Green Heart' which has, in essence, a pure urban function) no longer as an agricultural belt but more or less as an open green park. The region is not only filled with buildings (the so-called Vinex areas) and industrial parks, but is cut across by infrastructure, all for the benefit of the private car owner and public transportation. However, the infrastructure is, in many ways, an autonomous system that connects the nebula city with other urban fields. Instead of a clearly shaped structure, the urban system is now becoming a huge urban field composed of multiple urban centres connected by various flows of persons, information, money and goods (Brand, 2002). From spatial point of view, one may speak of an urban field that is marked by floating borders and criss-cross movements of individuals, information, goods and money taking place between several centres and hubs. In addition, commuting flows of individuals are becoming more complex and multifarious, with different destinations and increasing numbers and length of trip.

Moreover, the density of interactions between individuals no longer coincides with the spatial density of population. In increasing globalisation, there are many possibilities for long distance communication and personal contacts on an international scale. A typical example in this context is the increased importance of the so-called 'creative class' (i.e. highly qualified knowledge workers) that show quite different patterns of mobility, communication and interaction than the usual urban population. In this sense, one may argue that, as a result of the growing heterogeneity and variety in lifestyles and (sub)cultures, the population of the nebula city has also dramatically changed. Figure 1.3 illustrates a conceptual framework of the urbanisation process, in terms of the typology of urbanisation, and the corresponding changes in the urban structure of cities and regions.

Finally, it is important to mention that the concept of the urban field (or city-region) may be confusing, especially with regard to the issue of the optimal city size. More generally, the spatial boundary of the city-region depends on the criteria chosen to study a specific urban space (e.g. spatial level). Consequently, there exists no clear definition about what precisely the city-region means. One reason for this confusion lies in the difficulty of identifying the functional differentiation between core-centres and the suburban areas.

In the Netherlands, the term city-region appeared for the first time in the second spatial planning scheme of 1996. However, a precise definition and operationalisation of this concept remain unclear. In this official document, the city-region was described as 'a spreading system of one or more big centres (cities or agglomerations) into their surrounding small nucleus centres that are

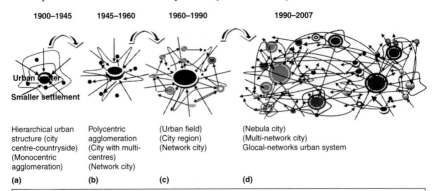

Figure 1.3 A typology of urbanisation and urban structure of cities and regions.

linked together by functional relations, and together form an integrated functional urban system' (translated from Brand, 2002: 8–9).

Moreover, the Dutch spatial planning schemes did not clarify either the precise nature of these functional relationships between urban centres, or more specifically the way these can be spatially separated from each other, i.e. their spatial boundaries.

One of the first tentative attempts to study the nature and scope of the functional relationships between different urban centres in the Netherlands was conducted by Manshanden and Knol in 1990 and concerned the northern wing of the polynuclear Randstad-Holland. In their empirical study, these authors did not find any strong evidence in favour of functional relations between the different parts of this urban region. The authors used a proxy variable of the spatial functional economic relations based on commuting relationships linking the different cities of the northern-wing area (e.g. as living and working places), and concluded that only the industry located between the Haarlem-Zaandam and Ijmond region showed a strong relationship with Amsterdam. Furthermore, their results showed that the functional entity of the city-region exists only with regard to demographic processes, such as differentiation, segregation and housing construction, and to a lesser extent with regard to functional commuting relationships (ibid.: 86). What this study clearly shows is that the functional relationships taking place at the spatial level of the northern wing of the Randstad are strongly dependent on the economic functions of the mainport[1] at Schiphol and the functioning of the housing and labour markets. However, at a higher spatial level, i.e. the southern and northern wings of the polynuclear urban structure of the Randstad-Holland, functional economic relations take place mainly at the city region.

More recently, these results were confirmed by another study of the functional economic relations at the metropolitan region and the Randstad-Holland levels (Oort *et al.*, 2006). This study shows the existence of strong inter-firm relations which are mainly oriented towards the centre of the city and its suburban areas. This means that the traditional hierarchical urban system and the diffused model still coexist at the city-region level. For example, within the greater Amsterdam region, more than 75 per cent of inter-regional firm relations are oriented towards the city of Amsterdam, and more than 40 per cent of the inter-firm relations take place within the city centre. In the case of the Arnhem-Nijmegen region, more than 60 per cent of inter-firm relations take place outside the city of Nijmegen. These results indicate the existence of a network city system at the level of the city-region.

1.4 Spatial level

The choice of spatial level is critical when studying the nature and origins of the spatial and economic transformation of cities and regions. This is because many of the empirical studies conducted on the same subject show different outcomes as a result of using different spatial aggregation levels (for example, the micro-spatial level of municipality or zip code, the regional city level, etc.), and different analytical method and/or models.

Researchers, planners and policy-makers use different terminologies (although they often agree about the definitions) to describe the variety of the topological urban landscapes that have evolved within the city's countryside such as 'fringe', 'inner fringe', 'rural–urban fringe', 'urban shadow', 'the exurban zone', 're-urban fringe', etc. Still, the reasoning often progresses from the city to focus on an analysis of the relationship of the city to the countryside instead of the other way around, i.e. of the countryside to the city. Accordingly, the urban fringe is considered a transition area lying between the continuously built-up areas and suburban areas surrounding the central city, characterised by low density of occupied areas and mostly devoted to agricultural or recreational activities. This transition area then develops into an area of mixed use which will ultimately be transformed into continuous urban use as the suburbanisation process develops further. This categorisation of the city–countryside hierarchy changes the relationships between a whole series of indicators such as property structure, land use, economic structure and social and community structure at the urban level.

Geographically, when analysing the urban structure of cities and regions different zones may be identified that result from a very complex and dynamic set of processes. They simply reflect different urban forms of continuous and discontinuous use of land in the urban space. In this perspective, specific geographic definitions or spatial levels of urban space remain rather subjective because they are based on a particular choice of criteria (e.g. degree of mixture of land use, level of farm vs. non-farm ownership, ratio of urban to non-urban population, commuting zones, etc.).

The urban spatial structure in which different areas of transition develop may vary significantly between different cities and regions. The variety of situations/ structures for the case of Schiphol and the Schiphol-Amsterdam region may be portrayed schematically as shown in Figure 1.4.

Note that the typology of spatial urban structure presented in Figure 1.4 is rather a simplistic representation of the possible continuity and change in land use at the levels of the core city, its (outer) fringes and the periphery. The rural–urban fringe is a discontinuous spatial phenomenon around most cities. The existence of an urban fringe depends upon the pressure on urban growth which often follows major accessible corridors or is concentrated in areas that are highly attractive for economic activity, i.e. high density, a diversity of activities and functions, and other advantages of agglomeration. In this sense, there is a little doubt that the basic phenomena underlying changes in the spatial structure of urban areas are the growth of urban population, the increase in mobility of the population and other economic factors such as the cost of land and housing, income, local taxes and the level of public services and amenities. A more important factor is the change in land use resulting from shifts in land ownership and the dynamics of the housing and real-estate markets. Consequently, it is important, at this level, to investigate the structure and change of land ownership in

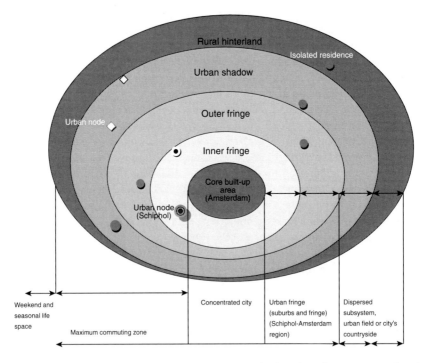

Figure 1.4 Typology of spatial urban structure and urban form in a monocentric urban system.

order to appreciate the magnitude of the metropolitan influence on the suburban areas and the countryside.

As mentioned above, the focus in this study is on the continuity and discontinuity in the spatial and economic development of the Schiphol region. Spatially and chronologically, this study concentrates on the urban field that acquired its shape during the nineteenth and twentieth centuries and is nowadays called the Schiphol-Amsterdam region, i.e. the area from Haarlem and Zuid-Kennemerland via Hoofddorp and Schiphol to the Amsterdam agglomeration.

Based on Figure 1.4, we make a distinction between the following different spatial levels:

1. the Schiphol airport area (i.e. urban node): formed by Schiphol Centre, and Schiphol West, East, North and South;
2. the Schiphol region (i.e. outer fringe): refers to the municipalities of Haarlemmermeer (Hoofddorp, Nieuw-Vennep, Badhoevedorp and Zwanenburg) and all surrounding municipalities (Haarlemmermeer comprises 26 centers and shares its boundaries with 13 surrounding municipalities);
3. the Amsterdam-Schiphol region (i.e. the core built-up area + the inner fringe + the outer fringe): formed by Amsterdam, Nieuwe-Amstel, Amstel-Meerlanden (e.g. Aalsmeer, Amstelveen, Diemen, Haarlemmermeer, Ouder-Amstel and Uithoorn), Zaanstreek (Wormerland, Zaanstad), IJmond (Beverwijk, Castricum, Heemskerk, Uitgeest, Velsen), the agglomeration of Haarlem (Bennebroek, Bloemendaal, Haarlem, Haarlemmerliede c.a., Heemstede, Zandvoort), the Gooi en Vechtstreek (Blaricum, Bussum, Hilversum, Huizen, Laren, Muiden, Naarden, Weesp and Wijdemeren), Almere and the Waterland region (Beemster, Edam-Volendam, Graft-De Rijp, Landsmeer, Oostzaan, Purmerend, Waterland and Zeevang);
4. the province of North Holland (i.e. 1 + 2 above + the urban shadow + the rural hinterland);
5. the northern wing of the Randstad-Holland (3 above + the rest of the rural areas): formed by IJmond, the agglomeration of Haarlem, Zaanstreek, Greater Amsterdam and Gooi en Vechtstreek, in addition to the sub-areas of Utrecht West, and the agglomerations of Utrecht, Amersfoort and Almere;
6. the Randstad Holland (5 above + the southern wing): formed by the northern wing, the southern wing and the two provinces of Flevoland and Utrecht.

More specifically, we refer to the Schiphol region as the urban space formed by the municipality of Haarlemmermeer and the municipalities of Aalsmeer, Uithoorn and Amstelveen. The Amsterdam region is formed by Greater Amsterdam, which is formed by the city of Amsterdam and its surrounding municipalities, and the Amsterdam-Schiphol region refers to both regions (see Map 1.1). Together, the Schiphol and Amsterdam regions form the metropolitan region which also integrates the northern wing of the province of North Holland, i.e. Greater Amsterdam, IJmond, Haarlem, Zaanstreek, 't Gooi and Vechtstreek (and part of Flevoland).

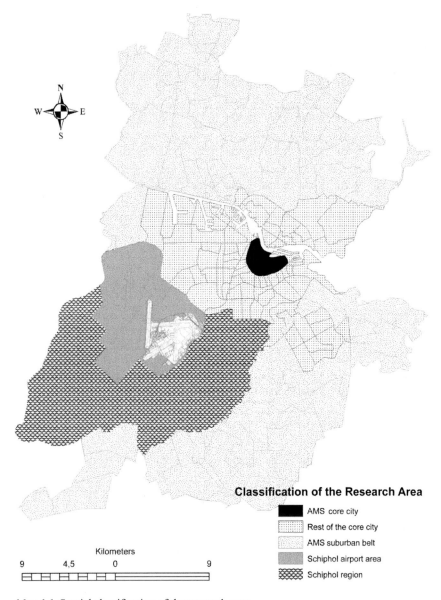

Classification of the Research Area

- AMS core city
- Rest of the core city
- AMS suburban belt
- Schiphol airport area
- Schiphol region

Kilometers

9   4,5   0   9

Map 1.1 Spatial classification of the research area.

1.5 Research methodology

The primary aim of this study is to understand regional development in general and the rise and development of an urban nebula in particular from a historical and institutional perspective. The main novelty of this study is that it does not solely rely on existing research on the 'institutional turn' that has heavily influenced the study of urban and regional development since the 1990s and which has resulted in a substantial body of literature looking at regional development and planning from an institutional perspective. Instead it applies an eclectic approach to integrating different disciplines (urban planning and geography, urban history, the sociology of institutions, institutional and urban economics) and research methods (quantitative and qualitative) in the study of a complex spatial phenomenon, i.e. the spatial and economic transformation of a region.

We consider the spatial and economic transformation of Schiphol and the Amsterdam region as strongly dependent on each other, and in this sense they must be integrated by means of a more unified analytical approach that takes into account various spatial and economic dimensions and spatial levels. In order to analyse this complex spatial phenomenon, a mixed-discipline approach and a rich methodological insight (i.e. a study in great depth of a particularly dynamic region) are used to shed light on the multiple dimensions and social-spatial entanglements of urban development. In both respects this study offers excellent opportunities to showcase the strengths and weaknesses of applying an institutional approach to analysing regional development.

Methodologically, we conduct first an extensive literature study of existing institutional theoretical approaches and applied research on (sub)urbanisation and spatial-economic changes. Second, we combine quantitative research methods (applied spatial statistical analysis and GIS analytical techniques) and qualitative analysis methods (archives (Schiphol and KLM, municipalities), interviews, policy and planning documents analysis, etc.).

First, with regard to the quantitative research methods, the analysis set out in this study uses data published by the Central Bureau of Statistics (CBS) in various editions of the population census from 1900 until 2001, the historical data of the Netherlands municipalities (HDGN) and, from 1970, the Annual Regional Economic Data (the so-called REJ). In addition, various time series data are constructed from the historical databases of Schiphol Airport (from 1926 until 2007), KLM, and the municipalities of Amsterdam (from 1900 to the present) and Haarlemmermeer (from the 1970).

From the Dutch Office of the Land Administration (Kadaster), we use topographical and cadastral data at the level of the airport area, Haarlemmermeer and the surrounding areas, and Amsterdam, where land property, ownership, charges and land use are recorded over the long term. This data is further analysed using GIS analytical methods to map changes in land use, and hence the spatial development of Schiphol and its surroundings in comparison to changes in land use at the levels of Haarlemmermeer and the Greater Amsterdam region.

Because GIS is a powerful tool for handling, analysing and visualising spatially referenced data and thus provides a comprehensive investigation of processes of regional and urban economic development (see Healey and Stamp, 2000), we use various GIS techniques to analyse, map and visualise the process of transfers in land use in terms of transformation and continuity at the level of the airport area and the Schiphol-Amsterdam region.

GIS has been defined as 'quantitative [*mainly statistical*] procedures and techniques applied in locational analytic work' (Gregory, 2000: 474).

One aspect of using GIS to map socio-economic and spatial (land use) changes is its ability to generate additional spatial data which may be used as inputs for further statistical analysis. The application of GIS to trace the historical change in spatial patterns and economic structure of cities and urban areas presents the advantage of combining various techniques of visualising these spatial changes with more advanced methods of spatial analysis (models).

One can often perceive changes in urban form better and more quickly through visual comparison than through other quantitative methods of analysis because visualisation may reveal relationships and patterns that are otherwise undetectable. This is particularly true when the researcher is interested in detecting and following historically the nature, direction and the level of changes in spatial patterns of urban areas. In this case, GIS enables us to see the elements of urban structure and function both in isolation and in their wider geographic context. As Jackson argues: 'Data that lends itself to textual and visual representation becomes a privileged source of information. [...] text takes priority over sound, charts and graphs over prose [...] seeing is believing [...] the power to make data compelling resides in the power to visually enhance it' (2008: 330).

Furthermore, the application of more sophisticated spatial analysis methods is possible once the data gathered is constructed in the correct format and made ready to use in combination with other data sources (for example, economic data with spatial references). This allows new forms of analytical synthesis, modelling and visualisation to be undertaken across different geographical units. Additionally, it is possible to identify and investigate the variety of linked dynamics identifiable at various temporal and spatial scales.

More generally, it is the ability of GIS to combine socio-economic data from different sources at different spatial units, such as data sources from remote sensing data (from either satellite or aerial photography), data on land cover and land use, soil type, geological and landscape features, elevation and climate, etc., that allows the description of different features of the spatial and economic landscape and their change in time that one might seek to explain (Overman, 2006: 3). Note that GIS is concerned very largely with representation. However, representation is not enough to identify the dynamic relationships among factors for change. Hence we need to go beyond representation to dynamics and change. This means that we need to involve not only patterns of change but also the processes of change. Consequently, a further unification of the spatial analysis of stochastic processes with the representation of urban spatial and economic changes within GIS must be stressed in urban and regional research (Longley and Batty, 2003; Batty, 2005; Rosenthal and Strange, 2005).

A final point that we want to stress here concerns the application of GIS techniques in economic historical study, or what is commonly known as 'historical GIS' (see, for example, Knowles, 2002). Historical GIS is often hard to deal with because of the need to combine a diverse range of data sources, such as maps (with various scales, cartographic styles, levels of detail, degrees of accuracy), urban plans, photographs (aerial and ground-level), economic data, historical data and socio-institutional records. Comparing spatial information between these sources or with information from the same type of source at different time periods may be difficult (Siebert, 2000: 538).

With regard to the statistical data, it should be noted that the data used are often not fully comparable, partly because the different data sources are serving different purposes. Even when using a single data source (for example the CBS data), there are differences because of regular revisions that might be made to the system of National Accounts, so that the figures before and after revision, for example, are difficult to compare. For example, regional data are only available from 1970 and are difficult to compare with regional data after 1993 because of changes in the definition of activities and sectors and the existence of potential breaks in the data. However, by focusing on growth rates rather than levels, and given the level of aggregation at the regional level, it is possible to construct time series at the levels of cities and regions. Note, however, that while the 40 agglomeration regions (NUTS-2) allow some regionalisation of the data, with some exceptions concerning the four big cities, it is still difficult to pinpoint any divergences between the cities themselves and their surrounding areas.

Second, the qualitative analysis focuses mainly on the case study method, which provides a systematic way of looking at interdependent events, actors and mechanisms in their real-life contexts (Yin, 2002). The qualitative study is based on multiple data sources, which enabled us to obtain stronger evidence from several sources. The first type of information was gathered from a systematic review of the literature and research publications, research reports, journals, company annual reports and publications, and policy reports (regional and national). These data are used to provide background information and to sketch an overall picture of the research subject of this study. The second type of information came from the analysis of archives, interviews and discussions with a number of individuals working in various sectors, e.g. former employees of and a number of key figures in the Schiphol Group and KLM, policy-makers of the province of North Holland and the municipalities of Amsterdam, Hoofddorp and Aalsmeer, a number of key figures in architect bureaus (NACO-Bentham Crowell), and researchers from various Dutch universities and research institutes (University of Utrecht, University of Amsterdam, RPB/PBL, etc.).

1.6 Plan of the book

The book consists of two parts divided into nine chapters. Chapters 2 and 3 present and discuss the main theoretical contributions of urban and regional economics and institutional economics that are relevant to our study.

The focus in these two chapters is to fill in the gap between these two different traditions of research by linking institutional approaches to urban economic theories. The aim is to construct a conceptual framework that allows us to shed light on various aspects of the urbanisation process and the determinant factors of change in urbanisation patterns and the economic structure of urban spaces.

This conceptual framework will then be put to the test in the remaining chapters where we elaborate extensively on the issue of the spatial and economic transformation of Schiphol and the Amsterdam-Schiphol region during the twentieth century.

Chapter 2 presents an overview of the main urban and regional economic theories that have contributed to our understanding of the formation, structure and evolution of cities, and more particularly the determinant forces of agglomerations underlying the spatial and economic transformation of cities and regions. Special attention will be given to the introduction and examination of major key ideas from the theories of urbanisation and urban sprawl, the theory of agglomeration economies and networks theory and their empirical application to urban phenomena. Based on this theoretical background and by using the concept of co-evolution, we construct a multi-space and multi-level conceptual framework that takes into account the dynamic interrelationships between the territorial, economic and institutional space at the micro and meso levels. This enables us to explain the dynamic processes of economic and spatial transformation and the configuration of cities and regions.

Chapter 3 deals with the concepts of institutions, the institutional environment and institutional arrangements. In this chapter, we provide a survey of the most important strands of institutional theories to economic analysis with special focus on the nature, role, formation and change with regard to institutions and institutional arrangements. The following strands of institutionalist economic approaches are reviewed in this chapter:

- the historical German School approach to institutions and institutional arrangements;
- the old American institutionalist school;
- the (neo-) new-institutional economic approach;
- the regulation approach; and finally
- the sociological/planning institutional approach.

Next, the concept of 'collective arrangement' will be introduced and extended in our discussions about the role and importance of the institutional environment in spatial and economic contexts. In addition, we will develop a conceptual framework of collective arrangements that addresses both the influence of the institutional environment on interactions among actors and factors in a spatial-economic environment. The development of this conceptual framework is based on a multi-actor, multi-level approach to urban transformation and governance, which allows the capture of the various actors and factors that may affect, directly or indirectly, the processes of spatial and economic transformation of the Schiphol region during the twentieth century.

The second part of this book comprises five chapters. Chapter 4 offers some stylised facts regarding the main driving forces of economic transition, industrialisation and urbanisation in the Netherlands during the last half of the nineteenth century and the first half of the twentieth. It stresses, on the one hand, the quantitative and qualitative importance of the industrialisation process and, subsequently, the sectoral shift and change in economic structure and, on the other, the massive urbanisation and spatial polarisation of economic growth in the Netherlands. Specific attention will be given in this chapter to the analysis of the demographic, spatial and economic transition of local economic structures and spatial patterns of the Amsterdam-Schiphol region, and more particularly the historical spatial development of the city of Amsterdam and the Haarlemmermeer region.

We turn then in Chapter 5 to the historical emergence and development of Schiphol airport by focusing on the interactions between the main actors and factors that have dominated the early history of Schiphol and played a key role in its future development. In particular we will explore the institutional and economic relations between the airport and the city of Amsterdam and Haarlemmermeer, as well as the relations between Schiphol and other actors. This chapter elaborates further on the specific role of the key actors involved in the development of Schiphol, their motivations and objectives as well as their formal and informal position vis-à-vis other actors, and explore how collective arrangements contributed to the emergence and transformation of Schiphol from a muddy military airfield into a modern municipal airport by the end of the 1930s. Conflicts between actors arising from the political decision-making process, for example the decision of the government to create a central national airport, will be examined in depth. Next, the economic performance of Schiphol during its early development period (i.e. the 1920s and the 1930s) will be examined using key economic performance indicators. Furthermore, applied policies and strategies for the future expansion of Schiphol in particular and of civil aviation in general, as manifested in spatial planning concepts, airport configurations and designs, and management, will also be discussed when we elaborate on the airport planning, airport configuration and management and operation of airport facilities by airport authorities and the municipality of Amsterdam.

Chapter 6 studies the postwar reconstruction and development of Schiphol airport in relation to the spatial and economic changes to the airport itself and the wider surrounding areas of Haarlemmermeer and the region. Special focus will be given to the question of how existing arrangements could be transformed and/ or created in order to ensure and sustain the future economic and spatial development of Schiphol and its surroundings, and the implications these new collective arrangements will have for the spatial planning and business operations of the airport activities. More attention will also be given to the various airport expansion plans developed and implemented by the Schiphol authorities, and the role of the different actors involved in influencing the decision-making process concerning the implementation of airport spatial planning. Next, we will turn to the examination of the effects of external factors in determining the spatial expansion of Schiphol and its surroundings, before elaborating further on the economic performance of Schiphol airport and the shift in the commercial strategies of Schiphol toward a more uniform market-oriented strategy. Finally, this chapter concludes with an extensive discussion of the implications of the spatial expansion and economic development of the airport for the surrounding areas, more particularly in terms of restrictions on urban spatial expansion and environmental effects like noise nuisance, pollution, etc.

In Chapter 7, we turn to the examination and analysis of the main urbanisation processes and economic changes that took place during the postwar period, particularly from 1945 to the end of the century. The aim of this chapter is to identify the key determinants that are grounded in the alternation of relative continuity and discontinuity of changes in the spatial patterns and economic structure of the Amsterdam and Schiphol regions. Various determinants of spatial and economic changes like the socio-cultural and demographic changes, and other factors affecting economic change at national and regional levels, will receive needed attention in this chapter. We will dig deeper in order to identify the main factors explaining the shift in spatial and economic structure from an industry-based to a services-based economy during the postwar period. Our (quantitative) analysis will be extended to the case of the Amsterdam region and the Haarlemmermeer-Schiphol region, with special focus on the analysis of the spatial structure and spatial transformation of these two regions between 1945 and 1990.

Chapter 8 extends the previous analysis in Chapter 6 concerning the economic and spatial development of Schiphol airport and the Schiphol region from 1980 until now. The chapter starts with a brief discussion on the nature, cause and consequences of the restructuring processes in the air transport sector in Europe and their implications for the development of Schiphol airport since the 1980s. Next, a quantitative assessment of the economic performance of Schiphol airport during the period 1980–2009 will be presented before we turn to an examination of the main causes explaining the adoption of the mainport strategy by Schiphol airport and its implications for airport spatial planning and the economic position of Schiphol from a regional perspective. Subsequently, the role of actors in the decision-making process concerning the implementation of various airport planning measures such as the master plan and/or other spatial-economic development policies of the airport will also be discussed.

Finally, we will discuss the shift in the policy vision for Schiphol from mainport to airport city, and in particular how this policy was developed and implemented. In close connection to this issue, we will provide an extensive analysis of the economic performance of Schiphol and its economic position as a strong cluster magnet for economic activities and a top location for high-end business services in the metropolitan region and the Netherlands. In addition, the negative effects of Schiphol in terms of noise nuisance and other environmental issues are also examined in this chapter. Chapter 9 concludes.

1.7 Reader's guide

This book is primarily aimed at researchers and students in urban geography and planning, urban history, and urban and regional economics, as well as policy-makers interested in the history of the spatial and economic transformation of cities and regions in general and the Schiphol and Schiphol-Amsterdam region in general. The book could also be used as supplementary reading in courses focusing on airport city complexes or multidisciplinary approaches to studying urban development.

Readers interested in theories of institutions, institutional arrangements and urban economics theories will find interesting reading materials in Chapters 2 and 3. These two chapters form what we consider to be the theoretical core of our study. Readers interested in how existing theoretical approaches are used in this study to construct a conceptual analytical framework centred on the concept of collective arrangements should read these two chapters in combination with the present chapter where our research questions and research design are presented.

Chapters 5, 6 and 8 may be grouped into a large block where the focus of the study is on the historical analysis of the spatial and economic development of Schiphol airport and its surrounding areas during the twentieth century.

Chapters 4 and 7 are devoted to an examination of the spatial and economic transformations at the level of the Amsterdam and Amsterdam-Schiphol regions, which are both much larger than the airport area and its surroundings.

2 Spatial-economic transformation and the rise of the nebula city

Theoretical considerations and conceptual framework

2.1 Introduction

In this study, we approach the sequence of spatial transformation of cities and regions from three perspectives corresponding to three specific notions of space: the economic space, the geographic space and the institutional space.

First, from an economic point of view, urban transformation can be understood in light of accompanying changes in economic structure, e.g. sectoral shifts from agriculture to industry and from industry to services, and the corresponding changes in existing modes of production, e.g. from a Fordist or mass-production system to a post-Fordist or flexible production system.

Second, from the geographical point of view, urban transformation is closely related to changes that take place at the level of the 'geographic space', e.g. the shift from a traditional monocentric hierarchical urban system to a more polynuclear urban network.

Third, from the institutionalist point of view, urban transformation can be understood in light of changes taking place at the level of the 'institutional space', which involve changes in institutional arrangements and institutions ranging from the formal to the informal, e.g. law and regulations, conventions, norms, traditions, etc.

Having said that, since the 1970s urbanisation patterns in industrialised countries have been affected by changes in territorial, economic and institutional spaces which have manifested themselves in increasing spatial specialisation and differentiation of economic activities and an increase in geographical concentration and dispersion of population and activities on a much larger urban scale than before. As a result, traditional hierarchical urban spatial patterns shifted from monocentric hierarchical urban system into a polynuclear urban system where traditional big cities and their suburban fringes show more spatial, economic and functional integration. Some authors identified this new urban pattern as a network of cities, a city-region, an urban field (Friedman and Miller, 1965) and/ or a megalopolis (Gottmann, 1961).

Note, however, that despite the great diversity of cities and regions in terms of their economic and institutional structures and social-cultural conventions, they all consist of relatively stable homogenous spatial entities. The viability and temporal stability of urban forms depend on the capacity of the local actors to develop dynamic collective proximity, which is a complex process of strategic interactions between actors that stimulate the constitution of local specific knowledge, practices and collective identity (Dupuy and Torre, 2004).

Today, the increased specialisation and regional division of labour between cities and regions push further the formation and development of urban networks beyond the traditional territorial scale, both nationally and internationally.

First, at the national scale, the emergence of the city-region is, on the one hand, the result of the delocalisation of industry and services and employment from the inner city to the suburban areas in the search for less costly and more abundant land and to escape the locational disadvantages of agglomeration such as congestion, pollution and the high cost of the labour force, land and housing, etc. On the other hand, improvements in transportation and communication technologies have eroded the traditional separation of working places from the living places. Both tendencies have direct consequences on the spatial organisation of activities and households and, indirectly, on the emergence of the city-region as a new space of production (Storper, 1997).

Second, at the international scale, metropolitan areas are now connected to global markets and are highly dependent on the free movement of capital, a highly skilled labour force, and information and knowledge. They represent the juxtaposition between local areas with specific resources and the global network economy, i.e. the so-called 'glo-location networks'.

Recent discussions on the resurgence of the metropolitan areas are fuelled by renewed attention to their attractiveness for economic activities and population in terms of diversity of products and markets, accessibility to amenities and the high quality of infrastructure, competitiveness and growth in contexts of spatial and cognitive proximities. Spatial proximity is regarded as essential to the growth of cities and regions because it stimulates knowledge spillovers and collective learning, which in turn lower transaction and search costs and enhance coordination between actors. This can be achieved through: (1) the mobility of human capital, e.g. knowledge workers as the carriers of knowledge transfer (tacit knowledge); (2) the diffusion of information through dense (mainly informal) networks of local actors; and (3) a common local culture of trust based on shared practices, rules and conventions.

In this perspective, big cities are portrayed as open and complex systems with strong specialisation, variety and complementarity of activities generating growth. Growth tends then to converge between cities and urban edges, including distant urban centres (Erickson, 1983; Garreau, 1991). In many situations, this tendency may lead to the formation of new production centres that possess strong relational networks and functional complementarities with cities and their suburban areas, depending on the 'social properties of networks in which economic agents are implicated' (Amin, 1999: 369).

Various studies on urban and regional economics, geography and planning, and sociology and political science have conducted extensive analysis on the emergence and growth of cities and the urbanisation and urban transformation of cities and regions from different perspectives. Economists approach the spatial transformation of cities and regions from rather a deterministic view of urban space. To them, urban space is considered often as the product of socio-economic dynamics governed by the principles of production, distribution, innovation, organisation and coordination (Lambooy and Moulaert, 1996). This view of urban space corresponds to different images of cities such as the innovative city, the consumer city, the informational city, the transactional city, the network city, the global city, etc.

However, what is usually missing in existing studies on the spatial transformation and growth of cities is a fundamental understanding of the nature, role and importance of existing institutions and institutional arrangements and their underlying interactions with the functional and spatial organisation patterns of cities and regions. In this sense, and to our knowledge, few studies have approached the spatial and economic transformation of cities and regions by linking the nature and dynamic of institutional and collective arrangements to agglomeration, urbanisation and growth.

The aim of this study is to fill this gap by linking various institutional approaches to urban economic theories, and more specifically to urbanisation and urban sprawl theories, the theory of agglomeration economies and the networks theory. Our goal is to construct a conceptual framework that will enable us to identify the main determinants of change in urbanisation patterns and the urban economic structure of cities and regions. In other words, we take as our starting point the historical and time-specific factors and processes underlying the spatial-economic structures of cities and regions, where various actors are directly or indirectly involved in the process of economic development and spatial organisation of activities and population. To achieve this goal, we focus our attention on the concept of institutional and collective arrangements, which we consider as determinants in (re)producing (and are (re)produced by) specific spatial and economic outcomes in cities and regions.

We apply this theoretical approach to study the spatial and economic metamorphosis of Schiphol airport and Schiphol region during the twentieth century. The structure of this urban nebula is shaped through the flows of people, goods, money, knowledge and information, with accompanying social-economic and territorial interventions, arrangements and regulations, which influence (directly and/or indirectly) the development trajectory of the nebula city and its spatial and economic configuration.

Our argument is that collective arrangements that are developed within a specific institutional framework allow economic agents to minimise costs, particularly coordination and transaction costs.

The organisation of this chapter is as follows. The next part of this chapter presents a survey of the most relevant theories of urban and regional economics, especially the literature on monocentric and polycentric urban systems (section 2.2), and suburbanisation and urban sprawl (section 2.3). Then we introduce and discuss the major key ideas of the theory of agglomeration economies and the networks theory and their empirical application to urban phenomena, more particularly the spatial implications of these theories in terms of key determinants triggering the spatial and economic transformation of cities and regions (sections 2.4 and 2.5). This will help us to understand the most important factors underlying the spatial transformation of cities and their economic structure from an economic point of view.

Next, we elaborate on the dynamic interrelationships between the territorial, economic and institutional space at the micro and meso level by using the concepts of co-evolution, local production systems, embeddedness and interrelatedness. This will enable us to construct a conceptual framework that will help us to shed light on the dynamic processes of economic and spatial transformation of urban areas in general and the Schiphol region in particular (section 2.6). The examination of the interrelationships between these three types of space is crucial to our analysis, because they co-evolve in time and space and determine the emergence of new urban patterns and functions, e.g. the transformations taking place in one space affect directly or indirectly other spaces and hence the spatial and economic configuration of cities and regions.

2.2 From a monocentric to a polycentric model of urban forms: a brief review

The field of urban economics has evolved rapidly from the beginning of the 1970s, developing a variety of theoretical concepts and an increasing number of applied empirical studies. Most urban economic theories emphasise the importance of agglomeration, production, transaction costs (including transport costs) and the unequal distribution of resources in shaping the structure of urban systems. The comparative advantage of cities depends on their capacity to reduce the costs of production and interactions through spatial proximity. However, the role that cities play in facilitating non-market interactions may be just as important as the costs involved in market transactions.

Traditional urban economic theories are based on the assumption of the monocentricity of metropolitan urban morphology comprising the central city and suburbs/hinterlands. Commuting and labour flows within such monocentric urban systems are assumed to be unidirectional, i.e. from the suburb to the centre of the city, and the residential and employment centres are spatially fixed, i.e. in the central city (Richardson, 1988).

With the increase in suburbanisation of employment and population during the postwar period, the monocentric assumption was relaxed to account for the rise of polycentric urban systems where suburb cities are considered as destinations as well as origins of labour flows (Richardson and Kumar, 1989; Margo, 1992; Gordon and Richardson, 1996; Greenwood and Stock, 1990).

2.2.1 *The monocentric city models*

The classic monocentric urban model can be traced back to classical location theory, especially to the land use model developed by von Thünen to study the spatial organisation of economic activities in the context and reality of northern

Germany during the nineteenth century. This model is based on the assumptions of the featureless space, isotropic transport and the instantaneous formation of perfectly concentric spatial arrangements around a single point[1] (Bailly and Huriot, 1999).

In line with the von Thünen model, monocentric models (Alonso, 1964; Mills, 1967; Muth, 1968) consider transportation technologies, and hence transport costs, as the main factor explaining changes in urban patterns. This view of the world is consistent with the historical reality of the first half of the twentieth century when only railway infrastructure and public transportation were relatively developed, transport costs were relatively high and the use of private cars was still in development. In other words, this view of the world corresponded to the daily urban system which is limited in time and space and where living and working take place within the same geographical space, i.e. at a distance between 15 and 30 minutes from the city centre.

Alonso (1964) extended the central concept of *bid-rent curves* to the urban context by replacing the concept of market place by the employment centre (CBD).

In the same vein, Lösh (1940) developed a model of monopolistic competition à la Hotelling-Kaldor and showed that economies of scale in production, as well as in transportation costs, are essential ingredients to understand the formation of economic space (an idea which was put forward by Alfred Weber in 1929). The core idea is that without increasing returns, there would be no trade and no interactions in economic and geographical spaces. Consequently, the economy would be condemned to the backyard (for detailed discussions on the non-convexities issue, see Koopmans and Beckman, 1957). More generally, the monocentric city model assumes that employment takes place at a single urban centre: the central business district (CBD). Residential development around that centre is determined by the trade-off between land costs or land rents (bid-rent) and travel or commuting costs.

Because transport costs dictate the existence of the hierarchy of cities, the CBD is considered a hub for transportation technologies in the sense that public transportation brings people to the city centre from which point they can walk to their workplaces. Goods produced in the city are shipped from the CBD to other areas, e.g. the consumers, by rail and water transport (Glaeser and Kohlhase, 2004).

Beside the development of infrastructure, the great force that has reshaped the cities of the twentieth century lies in the technological innovations such as powerful steam engines, electrical machines and transport technologies. With the improvements in transport infrastructure networks, the exchange of goods and services between regions increased substantially, and movement of people between distant regions and countries became much easier than before. As the real costs of moving goods declined by more than 90 per cent during the twentieth century, the need to agglomerate around rivers or coalmines became less important.[2]

Furthermore, the development of infrastructure implies a decrease in the distance between cities and regions and hence an increase in the daily urban system and an increase in the freedom for people and firms to choose from a wide array of distant locations. The basic assumption underlying this argument ultimately rests on the combined effect of increasing income and lower transportation costs to explain the phenomenon of suburbanisation and urban sprawl.

In short, the monocentric city model highlights the role of declining transportation costs to explain the general decline in city density and urban sprawl experienced by major industrial countries over the second half of the twentieth century. Following this view, the increasing use of the automobile and the accompanying decrease in transportation costs are the primary catalysts of urban sprawl and the increasing economic importance of suburban areas (Glaeser and Kahn, 2003).

More recently, Puga *et al.* (2005) have reviewed the monocentric city model and urban sprawl literature. The authors stress the fact that cities specialising in sectors with stronger agglomeration economies have more expensive land. This is because high land prices offset higher wages resulting from agglomeration economies. Thus cities specialising in sectors where employment tends to be more centralised tend to be more compact than other cities. In addition, commuting costs to the city centre have a direct effect on urban sprawl in the sense that cities that are built around public transport networks are generally more compact than cities that are built around the automobile.

Finally, it is worth mentioning that one important limitation of the monocentric models is their failure to account for the effects of firms' production decisions as well as the nature of agglomeration externalities in shaping urban forms. Furthermore, the extent to which metropolitan areas may be characterised as monocentric has declined over time[3] as they have become increasingly polycentric (Anas *et al.*, 1998). In this respect, the transformation of the urban form of the monocentric city model to the polycentric city model poses the question of how do the relationships between urban economic aggregates in monocentric cities extend to polycentric cities? To answer this question, we have to look at the main determinants and processes at work in the polycentric city models.

2.2.2 The polycentric city models

In opposition to the monocentric city model where land rents are determined only by accessibility for residents (land rent and commuting costs), these are determined in the non-monocentric city model also by the productivity of firms in different locations. Instead of the distance to the CBD, the accessibility and the variation of wages and productivity between alternative locations became the key to explaining elements of new urban forms. Thus not only do differences in transport costs matter but also differences in wages and productivity are also capitalised into land rents. The economics of this process was considered by Fujita and Ogawa (1982), Roback (1982) and Sivitanidou and Wheaton (1992).

The polycentric models explain the endogenous formation of secondary employment centres by stressing the important role of the forces governing employment dispersion related to transport and labour costs (see Fujita and Thisse, 1997). In these models, firms compete with other firms in both the labour market and the land market of a city. The commuting costs for its workers lead this firm to locate outside the CBD to avoid high commuting costs and be able to pay lower wages. This may be interpreted as the direct effects of centripetal forces working at the level of the agglomeration as described in the theory of agglomeration economies.

In the polynuclear urban system, cities are considered complex economic systems where specialisation and diversity of economic structure coexist side by side. Henderson's (1974) model of city systems provides an early explanation of factors explaining the structure of cities. In his urban growth model, Henderson stresses the importance of localisation economies for the industries in small cities and urbanisation economies in larger cities. Industries that exhibit urbanisation economies always choose cities where the productivity advantages of agglomeration are higher than diseconomies of agglomeration, e.g. congestion and other high-density costs.

In his multi-sector urban growth model, Abdel-Rahman (1990) shows that the basic causes of industrial agglomeration and city formation are the increasing returns to scale, which result from the existence of fixed costs in production and the preferences of firms for variety in intermediate inputs.

Similarly, Abdel-Rahman and Fujita (1990) examine the formation of a system of cities where each city specialises in the production of differentiated traded goods.

More generally, most polycentric urban models consider agglomeration economies as the main cause of the clustering of people and activities and hence of the formation and growth of cities. The idea is that workers and firms interact in an urban economy to generate joint economies of scale, e.g. advantages of specialisation and diversity/differentiation. However, although agglomeration economies are the *raison d'être* of most cities, their exact nature is unclear and only partially understood. What is known from the literature and empirical evidence is that agglomeration economies tend to create clusters of economic activities within a city, and that these clusters have direct effects on the surrounding residential densities. In addition, suburb centres, like cities themselves, emerge from the interaction between the centripetal and centrifugal forces. Both sets of forces entail strong externalities, e.g. external economies producing agglomerative tendencies, and congestion or nuisance externalities limiting the size and density of agglomeration.

Since different externalities operate at different spatial scales, it is quite possible that the spatial patterns of economic activities will be too centralised at one or a few locations (e.g. cities that are too big) and too decentralised at others (e.g. multiple small-suburb cities). This raises the question about the optimum size of the city and the 'market-determined' spatial structure.

Despite the fact that there is some room for public intervention in the organisation of space through government actions, a precise prescription of good planning remains difficult and in many cases even elusive. For example, externalities (crowding, congestion, pollution, etc.) may give rise to excessive employment decentralisation, which in turn may spawn excessively large suburban secondary agglomerations.

2.3 Urbanisation and urban sprawl theories

Historically, the development of cities in western countries may be characterised by three major stages: (1) the pre-industrial cities that were dominated by the economic power of landowners and the activities of merchants and craftsmen; (2) the industrial cities characterised by increasing specialisation and integration of production in manufacturing industry; and (3) the post-industrial cities that have emerged from the shift from industry to services and a knowledge-based economy (Huriot and Thisse, 2000: ix–x).

In most historical writing, the process of urbanisation refers to the growth and decline of cities. Urbanisation itself results from strong spatial patterns of concentration and density of resources, factors of production, population, wealth and economic activities.

More generally, studies on the growth and decline of cities have proceeded along a number of theoretical strands. One of these strands has emphasised the historical aspects of urbanisation. Massive population movements from rural to urban areas during the Industrial Revolution have fuelled urban growth and the urbanisation of cities throughout the world (see De Vries, 1984 and Bairoch, 1988). Technological innovations were facilitated by urban concentrations of population and activities and associated technological improvements, especially in transportation infrastructure.

Another related theoretical strand focuses on changes in the physical structure of cities as they grow. The changes in commuting costs and in the industrial composition of production and other technological changes are considered as the main explanatory variables of the growth of cities. The spatial concentration of population and economic activity in urban areas increases either because agents migrate from rural to urban areas in the search for jobs or because economies grow both in terms of population and output, which results in the growth of urban as well as rural areas.

A third theoretical strand has focused on understanding the evolution of systems of cities. The following two key questions have been subject to extensive analysis:

- How do cities of different sizes interact, accommodate and share different functions as the economy develops further?
- What are the properties of the size distribution of urban areas at different stages of economic development?

More generally, two opposite tendencies have been observed in the evolution of urban systems in developed countries during the nineteenth and twentieth centuries: a tendency toward concentration in larger cities and an opposite tendency (since the 1970s) toward the dispersion of population through the expansion of cities into their surrounding rural areas (Goffette-Nagot, 2000: 318). The first tendency was triggered by the increased division of labour and specialisation in industries and manufacturing firms, and hence increasing returns to scale.

Note that increasing returns appear at the level of specific activities, either public or private, as well as at the level of cities. The external effects of increasing returns foster the process of concentration of human activities and, subsequently, specialisation of cities and regions.

During the second half of the twentieth century, a growing number of modern polycentric urban agglomerations have evolved into 'network cities' enjoying a greater diversity and creativity (Hall, 1984). The network cities show a more highly diffused structure of flows, with criss-cross relationships between cities and outlying regions. These network relationships involve not only the larger cities, but also municipalities of equal or lower position in the urban hierarchy (Batten, 1995; Knaap, 2002). Economically, the central cities and suburbs show more complementarities (than competition) and specialisation of their economic structure. In this respect, a lot of attention has been devoted to the effects that urban growth has on urban structure. The main idea is that urban growth leads to suburbanisation, and is therefore associated with urban sprawl.

Urban sprawl involves households (as indicated by a flattening of the population density curve) as well as employment, either through continuous sprawl of jobs from the city centre to suburban areas or through the emergence of secondary centres (the so called edge cities) (Garreau, 1991; Henderson and Mitra, 1996).

Mills (1999) describes sprawl as 'excessive suburbanization', while Clawson (1962) describes it as 'the lack of continuity in expansion'. Other authors define urban sprawl as low-density forms of settlement, decreasing density and functional decomposition of cities (Glaeser and Kahn, 2003) or as de-concentration processes of urban functions combined with the spatial expansion of urban uses into rural areas (Pumain, 2003).

More generally, urban sprawl is associated with the tendency toward excessive spatial growth of cities and unplanned urban development that runs counter to the objectives of spatial development (Brueckner, 2001).

One of the characteristics of urban sprawl is the 'leapfrog development' which occurs when development takes place in areas that are disjointed from existing built-up area. When leapfrog development takes place in many areas, the spatial configuration may take the form of 'scattered development'. Hence, a key characteristic of urban sprawl is fragmented leapfrog development.

Various factors explaining urban growth and urban sprawl were proposed in the literature, such as the development of transportation infrastructure, technological innovations, population growth, sectoral shift, e.g. the fast growth of industry and services, and economic prosperity leading to socio-demographic shifts, e.g. the higher standards of living, increase in wealth, improvements in health care, sanitation, water, electricity, etc.

Indeed, during the late nineteenth and the twentieth centuries, changes in transportation technology resulted in massive changes both within urban areas as people fled from the central cities to suburbs and between regions. Conceptually, this argument is closely related to the monocentric urban model stating that sprawl can arise from three forces: declining transport costs, increasing incomes of households and population growth.

Note, however, that there is a difference between two different patterns of urban sprawl: a movement towards *decentralisation* consisting of a shift of population and activities from the inner city centre to the suburbs, and a movement towards *deconcentration* consisting of the relatively rapid growth of small urban areas, e.g. in term of population, employment and economic growth, in comparison to the larger areas (Carlino, 1985).

As a nation's population expands and incomes rise, cities must grow spatially to accommodate additional urban population due to the increase demand for new residential locations and spacious homes. This is because of the increasing demand for greater housing consumption in a location where housing is cheap, namely the suburbs, especially by the middle class. As a result of increasing demand for land, urban density declines near the CBD and increases in the outer fringes of the city. Similarly, investment in transportation infrastructures and transportation innovations stimulates inter-regional mobility, thus reducing the cost of commuting. As a result, suburban locations became attractive for single-family households as commuting costs fall, and this spurs further suburbanisation and urban sprawl. Moreover, the relocation of jobs to the suburbs increases as a result of changes in the transport orientation of industry and businesses. This is because firms increasingly rely on road transport and thus prefer the easy access to suburban locations by means of highways rather than shipping their output through centrally located rail depots and port facilities.

Given the exodus of the middle class, it is not surprising that commercial and related businesses followed them to suburban areas. Thus, unlike the fundamental forces driving urban expansion, job suburbanisation is partly an effect rather than a cause of this growth.

Finally, the suburbanisation and spatial expansion of cities may also be driven by fiscal incentives in suburban areas which are attractive to high-income households (Tiebout, 1956).

There are several negative side effects of urban sprawl on urban growth. According to Brueckner (2001), excessive urban sprawl may distort the urban growth process because of the rise of several market failures, e.g. the failure to account for the amenity value of open space around cities, the failure to account for the social costs of freeway congestion and the failure to account for the infrastructure costs of new development. In each case, the remedies for the market failure, as suggested by Brueckner, may range from regulation, charging for externalities, congestion tolls and increasing the price of gasoline and taxing low-density housing, in contrast to more direct control through physical planning and construction permits.

In contrast to Brueckner's point of view, Mills (2001) considers the problem of government failure instead of market failure to be the main distortion factor in urban growth (see Mills' comment in Bruekner, 2001). In his view, the government uses its power to confiscate the ownership rights of landowners to preserve open spaces. Yet government actions promoting excessive suburbanisation find their way through local government land use controls. Both central city and suburban authorities may impose restrictions on the business and housing market (such as, for example, a prohibition on the residential density of multi-family dwellings, minimum lot size requirements, height limitations, etc.). According to Mills, such restrictions may lead to excessive decentralisation of households and activities in metropolitan areas.

Finally, it is worth mentioning that suburb areas become intertwined with central cities and together they form a complex system organised around a large metropolitan region or city region, which comprises various dimensions: geographical, economic, cultural, social and political. Each dimension involves many different components of the system. In this respect, to understand the morphology of the regional city, one must take into account the most important aspects characterising the city such as its forms, functions and structure (Bryant *et al.*, 1982). First, the forms refer to the locational aspects of urban systems, i.e. the physical patterns of land use activities, population distribution and the networks linking them. Secondly, the functions refer to the activities themselves and the flows necessary for those activities, and finally the structure refers to the combination of forms and functions, i.e. the total environment formed by the interlocking parts of various locations and their interrelationships.

Note that regional cities are post-industrial cities characterised by the high mobility of people, resources and information, better communication technology, wider leisure and cultural amenities and creative industries. The differences between industrial cities and post-industrial cities is that industrial cities were mainly dominated by the traditional advantages of concentration stemming from localisation economies (e.g. specialisation), while post-industrial cities are more dominated by urbanisation economies (e.g. diversity of economic activities) (Moulaert and Djallal, 1995). This last observation leads us to investigate the next theoretical approach, which is of great relevance to an understanding of the processes of spatial and economic transformation of cities and region, namely the theory of agglomeration economies.

2.4 Theory of agglomeration economies

As mentioned above, a basic property of economic activities that thrive in agglomerations is increasing returns to scale. This concept is closely related to positive externalities accruing from increased variety and differentiation of economic activities that enlarges available inputs, goods and other resources in cities and regions. The focus is then on the synergy of external economies and advantages of scale which give rise to agglomeration economies (Lambooy, 1988; Lambooy and Oort, 2003).

There are different aspects of agglomeration economies. Whereas Marshall emphasises the benefits of agglomeration for industries operating in the same sector and being located within the same region, i.e. localisation economies, Jane Jacobs (1969) stresses the benefits of agglomeration stemming from differentiation or the diversity of economic activities in the city or region. For her, urbanisation economies are the basic ingredient of agglomeration economies at the city level. More recently, some authors like Storper (1997) and Nelson *et al.* (2001)

have added the institutional structure as a key feature of regional agglomerations, e.g. the existence of growth-inducing institutions and cultural and entrepreneurial attitudes. Close to this argument is the point of view expressed by Malmberg and Maskell (1997) who argue that the mechanisms leading to agglomeration economies are of a socio-cultural nature. Thus 'the key to explaining the sustained existence of agglomerations of related industries lies in their superior ability to enhance learning, creativity and innovations, defined in a broad sense' (ibid.: 32).

The German economist Alfred Weber (1929) was the first author who systematically (though rather restrictively) focused on the concept of agglomeration economies in his analysis of the localisation of industrial firms in relation to the process of regional economic development. Building on Weber's work, Hoover (1937) makes a distinction between three determinants of agglomeration economies:

- *scale economies* at the firm level, which depend on the size of the firm's scale at a specific point in time;
- *localisation economies* which refer to localised economies that benefit all firms operating in a specific industry such as the sharing of common inputs, intermediate goods, labour market and so on;
- *urbanisation economies* which refer to localised economies that benefit all firms operating in all sectors and activities.

This classification of agglomeration economies was later considered in some detail by Walter Isard (1956) and since then has become widely accepted among economists and geographers when referring to the concept of agglomeration economies.

Paul Krugman (1991a, 1991b, 1995), for example, emphasises the central role of agglomeration economies and 'increasing returns to scale' for spatial economic development. According to this author, these two concepts need to be related to the market structure (e.g. home market effects) in order to understand the spatial organisation of activities and the emergence and growth of cities. He argues that 'In spatial economics [...] you really cannot get started at all without finding a way to deal with scale economies and oligopolistic firms' (Krugman, 1995: 35).

Krugman stresses the fact that structural differentiation and specialisation of economic activity has a variety of compositions resulting in the fragmentation of regions and cities within regional, national and international boundaries (Fujita and Krugman, 2004). The main contribution of Krugman's work on regional and urban economics is his development of sophisticated and attractive models that explain the formation of a large variety of economic agglomerations (or concentrations) in geographical space or the so-called 'core-periphery model' (CP model).

Methodologically, Krugman's approach emphasises the three-way interaction among *increasing returns* at the level of the firm, *transport costs* (broadly defined) and *the movement of productive factors* (as a prerequisite for agglomeration) in a general equilibrium model, combined with non-linear dynamics and an evolutionary approach of equilibrium selection, e.g. market structure characterised by imperfect competition (ibid.: 142). Nevertheless, most of Krugman's arguments on the formation of cities and the unequal spatial distribution of economic activities between regions are closely related to the theory of external economies of Marshall (1920), the concept of cumulative causation of Myrdal (1957) and the concept of backward and forward linkages of Hirschman (1958).

In the historical context of the nineteenth century, Alfred Marshall noticed that many craftsmen and tradesmen operating in the same sector were spatially clustered in the same location where they could keep well informed about products and markets, and where they could easily imitate successful entrepreneurs without extra investment costs. Spatial proximity to the other firms is then regarded as an economic asset offering comparative advantages ('external economies') to firms that are involved in a process of 'collective learning' in spatially localised networks (Lambooy, 2002).

Marshall (1920) was clear about this point when he argued that the advantages of external economies are the result of not only the spatial proximity of economic actors but also the presence of a 'specific atmosphere' stimulating the exchange and the emulation of knowledge, learning effects and trust. He makes a distinction between four sources of external economies, namely: (1) scale economies internal to firms; (2) the pooling of a (large) local labour market of specialised skills; (3) the provision of various intermediate inputs at relatively low costs; (4) the local information flows or local knowledge spillovers, which lead to an increase in efficiency and innovations through costless mutual learning and sharing of knowledge.

Since Marshall, the concept of externalities (also called external effects) has been used in the literature to describe a wide variety of situations. Following Schitovsky (1954) there are two categories of externalities:

- *pecuniary externalities* – referring to the benefits of economic interactions that take place through the market mechanisms via the mediation of prices;
- *technological externalities* (knowledge spillovers) – that deal with the effects of non-market interactions taking place through processes affecting the utility of individuals or the production function of firms.

Recent empirical research in economic geography confirms the important role of Marshallian externalities in explaining the spatial clustering of firms in large cities and regions. Several studies show that the localisation advantages from the spatial proximity of firms in big cities result in lower production, transaction and transportation costs in comparison with other localities or regions (El Makhloufi, 2001). For example, Baldwin and Martin (2003) examine Marshall's (1920) idea stating that local innovation depends on local stocks of knowledge and point to the importance of face-to-face contacts in stimulating the transfer of knowledge between firms. According to these authors, there exists a strong relation between agglomeration and growth when knowledge and production are co-located. This is in line with the spatial variant of endogenous growth models developed by, among others, Romer (1990) and Grossman and Helpman (1991).

Krugman (1991b, 1995) explains the uneven distribution of economic activities between regions by the existence of agglomeration economies, which he considers as determinant elements of spatial configuration. Recent contributions to the economics of agglomeration make a distinction between two basic causes of agglomeration. *First nature* causes are land, climate, navigable waterways, immobile labour, etc. These regional endowments cannot be easily changed. *Second nature* causes refer to circularity in locational choice, e.g. firms want to be located where large markets are, and these large markets are where many firms are located.

The general principle that lies behind most modern contributions to geographical economics is that the observed spatial configuration of economic activities is the outcome of a process involving two opposing forces: agglomeration (or centripetal) forces and dispersion (or centrifugal) forces. The centripetal forces are generated by a circular causation of forward and backward linkages.

- Forward linkages stem from the proximity advantage where transaction costs are lower inside the agglomeration than outside the region. Firms then locate in big cities where the demand from input-buyer firms is larger, and for workers the incentive is to be close to the producers of consumer goods.
- Backward linkages (also known as input cost externalities) arise from a firm's spatial location relative to suppliers providing inputs with lower transaction costs and lower prices, and where the market is larger, e.g. big cities.

As a result of a complicated balance between these two opposing forces of forward and backward linkages, a type of local agglomeration of economic activities may emerge (Fujita and Krugman, 2004: 141).

The main idea is that the local production environment has a strong influence on the location of firms and industries through localisation economies and urbanisation economies. Because of these two conditions of agglomeration economies, lock-in effects may occur whereby localised firms in a specific region may persist in the long run. In this sense, increasing returns to scale constitute a strong centripetal force and are critical for the emergence of agglomerations, and hence the formation and growth of cities (Arthur, 1994: 46).

2.4.1 Spatial implications of agglomeration economies

Agglomeration economies, by their very nature, involve an obvious but important spatial aspect, namely concentration. Historically, agglomerations of economic activity were determined by 'first nature advantages' such as access to water, natural resources and other features of the geographic landscape, and the interrelated development of trade routes. The benefits of such spatial concentration of economic activity resulted into lower transaction and coordination costs, e.g. localisation externalities. Other types of externalities are externalities of urban scale and density or 'second nature advantages'. An increase in the urban population, for example, increases aggregate demand and enables firms to expand output without a corresponding increase in efficiency or productivity. In this sense, scale and density are interrelated but not identical. Their effects are manifested in urbanisation externalities.

Depending on the size and scale of the geographical urban space, the effects of agglomeration economies may be stronger at one spatial level and weaker at another. At the intra-urban level, for example, the proximity of firms to other activities is crucial to the growth of industries (Scott, 1988a, 1988b). At the level of the city region, agglomeration economies are more related to the diversity of economic structure, the quality of intra-regional transportation and communications networks, and the functional complementarity between the central city and its suburban areas. A typical example is the emergence of the urban nebula organised around a major mainport and several urban sub-centres where specialised activities such as financial and business services are concentrated. The exploitation of the benefits of agglomeration economies does not depend necessarily on the geographical proximity of firms, but merely on the accessibility and connectivity of such urban areas. This is because nowadays benefits generated within the big agglomerations are spreading over larger spatial scale levels, e.g. from agglomerations to suburban centres and to the hinterland.

The great advantage of agglomerations lies in the spatial manifestation of agglomeration economies through the potential benefits accruing from differentiation and specialisation. Larger cities provide individual firms with various opportunities for both local sourcing of inputs and the distribution of output as well as the production of knowledge and knowledge spillovers, either through face-to-face contacts or through inter-firm mobility of high skilled workers (Lucas, 1988; Rauch, 1993; Almeida and Kogut, 1999) – in other words, larger cities have a greater variety of consumer products and producer inputs and high levels of knowledge spillovers. The greater variety of economic activity and the diversity of consumers in larger cities increase productivity levels and the welfare of the urban population compared to smaller-sized competitor cities (Johansson and Quigley, 2004).

Larger cities, where agglomeration economies are the strongest, have thus better opportunities to develop a strong knowledge base and to nurture new growth opportunities. The idea behind these dynamic externalities of agglomeration was first put forward by Jacobs (1969), who states that the growth of cities is determined by the diversity of economic structure, which both sustains and is sustained by the cross-fertilisation of knowledge between firms. According to Jacobs, cities decline not because industries leave them but because new industries do not spring up in their place. Furthermore, differentiation of urban economic structure leads to an increased need for complementarities between activities and hence to mutual dependency in specialisation. Thus both differentiation and specialisation take place at the level of the city-region but also, through the increase in economic relations, at much higher spatial scale levels.

Beside the spatial dimension of specialisation and differentiation, these two categories of agglomeration also involve economic and socio-cultural dimensions in the sense that they create specialised clusters of activities that give urban areas specific characteristics, e.g. the financial centre, the cultural centre, the industrial centre, etc.

Finally, agglomeration economies also have an institutional dimension that takes place in a specific time (evolutionary development) and place (emergence of new activities and new places). It is now widely acknowledged that certain types of institutional environments facilitate economic growth through the agglomeration of firms that, in turn, attract and retain highly skilled labour (Lambooy, 2002). The spatial implication of this is a continuous spatial growth of urban space and the rise of complex polycentric urban forms.

2.4.2 Empirical evidence of agglomeration economies

In most applied studies, agglomeration economies refer to externalities stemming from the interaction of agents across space that positively affect local productivity and growth. Three dimensions of agglomeration externalities have been identified: industrial, temporal and geographic. The industrial dimension extends across firms within an industry or across industries and is the subject of most empirical work on agglomeration economies (Rosenthal and Strange, 2004).

Most earlier empirical studies on agglomeration economies examined the general relationship between city size and productivity (Sveikauskas, 1975; Moomaw, 1981; Beeson and Husted, 1989).

Henderson (1986) investigated the nature of agglomeration economies in two-digit SIC code manufacturing industries in Brazil and the United States. In both countries, localisation effects dominate most industries. In Brazil, there is strong evidence of urbanisation economies in only one of ten industries considered. Out of 16 US industries examined, only one industry has significant urbanisation effects whereas localisation economies are prevalent throughout many of the remaining industries. These findings are close to Moomaw's study based on an estimation of industry labour demand for 18 two-digit US manufacturing industries (Moomaw, 1988). In Moomaw's study, seven industries exhibit only specialisation effects, two industries exhibit only diversity effects and two industries exhibit both. In conclusion, localisation economies are dominant in the industry as only a small number of industries exhibit significant urbanisation effects.

Since the early 1980s, more attention has been given to empirical investigations into whether localisation economies (own-industry) or urbanisation economies (cross-industry) dominate an industry and/or which types of externalities are responsible for the economic growth of cities and regions.

Economists were inspired not only by the recent work of Lucas (1988) who sketched a framework where such spillovers were spatially localised and part of an urban growth process, where cities drive national economic growth, but also by the recent works of Romer (1986), Krugman (1991a, 1991b, 1995) and Arthur (1994) on increasing returns which in turn lead to path dependency and potential lock-in effects, and by the reformulation of growth models where knowledge accumulation and spillovers are considered the basis for endogenous growth in an economy (Romer, 1990).

In short, these growth theory frameworks suggest two lines of investigation. One is a more macro or aggregative approach where the focus is on a citywide level that knowledge spillovers lead to either growth in productivity or city size. The other line of investigation focuses on the micro-foundations of knowledge spillovers and the process by which knowledge spreads (for a review of urban models, see Duranton and Puga, 2004).

In a seminal paper relating city diversity and industry growth, Glaeser *et al.* (1992) use a panel of 170 Metropolitan Statistical Areas (MSAs) from 1956 to 1987 and examine the determinants of employment growth for each city's six largest industries. Their results show that cities with higher levels of specialisation and lower levels of diversity grow slower, providing strong evidence for the existence of Jacobs' externalities (urbanisation economies) over Marshall-Arrow-Romer (MAR) externalities (localisation economies).

Ellison and Glaeser (1997) used data for the 50 US-states at the four-digit classification level to analyse the effects of dynamic information externalities on urban economic growth. Their results show that dynamic externalities are weaker at the county-level than at the level of the state. This leads to the conclusion that while within-county spillovers are stronger, localised spillovers are still quite substantial at a higher spatial level than counties.

Henderson *et al.* (1995) examined the effect of past concentration and diversity on industry performance in 224 MSAs between 1970 and 1987. Their results show no evidence supporting the existence of Jacobs' externalities (diversity) in the case of traditional industries but strong evidence of both Jacobs' externalities and MAR externalities (specialisation) in the case of high technology sectors, e.g. new industries.

In a subsequent paper, Henderson (1997) extended this analysis and examined the lag structure of the dynamic externalities by employing annual data sets for the years 1977–90 of five capital goods industries at the two-digit level for the 742 urban counties of the USA. Again, his results suggest the presence of both MAR and Jacobs' externalities and their persistence over time.

In their efforts to control for endogeneity, Black and Henderson (1999) explored the nature of agglomeration economies using panel data drawn from the US Census Bureau's Longitudinal Research Database (LRD). The authors reported no evidence of agglomeration economies of any kind in capital goods industries, though MAR economies were present in high-technology sectors.

Jaffe *et al.* (1993) showed that spillovers between inventors (as proxied by patent citations) take place more often within regions than across regions. More recently, Breschi and Lissoni (2001) confirmed this finding and showed that the local nature of knowledge spillovers is caused by dense local social networks between inventors, which function as channels for informal knowledge exchange.

Finally, Rosenthal and Strange (2003) provided clear evidence of the diminishing of agglomerative effects as the physical distance between firms and industries increases. Their findings show that localisation economies decrease rapidly after just one mile, although the effect is significant up to 15 miles.

To summarise, studies on dynamic externalities suggest that diversity is important and that central city growth aids growth in the suburbs, and vice versa. However, empirical studies show that agglomeration externalities diminish rapidly with distance, suggesting that the relationship between cities and their suburban areas may be one of rivalry.

It should be noted that with the exception of Glaeser *et al.* (1992), who provided evidence in favour of urbanisation economies, most empirical studies concerning the nature of agglomeration externalities focus solely on manufacturing industries. It is likely that the relative importance of localisation and urbanisation economies depends on industrial sector and that manufacturing may exhibit location economies while service industries experience urbanisation economies. Today, the economies of most industrialised countries is knowledge based and services oriented, suggesting that the importance of urbanisation economies, especially dynamic externalities, are much more important for the economic growth of larger cities as has been shown by most empirical studies.

2.5   Networks theory: agglomeration and networks in spatial economy

More generally, networks are self-organised systems that are organised around a hierarchy of connected nodes and links taking place at various levels of connectivity. The most important hub, i.e. the one with most nodes, experiences the strongest attraction to other networks. However, there exist strong and weak hubs, depending on the number of links and their connection to other nodes, as well as the existence of certain complementarities and hierarchy between nodes.

More specifically, networks may be defined as sets of loosely connected relations linking individuals or organisations (firms), often without formalised structures or organisation. Williamson (1985) identifies networks as 'hybrid organisations', that is networks are viewed as an alternative coordination mechanism for the organisation and the market.

According to Lambooy (2004), the concept of networks is used in many ways according to the research field and the purpose of study, e.g. urban and regional economics, sociology, political science, planning, etc. This view is supported by Genosko (1997: 285) who argues that 'the network concept is "enigmatic" and appears in many shapes and forms. [...] In economics synonyms for networks are "strategic alliances", "joint ventures", "round tables" and such nomenclature.'

Indeed, in sociological and geographical literature, for example, the vehicles for the relationships between actors are trust, reputation and social capital, which clearly cannot be considered market relationships, i.e. expressed in prices and quantities. However, many relations that are described as networks can be perceived as market relations, either between individuals or between organisations (firms).

In an urban economy, both localised and non-localised networks exist. François Perroux (1955) gave a more precise description of networks of firms, and explained their contribution to the growth of sectors and regions. Perroux made clear the distinction between pure geographical space (concrete space of real estate, transport infrastructure and built-up areas) and economic space, which is a space of relationships linking economic actors, i.e. networks. Based on this categorisation of space, Perroux argued that networks should be organised around strong centres (the growth poles) that must act as coordination and organisation centres spreading growth to all participants in the networks (Lambooy, 1993).

More recently the concept of (spatial) 'clusters' has received more attention in urban and regional studies. Clusters denote a set of firms sharing a common history, maintaining strong inter-firm relationships and strong local embeddedness in term of their relation to local and regional institutions. Porter defines the concept of clusters as 'geographic concentrations of interconnected companies and institutions in a particular field' (Porter, 1998: 77).

The concept of spatial clusters is strongly related to the concepts of 'industrial complex' (Chardonnet, 1953) and 'industrial district' (Marshall, 1920). They all share an emphasis on spatial proximity, intensive relations in networks, externalities and non-market relations. In addition, spatial clusters, industrial complexes and industrial districts can be linked to the concept of agglomeration economies by considering the spatial linkages of firms in terms of locational advantages of proximity that result in economies of scale, scope and learning. In this respect, there exist strong complementarities between agglomeration and networks in the sense that networks may lead to similar external benefits arising from agglomeration economies, i.e. the provision of some or all of the utility gain and productivity in areas derived from agglomeration.

In a spatial context, networks play a crucial role in facilitating the exchanges of goods, capital, information, innovations and knowledge, both within and between regional agglomerations. Note, however, that there exist different activities and different networks that have different spatial effects. Therefore there are different combinations of hierarchical networks between cities and regions with different functions. For example, the polycentric urban system may be viewed as result of the development of a variety of functions per network, which encompass their own spatial patterns and their own logic of agglomeration. Networks organised around the mainports, for instance, have been developed outside urban agglomerations and within polycentric urban system. In addition, most of the mainport locations have followed their own development path and their own logic of economic and spatial growth within specific local and regional contexts. The result of this is the emergence of what some authors designate as splintering urbanism (Graham and Marvin, 2001), which is a logical consequence of the development of a new spatial structure based on a strong integrating process taking place at the level of the existing urban system (Lambooy, 2004).

Networks and agglomerations can also be approached from an institutional perspective by making a distinction between physical networks and economic networks in agglomerations (in the sense of Perroux). This last type of network includes transactions agreements and collective arrangements, a concept that forms the cornerstone of our argument in this study (see Chapter 3).

Accordingly, physical networks of agglomeration benefit all actors localised in agglomeration, while economic networks benefit only those actors participating in specific networks. In other word, economic networks arise from collective actions based on individual decisions made by group members of a network, which generate collective and institutional arrangements.

Finally, it is worth mentioning that because of the temporary character of the network structure, economic networks are subject to frequent changes, although the basic structure may remain the same. This is because actors in networks may switch easily between different networks, and in doing so, they give networks a more fluid character. To illustrate this point in a spatial context, one may think, for example, of shopping centres located in different urban areas which have a relatively stable spatial structure and where people have great freedom to choose where to do their shopping.

2.5.1 Networks of firms and their boundaries

In his seminal work on the nature of the firm, Coase (1937) suggested a set of criteria indicating when it is efficient to decompose an organisation into sub-units that may interact through the market instead of interacting as integrated parts within the same entity.

Although Coase's insight does not involve space, it helps explain why integrated firms can perform more efficiently than sub-units that integrate through the market. The idea is that when interactions through the market increase transaction costs, it is advantageous to organise interactions within organisations or firms. This raises the question of the efficiency of internalisation and/or externalisation of production through the organisation or through the market. The same argument was reformulated by Alchian and Demsetz (1972) and Williamson (1979) by introducing transaction costs as an explanatory factor in the organisation of firms and the formation of markets among different types of products, e.g. products with high and low transaction costs. The variation in transaction arrangements across products is explained by the existence of transaction networks.

The basic idea is simple: when transactions between firms take place on a regular and frequent basis, actors (buyers and sellers) will have the incentive to (re)organise their transaction arrangements to reduce the costs associated with establishing specific relationships or links.

Because firms are organised into nodes connected by specified linkages, transaction costs can be reduced if firms are spatially concentrated in the same area. In this case, firms may benefit from co-location within the same area and from their proximity to the markets which are usually found in larger cities or urban areas.

The incentives to form networks of firms stem from the possibilities to reduce transaction costs, to acquire information, to learn and/or to develop specific knowledge. However, networks are often instruments of imitation and diffusion of knowledge. Imitation between firms, especially small and medium-scale companies, is a lower-cost solution to innovation by using existing knowledge instead of investing in research and development by the firms themselves.

2.5.2 Spatial content of networks

In modern societies, networks connect different actors in different places (local, regional, global). Depending on the nature of their activities,[4] networks show different spatial patterns. In this sense, there exists a certain territorial congruency between economic networks and spatial networks. Both types of networks encompass dynamic processes of differentiation and specialisation of activities and agglomeration. This is the reason why urban structures show patterns of splintered urban structure (Graham and Marvin, 2001). In fact, one may consider splintering of urban areas as a new form of urbanism resulting, among other things, from the economic dynamics of urban space.

During the last three decades of the twentieth century, many European countries experienced dramatic changes in their urban space, which was manifested in the relatively rapid transition from a more traditional hierarchical monocentric urban system into a network of cities or an archipelago urban system (Castells, 1995; Veltz, 1996). In the USA, the change in the urban system took place several decades earlier than in Europe. In his book entitled *Megalopolis*, Jean Gottmann (1961) described the development of inter-metropolitan functional integration in an increasingly fragmented metropolis, an area that contains the metropolitan areas of Philadelphia, New York and Boston. Gottmann gives an extensive and detailed description of change in the economic structure of this metropolis, which has resulted in the shift of the economy from industry-based to transactional-based activities.

Jane Jacobs (1969) developed Gottmann's idea a step further by introducing the two concepts of differentiation and specialisation, which may be linked to the concepts of concentration and deconcentration in studying the formation and growth of cities.

Note, however, that the hierarchy of urban structure is not necessarily determined by the subordination of the urban fringe to the dominant central city, but by the existence of a coherent network structure and connections linking urban centres to specialised clusters within the metropolitan region. In this respect, some authors prefer to use the concept of complementarity between urban spaces instead of the concept of hierarchical systems (Lambooy, 2004; Knaap, 2002). Note that complementarities and hierarchies between cities and suburban centres exist side by side.

Since the 1980s, there has been a clear increase in the economic importance of suburban areas accompanied by spatial diffusion of (new) functions across many specialised clusters of activities in urban and non-urban centres. As a result, the metropolitan regions became more and more connected with their surroundings, and showed new forms of complementarity instead of hierarchy as was the case during the 1960s and 1970s. Recent studies on this subject offer convincing evidence that agglomeration economies are stronger at the level of the metropolitan region than at the city level. This suggests that suburban areas became very attractive locations for activities (working place) and workers (living place).

The concept of the 'polynuclear urban system' is often used to point out the development of these particular spatial patterns, while the concept of 'networks of cities' refers to the existence of functional relations between cities and their coherence through infrastructural connections. In other words, each network of functions has its own spatial dimension, depending on the nature and types of actors and activities (scientific research networks, R&D networks, marketing and logistic networks, etc.). In addition, networks may take place at global level while (small groups of) actors are concentrated in specific urban areas (city or region). Networks of cities are in fact networks of communication, which develop a high level of connectivity involving different levels of spatial scale, e.g. international airports and exhibition centres.

2.6 Linking spatial economics approaches to institutional theories: a perspective

The spatial organisation of activities and the spatial-economic transformation of cities and regions may be considered by developing a unified approach linking institutional aspects to the theories of agglomeration economies, urban sprawl and networks as described above.

The notion of agglomeration economies is most useful when focusing on the spatial implications of localisation and urbanisation economies in a system of city networks. More recently, substantial efforts have been made by economic geographers to integrate some key ideas developed by neo-institutional economic theory, especially Coase-Williamson's transaction cost analysis, in the analysis of agglomeration economies to bypass the Hooverian logic of production and distribution costs (Scott, 1988a, 1988b; Storper and Scott, 1989; Cappellin, 1988). In this respect, Williamson's idea of modes of coordination (e.g. internalisation vs. externalisation of costs and the minimisation of transaction costs associated with inter-firm linkages) revive at least some dimensions of agglomeration economies like, for example, externalities attributed to urban clustering and the spatial organisation of networks of actors and activities (Camagni, 1993).

Another interesting perspective that we propose in this research is the integration and enlargement of existing ideas developed by the French regulationist school, historical institutionalism and the new-institutional economics in a spatial context, aiming at an explanation of the spatial-economic transformation of urban areas. In particular, North's (1990, 2005) version of institutional economics is most instructive with regard to the structure of urban land use and local production and the spatial economic transformation of urban space. North's explanation of the rise of institutions – and implicitly of institutional arrangements – to control the uncertainty and opportunistic behaviour of actors may help us understand why rules, regulations, norms and conventions in specific markets are necessary for the efficient functioning of the market economy. In the real world, however, many institutions and institutional arrangements emerge and grow from spontaneous behaviour and interactions between market agents.

In addition, the analysis of special transformation can be enriched by integrating the proximity approach, stressing the importance of potential local resources of territories in stimulating local networks through collaboration and coordination between actors, e.g. the resolution of conflicts or the realisation of common projects. According to this approach, three types of proximities can be distinguished: the spatial proximity, the organisational proximity and the institutional proximity. Economic geographers focus attention on the geographical dimension of proximity and the institutional proximity (Pecqueur and Zimmermann, 2004).

Institutional proximity is based on the analysis of economies of governance (conventions) or the economies of interactions where some elements such as trust, bounded rationality, norms, rules and common representations and values are presented as key elements to explain the role and importance of institutional proximity to the spatial evolution of cities and regions (Dupuy and Torre, 2004).

Accordingly, the spatial and institutional proximities may foster the creation and exploitation of local production resources and stimulate inter-relationships between local actors and the development of collective learning through the exchange of (tacit) knowledge between those actors. In addition, institutional proximity may be considered a precondition to the emergence of collective arrangements. In other words, collective arrangements may become institutionally embedded in institutions when institutional proximity offers an adequate environment in which actors can interact easily with each other and form networks of collaboration aiming at developing common projects which benefit the whole local production system or the community. We will elaborate further on this issue in Chapter 3.

For now, the question that we want to raise here concerns the different modes of territorial development and trajectories in terms of their assets and resources, including the development of collective arrangements. In this respect, we borrow the following distinction between the three modes of territorial trajectories that were put forward by Colletis and Pecqueur (1993). These are: agglomeration, specialisation and specification. According to these authors:

1. The dynamic of agglomeration, synonymous to growth, is limited to the dimensions of spatial proximity and institutions. The origins of the territorial accumulation process are difficult to trace back to a specific activity or particular competency.
2. Specialisation is a trajectory that encompasses all three types of proximities described above, and is associated with clusters of activities or particular sectors such as industrial districts or specific local production systems.
3. Specification can be defined as a local mode of development founded on the rearrangement of competencies between actors operating in different sectors or activities and sharing common representations, conventions, norms and values.

The relational approach to space and place sketched above, which is inspired by the combination of some key ideas from institutionalist and spatial economic approaches, offers a promising theoretical avenue to encapsulate a more comprehensive analysis of the dynamic of institutional arrangements and institutions and their relationship to the long-term spatial economic transformation of urban space. The next step is then to connect, in a more systemic way, those various theoretical approaches, where the multi-dimensional facets of urban transformation can be identified and systematically analysed. This is because the spatial transformation of cities and regions is subject to simultaneous different processes which are at work, e.g. demography, economy, technology, planning, infrastructure and institutions, that cause and accelerate urban and regional transformation, not only at the levels of the geographical and economic space but also at the level of the institutional environment.

Indeed, the spatial and economic transformation of urban areas is directly affected by institutional arrangements such as formal and informal rules influencing the behaviour of individuals, and norms and values influencing the way people and actors interact with each other. In dynamic societies, norms and values are subject to change, wither gradually (incremental change) or/and radically (abrupt shocks from within and/or from outside the system).

Our argument is that two of the most important institutional factors influencing the spatial-economic transformation of cities and regions are collective and institutional arrangements. Collective arrangements are strongly linked to the organisation and elaboration of (formal and informal) contractual relations and conventions, such as cooperative agreements between private actors and between public and private actors. In other words, collective arrangements are created and used by actors to organise and coordinate their (collective) actions in economic, social and political systems. When they are accepted and respected by the majority of actors, and enforced by law and jurisdictional rules, they became part of existing institutions such as, for example, the protection of property rights and the regulation of markets and financial systems in modern societies.

This conception of spatial and economic transformation of urban space complements and enlarges the existing conception of urban spaces as sites (fixed points) in a composition of geographical networks, to encompass a conception of urban spaces as spaces of movement and circulation of goods, technologies, knowledge, people, money and information. In this sense, our application of the institutional approach to study the spatial and economic transformation of urban areas departs from the idea that territorial space is primarily a configuration of functions and arrangements that have been institutionalised in particular historical moments and become bounded in the spheres of economics, politics and culture of the territory (Paasi, 2001).

Recent empirical research in economics increasingly recognises the decisive importance of the spatial variation of institutional arrangements and the organisational features of policy mechanisms as background variables of urban economic growth (Amin and Thrift, 1995; Storper, 1997; Amin, 1999). Hall and Jones (1999) label these variables as social infrastructure. This body of empirical work in economic geography relates institutional and evolutionary approaches to institutional change. It focuses on institutional, cultural and social processes in order to understand the economic evolution of regions.

The evolutionary economic theory, for example, conceptualises the production system by emphasising the role of the learning agent (e.g. learning firm) involved in a process of technological and organisational innovation within a world characterised by the increase in uncertainty. Other theoretical approaches stress the role of the functional and spatial aspects of network organisation among firms as the trigger for the competitive advantage of learning regions and regional innovation systems (Perrin, 1991; Cooke and Morgan, 1998).

Following this line of research, the differentiation of urban forms is attributed to specific trajectories of organisation of production, inter-firm agglomeration and local specific stock of institutional assets (Storper, 1997), innovation and learning processes within and between economic and non-economic agents.

Having said that, we argue that the dynamic change in the functions and economic structure of cities and region, the power relations between actors and the spatial scales must be included in the analysis of the transformation of the urban landscape, including the institutional factors underlying this change. In other words, the dynamic change of urban economic structures and functions should be considered in the light of historical, spatial and socio-institutional changes taking place in the long run and must be theorised as such.

In this perspective, the (local) urban production environment provides both generic resources (capital, labour, etc.) and specific resources (knowledge, skills, institutions) which are very important in order to establish the local economic structure. In turn the local economic structure is the result of a long process of historical accumulation of resources, capital, knowledge and institutions. This is why some regions with important specific assets/resources are more attractive than regions providing only generic resources. Therefore the study of the urban transformation of the Amsterdam and Schiphol regions serves usefully to illustrate the unending processes of destabilisation and re-stabilisation through which regions and territories are institutionalised, demarcated, contested and restructured in particular historical moments.

In what follows, we present the analytical contours of a conceptual framework which will guide us in our study of the spatial-economic transformation of Schiphol and the Schiphol-Amsterdam region during the twentieth century.

2.6.1   *A conceptual framework to study the spatial-economic transformation of urban spaces*

Most recent literature on industrial districts and clusters consider space and trust as key factors of growth.[5] Storper (1997) argues that not only market relations but also traded and untraded interdependencies are important ingredients of regional growth. Untraded interdependencies are based on experience, trust and conventions. According to Storper, firms cannot survive in increasingly uncertain markets without non-market interdependencies. These interdependencies are conditioned by (and result from) the spatial and economic embeddedness of actors in regional structures.

Close to Storper's idea is Boschma and Lambooy's (1999) methodological approach based on the two concepts of routines and path dependency that highlight the spatial forms of increasing returns on the capacity of regions to adjust to increasing variety and uncertainty. According to these authors, such an evolutionary approach to urban space enables co-evolutionary processes between technologies, organisations and territories to unfold.

In the same vein, Lee and Saxenian (2008) suggest a meso-level approach that links rules, routines and institutions to their co-evolutionary outcomes. Three different types of spaces are distinguished by these authors: (1) the technological space; (2) the organisational space, e.g. economic; and (3) the territorial space. Together, these three types of space give a structural coherence to a series of intentional and collective actions that enable us to grasp the multi-faceted nature of co-evolution and hence the complexity of the dynamic of the spatial-economic transformation of urban space.

Drawing on Storper's world of production and in line with the recent study by Lee and Saxenian, we first extend this meso-level context by adding a third type of space which forms the focus of our study, namely the institutional space. Second, we choose a more desegregated level of analysis, which is the local production system of cities, instead of the industrial system at the meso level as in the Lee and Saxenian study. More particularly, the focus of our conceptual framework will be on the institutional space itself and its interconnectedness to other types of space to explain the multi-faceted nature of co-evolution of urban space, and hence the spatial-economic transformation of urban space in general and Schiphol and the Schiphol region in particular.

2.6.2 Co-evolution, local production system and urban economic transformation

One way to address the issue of the spatial-economic change of local urban space is to use the concept of co-evolution, which may replace any simple notion of a single directional impact. The term 'co-evolution' has been used in evolutionary economic geography to denote the mutual reinforcement of interactions between the path-dependent trajectories of various interlinked effects that trigger synergies among spatial-economic, technological and institutional fields in local production systems (Martin and Sunley, 2006). These links may take various forms such as a set of interrelated activities connected by traded and untraded interdependencies, or a wide range of firms, technologies and institutions intertwined into a complex web of networks and structures.

Since the system of fields or environment is composed of many adapting fields, each field of this system may be considered a complex adaptive sub-system in the sense that internal change in one field affects directly or indirectly the (internal) change in other fields. In this sense, the process of interaction between sub-fields of a system is a co-evolutionary process involving temporality (e.g. the process of change takes time) and selection (e.g. choice out of a range of external phenomena to be responded to).

The spatial manifestations of co-evolution have been highlighted in the complex interactions among developmental trajectories (or paths) of territories, technologies, organisations and institutions. In this perspective, two contrasting views could be advanced to clarify this point. The first view, drawing on studies of technological evolution, considers that a trajectory, once selected, may generate self-reinforcing processes that determine the future direction of development, which is, by definition,

beyond the control and the capabilities of actors. The second view, drawing on studies of institutions and institutional change, considers trajectory as both the outcome
and constraint of collective actions of actors (North, 1990).

More generally, the contrast emerging from these two points of view lies in the
scope and direction of a trajectory or path. While some trajectories that are based
on earlier decisions are difficult to modify or transform, other trajectories based
on a set of rules, standards, norms and conventions could be reproduced and
changed to start a new path of development. This last remark is crucial in studying the nature of the relationship between collective arrangements and urban
transformation processes in the sense that collective arrangements can also be
changed, reproduced and remodelled along a specific development trajectory.

In this perspective, an interesting question that should be clarified concerns the
way development trajectories – for example, the spatial-economic transformation
of cities and regions – emerging from the interaction between different types of
spaces converge and reinforce each other in shaping the economic and spatial
landscape of cities and regions.

Recent discussions on agglomerations focus on territorially bounded contexts
in the sense that local specific institutions, particularly appropriate institutional
arrangements, guide collective actions towards successful adaptation in a context
of increasing uncertainty. Accordingly, building strong sets of local institutions
in both the public and private sectors not only reinforces existing agglomerations,
but also reduces uncertainty, lowers transaction costs and improves the interconnectedness of firms within embedded networks and hence increases the competitive position of activities and regions.

When using the term embedded networks, we refer mainly to local networks
ranging from social ties, business networks and production networks to formal and
informal societal associations, and to how these relations promote resource sharing,
information flows and decentralised learning as well as other forms of synergies
and agglomerations (Grabher, 1993; Amin and Cohendet, 1999). Below, we will
elaborate further on this issue by proposing a micro-meso-level context that links
collective arrangements to different types of spaces and to their co-evolutionary
outcomes. Our conceptual framework starts with the premise that locally specific
spatial, economic and institutional contexts are very important in understanding the
spatial and economic development trajectories of cities and regions.

There is no doubt that, for the development to take place, a region must benefit from economies of scale and scope derived from agglomerations as well as
from other benefits stemming from the exploitation of the existing stock of relational assets, or what Storper (1997) has labelled 'untraded interdependencies'.

Figure 2.1 extends Storper's (1997) notion of the 'holy trinity' to suggest a
context comprising four spaces or environments: the technological, the organisa-
tional/economic, the territorial/geographic and the institutional. It gives an overview of the interrelationship between these different types of environments/
spaces at different levels of scale.

It is worth mentioning that the concept of environment or space in economic
theory is very diffuse. It is used here as a matter of geographical location where

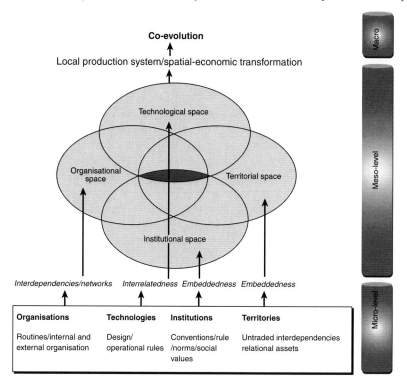

Figure 2.1 Coevolution of urban space: a micro/meso level.
Source: adapted and extended from Storper (1997) and Lee and Saxenian (2008, p. 60).

the four types of environments or spaces are acting simultaneously to influence the behaviour of (economic) actors, the institutional arrangements and the physical structures of locations.

Because people and actors are 'embedded' in their physical environment, we use the concept of embeddedness to denote the idea that economic actors do not only base their behaviour on information about prices and quantities, but also on other non-market relations, like norms, trust, social habit and social values (Granovetter, 1985).

The emphasise in this study will be on the micro-meso units of analysis in the sense that our focus will be on the role and evolution of market and non-market interdependencies underpinning the collective arrangements that sketch the evolutionary process of territorial, economic and institutional environments (Nelson and Winter, 1982).

The technological space

The technological space refers to the technological opportunities that may either guide or constrain the innovative capacity of firms and sectors and, therefore, determine which technology and technological innovations will ultimately be adopted.

Technological innovations, whether at firm or sectoral level, may be conceptualised in terms of a learning process which leads to various technological capabilities and, hence, to the economic success of cities and regions. Silicon Valley and the Third Italy are typical examples of these successful regions.

Note, however, that in the spatial context of an economic system, locational changes and changes in the economic structure and spatial patterns of urban space caused by the evolution of technology and markets are most frequent. The history of industrialised countries shows clear evidence of such dramatic shifts in economic structure and urban growth during the nineteenth century as a result of major technological innovations, especially in transport and infrastructure.

At the firm level, there exists a high level of uncertainty because the production environment in which firms operate is complex and unstable, and the information that is needed is not often freely available and readily accessible. This is the reason why the search process for new technologies is likely to be directed to routinised and familiar technologies and markets rather than adopting superior alternatives which deviate from existing routines, e.g. technology (Nelson and Winter, 1982). This applies also to the competition between new and existing technologies such as, for example, between the standard VCR recorder and the newer DVD recorder. Arthur (1994) shows that small and unpredictable arbitrary events may lead to the adoption of a new technology which rules out other outcomes, e.g. technologies. This is due to the mechanisms that lie behind increasing returns which generate lock-in and path dependency.

Dosi (1982) has proposed the notion of technological trajectory to stress the importance of history when describing the evolutionary nature of the innovative behaviour of firms, which he considers to evolve along specific trajectories based on technological and economic principles.

The organisational/economic space

The economic space evolves from organisational routines of production and exchange processes that are linked by interdependencies or networks at the regional, national and global scale. In this sense, the economic space is embedded in a regional spatial context for the simple reason that firms and organisations are 'context-dependent' and 'path-dependent'. This conception of organisational space is closely related to the French Groupe de recherche européen sur les milieux innovateurs (GREMI) (Aydalot, 1986; Camagni, 1991) who refer explicitly to the role of path-dependency in explaining the spatial clustering of vertically disintegrated firms in specific regions in Europe (e.g. Third Italy) and the United States (e.g. Silicon Valley).

Indeed, in many economic sectors but more specifically in the industry sector, the change in the technological space caused a shift in the organisational space. For example, after the Second World War, the organisation of the production system has shifted from the mass production or Fordist system to a more flexible production system (Piore and Sabel, 1984) in which flexibility and specialisation of vertically disintegrated firms have replaced the vertically integrated mass production firms. Flexible specialisation enables firms to achieve higher economies of scale and gain in competitiveness in an era of increased globalisation and internationalisation of economies. Furthermore, the post-Fordist production system has been resistant to external shocks and volatile economic cycles, as many studies have shown for the case of localised industrial clusters. On the one hand, the advantage of flexible specialisation is that firms with fewer resources have been able to specialise in specific components to reap economies of scale at the level of the whole industry. On the other hand, vertical and horizontal specialisation of firms facilitates the rapid transmission of information regarding product, market and process specifications between firms as well as knowledge spillovers, especially when firms are spatially clustered within the same region. In this case, information and knowledge become highly formalised, which gives this production system its essential character: specialisation, flexibility and economies of scale that accrue to territorially bounded industries.

The territorial/geographical space

The territorial space may be conceptualised as a stable homogenous entity in terms of collective knowledge, institutional structures and social conventions (Storper, 1997). Urban economic literature pays more attention to the potential effects of economic processes on the spatial structure, particularly the location preferences of firms and households, when explaining the processes behind the spatial-economic developments of cities. However, the territorial space is formed around a regulation system and evolves from institutional arrangements providing the embeddedness for economic actions. According to regulation theory, 'regulation' refers to a historically specific institutional regime for coordinating, stabilising and reproducing socio-economic relations, particularly the legal forms of financial management, labour relations and competition (Boyer, 1990). Economic geographers have extended this framework to include a wide variety of locally specific formal and informal institutions.

In addition to changes in the technological and economic spaces, a restructuring process takes place at the level of the territorial space in terms of territorial order or hierarchy that shapes the relationship between the core and the peripheral regions or between cities and their hinterlands. For example, during the 1960s and 1970s, most economic activities were concentrated in core cities but since the 1980s, a delocalisation movement of industrial firms and other activities took place from the city centre to suburban areas and to the peripheral regions, often in the proximity of infrastructural networks, e.g. highway corridors, or the border regions.

The suburbanisation process of jobs and activities was followed by an increased deconcentration of population to new suburban centres, which resulted in an increase in commuting flows between urban centres and regions. As a result, the urban system hierarchy shifted towards a more polynuclear urban system or network city system where the city region became the new urban centre of the urban system.

The institutional space

The institutional space may be considered a dynamic and complex structured set of institutional and collective arrangements influencing the organisation of firms and markets and the social, political and cultural systems of cities and regions.

In order to understand the meaning and role of the institutional space in the urban development process, a more dynamic conception of the institutional space is needed. In the analysis of the spatial-economic transformation of urban space, special focus should be given to the way in which different groups of actors and institutions are related to each other, to the coordination between actors (firms, individuals, developers, local governments, etc.) and to the role and nature of institutional arrangements in stimulating the growth of cities and regions.

More specifically, this conception of institutional space relates the strategies and interests of actors to the material resources, institutional rules and organising ideas which, together, trigger the cumulative process of agglomeration. However, this logic remains virtual if institutions and institutional arrangements do not permit their effective running, e.g. the ways through which individuals and institutions (public and private) plan and manage their common affairs.

From the categorisation of different spaces as outlined above, an examination of the nature and forms of the interrelationships between the four categories of environment or space, especially the relationship between the institutional, economic and territorial spaces, represents the focus of our analytical framework, which is built around the concepts of co-evolution, interdependencies, embeddedness and collective arrangements. When these four spaces are put together in the meso-level context, e.g. the local production system, it becomes possible to clarify the underlying forces explaining the role and importance of institutional and collective arrangements for coordinating evolutionary processes in a single space and/or at the junctures of two or more spaces. In this perspective, our analytical approach may be considered as tentatively connecting various theoretical and empirical works centred around the issue of the transformation of spatial structure and urban patterns of cities and regions. More specifically, the main aim of our study is a re-reading of the spatial and economic changes of urban areas from an institutional perspective in light of various attempts that have been made so far by several authors such as, among others, Storper (1997), Scott (1988) and Lambooy and Moulaert (1996). In following these authors, who borrow some key concepts from new institutional economics to explain the spatial and economic transformation of cities and regions, we believe that this conceptual approach is of great relevance when examining the relationships between institutional, economic and territorial space and taking into account the following three elements of analysis: (1) the identification of agents and institutions involved in urban development processes, their different goals, visions/ideologies and power; (2) the nature of the interactions between diverse agents and institutions and the kinds of constraints they impose on each other; (3) the effects of these interactions on the spatial and economic development processes of cities and regions (Krabben and Lambooy, 1993).

In the case study of Schiphol and the Schiphol region, for example, the form of governance relating actors and institutions derives from various tied institutionalised (formal and informal) arrangements, such as norms, values, trust, reciprocity and reputation, that facilitate coordination and cooperation among actors.

In addition, state intervention through a variety of industrial and economic policies and spatial planning policies not only stimulates the development of economic activities and industries, but also governs the rules that shape the market and non-market coordination mechanisms.

We are particularly interested in how coordination mechanisms take place between actors in localised production systems organised around territorial, economic and institutional spaces. Each of these categories of space is organised around a set of rules, routines or norms, providing the platform for the coordination of collective actions therein. For instance, collaboration among local actors or a group of pioneers and the coordination of their collective efforts may give rise to collective arrangements that set in motion co-evolutionary processes along a specific trajectory. According to North (1990), the orchestration of collective efforts (arrangements) is mediated through various institutions, where actors can exercise their power to mobilise resources and put coordination mechanisms into use.

Note, however, that there is a variety of locally and regionally based institutions supporting coordination and collaboration agreements between actors and organisations, including government, local and regional agencies, local business organisations, societal organisations and so on. Each institution has its own coordination mechanisms and specific actors associated with it.

2.7 Summary and conclusions

The emergence of the nebula city in the contemporary urban system can be approached from different theoretical perspectives. However, because the evolution of urban systems is based on incremental and sometimes radical changes in economic, territorial and socio-institutional structures of cities, the focus of the analysis should then be oriented towards theories describing the processes of urbanisation and urban change occurring in different environments or spaces and at various spatial scale levels.

Today, there exists a large and rich literature treating the causes and mechanisms leading to the emergence and growth of cities and regions. Most of the studies conducted so far stress on the one hand the spatial and economic impact of continuous processes of specialisation, differentiation, complementarities, organisation and coordination of spatial and economic networks, and on the other hand the restructuring effects of spatial, institutional and economic relationships within and between cities and regions.

Various theoretical approaches and models have been developed within the fields of urban and regional economics to explain the territorial and economic transformation and growth of cities. However, in this chapter, we have focused on theories that we consider most relevant to our study concerning the spatial and economic transformation of Schiphol and the Schiphol-Amsterdam region.

These are: the traditional monocentric city model and the polycentric city model describing the rise and change of urban forms or urban systems, (sub)urbanisation and urban sprawl theories, the theory of agglomeration economies and the theory of networks.

The first theoretical approach concerns the theoretical studies of traditional and modern urban models. These urban models are crucial to an understanding of the basic sources of changes in the urban patterns and economic functions of cities. The monocentric city model is based on the combined effects of lower transport costs, increased incomes and accessibility to residents (e.g. land costs and land rents, and commuting costs) as explanatory elements of the spatial (de)concentration of population and employment in cities. Together, these effects give rise to the traditional hierarchical urban system dominated by larger cities and various dependent small and medium cities.

In contrast, the modern version of the polycentric city model considers the spatial distribution of economic activities and the variation in labour costs (e.g. wages and productivities) between locations as major determinant factors of the formation of new urban forms, e.g. secondary employment centres.

Both city models can easily be related to the theory of agglomeration economies to explain the shift of the urban system from the monocentric to the polycentric form. These two city models are implicitly relying on the assumption that the interaction between (some) centripetal and centrifugal forces are crucial in creating clusters of economic activities within a city or region.

The second strand of theories presented in this chapter, which is complementary to the theories of the evolution of systems of cities and urban forms, concerns the theories of urbanisation and urban sprawl of cities. These two theories use various common explanatory variables to explain the growth of cities in relation to suburbanisation and urban sprawl, such as the shift in industrial composition of production, technological changes, transport costs, dynamic of migration of population and firms, etc.

Urban sprawl theory explains suburbanisation and the emergence of secondary cities by the shift in the balance of spatial densities of household, production and employment. In this sense, the process of suburbanisation takes place mainly through a continuous sprawl of jobs, households and activities, which tend to decrease in the traditional city centre and increase in suburban areas or secondary cities. In addition, special attention has been given to complementarities and the competition between urban centres within the metropolitan regions.

The third strand of theories concerns the theory of agglomeration economies. The basic argument of agglomeration economies is that spatial concentration of activities in a particular locality is strongly related to increasing returns to scale or externalities accruing from increasing specialisation, variety and differentiation of economic activities. Note that the effects of agglomeration economies are not uniform and depend on the size and scale of the geographical space where these effects are studied. The benefits of agglomeration economies are much stronger at a higher geographical scale than at the city level for example, simply because of the existence of positive net effects from the synergy with external economies, e.g. differentiation and specialisation, and advantages from the increase in economic relations.

The theory of agglomeration economies can be used in combination with the first two theories to clarify various dimensions of the spatial and economic changes of cities and regions. The economic and spatial dimensions of agglomerations involve the concepts of specialisation and differentiation, clustering and spatial proximity but also a socio-institutional dimension in terms of the creation of a specific institutional environment that facilitates the economic growth of cities and regions.

Close to the theory of agglomeration economies, the theory of networks further enlarges and enriches the analysis of both localised and non-localised networks of firms and their contribution to the economic growth of cities. Conceptually, these two theories can be related in a more systematic way by considering the spatial linkages of firms in terms of the locational advantages of proximity that result in economies of scale, scope and learning, the intensive relations in networks, externalities and non-market relations. In this sense, networks may lead to similar external benefits to those that arise from agglomeration, and together they offer powerful theoretical concepts that can be used to explain the rise and development of hierarchical networks of cities in a polycentric urban system.

In addition, networks and agglomeration can be approached from an institutional perspective. This can be done, first, by distinguishing physical networks from economic networks in agglomerations, and second, by introducing the concepts of transaction costs and collective/institutional arrangements in localised networks and spatial agglomerations to explain the spatial organisation of activities and the geographical transformation of cities and regions.

We believe that a unified theoretical approach linking the institutional aspects to the theories of agglomeration economies, urban sprawl and networks offers the basic explanatory variables for the spatial and economic transformation of cities and regions.

First, one of the main arguments put forward in this chapter is to link the notion of agglomeration economies to the concept of proximity in its different dimensions, e.g. spatial, economic and institutional. The aim is then to study the spatial implications of localisation and urbanisation economies in a system of city networks, and to stress the importance of the potential local resources of a territory and the economies of interactions in stimulating local networks through collaboration and coordination between local actors.

Second, special attention should be given to the non-market interactions and institutional proximity in order to identify and explain the main factors and actors triggering the mechanisms of change and (dis)continuity of spatial and economic development of cities and regions. In this perspective, the creation, development and exploitation of local production resources in the context of institutional proximity is strongly dependent on the ability and efficiency of existing institutions and institutional arrangements to facilitate market and non-market relations between local actors, and ultimately to stimulate growth. In turn, institutional proximity is a precondition to the emergence of collective arrangements and offers an adequate environment in which collaboration and coordination of collective actions may benefit the whole community, e.g. cooperative agreements between private actors, between public and private actors, etc.

Therefore our conception of the spatial and economic transformation of cities and regions is based on the idea that considers the territorial space to be configured as a mosaic of functions and arrangements that shape the economic structure and urban patterns of cities and regions. Change in and continuity of this configuration may result in an equivalent change in urban patterns and the economic position of cities.

More specifically, we propose a conceptual framework based on the concepts of co-evolution, embeddedness, routines and path-dependency to highlight changes in the spatial forms of cities and their capacity to adjust to increasing variety and uncertainty. This conceptual framework is largely inspired by the work of Lee and Saxenian (2008) and Storper (1997) who suggest a meso-level approach that links rules, routines and institutions to their co-evolutionary outcomes.

However, to grasp the complexity of the evolutionary processes of spatial-economic transformation of urban space, a distinction is made between four conceptions of space or environment: the technological space, the organisational space (i.e. the economic space), the territorial space and the institutional space. Our goal is to focus on the mutual reinforcement of interactions between these fields in order to explain the multi-faceted nature of co-evolution among spatial, economic and institutional fields within a local production system, and ultimately the spatial-economic transformation of urban space in general and Schiphol and the Schiphol region in particular.

It is within the territorial or geographical space that these environments are acting simultaneously in influencing the behaviour of (economic) actors, stimulating the rise of various forms of interrelated activities and arrangements and the physical structures of locations. When these four spaces are put together, it becomes possible to clarify, at the meso level, the main forces explaining the evolutionary processes of transformation in a single space and/or at the juncture of two or more spaces.

3 Institutional foundations of spatial-economic changes

A theoretical framework

3.1 Introduction

Regions and cities may be conceived as specific places where population, resources, information, technologies and opportunities, constituting the structural aspects of relationships, are concentrated. The wealth and prosperity of these specific locations result from a wide variety of accumulated agglomeration advantages and opportunities that permit access and transfer of locally bounded resources.

In the long term, it is likely that economic agents located in different regions will develop distinct characteristics, institutional arrangements and routines that result in increased differentiation between regions in term of the mix of economic activities, the form and nature of institutions, organisational forms and other place-bounded resources. Therefore one may argue that the differences in economic performances of cities and regions result from the differences in their geographical and institutional characteristics, technological variations and economic structure. Consequently, urban forms and patterns of cities and regions follow different logics and development paths, although the basic principles of urbanisation and urban development show strong similarities between regions at the international level. In addition, the learning processes and search and knowledge flows tend to be highly localised. These last aspects reflect a certain familiarity with the existing knowledge base, technological interdependencies and network relations. In this sense, the regions that develop competitive locational characteristics and an appropriate institutional environment that are more adapted to the needs of new activities have a strong competitive advantage compared to other regions.

Despite increasing interest during the last few decades in the historical and spatial peculiarities of institutions and institutional arrangements for understanding socio-economic states of localities, regions and nations, few studies have surveyed in a systematic way the theoretical and empirical works of existing strands of institutionalist approaches to spatial economic analysis. Filling this gap can only be accomplished by articulating an eclectic mix of methodologies and theoretical ideas from existing institutionalist literature that permits the deployment of a framework that is suitable for the analysis of spatial and economic changes in cities and metropolitan areas. In this chapter, we sketch the main contours of this eclectic mix of theoretical ideas that will help us to develop a suitable conceptual framework for analysing the spatial and economic transformation of urban areas in general and Schiphol and the Schiphol-Amsterdam region in particular.

Indeed, rethinking the spatial and economic transformation of metropolitan areas requires a fundamental understanding of the nature, role and importance of existing institutions and institutional arrangements, especially in economic and spatial planning domains, and their underlying interaction within functional and territorially organised patterns. This is a different institutional dynamics approach to the spatial and economic transformation of urban spaces than existing institutional deterministic approaches that consider the spatial-economic change of cities and regions as the result of pure socio-economic dynamics governed by the principles of the market, e.g. production and distribution, innovation, organisation and coordination. The application of this institutional dynamics approach aims at understanding the determinant factors of change in urbanisation patterns and the urban economic structure of cities and regions. It takes institutional and collective arrangements as the main cornerstones of the institutionalist analysis of urban forms and the economic structure of cities and regions.

More specifically, our conceptual framework is centred around the concept of collective arrangements as the coupling elements of various factors and processes determining the spatial and economic metamorphosis of Schiphol and the Schiphol region and their development into an urban nebula. The argument presented here is that an urban nebula may be considered a heterogeneous and fragmented urban configuration emerging from (and governed by) different, often contradictory, collective arrangements which are specific in time and space. The coherence of the internal structure of an urban nebula is determined by conscious planned and unplanned collective interventions, conventions and regulations reflected in economic and planning policies, planning designs, investment policies, perceptions and the daily rituals of using public space. In other word, the nebula city is a spatial phenomenon formed by different layers: the morphological, economic, political and socio-cultural. Moreover, the spatial configuration of the nebula city is supported and sustained by sets of collective arrangements which are deeply embedded in the local institutional environment.

From the above, we may conceive of collective arrangements as a set of resources, technologies, ideas, knowledge and factors that result from the interactions between different actors influencing the development trajectory of the nebula city.[1]

In the case of Schiphol airport and region, for example, collective arrangements consist of the relationships that Schiphol maintain(ed) with the representatives of the local, regional and national politics, KLM and other airline companies (Air France) and various economic sectors at the local, regional and international level, e.g. transport and logistics, project development companies, private firms, etc.

In the long term, the initial collective arrangement may develop into various sub-arrangements, each with its own logic of development and trajectory in which different actors may be involved. This natural and logical development of collective arrangements may lead to the emergence and persistence of structural problems of governance and coordination.

Note that collective arrangements have cognitive aspects and in this sense they may be conceived as carriers of collective representations and perceptions of the world. In our case study, this concerns mainly the meaning of the urban nebula as a mental horizon (e.g. capacity to find solutions to concrete problems) and a conceptual universe (e.g. thoughts, culture and paradigms). Examples of such cognitive aspects of collective arrangements are visions expressed by actors about the future development of Schiphol and the region that are often concretised into spatial planning concepts and designs, marketing concepts and PR campaigns, etc. All of these aspects may have direct and/or indirect impact on the decision-making process concerning the future development of Schiphol and the region.

The organisation of this chapter is as follows. Section 3.2 deals with the institutional environment, where we present and discuss the meaning, definition, role, formation and change of institutions and institutional arrangements as presented by various institutionalist approaches. The aim of this section is to position the concept of collective arrangements in the discussion about the role and importance of the institutional environment – and particularly the notions of institutions – in spatial and economic analysis. Most of the ideas that we discuss in this chapter are drawn from existing theoretical approaches to institutions and institutional arrangements that deal with a variety of features of the institutional environment within the market economy, the allocation systems and their governance.

Next, we review and discuss the relevance of the most important strands of institutional theories to economic analysis, strands which we consider most valuable in studying the economic and spatial transformation of cities and regions. The main goal of this survey is to identify the most important elements that may help us to understand the sources, nature and effects that institutions and institutional arrangements may have on the transformation processes of urban space.

The following strands of institutionalist economic approaches are reviewed in this section: the historical German School approach to institutions and institutional arrangements; the Old American Institutionalist School; the (neo) new-institutional economic approach; the regulation approach; and, finally, the sociological institutional approach.

Based on this wide-ranging and rich theoretical background, we then develop a conceptual framework centred around the concept of collective arrangements addressing both the influence of the institutional environment on interactions among actors and the influence of actors and collective arrangements on the spatial-economic environment (section 3.7). This framework will enable us to capture the main actors and factors that affect the process of the spatial and economic transformation of Schiphol and the Schiphol region during the twentieth century.

In the sections 3.8 and 3.9, we extend this conceptual framework to the study of various governance regimes with respect to urban regeneration and the spatial development of urban spaces. Furthermore, a multi-actor, multi-level approach to urban governance is presented. Section 3.10 then concludes.

3.2 Institutions, institutional arrangements and urban economic transformation

Since its infancy at the turn of the twentieth century, institutional economics has been developed into a rich stream of economic thought. Today, it comprises a wide range of theoretical approaches, all of which highlight the important role institutional structure plays in the economy, and adopt institutions as the centre-piece of economic analysis (Miller, 1978; Matthews, 1986; Langlois, 1986; Hodgson, 1988; Rutherford, 1994; Eggertsson, 1990; Nelson *et al.*, 2001).

Powell and DiMaggio (1991) provided a comprehensive survey of institutions and institutional analysis in economics and sociology, while Hall and Taylor (1996) surveyed the varied meanings of institutions in political science. In this chapter, we review and discuss most of the existing institutional theories by following the line that have been charted by these surveys, although our focus will be on institutionalist approaches in economics rather than other scientific disciplines.

Most reviewers of institutions identify the new institutional writings as attempts to enrich the assumptions about human and organisational behaviour contained in neoclassical theory, for example that economic actors behave rationally and choose actions that are appropriate to achieve their objectives, given the opportunities and constraints they may face (Eggertsson, 1990).

However, there is another stream of institutionalist thought that rejects the neoclassical idea of bounded rationality. Their argument is that the belief systems and preferences of agents need to be explained, not assumed or taken as given. Therefore human rationality needs to be understood as a social and cultural phenomenon (Hodgson, 1999). A similar divide can be found in political science between rational choice institutionalism and historical institutionalism (see Hall and Taylor, 1996), while the dominant position in sociology is that beliefs and values are socially constructed, at least to some degree.

More generally, there exists a variety of different traditions of institutional analysis in economics, sociology and political science that are concerned with the structures that induce and govern coordination and collective decision-making. Very often, a reference is made to the pioneering theoretical work of the American institutional (economics) tradition, especially the works of John R. Commons (1934) on transactions and Thorstein Veblen (1899/1919) on institutions. Both authors define institutions in terms of widely common and predictable patterns of behaviour in a society, including shared 'habits of thought' as well as actions.

Close to the tradition of the American institutional economics is the long-standing theoretical legacy of German and Austrian institutional analysis, which is much closer to Veblen than Commons.

A close look at the existing literature on institutions and institutional change reveals a wide range of definitions given to the concept of the institution, which leads to some confusion about its precise meaning. For example, the line separating the concept of the institution and the concept of culture is very fuzzy in sociological and anthropological analysis in the sense that both concepts are used to describe the same phenomenon or subject (Nelson *et al.*, 2001: 36). Sociologists argue that the patterns and behaviour of the organisation (firm) reflect the relevant business culture (Powell and DiMaggio, 1991). Scott (1991), for example, adds the notion of 'symbol systems' as part of the concept of institutions.

From the economic point of view, one may identify different categories of economic institutional approaches that have set the research agenda at the beginning of 1980s, building on the earlier works of the Historical German School (especially the work of Schmöller), the old American Institutionalism and/or the work of Coase on transaction costs.

A major difference between these approaches lies in the theoretical foundation of institutions, the choice of specific analytical tools and the applied methodology to investigate institutions. Indeed, while North and his followers made great efforts to integrate economic theory into economic history, those affiliated to the comparative institutional approach, for example, not only rely on historical information but make also extensive use of game theory as well.

A good starting point for discussion is to define institutions and investigate their meaning and application by each of these different institutionalist approaches.

3.2.1 Institutions

Broadly defined, institutions are (collective) arrangements that structure repeated interactions among actors and between actors and their (natural) environment. In other words, institutions are created and designed to structure and regulate the way people think, act and react to various changes taking place in specific time (historical context) and space (cities, regions, etc.). Institutions interact mutually with individuals in a dynamic way in the sense that they affect the actions and behaviour of individuals and emerge from, or are created by, human actions (Frey, 1990: 445). While institutions shape and constrain the strategies and options of actors, they determine largely the outcome of those actors' strategies and their practices. In doing so, they empower some actors and perspectives at the expense of others. Conversely, institutions can be challenged, altered or reproduced by actors by means of (strategic) interactions taking place at the economic and political levels.

However, institutions and institutional arrangements are unlikely to change in the short term, with the exception of situations when unexpected external shocks may take place, such as wars and revolutions for example. In this sense, both institutions and institutional arrangements are regarded as relatively stable parameters.

Institutionalist theories have used the concept of the institution in two ways: some institutionalists use institutions to stress the habitual and *routinised mode of institutions*, e.g. the idea that people's expectations, behaviour and interactions are shaped by and reflect both the humanly devised rules and regularities of behaviour. Others use institutions to stress the role and nature of institutions as *rules*, *patterns* or *procedures* that structure behaviour and interactions. These rules can be informal – norms, habits and customs – or formal – written laws, regulations and standards (Hall and Taylor, 1996; Scharpf, 1997).

In economics, broader notions of economic institutions are used to encompass concepts of rules, beliefs, norms, equilibria[2] and strategies or organisations and/or regularities of behaviour[3] (Greif, 1994). For example, Ullmann-Margalit (1977) and Coleman (1990) have articulated an 'institution as norms' approach, while Commons (1924), North (1990) and Ostrom (1986, 1990) define institutions by means of a rules (of the game) approach. Rules develop into conventions, social norms, private contracts and government laws that determine the decision-making mechanisms involving interacting actors.

These different conceptions of institutions offer an institutional explanation of observed regularities in the patterns of human behaviour. An examination of the interactions between individuals in the real world shows that the configuration of rules, norms and shared strategies influence the choices of individuals and that institutional configurations are nested within enforced regulations.

3.2.2 A variety of definitions

A key element of institutional analysis is the identification of common aspects of the various definitions given to institutions and the exploration of their relationships from different perspectives.

Veblen, for example, defines institutions as a set of norms and ideals that are difficult to reproduce through habituation by individuals. He states that institutions are

> in substance, prevalent habits of thought with respect to particular relations and particular functions of the individual and of the community; and the scheme of life, which is made up of the aggregate of institutions in force at a given time or at a given point in the development of any society. (Veblen, 1919: Chapter VIII)

Similarly, Hamilton (1932: 84) defines institutions as 'a way of thought or action of some prevalence and permanence, which is embedded in the habits of a group or the customs of a people', while Hodgson (1988: 10) defines an institution as a '… social organization which, through the operation of tradition, custom or legal constraint, tends to create durable and routinized patterns of behaviour'.

Schotter (1981: 11) considers institutions as general '… regularities in social behaviour … agreed to by all members of society', while Bush (1987: 1076) defines them as sets of '… socially prescribed patterns of correlated behaviour'. From the above, then, institutions are presented as habits and social organisations operating through traditions, customs and legal constraints that shape patterns of behaviour.

In following Hayek (1960), other institutionalists have emphasised the constraining character of institutions as a device to cope with uncertainty or ignorance. The constitutional element of this device is made up of the rules regulating the conduct and behaviour of individuals (Hodgson, 2006: 4).

Commons (1934: 69), defines institutions as '… collective action in control of individual action' and recognises at the same time that collective action may involve the strengthening of 'liberation and expansion of individual action' (ibid.: 73). In this sense, institutional structures both produce human behaviour, e.g. the (un)intentional and calculative actions of actors, and are produced by it. Thus institutions are shared meanings and practices that structure the actions of individuals and communities (Jessop, 2000).

The manifestation of institutions as a stable set of rules, norms and conventions shaping patterns of behaviour is also stressed by Claude Ménard (1995: 167). According to Ménard, institutions are '… manifested in a long-standing historically determined set of stable, abstract and impersonal rules, crystallized in traditions, customs, or laws, so as to implement and enforce patterns of behavior governing the relationships between separate social constituencies'.

Another definition is given by Scott (1995) who argues that institutions 'consist of cognitive, normative, and regulative structures and activities that provide stability and meaning to social behavior. Institutions are transported by various carriers – cultures, structures, and routines – and they operate at multiple levels of jurisdiction' (Scott, 1995: 33). In the same vein, Greif argues: 'An institution is composed of man-made, non-technological factors and the regularity of behavior they generate. These factors are exogenous to each individual whose behavior they influence' (Greif, 2002a: I.6).

In the tradition of transaction cost theory, Greif (2002a) relates institutions to transactions by arguing that institutions determine the cost of transactions and hence, as argued by Adam Smith, the division of labour, the extent of the market and the resulting efficiency gains from the specialisation of activities. In this respect, Greif relates institutions to institutional development as a result of the functioning of the economic system while North sees them as resulting from the political system. Indeed, and in opposition to Greif, North (1990: 3) considers institutions as '… the rules of the game in a society or […] humanly devised constraints that shape human interaction'.

Matthews (1986: 905) views institutions as 'sets of rights and obligations affecting people in their economic lives', while for Mirowski (1987: 1020) institutions are '… transpersonal rules that endow individual economic actors with the ability to cope with interpretations of action and with change'.

Institutions as 'the rules of the game' mean that all formal rules, including contracts and political and economic rules, and informal norms, e.g. conventions, codes of conduct and norms of behaviour, that individuals conceive to regulate their relationships (through enforcement mechanisms) define the set of existing institutions in a society at a certain point of time. In other words, institutions define and limit the set of choices of economic agents, determine the form of economic organisations and influence economic efficiency. They favour or discourage exchanges and all other forms of interactions, especially those needed for the coordination of economic activities.

The notion of institutions as rules of the game is used often to analyse the nature and level of interactions among individuals when addressing the issues of contractual arrangements and organisational interactions. Such interactions can be voluntary (buyer and seller in the marketplace) or involuntary economic transactions (a dictator and his or her subjects), political (as between parties or a party and its members) or social interactions (such as the relationships between parents and children or neighbours) (Greif, 2002a).

An important distinction in North's theorisation is between institutions (the rules of the game) and organisations (the players) constituted by groups of individuals – such as political, economic, social and educational bodies – bounded by common purposes to achieve certain objectives. More specifically, institutions and organisations are two interdependent entities. Institutions lead to the emergence and evolution of certain organisations and, in turn, these organisations influence how institutions evolve and thus are agents of institutional change.

More generally, the wide array of definitions of institutions makes it difficult to conciliate between the various meanings as to what exactly institutions are. However, the conventional institutionalist literature tends generally to conceptualise institutions as configurations of rules (of the game) and resources either inherited from the past or constructed to solve collective action or decision-making problems (Thelen and Steinmo, 1992).

3.2.3 Role, formation and change of institutions

The variety of definitions of institutions reflects the differences in points of view between the protagonists of institutionalist analysis, which invoke contradictory assumptions regarding human interactions and the functions institutions should fulfil in a society. For example, North (1990: 6) is clear about the major role of institutions in reducing uncertainties, while for Williamson and many others, institutions foster (economic) efficiency. They are the 'means by which order is accomplished in a relation in which potential conflict threatens to undo or upset opportunities to realize mutual gains' (Williamson, 1998: 37).

More generally, two views of institutions may be derived from a reading of institutionalist approaches: one view considers individuals as constrained by existing institutions, while according to the other individuals create institutions to achieve their goals (Greif, 2002a). In both cases, institutions entail rules and conventions that are collectively acknowledged and reproduced. Conventions are what North (1990) would call *informal* and *formal* institutions. Note, however, that there are disagreements within and between new institutionalist approaches about the role of informal and formal rules, norms, procedures, etc., and the significance of the cognitive, as opposed to normative, properties of institutions (see Hall and Taylor, 1996; DiMaggio, 1998; Powell and DiMaggio, 1991).

Formal rules of the game include the political and legal rules and economic rules relative to property rights and contracts. The main role of formal institutions is to facilitate exchanges and cooperation, through the enforcement of contracts and full respect of property rights. Informal institutions include norms of behaviour, tradition, conventions, etc., that serve as codes of conduct structuring the way individuals behave and interact with each other.

One important aspect of institutions is to generate trust for the carrying out of exchanges. North argues in this respect that one of the most important sources of both historical stagnation and underdevelopment is the inability of (some) societies to develop effective and low-cost enforcement mechanisms for contracts and respect for property rights (North, 1990).

Another disagreement between institutionalist theories concerns the way institutions emerge and change over time. North (1990) states that some institutions evolve by themselves while other institutions are deliberately created. In opposition, Hayek (1960) considers the creation of institutions as an unplanned consequence of human action that has influenced their development.

Commons (1924, 1934) recognises the spontaneous rise and development of customs, norms and rules but emphasises at the same time the important role of conscious collective governmental action in resolving conflicts that might arise from such institutions through the law and/or governmental policies.

Beside the difference between institutionalist theories that posit the idea that institutions involve conscious coordinated planning and those that consider institutions as the result of a largely uncoordinated evolutionary process, the question of whether institutions are efficient or not enlarges further the gap between the institutionalist theories (Nelson *et al.*, 2001). North claims that institutions evolved in a way that make them efficient (see Davis and North, 1971; North, 1981). In contrast, other intuitionalists claim that institutions do not need to be – and often are not – efficient. The argument put forward by these authors refers to the existing differences in economic performance across countries as a result of the differences in institutions, particularly efficient institutions.

Concerning the causes of institutional change, institutionalists believe that institutions can change because of endogenous processes, exogenous shocks and/or a combination of both. Central to endogenous institutional change are therefore the dynamics of self-enforcing beliefs and associated behaviour. This view of institutional dynamics considers endogenous institutional change within the context of the heritage of past institutions.

Historical institutionalism analyses endogenous institutional change through positive and negative feedback loops rather than equilibria as in the case of rational choice analysis (Thelen, 1999). By contrast, the sociology of culture stresses the hypothesis that institutions are the concretisation of the way individuals view the world, e.g. institutional order, and in this sense, institutional change corresponds to the change of one representation of the world by another.

Individuals use their perceptions about the world to structure their environment. They do not reproduce the reality, rather they construct systems of classifications to interpret the external environment, which is a human construct of rules, norms and conventions that define the framework of human interaction (North, 2005: 11).

In his recent work, North (2005) place institutions at the centre of economics and economic change because – as he argues – they are the incentive structure of economies (ibid.: VII). The content of institutions can change over time as a result of changes in formal rules and informal norms.

Within the constraints imposed by particular technological or economic configurations, actors can modify institutions to solve new problems, facilitate network-based collective learning or achieve increasing efficiency (Powell, 1996). In contrast, economic change is an ongoing process, guided by the perceptions of the players to produce outcomes that reduce uncertainty and transaction costs. The source of change in the perception of individuals and actors may be exogenous to the economy, but the fundamental source of change is learning.

Economic actors learn in different ways, and the rate of learning determines the speed of economic change, while the kind of learning determines the direction of economic change. In this sense, the learning effects of individuals and organisations and changes in the stock of knowledge are of major importance to the evolution of institutions. In other word, institutional change is likely to happen if there is a shared interpretative framework, e.g. shared knowledge, among actors believing in the urgency of change, which can arise only through the interaction between economic and institutional change (North, 2005: 63).

Although economists are in broad agreement that institutions are important for economic growth, there is disagreement about which institutions and which aspects of institutions are determinants for such growth. The broadly shared view is that institutions influence, or define, the ways in which economic actors behave and transact with each other in a context involving human interactions. Because economic agents are not fully rational and not equally powerful, economic growth cannot be explained only by the functioning of the economic system in terms of information and transactions, coordination processes, modes of communication and modes of governance (Lambooy and Moulaert, 1996).

More recently, there has been an increase in the number of empirical works investigating the relationship between institutions and economic growth. These empirical works involve the measurement of the cost of institutional inefficiency or poor governance by taking proxy measures of transaction costs (Knack and Keefer, 1995; Hall and Jones, 1999; Acemoglu *et al.*, 2001). The primary contribution of this body of empirical work is to demonstrate that institutions do matter for economic development.

Rodrik *et al.* (2002) estimate the respective contributions of institutions, geography and trade in determining income levels around the world. Their results show that the quality of institutions is a determinant in explaining economic development and growth. Similar studies report strong evidence to support the important role of institutions in the organisation of economic activity. However, this body of empirical research suffers from a lack of information on countries' institutional quality, which makes measurement of the quality of institutions difficult.

Knack and Keefer (1995) constructed from the International Country Risk Guide (ICRG) dataset five indexed average variables: rules of law, bureaucratic quality, corruption, risk of expropriation and government repudiation of contracts, for the years 1986–95. Their results showed a positive significant correlation of the ICRG index with growth, even after controlling for other variables such as education, initial income and other variables typically used in growth regressions. Their conclusion supported the idea that institutional environment is a determinant of a country's economic performance.

Using the same index as Knack and Keefer (1995) across 127 countries, Hall and Jones (1999) examined the relationship between institutions, capital accumulation and productivity. Their analysis confirmed once again the existence of a strong relationship between productivity, the quality of institutions and public policies. In particular, countries with favourable policies towards productivity growth and with efficient institutions show the highest productivity levels.

More recently, a different approach was provided by Acemoglu *et al.* (2001), who proposed a theory of institutional diversity among countries that were colonised by European countries.[4] They estimated the impact of institutions on economic performance and focused their attention on the mortality rates expected by European settlers in the colonies between the seventeenth and nineteenth centuries. The authors assumed that the choice of colonisation policy depended upon the value of this rate, and that current institutional patterns and economic outcomes were the result of past patterns and outcomes. They used a sample of 75 countries and regressed current GDP per capita against current institutions, and instrument the latter by settler mortality rates (i.e. they used settler mortality rates as an instrument of [the variable] institutions). The empirical evidence seemed to provide (some) support for the idea that current institutions, inherited from the past, have a significant effect on current income per capita. Their conclusions supported the idea that substantial economic gains may be realised through the improvement of efficient institutions.

In contrast to Acemoglu *et al.* (2001), Mauro (1995) proposed a different empirical approach. He used bureaucratic corruption and efficiency as key indicators of institutional quality and investigated the relationship between institutions and economic growth. He used data from the Business International indexes on corruption and efficiency of the judicial system for 70 countries in the period 1980–3. Again, his results pointed to the existence of a positive relationship between institutions and economic growth. In particular, the results provided clear evidence in favour of the idea that bureaucratic efficiency and political stability stimulate investment and increase economic growth.

In the same vein, Keefer and Shirley (2000) used a panel of 84 countries in the period 1982–94 and investigated the effects of the quality of institutions on the growth of government consumption, public investments and public debt. Their results suggest that macroeconomic policies are insufficient to foster growth.

3.2.4 *Why institutions matter*

In addition to existing divergences in the definition of institutions, there exist also different point of views concerning the question of which and why institutions matter. According to a widespread and accepted idea among economists, institutions matter because they contribute to the solution of problems of coordination, help to promote cooperative behaviour and overcome opportunism, offer many possibilities to internalise externalities and reduce uncertainty. Furthermore, institutions support the formation of social capital and facilitate an efficient use of accumulated collective historical experience of actions which, in turn, affect positively the likelihood of actors to commit to cooperative strategies.

One interesting account of why institutions matter was the structuration approach put forward by Giddens. Giddens (1984) treats institutions as sets of chronically reproduced, deeply sedimented rules and resources that constrain and facilitate social actions and bind them in time and space so that more or less systematic action patterns can be generated and reproduced (Giddens, 1984: 17–25).

Giddens' treatment of institutions presents two key innovative ideas. First, he explicitly introduces time and space into the analysis of institutions. Second, he connects institutions to specific forms of power and domination over individuals and their actions (ibid.; Jessop, 2000).

Furthermore, institutions do matter because of their role and capacity to select behaviours, without determining the course of action (see March and Olsen, 1996: 251–5). This implies that actors are free to choose a predetermined path for their actions. In this way, actors not only engage in action within a given institutional matrix, but can, in certain circumstances, deliberately reconfigure institutions and the resulting matrix.

3.2.5 Institutions and path dependence

Path dependency describes the process by which a specific event in the past induces a chain of subsequent events according to a deterministic pattern. In general, the concept of path dependency implies that 'events occurring at an earlier point in time will affect events occurring at a later point in time' (Djelic and Quack, 2007: 161).

Institutional path dependency involves the phenomenon that previous institutions are locked-in in earlier stages of the policy process and affect present and future decision-making. In this sense, historical institutional legacies may limit the possibilities of institutional innovation. However, social, political and economic forces could intervene in current conjunctures and actively rearticulate institutions so that new trajectories become possible.

Critical junctures related to institutional change refer to moments when significant shifts open up the possibility of moving along a new development path. In this sense, the formation and evolution of institutional arrangements may be affected by different patterns of interactions between ongoing social, political and economic processes (Thelen, 1999: 388). In turn, the complex sets of interdependent variables that are rooted in institutional arrangements influence the development path of institutions and consequently of other domains, e.g. the economic, geographical, social and cultural domains, spatial planning and environmental policy, etc. (Hall and Soskice, 2001).

From a spatial perspective, path-dependency and lock-in effects are crucial elements in understanding urban processes and forms of economic and social relations. Key to this understanding is the spatial-temporal inheritance of institutions and institutional arrangements. By that, we simply mean that arrangements and institutions have a definite spatial and temporal extension. They emerge in specific places and at specific times, and operate at one or more particular scales with specific temporal horizons of action (North, 2005).

3.3 Are institutions conventions, norms or (collective) arrangements?

According to Boltanski and Thévenot (1991), conventions are the analytical framework through which actors perceive, analyse and solve their problems. They facilitate cooperation and contractual exchange between actors. Therefore conventions may be conceived as equivalent to collective arrangements. This is the viewpoint that we adopt in this study.

In a market economy, institutions act as conventions that have evolved in time and have not been a priori deliberately designed. Think, for example, of the contractual arrangements that relate buyers and sellers in specific markets. Although markets may work more smoothly when property rights are clearly defined and enforced by law, there are many other cases where contractual arrangements persist without any external support or intervention. As Greif (2002b) shows, many of the institutional foundations of exchange are not provided by the state, but are organised through private institutions, especially in cases involving asymmetric information, incomplete contracts, complexity and the cost of and time for resolving conflicts through legal procedures. Note that this idea is different from that of Hayek, who argues that conventions, supported by moral beliefs, create order in a free (market) society because people believe that they ought to keep to these conventions.

In following Hayek's idea, Orléan (2004) used the concept of 'collective belief' to analyse conventions. He made a distinction between 'shared belief' and 'common belief'. These two notions of collective belief refer strictly to individual beliefs. They become collective belief only when they are accepted and adopted by all individuals in a society.

An interesting interpretation of conventions in the economy is given by the French 'théorie des conventions' which focuses on the analysis of concrete forms of coordination, the plurality of possible arrangements and their positive and normative evaluation (Favereau, 2002; Orléan, 2004; Dupuy *et al.*, 1989). The protagonists of the conventions approach consider individuals as making up part of collective objects such as institutions or situations. The main hypothesis of this theoretical approach is that market exchange between actors is dependent on constitutive conventions that structure individual actions (Dupuy *et al.*, 1989: 142). Consequently, conventions are the results of cognitively coordinated individual and collective actions, e.g. depend strongly on existing arrangements, values and beliefs.

If conventions are the result of deliberate collective choice, we might expect that inefficient conventions would simply be rejected by actors. However, because conventions evolve, they do not necessarily need to be chosen. A convention starts to evolve once the majority of individuals adopts and uses it rather than any other convention. This sets in motion a self-reinforcing process resulting in the establishment of this convention as the most successful one and the elimination of other alternative conventions. In the long term, the convention becomes the rule when people come to believe that they ought to act in a way that maintains established patterns of behaviour or rules. This is also the viewpoint expressed by

David Hume (1740: Bk 3, part 2, sec. 1–3) who explained how conventions can become norms. Hume argued that rules of property are conventions that evolve spontaneously; if we are to explain why these rules take the particular forms they do, we must look to 'the imagination' rather than to 'reason and public interest'.[5] The mechanism that can transform conventions into norms or rules is the human desire for the approval of others (Sugden, 1989: 95).

Ostrom (1998) extends this idea further by giving another interpretation of norms. Ostrom believes that norms are learned in social milieus. That is why they vary substantially across cultures, between individuals of the same culture and between historical periods. Ostrom (2000) compiled an analysis of the evolution of social norms and spontaneous cooperative behaviour. According to her, the development of social norms may be considered as shared understandings about actions that are obligatory, permitted or forbidden.

Contextual factors, such trust, reputation and reciprocity, are the key attributes of human behaviour that influence the establishment of long-term cooperation and the adoption of norms reflecting internal values (Ostrom, 1998). In this sense, trust, reciprocity and reputation feed one another and help to explain why repeated interactions within the group and face-to-face communication between individuals and actors have major effects on economic performance. Investment and cooperative participation in such networks of relations become more profitable in the presence of closure and appropriability (Ostrom, 1998).

When individuals reciprocate each other, there exists for them an incentive to acquire a reputation by keeping to their promises and carrying out actions whose benefits in the long term will outweigh the short-run costs. This mechanism allows individuals to establish mutual beneficial relationships that are based on trust. In addition, trust lowers transaction costs in the sense that trust reduces the cost of contractual arrangements, i.e. resources spent on contractual safeguards, litigation and protection from violations of property rights. The sociological institutional theories have elaborated extensively on this issue by using the concept of social capital and trust in economic transactions.

Following this institutionalist approach, developing trust in an environment in which others are trustworthy may be considered a major asset for economic growth (Fukuyama, 1995; Gambetta, 1988; Putnam, 1993). However, Greif (1994) is clearly in favour of the importance and superiority of formal institutional arrangements and formal institutions over informal institutions in strengthening trust because they support the openness of organisations towards new opportunities in trade and towards new members. In short, Greif considers formal institutions as essential for economic performance and believes that networks based on informal institutional arrangements are inefficient in the long term.

3.4 Theoretical approaches to institutionalism: a brief review

In social science, institutions evoke different readings according to the domain or approach of the research. Various forms of institution exist when analysing institutions, institutional order, conventions and rules, and organisations (Boyer and

Saillard, 2002: 531–50). Hall and Taylor (1996) provide a comprehensive survey of the literature on institutional theories in social science. Three theories of institutionalism dominate the mainstream schools of thought: the historical approach, the rational choice approach and the sociological approach. These different schools of thought have differences and similarities in interpreting the emergence and persistence of institutions (Thelen, 1999: 371). The differences concern the issues of theoretical versus empirical work, the exogenous or endogenous formation of institutions, micro-foundation versus macro-historical research, and finally the difference between a functional and a historical view of institutions (for a detailed survey of these three institutional theories, see Hall and Taylor, 1996; Thelen, 1999).

In economics, institutions are now widely recognised as determinant factors of economic performance and development. The idea is that people engage in economic transactions and seek cooperation in order to lower transaction costs – especially in cases when markets are imperfectly competitive – and the uncertainty and the frequency of repeated transactions is high.

Trust between actors is the binding factor in successful cooperative behaviour and a fundamental building block in the formation of social capital (Fukuyama, 1995; Granovetter, 1985; Coleman, 1988). For example, the literature on industrial districts stresses the fact that cooperation and collaboration between local actors imply the existence of relationships based on trust. Both trust and trustworthiness are based on moral values as well as on an objective valuation of cooperation (Linders at al., 2004: 6).

In a spatial context, trust feeds from repeated and regular interpersonal contacts between local actors. There is strong evidence of the existence of a positive relationship between the durability of interactions, relations of proximity and reciprocity, and trust among actors and the economic performance and development of some localities and regions.

More generally, the foundation of institutional economics can be traced back to the principal schools of heterodox economic thought which prevailed at the beginning of the twentieth century. At that time, institutional economics, with special reference to the Old American Institutionalism and the German Historical School, was a leading school of economic thought before it was displaced by the neoclassical school. The principal reason behind this turn was the methodological shift in economics in favour of the neoclassical paradigm. This methodology favoured prediction over understanding, mathematical formalism over analytical description and generality over historical and spatial explanation (Hodgson, 1998). Institutionalist theories steadily declined since then to become heterodox, marginalised and less recognised in the discipline and practice of economics.

Despite the fact that the institutional paradigm in economics is a very broad field historically, ideologically, theoretically and methodologically divided, it is still united by relatively common sets of beliefs and attitudes emphasising the importance of institutions for the economic organisation (Lambooy and Moulaert, 1996). The emphasis is made not only on the conventional problems of resource allocation, income distribution, output, prices, employment, etc., but also on other issues related to the organisation and structure of the economy.

From this perspective, the interpretation of institutions by economists is somewhat different from other social scientists. Economists believe that the main function of institutions lies principally in their ability to correct the market failure, that is they are analysed in term of efficiency. Accordingly, the analysis of the role of institutions in economics is somewhat polarised toward the questions of the existence and efficiency of institutions, with little (or no) attention to their dynamic change. The widespread idea is that institutions are created by human inventions to improve the functioning of the economic system through the coordination of economic actions (North, 1990; Medema *et al.*, 1998). Based on this reading of institutions, one may then argue that institutions are created to protect the interests of the majority and to control and prevent (political, economic) conflicts between the elite and the mass population.

However, when the focus of studies is oriented towards institutional change, reference is very often made to changes in the markets, e.g. price mechanisms, and to the competition between and within organisations. Consequently, the thickness of institutions is then explained by the existence of discrepancy between the relatively fast and dynamic change of technological innovations and organisations and the slower change of institutions (Boyer, 2004: 10).

In contemporary economics, much attention has been devoted to neo-institutionalist and new-institutionalist (NIE) theories. Although the similarity in the terminology of the neo-institutional economics and NIE is quite confusing, distinctions between both approaches are quite significant. In what follows, we elaborate further on both institutional theories, in addition to the German Historical School (for an excellent survey of the German Historical School, see Nussbaumer, 2005), and the French regulation theory (see Boyer and Saillard, 2002).

3.4.1 The German Historical School

At the beginning of the twentieth century, the German Historical School provided challenging insights into the relationship between the localisation of economic activities, territorial development and the role of institutions. The first spatial reading of institutions can be found in Gustav Schmoller's analysis of the formation and design of local institutions. According to Schmoller (1897/1905), the capacity to face the basic needs of individuals depends on the quality of the collaboration between local authorities and the (national) state.

During this period, fierce intellectual debates took place between the protagonists of the German Historical School and the Austrian School of Economics (e.g. Schmoller vs. Menger) concerning the theoretical foundations and the methodological aspects in economics.

Carl Menger (1871) was a strong protagonist of isolating strictly economic causes in order to construct a theory that is suited to specific economic subjects. His methodological approach is deductive in the sense that it establishes causal law in economics. In contrast, Schmoller (1897/1905) contested this methodological approach in favour of the historical approach, which takes into account different factors influencing economic life. However, Schmoller did not provide a rigorous empirical method that could sustain his theoretical approach, and this was the main reason why the mainstream economists involved in this debate accepted Menger's hypothetico-deductive approach as the standard methodology of economic analysis (Nussbaumer, 2005).

Methodologically, Schmoller was concerned by the historical contextualisation of economic analysis, that is he tried to answer a set of questions specific to a particular historical context. His main ambition was to construct a universal theory based on methodological individualism that considers norms and rules as the most important coordinating forms of the behaviour of economic actors (Hodgson, 2000).

Theoretically, Schmoller's aim was to understand the role of local institutions in relation to the organisation of space by local communities (or what he called 'territorial corporations'). He showed that the dialectic between economic relations and the social and political organisation of territories is strongly determined by the balance of power and tensions between different actors, that is the local balance of power within institutions (internal balance of power) and between institutions (external balance of power) (Nussbaumer, 2005: 59).

Schmoller considered the territorial communities as human communities reflecting collective achievements in the sense that: 'Each [village] circle or province is a visible expression of mental and material community, where the construction of different sort, roads, boundaries, defense are rooted in space' (Schmoller, 1905: Book 1, p. 130; Nussbaumer, 2005: 20). By mental community, he means that historically constituted arrangements or local institutions – reflected in norms and customs – make up a collective memory of historical events.

In short, Schmoller offers a pragmatic approach to institutions where the relationship between institutional actions and their evaluation goes through their capacity to respond to local needs, that is local culture. More precisely, his institutional approach is based on individuals and actors, their needs and their power to influence the decision-making process.

The intellectual debates that took place between Schmoller and Menger have also influenced discussions among economists working on spatial and economic issues. As result, two theoretical approaches emerged. The first approach focused on the economic causes of localisation and urbanisation, while the second focused on the historical aspects of the spatial configuration of economic activities.

Von Thünen (1875) was one of the first economists to construct a theory of localisation and urbanisation. His work *Der isolierte Staat in Beziehung auf Landwirtschaft und Nationalökonomie* is extensively studied by economic geographers and economists, and is subject to different interpretations.

The isolated state gives a simplified and abstract representation of space, characterised by a uniform plain, with one city centre and many concentric rings around it. The spatial dispersion of activities is determined by the price level of land (from which transport costs are deducted), known as the 'bid-rent'. The bid-rent theory explains the spatial localisation of activities by transport costs, (market) prices and rent.

Beside Von Thünen, other German scholars have made important contributions to the analysis of localisation and urbanisation, such as, for example, Wilhelm Roscher (1865)[6] and Albert Schaeffle (1873).[7] These two authors retained a historical approach in studying the historical movements and evolution of land-use to explain the determinant factors of localisation of economic activities.

Alfred Weber (1909) was the first economist to introduce a systematic analysis of agglomeration economies to explain the localisation of economic activities in space. His methodological approach is a combination of the economic analytical method (e.g. costs/prices and quantities) and a historical approach that integrates social factors.

Weber stressed the importance of prices (market), endowment of resources and labour force and transport costs as the main factors in the localisation of activities and firms. However, the focus in his analysis was centred around two determinants of the localisation of firms: the importance of transport costs and the economies of agglomeration.

The most important theoretical aspect of Weber is his explanation of the spatial configuration of economic activities in term of agglomeration economies, concentration and dispersion. According to Walter Isard (1956), Weber's approach may be considered evolutionary in the sense that his theory of localisation presents a clear reading of the transformation of spatial structures of cities and regions.

The scientific legacy of Weber inspired many other scholars such as Ruud Hammer (1922), Carl Christiansen (1922) and Werner Sombart (1910) (for an excellent survey and discussions of the contribution of the German Historical school to local development, see Nussbaumer, 2002).

Hammer (1922) applied Weber's ideas in his study of the localisation of the jewellery industry in Germany. His analysis elaborated on the historical factors of localisation in relation to the agglomeration of industry. According to Hammer, the application of localisation theory to specific industry necessitated an analysis that combined the social and economic aspects (such as the role of actors, the forms of firms) with historical events and the cultural characteristics (for example, the behaviour of actors organised in professional groups, kinship relationships or religion).

Christiansen (1914) studied the development, localisation and spatial organisation of the chemical industry at the end of the eighteenth century. According to this author, the spatial agglomeration and development of this industry can be explained by the role of the 'first-mover' firms and their capacities for innovation. In his view, technological development is the key factor of change in the forms of spatial organisations.

In the same vein, Werner Sombart (1910), who studied the localisation of clothing industry, criticised the work of Weber by pointing to its inconsistency in constructing the micro-foundations of the economic system based on the analysis of the rational behaviour of individuals. Sombart stressed the fact that the analysis of spatial configurations and localisation is pre-conditioned by understanding first how the capitalist system itself works, and how actors transform the system in the long term. His main criticism of Weber's localisation theory is its focus on cost minimisation. According to Sombart, other qualitative advantages of localisation expressed in terms of proximity facilitating network relations between firms and between firms and their direct environment are very important (Sombart, 1910: 755). After all, the localisation of firms depends on various factors related to the quality of the environment (note that Sombart used the term quality instead of agglomeration economies).

To return to our argument, the scientific legacy of the German Historical School presents two approaches to space: (1) a spatial approach concerned by the use of space by economic actors; and (2) a territorial approach concerned with analysis of the appropriation of space by existing institutions. These two complementary approaches show that there exists a direct connection between the spatial evolution of economic systems (spatial approach) and the territorial evolution of cities and regions (territorial approach). However, to understand the sources and nature of the evolution of spatial and economic environments, the importance and the role of actors and institutions should be stressed.

Recently, the localisation theory was revived and put on the research agenda by the French regulation school through its focus on the issues of spatial localisation and the development of economic activities.

3.4.2 Old Institutional Economics

The Old Institutional Economics emerged at the turn of the twentieth century out of a critical assessment of the orthodox assumptions. The multidisciplinary theoretical work of the old American institutional economics (OIE hereafter) is centred on the role of institutions in the economy and in economic behaviour.

John R. Commons (1924, 1934) established the theoretical background of 'legal economics' with a focus on economic transactions as the most elementary building blocks of economic institutions. In Commons' theory, there are three dimensions to a transaction: an *exchange dimension*, a *hierarchical dimension* and a *scarcity dimension*. Together, these three dimensions provide an analytical framework of transactions that clarify the role of institutions in the economy.

Commons' theoretical approach to institutions and institutional change is problem-centred, e.g. institutions and institutional structures are considered problem-solving instruments of conflicts of interests between individuals. In Commons' words, institutions are the 'working rules' that determine '... what the individual can, cannot, must, must not, may or may not do' (Commons, 1931: 650).

Commons was particularly interested in the question of how working rules affect economic behaviour and economic outcomes, and how they change over time. According to this author, working rules drive the development, provide cooperative solutions and establish order and certainty in the course of economic life. They are codified in the legal framework, decisions of the courts and administrative bodies, or in a less formal sense in the prescribed behaviour of individuals within a community, that is its customs (Rutherford, 1994).

In short, Commons' institutionalism: (1) places emphasis on the transaction as the basic unit of economic analysis; (2) recognises the significance of customs and ideology in the development of (working) rules; and (3) highlights the importance of property rights, legal framework, pressure groups and political institutions in economic organisation.

In contrast to Commons, Thorstein Veblen (1899/1919) was strongly influenced by the evolutionary theory, and in this sense is considered by some authors as the founder of the evolutionary strand in institutional economics.

Veblen (1919: 74–5) argued that: 'The economic life of the individual is a cumulative process of adaptation of means to ends that cumulatively change as the process goes on, both the agent and his environment being at any point the outcome of the last process.' This means that alongside the exogenous 'shocks' to the system, endogenous institutions and human agency largely determine the course of socio-economic change in a accumulative incremental way.

In other words, Veblen and his followers view the socio-economic evolution of a society as a selection process, which is similar to the broader Darwinian conception of biological evolution (Zingler, 1974; Hodgson, 1988, 1999; Foster, 1991). Seen from this perspective, institutions are viewed as units and replicators of socio-economic evolution, similar to the role of genes in biology. This is because institutions have stable and self-reinforced qualities that allow them to sustain and 'pass on' their important characteristics as circumstances change through time. More particularly:

> The life of man in society, just like the life of other species, is a struggle for existence, and therefore it is a process of selective adaptation. The evolution of social structure has been a process of natural selection of institutions. (Veblen, 1919: Chapter VIII)

Thus the old institutionalists recognise the idea that the institutional environment has a significant effect on human perception, preferences, expectations and behaviour. Because economic processes are embedded in social relations, economic institutions constitute only a small part of the wider set of socio-cultural institutions, comprising values, beliefs, customs, norms and so on, which cannot be fully explained in purely individualistic terms. One of the important forces in the process of evolution in socio-economic systems is technology. In this respect, Veblen made a distinction between two tendencies that are present to a different degree in all human societies:

- *echnological or instrumental frames of mind* that are connected to the intrinsic human propensity for 'workmanship', 'idle curiosity'[8] and creative innovation of knowledge;
- *pecuniary frames of mind* that are related to the predatory aptitude of human behaviour to serve 'leisure class' interests, legitimate dominance and abstention from productive work, and the exploitation of the established status quo and traditions to defend own interests.

Instrumental frames of mind are considered conducive to economic development while the pecuniary frames are resistant to progress and change and are thus restrictive and sometimes even destructive to economic development (Ayres, 1962). The result is an evolving socio-economic system, driven by status emulation, conflicts and power relations, where old institutions break down and new ones emerge in a continuous process of adaptation to changes (e.g. the Veblenian dichotomy) (see Dugger, 1979; Wisman and Rozansky, 1991).

To return to our argument, the OIE approach considers institutions, like all other social structures, to be products of human society. Institutions are perceived both as structural entities that define the cognition and behaviour of individuals and as a social heritage of collective mental and spiritual products, that is the cultural dimension of institutions. In this sense, the basic function of institutions is to ensure certainty and continuity in social and economic life and, as such, they are characterised by relative stability, self-reinforcement and the capacity to replicate (Arvanitidis, 2006: 13).

3.4.3 Neo-institutional economics theories

There are several versions of neo-institutional economics, ranging from the transactional approach of Coase (1937) and Williamson (1975, 1985) to a broader interpretation of institutional dynamics by North (1990) and his followers.

Neo-institutional economics is defined here as the broader transaction approaches that have tried to complete or replace the price allocation system theory with much broader allocation logic based on the exchange of property rights under the regime of minimising transaction costs.

More specifically, the neo-institutionalists reject the neoclassical assumption of rationality in terms of individual utility maximisation. In contrast to the neoclassical assumption of independent, subjective and individual consumer preferences, neo-institutionalists view consumption as determined by social and cultural considerations or as a social act of learning. This means that what is rational is not just a matter of individual calculation of an optimum, but rather a matter of developing common perspectives and generating norms and rules of what is preferable and appropriate.

Coase defined the maximising boundary of a firm as the division between the set of things it could do better or cheaper than when it hires or buys. The contractual arrangements are ordinarily agreements about future performances. It is this fact that makes the non-contractual part of contracts central, since the parties' predictions of each other's future behaviour depend on predictions about each other's future morality.

However, there is no agreement between neo-institutionalists about the precise definition of institutions and their relation to transactions, but most authors seem to agree that 'when it is costly to transact, institutions matter' (Coase, 1937). Seen from this perspective, institutions are viewed as devices to reduce uncertainty and improve economic efficiency (North, 1990).

The focus of the neo-institutionalist approach is on understanding and explaining the organisational structure of the economy by taking into account the opportunistic behaviour of agents, information asymmetry and transaction costs.

Coase (1937: 336–7) was probably the first to emphasise that uncertainty and lack of information led to market failure.[9] He argued that uncertainty in market exchanges leads to economically inefficient outcomes, that is sub-optimal outcomes.

Inspired by the work of Coase (1937), a broader strand of economic institutional analysis has emerged since the 1970s treating a variety of topics, ranging from the boundaries and ownership of firms and internal problems of agency and their management to corporate culture (Kreps, 1990).

The concept of transactions constitutes the key element of neo-institutional economic analysis. The notion of the transaction is not confined just to the transfer of goods and services but also to the transfer of property rights, that is their creation, maintenance, use and change (Coase, 1960; Demsetz, 1967; Alchian and Demsetz, 1973). In this sense, transactions in modern societies take place within a framework of rules and rights, which is not only economically but also politically, legally and socially determined and enforced.

Transaction costs are costs associated with the coordination of economic activities within and between firms and the economy. In his survey of neo-institutional economics, Eggertsson (1990) defines transaction costs as 'the costs that arise when an individual exchanges ownership rights to economic assets and enforce their exclusive rights', and adds: 'When information is costly, various activities related to the exchange of property right between individuals gives rise to transaction costs' (Eggertsson, 1990: 14–15). Similarly, North (1990: 27) identifies transaction costs as 'the costs of measuring the valuable attributes of what is being exchanged and the costs of protecting rights and policing and enforcing agreements'.

The transaction cost theory relies on two important assumptions about human behaviour in explaining the emergence of transaction costs in economics, namely: (1) individuals are subject to bounded rationality – this means that the knowledge of a decision-maker is limited because of uncertainty and the complexity of the environment, i.e. the markets; (2) individuals displays opportunistic behaviour.

According to North (1990: 25): 'These uncertainties arise as a consequence of both the complexity of the problem to be solved and the problem-solving software […] possessed by the individuals.' This is why institutions are considered by neo-institutionalists to be a means of reducing uncertainty involving human interaction. That is: 'Institutions provide the structure for exchange that (together with the technology employed) determine the cost of transacting and the cost of transformation' (North, 1990: 34).

Because of these two assumptions, transactions and economic organisation are allocated either to market relations or to arrangements within organisations, depending on the circumstances (Coase, 1937, 1992; Demsetz, 1967, 1997; Williamson, 1975, 1985, 1993). Consequently, the choice between make or buy, that is internalisation or externalisation, depends on the size of the transaction costs, which in turn are determined by three factors: the *frequency* of transactions, *uncertainty* and the *specificity of assets*.

The specificity of assets involves three types of asset: (1) the *site specificity* – that is proximity to certain physical elements like infrastructures; (2) the *physical asset specificity* – that is specific machines or equipment in the production process; and (3) the *human capital specificity* – that is knowledge and skills.

Globally, transaction costs take on a different nature depending on the various contexts in which they appear. When considered with regard to existing property rights, for example, transaction costs consist of the costs of defining and measuring the characteristics of goods and services in addition to the costs of using, enforcing and monitoring specified rights.

When applied to the transfer of existing property rights and/or transfer of contract rights between individuals (or legal entities), transaction costs include the costs of information, negotiation, decision-making and enforcement (Furubotn and Richter, 2000).

As we have mentioned before, the size and structure of transaction costs influence the choice of the 'governance structure', the organisational form and the management structure. Consequently, institutions and organisational structures minimise transaction costs associated with the running of the political and economic systems.

Note, however, that debate within transaction theory is focused on the tension between different modes of coordination or governance, that is market, hierarchy and networks.

The market, hierarchy and networks are comparable categories of coordination and governance of economic functions. For example, market refers to allocation and exchange, firm refers to production, exchange, investment, etc., and households refer to consumption and exchange. Therefore various types of functional organisation have their own logic and own principles of organisation, governance and coordination. These principles are not necessarily determined by the nature of the economic or social functions, but by human interactions such as cooperation and competition, or solidarity and exploitation.

Another key element of transaction costs refers to information. In the real world, information is substantially incomplete and people are not always perfectly informed. This leads to asymmetry of information between the transacting parties where the holder of superior knowledge, i.e. information, could use it opportunistically (Sykuta and Chaddad, 1999). Based on this assumption, neo-institutionalists recognise that contracts are always incomplete.

One last remark that we want to stress here is the fact that neo-institutional economics highlights the important role of the political and legal institutions and their organisational structures in explaining the economic organisation and, ultimately, the factors that account for economic development and growth. The idea is that economic growth and economic change cannot be explained by focusing solely on markets and exchange relations, since markets and market processes do not operate in a vacuum but are embedded within an institutional structure that defines rights and duties, obligations and opportunities.

3.4.4 New institutional economics theories

New institutional economics oppose neoclassical theory in that it focuses on the benefit of institutions in terms of the transaction costs. The main concern is clearly oriented towards institutions – including government institutions – that are of great importance to the functioning of markets such as legislation and rules regulating market behaviour and so on.

In this sense, institutions only matter if they can reduce the costs of economic transactions (information, contracts, etc.), and especially the costs related to property rights. The argument advanced here is that under the effective rule of law, the protection of contractual and property rights and the absence of disruptive market factors reduce uncertainties and increase the confidence of individuals and firms in the future developments.

North (1990, 2005) sees a clear relationship between the rule of law or institutions and the economic prosperity (e.g. growth) of Western countries. According to North, institutions are in large measure 'path-dependent': they came into being in a specific setting, partly as result of established interests, and are difficult to change in a particular institutional framework. Putnam (1993) shares this point of view in his study of the administrative reforms in Italy. Putnam makes a distinction between weak and strong embeddedness of institutional structure in societies[10] and argues that devolution works much more successfully in regions with a traditionally strong institutional structure than in regions with a weak institutional structure.

More generally, the new institutional approach starts with the incorporation of transaction costs and property rights analysis but goes a step further in challenging the conventional assumptions of long-run equilibria and rational economic logic.

Institutions are seen in the light of formal rules and informal constraints and their enforcement in shaping human interactions. North (1990) distinguishes between these three elements as follows:

1.   Formal rules include political (and judicial) rules (that is hierarchy and the structure of polity), economic rules (property rights) and contracts.
2.   Informal constraints like taboos, customs and traditions are part and parcel of the social and cultural frameworks. They include self-enforcing social conventions, self-imposed codes of conduct (such as ideology) and social norms of behaviour.
3.   Third-party enforcement implies the development of the state as a coercive force able to monitor property rights and enforce contractual arrangements.

Note that there exists a clear distinction between institutions and organisations. Institutions are the rules of the game of a society or constraints that structure human interactions. Organisations are the players or groups of individuals bound by a common purpose to achieve specific objectives like political parties, the senate, a city council, a regulatory agency, firms, trade unions, family farms, cooperatives, sport clubs, schools, colleges, vocational training centres, etc. Therefore modelling institutions is in the first place modelling the 'man-made' constraints on human interactions, and modelling the organisation is theorising about structure, governance and policies of purposive social entities.

Based on this distinction, both North (1990, 2005) and Greif (1998, 2006) argue that empirical investigation of institutions and organisations should focus on the following issues:

- the costs of transactions with regard to the functioning of (political and economic) markets;
- the formal rules in an economy, and in particular political structure, property rights and legal system;
- the informal constraints, that is the social rules that shape human interactions;
- institutional evolution and change, using the concepts of path-dependence and considering the interconnectedness between informal and formal institutions;
- the organisational structure of a political economy, with a particular focus on the issue of the bargaining power of actors.

Concerning the path-dependency of institutions, one may argue that institutions result from a historical path that is punctuated by acts of purposeful design and development/change (Weimer, 1995). In this sense, the development of institutions is path-dependent, that is determined by past experiences, conventions, culture, etc., and place-dependent, that is determined by geopolitical contingencies.

According to Vromen (1995: 212–13), path-dependence and lock-in are phenomena that are themselves the result of more 'fundamental' evolutionary mechanisms, such as selection and adaptive learning. This means that institutional change is an interactive evolutionary process in the sense that it takes place in an incremental way and delivers increasing returns to institutional learning processes, which in the end may lead to institutional change.

North's approach holds a broader view of institutional dynamics in the sense that it recognises institutional change as path dependent and that does not always contribute to more efficiency. Moreover, once an institutional strand in an 'inefficient' path produces stagnation, it can persist because of the nature of the path-dependence and institutional lock-in, due to the difficulties of overcoming the high transaction costs of new institutional arrangements and the learning capacity of existing arrangements.

More recently, North (2005) has argued that institutions are not necessarily, or even usually, created to be socially efficient; rather they are, at least in the case of the formal rules, created to serve the interests of individuals and groups that use bargaining power to create new rules. In a zero transaction costs world, bargaining power does not affect outcomes. However, in a world of positive transaction costs, it does affect outcomes in the sense that it shapes the path and the direction of the long-term economic change.

3.4.5 *The regulation theory (théorie de régulation)*

The regulation theory (hereafter TR), stemming from the French regulation school, integrates the analysis of political economy with societal economics and the state to examine the social processes and (socio-political) struggles that define and stabilise the modes of economic calculation and norms of economic conduct (Boyer, 1987).

The notion of the 'mode of regulation' is used to cover the social and economic modes of regulation that secure the conditions for the reproduction of a specific regime of accumulation, that is the particular dynamic configuration of production and consumption.

Regulations are conceived by this theoretical strand to be the domination of one group among other groups. The regulatory power of institutions or the state (that is the law and norm setting, penalties and incentives, etc.) reflects the unequal distribution of power and resources. Institutions, whether formal or informal, are then considered to be the codification of fundamental social relations, which are related to political decision-making, that is jurisprudence and the law (Coriat, 1994).

Note that the notions of *régulation* (regulation) and *réglementation* (rule-making) have different meanings. Jessop (1995) illustrated this difference by arguing that *réglementation* refers to direct economic rule-making by the state, while *régulation* refers essentially to the regulatory effects that arise through the social interactions of actors within the economic field. In this perspective, *réglementation* contributes to regulation in the same way as other social activities and collective arrangements.

According to Lambooy and Moualert (1996), the regulationist approach is more realistic in dealing with the strategic role and the effects of power relationships, social inequality and political dynamics.

The TR recognises the limits of instrumentalist economic regulation and the necessity of defining a much broader world of regulatory dynamics interfering with the organisational and material reality of urban space or urban production system. In addition, the TR makes a clear distinction between state and non-state regulation, informal and formal regulation, in identifying the regulatory dynamics at the local level. In this sense, regulation is the outcome of socialisation processes which codify individual and collective behaviour in subsystems of urban society.

Note that the regulationists reject the neoclassical idea of rational economic men and self-regulating market phenomena in favour of a socially embedded and socially regulated economy. Following the regulationist approach, capitalist expansion and/or economic development comprises economic factors as well as non-economic factors. The latter include institutions, collective identities, shared visions, common rules, norms and conventions, networks, procedures and modes of calculation. All these factors play a determining role in structuring, facilitating and regulating (regimes of) accumulation. Accordingly, changes in the mode of production, that is the regime of accumulation, produce new contexts for economic development which lead to spatial reorganisation through the processes of decentralisation and consolidation. The central argument put forward by the TR is that regimes of accumulation have inherent tendencies towards crisis and instability. This is because regulatory crises arise whenever a regime of accumulation and the mode of regulation change. Therefore minor successive crises of the regime of accumulation may result in major breaks with old tendencies and hence to discontinuities of regularities. The second industrial divide identified by Piore and Sabel (1984) is one example of such a moment of breakage in the evolution of the capitalist system. The result was then a clear shift in the dominant modes of production that took place in the capitalist world since the second half of the 1970s, that is a shift from the Fordist production system to a flexible production system.

In short, the main idea of the TR is that a new regime of accumulation and a new mode of regulation produce a new context for economic development. In their seminal work based on the TR, Salais and Storper (1993) analyse different modes of economic coordination between actors, products, forms of actions, forms of uncertainty and the possible 'worlds of production'. According to these authors, there exists a variety of production worlds that are determined by different possible actions of actors, including the interventions of the state in coordinating collective actions.

However, one may note that the regulationist theory does not offer satisfactory answers as far as the analysis of urban and regional development is concerned. The TR focuses primarily on the role of the state and not on the role of collective autonomous entities such as cities or regions. Furthermore, the structuration of the nation is hierarchical in the sense that the state is considered as the sole carrier of institutional legitimacy. Finally, competition is regarded as exclusively global, that is the nation against the global market and its anarchy.

3.4.6 The sociological institutionalist approach

Sociological institutionalism interprets institutions in a much broader context than economists do. Because institutions are embedded social codes of conduct that shape the behaviour of individuals, the sociological approach to institutions is more concerned with cognitive, cultural and normative explanations of institutions.

According to this view, institutions involve shared cultural understandings, either explicit or taken for granted, of what is 'good', efficient and legitimate. The focus in sociological analysis is oriented towards the study of the relationship between institutions and individual interactions in terms of 'embeddedness' and the role of social networks and other 'common circles' (Grossetti and Bès, 2003). In addition, sociological institutionalist approaches reject the idea that institutional change is guided only by technical rationality, but is also guided by social rationality based on cognitive processes, interpretation of events, beliefs and values. In this sense, the categories of trust and cognitive capital are very important in understanding networks of (local) actors, the meta-value of social utility and collective interest.

Recent works on the social embeddedness of interpersonal economic relations emphasise the role of strategic interdependency between actors in inducing cognitive processes. Granovetter (1985) suggested an analysis of networks in terms of embeddedness by making a distinction between two visions: the 'over-socialisation' (norms, influences of social and cultural behaviour) and the 'under-socialisation' (atomisation of behaviour based on individualism and utilitarianism). He defines a network as 'a set of actors who know each other's relevant characteristics or can learn them through referral'.

Networks generate trust and consequently reduce the transaction costs of inter-action. Paldam (2000) stressed the importance of trust (following from effective social norms) for self-enforcement of cooperative behaviour.

Embeddedness means that every productive activity is based on interpersonal trust (necessary in the delegation of authority) and social affiliation, which create the necessary conditions for the acceptance of conventions. According to Granovetter, formal institutions do not produce trust but instead are a functional substitute for trust, and that 'institutional arrangements alone could not entirely stem force or fraud' (Granovetter, 1985: 489).

More generally, the sociological approach to institutions considers the adop-tion of institutions in term of their social appropriateness and legitimacy rather than a 'logic of instrumentality' (March and Olsen, 1989). A key element in institutional development is the process of institutionalisation, which is 'a process in which fluid behaviour gradually solidifies into structures, which subsequently structure the behaviour of actors' (Arts and Leroy, 2003: 31). This process is accompanied by the development of particular discourses, power and resource relations. Institutionalisation is itself a process guided by institutions and influ-enced by preceding solidifications of structures (Hodgson, 1999).

Recent studies in urban economics have examined many attributes of the sociological interpretations of transaction costs theory in relation to regional characteristics, such as the significance of social capital, spatial networks, tangi-ble and intangible assets and professional connections. It is now widely acknowl-edged that institutional conditions are much stronger in a regional economy than the dominant tendency of internationalisation (Storper, 1997).

The concept of social capital is therefore relevant to understand the role of insti-tutional and collective arrangements at the regional level. A spatial interpretation of the concept of social capital can be found in the contributions of the 'old' Italian school of economic sociology to the analysis of industrial districts. Social capital refers to features of social organisation such as networks, norms and trust that facilitate coordination and cooperation between actors in seeking mutual benefits. As such, social capital enhances the benefits of investment in physical and human capital at the local, regional and national levels (Putnam, 1993).

3.5 Collective arrangements, institutional arrangements and institutions

The concepts of institutions and institutional arrangements have been defined in many ways, depending on the theoretical orientation, the applied methodology and the focus of the study.

Most institutionalist theories focus principally on the nature and forms and the formation and changes of institutions but do not offer satisfactory answers concerning the nature, formation and development of institutional and collective arrangements in relation to institutions. In addition, the role and importance of institutional and collective arrangements in a spatial context is ambiguous, if it exists, and is practically absent in most studies on urban development and urban growth. However, from various institutionalist theoretical approaches presented in this chapter, one may distil some key ideas to sketch the nature, forms and dimensions of collective arrangements. More often than not, institutionalist scholars do not define the concept of collective arrangements in any consistent, clear and precise way.

Our purpose is to identify, examine and discuss the meaning and forms of collective and institutional arrangements, particularly as they relate to institutions, the institutional environment and institutional change, and subsequently to apply the concepts of collective arrangements in a spatial context.

In this perspective, the following question becomes relevant. Are collective arrangements conventions, modes of governance, models of coordination, sets of institutional forms, laws, traditions, etc., or just a combination of all these elements?

In economic geography, institutional analysis is concerned with the study of the interactions between structures and agency, and between the institutional environment and institutional arrangements in the economic space (Martin, 2000). The institutional environment refers to all kinds of formal rules (legal codes, laws and constitution) and informal conventions (norms, habits, culture) at work in the economy.

Institutional arrangements refer to organisational forms such as firms, states, public-private partnerships, business associations, etc., that are shaped by the institutional structure. As we have argued before, the institutional structure stimulates or/and imposes constraints on the social behaviour of organisations and the way they conduct their operational activities to gain in economic performance. These organisations can also produce and reproduce existing institutions and institutional arrangements by modifying them, either deliberately or unintentionally, over the course of time. Consequently, collective arrangements may be conceived as the basic building blocks of institutional arrangements and institutions. In other word, collective arrangements may result in institutional arrangements, and both operate within an institutional regime and/or institutional structure. Although the concept of institutional arrangements is frequently used more in the institutionalist literature than the concept of collective arrangements, the difference between them is rather fuzzy. Both concepts are used synonymously, and this applies to a certain degree to the concepts of institutions and institutional arrangements.

In the light of all this, we consider collective arrangements as the basic elements of construction for institutional arrangements. In turn, institutional arrangements have a strong institutionalised character and are strongly embedded in institutions. Consequently, collective arrangements, which may or may not be institutionalised, evolve over time and may became institutional arrangements when they are collectively accepted and standardised through laws, regulations and formal arrangements within the institutional environment. To illustrate this idea, imagine the institutional environment as a pyramidal construction composed of three basic construction blocks: the basic infrastructural block, i.e. the micro-level, is formed by collective arrangements; the second intermediate level, i.e. the meso-level, is formed by institutional arrangements; and finally institutions form the upper top level, i.e. the macro-level. Together, these three building blocks shape the institutional environment and its arrangements, which are specific in space and time depending on different kinds of contingencies.

Strictly speaking, an examination of the role of the institutional environment from this perspective has serious theoretical and empirical implications for the study of the spatial-economic transformation of cities in a sense that individual choices, preferences, norms, culture, values and individual actions are the princi-pal ingredients of collective arrangements that shape the spatial and economic structure of urban spaces.

Figure 3.1 provides a graphic illustration of the relationships between institu-tions, institutional and collective arrangements and their level of analysis.

More specific, institutional arrangements operate within the governance system, which is the sum of the many ways that individuals and organisations (public and private) manage their common affairs. It includes formal institutions and regula-tions (formal institutions of governments, markets, the law and constitution, and organisations), as well as informal arrangements that serve the interests of people and organisations such as traditions, values and norms.

We define collective arrangements as 'sets of rules, norms, values and public policies taking place in an institutional setting, i.e. mode of governance and coordi-nation. They result from a negotiated and accepted inter-institutional (and organisa-tional) process between different actors, which are bounded in time and space.'[11] In other word, collective arrangements are essentially 'rules' and conventions, both

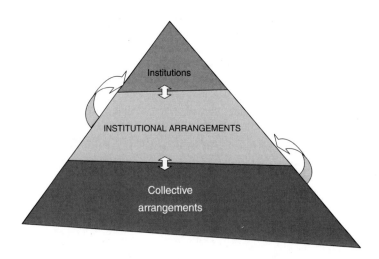

Figure 3.1 Typology and levels of analysis of institutional and collective arrangements.

formal and informal, aiming to reduce uncertainty, and the mode of conduct and attitudes structuring human behaviour. Formal collective arrangements are codified in institutions, regulations, plans and policies, etc. They involve a democratic setting which facilitates consultation, control of power and the preservation of (property) rights, through different schemes such as political rights (voting in elections, referendums) and economic and social rights. Other collective arrangements include traditional laws and customs, which may be formal (traditional law) or informal (tolerance, consensus model, love for trade and discovery, etc.).

Institutional and collective arrangements are institutionally structured, and directly affect the way in which social, economic and political actors behave. Alternatively, one may speak then of collective-choice arrangements when all stakeholders are included in the formation of appropriate rules and in rule adaptation over time.

The different levels of forms of institutional and collective arrangements are governed by the rule of law and/or conventions concerning the arbitrage between parties by public actors, or by negotiations between private and collective actors, or by selection (routine) (see Table 3.1). For example, the urban regime theory considers institutional forms (regimes) as key elements in analysing how certain coalitions maintain the power to act and the capacity to govern. It takes as its point of departure the idea that the processes of governance reflecting authority and ownership are distributed between different organisational bodies at different scale levels, e.g. the global, national, regional and local. Successful governance structure therefore depends on the availability and efficient mobilisation of resources and actors that are not formally part of the government (Painter, 1997; Stone, 1993).

Another interpretation of institutional and collective arrangements in economics is given by Lambooy (2005), who states that the concept of institutional arrangements may be related to the organisational elaboration of contacts resulting in arrangements such as public-private collaborations and other contractual relations. This interpretation of institutional and collective arrangements is similar to the point of view expressed by the heterodox analysis, which argues that organisational governance is based on the mode of coordination between actors in various fields of action, e.g. in the domains of territory, economics and politics. The main driving force of coordination is the realisation of common collective

Table 3.1 Rules governing institutional and collective arrangements

Rules of law	Political rules (order)	Collective conventions dictated by public power	Common law (jurisprudence)
Conventions	–	Collective arrangements (conventions)	Individual arrangements (conventions)

Source: Billaudot (2006, p. 18)

projects that are based on voluntary and solid engagement between local actors (Draperi, 2003). The realisation of these collective projects depends on the articulation between actors within or outside the market, usually in organised networks. The decision process underlying the coordination between actors is founded on participatory democracy and results in the production of specific resources (goal) established from the collective action and learning (Enjolras, 2002).

Two examples illustrate the specific meaning of collective arrangements in an urban context: first, land property rights, and second, the management of economic and financial resources in urban areas. In these two cases, collective arrangements are usually guided by formal arrangements, targeting specific resources such as water management, agriculture, industrial parks, transportation networks, production, distribution, trade, cultural heritage, etc., as well as by informal arrangements such as social expectations of the accessibility and use of resources (Smajgl *et al.*, 2003).

In summary, collective arrangements are an important element of the existing institutional structure and a major building block of institutions. To understand the nature and meaning of institutional arrangements in shaping and sustaining institutions, we need first to know what they are, which characteristics they have, how and why they are crafted and sustained, and which effects they may generate in diverse institutional settings.

3.6 Collective arrangements: definition

A careful examination of existing institutionalist theories shows the scarcity of research focusing on the concepts of institutional and collective arrangements in studying the emergence and development of institutions and institutional structures. An exception to this observation is Ostrom, whose research work shed some light on the definition of the concept of collective arrangements. According to Ostrom, collective arrangements may be defined as 'the prescription (rules of the game) that individuals use to organize all forms of repetitive and structured interactions including those within families, neighborhoods, markets, firms, sports leagues, churches, private associations, and governments at all scales' (Ostrom, 2005: 3).[12]

The closest counterpart to the most widely used definition of the term 'institution' is institutional arrangement. Davis and North (1971) make the distinction between 'institutional environment' and 'institutional arrangement'. They define institutional arrangement as 'an arrangement between economic units that governs the way in which these units can cooperate or compete'.

Both collective and institutional arrangements take the form of formal or informal arrangements. They may involve a group of individuals or actors and organisations, and they may be temporary or long-lived.

From an economic point of view, the formation of new arrangements will alter the way economic units can cooperate or compete, but the change of an arrangement may involve a single individual, a group of voluntarily cooperating individuals, or public and public-private parties. This latter type of arrangement involves some legal change, but the former type of arrangement, while resting on the legal structure that constitutes the environment, involves only the private sector.

In this study, we consider collective arrangement as 'a set of structured rules and conventions that covers the particularity of the development and growth of the urban space in the long run, including the analytical and methodological instruments describing the inherent arrangements, organisation and transformation of the whole region'. In other words, collective arrangements are structures formed by many layers from which *the rules-structured situations* govern the (inter)actions between multiple individuals and multiple actors, and affect their strategies and outcomes. Some of these rules are crafted within existing institutions that are used to structure an individual's deliberations and decisions such as, for example, the rules people use when driving a car.

Note, however, that the diversity and the complexity of situations where time and space are involved make the analysis of institutional and collective arrangements very difficult (Ostrom, 2005). Following Ostrom, the diversity of regularised social behaviour, observed at multiple scales, is constructed from universal components organised into many layers. These layers create the structure affecting their behaviour and the achieved outcomes.

Developing a multi-level taxonomy of the underlying components of situations that human actors face may help us to understand the functions of institutions and how collective arrangements come into existence. A key step in this perspective is to focus attention on the goals of actors, their objectives and the specificities of time and place in creating and sustaining collective arrangements in the long run.

More specifically, collective arrangements have many dimensions and ramifications which make them very difficult, if not impossible, to be transmitted between spaces and sectors or domains. In fact, there is no single collective arrangement which works across diverse spaces and policy areas or even between diverse sub-types within a broad policy area. Therefore each collective arrangement is specific in time and space.

Collective arrangements come into existence and develop a particular history from which they persist and maintain their structure and configuration in the long term. In the case of Schiphol airport for example, the basic arrangement was very simple, namely the decision of the government in 1945 to make Schiphol the sole international airport of the Netherlands. As result, Schiphol become the national base for the Dutch national airplane company KLM. Also, the decision to change the ownership of the airport from a local-municipal airport into a (national) private company with the majority of shares in public hands, i.e. the state and the municipality of Amsterdam, is another example of how existing collective arrangements may be substituted by new ones. The substitution of old collective arrangements by new ones had multiple consequences for the airport itself (a public company with commercial objectives) as well as for the spatial organisation (planning, extension, etc.) and the economic development of the Schiphol region. This meant that a great part of the Schiphol airport became an open public space. However, if Schiphol had been privatised in 2006 as the airport authorities wanted, then this over-coupling arrangement could have been replaced by a new arrangement.

Note that the actual arrangement gives Schiphol a unique position as a spatial phenomenon, that is an urban centre and powerful global player or actor at the local, regional and national level. This unique position evokes great tensions (economic, environment, ecology, etc.) between Schiphol airport and its surrounding urban areas, albeit the economic and political support for the future growth of Schiphol is still strong. This is because there exists a majority of actors outside the collective arrangements that are generally more loyal to Schiphol and supportive of the existing arrangements.

3.6.1 Criteria, dimensions and characteristics of collective arrangements

Criteria

As mentioned above, collective arrangements may be viewed as building blocks and a 'hybrid form' of institutional arrangement within an existing institutional setting. They are context dependent and spatially embedded and need time and resources to settle in and transform into institutional arrangements, and possibly in the long run into institutions.

In this sense, collective arrangements are subject to various criteria:

1. They must be accepted, respected and adopted collectively by all parties involved in public policy domains.
2. They are spatially embedded and dependent on the context and the specificity of localities where they take place.
3. They make part of the law of conduct and shape the behaviour of individuals/actors.
4. Finally, they are 'path-dependent' and historically determined (history matters!).

Collective arrangements meeting these criteria give shape to a specific mode of governance of urban spaces and specify the way the actions and behaviour of actors are structured and coordinated when acting individually or collectively to serve common goals.

Note, however, that uncertainty, administrative and jurisdictional boundaries and the difficulty of measuring the impacts of economic activities on the environment when pursuing sustainable spatial and economic development policy pose great challenges at the level of urban governance, more particularly with regard to the ongoing deregulation and decentralisation of the decision-making process in planning and designing urban space. This view of urban governance that seems to gain more support in several industrialised countries emphasises systems approaches, flexible and adaptive institutions, decentralisation and empowerment, collaborative governance and communicative planning.

Characteristics

Different characteristics of collective arrangements may be identified which distinguish them from other types of institutional arrangements and institutions.

First, every arrangement is sealed by legislation or a basic document in which agreements and long-term objectives are determined. This leads to the emergence of various alliances, conventions and agreements. Conventions, whether planned or unplanned, arise from standardised arrangements, which facilitate interrelationships between actors (alliances, agreements, contracts, etc.). National and regional policies, spatial planning concepts/documents and planning design, and investments may be seen as conventions with accompanying representations and the ritual use of public space. In this sense, collective arrangements may be considered a specific element of the local institutional environment supporting local business culture and facilitating interconnections between various local actors.

In the Dutch governance culture, for example, Schiphol may be seen as a unique phenomenon. All collective arrangements developed so far around Schiphol are formed around various concatenations of interconnected and parallel agreements and contracts involving various independent actors, with different interests, objectives and decision-making powers. However, the bifurcation of the initial arrangement into various parallel arrangements involving increasing numbers of different actors may lead to conflicts and inertia in the sense that some autonomous actors may not accept some of the existing arrangements and resist. To clarify this point, we take as an example the case of Schiphol airport and KLM. Both actors have different interests and objectives but are ultimately condemned to cooperate with each other. However, agreements between these two actors are not always obvious because of differences in business culture and sector specificities. As a result, conflicts between such actors may jeopardise the durability of existing collective arrangements. This was the case, for example, when these two actors had divergent point of views concerning the construction of a new airport in the North Sea during the 2000s. Another complex factor, which may hamper the continuity of collective arrangements, is the case when some autonomous actors within the region do not comply with the widely accepted common decision-making processes and procedures governing spatial planning objectives. In this case, the collective arrangement may become, to a certain extent, a specific world in itself.

Second, the initial arrangement becomes more and more complex as it develops and bifurcates into various sub-arrangements which may be complementary to the initial one or develop into new arrangements that open up new trajectories along the existing development path. The replacement of this arrangement by a new one or its redesign may occur under unexpected circumstances or internal and external shocks. Bifurcation through the reconfiguration and/or refinement of existing or new arrangements is sustained through a network of actors and institutions sharing the same social, economic and cultural background. For example, since the 1950s, Schiphol has developed into one of the most important growth centres, not only for the region but also for the Dutch economy. As result, Schiphol received special attention from the state and was, for the first time in its history, integrated into the national spatial planning scheme. This shift in the economic position of Schiphol was accompanied by the development of new arrangements and/or the reconfiguring of old ones.

Third, arrangements are initiated, in the first place, to serve specific objectives, but may also be enlarged and applied to other domains and other contexts as well, that is collective arrangements elaborate general procedures which are applied in various domains without losing their efficiency. For example, arrangements structuring the functioning of existing networks of firms operating in different sectors have strong links to the activities of Schiphol airport, such as logistics and distribution, transportation and communication, etc.

Consequently, the arrangements take place at multi-scale levels. They are not limited to a specific local geographical level but cross many such levels at the same time. In the case of Schiphol, arrangements developed around the airport apply also to regional as well as to national levels when considering the economic functions of Schiphol in terms of the region and the nation. In this sense, these arrangements act as important elements of change in the social and spatial-economic structure for the whole region.

Fourth, conventions, whether planned or unplanned, emerge from existing arrangements and entail a collective visual representation, which may be concretised in urban planning concepts, architectural forms, marketing and PR campaigns and artistic impressions. In addition, these collective representations of arrangements may raise resistance from groups of individuals and/or non-governmental groups (regarding environmental and health issues for example). Examples of such conventions are policy plans/documents, designs, investments, conventions concerning image building (representation) and the everyday and ritual use of the public space.

Fifth, the arrangement is spatially bounded and time specific. However, the arrangement criss-crosses different spatial levels and is not necessarily specific to a particular locality. For example, Schiphol affects directly and indirectly the social-economic and spatial structure of the whole city region and not only the surrounding urban localities, e.g. the Schiphol region.

More generally – and from the point of view of the objectives, commitments and responsibilities of major actors such as the Schiphol group, for example, and the accompanying discourse – collective arrangements acquire, eventually, clear physical and economic features and constitute parts of the emerging nebula city within the urban nebula. These parts manifest themselves as:

- a cognitive formation that gives shape to existing representations and rational considerations behind the over-coupling of collective arrangements and existing sub-arrangements;
- a mental horizon like, for example, the association of KLM airplanes with swans or the association of Schiphol with different images in the imagination of the public (adventure, discovering the world, etc.);
- a conceptual universe, such as, for example, the conceptual world of Schiphol airport in the past (hub transport node), and the new version of Schiphol as an airport city or a nebula city.

Even if Schiphol shows an urban form similar to an average downtown city-centre, in term of its existing facilities and services the airport has its own specific and alternative urban patterns and structures to the traditional city centre. This becomes clear when considering, for example, the functional design of the airport, which integrates performance (hyper-functionality) of the built-up area with knowledge about the behaviour of its users.

More generally, perceptions about Schiphol as a nebula city are reflected in the development of visions about the future spatial development of the airport, of the marketing concepts, urban planning, landscape and infrastructure and architectural design, and the graphical concepts in advertisements (websites, posters, logos, etc.). These fictional concepts, with their discursive, visual and graphical elements as well as the numerical-conventions and traditions, represent a pure concretisation of existing arrangements. Similar representations give sub-arrangements the status of the visionary, the obvious, the comprehensible and the sympathetic. Instructions for these fictional concepts are not given, but are intended to reassure people, and to canalise their emotions and behaviour toward an easy acceptance of (necessary) interventions in the direct environment of Schiphol.

In contemporary urban life, perceptions play a decisive role in shaping public opinion and gaining acceptance of and support for policy measures and future development. The image of the world is a reflection of the real world as understood in our imagination, that is the culture of perception or image competes with other realities to produce an image of the world that we perceive as real. In this sense, (multi)media and the internet have a strong influence on the way individuals shape their perception of the external world. These perceptions about objects are by definition not embodied in culture but are very important in shaping or (re) producing identities, power and markets.

Dimensions

Beside their different characteristics, collective arrangements also have different dimensions.

- A collective arrangement comes into existence and develops its own history from which it persists and maintains its structure and configuration in the long term. In the case of Schiphol, for example, the basic arrangement was very simple and straightforward, namely the decision of the government in 1945 to make Schiphol the sole national airport of the Netherlands. As a result, Schiphol also became the permanent base of the national home carrier KLM. Similarly, Schiphol has been operating as a public company for almost a half century now. This means that a great part of the airport Schiphol is public open space. But should Schiphol ever become a private company, this over-coupling arrangement will be changed and the public open character of Schiphol will disappear. This will have direct consequences for the users of this space and for the surrounding urban areas.
- Collective arrangements involve a cognitive aspect (e.g. imagination, information (its acquisition and interpretation), learning and knowledge spillover), a mental horizon (e.g. the association of KLM airplanes with swans) and a conceptual universe (for example, the airport city concept). These serve as the

main support for building a representation of existing arrangements and hence for interpreting the reality of the urban nebula. Examples of such a mental horizon and conceptual universe are the different forms of vision regarding the future development of the region, the designs (town planning, architectural and infrastructural designs) and marketing campaigns (posters, advertisements, films, photos, etc.). These 'soft aspects' of interpreting the urban nebula phenomenon are embodied in fictive perceptions (discursive, visual, graphical, data) of existing collective arrangements on which decision-making has to be made. These fictional concepts – with their discursive, visual and graphical elements as well as the numerical conventions and traditions – represent the concretisation of arrangements. Similar representations give (sub-)arrangements the status of the visionary, the obvious, the comprehensible and the sympathetic. This may sometimes be misleading when thinking about the future development of Schiphol (for example the possible advantages of combining the mainport strategy with the airport city concept).

- Perceptions play an essential role in the way individuals interpret the nebula city (for example, the strong association between the Dutch company KLM and Schiphol). In urban life, perceptions about the external world are in fact a translation of the world as understood through images. In this sense, the media, (political) power and the market reproduce the identities and perceptions of individuals.

3.7 A conceptual framework of collective arrangements

Collective arrangements are not deterministic because they are subject to change in their reconfiguration through negotiation and the decision power of actors or by exogenous change induced by the context (Reynaud, 2002). Each possible arrangement, although viable in some places, can be irrelevant when applied in other places structured by specific institutional environment. The capacity of adaptation and the reactivity to the change constitute an integrated part of the viability of existing institutions and collective arrangements. Consequently, the viability of collective arrangements depends on the generative capacity of their configuration and potentialities to change and to adapt to different contexts in time and space.

By identifying and describing the evolution of collective arrangements and their interventions in determining the spatial and economic transformation of cities and regions, we develop a conceptual framework of collective arrangements based on the recent work of Thelen (2003) and Boyer (2004).

More specifically, we follow the general line described in Boyer (2004) and introduce some modifications, which we consider in light of the objectives outlined in this study. We make a distinction between three determinant processes that explain the evolution of collective arrangements in time and space. These are: the process of accumulation/bifurcation (Boyer called it 'sedimentation'), the process of transformation and the process of reconfiguration or recombination.

3.7.1 Accumulation/bifurcation

The process of accumulation is a process of adding new arrangements to the existing ones. New collective arrangements often emerge from relatively stable arrangements that are sustainable in the long term.

The process of accumulation of collective arrangements, eventually associated with the transformation of some arrangements, gives a repertoire of procedures and mechanisms of coordination among which various actors can make their choice when planning strategies. In addition, the heterogeneity of arrangements allows actors to find the right arrangements that may fit within a specific local and historical context (Boyer, 2004: 34).

The analysis of the evolution of collective arrangements through the process of accumulation should take into account the following two important elements: (1) the heterogeneity of the preferences of actors (Hildenbrand, 1997) and existing technological possibilities; and (2) the time-horizon, in the sense that a long-term historical view must be considered in order to understand the formation of collective arrangements within a specific institutional context, their transformation and progressive evolution or disruption, that is disappearance in the long run.

3.7.2 Transformation

The process of the transformation of collective arrangements can be defined as the process by which a collective arrangement achieves a new configuration by changing one or many of its constituent components. For example, the basic arrangement – or more precisely the predetermined objectives of the arrangement – may turn out to be difficult to realise. As result, a new and better arrangement adapted to the changing context (environment) aiming to realise the same objectives may emerge, often with different actors or organisations. The new arrangement may pursue the same objectives as in the basic arrangement, but with the advantage of developing a new arrangement instead of reforming the old one.

Because of the increased pressures from a changing environment, collective arrangements may be subject to a mechanism of internal recomposition/redefinition of existing relations linking actors to each other and to their environment. However, this reversal is not mechanistic by nature, but a direct result of strategic interactions between actors that may open up a window of opportunity to new configurations (Boyer, 2004: 31). Technically, the transformation process from one collective arrangement to another takes place through a converter or a switcher, which could be a powerful actor or a group of pioneers or actors, as we will show later on in the case of the Schiphol airport during the 1920s (Boyer and Orléan, 1992).

3.7.3 Reconfiguration

In addition to the processes of accumulation and transformation, reconfiguration is also determinant in explaining the changes in the configuration of collective arrangements. The main idea of reconfiguration starts with the fact that collective arrangements are linked to each other, and that the linkages between them depend on the nature and the intensity of the relationships that bind them together. Consequently, the reconfiguration of different collective arrangements is of great importance for the evolution of the (local) institutional configuration, which takes as a point of departure the heterogeneity of arrangements constituting the institutional environment. Furthermore, the relationships between collective arrangements may take the form of complementarity or hierarchy (Boyer, 2004: 35).

Because of the richness of institutions and institutional arrangements, some collective actors and groups of individuals may try to redefine their position and status and improve their power position by entering into new networks or abandoning old ones that no longer represent any advantage to them (ibid.: 34). Accordingly, political and economic networks can be rearranged and reconfigured to secure their existence and durability in the long term. The regulationist approach, for example, applies the idea of reconfiguration to the evolution of institutions in order to explain the change in the hierarchy of the state apparatus and the organisational forms of firms under the Fordist and post-Fordist production systems (for a more detailed analysis, see Boyer, 2004).

In summary, the mechanisms of accumulation/bifurcation, transformation and reconfiguration take place at different (spatial) scale levels. Accumulation concerns the creation of new arrangements complementary to the old ones in the same field. The process involved at this stage is similar to the process of selection in evolutionary economic theory.

The transformation of collective arrangements defines the process of reorganisation and restructuration of procedures, organisation and the interpretation of the rules by actors within a specific collective arrangement. The dynamic process of transformation is related to learning and experimenting by individual or groups of actors within existing possibilities offered by collective arrangements.

The reconfiguration of collective arrangements concerns the redefinition of the relations between collective arrangements within the same local institutional configuration or institutional system. This process is beyond the control of individual actors because it involves strategies of mobilising local powers and the intervention of the state and/or local government bodies such as the provinces, municipalities, etc.

Put together, all these three mechanisms, which are complementary and may take place at the same time, effect the spatial transformation and economic development of cities and regions. Each of them, whether separately or in conjunction with other mechanisms, opens up a window of opportunity to new spatial and economic configuration of urban spaces. The adoption of this approach, when dealing with the nature and conditions of the spatial economic transformation of regions, reveals the existence of a variety of evolutionary institutional forms and arrangements that affect the existing institutional configuration.

The transformation of collective arrangements changes the initial objects, routines, norms and conventions adopted by actors operating in the same economic, political and social fields. The process of accumulation constitutes one of the most important factors of institutional change in the sense that within the same field new and old collective arrangements may compete, and in doing so they may accelerate or slow the transformation processes at work. In this perspective, the conjunction between transformation, accumulation and bifurcation may be understood as key elements of adaptation and innovation in the evolution of the institutional and collective arrangements, and ultimately of institutions. Additionally, the characteristics of local institutional configuration depend on the nature and intensity of the relations between its constituent components, especially the different types of collective arrangements. In this sense, the reconfiguration of existing collective arrangements is very important in understanding the institutional, spatial and economic transformations in the long term.

Finally, our approach adopts a conception of collective arrangements that takes into account the degree of coherence of spatial, economic and institutional configurations of cities, and factors and actors that govern their evolution in the long run. The next step then is to address the characteristics of the relationship between collective arrangements and the transformation of spatial-economic environments. We focus here on three main characteristics to explore the role and importance of collective arrangements in a spatial context, i.e. cities and regions, namely the path-dependent character of collective arrangements, their degree of complementarity and hierarchy, and their constituent entities.

First, the concept of path-dependency may shed more light on variety and specificity in the evolution of collective arrangements in a spatial context. The long-term stability of collective arrangements may be disturbed by short periods of unexpected – exogenous or endogenous – shocks giving birth to new arrangements that may shape the path to new (spatial and economic) regularities. Note that the accumulation of a series of minor transformations of collective arrangements may lead to big transformations of localised institutional configurations.

Second, another important element of the analysis is the hierarchy and complementarities between different forms of collective arrangements within an institutional configuration. The homogeneity of the behaviour and strategies of actors is not conditional on the stabilisation of the institutional configuration and collective arrangements. This is because the diversity of rules and conventions adopted by actors guarantees the reactivity of and capacity for reinterpretation and redefinition of existing rules that govern arrangements.

Third, the diversity of mechanisms mentioned above makes it clear that there is a necessity to define clearly what we mean by collective arrangements and what their constituent entities are (see our discussion above about the criteria, characteristics and dimensions of collective arrangements). In doing so, it becomes possible to set the principal object of analysis within an urban-institutional economic framework. Because institutions follow 'conscious' and 'unconscious' processes of creation and adjustment to the context, collective arrangements should also follow the same path. However, this makes it very difficult to give the same meaning of continuity and change to what we define as convention, routines, norms, habits and rules governing the relations between actors involved in generating collective arrangements.

Having said that, and from a spatial-economic point of view, institutional and collective arrangements can facilitate spatial and economic change when they are not in conflict with a related institutional environment. As we have argued before, in the long run, some collective arrangements may be formalised into full institutional arrangements that guide the development trajectory of the local production system in all its dimensions and spatial scales.

From an (urban) policy point of view, formal collective arrangements facilitate policy intervention and define the responsibilities and roles of the different public and private actors involved in the application of policy. However, problems of design and reconfiguration of collective arrangements may arise when they are in conflict with specific policy objectives. In this case, the government may set specific goals and design new (formal) arrangements, for example through the process of transformation or reconfiguration, that can facilitate strategic action among actors in order to obtain intended outcomes.

In urban and regional contexts, one may identify different types of collective arrangements structuring the territorial and functional organisation of economic activities.

First, collective arrangements can be related to two organisational forms: competition and cooperation. Some types of collective arrangements may foster regulated interactions and limit others, while other types of arrangements may favour some actors and constrain others. In this sense, the choice in favour of certain types of collective arrangements in particular locations affects the nature and type of interactions between actors and their outcomes, e.g. increasing competition and/or more coordination among actors. This choice generally depends on the choice of the optimal coordination mechanism, e.g. coordination through the market or the government. For example, the preference for state interventions in the process of economic development and spatial planning may or may not stimulate networks of cooperation between private and public parties around common projects of national importance.

Second, the interactions between actors are often territorially organised, either horizontally, i.e. between actors from the same layer, or vertically, i.e. actors from different layers. Vertical forms of interaction occur when different government layers bundle their efforts around one or more policy-issues crossing different jurisdiction and spatial levels (municipalities, provinces, regions). Horizontal forms of interaction involve different actors belonging to the same jurisdictional and spatial level working together to reach common collective objectives, e.g. local and regional economic growth.

This brings us to the important issue of the spatial scale of collective arrangements because a single policy may have important unintended side effects arising from the operation of institutional and collective arrangements at different spatial levels.

Indeed, spatial scale levels are constructed through the struggles of actors, movements and institutions that influence locational structure, territorial extension and spatial organisation of activities. In other word, the geographical boundaries of cities and regions are produced and transformed through a range of various socio-political and economic processes and strategic interactions between actors. McGuirk (2003) placed urban governance in a multi-level and multi-system framework which views social, political and economic processes as co-evolving layers of the territorial organisation. Based on this point of view, the spatial scale of collective arrangements refers simply to both the formal and informal processes and institutional channels that are involved in governing a bounded territory such as a municipality, city, metropolitan region or the nation-state. Building on Ostrom's (1990)[13] categorisation of the levels of rules/arrangements that cumulatively affect the actions taken and outcomes obtained in using 'common property resources', we distinguish four levels of institution where collective arrangements take place:

- The first level contains the institution of social relations founding the political (and legal) and economic institutional arrangements regulating transactions between organisations or between individuals and organisations.
- The second level concerns the institution of territorial institutional units, e.g. formal organisations such as financial firms, the administration, the family, associations, etc.
- The third level contains the institution of rules of the function of organisations (internal organisational rules).
- The fourth level contains the institution of rules of the function of individuals or citizens, e.g. informal rules, norms, values, traditions, etc.

3.8 Governance regimes and urban regeneration

The presence of natural resources, differentiated urban production systems and specialisation of activities in combination with the presence of local institutions that stimulate growth are necessary conditions for a city or region to gain comparative advantage.

In the digital era, local institutions also include what Sassen (2001) calls 'social connectivity'. This represents all forms of governance formed by sets of individuals and organisations that plan, coordinate and manage their common affairs with the ultimate goal of controlling the way the economy is functioning and the spatial domain is organised.

Since the 1970s, regional and urban policies have shifted from hierarchical (institutions), normative and sectoral approaches to strategic, consensus and integrated approaches. The shift of urban and regional policies strengthened local networks and their inter-organisational forms as seen in the increase in urban public-private partnership initiatives (Camagni and Gibelli, 1994). More particularly, strategic planning and flexible governance arrangements in overlapping polycentric jurisdictions became the catalyst for cooperation and relationships where reciprocal learning and knowledge sharing occur through communications.

Inter-urban issues are often related to spatial conflicts, while intra-urban issues refer to social aspects. In each case, many actors are perceived to be stakeholders, including public and private organisations and various societal groups and organisations. The intricacy of the problems associated with flexible governance arrangements is such that the involvement of so many stakeholders does not necessarily lead to adequate policy. However, there seems to be a general agreement that top-down and command-and-control models of governance are no longer appropriate, or at least not as appropriate as they previously might have been (Healey, 1998). In this sense, urban governance differs from traditional forms of government by including actors representing not only the public sector, but also the private and other societal sectors. These actors are engaged in different networks of partnerships that are autonomous with respect to the state and independent of each other. The participation in such networks is very often based on mutual interests, exchange of resources and commitment.

Note, however, that such governance structures also generate tensions and conflicts between various partners in networks and partnerships with respect to accountability, legitimacy and power, especially in situations where there is devolution of responsibility without proper devolution of decision-making authority, competence or (budgetary) power (Dekker and Kempen, 2004: 111).

Central to urban regeneration practice is cooperation between different tiers of the government and external agencies in urban planning and local and regional economic policy. Cooperation can be between central, municipal and sub-municipal levels.

From the 1990s, many Western central governments, including the Dutch government, increased the burden of local governments through the devolution of tasks previously in the hands of the state, that is decentralisation and the stimulation of self-organising networks and bottom-up initiatives. However, it is important to note that new governance structures could succeed only if they provide a framework in which relevant actors can reach agreement over spatial and temporal horizons of action vis-à-vis their environment. In other word, such governance structures must first stabilise the cognitive and normative expectations of actors by shaping and promoting common goals as well as developing adequate solutions to sequencing problems, that is predictably ordering various actions, policies or processes which have different temporal logics (Jessop, 1999). This last observation brings us to examine the question of the multi-actor and multi-level approach of urban governance that dominates in many European countries and in the USA.

3.9 Multi-actor, multi-level approach to urban governance

The fundamental structure of urban governance is formed by administrative networks, financial flows and authority relationships between the state and local and regional authorities, e.g. municipalities and provinces.

On the one hand, the contemporary government systems are deeply institutionalised through formal rules and expectations about how each government tier should perform its tasks, responsibilities and decision-making power in a democratic and legitimate governance structure. On the other hand, local and regional organisational governance takes place within the context of intra- and inter-local and regional relations.

To understand the nature, role and importance of collective arrangements in the spatial and economic transformation processes of cities and regions, one should start with the identification of key local actors, as they are the key building blocks of local institutional arrangements.

Taking into account the differences in urban and regional governance structures between countries, four principal actors can be identified in any urban setting. These are:

- *individuals and organisations* – which include individuals, local businesses, other users of metropolitan services and those providing financial resources to governments;
- *local government bodies* – such as municipalities, city councils, chambers of commerce, etc.;
- *provincial bodies* – e.g. provinces and inter-province entities; and finally
- *the state* – including state government entities such as ministries, (quasi) public entities, etc.[14]

This categorisation of key actors in any urban setting suggests a typology of metropolitan regions in terms of vertical and horizontal relationships. In vertical relations, the state can retain control and decision-making power at the local and regional level, i.e. centralisation, or elect local and regional entities to create empowered local governments, i.e. decentralisation. Conversely, horizontal relations can be concentrated in the metropolitan area or diffused broadly through multiple regional entities integrated in the metropolitan area.

Note that the identification of the key actors is, in itself, not sufficient to understand the main factors affecting the territorial and economic development of cities and regions. One should rather focus attention on other dimensions such as the specific role and position of power of actors within networks (e.g. key actors or dependents), their governing position (e.g. inter-governmental, intra-governmental, public-private, etc.), their motivation (e.g. cooperation or competition) and their goals and objectives (e.g. production, exchange, regulation, etc.). Other dimensions such as the competency, aspirations, intervention and legislative or operational powers of actors must be taken into account when analysing institutional and collective arrangements in an urban context.

Different governance regimes have been identified such as public governance, partnership governance and merchant or competitive governance that correspond to different coordination forms. These governance regimes are composed of three principal elements: actors, applied instruments of public policy serving collective interests and the institutional modality of interactions within public policy networks (Enjolras, 2004). However, different combinations of governance regimes are possible, depending on the territorial scale level and sector of activity, e.g. organisation, market (private sector) or the state (public sector). For example, if a local government wants to sustain the competitive position of the region, the regional economy must be flexible enough to respond adequately to changes occurring inside the region and/or resulting from changes occurring outside the region. In this way, the region can absorb external shocks and respond adequately to external changes when local authorities operate in networks aiming to coordinate the actions of public and private actors.

Recent empirical studies on the governance structures of metropolitan regions in the USA indicate that decentralised local government does not generate a more effective or competitive regional economy than centralised local government (Dolan, 1990; Lewis, 1996). Accordingly, there exists no ideal form of governance structure that meets all requirements and demands of the community with respect to different sets of responsibilities. Therefore understanding regional governance requires a sense of the relationships of authority, the distribution of power, the competencies and resources between the state and local governing institutions at the local and regional levels.[15] However, the representation of the power relationships between different actors involving institutional arrangements is much more complex than just the relationships between state and local governing institutions. This means that the distribution of power reflects only one dimension of a region's ability to control its own fate that is set in the context of state–local power relations. In fact, every collective actor at the level of the family, firm, state and municipality, for example, is crossed by other logics of action at the level of individuals or economic or political actors. Accordingly, institutional and collective arrangements may be viewed as instruments of the codification of authority and at the same time as important elements sustaining social mediation between different parties/actors that are involved in voluntary cooperative activities. Especially at the level of the city and the metropolitan region, there are various actors and organisations that work together in partnerships and networks of relationships taking place through exchange systems that are based on reciprocity and association. These community-oriented exchange systems blur the sectoral, jurisdictional and geographical levels. This is the reason why some authors view cities as collective economic actors or decision-makers that have the authority and power to implement specific policy decision-making (Pompili, 2006: 10).

In fact, the city can be considered a society structured around civic, economic and political leaders and the circles where they meet. Such leaders have a functional legitimacy, and their individual decisions, or lack thereof, are very influential in terms of their impacts on the spatial and economic development of the city. Based on this view, cities can be analysed as sets of economic decision-makers sharing collective interests, exploiting collective resources and undertaking collective actions.

It is worth mentioning that partnerships and networks of relationships between local actors may be structured vertically around the existing state–local relationships and/or horizontally around the existing relationships between local actors within the metropolitan area (municipalities, provinces). However, the effect of the interaction of state centralisation and metropolitan governance on competitiveness indicates that, on average, the metropolitan areas that are the most competitive are centralised regions in decentralised states.

Actors involved in networks and partnerships gain different benefits from a partnership. Conflicts may also occur between actors that may result from the political, cultural and/or ideological dimensions of institution building. More often, consensus between actors is regarded as an important condition for success in situations where variations in interests and policy cultures may hamper the functioning of networks (Raco, 1999). In cases where the institutional environment in which a communitarian network develops is democratic, it should act as a catalyst for cooperation and interaction with other networks, and as a coordination mechanism for fine-tuning agendas and actions between networks. Actors in the networks are individual, collective and public actors representing the various logics of capital (business, ecological, institutional and human). Communication take place through horizontal flows and collective meetings where information is exchanged and proposals for further actions are prepared.

More globally, measures of regional coordination depend largely on cooperation between different actors belonging to different fields and geographical scales. This cooperation principle enables customised solutions according to content, space and time. In addition to the public-public collaborative arrangements, many private and public-private associations and coalitions arrange their own version of regional coordination whether or not they operate in collaborative arrangements based on mixed responsibilities that are supported (or not) by the government in performing their tasks.

3.10 Summary and conclusions

Institutional economics comprises a wide range of theoretical approaches and methodologies that investigate the importance of institutions and institutional structures in governing the coordinated and collective decision-making of agents in specific economic, social and cultural contexts.

However, a comparison between various institutionalist traditions may lead to some confusion when analysing the different meanings and definitions that are given to the concepts of the institution and institutional arrangements. These differences are motivated principally by the theoretical foundations of various institutionalist traditions, the contradictory assumptions regarding human interactions, and the choice for specific analytical tools in investigating the formation, evolution and change of institutions and institutional arrangements.

More generally, the common link between all institutionalist approaches is the conceptualisation of institutions as a configuration of arrangements, rules and procedures that structure people's expectations and their behaviour, and the interactions between actors and between actors and their environment, including the socio-cultural, political, economic and spatial. In turn, institutions are reproduced and transformed through the strategic interactions, actions and reactions of actors to various changes in their environments. In this sense, institutions, whether formal and/or informal, are economic and social organisations and practices operating through rules, beliefs, traditions, customs, norms, equilibria, strategies and regularities that, together, shape patterns of behaviour.

Institutions as 'the rules of the game' define and limit the sets of choices of economic agents, determine the form of economic organisation and influence economic efficiency. They favour or discourage exchanges and other forms of interactions, especially those needed for the coordination of economic activity.

Contemporary institutionalist approaches disagree about the role of informal and formal institutions in economic and social life, the significance of the cognitive properties and efficiency of institutions, and the way institutions emerge and change over time. Some institutionalists believe that institutions involve conscious coordinated planning. In opposition, other institutionalists consider institutions to be the result of a largely uncoordinated evolutionary process. This last point of view is shared by most economists, who consider institutions as conventions that have been evolved over the long term and not deliberately designed. This view of institutions fits well with the idea that economists have put forward to explain the sources of economic change. According to this view, economic change is an ongoing process that is guided by the perceptions of the players to produce desired outcomes that reduce uncertainty and transaction costs. The fundamental source of economic change is learning, and the rate and the type of learning determine, respectively, the speed and the direction of economic change. In short, the learning effects of individuals and organisations and the dynamic change in the stock of knowledge are fundamental to the evolution of institutions. Recent empirical work investigating the relationship between institutions and economic growth provides clear evidence supporting this statement.

Our argument is that institutions evoke different readings according to the domain of research and the type of institutional strand taken into consideration. This applies not only to institutionalist approaches in the broader field of social sciences, but also to a specific but divided field such as economics. However, one may note that within the institutional paradigm in economics, there exists a unifying common belief between economists that emphasises the importance of institutions, in terms of efficiency, for the economic organisation of markets, firms and networks.

Institutional change is viewed in the light of changes in technological innovations, organisations and competition between economic agents in the market economy. Although economic institutional approaches are partly inspired by the old American institutional economics in terms of their focus on economic transactions as the most elementary building block of economic institutions, the undervalued German Historical School provides the most attractive and consistent explanation of the relationship between the localisation of economic activities, territorial development and the role of institutions. Therefore the argument that we have put forward in this chapter is our firm belief that reviving the scientific legacy of this (marginalised) school of thought would enormously enrich and deepen our understanding concerning the formation, the self-reinforcement and the dynamic change of institutions and institutional arrangements from historical and spatial perspectives.

In addition, major efforts should be made, as we have tried to do in this chapter, to produce a synthesis of the major ideas from existing institutionalist theoretical strands and link them to urban and regional economics and spatial planning in order to understand and explain the organisational structure of the economy in a spatial context. This can be realised by taking into account the nature and role of collective and institutional arrangements in shaping political, social and legal institutions and their organisational structures in explaining the economic organisation and, ultimately, the effective factors accounting for economic development and growth.

Building on several versions of institutional economic theories, such as the neo- and new-institutional economics, regulation theory and sociological institutional- ism, and borrowing from them the main theoretical ideas, is crucial in developing a conceptual theoretical framework centred on the concepts of institutional and collective arrangements in relation to institutions. Because we are interested in positioning the role and importance of collective arrangements in a spatial context, a careful examination of the meaning of collective arrangements should take into account the nature, forms, criteria and various dimensions of this concept.

The first challenge is to define in a consistent and precise manner what we understand by collective arrangements and how they are integrated within exist- ing institutional environments. We conceive collective arrangements as the basic building blocks or infrastructure of institutional arrangements and institutions. These latter are considered as the superstructure of the institutional field or institutional regime.

Strictly speaking, institutional and collective arrangements operating in a specific institutional regime are not synonymous. Institutional arrangements are institutionalised 'rules of the game' that are embedded within various societal domains (economy, spatial planning, politics, culture, etc.), but collective arrangements may or may not be institutionalised (yet). They evolve over time and at a given moment in time they may transform into institutional arrangements after being institutionalised through law, regulation and other formal arrange- ments. More specifically, collective arrangements are context dependent and spatially embedded, and need time and resources to settle and to transform into institutional arrangements, and in the long run into institutions.

Viewed from this perspective, institutional arrangements are essentially rules and conventions operating within institutional settings, and include formal insti- tutions and regulations as well as informal arrangements that include traditional laws, values and norms and customs. These may be formal such as the traditional law, for example, or informal like tolerance, a consensus model, a love for trade and discovery, etc.

Moreover, collective arrangements are subject to various criteria, possess different characteristics and have many dimensions. What is important for the purpose of our study is to identify and describe the evolution of collective arrangements and their interventions in the spatial and economic domains in general and the spatial and economic transformation of cities and regions in particular. In this respect, we develop a conceptual framework based on three determinant processes that explain the evolution of collective arrangements in time and space. These are: the process of accumulation, the process of transfor- mation and the process of reconfiguration or recombination.

The process of accumulation concerns the creation or selection of complemen- tary (new) arrangements within the same field, while the process of transformation of collective arrangements defines the process of reorganisation and restructuring of procedures, organisation and interpretation of the rules by actors within exist- ing possibilities offered by collective arrangements. Finally, the reconfiguration of collective arrangements concerns the redefinition of the relations between different collective arrangements within the same local institutional configuration or institutional regime.

Our conceptual framework reveals the possibility of the existence of a variety of evolutionary institutional forms and arrangements that follow different progressive development trajectories affecting the institutional configuration. It takes into account the degree of coherence of spatial, economic and institutional configurations on cities and regions, and factors and actors that govern their evolution in the long run.

In urban and regional contexts, collective arrangements structuring the territorial and functional organisation of economic activities may be reflected into two spatial organisational forms: competition and cooperation, that is either horizontal or vertical interactions between actors. Note, however, that the complexity and dynamic of collective arrangements may result in a complex urban governance structure, especially when large and growing number of interacting independent actors are involved in the decision-making process. In this case, it is important to identify the relevant key actors, their specific role and position of power within networks, and their goals and motivations in order to understand the nature, role and importance of collective arrangements in the spatial and economic transformation processes of cities and regions. This is because collective arrangements form the key building blocks of local institutional arrangements, and therefore any good governance structure could succeed only if it provides a framework in which relevant actors can reach agreement over spatial and temporal horizons of action vis-à-vis their environment. Note that there exists no such thing as a good or ideal governance regime, because this depends on the territorial scale level and the sector of activities such as the organisation, the market (private sector) or the state (public sector).

At the level of city or the metropolitan region, various actors and organisations work together in partnerships and networks of relationships that take place through market exchange systems. Cooperation and market transactions are two alternative modes of coordinating economic activities. In this sense, coordination can be fulfilled through the organisation, i.e. the hierarchy, the market, or through hybrid coordination forms such as networks for example. These three modes of coordination are especially relevant when examining the different models governing inter-firm arrangements and/or land use planning and their effects on the spatial configuration and transformation of urban areas or city regions.

Part II

Application

Spatial-economic transformation of Schiphol airport and Amsterdam-Schiphol region during the twentieth century

4 Urbanisation and industrialisation of Schiphol and the Amsterdam-Schiphol region 1900–45

4.1 Introduction

Few studies have been conducted on the relationship between urbanisation and airport development, not only for the early years of airfield development in the 1920s and 1930s, but also during the opening decades of the post-Second World War period. In this chapter – and in Chapter 5 – we analyse the causes and consequences of the rise and development of Schiphol airport in relation to urbanisation and urban development of the Amsterdam-Schiphol region. In doing so, we hope to fill this gap in the literature.

From a historical perspective, the rise and development of airports are closely related to urbanisation, urban sprawl and economic growth in the sense that airfields are strongly associated with the cities where they are located. In this perspective, thinking about airport development as an integral part of the urbanisation and economic transformation of cities and regions, instead of the traditional view which considers airports only as point and line infrastructure, transport nodes or transportation locations, can shed more light on underlying factors of urbanisation and economic growth of cities and regions.

The historical spatial transformation of cities and their suburbs is strongly related to changes in land use patterns and activities that are accompanied by movements of people, goods, capital, services, money transactions, information and innovation. As a result, complex patterns of flows occur, which vary with the forms, functions and structures (Daniels, 1999).

To understand the historical changes of urban forms and the spatial and economic organisation of cities and surrounding countryside in Europe, one may go back to the nineteenth century when most European countries were structurally affected by the urbanisation and industrialisation processes that triggered these changes. More specifically, from the late nineteenth century until the Second World War, industrialisation and urbanisation generated a strongly polarised hierarchical urban system dominated by monocentric agglomeration. Urban centres attracted a continuous flow of people, goods and capital from other regions and from the small towns and villages surrounding them. The continuity and change in land use between city centres and their suburban areas and the periphery (outer fringes) is often considered a discontinuous spatial phenomenon.

In this sense, urban sprawl and the urbanisation of the urban fringe depend upon the pressure on growth such as high density, diversity of activities and functions, other agglomeration advantages and the intensity of human activities that use the geographic space (or the topographic space). These activities generate the forms and functions of urban areas (or the topological space). Consequently, the transformation of the topographic space may be seen as the representation of the transformations occurring in the topological space. In other word, there is not only a transition in terms of forms, but also a transition in the functional relationships between cities and their surrounding areas and between cities in the wider territorial area, e.g. at the inter-regional level. Note, however, that human activities themselves result from the interaction of the human decision-making units, namely individuals, households, firms and institutions.

History shows that industrialisation and urbanisation are intimately related. The first wave of urbanisation, for example, was closely related to the development of agriculture and the increased concentration of economic activities in the major urban cities. In the Netherlands, the growth of cities took place in the second half of the nineteenth century. The first migratory movements of the population from the countryside to big cities, especially to the western part of the country, began around 1875 with the industrialisation of the country. The agriculture sector experienced a major development in terms of technological development and forms of production. As a result of the substitution of labour by capital, a large part of the workforce was released from the agriculture sector. Most of the unemployed labour force then sought refuge in the cities where the opportunities to find a job in industry was much higher than in other sectors. Cities then grew relatively faster with the increase in industrialisation and, therefore, the demand for labour released from the agricultural sector increased. In addition, the construction of railroad infrastructure networks further stimulated the movement of people, goods and information between regions formerly isolated. Intra- and inter-regional infrastructure brought about the first real suburbs and the rapid growth of cities, by providing cost-effective and reasonably swift links between cities and the countryside.

The first wave of suburbanisation, which took place at the end of the nineteenth century and the early years of the twentieth, had an elitist origin, in the sense that suburbs were mainly 'refuge settlements' for rich people escaping the crowded, polluted and unhealthier cities. At the same time, the mobility of people, e.g. commuters between cities and the countryside, increased as the technological advances in transportation technology made considerable improvements. As a result, the daily urban system of the working class increased considerably, and in turn this resulted in a further increase in suburbanisation and the urban sprawl.

In the historical context of the beginning of the twentieth century, the first signs of the development of the aviation industry became apparent, although it was restricted at first to the military domain and civil aviation did not take off until after 1919 and into the 1920s (we will come back to this issue in Chapter 5). Beside the spatial effects of urbanisation and industrialisation, the development of airfields and civil aviation also changed the spatial and economic structure of the cities and the region considerably. In this sense, the historical changes that took place in the Netherlands during the late nineteenth and the first half of the twentieth centuries, in term of spatial and economic changes, are of great importance in understanding the long-term spatial-economic transformation of Schiphol and the Amsterdam region.

In this chapter we focus on the historical background underlying the industrialisation and urbanisation processes during the first half of the twentieth century in the Netherlands, as well as at the regional level, especially that of the Amsterdam-Schiphol region.

This chapter is organised as follows. In section 4.2, we discuss the main driving forces of economic transition, industrialisation and urbanisation in the Netherlands during the last half of the nineteenth and first half of the twentieth centuries. A detailed quantitative and qualitative analysis of the industrialisation process and the subsequent sectoral shift and change in economic structure is approached from different perspectives in subsection 4.2.1. The aim is to identify, describe and explain the main driving forces behind the industrialisation and urbanisation of the country during one of the most critical historical periods in the recent history of the Netherlands. In section 4.3, we analyse the demographic, spatial and economic transition during the first half of the twentieth century at the meso-level, with special attention to the economic transformation of the local economic structures and spatial patterns of the Amsterdam-Schiphol region and the Randstad-Holland. Next, a detailed analysis of the historical spatial development of the city of Amsterdam and the Haarlemmermeer region is provided in sections 4.4 and 4.5. More attention is given to urban spatial planning and urban development in relation to geographical and economic changes in these two locations from 1900 until 1940. Section 4.6 concludes.

4.2 Economic transition and industrialisation in the Netherlands 1850–1945: a brief review

Compared to other European countries such as the UK and France, the Netherlands almost missed the Industrial Revolution as industrialisation did not reach the country until around around 1870. However, when industrialisation started, rapid economic growth took place whereby the economic structure of the country changed drastically. Industrialisation, which was based on the extraction of natural resources (mining and the coal industry) and the low cost of the labour force, has been strongly related to increased urbanisation. Dutch cities, especially the four big cities in the western part of the country, grew relatively faster and the Netherlands was able to catch up with other industrialised countries such as Britain, France and Germany. Between 1870 and 1917, the GDP per capita in the Netherlands increased even faster than in France and Germany and reached the same growth level as in the UK between 1920 and 1930. Together with France, the economic growth in the Netherlands was among the highest in European countries during the postwar period 1961–78 (see Figure 4.1).

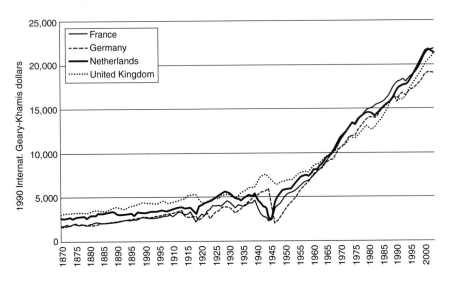

Figure 4.1 Growth per capita GDP of the Netherlands: 1870–2002.
Source: Maddison, A. (2008) *Historical statistics for the World Economy* (1–2003 AD).

Emerging urban cores such as Amsterdam and Rotterdam attracted thousands of people from the countryside who had been released from agriculture. As a result, the size of the cities and the urban population density reached unprecedented levels. For most of these working-class immigrants single home occupancy in the city proper was either unaffordable or unavailable, therefore the city fringes provided a location where the new inhabitants could construct new homes. In the meantime, manufacturing industries also moved to these unplanned suburbs, partly because of the proximity to a potential labour force and partly because of the abundance of low-priced land in these areas. As a result, an increasing number of land development companies emerged in the construction market, and speculation in land and building construction took unprecedented forms, especially in Amsterdam.

More generally, the industrialisation and urbanisation of the country were accompanied by a relative faster increase in the population from 1875. In 1900, the total population of the Netherlands stood at about 5 million inhabitants. This number increased to more than 8 million during the 1930s and 10 million in the 1950s, before reaching 16 million in 2000–1. The distribution of population by age shows a high growth rate in the categories 0–20 years and 20–45 years, especially during the first three decades of the post-Second World War period. More particularly, the period 1960–75 may be characterised as a 'baby boom' period because of the high growth rate of the population under 20.

However, the cause of the revival of the Netherlands and the Dutch cities has its roots in the structural improvements in infrastructure (railroads and public services) and the tremendous growth in the construction sector, which, together, triggered the processes of industrialisation and urbanisation. This has resulted in an increase in employment in the manufacturing industry and services, and consequently an increase in real wages, incomes, consumption and productivity. According to Zanden and Riel (2000: 350), economic growth in the Netherlands is related to two waves of investment that took place at the end of the nineteenth century. The first wave took place in rail transportation technology between 1866 and 1882, as a result of investments in railroad networks and housing construction. The second wave took place between 1894 and 1913 and was caused by the substitution of labour by capital in agriculture, an increase in investment in fixed capital in the manufacturing sector after 1870, e.g. steam machines, gas power, electric motors, etc., and investment in the construction sector, e.g. infrastructure and housing.

Beside the rapid increase in technological innovations, specialisation and division of labour in the manufacturing industry increased the size of the market, which, in turn, resulted in an increase in production (i.e. the scale of production) and investments. The increase in investments in the manufacturing sector was sustained by two main factors. First there was a high level of capital accumulation by the Dutch financial and banking sector gained through trade with the Dutch colonies. Secondly, there was a high level of saving as a result of high interest rates and a gradual decrease in the long-term interest rate in the capital market. For instance, between 1876 and 1915, the long-term interest rate was around 3–4 per cent while in 1925 it was about 5 per cent before decreasing to approximately 3 per cent in 1938. Savings increased by almost 66 per cent between 1814 and 1853 (from 36 million to 60 million guilders), and by more than 114 per cent between 1854 and 1863 (from 60 million to 128.9 million guilders), before stabilising at 296.6 million guilders between 1884 and 1893.

4.2.1 *Industrialisation and transformation of economic structure: the sectoral shift*

With the industrialisation of the Netherlands, structural transformations of the Dutch economy took place between 1860 and 1945. One characteristic of these structural changes was the shift in the economy from agriculture towards the manufacturing industry and services. To understand these changes, one has to take into consideration the circular cumulative processes occurring at the demand and supply sides of the national economy, more particularly the changes occurring at the level of employment, wages and incomes, production, investment and productivity, and the demand for goods and services. For example, total employment in the manufacturing sector doubled *between 1850 and 1900*. By the end of the nineteenth century, more than 30 per cent of employees had a job in the agriculture and fishing sectors, 25 per cent in industry and 13 per cent in the service sector while only 10 per cent of the Dutch labour force had a job in domestic service, i.e. as a household employee (see Table 4.1). In 1920, the share of employment in the agriculture sector decreased to 23.5 per cent but increased

Table 4.1 Share of labour force by sector (as % of total labour force)

	1899	*1909*	*1920*	*1930*
Agriculture and fishing	**30.4**	**27.5**	**23.5**	**20.2**
Extraction of minerals	1	1	2	2
Manufacturing industry	**25**	**26**	**28**	**28**
Public services	0	0	1	1
Construction and installation firms	7	7	7	8
Trade, hotels and catering industry	11	11	12	14
Transport, storage and communication	6	7	8	8
Banking, insurance and business services	2	3	4	4
Total services	**13**	**13**	**13**	**13**
Domestic services	10	10	8	8
Others	3	3	2	2

Source: CBS (200 jaar statistiek in tijdreeksen, Historie Arbeid: 1899–2005).

to 28 per cent in manufacturing industry. The manufacturing sectors and services registered relatively high increases in employment, especially in trade, the hotel and catering industry, transport, storage and communications, and banking, insurance and business services. The share of the labour force in the 'domestic services' sector decreased further from 10 per cent in 1899 to 8 per cent in 1930. This was mainly due to the absorption of the female labour force by the manufacturing industries and the services.

First, the agriculture sector in the Netherlands was characterised by large variations in production and productivity levels between the fertile clay regions along the great rivers Rhine, Meuse and Scheldt in the west, the sandy regions in the east and the low-productive regions in the proximity of the North Sea (Zanden, 2002: 2). Between 1882 and 1896, the Dutch agriculture sector was severely hit by a decrease in prices, due, among other things, to the increase in imports of agriculture products, especially from the USA. As a result, the level of employment, wages, incomes and land prices decreased significantly. Between 1904 and 1930, the agriculture sector recovered and the number of firms increased from 183,000 in 1904 to 234,000 in 1930. The average relative change in the number of new firms was around 5.5 per cent between 1921 and 1930, and 40.31 per cent between 1930 and 1950. This tendency was then reversed from the 1960s onward, as the economic transition from an industry-based economy to a more services-oriented economy began to take place in the Netherlands. (The average relative change over the whole period 1960–99 was –23.78 per cent and –28.9 per cent between 1960 and 1980, and –17.9 per cent between 1980–99.)

Note that the modernisation of the agriculture sector at the end of the nineteenth and throughout the first half of the twentieth century took place through capital intensification, rationalisation and restructuring of the production process. Because of economies of scale in production and the efficient use of resources, productivity and production increased substantially at the end of the nineteenth century and in the first decades of the twentieth.

The modernisation of agriculture was supported by new institutions such as cooperative organisations, education centres, cooperative banks and insurance companies, as well as the accessibility information about markets, technologies and production methods. Furthermore, the increased scale of production and the specialisation of firms resulted in a significant decrease in transaction costs and an increase in efficiency in production in terms of optimal use of land, the introduction of new production methods, and the diversification and intensification of production process, etc.

Second, manufacturing industry was highly concentrated and oligopolistic during the second half of the nineteenth century. A few large-scale family companies dominated the manufacturing industry producing for large markets, for example Philips in Eindhoven, the Van den Bergh butter company and Douwe Egbert (coffee) in Utrecht, food companies in Zaanstad and shipbuilding firms in Rotterdam. Investments in the manufacturing sector were particularly concentrated in the heavy industries such as shipbuilding, metallurgy and coal mining, the electrical engineering industry and the food industry.

However, in the 1870s, small and medium-sized enterprises (SMEs) began to emerge in manufacturing. The majority of SME firms were supported by low labour costs and low land and rental costs in cities (Wagenaar, 1990: 180–4). Furthermore, the Dutch manufacturing industry was stimulated by a liberal industrialisation policy based on low-cost competition, international specialisation and the development of modern physical infrastructure aiming to extend the size of the national market.

Although the number of firms decreased between 1890 and 1930, production levels increased substantially, together with considerable improvement in the competitive position of Dutch industry. The economy of increasing scale resulted in the geographical concentration of production in a limited number of regions, very often in and around the urban centres of the western region. The selective spatial concentration of the population in the four cities of the Randstad-Holland was the result of the relative decrease in agriculture in the specialised agrarian areas along the borders of this region, and the increase in nominal wages in the manufacturing sector, especially since the 1860s. During the period 1868–1900, for example, real wages in the Netherlands increased by 150 per cent (from less than 500 million to 796 million guilders) and by more than 170 per cent between 1910 and 1921.

Another major change in manufacturing industry was the introduction of new management forms. Most big companies changed their family-based management style to a more Taylorist style, that is a separation of management from production and distribution activities and the creation of an intermediate controlling layer within the firm. This change in the internal management of manufacturing firms is also associated with the second wave of industrialisation and the emergence of the industrial society based on the Fordist production system (Toffler, 1980). The main principles of this production system lie in the standardisation of the production process (mass production), specialisation (technical and social division of labour), synchronisation of tasks (e.g. chain work, concentration) and efficiency in the organisation of activities (e.g. separation of management from standardised work processes).

In summary, the transformation of the industrial structure in the Netherlands was accelerated by the introduction of innovations (in products and processes), the development of steam engines (from 1880), improvements in transport technologies and the use of new materials and new energy resources such as gasoline, oil and electricity. In particular the introduction of new electrical engines into the production process enabled firms to concentrate their production in a few large firms, to produce more efficiently and to realise economies of scale and scope. The analysis of productivity levels in manufacturing industry shows the clear domination of the food, textile and extraction and mining industries, which registered high levels of productivity between 1890 and 1937. However, a substantial increase in industrial sector, in terms of productivity, took place after 1915. The value added increased in almost all industries, which supports the fact that the country reached a high level of industrialisation and that the manufacturing industry became the most important driver of economic growth of the Dutch economy.

Third, besides the growth of manufacturing industry, the growth of services was one of the main driving forces of economic change in the Netherlands. The service sectors which underwent the greatest expansion during the period 1840–70 were trade, tourism, repair and renovation work, transportation, storage and communication. In contrast, the construction industry and public services lagged somewhat behind other sectors.

Services became important sources of economic growth, especially with the increase in trade and transport activities between the Netherlands and its colonies, and the increase in public expenditure on public amenities, e.g. education, health care, housing, etc.

More generally, the institutional and economic reforms, which took place at the end of the nineteenth and beginning of the twentieth centuries, resulted in structural changes in the Dutch economy. These changes were manifested, first, by a shift from an agriculture-based economy into industry-based economy and then by a rapid increase in economic growth after 1870. Secondly, the modernisation of the agriculture sector was accompanied by important institutional reforms and restructuring of the sector. Thirdly, because of strong expansion in the manufacturing industry and services, mainly trade with the Dutch colonies after 1870, the Netherlands was then able to catch up with other industrialised countries such as France, Germany and the UK. The industrialisation of the country was pushed further ahead by the second industrial revolution, which took place around 1890, that was based on technological innovations and the use of new resources such as oil and electricity.

4.2.2 *Main triggers of industrialisation and economic growth in the Netherlands*

The development of high-quality transportation systems in the Netherlands was, without doubt, of crucial importance for the industrialisation and urbanisation of the country and its economic growth. Historically, different transportation systems existed in the nineteenth century. The inland waterway transportation system played a key role in the economic growth of cities like Amsterdam and Rotterdam during the golden age, that is the seventeenth century. All larger Dutch cities in the west, north and south of the country were connected with each other through a sophisticated waterway transport system of passengers and goods.

Up until 1870, Dutch provinces were not economically integrated because of the poor physical state of the transport infrastructure, the higher cost of inland navigation and transit trade along the River Rhine, the high taxation on river crossings and bridges, and the monopoly power of some powerful actors that dominated the inland water transport sector, i.e. 'beurtvaarten' (inland water transport between cities) and 'trekvaarten' (canal-boat transport) (see Knippenberg and de Pater, 1988). However, the great turning point in infrastructure construction took place during the reign of King William I of Orange. A major part of public investments were spent on infrastructures such as the improvement of existing waterway transport systems, the construction of new railroad transport networks and the winning of new land such as the reclamation of the Haarlemmermeer polder in 1852. However, investments in large infrastructure projects changed according to the priorities and needs of the Dutch economy. Up until 1850, for example, public investment was concentrated merely on the reclamation of land from the sea and lakes, the improvement of waterway transport through rivers and canals and the improvement of the costal defences. Between 1850 and 1870, a large part of public investment in infrastructure projects concerned the construction of the railroad network system. From 1902 until the 1920s, public investments in infrastructure were oriented towards the expansion of existing local and intra-regional railroad networks, and towards public services such as the gas and water supply and electricity network.

As Figure 4.2 shows, approximately, 77 per cent of investments in infrastructure concerned the construction of the railroad transport network in 1870, more than 20 per cent of total investments were spent on the construction and improvement of roads in 1850 and more than 55 per cent of investments in 1897 concerned improvements to the waterways infrastructure, e.g. canals and rivers.[1]

During the 1930s and 1940s, the largest part of public investment in infrastructure concerned road construction, waterways and harbours, while during the post-Second World War period, the greatest share of public investment was oriented towards the reconstruction of vital physical infrastructure that was destroyed during the war (i.e. category 'others'), and towards further enlargement and improvement of roads/motorways, canals and the coastal defences. Note that, during the 1950s and after the devastating 'water disaster' of 1953, substantial amounts were spent on coastal defence construction projects, and since the 1970s on the improvement of the water supply system and (social) housing construction.

Dutch economic historians agree that the construction of the railway transport networks played an important role in triggering the process of industrialisation and urbanisation in the Netherlands, and hence the integration of regions formerly disconnected from each other.

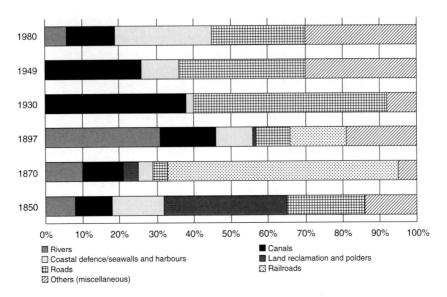

Figure 4.2 Investments in infrastructure between 1850 and 1980 (%).
Source: compilation based on Bosch and van der Ham (1998, p. 76 and p. 153).

Up until 1860, the railway network system in the Netherlands was composed of a very limited numbers of railway tracks. By the end of the nineteenth century, however, a completely new and coherent railway network system connecting all regions of the country had been realised. The railroad network was filled by numerous additional local tracks for trams and regional trains. Since then, only minor improvements have been implemented, and it was not until the late 1970s that important changes in the initial configuration were made, in particular the construction of new connections between Amsterdam and The Hague through the Schiphol airport and between Schiphol and the rest of the country.

In 1860, for example, there was only 335 km of railroads in the Netherlands, of which 32 km were electrified. Ten years later (1870), the total length of the railway network reached more than 1,500 km, of which 133 km were electrified services. In 1995, the total length of the railways reached 2,813 km, of which 1,939 km were electrified services (see Map 4.1). In terms of economic performance, the railway sector showed a large increase in the total number of passengers between 1900 and 1916 (from 33,000 to 76,000 passengers), followed by a slight, but continuing, decrease between 1917 and 1936.

It is widely recognised now that at the beginning of the twentieth century, the dwelling patterns of the Dutch population changed dramatically due to the advances in transport technology, decreasing transportation costs, increasing incomes and increasing amounts of free time. As Schmal (2003: 67) argues, trams and trains were very important elements in explaining the expansion of the daily urban system and the convergence of the time-space and cost-space.[2]

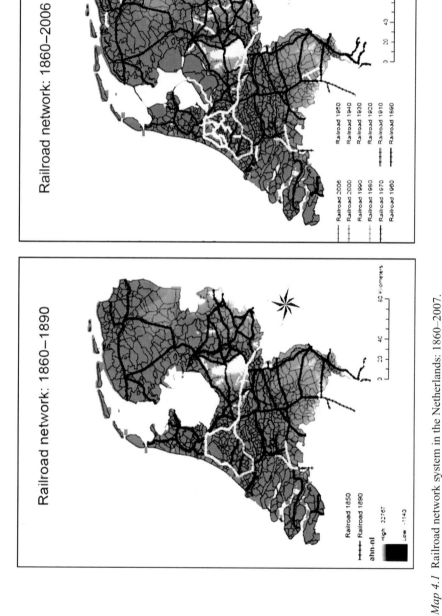

Map 4.1 Railroad network system in the Netherlands: 1860–2007.
Source: based on various historical maps from archives and from the Ministry of Transport and Waterworks (min. VWS).

The development of the railroads enabled workers to follow jobs to the cities. At the end of the nineteenth century and during the first half of the twentieth century, employment was concentrated in the downtown centre of central cities and around harbours. The accessibility of the city centre posed many problems as it became increasingly filled with horses, carriages, salesmen and pedestrians. Most people could only reach their destination by walking through crowded streets. At that time, the lack of appropriate public transportation limited the range of regular activities to the city centre and immediately surrounding areas.

Because the population and work activities simultaneously followed each other, high urban density meant that the quality of life in many Dutch cities was deteriorating rapidly. Various reports and studies that were conducted at the end of the nineteenth century and during the first half of the twentieth described Amsterdam and other big cities of the Randstad as overpopulated, unhealthy and relatively expensive for the working class (see Klerk, 2008). The improvement in various modes of transportation was then expected to improve the mobility of the population and solve, at least partly, the housing shortage and the sanitary and health problems in the cities (Schmal, 2003: 68).

On one hand, the development of the public transport and the expansion of national and local railway networks expanded the daily urban system from 5–10 km to 20–30 km. On the other hand, the improvement in transportation infrastructure, together with the developments in transport technology, provided workers with greater flexibility in their choice of living and working places. Suburban areas such as Kennemerland, the Gooi, the Utrechts Heuvelrug and the Veleuwezoom (including Arnhem) became popular settlement areas for the urban elite. Most of these suburban areas, which were first popular holiday and recreation places during the last decade of the nineteenth century, became permanent residential settlements for the middle classes. Beside the towns of Baarn, Hilversum and Bussum in the Gooi and Bloemendaal and Heemstede in Kenemrland, small towns such as Laren, Blaricum and Huizen and the villages of Badhoevedorp and Diemen also became very popular settlement areas for commuters.

At the city level, however, the replacement of the old-fashioned and costly horse-drawn trolleys (operated by private companies) by electric trams opened up larger urban areas for the construction of new residential districts. Cities took over the running of the intra-urban tramway services from the private operators, as in, for example, the case of the Amsterdamsche Omnibus Maatschappij (AOM) in 1900.

Tramways and inter-regional tramway lines became the preferred means of public transportation for the working classes because of the low and falling price of tickets (from 10 cents in 1900 to 5 cents in 1913) and the introduction of special low rates for subscribers (Schmal, 2003: 76).

Between 1889 and 1910, the prices of public transportation (tram and train) as well as the travel time between cities have decreased substantially. As a result, the accessibility of Dutch cities and regions was substantially improved. Figure 4.3 shows the combined effects of decreasing travel costs (in value) and travel time (in minutes) between Amsterdam and some other Dutch cities between 1880 and 1980.

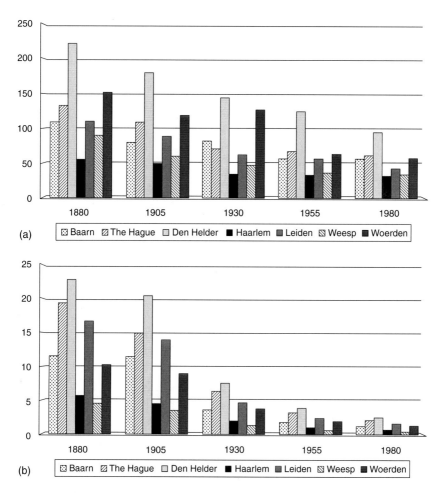

Figure 4.3 Transport costs (above) and travel time (below) from/to Amsterdam: 1880–1990. *Source*: based on Musterd and de Pater (1994, p. 23).

Taking 1880 as the base year, travel costs in the public transportation sector (i.e. prices of tickets calculated as a percentage of incomes) have dropped from 85 per cent in 1905 to 41 per cent in 1930, and from 18 per cent in 1955 to 12 per cent in 1980. The highest decrease in transport costs occurred between 1905 and 1930, due to the improvements in transport technologies and the introduction of new transport means such as the automobile and the airplane. Similar decreasing patterns of travel time between cities are also shown in Figure 4.3. For example, the travel time from Amsterdam to The Hague decreased by 25 minutes between 1880 and 1905 (from 133 minutes to 108 minutes) and by more than one hour in 1930 (71 minutes). From 1955, the same distance could be made in less than 1½ hour by train (86 minutes in 1955), and just over one hour (61 minutes) in 1980.

More globally, the combination of changes in transportation technology and the development of transportation networks produced the basic ingredients of suburbanisation and urban sprawl, e.g. dispersed residential areas and industry. For example, in 1928, only 5 per cent of the working population commuted between cities and regions. This percentage increased to 15 per cent of the total working population of the Netherlands in 1947, 27 per cent in 1960 and respectively to 35 per cent and 52 per cent in 1971 and 1986. Furthermore, the combined effects of the decreasing transport costs and travel time with the expansion of intra- and inter-regional public transportation (train, tramways and regional trams) and an extensive public housing policy supported the suburbanisation process at the regional level. In Amsterdam, for instance, new settlements of commuters were dispersed along the tramlines connecting the satellite locations of Sloterdijk and Diemerbrug to Amsterdam city centre. Interventions of the central government were restricted to water management, including the extensive reclamation of land from under water, and the improvement of infrastructure and public services. Spatial planning was the domain of local authorities (Bertolini, 2001).

Beside investments in infrastructure such as railway networks, great efforts were also made by the Dutch government in the construction and extension of telecommunication networks and public services. In 1852, for example, there were only five telegram offices in the Netherlands, one in Amsterdam and the other four in the cities of The Hague, Rotterdam, Dordrecht and Breda. In 1867, the number of offices was extended to 90 locations. In 1895, only 31 local telephone networks existed in the country, which were used mainly by public services units. Gradually, the use of telephone communications expanded to almost all regions. Between 1895 and 1943, the use of telephones by Dutch citizens and public services increased from 12.7 per cent to 1,041 per cent. In 1938, the total number of telephones used in the Netherlands reached 306,000, and in 1943 approximately 345,000 phones.

In the first instance, the private initiative took the lead in investing in new transport, communication and public services. Gradually, the municipalities began to compete with private firms in the supply and distribution of gas, electricity and water to their inhabitants. At the same time, the electrification of the Netherlands took place at a larger scale. In 1922, two-thirds of all Dutch municipalities (about 357) were able to produce and distribute electricity. Seventeen years later (1939), only six municipalities were not in possession of their own central electricity supply.

The major part of the production of electricity came from thermal energy centrals owned by the municipalities.

More generally, the electrification of the Netherlands gave an additional boost to the industrialisation of the country and to the improvement of public transportation, e.g. the electrification of trams and trains. Firms were able to use new electricity-driven equipment in their production processes. As result, the size and scale of production increased considerably, and craft firms gave place to big manufacturing firms producing on a greater scale and for a much larger market.

In addition, investments in the construction sector were closely related to the improvements in the infrastructure networks, which resulted in the spectacular expansion of large Dutch cities from 1860. Consequently, construction activities increased substantially between 1866 and 1883. The levels of investment in the construction and installation sector were very high during the period 1917–30. The value added increased from 2 million guilders in 1900 to 75 million in 1920 and to 100 million in 1929. However, the economic crisis of the 1930s had clear negative effects on the construction sector, especially between 1934 and 1936. It is worth mentioning that the introduction of the Housing Act in 1901 had direct effects on housing construction in the Netherlands. Before 1900, about 27 to 30 per cent of new housing consisted of small-sized houses comprising one and two rooms. Between 1900 and 1910, large numbers of newly constructed houses were 'social housing' with two or more rooms. After 1910, the majority of new housing consisted of large houses comprising three or more rooms. It seems that the focus of the government was mainly oriented towards the accommodation of an increasingly urban population in general and of households with two or more children in particular.

Last but not least, important political and institutional changes that took place in the Netherlands during this period could be considered one of the main triggers of economic growth. Historically, the political structure of the Netherlands has had a long tradition of decentralisation. One of the most characteristic features of the Dutch republic was its federal nature and the strong autonomy that was given to local (urban) authorities (Wagenaar, 1998: 209). The New Municipality Law of 1851 stated that all cities, towns and villages were equal in law and their local governance was the responsibility of the local authorities. Thus local authorities enjoyed great financial and fiscal autonomy, for example with regard to local taxes on land, patents and private incomes. However, several changes in the Dutch political system took place during the second half of the nineteenth century. Thorbeck's constitutional reforms of 1848, for example, increased the power of democratic political institutions at the expense of the power of the monarchy. Under the new Dutch constitution, the law improved the participation of citizens in political life. For example, until 1830, less than 5 per cent of the Dutch population had voting rights. By 1917, all adult men had the right to vote; five years later (1922) adult women were also given the same right.

Furthermore, in 1865, under pressure from liberal politicians, large numbers of local taxes were abolished and replaced by a centralised taxation system. As a result of fiscal reforms, local authorities became fully dependent on the state municipality's funds and other state subsidies that were directly managed by the central government. The state intervened actively in the social, cultural and economic affairs of cities and regions. Beside the financial reforms, the central government had to respond actively to increasing demands from new political movements, especially from the Confessionalist (at the national level) and the socialist movements (at the local level). As result, a series of social reforms and policy measures aimed at improving education (e.g. the introduction of compulsory learning), health care, housing and public services were applied both at national and local levels.

In short, from the 1870s, the Netherlands became a modern nation, with clear domination of the so-called 'pillars' (or the 'pillarisation of society') across existing religious beliefs and political ideologies. This pillarisation has largely determined the social, economic and political life of Dutch society. After the First World War (1914–18), the political administrative system in the Netherlands changed fundamentally with the introduction of universal suffrage. The Confessionalist and socialist political elite took the power from the liberals at the national level, but at the local level the socialists held the reins after 1918, albeit in a coalition with other parties as in the case of Amsterdam for example.

4.3 Economic and demographic transition at the regional level: the Amsterdam-Schiphol region 1900–40

A direct consequence of decreasing employment in the agriculture sector between 1880 and 1913 was the increase in intra-regional migration, especially from the periphery regions to the four big cities of the Randstad-Holland where the expansion of manufacturing and services provided sufficient growth to mop up the labour force released from the agriculture sector. It was in this context that public investments in infrastructure and housing construction were used to trigger economic growth in cities and regions.

From 1900, a period of unprecedented economic expansion and growth took place in the Randstad region. For the first time in a long period of economic decline (the sixteenth to the seventeenth centuries), the urbanisation and urban concentration of population and activities in Amsterdam and Rotterdam produced both positive agglomeration benefits and increasingly negative agglomeration effects, e.g. congestion, pollution, housing shortage and overcrowding. The priorities of local governments were then oriented towards the improvement of the quality of life and the accommodation of a growing urban population. Under the pressure of population growth, existing medieval city walls around the traditional cities such as Amsterdam and Utrecht were demolished in order to create more space for the realisation of cities' expansion plans.

More generally, the tendency during this period was rapid industrialisation followed by successive and continuous migration of the population from peripheral agrarian regions in the direction of large industrial cities.

4.3.1 Demographic transition

In 1622, the total population of the Netherlands was 400,000, of which 60 per cent lived in cities and 40 per cent in the countryside. Among the 33 existing cities, 18 had a population of less than 5,000. Amsterdam was the largest city in 1670, with approximately 200,000 inhabitants, corresponding to approximately 50 per cent of the country's total population. Besides Amsterdam, the most important cities at that time were Leiden, Haarlem, Delft, Gouda, Hoorn, Enkhuizen, Rotterdam and Middelburg. As a result of urban resurgence during the seventeenth and eighteenth centuries, Amsterdam and Rotterdam, and to a

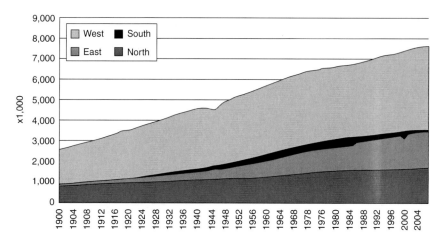

Figure 4.4 Population growth by region between 1900 and 2007.
Source: CBS (HDNG and Volkstellingen, 1899–2007).

lesser extent The Hague and Utrecht, grew rapidly, while previously important towns in the South and East of the country stagnated or declined with respect to their rank and size within the Dutch urban city system. A new geographical pattern of several large towns, a number of medium-sized towns and many small towns emerged. In 1849, more than 40 per cent of the Dutch population lived in these towns. By 1930 this percentage had grown to 65.6 per cent, before falling to below 53 per cent in 1970 (Deurloo and Hoekveld, 1980).

However, at the beginning of the twentieth century, the Netherlands was still largely rural. However, over a period of just one century, it has changed into one of the most urbanised countries of Europe. The Industrial Revolution prompted the development of new infrastructure (harbours, rail infrastructure, roads), which, in turn, stimulated the growth of the most accessible urban centres. The largest concentrations of urban population have always been in the western regions of the country, where the largest four cities – Amsterdam, Rotterdam, The Hague and Utrecht – are located.

While the population of the country as a whole and of the provinces of North Holland, South Holland and Utrecht have shown continuous growth since 1900, the growth was less straightforward in other regions of the country, and more particularly in the small and medium-sized cities (see Figure 4.4). However, the picture is somewhat different between the cities of the province of North Holland: while the population of Amsterdam grew continuously between 1900 and 1950, the population of small and medium-sized cities remained largely unchanged over the same period.

If we divide the metropolitan regions into the central city Amsterdam and its surrounding municipalities the following picture emerges in terms of spatial density of the population per km²: the peripheral urban centres of the province, i.e. the outer-fringe areas, experienced a continuing decrease in population, while

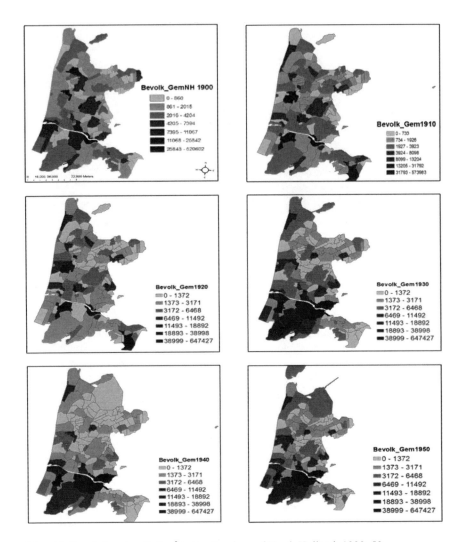

Map 4.2 Population density/km² in the Province of North Holland: 1900–50.

Amsterdam and its immediately surrounding urban areas experienced an increase in population density throughout the period 1900–1940.

Looking at the population structure by age between 1900 and 1930 at the level of the Amsterdam-Schiphol region and the province of North Holland, one may notice the dominant population category aged 14–64 years (see Map 4.2). This category increased between 1900 and 1930 from less than 38,000 to more than 400,000, while the population category 1–14 years showed a moderate increase in the region Amsterdam-Schiphol (between 18,000 and 20,000) and high growth in the rest of North Holland (from more than 68,000 to almost 120,000). The category 65+ was stable during the whole period.

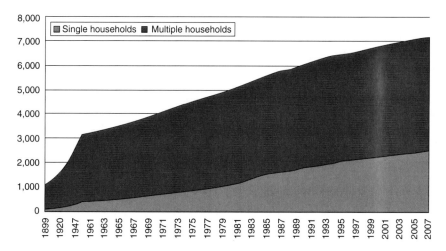

Figure 4.5 Categories of households in the Netherlands (×1,000): 1900–2007.
Source: CBS (HDNG and Volkstellingen, 1899–2007).

More generally, analysis of the demographic figures shows an absolute domination of the city of Amsterdam in terms of urbanity and urban density at the level of the province of North Holland. Also, Amsterdam has the highest levels of the workforce (15–64 years), and almost half of the potential workforce (1–14 years) of the province in 1900–30. Finally, the population of Amsterdam and the Schiphol region are relatively young, i.e. a low share of the population aged 65 or more in the total population of the region.

Concerning the change in structure and composition of households, one may notice that before the 1960s, the nuclear family in the Netherlands was the dominant type of household. This is because Dutch society was strongly based on traditional family values, at least before the 1960s. However, the transformation from traditional family to a more individualised society had a more revolutionary character, given the fact, as we have mentioned before, that Dutch society was more embedded in a societal system of 'pillarisation'.[3]

Figure 4.5 shows the distribution of the Dutch population by categories of households during the twentieth century. Between 1899 and 1950, the dominant category of household was the 'multi-persons household'. However, the single households increased relatively faster from the 1970s as a consequence of the changing lifestyles of the population and the revolutionary societal changes that took place during the 1960s and the 1970s with the depillarisation of Dutch society.

At the regional level, the average number of persons per household in 1930 in big cities like Amsterdam, The Hague and Rotterdam shows the predominance of households made up of two to three persons, including one to two children. This can be interpreted as an indication of the decrease in the size of households compared to the earlier period of 1900–30 for example. The average number of persons per household and the average number of children per household is generally much higher in the countryside and less urbanised areas than in the big cities.

The changes, in the structure and composition of households and population growth have direct effects on the functioning of the housing market in large cities. On the one hand, the population growth and the development of transportation expanded the residential areas. However, the growth of the urban population was more driven by the excess of migration flows than by the natural increase of the urban population, i.e. an increase in the birth rate. The excess of migration flows was quite high between 1881 and 1895 in the case of Amsterdam, and from 1950 in the case of the Schiphol region. Note that the largest part of migration movements had an intra-regional character, in the sense that they took place mainly between the municipalities of different regions, and to a lesser extent between the municipalities belonging to the same province or region. Intra-regional migration reached high levels between 1900 and 1920s, although with a slight decrease during and after the First World War.

On the other hand, changes in the structure and composition of households, combined with the change in the economy from handcraft activities to large-scale manufacturing industry, altered the housing market and the structure of the city centre. The restructuring of the previously manufacturing-based urban labour market resulted in the decentralisation of employment from the traditional city centre to the urban fringes. At the same time, the ongoing process of urbanisation resulted in increasing pressure on the housing market.

To accommodate the ever-growing numbers in urban population, local authorities engaged in the construction of new neighbourhoods for the working classes in the city fringes. The large-scale construction projects of new housing were made possible by the application of the Housing Act 1901, that gave local authorities a powerful jurisdictional instrument to control land use and the housing market, and hence the urban expansion of cities. As a result, the share of the population living in the urban fringes increased much faster than the share of the population living in and around the traditional downtown city, as the case of Amsterdam clearly shows (see Figure 4.6).

At the end of the nineteenth century, the total population of Amsterdam living around the city centre increased substantially. In 1909, the majority of the population of the city were located in the inner city areas. By 1920, more than half of the inhabitants of Amsterdam lived in the urban fringes, while the share of population living in the city centre registered a continuing decrease, especially during the 1930s.

4.3.2 Economic transition and change of economic structure

The declining growth rates in the 1900s, the stagnation of the 1914 and the subsequent recovery of the Dutch economy are clearly reflected in employment (and value added) figures for the country as well as for the major cities of the western region. However, the gap in growth rate between the provinces of North and

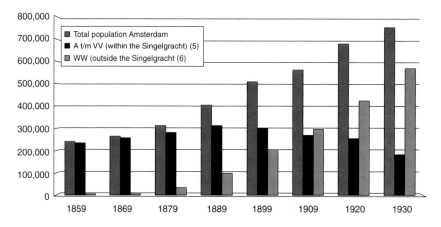

Figure 4.6 Population growth within and outside the city centre of Amsterdam (1859–1930).
Source: based on data from O+S (Onderzoek and Statistiek) Amsterdam.

South Holland and the rest of the country has since merely increased. In 1899 for example, 41.6 per cent of the total labour force was concentrated in the three major cities of Amsterdam, Rotterdam and The Hague.

The cities of North and South Holland provinces dominated by far all other cities of the country in terms of economic performance, with 21.36 per cent of the total labour force in the agriculture and fishing sector, and respectively 45 per cent, 50 per cent and 57.5 per cent of the total labour force in industry, services, and trade and export. The growth of all sectors in North and South Holland is even more striking between 1899 and 1930. Compared to the growth rate of employment in the Netherlands as a whole, the growth rate of employment in the agriculture and fishing sector in North Holland was very high. The manufacturing industry grew by 93 per cent in North Holland and 89 per cent in South Holland, while the growth rate of employment in services, and the trade and transport sectors were both much higher than the national average during this period (respectively, 147 per cent, 170.3 per cent and 96.4 per cent and 81.4 per cent) (see Table 4.2). This reflects clearly the rapid growth of industry and services in the Randstad during the country's industrialisation period.

Table 4.2 Employment growth in Randstad-Holland between 1899 and 1930 (%)

		Agriculture and fishing	*Industry*	*Services*	*Trade and transport*
The Netherlands:	1899–1930	2.04	56.42	54.71	57.34
North Holland:	1899–1930	462.60	92.85	147.01	170.34
South Holland:	1909–1930	33.92	88.82	96.42	81.49

Source: CBS (HDNG and Volkstellingen, 1899).

However, employment growth is much more pronounced at the regional and city levels during the period 1920–30, especially in the greater Amsterdam-Schiphol region, The Hague and Rotterdam.

In 1899, Amsterdam had 408,601 inhabitants, of which 129,654 were occupied workers. About 50 per cent of the active population (men) worked in manufacturing industry, while only 18 per cent of the population worked in the fishing and hunting sectors. The increased employment in manufacturing industry sustained the increase in the population for a long time. The opening of the North Sea canal in 1876 resulted in an increase in the number of firms operating in the transportation sector, in banking and in the equipment/machinery industry. By the end of the nineteenth century, because of the increased diseconomies of agglomeration such as pollution and congestion on the one hand and substantial improvement in transportation networks on the other, manufacturing industry became geographically more dispersed. As a result, a new spatial organisation of urban space began to emerge during the 1920s and 1930s as living and working places gradually became separated from each other. The delocalisation of manufacturing industries – for example, the tobacco industry from Amsterdam to Zaanstreek – resulted in an increase in commuting movements (out-commuters) from city centres in the direction of suburban areas.

Note, however, that while the metropolitan core generally experienced an ongoing gain in the number of jobs, growth in employment in the urban fringe and beyond was far below the national average. This was due to the growth of the service sector in large cities, more particularly in trade, transport, finance and the banking sectors.

More generally, the geographical pattern of economic growth from 1900 onwards is one of high increase in the major large cities of North and South Holland and their immediately surrounding urban areas. The spatial concentration of firms was more or less evenly distributed over North and South Holland and between the Randstad and the rest of the country. Some manufacturing industries were spatially concentrated in the western and southern parts of the Netherlands like the textile and shoes industries, shipbuilding, and the food and clothing industries. However, with the improvements in the transport infrastructure, the decreasing transportation costs and the relatively low wages at the periphery, industrialisation began to spread through the rest of the Netherlands. In the shoes and textile industries, for example, the region of Brabant produced 50 per cent of the total production in this industry in 1858, and about 80 per cent in 1906 (Jansen and de Smidt, 1974).

If we now focus on the Amsterdam-Schiphol region, analysis of employment density by sector during the period 1899–1960 reveals interesting patterns of spatial concentration of employment at the municipality level.[4] Nineteen sectors have been aggregated to four:

- agriculture and fishing;
- industry;
- trade, transport and communication; and
- services.

A high ratio of employment density indicates a high concentration of the sector in the municipality's economic structure. The results shows that the Amsterdam-Schiphol region registered the highest employment density in 1930 and 1960, and to a lesser extent in 1947. At the regional level, however, employment density is much more dispersed across municipalities, indicating that employment is much more spread across urban areas of the province.

At the sectoral level, the results show strong evidence in favour of a high concentration of employment in the manufacturing industry, the trade and transport industry and services in the Amsterdam-Schiphol region in 1900 and 1930. Other observations that should be made include the increasing spread of industry and trade and transport activities across the region between 1900 and 1930. In contrast, agriculture is mainly concentrated in the northern agrarian areas of the province and to a high degree in the Amsterdam-Schiphol region between 1900 and 1930. This may be attributed to the importance of agriculture, especially horticultural activities, in Haarlemmermeer, Aalsmeer and Uithoorn. However, a clear decrease in the agriculture sector in this region is registered from 1947 onward due to the rapid development of the Schiphol airport, transport and logistics, and service activities in this area.

A much better indicator of the spatial concentration of economic activities is the specialisation index. This index is measured as the share of employment in sector *s* in a local economy (in our case municipality *z*) divided by the share of employment of the same sector in the national economy.

Since different cities are specialised in different sectors, certain sectors account for a larger share of overall (say, national) employment than others. This leads naturally to the following specification of the specialisation index:

$$S_{z,s,t} = \frac{\text{emp}_{z,s,t}/\text{emp}_{z,t}}{\text{emp}_{s,t}/\text{emp}_t}$$

where:

- $S_{z,s,t}$ is the specialisation index in sector *s* in municipality *z* in time *t*;
- $\text{emp}_{z,s,t}/\text{emp}_{z,t}$ is the share of employment in municipality *z*, sector *s* in time *t* to the total employment in all sectors in municipality *z* in time *t*;
- $\text{emp}_{s,t}/\text{emp}_t$ is the share of the total employment in sector *s* at time *t* to the total of employment in all sectors at national level in time *t*.

The specialisation index is constructed such that higher values of the variable reflect higher levels of spatial concentration in a particular location/sector. A high specialisation index in a given sector is considered an indication of the economic weight of that sector in the economy of the city or region. The calculation of this index in different periods of time gives an idea about the dynamic of change in the distribution of economic activities between cities and regions. For example, a specialisation index equal to 1 (or 100) indicates the presence of a sector with the

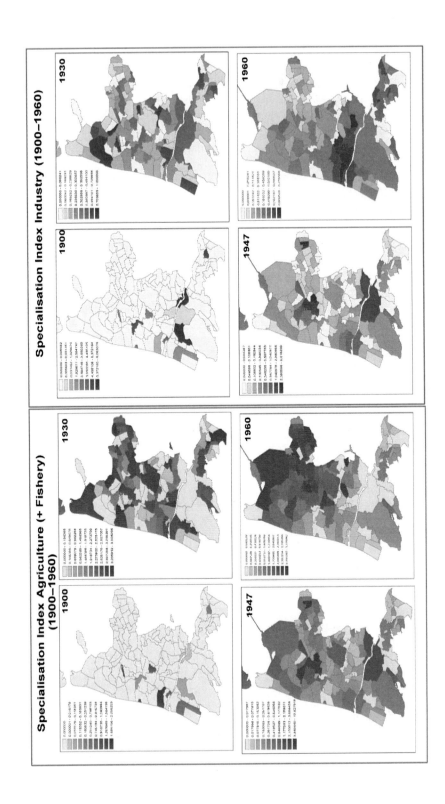

Specialisation Index Industry (1900–1960)

1930

1960

1900

1947

Specialisation Index Agriculture (+ Fishery) (1900–1960)

1930

1960

1900

1947

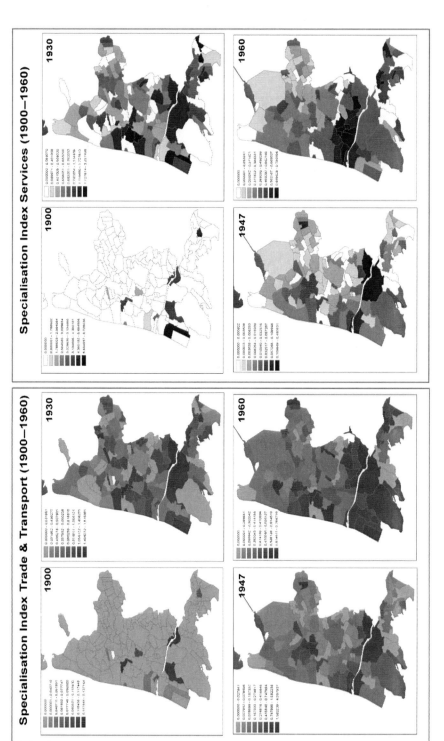

Map 4.3 Sectoral specialisation in the North-Holland region from 1900 to 1960.

same share in local employment as in national employment, while a specialisation index above 2 (or 200) indicates the presence of a sector with a share in local employment twice as large as its share in national employment, i.e. a higher sectoral specialisation at the spatial level.

The specialisation index shows clear differences in the concentration of sectors between the municipalities within the Amsterdam-Schiphol region and the province of North Holland, especially from 1930 onward (see Map 4.3). The concentration of agriculture is clearly higher in the northern areas of the province with industry in the Amsterdam-Schiphol region and more particularly the Zaanstreek region.

From 1900 to 1947, the Amsterdam region showed a high spatial concentration of trade, transport and communications, and services. Industry, trade, transport and distribution are strongly concentrated within the boundaries of the Amsterdam region along the main waterway transport nodes to the west and to the southeast parts of the North Sea Canal.

From 1947 onward, however, trade and transport activities became much more concentrated in the Schiphol region as agriculture became less dominant. In this sense, the linkages between manufacturing industry, trade and transportation largely determined the development of economic activities in the Amsterdam-Schiphol region.

In summary, the most striking features that can be observed from analysis of the specialisation index are as follows. First, there was a clear sectoral shift from an industry-based economy to business services, trade, transport (logistics) and communications activities in the Amsterdam-Schiphol region. The shift in economic structure of the Amsterdam-Schiphol region may be explained by the increasing investment (public as well as private) which stimulated on the one hand employment and job creation in industry and services, and on the other improvements to production processes (efficiency), innovations (of products and process) and the competitiveness of local firms. Evidence supporting this explanation could be measured by the regional growth potential such as the value of investments or the level of productivity (e.g. value-added).[5] Second, a clear shift from agriculture to industry, trade and transport activities took place in the Zaanstreek and the Kop of Holland areas. Finally, the agriculture sector is still concentrated in the periphery areas of the province of North Holland.

4.4 Urbanisation and spatial change in the Amsterdam-Schiphol region during the first half of the twentieth century

Historically, the development of Amsterdam has been strongly connected to trade and related commercial activities. Because of insufficient productive arable land in and around Amsterdam, and hence the limited possibilities for wheat farming, the city has developed a strong basis of commercial activities, especially importation and storage of natural resources and agricultural goods such as dairy, wheat, corn, beer, wood, iron ore, fish and salt. The increase in commercial activities resulted in the development of service activities such as insurance, banking, transport and port activities.

The accumulation of capital by Amsterdam's wealthier merchants and traders reached high levels during the seventeenth century. Amsterdam became the undisputed trade and the financial centre of Europe (Mak, 2003). Wealth and economic growth attracted more people searching for jobs, fortune or a safe haven in the city. With the increased wealth, other activities also flourished in Amsterdam, for example painting, the arts, printing and cartography.

After the liberation of Amsterdam from Spanish occupation (following 80 years of war against Spain (1578–1648)), Amsterdam managed to expand its trade networks further in Europe, and later with many trading posts in Asia, Africa and America. For the first time in the history of modern capitalism, multinational corporations controlled by private shareholders appeared in the Netherlands, the VOC (1602) and the West Indies Company (1621). These two companies played an important role in the Dutch colonial expansion in Asia (Indonesia) and the Americas (New Amsterdam, later New York, the Caribbean and Brazil), and in the organisation of trade between Amsterdam and the rest of the world.

The glorious period of Amsterdam's economic domination has left its trace in the existing buildings and the spatial patterns of the city. Amsterdam's first expansion plan dates from 1610, when the authorities began to study the plan envisaged by the city carpenter Hendrick Jacobszoon Staetes. This first urban expansion plan envisaged the creation of three islands in the western IJ river (Bickerseiland, Realeneiland and Prinseneiland), and adjacent to them a large new district to house workers, craftsmen and small traders (known currently as the Jordaan neighbourhood).

Amsterdam expanded with its famous 'horseshoe' ring of canals filled with commercial and residential buildings. Due to the egalitarian values of the Dutch, the wealth of the traders and bankers was more to be found within the city centre than without. The focal point of activities was Amsterdam harbour located on the river IJ and several service activities related to trade and commerce (banking, finance, insurance, trade houses, etc.) in the city centre.

According to the Dutch historian Taverne (1978), Amsterdam's famous Canal Zone acquired its archetypal shape without any conscious planning. Building construction followed the original patterns of the polder ditches, which had served perfectly the requirements of the medieval military city. In addition, the canal belt was 'the best conceivable infrastructure for making the city a perfect circulation machine' (Wagenaar, 1998). The canal system was built in phases, starting in 1613 with the extension of canals to the Amstel and later in 1675 with the digging of additional sections to the east of the Amstel.

With the resurgence of Amsterdam, a couple of neighbouring towns and villages on both banks of the Zaan river grew into a modern industrial region. Dutch economic historians give various explanations for the revival of industrial development in this area. Some of the most important lie in the existence of a specific local business milieu which sustained strong local networks among local entrepreneurs and the introduction of new technological innovations, particularly the windmills (1596) and the pumping mills to drain the polders (Davids, 1997).[6] The Zaan region grew into an important industrial area specialising in food processing activities, and trade and logistics activities, with strong industrial ties to Amsterdam's trade and financial sectors. To the west of the city, Haarlem became the second largest city in the region as it managed to develop a strong industrial basis centred around the textile and printing industries (the world's first daily newspaper was published in Haarlem in 1656!). However, most of the founders of the textile industry in Haarlem were Flemish migrants who had escaped the Spanish occupation.

During the eighteenth century, the Dutch Republic gradually lost its economic position to England and France. As a result, the economic growth of Amsterdam stagnated. The region lost much of its economic vitality and missed the Industrial Revolution of the eighteenth and most of the nineteenth centuries. While England built up entirely new industrial production processes based on steam and coal, the industries in the Amsterdam-Zaan region were still dependent on wind and water power. Reasons for this economic stagnation were the lack of innovation, the low levels of investment in firms, the limited capacities of the natural resources (natural endowments), the limited size of the national market, increasing competition from abroad and the continuous struggles between local authorities in the absence of a strong central authority in the Dutch Republic. In addition, the inaccessibility of the Amsterdam harbour from the North Sea and the weak economic position of the Dutch hinterland compared to emerging rivals like London and Hamburg weakened the economic position of Amsterdam and the region (Mak, 2005). The economic position of Amsterdam became worse in 1813 when the city lost its political functions to the emerging political centre The Hague. The monarchy and the political institutions settled in The Hague and with them many civil and political servants, firms and services. In addition to the city of Rotterdam, Amsterdam acquired a new rival – The Hague (and later the city of Utrecht).

The degradation of the former financial centre and symbol of capitalism was also reflected in the spatial structure and physical state of the buildings in the city. In contrast to other European capital cities such as London, Paris, Vienna and Berlin, Amsterdam was not able to realise the large construction and urban expansion projects along the lines of Haussmann because of high structural financial deficits. It was only at the end of the nineteenth century, with the modernisation of the Netherlands, that Amsterdam was able to realise several major urban expansion projects thanks to the capital accumulated by the new industrial and colonial elite.

Nevertheless, roughly between 1870 and 1915, Amsterdam enjoyed a 'second golden age' as a result of an increase in colonial trade and the accumulation of wealth from trade with satellite colonies of the Dutch metropolis, made possible by the opening of the Suez Canal. In addition, German unification gave a significant economic impetus to the Netherlands, in the knowledge that Germany was (and still is) the most important trading partner. And we must not forget, in this respect, the positive effects of the opening of the North Sea Canal for trade and the industrialisation of Amsterdam and the surrounding region. With the opening of the North Sea Canal, the accessibility of Amsterdam from the sea was improved (see Map 4.4). However, the positive effects in terms of trade and economic growth were rather below expectations because the rival city of Rotterdam managed to attract most of the trade activities and related industries, such as shipbuilding, to its harbour.

More generally, the economic growth of Amsterdam from 1900 was accompanied by the rapid growth of the urban population, and for the first time in its history the city expanded beyond the existing historical boundaries. The medieval city walls disappeared from the city urban landscape and new large suburban areas were annexed to the city in order to provide new neighbourhoods for the working classes, for example the Pijp and Oud West neighbourhoods.

However, the population growth was much more moderate when compared to fast-growing rival cities such as Rotterdam, The Hague and Utrecht. As a result, a polynuclear spatial structure based on the 'social division of labour' between these four largest cities of the Netherlands emerged. Amsterdam developed into the cultural and financial centre of the Netherlands, Rotterdam grew into an industrial and logistics centre encompassing the largest harbour in the country, The Hague became the political centre of the country and the primary location for international diplomatic relations, while Utrecht became the main central node in the Dutch infrastructural networks (roads/highways and railways).

In short, the structural patterns of the Dutch urban hierarchy, in terms of size and rank of cities, was much more affected by urbanisation than industrialisation. This is because the urbanisation character of big cities, especially in the western part of the Netherlands, was more spread between various cities. This spatial structure explains largely why the Netherlands lacked a dominant metropolis or city region as was the case, for example, with the Île-de-France region in France and Greater London in the UK.

4.4.1 (Un)planned urbanisation: spatial expansion and urban planning

During the period 1850–1900, the population density in Amsterdam was very high, due to the combined effects of a dramatic increase in urban population and the structural scarcity of open space in the city. The overpopulation of Amsterdam and the lack of sanitary infrastructure resulted in high numbers of deaths caused by cholera and other infectious diseases. Water and sewerage were non-existent, garbage, faeces, slaughterhouse trash and animal cadavers were dumped on the streets. The construction of sewerage and drinking water installations were among the highest priorities of local authorities. Things got even worse with the increased industrial activity in the city. The introduction of steam machines in manufacturing factories increased pollution, noise nuisance and risk of fire (Wagenaar, 1998: 23). Because industrial production required higher frequency of supplies and deliveries of goods and raw materials, traffic to and from the city centre increased substantially to the point where the main streets around the city centre became highly congested and almost inaccessible for pedestrians.

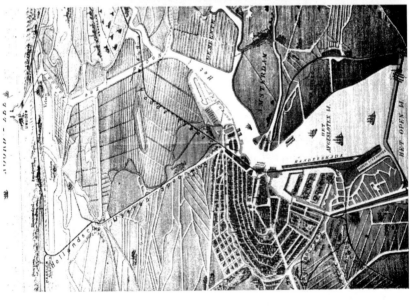

Map 4.4 Panoramic view of the city of Amsterdam and the North Sea Canal (nineteenth century).
Source: DRO (DIA's Archives), Municipality of Amsterdam.

However, these problems were not specific to the city of Amsterdam but also affected the other large Dutch cities. More generally, by the end of the nineteenth century, almost all large Dutch cities were overpopulated, highly congested and unhealthy, and were registering high death rates caused by the deteriorating living conditions of the working class and regular outbreaks of diseases. Interventions by local and public authorities were inevitable.

The spatial structure of Amsterdam changed radically with the application of various urban expansion projects such as the construction of the Rijksmuseum (1885), the Central Railroad Station (1889), the extension of Amsterdam's port area and the expansion of the residential areas within the old seventeenth-century city-centre area. The extensions of residential areas were intended to accommodate the growing population of Amsterdam caused by continuous migration flows from the countryside.

However, because the municipality of Amsterdam was lacking the financial means to realise large-scale and ambitious city expansion plans, the housing construction and land markets were controlled by private land speculators and rapacious property owners (most of them were magistrates!) that were seeking to make high profits from land exploitation and housing construction. Most were not interested in urban design and/or the realisation of large-scale urban expansion projects, but in the development of lower-middle-class housing, for which there was a much higher demand than for upper-class housing (for example, the Pijp and Oud West neighbourhoods). In short, the land use and housing markets were devoted to the principle of free market property development and land speculation by private project developers. Nevertheless, despite the structural financial deficit, Amsterdam's local authorities were successful in realising some important urban projects. For example, besides the construction of the central railway station in 1868, many canals – like Spui and the Niewezijds Voorburgwal – were filled in in 1881 to resolve the increased traffic jam in the city centre.

In 1866, Amsterdam city council, with a majority of liberal democrats, used existing expropriation law to realise some urgent expansion projects by demolishing existing houses in the Haalsteeg and the Oude Doelenstraat (later Damstraat) areas. During the same year, a new expansion plan was proposed to the city council by the architects Cornelis Outhoorn (the architect of the Amstel Hotel and the Paleis voor Volksvlijt) and Kuinders to construct a new neighbourhood for the working class between the city centre and the Muiderpoort area. This plan was the first urban expansion plan in a long list of unrealised city expansion plans such as, for example, the Ousthorn and Leliman plan to link Westermarkt with the Dam Square and Niewmarkt-Plantage, and the Gosschalk (1872) traffic plan aimed at improving the accessibility of Amsterdam by road.

As mentioned before, the deteriorating living conditions in the city, the uncontrolled suburbanisation, the increase in speculation in the land and housing markets and the exodus of the wealthier inhabitants from Amsterdam to suburban areas, particularly to the coastal region of Haarlem and the sandy areas of the Gooi-Hilversum, pushed local authorities to embrace the idea that urban design and city planning should be brought once and for all under the control of the city council.

1900   1915   1930

Map 4.5 Spatial expansion of Amsterdam between 1900 and 1930.
Source: Cadastral historical maps (Historical Bonne maps).

In fact, Amsterdam's spatial expansion took place step by step and very selectively, often under great pressure from traffic congestion, pollution and the degradation of living conditions in the old neighbourhoods around the city centre (see Map 4.5). The first city expansion works were executed in the city centre, where some canals were filled in and added to the existing streets to improve accessibility to the city centre. The old buildings in the city offered enough space to build new houses for the working class, e.g. the Marnixstraat to the east of the city border, as well as new dwellings for the local elite in the Plantage area in the eastern part of the city centre.[7] However, these small and often restricted spatial changes were not an adequate response to the existing urban problems. Amsterdam needed more land to realise large-scale expansion plans. One way to achieve this goal was the annexation of large suburban areas. The first annexation took place in 1877 while the second and third annexations took place respectively in 1896 and 1921. In 1921, the municipalities of Wategraafsmeer, Sloten and parts of Westzaan, Zaandam, Oostzaan, Diemen, and Ouder and Nieuwe Amstel were added to Amsterdam. As a result, the total area of the city increased from 4,600 ha to 17,450 ha and its population grew to 35,700.

From 1918, Amsterdam and the Netherlands adopted a collectivist approach to society. Health care, education and the housing shortage dominated public policy in the 'welfare state'. Great efforts were made to implement the Housing Act, which gave cities the power to dictate housing planning, control of housing stock, the quality of public amenities and the social composition of the city districts.

It is worth mentioning that many city planners and architects such as Samuel Sarphati, van Niftrik, Kalff, Berlage, and van Esteren have left their mark through the city buildings and urban expansion of Amsterdam. Most of these city planners set out the pattern and direction of city expansion through planned interventions and the choice of specific arrangements of streets, infrastructure, buildings, parks and recreation areas. The way this was accomplished affords us an impression of the dominant planning doctrine and functioning of the local governance regime that gave them the opportunity to develop and design their unique spatial planning strategies. For example, the topographical contrast between Paris, London and Amsterdam largely reflects the divergence in political regimes, housing preferences and culture, and lifestyle. For example, the British prefer garden cities, while the French prefer the big central city as a living place.

Today, most of these of city planners are still alive in the collective memory of Amsterdam because of the realisation of their impressive urban projects, specific neighbourhoods and/or design of unusual expansion plans such as the construction of the Paleis der Volksvlijt and the Amstel Hotel by Samuel Sarphati (1813–66), the expansion of the Pijp neighbourhood (the so-called Plan YY) by J. G. van Niftrik (1866–7) (for more details, see Wagenaar, 1990), the expansion plan by J. J. Kalff (1873–81) and Berlage's expansion plan for the South Amsterdam neighbourhood (Berlag, 1905–18).

However, the Amsterdam General Expansion Plan (AUP, 1934), developed by the city planning department (L. S. P. Scheffer, T. van Lohuizen and C. van Esteren), constituted a new approach to city planning known as the 'lobe-city model' or finger city, and has served as the main guiding document for the planners and as a blueprint for the city's spatial development after the Second World War till today. The AUP was the first systematically compiled urban expansion plan based upon a combination of extensive statistical analysis and forecasts of urban population. In opposition to existing standard practices of that time in Europe, research, planning and implementation of the AUP were all in the hands of the city of Amsterdam (Dijkink and Mamdouh, 2003: 168). The planning of the airport was not fully integrated into regular city planning, but a close look at the AUP clearly shows that the compilers of the plan had thought about the future development of airports. (Beside Schiphol airport, another water airport at the IJ-over was also projected on the map – see Map 4.6.) This clearly shows the municipality's great interest in Schiphol airport and hence explains why Schiphol was integrated into Amsterdam's urban expansion planning. Our argument here is that the relationship between airport planning and city planning – which were in fact worlds apart – was stronger by the end of 1920s and the 1930s, as we will clearly show in the following chapters. The AUP clearly shows the integration of city planning and airport planning during the 1930s, at least in the case of Amsterdam.

4.5 Haarlemmermeer and Schiphol: a brief historical overview

The name 'Schiphol' appeared for the first time in 1447 on a land property document that points to a location in the 'Aelsmerbanne in Schiphol'. The historical chart of Rijnland of 1610–15, drawn by the Dutch cartographer Balthazar Floritz van Berckenrode (1591–1644), shows the location of Schiphol at the northeast corner of the great lake of Haarlemmermeer. Various names were given to this location such as 'Sciphol', 'Schip Holl', 'Schipsholle' and 'Schipshol'. However, the name Schiphol came probably from the Dutch term 'Schipsholle', which means ships' graveyard. The location of Schiphol was known to the inhabitants of the region as a dangerous place on the Haarlemmermeer lake, because with strong southeast winds, many wrecked ships wound up in this corner of the lake (see Map 4.7).

For a long time, the Haarlemmermeer polder, with its immense lake, formed a natural defensive barrier for the city of Amsterdam and the surrounding area. After the reclamation of the Haarlemmermeer polder in 1852, a defensive waterfront line, with many military batteries and towers – such as the fort Schiphol at the northeast corner of the Haarlemmermeer polder, the fort of Heemstede and the fort of Leid – was created around the North Holland province. The idea was that in the case of a military invasion, the whole waterfront line could be inundated to slow down and/or stop the advance of the enemy.

The reclamation of the Haarlemmermeer lake was one of the major infrastructural projects of the nineteenth century. The decision to reclaim new land from the lake was made by a royal decree issued by King Willem I. The state appointed a commission, under the chair of Gevers van Endegeest, to supervise and report on the progress of this large project. Many pumping mills, driven by steam engines, were put to work around the Haarlemmermeer polder.

Map 4.6 General Extension Plan of Amsterdam (AUP, 1934).
Source: DIA's archives of DRO, Municipality of Amsterdam.

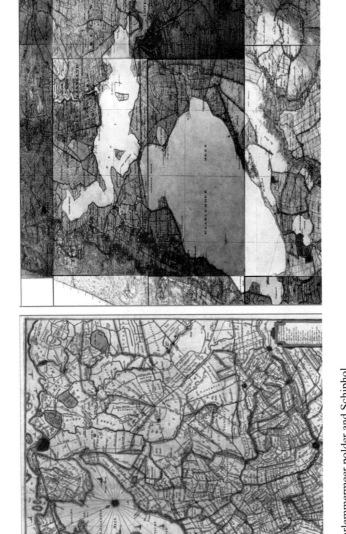

Map 4.7 Historical map of Haarlemmermeer polder and Schiphol.
Source: Cadastral historical map (TMK: Topografische en Militaire Kaart van het Koninkrijk der Nederlander). Scale: 1:50,0000, s'Gravenhage (1860–1905).

After 12 years, almost 800 million m^3 of water had been pumped from the lake and a total surface of almost 18,000 ha of land had been reclaimed. The land was subject to a careful parcelling system of 1 km by 1 km, separated by canals and roads from the northwest to the southeast within a radius of 3 km. Land plots were 200 m broad, delimited by roads at the front side and canals at the back (see Map 4.8). The total costs of reclamation of the Haarlemmermeer polder reached 13.8 million guilders.

Between 1853 and 1855, 16,822 ha of land parcels were sold to private owners for about 8 million guilders, and 32 ha of land were reserved by the state to build two new rural cores: 'Haarlemmermeer' in the province of North Holland and the 'Venneperdorp' (known today as 'New Vennep') in the province of South Holland. However, the Dutch state decided in 1855 to integrate the whole Haarlemmermeer polder into the province of North Holland.

A large proportion of the reclaimed land came into hands of the wealthier landowners from Amsterdam and the surrounding areas. Fifty-five per cent of the total land was sold to 32 private landowners who possessed land parcels of more than 100 ha. Of these 32 landowners, only four were settled in Haarlemmermeer itself. Together, they shared more than 6,728 ha of land (an average of 200 ha per landowner) in 1860, corresponding to 37.37 per cent of the total surface of Haarlemmermeer. Eighty-six per cent of the total arable land was leased and/or hired to farmers (leaseholders). Only 14 per cent of the total surface was owned by local farmers/inhabitants of Haarlemmermeer polder.

The first settlers of the new polder were immigrants that came from the regions of Friesland (2.1 per cent), North Brabant (45 per cent) and other areas of the province of North Holland (29 per cent) (see Table 4.3). The majority of these settlers were released from agriculture, and most of them were hoping to improve their living conditions by starting a new life in the new polder. Between 1915 and 1935, the number of settlers in the polder grew substantially when people from the surrounding areas of the province and from the North Brabant province found their way to the polder. After 1935, the majority of new settlers came from the northern regions, and to a less extent from the surrounding areas and from the province of North Brabant. Nevertheless, the majority of the inhabitants of Haarlemmermeer have their origins in the province of North Holland.

During the early years of Haarlemmermeer, the living conditions of the first settlers in the polder were extremely difficult. It was a hard struggle against nature to make the new land more suitable for agricultural activities. New settlers were confronted with various problems, for example regular high water levels, extremely muddy soil, shortages in the means of production and equipment, outbreaks of tropical diseases, plagues, poverty, etc.[8] It took many years before the soil of the polder was finally turned into suitable arable land and hence into profitable agricultural business activities. However, the relatively young population of the polder turned out to be decisive in the development of Haarlemmermeer into one of the most productive agrarian regions of the country. Compared to the Dutch population in 1589, the share of the population category aged between 30 and 40 was 35 per cent in Haarlemmermeer, in contrast to 14 per cent at the national level.[9] In addition, Haarlemmermeer registered an increase in the category of population

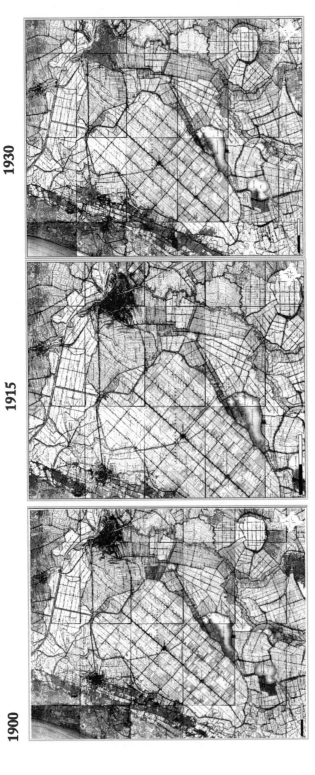

1900   1915   1930

Map 4.8 Historical map of Haarlemmermeer-Amsterdam region 1900, 1915 and 1930.
Source: Topografische Dienst; Cadastral historical maps (Historical Bonne maps). Scale: 1:50,0000.

Table 4.3 Geographical origins of settlers of Haarlemmermeer
polder (as % of total population)

	Before 1915	*1915–1935*	*After 1935*
Surrounding areas	29	30	35
North Brabant	45	30	14
Northern regions	2.1	7.3	15

Source: Schröder (1955, p. 144).

under 14 years between 1881 and 1885. The difference between the total number of new-born children and the total number of deaths was 1,566 during this period and 22,000 in 1910. Figure 4.7 shows the population growth in Haarlemmermeer and the surrounding areas between 1900 and 1971.

The two main determinant factors in the growth of the population were the increasing regional migration flows and the high birth rate in the Haarlemmermeer polder. The total population of Haarlemmermeer was 3,000 in 1855. Fifty-four years later, the total population had reached 16,627 inhabitants, and 23,340 in 1920. The majority of the population of Haarlemmermeer was concentrated alongside the borders of the polder. The spatial distribution of the population reflects nicely the social and economic differences between the inhabitants of the north, south, east and west of the polder. For example, the population of the border areas, like the small villages of Alsmeer, Lisse, Hillegom and Halfweg, were relatively poorer than the inhabitants of the midland areas.

With regard to land use in the Haarlemmermeer polder, the majority of culti-vated land was used as farmland because of the soil composition in the polder, e.g. sea-clay soil is more suited for farming activities than pasturage. Data on land

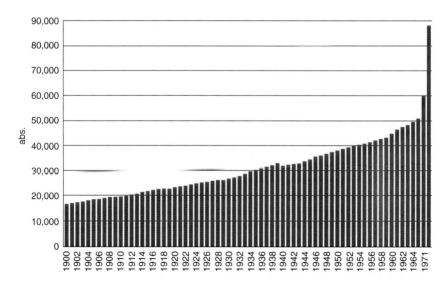

Figure 4.7 Growth of population of Haarlemmermeer: 1900–71.
Source: CBS (HDGN and Volkstellingen, 1899–1980).

use in Haarlemmermeer shows a continuing decrease in the total size of pasture areas between 1880 and 1923 (from 6,621 ha to 1,100 ha). However, despite the diverse character of agricultural activities in Haarlemmermeer, this sector was generally divided between the production of vegetables in the north, bulb cultivation in the west and floriculture in the east of the polder.

The modernisation of agriculture in Haarlemmermeer followed the same trends of modernisation and rationalisation in agriculture at the national level. However, in the case of Haarlemmermeer, local initiatives played an important role in accelerating the modernisation process in this economic sector. One local individual that played a major role in this respect was J. P. Amersfoordt, the mayor of Haarlemmermeer. Amersfoort, the son of a Amsterdam magistrate, was very interested in the new developments that were taking place in the agriculture sector in the UK and Germany, such as the use of new technologies and equipment and the application of new methods and processes in production. In his own farm 'de Badhoeve', which served as a laboratory for his experiments, he introduced new equipment and production methods aimed at increasing the scale of production and productivity in the polder. In doing so, he was hoping, through the organisation of frequent events, to convince local farmers of the (economic) benefits that might be generated from modernising their activities and the introduction of new equipment and products in order to improve their living conditions. Because of these local initiatives and the improvement in interactions between local actors, Haarlemmermeer became in 1875 one of the wealthiest agrarian areas of the Netherlands, where new (steam) equipment and artificial fertilisers were widely used by farmers. As a result, returns from the exploitation of land were relatively higher than the national average. Consequently, land prices increased from approximately 20 guilders per ha to 100 guilders per ha, and the price of land became much higher in Haarlemmermeer than in the fertile clay regions of Groningen and Zeeland for example.

Due to the increase in production and wealth in Haarlemmermeer, the weekly wages of land workers in Haarlemmermeer were on average more than 2 guilders higher than the national level between 1861 and 1898, and 1 to 3 guilders higher than the national wage in 1909 (see Table 4.4).

Unfortunately, Haarlemmermeer was deeply hit by the (international) downturn in the agricultural sector during the 1870s, with an increase in unemployment among land workers and difficulties among farmers to pay land rent. Because of the crisis and the increased prices of meat and sugar, some farmers

Table 4.4 Weekly wages of agrarian workers (in guilders)

	Haarlemmermeer	*The Netherlands*
1861	9	6
1890	6–80	4.50–5.85
1898	7.50	5.85
1909	6.75–11.50	5.65–7.7

Source: Schröder (1955, p. 143).

switched their activity to stock farming (especially horses and cattle) and the production of sugar beet. The total surface of cultivated sugar beet increased from 300 ha in 1880 to 1,000 ha in 1890.

From 1900 onward, the economic situation in the polder improved considerably due, among other things, to the increase in the prices of agricultural goods, the collective participation of farmers in local organisations and the creation of new institutions such as, for example, cooperatives of farmers and cooperative banks.

During the 1950s, 43 per cent of the total surface in the Haarlemmermeer polder was occupied by the production of grain (cereals such as wheat, barley, oats, rye and corn) and respectively 2.5 per cent and 1.1 per cent of the total surface was reserved for pasturage and other agricultural products. Cattle farming, which was concentrated in the northern and eastern areas, occupied 10 per cent of the total surface of the polder.

Besides farming activities, floriculture increased enormously in Haarlemmermeer during the 1920s and 1930s, especially within and around the municipality of Aalsmeer. During this period, the total returns from floriculture in the Netherlands have been estimated at 65 million guilders, of which 22 million guilders, corresponding to 33 per cent of the national value of flowers, was realised from the selling of flowers through the public auction at Aalsmeer. The proximity of Aalsmeer to the Schiphol airport is the most important factor explaining the rapid increase in floriculture in this area. In this sense, the development of the airport and Haarlemmermeer are closely related to each other since the early days of the development of the airfield in the 1920s and the 1930s.

The economic and spatial effects of Schiphol on the surrounding areas became more apparent during the 1930s. However, one may argue that the shift in the economic structure of Haarlemmermeer is partly determined by the increased importance of Schiphol airport as well as other factors that took place at the level of the Amsterdam region, i.e. the industrialisation and urbanisation of this region.

Figure 4.8 shows the sectoral shift in the economic structure of Haarlemmermeer, in term of employment, between 1899 and 1960.

What is important to note here is the rapid decline in the labour force in agriculture and the increase of employment in industry and trade and transport activities in Haarlemmermeer. In 1899 for example, more than 60 per cent of the labour force was employed in agriculture. This percentage fell to no more than 15 per cent in 1930, before stabilising at 19 per cent in 1960. The tendency for employment to fall in the agriculture sector may be interpreted as the result of the substitution of labour by capital, and the restructuring effects of the rationalisation and modernisation of agriculture on local labour markets, e.g. fewer people were needed as new equipment and technologies were introduced into this sector.

Another important observation is the increase in importance of service activities, in particular trade and transport, especially after the Second World War. This may be attributed to the increasing importance of airport activities. In this sense, the economic and spatial development of Schiphol airport has changed radically the spatial and economic structure of Haarlemmermeer from a 100 per cent agriculture-based economy to a more diversified local economic structure.

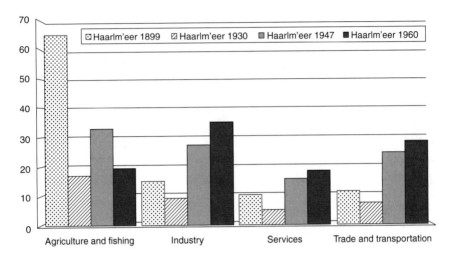

Figure 4.8 Labour force by sector in Haarlemmermeer: 1899–1960 (%).
Source: CBS (HDNG).

To summarise, the interwar period can be characterised as a period of (quantitative and qualitative) structural change in the local economic structure of Haarlemmermeer. Schiphol airport became the centre of economic activities and a growth pole par excellence, not only to the Haarlemmermeer polder but also to the Amsterdam region. In this sense, urbanisation and the economic growth of Haarlemmermeer are closely related to the development and growth of airport activities.

4.5.1 Urbanisation and urban planning in Haarlemmermeer (1920–45)

Up to the Second World War, Haarlemmermeer had preserved its agrarian character within the Amsterdam metropolitan region. Most of the villages of Haarlemmermeer were not very significant in terms of geographical size and number of inhabitants, except the semi-urban core centre of Hoofddorp. The countryside character of the Haarlemmermeer polder contrasted with the increasing urbanisation and urban sprawl of the Amsterdam region. In the spirit of the prevalent tradition of Christaller's hierarchical urban system, Haarlemmermeer was highly dependent on Amsterdam as a marketplace and primary provider of a wide range of high-quality services and public utilities. Accordingly, the functional relationships between Amsterdam and Haarlemmermeer can be described in terms of the relationships defined in urban studies concerning monocentric city models. However, the suburbanisation process that took place at the level of Amsterdam was accompanied by the subsequent urbanisation of several areas in the Haarlemmermeer polder.

On one hand, the urbanisation process in Haarlemmermeer was driven by the growth of the Schiphol airport itself, and more particularly by the growth of activities related to the airport. On the other hand, the urbanisation process was driven by the rapid increase in the number of Schiphol and KLM employees. Most of these employees were searching for housing close to their places of work, e.g. the Schiphol region. However, a clear tendency towards intensified urbanisation in Haarlemmermeer became apparent only by the end of the 1960s and the 1970s, although the first signs of urbanisation of some villages in the polder took place before the Second World War, as in, for example, the case of Zwanenburg, Badhoevedorp and Hoofddorp. In what follows, we give a brief review of the urbanisation of these three suburban centres in Haarlemmermeer.

Zwanenburg

As mentioned before, the urbanisation of Haarlemmermeer took place with the development of Schiphol airport, as the number of urban commuters established in the northern parts of Haarlemmermeer increased rapidly. During the 1920s, the village of Zwanenburg became a favourite suburban residential district for the working class. In this sense, Zwanenburg constituted the first visible example of urban sprawl and spatial expansion of Amsterdam in the direction of the empty Haarlemmermeer. The spatial development of this village was brought about by private initiatives without any intervention from local authorities. In this respect, many of the obligations related to the development of the spatial planning scheme or the zoning regulation plans that were applied by cities at that time were not taken into consideration by the developers of this new residential settlement. In this sense, Zwanenburg is a typical example of an unregulated and unplanned suburban centre, whose existence and development were dictated by the urgency to accommodate the workers of Schiphol (most of them commuters) from Amsterdam.

Badhoevedorp

Badhoevedorp was developed in the 1930s as a typical model of a garden city. As was the case of Zwanenburg, the aim of the policy-makers to develop this settlement was to accommodate the employees of Schiphol airport, KLM and Fokker, and other inhabitants of the municipalities of the Haarlemmermeer polder. In contrast to Zwanenburg, the expansion plan of this small village was subject to the requirements of the Housing Act, which meant that the expansion plan first had to be approved by the local authorities with respect to the quality of construction, design, green space, etc., before its execution. The expansion plan of Badhoevedorp was approved by the local authorities in 1934, and thereafter the first construction work began in the western part of the village (completed in 1937). Although Badhoevedorp was a semi-agrarian area, the village developed into a full suburban residential area for commuters working in Amsterdam and/or the airport area. After the Second World War, Badhoevedorp developed into a workplace location where many transportation and logistics firms, services and trading firms, and wholesale trading companies are located.

Hoofddorp

Hoofddorp is one of the two main suburban core centres of the municipality of Haarlemmermeer. The first expansion plan for Hoofddorp was designed in 1909.

This (paper) plan was revisited in 1922 because of the integration of two additional construction projects: the Haarlem–Hoofddorp–Aalsmeer railway line and the Hoofddorp–Nieuwe Vennep–Leiden railway line. However, with the increased activities in Schiphol and the rapid suburbanisation of Amsterdam, a new expansion plan for Hoofddorp was designed by the architect Wieger Bruintaking in 1941, which took into account future increases in the demand for additional new dwellings by new commuters as well as the demand for industrial sites by firms. Note that the delocalisation of Fokker from Amsterdam and the increasing number of employees of KLM and Schiphol were already subject to intense discussion between the local authorities of Amsterdam and Haarlemmermeer, and between these two parties and KLM and Fokker. As predicted by the designers of the expansion plan, after the Second World War the demand for new dwellings and industrial sites increased substantially in this suburban core area, especially from the 1960s. Since then, Hoofdorp expanded very rapidly and several large construction projects were completed at this location such as the 'Pax' and 'Bornholm' neighbourhoods that comprise some 4,600 new dwellings. We will turn to this subject in the following chapters.

4.6 Summary and conclusions

This chapter has dealt with the main causes and factors of industrialisation, urbanisation and economic growth in the Netherlands in general and the Amsterdam-Schiphol region in particular during the late nineteenth century and the first half of the twentieth century.

Although the Industrial Revolution reached the Netherlands much later than other major European countries like the UK, Germany and France, the industrialisation of the country, which started around 1870, took place at a relatively rapid pace so that the Netherlands was able to catch up with these countries within a few decades.

Firstly, the acceleration of industrialisation was caused by high levels without precedent of public investment in transport networks (waterways, rail and road networks) and public services (electricity and telecommunication networks), by innovative technological advances and by rapid growth in the construction sector. Industrialisation was accompanied by a structural economic transformation of the Dutch economy and fundamental changes in the spatial patterns of cities and regions. The most important consequences of the modernisation of the transport infrastructure and advances in transport technology were, respectively, the increase in accessibility of cities and regions, the decrease in transport costs between regions, the increase in people's mobility, the expansion of the daily urban system and the increase in inter- and intra-regional trade. People and goods could be moved over longer distances in less time and at lower cost than before. The first signs of the separation between working and living places and suburbanisation became visible at the level of the Randstad, albeit in a more selective way. The negative side of these developments was the high increase in urban density and the overpopulation of large cities, the increase in pollution and congestion within and around the traditional city centres, the increase in housing shortages, an increase in health and safety problems and, more generally, a deterioration in the living conditions of the urban population.

Second, political and institutional reforms also played a key role in guiding the modernisation process – in the political, social and economic fields – of Dutch society. Examples of such reforms were the introduction of a new governance structure in the Netherlands based on the strong financial and fiscal autonomy of local authorities, e.g. the municipalities and provinces, the application of a new municipality law (1851) and Thorbeck's constitutional reforms introduced in 1848, which limited the power of the monarchy and increased the political participation of Dutch citizens. In addition, the modernisation of Dutch society was accompanied by structural demographic changes, especially changes in the structure and composition of households, which were manifested in an increase in one- and two-person households in the total urban population and a continuing decrease in the number of persons and the number of children per household, especially in the big cities. Concomitantly, the demographic changes were closely related to the social and cultural changes that had a revolutionary character in terms of their effects on traditional family values and societal organisation around 'pillars'. It was from this system of societal organisation that the famous Dutch culture of consensus has emerged, which has dominated – and still dominates – political and socio-economic life in the Netherlands.

In short, the development of the infrastructure and the rapid urbanisation and industrialisation were closely related to changes in the economic structure and socio-demographic, political and institutional changes in the Netherlands. Note, however, that the rapid economic growth could not be reached without the presence of high levels of capital accumulation and investment. In this respect, two waves of investment (1866–82 and 1860–1945) were identified in relation to economic and spatial transformations in the Netherlands. The first investment wave concerned the development of new infrastructure networks, the introduction of technological innovations (especially the introduction of new technologies such as the steam engine and electricity-driven machines), capital intensification and the rapid increase of the construction sector. Economic growth was sustained by substantial expansion in the size of the market, by the specialisation and division of labour within as well as between firms and, subsequently, by the increase in production, productivity and investment.

The second investment wave mainly concerned investments that were oriented towards restructuring the Dutch economy. As a result, the economic structure shifted from an economy based on agriculture and traditional handicraft activities to a manufacturing industry and services-based economy. What most characterised this structural shift in the Dutch economy were the increased levels of employment, production, investment and wages in the manufacturing industry and service sectors. Note, in this respect, that the agriculture sector was fundamentally reformed and modernised through capital intensification and rationalisation and the optimal use of resources in the production process, which in turn resulted in an increase in economies of scale and scope. Furthermore, these reforms were facilitated by the creation and development of new institutions and institutional arrangements such as the creation of cooperative organisations, learning/education and innovation centres, financial institutions and insurance companies.

More generally, since 1870 the strong economic growth in the Netherlands and the expansion of the manufacturing industry may be explained by the development of new technologies such as the steam engines, the use of new resources and materials in production such as oil, electricity and steel, etc. and – let us not forget – the implementation of a market-oriented liberal industrialisation policy based on low-cost competition, international specialisation and the development of modern infrastructure networks. Furthermore, the Dutch manufacturing industry was transformed from a highly concentrated sector dominated by a few large-scale family companies into a more diversified sector dominated by competitive small and medium-sized enterprises.

In addition, the services sector grew substantially and became one of the main driving forces of economic growth, especially the trade and wholesale sectors, as well as repairs and renovation work, transportation, banking and insurance, storage and communication, and public services.

At the regional level, growth of manufacturing industry and services in cities like Amsterdam and Rotterdam exercised a strong pull-effect on workers from the countryside, especially the labour force that was released from agriculture. With the increase in urban population and urban density, large Dutch cities were confronted by two main problems: first the modernisation of existing urban infrastructure networks in order to improve accessibility to the inner cities; and second, the need for additional land to accommodate a fast-growing urban population and new industries within and around the city and its urban fringes. It was in this context that most large Dutch cities expanded beyond their historical medieval city walls. New neighbourhoods were built up around the city centre, mostly by private land development companies or private initiatives. The substantial growth of the construction sector was mainly driven by market mechanisms, i.e. were demand driven, and speculative motives. However, the Housing Act of 1901 gave local authorities a powerful jurisdictional instrument for controlling land use and the housing market by restricting the uncontrolled suburbanisation process while at the same time giving local authorities new powers to realise large-scale urban expansion plans. Following the implementation of this new collective arrangement, Dutch cities made considerable efforts to dictate housing planning and housing stock, to improve the quality of amenities and to control the social composition of city districts. Furthermore, local authorities embraced the idea that urban design and urban planning should be brought under the full responsibility of the municipal and regional planning departments. These units were managed by city planners that set out spatial planning strategies based on a specific planning philosophy, e.g. garden city, functional or organic city, etc. In the case of Amsterdam, some influential city planners such as Sarphati, Kalff, Berlage, van Esteren, Scheffer and van Lohuizen have left their mark on the spatial development of the city through the realisation of impressive designs for buildings, streets, gardens, etc., and the implementation of unusual urban expansion plans such as, for example, the famous 'General Extension Plan of Amsterdam (AUP)' of the 1930s.

One of the most striking features concerning the economic transformation of the city of Amsterdam and the Schiphol region was the growing gap in economic growth between the cities and the countryside. This reflects, however, a much broader tendency towards increasing discrepancies between the Dutch regions, especially between the four large cities of the Randstad and other cities and regions. In fact, this is not surprising, because the main large cities of the North and South provinces of the Randstad dominated by far all other Dutch cities in terms of urbanisation, industrialisation and economic growth. In 1899, for example, more than 21 per cent of the national labour force in agriculture and fishing, 45 per cent of labour force in manufacturing industry and 50 per cent of the labour force in services lived and worked in the Randstad. Trade and export firms offered more jobs to the active population than in any other region of the country (57.5 per cent of the national labour force). Over the whole period 1900–30, growth rates in industry and services were much higher in the Randstad-Holland than national levels.

Historically, the economic revival of Amsterdam started with the opening of the North Sea Canal in 1876 and the increase in colonial trade, which gave a boost to the transportation sector, banking and insurance, shipbuilding, food processing, the textile industry and the equipment and machinery industries. With the increase in employment in industry and services, the number of in-commuters to the city increased rapidly. From the 1920s, the out-commuter flows from Amsterdam to the suburban areas also showed a substantial increase as a result of the delocalisation of manufacturing industries to the surrounding urban areas, as in, for example, the case of the tobacco and food processing industries in the Zaanstreek areas (i.e. the northern part of greater Amsterdam).

Despite the growing importance of the manufacturing industry, the economic structure of the Amsterdam-Schiphol region is clearly service-oriented (trade and transport, commercial and financial sectors), while the rest of the province has a greater share of manufacturing and agricultural activities. Within the province, the three major cities of Amsterdam, Haarlem and Zaanstad tend to specialise in transport, communication, banking and business services. The rest of the municipalities in the province of North Holland are biased towards agriculture and fishing, public utilities, distribution and tourism (hotels and catering). Empirical analysis of the spatial concentration of economic activities in the Amsterdam-Schiphol region during the first half of the twentieth century shows clear evidence supporting the increase in specialisation of the Amsterdam-Schiphol region in business services and some specialised manufacturing industries rather than other cities and regions of the Randstad.

The spatial expansion and suburbanisation of Amsterdam during the late nineteenth century and the first half of the twentieth century was based on a selective urban planning doctrine. This gradual and selective urban expansion of the city can be explained by the structural financial deficit of the city and the shortage of land for the realisation of urban expansion projects. Together, these two elements limited the realisation of the large urban expansion projects that were accomplished in other major cities such as Paris or London. However, among the famous urban expansion plans realised by the city of Amsterdam were the urban expansion of Amsterdam South (Berlag) and the General Expansion Plan of Amsterdam (AUP) in the 1930s. These major urban expansion plans, and many other expansion projects, could be realised because of successive annexations of suburban areas around the city boundaries (in 1877, 1896 and 1921). As a result, the total area of Amsterdam increased substantially – from 4,600 ha by the end of the nineteenth century to 17,121 ha by the 1930s.

Close to Amsterdam, Haarlemmermeer was functionally and economically strongly dependent on the central city Amsterdam. The first settlers of this agrarian area were immigrants from the regions of Friesland, North Brabant and the province of North Holland. The majority settled along the border areas of the Haarlemmermeer polder like Alsmeer, Lisse, Hillegom and Halfweg. The relatively young population of Haarlemmermeer, the diverse character of agricultural activities in this area, the modernisation of the agriculture sector, and the creation of new institutions turned out to be decisive in the development of Haarlemmermeer into one of the most productive agrarian regions of the Netherlands. In 1875, Haarlemmermeer became one of the wealthiest agrarian areas in the country, where the use of new (steam) equipment, artificial fertilisers and returns from land exploitation were relatively higher than the national average. However, the development of the Schiphol airport and Haarlemmermeer became intertwined after the 1920s. The influence of Schiphol on the surrounding areas became apparent with the increase in activities that were related to the airport such as, for example trade and transport activities, especially after the Second World War. In this sense, the development of Schiphol airport has changed radically the spatial and economic structure of Haarlemmermeer from an agrarian economy to a more service-oriented and diversified economy.

In addition, the suburbanisation process that took place at the level of Amsterdam was subsequently accompanied by the urbanisation of Haarlemmermeer. The urbanisation process of Haarlemmermeer was to a great extent driven by the growth of Schiphol airport and its related activities, as the historical urban development of Zwanenburg, Badhoevedorp and Hoofddorp clearly shows.

Schiphol airport became one of the most important economic centres and growth pole par excellence, not only for the Haarlemmermeer polder but also for the whole Amsterdam region. In this sense, the urbanisation and economic growth of Haarlemmermeer are closely related to the development and growth of Schiphol airport. The example of Schiphol airport clearly shows the existence of strong relationships between the urbanisation process of the region and the economic development of the airport activities, and hence the importance and role of the airport in triggering spatial and economic processes that have strong long-term effects at the local and regional levels, as the following chapters clearly show.

5   The rise and development of Schiphol airport

From a military airfield to a municipal airport 1916–45

5.1 Introduction

Closely related to the industrialisation and urbanisation of the Amsterdam-Schiphol region, our investigation in this chapter centres on the historical causes, actors and motives explaining the rise and development of Schiphol airport during the 1920s and 1930s.

Despite the wave of studies on airport development in Europe and the USA published over the past two decades, research focusing on the wider implications and interdependency of airport and urban development has been scarce. Most studies deal with specific topics, such as airport design, architecture and engineering, infrastructure, the early history of single airports or the remarkable feats of aviation pioneers. From these studies, we refer, for example, to Brodherson's research on the construction and design of airport facilities and installations in the early days of the development of airports (Brodherson, 1993, cited in Bednarek, 2001: 4–5), Douglas' study on the evolution of technology and the increasing complexity of airports (Douglas, 1995), Myerscough's excellent survey of the provision of British airports during the interwar years (Myerscough, 1985) and Dierikx and Bouwens' extensive monograph on the history of Schiphol airport in the European context. This last study, however, focuses more particularly on airport architecture and design (Dierikx and Bouwens, 1997). Nonetheless, these studies have touched upon very relevant issues with regard to airport history. Bednarek (2001), for example, has posed one of the key questions concerning how and why most airports at first instance were run by municipal authorities. In both the USA and the Netherlands, in contrast to many other European countries, airport development was a local matter. The construction of airports was the result of the collective efforts of local politicians and some key businesspeople who believed in the positive effects that aviation could have on their cities and businesses. According to Bednarek, financial considerations explain the involvement of local actors in the construction of the first airfields. In the USA, local governments were not financially able to support the construction of airfields. Other institutional agencies such as the US Post Office, municipal governments and local (business) interest groups were the driving forces behind the construction of many local airfields in the country.

Fuelled by local boosterism aimed at improving the local economy, civic pride and/or a strong belief in the future of aviation, many cities took up the challenge. Although Bednarek's analysis cannot simply be applied to Schiphol airport because of differences in the financial system between the Netherlands and the USA, her study put forward the need to approach the early history of airport development from a wider perspective. After all, apart from their important economic and infrastructural functions, airports also possess important cultural and institutional aspects such as image, perception and collective governance, which involve various actors at different spatial levels – local, regional, national and international – and in different institutional settings. This is precisely the analytical approach that we follow in this study. In this sense, our approach is somewhat different from existing historical studies on the early development of airports with respect to the following three considerations. First, we consider the rise and the development of Schiphol airport as one of the key determinants of the (sub)urbanisation and spatial transformation of Haarlemmermeer and the greater Amsterdam region. Second, Schiphol is one of the main driving economic forces that has far reaching consequences on the transformation of the local and regional economic structure of the Amsterdam-Schiphol region during the twentieth century: more particularly we refer here to the role of Schiphol in sustaining the position of Amsterdam as the centre of traffic flows, commerce and industry. The accessibility and the proximity of the airport to the economic capital of the country has been explicitly mentioned by various key actors during the 1920s and 1930s as crucial in sustaining the economic growth of the city and the region. In other words, the presence of a commercial airport near Amsterdam was then considered important for the future economic development of the city: Schiphol needed Amsterdam as much as Amsterdam needed Schiphol. Third, Schiphol may be seen as a typical example of how a collective arrangement can evolve over the long term into an institutional arrangement within the local/ regional institutional field.

Historically, the development of civil aviation in the Netherlands has its origins in military aviation. The first pioneers in this new emerging sector were ex-military pilots, aeronautical engineers and enthusiasts from the business world and civil aviation circuits that took initiatives to invest in developing Dutch civil aviation using existing military airfields. The first effective commercial operations of civil aviation took place at the end of 1919 when the Dutch airline company KLM began its commercial operations at Schiphol military airfield.

As was the case with many airfields in the USA during the 1920s, the early development of airports in the Netherlands was a local issue. The construction of Schiphol airport was the result of the collective efforts of local politicians, military officers and the business elite who deeply believed in the idea that civil aviation could have great beneficial effects on their cities and businesses. In this sense, the airport construction involved various actors acting at different domain levels, e.g. local government, businesses and societal organisations.

During the first two decades of its existence (1920s–1930s), Schiphol airport changed drastically in size, function, land occupation and social and economic importance for the local and regional economy. Furthermore, the rapid development in aviation technology has put much pressure on airport design, planning, organisation and management of the airports. Consequently, the spatial requirements for airport expansion and improvements to airport facilities, in terms of land use and land reservation for future expansion, had clear effects on the city spatial planning (for example through zoning regulation), as the airport became vital for the economic development of the surrounding areas, particularly Haarlemmermeer and Amsterdam.

In our analysis of the interplay between the various actors involved in airport development, we focus our attention on the concept of collective arrangements to highlight the important role of the institutional environment in understanding the early development of Schiphol airport in relation to its surrounding areas. We consider Schiphol the result of collective arrangements stemming from a combination of policy, agreements, governance structure and economic support (for instance investments) aimed at the creation, improvement and transformation of the airport's economic and spatial structure in relation to its wider urban and regional environment. In turn, the (local) interactions between the different actors and factors influence – either directly or indirectly – the long-term development trajectory of the airport and its spatial and economic configuration. Note here that the term 'actors' refers to private and/or institutional individuals or groups of individuals and organisations that are directly and/or indirectly involved in (or affected by) airport development activities, such as, for example, individuals from civil aviation and the aeronautics industry, airport authorities, municipalities, provinces and the state, residential groups, business organisations and other commercial tenants, as well as socio-cultural, political and civic groups, etc. In this sense, the structure of collective arrangements is shaped through the interplay of people, goods, money, knowledge and information, and the accompanying spatial interventions, agreements and regulations. In short, the origins and development of Schiphol airport during the 1920s and 1930s may be viewed as the result of successive collective arrangements that have structured and determined the development and growth of the airport over the long term.

The public demonstration at Schiphol airport on Saturday, 2 July 1938, for instance, was part of the emergence of a new collective arrangement which eventually led to the establishment of Schiphol as a national airport after the Second World War. Different actors at the local, regional and national levels were involved in determining the main contours of this new collective arrangement. In this study, we make a distinction between the three principal actors that were involved in the development of Schiphol airport:

- *individuals* – key individuals from civil aviation or aviation enthusiasts, members of local business communities and users of airport services;
- *local government or representative entities* – such as municipalities, city councils and chambers of commerce; and
- *the state* – including regional and national bodies such as ministries and national (semi-)public institutions – the National Aviation Board for example.

The aim of this chapter is to describe and discuss the historical background to the rise and development of Schiphol airport through a focus on the interactions between the main actors, and on the role and importance of key political, spatial and economic factors that have determined the early history of Schiphol and other Dutch airports. We particularly explore the institutional and economic relations between the airport and the city of Amsterdam and Haarlemmermeer, as well as the relations between Schiphol and its competitors, e.g. the rival Dutch airports which competed with Schiphol to acquire the status of 'national airport'.

This chapter is organised as follows. In section 5.2, we explore and discuss the historical background to the origins and the development of the military airfield at Schiphol, and analyse the underlying causes, factors and actors who played important roles in its future development. We identify the key actors that played a crucial role in the development of Schiphol, elaborate further on their specific roles, motivations and objectives and explore how they contributed to the emergence and transformation of existing collective arrangements that directed the development of Schiphol from a military airfield to a municipal airport. Apart from their formal nature, collective arrangements also encompass certain collective representations and perceptions with regard to airport and urban development, as manifested in spatial planning concepts, airport configuration and design, and airport management strategies. These issues are discussed in the next section as we elaborate further on the issue of how Schiphol airport was managed and operated by the municipality of Amsterdam. Next, we turn our attention to the issue of economic performance of Schiphol during its early development period, i.e. the 1920s and the 1930s. In this section (5.6), we examine the key economic performance indicators and discuss the question of why Schiphol airport benefited from unconditional financial support from local authorities despite the fact that Schiphol was an extremely unprofitable business with regard to the generation of sufficient revenues to sustain its basic operational activities.

In section 5.7, we will elaborate further on the issue of the 'battle of the airports' between Amsterdam and Rotterdam, the so-called 'Leiderdorp affair', and their efforts to get support from the state to develop their airport into the country's single central national airport. The fierce debates between the various actors involved in this affair are extensively reviewed and critically assessed in the light of an in-depth study of historical records and official reports from the archives. Section 5.8 gives a brief historical overview of the situation of Schiphol under the German occupation and section 5.9 concludes.

5.2 The rise of a military airport in the polder: historical background

During the First World War, airplanes became frighteningly destructive military weapons that brought serious damage to the military capacity and civil infrastructure of the enemy. For the first time in the history of humankind, thousands of people could be killed with relatively high precision air bombardments. Soon after the First World War, the military needed to train pilots to carry out long-distance missions. To achieve this goal, new airfields were set up within or in the proximity of existing military facilities and artillery batteries.

In the case of Schiphol, the birth of this airfield in particular and of Dutch civil aviation in general can be traced back to the military decision to create a new airfield in the Haarlemmermeer polder. From a military point of view, this strategic decision was motivated by the need to strengthen the Dutch military lines of defence against eventual attack from Germany.

In 1914, a small unit of the Netherlands Air Force Command (hereafter the LVA) was created by the Ministry of War. The LVA operated from a central military base located in the airfield of Soesterberg near the city of Utrecht. With the outbreak of the First World War in August 1914, the LVA's main task was the observation from the air of the military movements of the enemy on Dutch ground. In the event of a military attack by Germany, the Dutch military forces could quickly retreat to the Fortress of Holland behind the inundation area, known as the water defence line stretching from the small town of Muiden to the cities of Utrecht and Gorinchem (Molenaar, 1968: 2). For this reason, on 1 August 1914, the Commandant in Chief of the land and navy forces, General C. J. Snijders, ordered his Commandant of the Department of Aviation, Captain H. Wallard Sacré, to search for a suitable location to construct a new military airfield in proximity to the main artillery batteries that defended the North Sea Canal from Amsterdam. Commandant Sacré found a number of plots of land in the vicinity of the existing artillery location in Hembrug (Achtersluispolder) in the northern area of the North Sea Canal. This terrain was then hired and made ready for use as a military airfield. A few months later, it became clear to the military officials that this very muddy terrain was not suited for military air operations. In his search for new terrain suitable for an airfield, commandant Sacré found another location in the Zeeburgerpolder close to the artillery fire terrain in the western side of Amsterdam that could be used by the Air Force and Navy departments of the Ministry of War. However, this new location was abandoned because the Navy department was not interested in participating in the construction of a combined Navy base and airfield in this location.

Table 5.1 The construction costs of the military airfield Schiphol (1915)

Construction of bridge	ƒ 1,000
Construction of four wooden sheds (20 × 20m) for 12 airplanes (ƒ 8,500 each)	ƒ 34,000
Shed for service cars	ƒ 8,500
Construction of a storage house	ƒ 7,500
Wooden shed (for 100 men)	ƒ 15,000
Hardening of the terrain	ƒ 1,500
Dumping and draining of (crossing) water channels	ƒ 2,500
Connection to electricity central, water supply, fuel station (+ PM post)	ƒ 10,500
Total costs	ƒ 80,000

Source: Molenaar (1968, p. 5).

Finally, on 2 November 1915, Wallard Sacré found eminently suitable terrain in the Haarlemmermeer polder (e.g. the 'Halfweg' location), which met perfectly the requirements of the military for the construction of a military airfield. This terrain was located within the fortress of Amsterdam and in the proximity of the Rijnkanaal waterway and the central electricity supply. The total surface of the terrain was 400 by 500 metres, divided into four nearly equal land parcels (see Map 5.1).

In order to make this terrain operational for military airplanes, Sacré estimated the total costs at *f* 180,000, including the total cost of acquiring the land parcels and the construction costs (i.e. 20 ha at *f* 5,000 per ha and *f* 80,000 for the preparation of the terrain) (Molenaar, 1968: 5) (see Table 5.1).

The Minister of War N. Bosbom rejected this proposal on 22 November 1915 because of the high acquisition costs (e.g. more than the maximum amount of *f* 100,000). However, General Snijders managed to convince the minister of the urgency and importance for the Dutch Air Corps to have its own airfield near Amsterdam, and not far from the Soesterberg air base. On 17 December 1915, the Minister of War approved the second proposal of the LVA to purchase only two of the four land parcels (200 by 600 metres) for *f* 55,229.40 (*f* 4,527 per ha). However, the preparation of the military terrain took longer than was expected. The airfield was 500 metres long and 250 metres wide with a total area of 16.5 ha, and was officially opened in August 1916 (see Map 5.1). Shortly after it became operational, it turned out to be too small for aircraft landing, especially in a crosswind. Aircraft landing and taking off needed a landing field at least approximately 80 by 80 metres. Fortunately, the new Minister of War B. C. de Jong was more receptive to the demands of the military command to improve and expand the airfield facilities. The Dutch government, which had noted the increasing military importance of aviation and the rapid advance in aeronautical technology, doubled the budget of the Air Corps to 5.7 million guilders (Dierikx and Bouwen, 1997: 48).

In order to extend the airfield terrain, the military expropriated 16 land parcels from various local farmers and part of a land parcel belonging to the Haarlemmermeer polder administration. The total surface area of the airfield increased from 16.5 ha to 60.3 ha (see Map 5.2). However, despite the increased surface of Schiphol, the poor physical condition of the airfield did not improve much until the 1920s, due to the absence of good drainage facilities and a supply of electricity and water. As result, during the rainy seasons, the airfield terrain – known as 'Schiphol les Bains' among foreign pilots – was practically inaccessible.

From 1919 onward, the military airport entered a new phase in its development when the military agreed to share the use of the airfield with the Dutch aviation company KLM. This decision can be seen as the prolongation of the basic collective arrangement that gave rise to the Schiphol airfield, namely the decision of the military to construct the airfield. As a result, Schiphol became a mixed airfield operating as a military airfield and as a civil aviation aerodrome.

However, to understand how this collective arrangement emerged, we need to look closely at the nature of the relationship between KLM and Schiphol airport between 1919 and 1926.

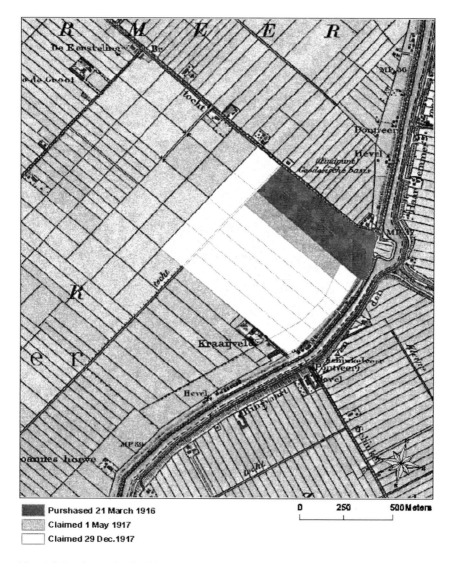

Purshased 21 March 1916
Claimed 1 May 1917
Claimed 29 Dec.1917

0   250   500 Meters

Map 5.1 Land parcels of Schiphol military airfield: 1916–19.

5.3 Royal Dutch Airline Company KLM and the rise of Schiphol

The famous transatlantic flight of Lindbergh from the USA to the French airport at Le Bourget had a great impact on the public and the aviation circuits in Europe. Aviation enthusiasts and professionals of the aeronautical industry had great expectations for the potential commercial possibilities of civil aviation as a business model and for the future of the air travel market. The aeronautic industry

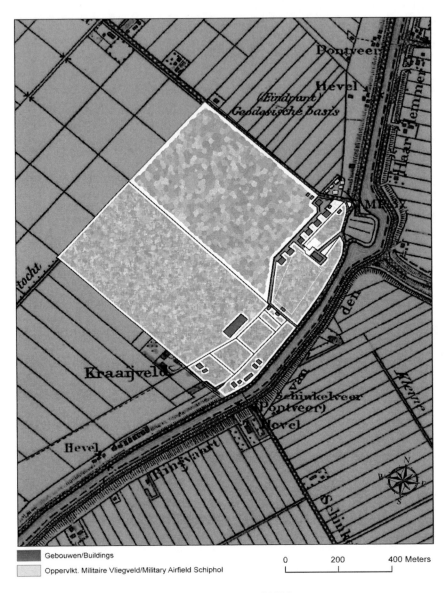

Map 5.2 Military airfield Schiphol between 1916 and 1926.
Source: based on Historical Bonne maps.

began to shift its emphasis towards technological innovation, design and commercialisation of aircraft (Gordon, 2004: 10).

It was in this context that in the Netherlands a group of individuals active in aeronautical circles, in cooperation with the chamber of commerce, aviation organisations, other individuals and (local) media, began to organise events with the aim of promoting commercial aviation, e.g. hosting flight shows and meetings, and publishing articles, studies and reports on the developments in aircraft technology, civil aviation and commercial airports. Many of these people were closely related to the military and/or active in aeronautical and aviation circles. One of them was the pilot Lieutenant Albert Plesman, a great advocate of the development of Dutch civil aviation. Plesman was aware of the position of the Netherlands lagging behind in the fields of aeronautic and civil aviation compared to other European countries, especially Germany and France. His main concerns were also shared by a number of prominent individuals from the aviation circle and the media. The aviation magazine *Het Vliegveld*, for example, published in 1918 a series of articles and studies focusing on the development of aviation technology and the emergence of commercial airports in Europe (Leeuw, 1989: 15). As result of these discussions, the Royal Dutch Association for Aviation (De Koninklijke Nederlandse Vereniging voor Luchtvaart (KNVvL)) formed the Commission of Air Traffic in 1918 to study the possibility of developing a Dutch airport for civil aviation. However, things became more concrete when Plesman and Hofstee published an announcement to organise the first international exhibition of air traffic in Amsterdam in 1919 (known as the Eerste Luchtverkeer Tentoonstelling Amsterdam, hereafter ELTA). Many aviation enthusiasts were involved in the organisation of this event, ranging from those belonging to the financial elite to members of the military circle and the city council of Amsterdam.

Plesman managed, in a relatively short time, to get the needed financial support from Amsterdam's private bankers (f 300,000 as guarantees) and the state (a subsidy of f 75,000) to organise this big event on 1 August 1919. Over a period of six weeks, more than 500,000 people visited the ELTA international exhibition, at which various participants from the European aviation sector presented their aircraft to the public and participated in air flight shows. The event was a great success, and total revenues generated by the exhibition were high enough to pay back all the financial loans and other costs.

Building on the successful organisation of the ELTA exhibition, a group of prominent business elite (financiers, bankers and businessmen) decided to join forces to create the Dutch airline company KLM.[1] Albert Plesman was appointed administrator (later director) of KLM, and the official documents of the creation of KLM Royal Dutch Company were signed on 7 October 1919.

In March 1920, KLM obtained a generous contract from the Dutch post office to transport the mail between Amsterdam and London. Plesman chartered two Havilland DH-16 airplanes from the British carrier Air Transport & Travel (AT&T) to schedule airmail flights from Amsterdam to London. Two months later, the first aircraft from London landed at Schiphol military airfield. In June 1920, Schiphol airfield was officially opened to commercial air traffic, albeit with a maximum of 30 flights per month.

On 15 August 1920, Plesman purchased two Fokker F-II airplanes from the Dutch airline construction company Fokker. This was the beginning of a long period of cooperation, but also of conflicts and disputes between Anthony Fokker (Fokker) and Albert Plesman (KLM).[2] The relationship between these two companies, and from 1926 with the airport Schiphol, was crucial for the development of Dutch civil aviation in general and Schiphol airport in particular. Fokker furnished new airplanes to KLM and the performance of KLM attracted the attention of other airline companies to the high quality and performance of Fokker airplanes. However, the prevailing commercial ambitions and market-oriented strategy of KLM, and especially of Albert Plesman, put an end to the close cooperation between KLM and Fokker. When Douglas developed the Douglas DC-I and DC-II in 1933–4, Plesman did not hesitate to substitute Fokker airplanes with the new Douglas airplanes. To Plesman, KLM was much more important than personal friendship, and this kind of thinking largely applied to the relationships involving KLM (Plesman) and Schiphol airport's managing director Jan Dellaert.

Note that from its early years (1919), KLM was financially supported by the national government, as was the case of most other national airlines in Europe during 1920s and the 1930s. From the start of its activities, KLM turned to the Ministry of Waterworks, which was responsible for civil aviation, for additional subventions and asked the government to play active role in setting up direct air service lines between Amsterdam and the Dutch colonies (Batavia). The Minister of Waterworks Adriaan König offered to cover two-thirds of KLM deficits to a maximum of f 200,000 in 1920 and 1921. However, financial support to KLM was more than doubled in 1921 (406,313 guilders), and after a short break in 1926, the Dutch government decided in the summer of 1927 to continue its financial support for a period of seven years in order to help KLM to expand its air services between Amsterdam and the Dutch colonies. As a result, KLM became a quasi-public firm with the state as the major shareholder in the company. The total financial support to KLM reached f 970,000 in 1930 when KLM started its regular air services on the Amsterdam–Batavia line, and despite the economic crisis, KLM received f 547,800 a year from 1934 onward (Dierikx and Bouwen, 1997).

However, despite the financial support from the state, KLM was not able to generate any positive results, with the exception of 1934 (113,819 guilders) (see Figure 5.1).

Although KLM was given full monopoly to exploit the Amsterdam–Batavia line, Plesman was concerned by the passive attitude of the Dutch government, especially when KLM's airline activities came under pressure because of unfair competition from the British Imperial Airways service on the London–Amsterdam–India and Amsterdam–Batavia lines. Plesman then turned to the Dutch authorities and asked for (political) help. In the end, KLM succeeded in strengthening its competitive position on the Amsterdam–Batavia line by using faster and much bigger aircraft, e.g. the Douglas DC-2 airliner.

Note that KLM's activities increased remarkably between 1926 and 1939, especially the post and freight transport activities (see Figure 5.2). As a result of the increasing activities by KLM and other foreign air companies, Schiphol developed into one of the most important air transport junctions in the European air transport network.

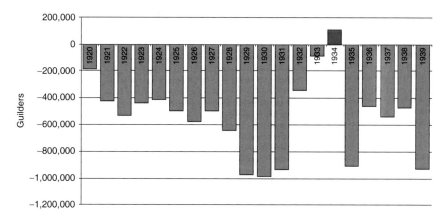

Figure 5.1 Net results of KLM between 1920 and 1939.
Source: KLM Annual Reports and Dierikx (1999, pp. 371–373).

KLM's great success in operating intercontinental air traffic services, especially on the Amsterdam–Batavia line, is closely related to the introduction of new aircraft technology during the 1930s, such as the Douglas DC-1 and DC-2 aircraft. However, the most important development in aircraft technology was the introduction of a larger version of the DC-2: the Douglas Sleeper Transport (with a capacity of 21 passengers) used to fly non-stop from coast to coast in the USA. The daytime version of this plane was the popular Douglas DC-3, used by KLM in 1936 on the Amsterdam–Batavia–Sydney route, that helped the airline companies make money from the transportation of passengers.

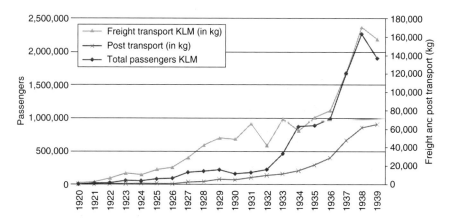

Figure 5.2 Total passengers, post and freight transported by KLM between 1920 and 1939.
Source: KLM Annual Reports (1920–1940).

More generally, the increased competition between KLM and its rivals on the Amsterdam–Batavia route during the 1920s and 1930s illustrates how civil aviation was used by countries as an instrument of political power and a means of preserving 'colonial' prestige (see Dierikx, 1991). However, this does not mean that commercial airplane companies were not interested in the profitability of their businesses. Most of them tried to become financially independent, but the limited market, low demand (i.e. number of passengers), the increasing price of new airplanes and the growing competition largely explain why most airplane companies were operating at loss. Without financial support from national governments, the majority of national airplane companies could probably not survive at that time.

In this respect, one may ask the following legitimate question. Why did European governments financially sustain their national airline companies but did not do the same in the case of emerging airports?

According to Bednarek (2001: 51), western countries exhibited a deep faith in science and technology as the means to control the often harsh environment, improve the living conditions of the population and generate wealth. In addition, many European countries were convinced by the fact that the development of air transport technology would strengthen the connectivity of the core metropolitan nations with their colonised satellite regions. In this sense, aviation was considered a symbol of (political and military) power and an instrument to expand the political and economic influence of countries far beyond their traditional national boundaries. Finally, from a local economic perspective, commercial aviation offered many opportunities to diversify the economic structure of regions through both commercial airline operations and aircraft manufacturing industry (Bednarek, 2001: 52).

More specifically, increased governmental involvement in the development of national civil aviation could be explained by the ambition of the metropolitan centres to establish direct connections by air with their colonial territories (Great Britain, the Netherlands, France and Belgium, for example). Some countries such as the United States and Japan used their international airlines as instruments for political, economic and military interventions in regions where they held strategic interests. Yet, as Dierikx and Bouwens (1997: 333) argue, the most important motives, common to all countries that supported their national aviation companies, were related to national pride and prestige. The provision of financial and diplomatic assistance to national aviation companies was decisive for their survival.

5.4 The great detour: from mixed airfield to municipal airport

During the period 1920–40, most of airfields in the USA and Europe were strongly associated with the municipalities in which they were located. Progress in the aeronautical field and air transport technology dictated largely the way airfields have been developed in terms of design, planning, organisation and management. For example, the spatial configuration of the first-generation airfields (e.g. military and mixed airfields) consisted often of a flat and well-drained landing terrain for safe landings and take-off. These basic requirements for airfields fitted the basic needs of the first generation of airplanes.

From this perspective, the emergence of the first airfields may be seen as the result of a basic and very simple collective arrangement in which a limited number of actors were involved, often the municipality and a limited number of private parties. Many of these actors were, directly or indirectly, involved in aviation activities and shared the same vision and belief in the bright future of civil aviation. They were pioneers and visionaries of the new aerial frontiers that were expected to establish a new world in the skies (Plesman believed that 'Aviation will unite all people around the globe'). However, with the development of commercial aviation, the public image of aviation – the heroic pilot as a frontiersman facing constant danger and sudden death – gradually shifted toward a more mature image as it became a normal business. The adventurer pilots became skilled professionals who cared very much about passengers, goods and the plane itself.

From this perspective, one of the most important questions about the emergence and development of airports in general and Schiphol airport in particular is: how and why they were developed and operated by local authorities (Amsterdam in this case)? More specifically, which underlying collective arrangements can be identified and which actors were involved in the development of the airport and why?

Since the start of KLM's commercial activities at the Schiphol military airfield, many questions were raised by the military authorities about the advantages and disadvantages of mixed military and commercial activities at the same airfield. The main issues were related to regulation, coordination, control and safety within the airfield zone. However, because of the difficulty in reaching agreement about which government department should get full control over the military and civil aviation activities, Schiphol airfield came officially under the control of two different ministries: the Ministry of War, which was responsible for the military activities, and the Ministry of Waterworks, which was responsible for the civil aviation activities.

The Ministry of Waterworks created a special office of aviation services that reported all commercial air activities to the military authorities. In 1930, this service was integrated with the National Air Traffic Board (hereafter the RLD).

The landing fees for commercial airplanes at Schiphol were fixed by the military authorities at one cent per horsepower. The payment of the landing fee gave airplanes the right to use the airfield services provided by the military staff, such as assistance with landing and departure, the filling of fuel and water tanks and the provision of weather information to the pilots. However, with the increasing scope and scale of services provided by the military corps to civil aviation, and the rising costs of the airfield services (e.g. lighting of the landing ground, fire control, medical services, passport checks, etc.), the coexistence of two different air activities within the same airfield came under pressure.

Two alternative options were then suggested by the military authorities. The first was the construction of a new airport for civil aviation. Alternatively, the municipality of Amsterdam had to take over the operation and management of the airfield from the military authorities. This latter option was most welcome from the point of view of Amsterdam's chamber of commerce which saw the airport as a potential contributor to the economic growth of the city, e.g. by attracting firms and activities.

Besides the chamber of commerce, aviation organisations, local media and the local political and economic elite lobbied actively to push local authorities to embrace the idea of having their own local airport for commercial aviation. These local actions clearly demonstrate the continued influence of urban 'boosterism'[3] and the 'winged gospel' (Bednarek, 2001: 64).

Convinced by the idea of the chamber of commerce and other local actors, the municipality of Amsterdam was then prepared to participate in the management of Schiphol and invest in the expansion of the airport facilities. Amsterdam was hoping to benefit from the future growth of commercial aviation activities, in compensation for the loss of harbour activities to its rival city of Rotterdam. After all, Rotterdam had its own commercial airport (Waalhaven) which was much better equipped than the airfield at Schiphol.

More generally, Amsterdam's local authorities were actively involved in acquiring and expanding the airport because of the great pressures from local aviation enthusiasts, particularly from the business elite (involved with KLM, harbour activities, etc.) who had taken risks in investing in creating the commercial aviation company. However, the role of the military in the early development of the airfield was very important for many reasons. First, they facilitated the mixed-use of the airfield for commercial aviation activities. Second, they facilitated its conversion to a full civil aviation airport. The main reasons why the military abandoned Schiphol were based on pure financial considerations and the decreased threat of war, which was after all the main reason the military airfield was built.

At the national level, the deterioration of the government's financial situation in 1921 pushed the Ministry of Finance to think seriously about the concentration of commercial air activities at Rotterdam's Waalhaven airport, and in doing so, Waalhaven would become the sole national commercial airport of the country. However, this plan was not realised for two main reasons. First, KLM had already established a scheduled service to London from Amsterdam. The company was prepared to participate in the exploitation costs (loss) of the airfield if the state would financially support the company (financing the deficit) for a period of five years. Furthermore, the Dutch post office signed an agreement with KLM to transport the post from Amsterdam to London and not from Waalhaven airport in Rotterdam. Second, both the Ministry of War and KLM pinned their hopes on the Amsterdam local authorities expanding and improving the airport facilities at Schiphol. They were supported by the Amsterdam chamber of commerce, which saw clear commercial interests in the development of Schiphol. The municipality, however, lacked the expertise, political power and financial means to effectively operate and manage the airport.

Amsterdam then came up with a proposition to take over the exploitation costs of the airfield on the condition that Schiphol should be operated and managed by the municipality for a period of 20 years. The cost of improvements to the airport facilities were estimated at ƒ 565,000. However, the negotiations between Amsterdam and the Ministries of War and Waterworks took six years (from 1920 to 1926) before an agreement was reached. This is because the two ministries could not agree about which of them had the effective authority to negotiate the transfer of the airport to the city of Amsterdam. The Ministry of War was officially the owner of the airfield terrain, while the Ministry of Waterworks was responsible for the maintenance of the airport.

The city council of Amsterdam voted almost unanimously in favour of taking over Schiphol airfield from the Ministry of Waterworks. Amsterdam was given full responsibility to manage and operate the airfield, except for a small part of the terrain for the military, for a period of ten years (from 1 January 1926 to 1 January 1936). Amsterdam managed to extend this agreement by another 30 years in 1925. In 1935, the military part of the airport terrain was leased to Amsterdam (for a period of 50 years) and in this way all of the airport terrain fell under the control of Amsterdam. In 1938, the state proposed the transfer of ownership of the airport terrain to Amsterdam for ƒ 600,000, but the final agreement could not be signed because of the rising tensions around the issue of the central national airport (ACA, 1323, Nr. 69/12).

The management of Schiphol came under the responsibility of the municipal department of commerce (*Dienst Handelsinrichtingen*), which was also responsible for the management of port activities, and the department of public works that drafted the first plans for the future expansion of the airport. Within the former department, the local authorities created a separate airport department called the *Dienst Luchthaven Schiphol*. From that point, the development of Schiphol airport received special attention from the Amsterdam planning department as an important element of the overall spatial and economic development of Amsterdam and the region. This is because the ongoing development of airplane technologies and the corresponding increase in commercial aviation resulted in a gradual spatial expansion of Schiphol airport, which in turn called for a more systematic approach to the future spatial development of the airport and its relation to Amsterdam urban areas.

In 1927, Amsterdam signed an agreement with KLM concerning landing fees and airport charges. KLM was charged to offer services to other airplanes in the airport area against financial compensation of ƒ 13,275 per year. From the total revenues of Schiphol airport, one-third of additional revenues and the net revenues from visitors' charges (after deduction of taxes) were paid by the airport authorities to the municipality of Haarlemmermeer and KLM, and two-thirds to the municipality of Amsterdam (ACA, 1323, Nr. 69/12).

More generally, a very limited number of actors were closely involved in the development of the airport during its early days. If we consider the rise and development of Schiphol airport as the result of a collective arrangement, then the identification of the key actors becomes easy. This is because of the simple character of this collective arrangement, which was in first instance the creation of a military airfield and its conversion into a municipal airport. The key actors that played a crucial role in creating the first collective arrangement that shaped the first contours of the development of Schiphol airport are, respectively, the municipality of Amsterdam, KLM, the Ministry of Waterworks and the Ministry of War, and to a lesser extent (indirectly) the municipality of Haarlemmermeer, the Fokker airplane construction company, the province of North Holland, the chamber of commerce and a very limited number of other local actors.

Figure 5.3 gives an overview of the key actors involved in the formation of the first collective arrangement that structured the development of Schiphol airport during the period 1919–40.

To sum up, many reasons can be given for why Amsterdam took the lead in the development of Schiphol airport from 1926 onward, although the municipality lacked knowledge, expertise and the financial means to operate the airport. Among these reasons, we cite the following:

- The military, the Dutch post office and other civic groups played an important role in stimulating and pushing the local authorities of Amsterdam to take over the former military airfield.
- Not only competition with the city of Rotterdam, but also prestige and local boosterism pushed Amsterdam into developing the municipal airport to keep up with rival cities such Rotterdam and other European cities such as Paris and London.

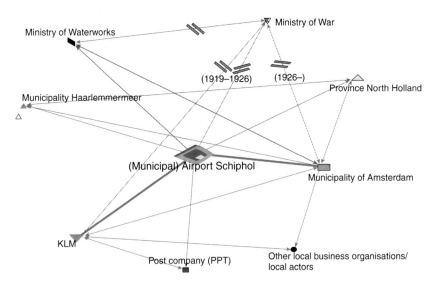

Figure 5.3 Networks of actors involved in the development of Schiphol during 1920s and 1930s.
Note: the thickness of the lines shows the density of the relationships between Schiphol airport and other actors. The lines marked with strips show the end of the relationships, e.g. the disappearance of actors.

- The local authorities of the four large cities were actively involved in promoting and marketing their cities as economic centres and attractive places for work and people. In the case of Amsterdam, this period coincides also with the emergence of a number of local key actors who believed in a new governance style aiming to defend and promote local interests and improve the economic position of the city nationally as well as internationally (Kaal, 2008). For example, the modernisation of Schiphol airport was important for the promotion of Amsterdam internationally during the organisation of the Olympic Games of 1928.
- Schiphol airport was considered by Amsterdam as the perfect alternative to strengthen the economic position of the city after the delocalisation of some key port activities to Rotterdam.
- There was a need to diversify the economic structure of cities through both commercial airline operations, aircraft manufacturing and related activities.
- Finally, there were global circumstances such as the faith exhibited in modern transportation technology to boost economic growth, and the high expectations of aviation technologies to improve the connectedness between people, cities and regions at an international scale (see Bednarek, 2001).

5.5 Managing and operating the 'freak aerodrome of the world'

Perhaps the most striking feature that made Schiphol airport famous in the world is its unique location situated four metres below sea level. The American journalist Lowell Thomas from the *New York Times*, who travelled around Europe in the 1920s reporting on European airports, described Schiphol as 'a freak aerodrome of the world, it takes the blue ribbon …' (Gordon, 2004: 18).

As mentioned before, the operation of the Schiphol airfield started in 1919 with very modest equipment and limited facilities, and a staff of seven who were responsible for the ground operations. KLM's commercial activities started at Schiphol airport with one chartered aircraft (a converted military plane) and a couple of hired pilots, before Fokker F-II and F-III aircraft were purchased from Fokker in 1921. Shortly after, foreign airlines began to use Schiphol airport as a destination and/or a transit (stop-over) airport to their final destinations.

Schiphol was developing into an important hub airport, with swift connections to all leading European cities such as London, Hamburg, Copenhagen and Brussels, although its equipment and facilities were still lagging behind in comparison to other European airports. Its importance and attractiveness for commercial air traffic was mainly due to its geographical location and the economic position of Amsterdam and the surrounding areas. As Gordon (2004) has rightly put it:

> The technological limitations of the day, and the geographical location of Amsterdam on the main air routes from London to Germany and Scandinavia, and those from Paris to Scandinavia, made Schiphol a favorable stop-over airport. (Gordon, 2004: 32)

Under the progressive management of the city of Amsterdam, the equipment and facilities of the airport were gradually improved in order to meet the increasing demand for airport services. Since then, Schiphol has been developed into a safe international airport for the biggest airplanes (ACA, 1323, 1010 S1935, 1471S1935 and 531).

In 1930, the most frequent destinations from Schiphol were London, Brussels and Paris (with three scheduled flights a day). Schiphol became the fourth busiest international airport in Europe, after London, Paris and Vienna, and by the end of the 1930s, it had jumped to third place. The home carrier KLM offered 116 out of 223 scheduled flights per week from Schiphol. Under the far-sighted leadership of Albert Plesman (director of KLM), the airport became one of Europe's most important aviation crossroads. A considerable proportion of the air traffic at Schiphol airport consisted of transfer passengers, freight and post transport (more than one-third of passengers and one-quarter of freight passed through Schiphol). Figure 5.4 shows the growth of Schiphol airport, in terms of passengers and freight transport between 1920 and 1938.

The number of passengers increased from 11,700 in 1931 to 50,000 in 1934. This tendency continued progressively from 1935 (50,125 passengers) to reach almost 65,000 passengers in 1937. The number of transit passengers grew substantially between 1931 (1,270 passengers) and 1938 (24,530 passengers). The airplane movements and the loading capacity grew proportionally between 1926 and 1932. Nevertheless, from 1934 the loading capacity showed a higher increase than the number of airplane movements, mainly because of improved aviation technology, e.g. aircraft became bigger and much faster.

Having said that, before Schiphol was able to realise these spectacular achievements, during the early years of the 1920s the airfield was very primitive. Infrastructure and facilities were either lacking or very basic in nature, and the

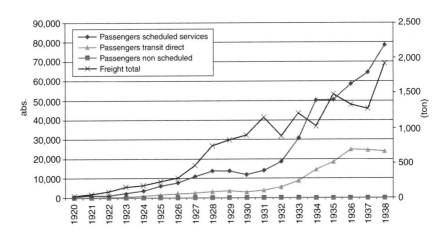

Figure 5.4 Growth of passengers and freight transport at Schiphol between 1920 and 1938.
Source: Annual Reports of the Municipal Airport Schiphol (1926–1938).

existing military facilities had deteriorated over the years. There were no such facilities as terminal buildings, hangars or passenger check-in desks. The only standings at the airfield were a couple of wooden barracks at the border of the airfield terrain, a hangar (35 m by 80 m that was partly used for passenger departures), and a hotel-restaurant building located on the southwest side of the airfield. This hotel-restaurant was used by KLM to accommodate pilots and crew members.

The physical state of the roads to Schiphol was deplorable. The only public transport service to Schiphol was the horse-tram connecting Amsterdam city centre to the small neighbourhood of Sloten in the western part of the city. From that point, a gravel road connecting Sloten to Schiphol was the only road to reach the airport. The only non-stop transport connection between Schiphol and Amsterdam was the KLM scheduled bus service for passengers. People travelling by car were forced to pass through two toll bridges and a narrow bridge at the Rijnvaart canal. The travel distance (about 12 kilometres) from Amsterdam to Schiphol took almost 30 minutes. After the passengers arrived at the airfield, they got special (leather) jackets, glasses, and water jars (to warm their feet) before takeoff. During the rainy days, passengers were carried out individually from the KLM waiting hangar to the airplane. The airplanes themselves were very noisy and smelly, with very little space between passengers.

However, improvements to the airport facilities and the airport terrain were soon to be initiated by the municipality of Amsterdam in 1926. The terrain was renewed and levelled, an underground drainage system was constructed and a big white circle, that served as an orientation point to landing aircraft, was put in the middle of the landing strip. Furthermore, a large concrete apron was constructed at the front of the KLM hangar, the office space was extended and a terminal building with a concrete platform for arriving and departing airplanes was built. The terminal building was completed before the start of the Olympic Games in 1928 and contained spacious halls for the handling of in- and outbound air-travellers and between them a waiting room, the offices of the municipal airport authorities, the radio service room, the weather office and the control-tower.

However, when compared to Le Bourget, Croydon or Tempelhof, all these improvements were much less impressive and very modest in size and scope, due to the limited financial capabilities of the municipality of Amsterdam and the absence of financial support from the state.

In 1929, the airport authorities developed plans for the construction of a new hangar (40 × 100 m) that was fitted with two electrically driven folding doors, and a concrete apron consisting of 5 × 5 m concrete plates. Next to this hangar, three side-buildings for essential workshops, storerooms, a buffet counter and offices, with a total floor space of about 3,000 m², were projected on the construction plan.

Because of the rapid increase of air traffic at Schiphol airport during the 1930s, substantial extensions of the terminal building were constructed. A new spacious restaurant for visitors was built on top of the waiting room, with a large roof-terrace from where sightseers had a panoramic view of the airport terrain.

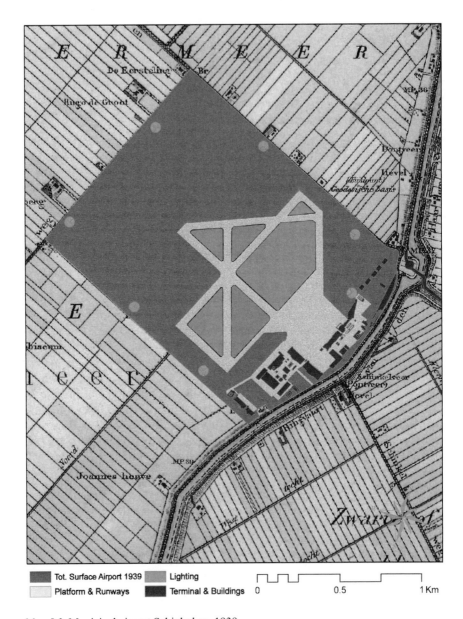

Map 5.3 Municipal airport Schiphol ca. 1939.

By the end of the 1930s, a fine system of runways (the second best in Europe) stretching in eight directions and a large concrete apron covering 31 acres were constructed, together with large hangars and workshops, a station building with a control tower, a restaurant with terraces and up-to-date night landing lighting and radio equipment (see Map 5.3).

Note that during this period, many airports were confronted with difficult technical problems for which the municipalities had to find adequate solutions. In this respect, the airport authorities began experimenting with the use of different materials in the construction of platforms and runways, such as cinders, gravel and asphalt. However, the breakthrough in the construction of airports was provided by Henry Ford's airport in Detroit where the first concrete runway (instead of the mostly used turf-covered landing strip) was constructed. From then on, paved runways became the norm in the construction of airports all over the world.

In the case of Schiphol airport, the composition of the soil – a firm foundation of fine sand mixed with clay – offered a good basis for supporting the construction of concrete runways, including a fine-meshed drainage system and good possibilities for maintaining the stability of the soil under bad weather conditions. A very intensive draining system was laid under the whole landing area which discharged water into the boundary ditches of the airport. These deep boundary ditches were drained by electrical pumping stations that kept the water level lower than in the adjoining land (e.g. the Haarlemmermeer polder). This was crucial to maintaining a proper carrying out capacity of the outfall sewers and to keep the water table of the airfield area down to a safe level.

The paving of the runways was provided with an inward slope to carry off the rainwater to the outside through the construction of special gutters and drains under the runways. The asphalted runways consisted of a 50 cm thick tamped sand-bed on which a heavily rolled packed stone base 25 cm in thickness was covered with a 5 cm thick layer of asphalt concrete. The reinforced concrete plates were 12.06 × 12.06 m, supported at the edges by extra reinforcement and under the corners by a supporting plate placed in the body of sand. Joints between the concrete plates were filled by copper strips placed in concrete and supported by edge-moulds, which remained in the construction while on top of the strips asphalt was poured into the joints to prevent the sand settling (ACA, 1323, No. 932a-b-S49).

With regard to the infrastructure, under pressure from the Amsterdam city council, the road access to Schiphol was integrated into the planning of the national motorway linking Amsterdam to The Hague through Schiphol and the provincial road linking Haarlem and the Gooi through Schiphol. The provincial road was built by the city of Amsterdam, in cooperation with the province of North Holland and the Ministry of Waterworks, while the national highway linking Amsterdam to The Hague was built by the Ministry of Waterworks.

The rapid development in aviation technology necessitated the construction of new runways and ground facilities such as radio communication and navigation equipment, lighting systems, beacon lights, day-and-night operations, etc. As airport activities became more complex, frequent interactions between airport operators became one of the most important sources of information, especially with regard to technical problems and issues related to airport construction and the operation and management of airport activities, i.e. the runway surfacing and drainage system, lighting, hangar construction, air traffic congestion, concessions, sales and advertising, standard accounting systems and other airport services. The exchange of information, experiences and knowledge took place mainly through regular meetings, correspondence, working visits, conferences and publications in professional aviation magazines. More specifically, networks of airport professionals and managers were the main sources of shared information and knowledge. This was very important in the development of international standards concerning the construction, design, management and operation of airports, and the implementation of standardised safety measures around the airport area.

As mentioned above, the expansion of and improvements to airport facilities became very costly with the rapid increase in aviation technology. Particularly during the great depression of the 1930s, the rising costs of airport improvements surpassed by far the revenues generated through airport activities. The airports proved far more expensive and far less profitable than was expected. With regard to Schiphol, and despite the growing costs and lack of revenues of Schiphol municipal airport, local authorities continued to support financially the airport's ambitious expansion projects. But why did local authorities continue to invest in such an unprofitable business?

Before answering this question, let us look at the total investment of the municipality of Amsterdam in airport facilities during the period 1926–39, and the total costs and net turnover generated by Schiphol airport during the same period.

As Figure 5.5 shows, total investment made by the municipality of Amsterdam in improving the physical state of the airport and facilities increased between 1927 and 1930 by more than 154 per cent (from 693,337 guilders in 1927 to 1,766,070 guilders in 1930). This increase was maintained during the 1930s (6,420,299 guilders in 1939). Over the whole period 1926–40, total investments by the municipality reached 44.39 million guilders.

Similarly, from an examination of the total costs, the net results from Schiphol airport show a continuing decrease while total costs of the airport rose. Thus

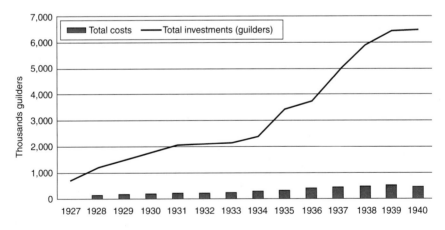

Figure 5.5 Annual total investments in the municipal airport Schiphol: 1926–39.
Source: Annual Reports of the Municipal Airport Schiphol (1926–1940).

Schiphol was clearly an unprofitable business during the 1920s and 1930s. The negative net result became greater from 1936 onwards (−160,477 guilders), due to the economic crisis. The total costs were clearly much higher than total revenues. The accumulated net result and total costs over the whole period were, respectively, −1,744,009 guilders and 4,006,962 guilders. However, the difference between costs and net results was proportionally compensated by the city subsidies as Figure 5.6 clearly shows.

In 1928, the total subsidy from the city of Amsterdam to Schiphol airport reached 76,707 guilders (113,288 in 1931 and 160,477 in 1936), rising to 342,370 guilders in 1940. Over the whole period 1926–40, total subsidies from Amsterdam to Schiphol reached 1.74 million guilders.

If we now turn to the question of why local authorities continued to support financially an unprofitable business, we suggest that the answer lay in 'local boosterism' and growing national pride and interest among the people in the achievements of Dutch civil aviation, especially the achievements of the airplane construction company Fokker and the national airline KLM.

Dutch pride in and great sympathy for civil aviation were high during the autumn of 1924 when a couple of businessmen (the 'Vlugtocht Nederland-Indië' committee) chartered a Fokker F-VII to make the first non-stop flight from Amsterdam to Batavia. A large crowd gathered at Schiphol to witness this unusual event. Unfortunately, the aircraft was forced to make an emergency landing in Bulgaria when its single engine cut out. A month later, the Fokker F-VII was able to continue the journey to its final destination and thousands of Dutch people followed the pilots' journey through daily radio reports. Nevertheless, Dutch pride was at its height in 1933 when the airplane *Pelikaan* made a historical special Christmas return flight from Amsterdam to Java. The pride of the Dutch people was once again very clear when the Douglas DC-2

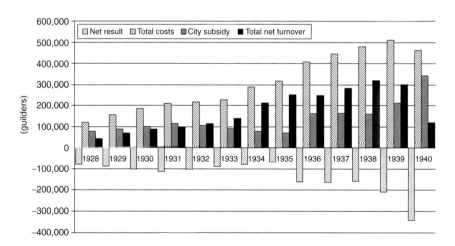

Figure 5.6 Net results, total costs, net turnover, and subsidies to Schiphol airport: 1926–40.
Source: Annual Reports of the Municipal Airport Schiphol (1926–1940).

Uiver (*Stork*) came in second place in the Melbourne race, beating all its rivals, especially the high-tech British airplanes.

Beside Dutch pride, the potential advantages of and great opportunities for air transport in linking countries and continents were widely shared by the public and civil aviation professionals. In the first transatlantic flight – made by Charles Lindbergh in May 1927 from New York to Paris – many saw the start of a new era in transcontinental air transport. In the same year, KLM was able to organise two successful return flights to Batavia. In short, long-distance flights increased the interest and the fascination of the public for the aviation sector. The media (radio, newspapers, etc.) played an important role in spreading news and information about the latest achievements in the aviation world, and by doing so exerted great influence on the development in the public imagination of aviation and aircraft technology (see *De Groen Amsterdammer*, 1927–32). Because of all these achievements and the great interest among the public for the heroes of the sky and the aviation sector, airports became very popular attractions. For example, the total number of visitors to Schiphol airport increased spectacularly during the 1930s. An important part of the revenue generated by the airport came from visitors' fees, which increased from 14,870 guilders in 1929 to 70,592 guilders in 1935 (the highest level) before stabilising between 1936 and 1937.

5.6 Economic performance: Schiphol as an unprofitable business

As mentioned above, the national airline became the symbol of the nation's pride and technological progress. In contrast to KLM, which enjoyed financial support from the state, Schiphol airport was financially more dependent on the local authorities.

With the growth of airport activities, additional land was needed to expand the airport. However, spatial expansion was possible only by purchasing or expropriating large parcels of land from private owners. As a result, land values in the areas surrounding Schiphol increased faster than in other suburban areas of the region. To compensate for the high costs of land acquisition and investments and to increase revenues, the airport authorities started to rent and/or lease parts of the existing airport buildings and land and to charge visitors to the airport. Another source of airport revenue was to increase landing tariffs and other airport fees to airline companies. However, such increases put extra pressure on the activities of KLM and was very often a source of conflict between KLM (Albert Plesman) and Schiphol (Jan Dellaert).

The rising costs of improving airport facilities surpassed by far the revenues generated from airport activities. Consequently, Schiphol continued to operate at a deficit and, in turn, the city of Amsterdam continued to subsidise this deficit and to finance airport investments, often by borrowing money from the state and/or the capital market. Figure 5.7 shows the airport's revenues between 1928 and 1940.

Revenues from rental and lease activities (buildings, hangars, shops, restaurants and land) in the airport area increased in absolute terms from 19,475 guilders

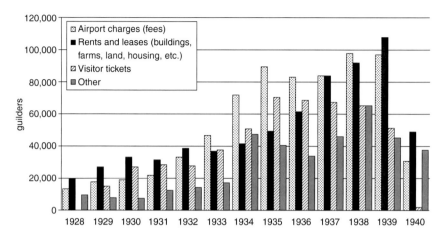

Figure 5.7 Net revenues of Schiphol from airport activities: 1928–40.
Source: Annual Reports of the Municipal Airport Schiphol (1926–1940).

to 61,218 guilders in 1928 and 1936, and to 107,861 guilders in 1939. This corresponded to an increase of 111.53 per cent between 1928 and 1934, and 119.30 per cent between 1935 and 1939.

Revenues from airport charges to airplane companies grew from 13,055 guilders in 1928 to 89,315 guilders in 1938. Over the whole period 1928–38, this represented 31 per cent of all revenues.

With regard to costs (Figure 5.8), a great proportion of the total costs concerned the payment of interest (31,870 guilders in 1928 and 194,804 guilders in 1940)

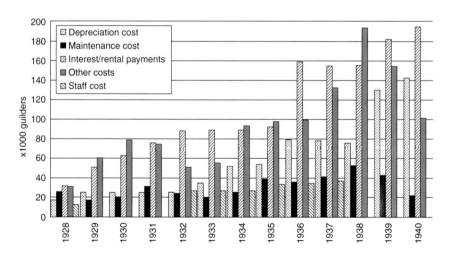

Figure 5.8 Annual costs of Schiphol airport: 1928–40.
Source: Annual Reports of the Municipal Airport Schiphol (1926–1940).

and personnel costs. This last category of costs increased by 191 per cent between 1928 and 1937 (from 12,577 guilders in 1928 to 36,630 in 1937). Note that in 1935, only 450 workers were employed by Schiphol, of whom 50 per cent lived in Amsterdam, 39 per cent in the surrounding areas of Schiphol such as Rindijk, Badhoevendorp, Amstelveen, Aalsmeer and Hoofddorp, and 11 per cent in other cities, more particularly in the Duinstreek area. In 1938, the total number of employees at Schiphol reached 1,200.

With the increased costs and in search of additional sources of revenue, the airport authorities experimented during the 1920s and 1930s with the idea of providing social and recreational facilities at the airport as a way to gain additional revenues. Visitors' fees formed an important source of additional revenues, but they were clearly not enough. The airport authorities then turned to the government in the hopes of gaining additional financial support. The most important reason the airport authorities took this path was the growing complexity and scale of airport infrastructure and facilities. Another reason was that airport activities had become too important economically to be ignored by the central government.

In this perspective, during the early 1930s, discussions about where the future national airport should be located dominated public debates in the Netherlands. As a consequence, the cities of Amsterdam and Rotterdam, and to a less extent The Hague, entered into a battle of prestige to upgrade their municipal airports in order to win the prize of being the only Dutch national airport. For the first time, the central government got the opportunity to intervene and to take the lead in the operation and management of airport activities. Arguments in favour of (but also against) public ownership become stronger when the government decided to designate the location of the Netherlands' national airport.

The issue of the national airport and the public ownership of Schiphol resulted in intense debates between those for and those against the idea that Schiphol should become the country's sole national airport. The decision about the national airport constitutes the first major break in the existing collective arrangement, namely the continuation of the arrangement (e.g. Schiphol as a municipal airport) or its replacement by a new one (e.g. Schiphol as the national airport). Thus the future development of Schiphol airport depended heavily on the final decision of the government concerning this issue.

5.7 Competition between Amsterdam and Rotterdam: the Leiderdorp affair

The issue of the central airport and the resulting competition between the two rival cities of Amsterdam and Rotterdam was mainly driven by prestige and economic motives, but also by the degree of involvement of the city councils of these two cities in the development of their municipal airport. The Rotterdam municipal airport Waalhaven was opened in 1921. From its early days, Rotterdam city council was actively involved in the development of the municipal airport. When it became clear that the city of Amsterdam was pulling ahead in the aviation sector, Rotterdam responded by offering substantial subventions (to Lufthansa for example) and exemption from landing fees (in the case of the French carrier Lines Farman) to attract airplane companies to Rotterdam.

Note that until the 1930s, Waalhaven airport was much more up to date in terms of airport facilities (such as terminal buildings) and equipment (radio communication station) than Schiphol airport, but was too small to realise any ambitious expansion plans.

The fear that Amsterdam might lose its competitive position to Rotterdam, in which case KLM would delocalise its activities to Waalhaven, pushed local authorities to engage in an extensive expansion plan of Schiphol in 1935. In this respect, a special commission was formed by the city council in September 1934 to develop Schiphol's future expansion plans (ACA, 1323, No. 531, 19–35). The members of the commission met 17 times between 20 September 1934 and May 1935. Different aspects of the Schipohl expansion plan were discussed in depth, including the expropriation of land parcels, the planning of airport facilities and infrastructure, the optimal spatial organisation of buildings and hangars, the size and configuration of the station complex and landing strip, the lighting equipment, the connection of Schiphol to public transport networks, housing for the employees of Schiphol, KLM and Fokker in the surrounding areas of Amstelveen, Aalsmeer and Badhoevedorp, and the determination of the areas of zoning regulation around the airport.

Note that the first expansion of the airport took place in 1932 with the expropriation of large land parcels from two private owners: the farmers Rombouts and Josepha Hoeve. In 1933, approximately 188 hectares of additional expropriated land was added to the airport grounds. After many successive expropriation operations, the total surface of the airport, which was 800 by 800 metres in 1934, became 1,200 by 1,500 metres in 1935. The landing area was expanded by 800 by 785 metres to accommodate larger aircraft (the total surface area of the landing field was 210 ha). Schiphol thus became one of the largest airports in Europe in terms of its total surface area (see Map 5.4).

However, the director of the national home carrier KLM, Albert Plesman, was not satisfied by the level and quality of airport facilities. In 1932, Plesman launched the KLM plan for the expansion of the airport facilities. In this plan, Plesman advocated the transfer of the central terminal building from its existing location to the northern perimeter of the airport area, in proximity to the railway and the motorway linking Amsterdam to The Hague.

Amsterdam rejected the KLM plan because of the high financial costs involved in the displacement of the central terminal building to the northern area. At the same time, Amsterdam launched its own plan, which focused on improving and expanding the airport facilities in the existing locations (see Map 5.5).

KLM's operational activities were at that time spread between Schiphol and Waalhaven. One of Plesman's aims was to concentrate all aviation activities in one national airport in order to save on the increasingly high operational costs of the airline company. To Plesman, the construction of a central national airport

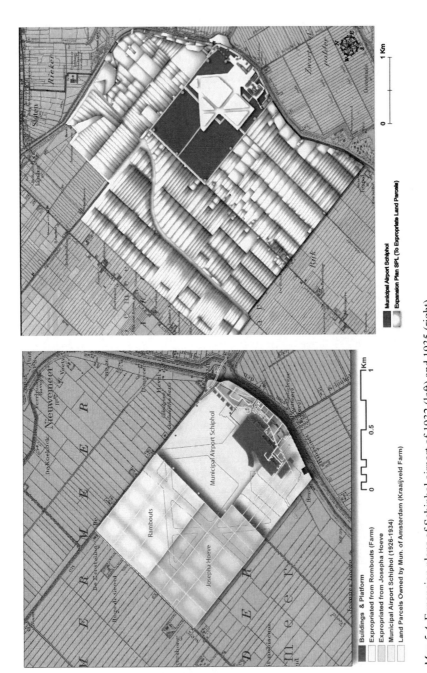

Map 5.4 Expansion plans of Schiphol airport of 1932 (left) and 1935 (right).
Source: based on historical maps from ACA/Aviodrom archives, projected on historical 'Bonne' maps.

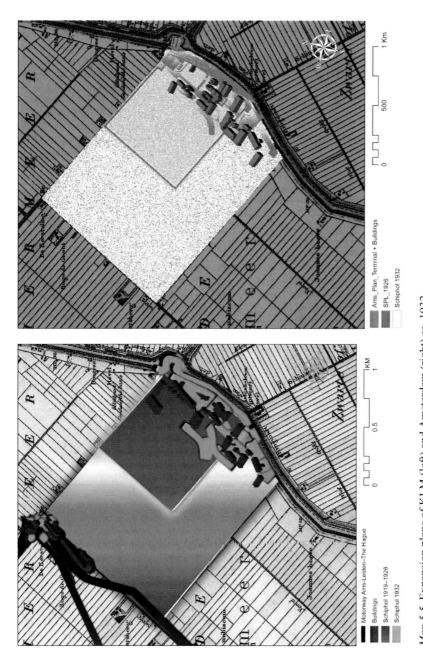

Map 5.5 Expansion plans of KLM (left) and Amsterdam (right) ca. 1932.
Source: based on maps from ACA archive. Both maps are projected on historical Bonne map of 1930s.

was a matter of national interest, given the fast development in aviation technology, the resulting increase in air traffic and the number of passengers.

Rotterdam city council was prepared to develop Waalhaven into an international airport while their counterparts in Amsterdam were convinced of the primacy of Schiphol over Waalhaven as the main air traffic centre for the Netherlands. In contrast to Waalhaven that suffered from a shortage of land for the expansion of the airport, Schiphol had the advantage of abundant land in the Haarlemmermeer polder for the future expansion of airport facilities. In addition, the municipality of Haarlemmermeer was prepared to cooperate with Amsterdam in facilitating the future expansion of Schiphol and related activities on its soil. Stimulated by this and the unconditional support from local actors, Amsterdam put its political and economic resources into defending its local interests vis-à-vis the city of Rotterdam.

However, the director of KLM, Plesman, came up with a radically new alternative: both Schiphol and Waalhaven should be closed or converted to a military airfield (in the case of Schiphol for example) and a totally new centrally located national airport should be constructed at Leiderdorp near the city of Leiden. His main argument was that the central location of Leiderdorp airport would reduce the operational costs of KLM by almost 300,000 guilders a year and, at the same time, reduce the financial costs of improving facilities at both Schiphol and Waalhaven. In other word, the construction of a new central airport would help KLM to rationalise its costs, increase its efficiency, increase its profitability and open up new growth opportunities to the airline company through the concentration of all its activities in one single location.

According to this alternative plan, the geographical location of the new airport in proximity to the main motorway linking the four big cities of the Randstad-Holland was considered crucial. The new airport in Leiderdorp could be easily connected to the future national highway as well as to the railway. Also, from a technical point of view, the geographical location of Leiderdorp was more suited than any other location because airplanes could land and take off in any wind direction. The total construction costs of this project were estimated to be 12 million guilders.

Plesman managed to convince the Minister of Public Works J. A. M. van Buuren of this plan which the minister defended successfully during the cabinet meeting of May 1938. Soon, the council of ministers had sent an information letter to the municipalities of Amsterdam and Rotterdam (and Leiden) concerning the intention of the government to support the Plesman plan. Because both cities were not consulted by the minister, this news from The Hague was unexpected and disappointing to Amsterdam. The city had invested almost 6 million guilders in improving and expanding the airport facilities in extremely difficult economic times (i.e. the financial crisis of the 1930s). For the Amsterdam local authorities it was out of the question that Schiphol could be closed or downgraded to a military airfield. The argument put forward by Amsterdam was that the airport and Amsterdam were intertwined and could not be separated from each other. The argument most heard was that the present and the future of Amsterdam depended on the future of Schiphol and vice versa. In other word, the future economic position of Amsterdam was strongly associated with the development of its airport. It was also a question of pride and local (economic) interests as Amsterdam had made huge sacrifices to make Schiphol one of the best-equipped modern airports in Europe. If this plan was to be carried out, Schiphol would then lose its status as the main Dutch airport indefinitely, a status that it had managed to establish over the previous two decades. In this sense, following Amsterdam's view, if such decision were to be made, then the country's sole central airport of the country should be Schiphol itself and none of others.

The city council united behind its mayor Willem de Vlugt (1921–41), himself a former local businessman, and protested heavily against the plan from the Ministry of Waterworks. An intensive period of political offensive, lobbying and mobilisation of the inhabitants of Amsterdam by the city mayor de Vlugt and the members of the city council, the chamber of commerce and the local elite followed (Greup, 1936). In a short time, the chamber of commerce had mobilised thousands of Amsterdam citizens to protest against the government's decision to close Schiphol airport. In June 1938, a committee for the preservation of Schiphol – known as 'S.O.S. Schiphol' – was formed by the chamber of commerce where the local elite, businessmen, politicians, intellectuals and many societal movements were represented. On Saturday, 2 July 1938, more than 15,000 people gathered at Amsterdam's Schiphol airport to demonstrate against the national government's plans for the establishment of a new national airport somewhere near the city of Leiden.[4]

According to one of the initiators of the protest, the citizens of Amsterdam were keen to prove that 'they loved Schiphol and considered the airport to be an integral part of their beloved city and could not accept the amputation of such an important part of Amsterdam life' (*Het Vaderland*, 1938).

Speeches were made by G. H. Crone, the chairman of the chamber of commerce, G. C. J. D. Kropman, the city's commissioner of commerce, and A. F. Bronsing, the director of an Amsterdam steamboat company, all stressing the importance of Schiphol to the city of Amsterdam. Moreover, the proximity of the airport to the economic capital of the country was explicitly mentioned as a prerequisite for airport development. In turn, the presence of the airport near Amsterdam was considered crucial for the future economic development of the city: Schiphol needed Amsterdam as much as Amsterdam needed Schiphol. Hence, the construction of a new central airport many miles away from the Amsterdam region was an example of a complete lack of understanding regarding airport development, according to those gathered at Schiphol.

Finally, members of the Amsterdam city council were embittered by the fact that the national government only started to show interest in airport development at a time when Schiphol finally had developed into a modern airport after many years of financial support by the municipal government. Eventually, Amsterdam managed to turn the tide in its favour, but only after the Second World War. Instead of constructing a new airport, the national government would decide to officially re-establish Schiphol as the 'Dutch National Airport'.

Under increasing pressure from Amsterdam and Rotterdam, the government plan defended by the Minister of Waterworks, van Buuren, was rejected by a great majority of the members of the parliament in December 1938 (with 72 votes against 14). However, the Minister of Waterworks did not give up the struggle completely. Shortly after the rejection of the central airport plan by the parliament, he appointed an independent commission to study the future of Dutch civil aviation. The main task that was given to this commission was to study all possible locations in the western part of the country and report to the minister about the most appropriate location for the construction of a central national airport.

At the same time, talks between Amsterdam and the state about a new form of organisation for the airport at Schiphol (e.g. founding a public company) were started. The idea was that Schiphol would become a public company with the state and Amsterdam as the major shareholders. Under the new organisational form, Amsterdam could enlarge the financial capacity of Schiphol through support from the state and the capital markets.

From the government's point of view, beside the financial considerations, participation in this new organisation would give the state the opportunity to control and manage the future development of one of the most dynamic and promising economic sectors of the country. Should the negotiations between Amsterdam and the state prove successful, the state would then contribute 60 per cent of the capital of Schiphol and the municipality of Amsterdam 40 per cent. However, before the commission began its work, the military tensions increased in Europe. The threat of another war resulted in the mobilisation of the Dutch armed forces in August 1939, and Schiphol became the centre of the Netherlands air defence system. Three fighter squadrons and one bomber squadron were then stationed at Schiphol. Once again, Schiphol became a military airfield.

5.8 When the 'night fell on Schiphol': the end of a collective arrangement

Before the German invasion, Schiphol figured among the main targets of the first raids that commenced on 10 May 1940. As a result, eight airplanes of the LVA were damaged or destroyed. Jan Dellaert (1947), the director of Schiphol, wrote about this event: '[…] when in the early morning of May 10th, 1940, the German bombers started their unexpected raid on our beautiful Airport, night fell on Schiphol' (ACA, 1323, No. 932-1949).

The German bombardment of Schiphol airport hit many targets but was not heavy enough to cause serious damage to the airfield. At that time, bombs were not as heavy or destructive as at the end of the war. In July 1940, Schiphol was occupied and used as the military base of the German Luftwaffe (known as Fliegehorst 561), where two German squadrons were stationed. The German occupying force repaired the damaged areas of the airfield, then shortly after the repair work extended the runways, constructed taxiways on the ground adjoining the airfield and erected a couple of small hangars for parking aircraft. Furthermore, a number of big, heavily reinforced concrete bunkers were built for the accommodation of the military staff and other personnel during raids while at numerous locations anti-aircraft batteries were set up around the airfield as a means of defence.

Municipal involvement with Schiphol was suspended and the whole airport became an officially closed military area. The key figures in Dutch civil aviation – the director of the airport Dellaert and the director of KLM Plesman – managed to escape German detention (though Plesman was later arrested in Eindhoven and put in jail in The Hague). However, during the occupation, many key figures from civil aviation and their personnel continued to meet regularly in Amsterdam to discuss different issues related to airport development such as the configuration and layout of the ideal airport, the type and size of the equipment required, airport facilities required and the best lighting system for a modern airport.

Under the occupation (August 1940), the Ministry of Waterworks appointed a commission (chaired by Dr D. A. P. N. Koolen) to study the possibilities for the construction of a national airport in the Netherlands. The commission continued its meetings from 1940 until 1944. Within this commission, three separate sub-commissions started discussions about different technical aspects related to the construction of an airport, such as the configuration of the airport in terms of a tangential or parallel layout, aprons, taxiways, the distribution of buildings, and lighting and radio installations. The members of these sub-commissions were the director of Schiphol airport Jan Dellaert, representatives from the Ministry of Waterworks, representatives of KLM and other members of the local authorities (ACA, 1323, Nr. 61II; Nr. DH1940; Nr. 272 S.1940; Nr. 3/35S (51-III); NA, 2.16.39, No. 25–32).

The discussions that took place within each of these three sub-commissions were either technical and/or theoretical in character. The technical issues focused on the latest developments in civil aviation around the world, more particularly in the USA. More interesting in all these discussions was the debate about the ideal layout of the new generation of airports. In this respect, the members of the commission developed many ideas and plans about the layout of new airports. One of these plans was the expansion of the prewar layout with a star-shaped system of eight runways that could be used in all wind directions. Based on these discussions, the director of Schiphol Dellaert was able to develop his first ideas about the tangential plan that would play an important role in shaping the future development of Schiphol airport during the post-Second World War period.

The strategic military position of Schiphol for the Germans in bombing Britain was very important. As a consequence, the Allies targeted Schiphol systematically between July and December. As a result of the increased air raids against the Germans, Schiphol was heavily damaged in 1943. Consequently, Schiphol was only infrequently used by the Germans.

From 'mad Tuesday' in September 1944, with the start of the Allied operations (code named Market Garden!) near Arnhem, the German 'Spreng Kommandos' started the systematic destruction of the airport to prevent the Allies from using it for their raids against Germany. The terminal building was blown up, hundreds of bomb craters ripped up the runways and the hangars were dismantled or destroyed. The pumping station was also blown up, and during the winter Schiphol became saturated with water. In short, the airport was completely destroyed. After the war, the state contributed 100 per cent towards the construction of the taxiways and 60 per cent towards the construction of the buildings, whereas the municipality of Amsterdam contributed to the reconstruction of Schiphol up to 40 per cent of the total costs.

5.9 Summary and conclusions

In contrast to existing views concerning the emergence and development of airports during the pre-Second World War period, we have shown that the rise of Schiphol airport was the result of dynamic collective arrangements that were subject to transformation and change by key actors involved in the development of the airport. Schiphol, first structured as a military airfield under the basic collective arrangement, was first transformed, between 1919 and 1925, into a mixed airport for both civil and military operations and then, from 1926, into a fully municipal airport for civil aviation.

During the early 1920s, with the increase in the scope and size of airport services provided by the military for growing numbers of civil aircraft, the coexistence of two different activities at Schiphol was questioned by the military authorities. Moreover, the military lacked the financial means to make necessary improvements to the airport infrastructure. Schiphol was at that time a very rudimentary airfield and lacked, among other things, appropriate terminal buildings, hangars and passenger check-in desks. Moreover, it was very difficult to access by road and rail from Amsterdam and the surrounding areas. Both the Ministry of War and KLM pinned their hopes on Amsterdam improving the airport facilities and equipment at Schiphol. They were supported by the Amsterdam chamber of commerce, which considered the development of Schiphol to be one of the main contributors to the future economic development of the city. The municipality, however, appeared to lack the expertise, political power and financial means to effectively operate and manage the airport. Despite the fact that almost none of the European and American airports and airlines were profitable at that time, Amsterdam municipal government was, nonetheless, keen to take over Schiphol and invest in its future development. In the end, and after relatively long negotiations, Amsterdam city council almost unanimously decided to take over Schiphol airport from the military in 1926.

The emergence of a conglomerate of local lobbyists and national businessmen was the key factor in turning the airport development into an economic issue using a rhetoric of progress and modernity which fed into the self-perceived need of the Amsterdam elite to improve the city's economic potential and competitiveness. Thus they managed to persuade Amsterdam city council to take over the airport. Schiphol was turned into a predominantly local, municipal project, albeit of national significance. Where the previous collective arrangement had lacked a catalyst actor, the municipal government became responsible for the future development of Schiphol. In other words, Schiphol primarily served the local interests of the city of Amsterdam. The success of the municipal approach to the development of Schiphol airport necessitated the involvement of the state. During the 1930s, the municipal airport turned into an airport with national appeal and significance. Moreover, in terms of the operation and management of airport activities, Schiphol had outgrown the capabilities of the local government.

In order to reach its desired status as the Dutch national airport, a new collective arrangement had to be established which involved the state as the key actor. Bringing the state back in, however, involved a risk for Schiphol, as our discussion on the Dutch airport battle has made clear. Only after long negotiations would Schiphol emerge as the main Dutch airport.

The early history of Schiphol has also shown that a basic collective arrangement can be transformed without losing its basic constitutive components. In the case of Schiphol, the relatively simple character of the first basic arrangement evolved, as time passed and the number of actors involved increased, into more complex multi-arrangements, especially during the postwar period. This growing complexity of arrangements mirrors the increasing economic importance of Schiphol at the local and regional levels. From the 1930s onwards, Schiphol turned into a real catalyst for urban and regional economic development. This was part of a long process of spatial-economic transformation that took place at the level of the Amsterdam-Schiphol region (see Chapter 4).

In this sense, the development of Schiphol can be understood in the light of the efforts made by Amsterdam's local authorities to diversify the economic structure of Amsterdam, which was centred on the development of harbour-related (petro) chemical industries and service activities. However, as our analysis in this chapter shows, the rise and development of Schiphol airport, as well as the development of civil aviation during the 1920s and 1930s, did not as yet act as an important boost for the economic development of the region. The early history of Schiphol is, therefore, related not so much to economic as to institutional developments. A number of factors were important during the early decades of its existence.

First, the close cooperation and the great influence of (some) key actors such as the KLM director Albert Plesman, the managing director of Schiphol Jan Dellaert, aircraft builder Anthony Fokker, the mayor of Amsterdam Willem de Vlugt and other local figures seem to have been decisive for the success of the airport in its early years. Each of these actors had their own vision, ambition and goals, but in the end they all played a crucial role in determining the future development of Schiphol. In fact, together, these actors formed an informal coalition organised around conventions, agreements and rules, which largely shaped the history of Schiphol during the interwar period.

As a true believer of the winged gospel, Amsterdam city council was willing to take risks and invest large amounts of money in the improvement and extension of the airport facilities, despite the economic crisis of the 1930s and knowing that Schiphol was not able to generate enough financial means to sustain its ambitious expansion plans. Rotterdam and The Hague lacked such a conglomerate of (powerful) local authorities, business people and aviation enthusiasts which could act as catalysts for the construction of an airport within or near their cities.

Second, the early development of Schiphol was guided by civic pride and local boosterism, urban competition, political considerations and great enthusiasm for civil aviation technology, airport infrastructure and heroism which surrounded the early history of aviation. From an economic point of view, Schiphol (and KLM for that matter) is a typical example of inefficient business activity that managed to survive the most disastrous economic depression of the twentieth century.

During its early years, economic rationality, however, seems not to have played a major role in the development of the airport. From the second half of the 1920s, the Amsterdam government conveyed a strong sense of urgency, and the necessity to grab the chance provided by Schiphol to make a significant leap in the development of their city. Major improvements in airfield facilities and construction works were carried out shortly after Amsterdam had taken over responsibility to operate and manage the airport. The municipal authorities managed to convince the national and provincial governments of the need to integrate Schiphol into the national and provincial road networks. Within the course of two decades, the rather primitive Schiphol airfield developed into a modern European airport. In turn, Schiphol played a significant role in local boosterism, as was illustrated by the use of the airport in marketing a 'modern' image of the city, and as an instrument in attracting investments and boosting the local economy. In 1928, when Amsterdam hosted the Olympic Games, Schiphol was used as a marketing instrument in promoting the city of Amsterdam as a touristic modern city and the economic capital of the Netherlands.

Third, Schiphol benefited from international development in airport construction, design, layout and airport equipment, which provided the basic framework for thinking about the future development of Schiphol. The authorities were actively involved in formal and informal networks of airport operators and professionals from civil aviation circles. For example, the exchange of information about the latest technological developments in the aviation sector and airport construction took place through direct (meetings, conferences, work visits) or indirect contacts (correspondence, professional magazines) within and between different official and informal organisational networks worldwide. The exchange of experiences and expertise between airport authorities was of great importance in resolving complex technical issues that confronted the Schiphol authorities in their search for effective ways to modernise and improve the airport's facilities and infrastructure in accordance with international standards. In this sense, the expansion and the improvements of technical standards at Schiphol airport were largely inspired by international experiences. For instance, two main technical issues which confronted Schiphol authorities were resolved partly by copying existing practices in other airports, especially in the USA, namely the construction of a sophisticated drainage system and of a system of paved runways.

From the early 1930s, the expansion plan of Schiphol was integrated into the Amsterdam Development Plan (AUP) and with the urban development plan of the Haarlemmermeer as a first step to coordinate the expansion of the airport and the surrounding areas. In this sense, the future expansion plans for Schiphol constituted an integral part of the overall urban expansion plan for the city of Amsterdam and the municipality of Haarlemmermeer, which clearly indicates once again the great importance of Schiphol for Amsterdam and the region.

A special municipal commission was created by Amsterdam to study and prepare the Schiphol expansion plan in 1935. This plan was developed by urban planners and designers of the city of Amsterdam, in cooperation with the airport authorities, the municipality of Haarlemmermeer and the province of North Holland.

The Schiphol expansion plan not only consisted of the development of the airport itself, but also dealt with several other issues such as housing for Schiphol and KLM employees, the forecasting of the volume of air traffic and the total amount of land needed for the future expansion of the airport, the spatial organisation of the airport facilities and equipment, and the zoning regulation around the airport area.

Fourth, compared to foreign airfields like Le Bourget, Croydon or Tempelhof, improvements to the airport facilities at Schiphol airport were, however, much less impressive and very modest in size, design and scope, due to the municipality's lack of financial means. It is, however, difficult to compare different airfields across Europe because of large differences between airports in terms of their construction, design, management and exploitation. While Tempelhof airport and, to a lesser extent, Le Bourget benefited from state financial support, Croydon and many other local airports in the UK – like Schiphol – were financially supported by less affluent local governments. As was the case for many European airports, Schiphol registered a continuing financial deficit.

The complexity of managing the airport and the increasing operational costs and funding for the expansion of airport facilities pushed Amsterdam to turn to the national government for financial support. However, this did not apply just to Schiphol but also to the majority of other European airports. In turn, for financial support, the Dutch national government aimed to strategically invest in an airport that appeared fit to face the future challenges of the aviation sector. This meant that a choice had to be made between Schiphol and its main competitor Waalhaven, or the possible construction of a whole new national airport in Randstad-Holland. In Amsterdam, these plans were met with fierce protests and eventually the national government was persuaded to turn Schiphol into the Dutch mainport.

Finally, the historical development of Schiphol shows that the long-term evolution of a basic collective arrangement may result in several sub-arrangements that may follow their own development path, but together they structure and determine the future development of the airport. Airport facilities and infrastructure may be destroyed by exogenous shocks (in the case of Schiphol the war), but the reconstruction of the airport may still be based on existing or complementary new collective arrangements. In this sense, the examination of the causes, motives and consequences of the rise and development of Schiphol during the pioneering era of the 1920s and the 1930s is crucial in order for us to understand the present importance of Schiphol airport at the regional and national levels.

6   Reconstruction and development of Schiphol airport 1945–80

6.1 Introduction

A few weeks after the liberation of the country in 1945, the new Dutch government set up an urgent reconstruction programme aimed at the recovery of the most vital economic sectors and the reconstruction of infrastructure networks in order to sustain economic recovery. In addition to the devastated economic situation in the Netherlands, reflected in the dramatic shortages in the supply of products, raw materials and equipments, the financial position of the government deteriorated. Fortunately, the Marshall financial aid, started in June 1947, gave a major boost to the recovery of the Dutch economy. In addition, the Marshall aid set up grounds for sustainable economic growth during the postwar period.

The government and local authorities started the reconstruction and restoration of ports and airports, roads and railway networks, electricity networks, water installations, and public services. The reconstruction of Schiphol airport received special attention from local authorities and the national government. In a few months after the liberation of the country, the airport was made operational for the air traffic activities.

However, during the reconstruction period, it became clear that the reconstruction of what had been damaged during the war and the recovery of the Dutch economy could only be realised by direct intervention from the state through strategic planning, and tight coordination and management of the major reconstruction projects. In contrast to the prewar period, direct intervention from the state in the economic and social domains was not contested by the population because of high expectations and the widely spread optimism about the future development of the country. The majority of the population believed that improvement in their lives could only be realised by state intervention. As a result, the Dutch economy recovered rapidly during the next two decades of the 1950s and 1960s. Production levels, exports, employment, and household disposable incomes increased considerably. Economic growth was accompanied by a shift in the demographic patterns of the Dutch population, alongside the resulting spatial changes and the increase of urban sprawl. This was mainly due to the changing patterns in household composition, the increase of individualisation of Dutch society, and the increasing mobility of people.

More generally, with the introduction of the welfare state and the recovery of the economy, life expectations and the level of welfare among the majority of the Dutch population improved substantially. This resulted in a further increase in consumption and expenditures, production, investment, and hence economic growth. Economic sectors – the industrial sector, services and the agricultural sector – showed spectacular growth, including the commercial aviation sector. For the first time in the history of commercial aviation, the market size of this sector grew very rapidly, and airplane companies and airports were able to realise substantial and increasing profits.

The commercial aviation sector grew even faster than some traditional manufacturing activities. The airline companies responded to these developments by introducing bigger and faster airplanes, cheaper flights, and at the same time, they started to apply clever marketing campaigns to promote the sector to the wider public. Airlines offered lower, affordable airfares and fully paid package tours to individuals and groups of travellers. The era of mass air transit was under way and 'Every level of society was represented in the "new democracy of the air"' (Gordon, 2004: 142).

With regard to Schiphol airport, the postwar period saw the rebirth of the new airport under a new collective arrangement based on the decision of the government in 1945 to designate definitively Schiphol airport as the sole international airport of the Netherlands. The municipal airport now became a national airport that served the national interest. However, before the definitive decision of the government, the State Commission on Airfields (the so-called 'Small Commission') was installed by the government to study the optimal geographical location of the Dutch international airport. Intense and long discussions about the optimal location of the central airport (Schieveen in Rotterdam, or Burgerveen or Schiphol (both in Haarlemmermeer)) took place between the members of the commission and the representatives of KLM, Schiphol-Amsterdam and Rotterdam. In the end, Amsterdam won the battle against KLM and its rival Rotterdam. From this, a new collective arrangement emerged in 1957 whereby Schiphol became a private company (Schiphol Airport Company) owned by public institutions: the state and the municipalities of Amsterdam and Rotterdam. This new collective arrangement replaced the prewar arrangement of 1926, whereby Schiphol was in the hands of local authorities (Schiphol as a municipal airport). This also marks a new era with respect to the organisation, coordination and management of the airport. Schiphol then became a commercial organisation operating in accordance with market mechanisms like any other private firm, albeit under the control of public stakeholders. Before the emergence of this new arrangement, Schiphol airport was considered a transport node and public utility providing (air) services to consumers (airliners and travellers). From 1960, however, and under increasing competition and the commercialisation of the air transport sector, Schiphol shifted its policy from being the provider of public services to a more commercially oriented strategy aiming to generate substantial profits and revenues.

Parallel to these developments, rapid structural changes took place in aeronautical technologies, especially at the level of airplane technology, with the successive introduction of newer, bigger and faster jet planes. These developments in aeronautical technology had a great effect on airport design, planning, spatial organisation, operation and management of airport activities. The second generation of airports built during the postwar period were mainly planned as 'transfer machines' and 'transport nodes' allowing swift and smooth circulation of passengers and goods. Cost-saving measures to reduce as much as possible the time between airplanes landing and taking off and increasing airport capacity became the key factors in determining the competitive position of airports.

The implementation of ambitious expansion plans became problematic as many airports lacked additional land for the extension of airport activities, especially with the introduction of bigger jet planes. However, in contrast to many European airports, the expansion plans for Schiphol could easily be realised due to abundant land available at a low price in the Haarlemmermeer polder. The first expansion plan for Schiphol was developed in 1948. This plan was extended further in the second expansion plan of 1952, which was based on the tangential system comprising four runways (two by two) around a large central traffic area (comprising new terminals, passenger area, commercial area, etc.).

In 1957, the Schiphol airport authorities began the construction of the new airport at approximately four kilometres from its original location (currently the freight area of Schiphol). The construction of the central traffic area took five years (from 1963 until 1967), and was ultimately opened by Queen Juliana in 1967. However, the accessibility of the new Schiphol airport lagged behind compared to the relatively fast increase in the size and scope of the facilities at the airport. The opening of the railway line linking Amsterdam and The Hague through Schiphol was accomplished only in the 1980s.

In the meantime, new airplanes were introduced at relatively short intervals. Air traffic entered an era of increasing scale and scope where price competition replaced monopolistic competition, and was based on quality of services and limited market share (business class). Most importantly, the democratisation of air travel, the rapid technological progress and the increase in living standards opened the doors to long-distance and intercontinental air travel for the middle and lower classes. In other words, the democratisation of air travel created a new geographical dimension in the sense that distant places no longer existed – the world became smaller. This was made possible by the progressive extension of air networks, intra-Europe as well as transatlantic/intercontinental (Gordon, 2004: 155). Also, decreasing transport costs, reflected in the reduction in the price of tickets, and the introduction of the tourist class made flying more accessible to all social classes.

By the end of the 1950s and the beginning of the 1960s, the jet era put more pressure on airport planning and the spatial expansion of Schiphol airport. The airport expanded gradually and became one of the main economic centres of the Amsterdam region and Randstad-Holland. The rising economic importance of Schiphol vis-à-vis the surrounding urban areas was strengthened further by its integration within the national planning scheme and the provincial economic programmes. This was necessary because Schiphol had developed into one of the most attractive locations in the Netherlands, the strong effects of which brought in people (employment) and activities (industrial firms and services). Schiphol was then considered by local and regional authorities as a valuable economic centre generating substantial economic growth through direct and indirect economic effects. The spatial and economic effects of the airport went beyond the traditional territorial and administrative boundaries.

More generally, the rebirth of Schiphol after the Second World War structurally changed the economic and spatial landscape of Haarlemmermeer and the region. The national airport was considered by some people as a symbol of national pride, prosperity and progress. Others contested the uncontrolled expansion of the airport and the negative effects that were generated for the surrounding area.

In this chapter we focus our attention on the postwar reconstruction and development of Schiphol airport, and more particularly on the emergence of the new collective arrangement, that is Schiphol as the world airport of the Netherlands, that would determine the future development of the airport and its surrounding areas (section 6.2). We discuss the role, motives and objectives of the actors involved in the decision-making process that gave birth to this new collective arrangement (section 6.3). Next, the implications of this new collective arrangement on airport planning, and the future spatial and economic development of Schiphol, are examined in section 6.4. A special focus is given to expansion plans that were developed and implemented by the Schiphol authorities, and subsequently the role and influence of external research in influencing the decision-making process concerning the airport spatial planning (section 6.5). Furthermore, we analyse different aspects of the replacement of the basic collective arrangement, i.e. the Schiphol municipal airport, with a new arrangement, i.e. Schiphol airport company, and the implications for airport planning and expansion plans in terms of runway construction and the construction of the new central terminal area, the airport as we know it today. In addition, the effects of external factors are examined in section 6.6. We turn then, to the economic implications of new collective arrangement as the Schiphol Airport Co. oriented its business focus toward a more market-oriented strategy (section 6.7). Next, the spatial implications and the environmental and safety issues stemming from the spatial and economic development of Schiphol airport on its surrounding urban areas are extensively analysed in section 6.8. Section 6.9 concludes.

6.2 Postwar reconstruction and the development of Schiphol airport

Schiphol airport was completely destroyed by Allied bombing and the deliberate demolition by the German military. The German demolition team placed bombs at the airport and let them explode all over the airport terrain. Runways, aprons, buildings and the drainage system, especially the drains under the paved area, were severely damaged. Rebuilding Schiphol airport and restoring its basic functions were among the highest of priorities of the Amsterdam authorities and

Dutch government. Schiphol was seen as a symbol of national pride and the ultimate example of challenge to the occupier, according to Prince Bernhard, who proudly announced that: 'Our great Schiphol airport has risen phoenix-like from the ashes and ruins of war' (Gordon, 2004: 158).

Despite the devastated financial position of Amsterdam, the city began the reconstruction work immediately after the liberation of the country. A number of road-construction firms and other local companies were contracted to start clearing away the rubble and remaining debris at the airport terrain.

The new Schiphol opened in July 1945 with a paved runway and a few temporary buildings (the air traffic control was set up on the back of a truck). Much of the remaining material from the old buildings and imported rubble from other regions were used to rebuild the foundations of the runways and the airport terrain. The Dutch airline company KLM began its operations at Schiphol directly after hostilities ceased. As a temporary measure, KLM director Albert Plesman purchased airplanes from the military to start KLM's operations.

During the first months of the postwar period, the Netherlands was hit by a bitterly cold winter and the scarcity of food products. Work progress at the airport was delayed because workers were frequently on strike. Most workers were weak and not able to toil eight hours a day. The working time was then reduced to 33 hours a week (approximately 6.5 hours a day), and substantial meals were served by the Allied kitchens in order to improve the physical condition of work-ers. However, the major problem that faced local authorities was the lack of the equipment and materials needed for the reconstruction of the airport. In this respect, the local authorities were grateful for the use of heavy machinery in the reconstruction of the airport provided by the Royal Corps of Engineers and the US Air Transport Command (National Archive (hereafter NA): 2.16.39, No. 10–14; No. 1–2; No. 25–32; letter 17 April 1946).

More generally, reconstruction work at Schiphol airport advanced rapidly. In 16 February 1946, the construction of the first two runways (2,150 × 60 metres) was started, under the supervision of Colonel Spainhour, the Commander of the IXth Engineering Corps. The reconstruction of runways was crucial to the American Overseas Airline Inc., because of the demobilisation of the American airforce. Bomb-craters along the runways were filled up with rubble and, after few weeks, a 1,000-metre long runway and a decent parking facility were completed. The 1,600 metres provisional northeast–southwest runway 05-23 was finished in July 1945, and was immediately used by the Allies for military transport (from 8 July 1945) and commercial aviation (from 28 July 1945).[1]

The NE–SW runway was extended by 700 metres in 1947 (to 2,335 metres), and the other three runways were repaired between September and October 1945. These were: the north–south runway 18-36, the runway 09-27 (extended in 1947) and the runway 14-32 (1,800 × 60 metres, finished in 1948) (see Table 6.1).

Favoured by nice weather, reconstruction work advanced with the utmost speed as a result of the abundant labour force and the sense of urgency to rebuild Schiphol airport. The total number of workers at Schiphol airport grew from around 500 in May 1945 to 800 by mid-June, and to more than 1,800 by the end

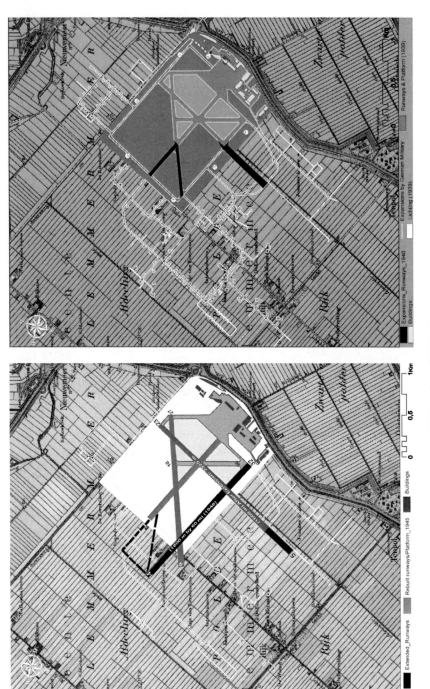

Map 6.1 Reconstruction of Schiphol airport between 1945 (left) and 1947 (right).

Table 6.1 Runways configuration of Schiphol airport in 1949

Runway No.	Length	Breadth	Remark
05-23	2,150 m	40 m	(Extended to 2,335 m in 1947)
18-36	850 m	40 m	–
09-27	1,800 m	40 m	(Before 1948)
14-32	1,800 m	60 m	(Extended and broadened in 1948)
01-19	1,800 m	60 m	(Completed and in use in 1949)

Source: ACA 1323 and Annual Reports Schiphol Airport (1946–1949).

of August 1945. By the end of November 1945, the complete runway system was repaired and made operational for air traffic. In the meantime, reconstruction work on the platform and aprons advanced fairly well.

The runways were constructed following the international requirements of the Chicago Convention and the International Civil Aviation Organisation (ICAO) for class-A airports, i.e. a runway length of at least 2,150 metres able to support a single wheel-load of 45 tons. The instrumental runway consisted of a 30 cm thick layer of rolled concrete of a meagre composition on a 35 cm thick sand-bed, and a 25 cm thick rolled foundation of packed stone, paved with a 5 cm layer of asphalt concrete. In December 1947, Schiphol began the construction of a new runway: the NE–SW runway 01-19, which was completed in 29 December 1949 (see Map 6.1).

During the reconstruction period, government institutions such as the National Air Traffic Board (*Rijksluchtvaartdienst* (RLD)), Weather Office and KLM departments were provisionally accommodated in a few wooden huts. KLM purchased two wooden hangars from Sweden, where four aircraft could be sheltered. Engine inspections and repair by KLM technicians took place in the open air, under removable small hoods (ACA 1232, No. 932-1949).

After the demolition of the remaining damaged buildings and the clearance work in the technical area, reconstruction works were then started in this space. New hangars (No. 1A, No. 4, No. 5 'Croydon' (was B) and No. 6 'Le Bourget' (E)) were built in 1947, taking into consideration the large tail-fin of new airplanes such as the DC-4 (Skymaster), which was 8.4 metres high.

The rapid increase in the number of passengers since 1946 pushed the airport authorities to reconsider the basic plan for the construction of the terminal building. Reconstruction work on the new station building area progressed very slowly during 1945 because of shortage of materials and qualified workers (Annual Report Schiphol Airport, 1945: 22). In contrast, construction on the platform and the terminal building area advanced rapidly. In 1948, a total surface of 22,000 m^2 (was 10,000 m^2 in 1947) of the platform was reconstructed and one year later (17 May 1949) the international section of the station building was opened. The terminal building was divided into two sections: (1) the domestic air-traffic section, where major parts of the cargo services were also located – this section was free from customs formalities; (2) the international air-traffic section (European and intercontinental), comprising large handling halls for incoming and departing passengers and the offices of KLM services. Between the two large

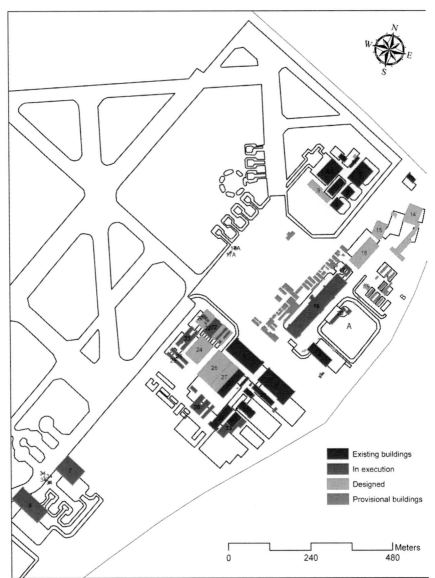

Legend: 1A, 2,3,..., 8: Hangars; 9: Garage; 10: New Hangar11 & 12: storage/depot; 13: Garage terrain service 14: Garage car service ; 15 : Civil service & coffee house; 16: station building national-expedition-airline company; 17: air traffic observation tower; 17A: provisional air traffic tower; 18: Station building Europe & Intercontinental; 19: movie theater; 20: Communication Service; 21: Central telephone; 22: Flight service; 23: Buffet /canteen); 24: Administration; 25: Administration & store; 26: Store; 27: Central workplace; 28 & 29: I.E.R.A; 30: Buffet/canteen; 31:Test-engines station; 32 & 33: Engine workplace; 34: provisional test-engine; A: Car parking terrain; B: public parking bicycles. Source: Schiphol Annual Report (1947).

Map 6.2 Airport facilities and buildings at the central terminal area ca. 1948.
Source: based on ACA-Schiphol archives and Aviodrom archives.

halls, a waiting room was constructed, which served as a restaurant (see Map 6.2). Next to these halls, the offices of the Government Aeronautical Services and the municipal management were constructed, and in front of them rose the five-storey control tower of the Air-traffic Control Service (Annual Report Schiphol Airport, 1945: 22).

During the first five years after its opening, Schiphol airport witnessed an increase in the number of visitors: 202,805 people visited the airport in 1946, more than doubling by 1947 to 604,356 visitors before reaching 912,650 visitors in 1949. The fascination of people for new airplane technology made Schiphol airport one of the most visited locations in the country.

Revenues generated from visitors' fees increased from 100,000 guilders in 1947 to half a million guilders in 1960 (an increase of 500 per cent) and to 800,000 guilders in 1967. The highest level of visitors was registered at the end of the 1950s when new jet airplanes were introduced, and after 1967 when the new central terminal area and the new Schiphol airport was officially opened (see Figure 6.1).

To accommodate the growing numbers of visitors, a large cafe-restaurant was built on the top of the waiting room. On either side of this restaurant were observation platforms extending along the whole front of the building. On the top of this restaurant, another observation terrace, with a small coffee room, was built. From there, visitors could follow the airplanes parking on the apron or landing and taking off.

The total reconstruction costs of Schiphol airport reached 49 million guilders. In addition, KLM invested about 10 million guilders in the construction of new hangars, repair shops and maintenance buildings. Three years after liberation (1948), Schiphol had again regained its prominent position in European air transport. Schiphol became one of the most important junctions for transatlantic and intercontinental air services and a gateway to Central and Western Europe. KLM,

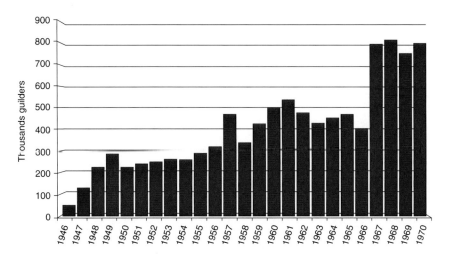

Figure 6.1 Net returns of Schiphol airport from visitors' tickets (1946–70).
Source: Annual Reports Schiphol Airports (1945–1970).

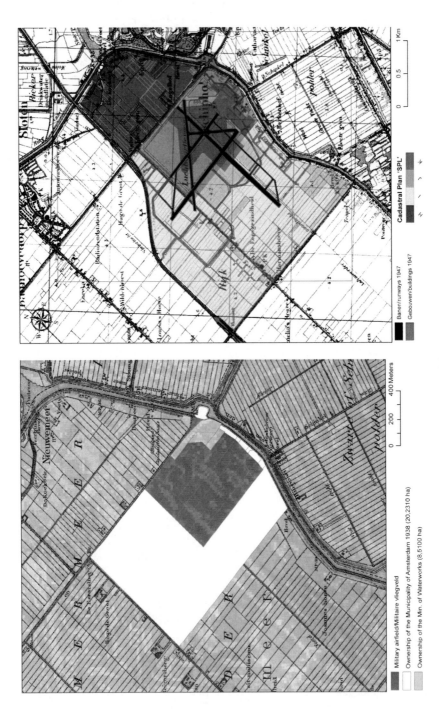

Map 6.3 Total surface of Schiphol in 1938 (left), and ca. 1947–8 (right).

and with it many other foreign airlines, found their way back to Schiphol.[2] More than 100 daily flights (i.e. incoming and outgoing scheduled aircraft) took place at Schiphol airport, and more than 50 European and some American charter companies (Breathens, SAFE from Oslo and Seaboard & Western from New York) opened regular airline connections to and from Schiphol airport.

The development of Schiphol into a major transfer hub in international and European air networks was due, on the one hand, to the destruction of the main European airports that had served as transfer nodes in international and European air traffic such as Berlin's Tempelhof. On the other hand, Schiphol airport activities had been historically developed around passenger transfer and cargo activities. In this sense, the development of Schiphol as a hub in international air traffic networks was based on a conscious policy aimed at improving the competitive position of Dutch commercial aviation internationally.

Sustained by the decision of the government to designate Schiphol as the international airport of the country in 1945, Amsterdam started repair work and the reconstruction of the most essential parts of the airport and adding land parcels that were confiscated by the German occupiers to the airport terrain. The total surface of the airport expanded from 210 ha in 1940 to 690 ha in 1950 (nine times the total surface of Schiphol in 1920), and to 700 ha in 1955–7. The area of surfaced runways and aprons was more than doubled (638,000 m²). Map 6.3 gives an overview of the spatial expansion of Schiphol before and after the Second World War.

6.3 A new collective arrangement: Schiphol as the world airport of the Netherlands

On June 1945, the Minister of Waterworks and Reconstruction (Minister Trump), the Minister of War and the Minister for the Dutch Navy installed the State Commission on Airfields (*Rijkscommissie Luchtvaartterreinen*, hereafter the RCL) to study the technical state and the long-term development of the Dutch airports (NA 2.16.39, No. 10–14; No. 1–2). The main task assigned to the RCL commission was to examine the technical and physical state of the terrain at all Dutch airfields and to make a selection of which airfields should be used for civil and which for military aviation. In addition, the commission was charged to advise the state about the most appropriate location for the international airport of the Netherlands, and on the organisational form of Dutch airports, e.g. military ownership, public ownership, private ownership or a combination of both.

The State Commission on Airfields was composed of six members chaired by the engineer H. W. Mouton (Figure 6.2). However, in July 1945, for some unclear reason, the Minister of Waterworks appointed a new chairman of the commission: Professor Ir. H. T. Zwiers from the Technical University of Delft (from 29 September 1945). Note that the new chairman of the commission Professor Zwiers had been a member of the municipal study commission that was charged by the city council of Amsterdam to develop the expansion plan of Schiphol municipal airport during the period 1934–5. In cooperation with Amsterdam's

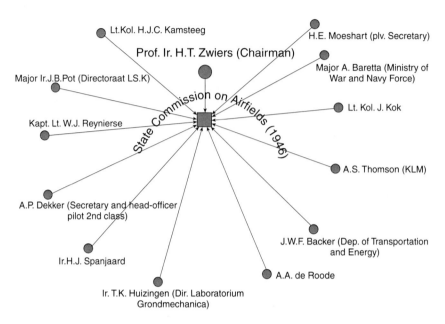

Figure 6.2 Composition of the State Commission on Airfields (RCL).
Source: Network graph is based on Networks Graph Analysis program UCINET v6.216.

famous designers of the 'General Expansion Plan of Amsterdam' (AUP) Messrs Scheffer, van Lohuizen and van Easteren, Professor Zwiers was directly involved in the discussions about the technical design of the runways, aprons and taxiways, the lighting, the buildings, the zoning regulations and the matter of housing for the employees of Schiphol, KLM and Fokker.

The commission was in favour of a central location for the international airport between the four big cities of the Randstad – that is, accessible to transport networks. More detailed technical issues and requirements for the construction of the international airport were discussed by the members of the RCL commission, such as the length of the runways (2,150 metres in case of three runways and 4,500 metres in the case of two runways), the atmospheric requirements of the location (wind speed and direction, vertical and horizontal sight view, distance to clouds from the ground, etc.), the type of soil and its suitability for an efficient drainage system, possibilities for future expansions and the accessibility of the location to infrastructure networks (railway and motorway). According to the RCL commission, a minimum size of at least 2,000 ha was required for the construction of the new central airport.

After long debates between the members of the commission, the local authorities and KLM representatives, the commission came to the conclusion that Schiphol was the best equipped Dutch airport and hence the most appropriate location for the trans-oceanic, intra- and intercontinental air traffic activities.

The final report of the commission was presented to the government on 15 September 1945 (NA 2.16.39, No. 10–14; No. 1–2 and No. 25–32).

The government followed the RCL's advice and designated Schiphol as the world airport of the Netherlands. The government decision was formalised by the resolution of the Council of Ministers, which was passed on 8 October 1945, and later by a decree of the Minister of Transport and Energy on 7 January 1946.

The city of Rotterdam, supported indirectly by KLM, tried to convince the government of the necessity to build its own international airport, without success. However, the main problem facing Waalhaven airport was the lack of space for further expansion because of its close proximity to the River Maas. As an alternative, Rotterdam proposed to build an airport at Schieveen, which is located to the south side of the city between Rotterdam and Barendrecht. The RCL was sceptical about the Schieveen location because the soil was less resistant to allow the construction of paved runways for larger and heavier airplanes. Beside this technical problem, KLM was against the construction of two class-A international airports in the Netherlands. However, Rotterdam was given the chance to build a class-D airport, with an open option to upgrade it into a class-A international airport in the future (NA 2.16.39, No. 25–32). Although very disappointed by the government decision, Rotterdam's authorities were forced to give up their ambition to construct a new international airport in Rotterdam.

Besides Rotterdam, KLM representatives were also against the RCL decision to designate Schiphol as the international airport of the Netherlands. On 24 October 1945, the managing director of KLM Albert Plesman sent a letter protesting against this decision to the RCL commission and to the Ministers of Waterworks, War and the Navy (NA 2.16.39).[3] His main argument was that the RLC commission had not paid much attention to the other alternatives such as the Burgerveen plan (known as the KLM South Plan (*Plan Zuid* or *HMP-Zuid*)). According to Plesman, the expertise and knowledge needed to conduct a detailed and more objective comparative study on the optimal location of the international airport was lacking in the Netherlands. In this respect, Plesman offered 100,000 guilders to the RCL commission to start a detailed study about the optimal location of the central international airport (ibid.).

In the meantime, the State Commission on Airfields installed the 'Small Commission' (also known as the 'Study Commission for Schiphol') in June 1946. The main tasks of this sub-commission were the study of the technical requirements, the spatial organisation and the spatial expansion plans of the international airport following the international standards, i.e. the requirements of the ICAO and the Montreal and Chicago Conventions (NA 2.16.39; 28th meeting of 16th April 1946). The Small Commission held several meetings between 1946 and 1948. More particularly, the following issues were examined in depth by the commission: the construction of the terminal area, the connection of the airport to national infrastructure networks, the technical and spatial organisation of the airport facilities, the future development of air traffic activities (i.e. forecasts of the numbers of passengers and visitors) and the future capacity of Schiphol airport.

Within the Small Commission, the visionary ideas and expertise of Plesman were of great value in enriching discussions about complex technical issues such as the optimal location of the central terminal building and the accessibility to airport facilities and public infrastructure networks. However, Plesman was participating in this commission to defend the interests of KLM. As an alternative solution to the costly reconstruction of Schiphol airport as an international airport, Plesman was in favour of constructing a completely new central airport in one of the following three locations: Schieveen (near Rotterdam), Ypenburg (to the east of The Hague) or Burgerveen (*Plan Zuid/HMP-Zuid*) in the southern part of Haarlemmermeer. The location itself was not of importance to Plesman because KLM in any case could then decrease its total exploitation costs and increase the efficiency of its operational activities if all activities of the company were to be concentrated in one central location.

Convinced by the idea that Burgerveen was the most optimal geographical location for the international airport of the Netherlands, Plesman contracted external research institutes to study the potential advantages of this location (Plan Zuid) compared to other three locations (Schiphol, Schieveen and Ypenburg). To Plesman, research was a powerful instrument in his attempts to convince the commission and the government of the cost-effectiveness and the opportunities that might be offered by Burgerveen as the central location for the Dutch international airport.

In June 1946, KLM published its report R47 entitled 'Exploitation Comparison Between Different Airports' (*Exploitatievergelijkingen der verschillende luchthavens*), which offered detailed estimations of the exploitation costs for the operators and the users of these airports (such as KLM and the NS).

According to the KLM report, Burgerveen (*HMP-Zuid*) should become the national airport of the country, in combination with a class-D airport in Schieveen. By concentrating all KLM's activities in one location, the total exploitation costs for KLM were estimated to be $f\,300,000$.

Furthermore, should Burgerveen be used without a second airport in Rotterdam, the KLM report claimed that the construction costs for road connections to the airport would be zero.

By comparing the total costs between the three alternatives, KLM subtracted the total costs for KLM (ground exploitation and commuters' service costs) from the total costs of the airport authorities. The estimated figures show a clear cost-effectiveness in favour of Burgerveen over Schiphol. In terms of cost-savings for KLM, estimated figures show a clear cost-effectiveness in favour of Burgerveen (with a class-D airport at Rotterdam) over Schiphol (about 30 per cent of total costs).

More generally, and from the estimated figures of total operational costs for KLM, Schiphol was clearly less desirable as a central airport compared to Burgerveen.

On 24 July 1946, KLM published the second KLM Report R86 entitled 'Airport Issue in the Netherlands' (*Vliegvelden vraagstuk in Nederland*). This report supported the conclusions of Report R74, and presented further details on the airport planning of HMP Zuid (the Burgerveen plan). KLM developed various planning concepts for HMP Zuid based on a parallel runways system ranging from three, four and six parallel runways, and a hexagonal central terminal building in the centre of the terminal area.

However, the Small Commission was highly sceptical of the KLM Report R74. According to Professor Zwiers (chairman of the commission), this report was clearly biased toward the Burgerveen plan. The RCL commission reacted to KLM claims by conducting its own study to verify the estimated KLM figures and the conclusions of both reports.

The RLC report in response presented new estimated figures. According to this report, the estimated total construction costs of Schiphol international airport and Burgerveen airport were nearly equal. The total construction costs for Schiphol were estimated at +/– ƒ 123,000,000 against those for HMP Zuid of +/– ƒ 126,045,000. In addition to the total construction costs, another ƒ 41,500,000 should have been added should the state decide to close Schiphol and construct a new airport, i.e. the HMP Zuid. If this possibility had been taken into consideration by the KLM report then the total costs would be ƒ 167,637,000. Moreover, the residual value of Schiphol, in case of closure, was estimated to be ƒ 2,700,000 (e.g. 400 ha land = ƒ 1,200,000 (+) buildings = ƒ 1,500,000). Consequently, taking into account all this elements, new estimations showed a negative capital expenditure for Burgerveen of approximately ƒ 42,000,000 (NA 2.16.39; No. 25–32; RCL contra-report, p. 5).

Thus the RLC commission estimated total costs to be ƒ 167,637,000 in the case of Burgerveen and ƒ 164,937,000 in the case of Schiphol. Note that the KLM report claimed that in case of Burgerveen airport, the construction of a national motorway would not be necessary. However, if the total costs of the construction of and improvements to roads (national and provincial) were added to the total construction costs of Burgerveen, the estimated figures for Schiphol and Burgerveen would be, respectively, ƒ 2,000,000 and ƒ 10,000,000.

More generally, the RCL report in response concluded that the total costs of the construction and exploitation of Burgerveen were nearly equal to the estimated construction costs of a four-runway system at Schiphol (see Table 6.2).

Table 6.2 Total costs of construction and exploitation of Schiphol and Burgerveen against other alternatives (values in guilders)

	Schiphol (SPL)	Burg'veen	SPL + R'dam D	Burg'veen + R'dam D	SPL + R'dam B	Burg'veen + R'dam B
Total expen- diture	4,236,920	4,293,920	5,565,124	5,62,124	6,531,800	6,588,800
Total incomes	1,138,920	1,138,000	1,272,000	1,272,000	1,423,000	1,423,000
Deficit	−33,098,920	−3,155,920	−4,293,124	−5,350,124	−5,108,800	−5,165,800

Source: NA 2.16.39, No. 25–32.

Furthermore, the total exploitation costs for the airport operators in the case of Schiphol were significantly less than in the case of Burgerveen.

Another major objection of the RLC to the Burgerveen plan was the limited possibilities for the future spatial expansion of airport activities, especially in the eastern direction of the Hoofdvaart because of the already planned urban expansion of the municipality of Nieuwe Vennep. The total land surface that was needed for the construction of the airport with three runways was estimated to be approximately 1,150 ha, 100 ha higher than was estimated in the KLM Report R-62.

During the discussions of the KLM reports and the RLC report in response, heated debates took place between the KLM representatives, and more particularly Plesman, and the members of the RLC commission, especially Professor Zwiers. The intense debate about the central location of the international airport in Burgerveen or Schiphol were of the same magnitude as in the prewar discussions concerning the Leiderdorp affair. However, in contrast to the Leiderdorp affair, new actors were now involved in the discussions, for instance the new mayor of Amsterdam (A. J. D'Ailly), who was fully supported by the members of the city council, the chamber of commerce of Amsterdam and other influential local actors and civil organisations. All these actors rejected the Burgerveen plan and refused Plesman's idea to downgrade Schiphol to a technical area of the Burgerveen international airport or to a military airport. For different reasons, the city of Rotterdam and the municipality of Haarlemmermeer were also against the Plesman plan. In the end, the Burgerveen plan was officially rejected by the Minister of Transport and Waterworks on 7 April 1948.

6.3.1 Identifying the key actors involved in the decision-making process

The period 1945–57

It is clear that the State Commission on Airfields played a crucial role in pushing the state to designate Schiphol as the international airport of the country. This decision may be considered as the official formalisation of a new collective arrangement, which would determine the future development of Schiphol airport in particular and the spatial and economic development of the Schiphol region in general. In this sense, the (future) development of Schiphol in terms of spatial planning, geographical expansion, the economic position of the airport at the local, regional and national level, and the discussions about the effects of air traffic activities for the surrounding area took place within the basic framework created by this collective arrangement.

We should note that various actors were directly or indirectly involved in the decision-making process which ultimately resulted into the emergence of this new collective arrangement. Beside the State Commission and the Small Commission on Dutch Airfields, many other actors were directly or indirectly involved in this decision-making process, among them being the Ministry of

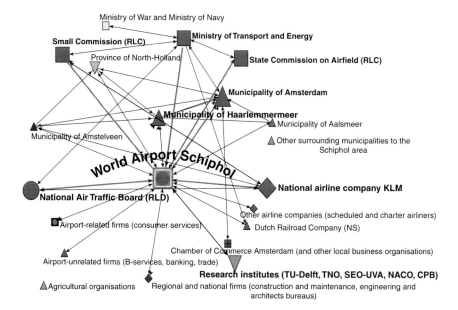

Figure 6.3 Key actors involved in the decision process: the first phase 1945–57.

Transport and Waterworks, the Ministry of War and the Ministry of Navy Force together with the city of Amsterdam, the Schiphol airport authorities, KLM, the National Air Traffic Board (RLD) and the city of Rotterdam. Other actors were also incidentally involved in the discussions (Figure 6.3) but most of them played a less significant role in determining the final decision about the future development of Schiphol, for example the province of North Holland, the National Railroad Company (NS) and the municipalities surrounding the airport. In addition, external research institutes played a crucial role in shaping the ground for further discussions between the parties, and in the end they played an important role in influencing the decision-making process. In other word, external research institutes may also be considered important parties acting behind the scenes, albeit without effective power to influence directly the decision-making process.

During this period, Schiphol airport itself was not a powerful player because officially it was still under the control of the municipality of Amsterdam. However, this situation would change radically with the change of ownership of the airport in 1958.

After the final decision of the government concerning the issue of the international airport, the State Commission (Small Commission) focused its attention on the issue of Schiphol's expansion plan and its future development. Long discussions took place about the most appropriate layout system and the spatial organisation of the airport facilities. In fact, the acceptance of the tangential runways system formed the basic arrangement that shaped the basic conditions for the future spatial expansion of the airport. This can be seen as a typical example of how a sub-collective arrangement (e.g. a tangential plan as the basic spatial plan for Schiphol) may emerge from the existing arrangement that, in turn, creates its own development path.

Note that different domains were not equally affected by these collective arrangements, e.g. airport planning, institutions, economic and socio-cultural domains. For example, the airport development had positive effects on the economic domain and negative effects on the urban planning domain, e.g. the increased noise nuisance for the surrounding area and the zoning regulations limiting urban expansion. In addition, the choice to apply the tangential plan demanded specific planning and spatial organisation of the airport terrain, more particularly with regard to the planning of the central terminal area, the distribution of buildings and runways, etc.

More generally, one may conclude that the decision to adopt the tangential plan for Schiphol airport is path-dependent, in the sense that once the actors involved had made their choice, they had consciously (or unconsciously) determined the future (spatial and economic) development path of the airport.

The period 1957–80

In 1957, Schiphol officially became a private organisation. This new collective arrangement replaced the existing arrangement dating from the prewar period, that is the municipal Schiphol airport. As a result, Schiphol became fully independent from the city of Amsterdam and emerged as one of the main powerful players at the local and regional levels. The powerful position of Schiphol was strengthened further during the 1950s and 1960s, when its spatial expansion gradually became contested by a wide range of actors in the region, including the city of Amsterdam and its reliable partner the municipality of Haarlemmermeer.

Another consequence of this new collective arrangement was the change in the role and position of existing actors, as new actors became more involved in the development of Schiphol after 1967. Among these actors were the Ministry of Finance, the Ministry of Spatial Planning, various societal organisations (including the residents of the surrounding municipalities) and environmental organisations. These last two actors played a major role during the 1960s and 1970s in influencing the decision-making process concerning the future development/expansion of Schiphol airport (Figure 6.4).

A typical example concerning the changing role and position of some key actors is given by the municipality of Haarlemmermeer. Before 1957, Schiphol was viewed as part of the city of Amsterdam within the Haarlemmermeer polder. The municipality of Haarlemmermeer had no other choice but to cooperate with Amsterdam because of the long-term economic advantages generated by the airport activities. As a result of the new collective arrangement, Haarlemmermeer came to consider Schiphol airport as a key economic sector, a business partner and one of the biggest private firms dominating the economic landscape of the municipality. Hence, the economic position of the municipality became more

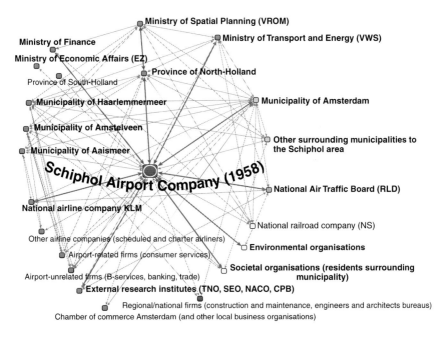

Figure 6.4 Key actors involved in the decision process: period 1957–80.

dependent on the airport's functions and related activities in terms of revenues, employment and the attraction of new firms (investments), as well as the most important source of economic growth in the region. Moreover, Haarlemmermeer could now negotiate directly with Schiphol without consulting the public works department or the city council of Amsterdam. In other word, Haarlemmermeer was in a certain way also decoupled from Amsterdam.

One major conclusion that should be put forward in this respect is that the prewar collective arrangement, which was very simple in its content and structure and involved a limited number of actors, became more complex, with various ramifications developing in different directions and involving an increasing number of actors. This is to say that, within the same playing field organised around Schiphol, the entry and exit of the players/actors increased considerably as well as the players' changing positions of power. As a result, the decision-making process concerning the future development of Schiphol airport became more complex. Furthermore, Schiphol no longer fitted within the existing Dutch governance structure, that is the tripartite governance structure formed by local, regional and national administrative bodies. By the end of the twentieth century, the position of Schiphol within the Dutch administrative and political landscape was subject to extensive discussions, especially through various studies and reports warning against the dangers of a lack of a clear governance structure that might control the decision-making process regarding the future development of Schiphol airport.

6.4 Implications of the new collective arrangement on airport planning

6.4.1 Which expansion plan for the international airport?

The first postwar expansion plans of Schiphol airport were designed by the Department of Public Works of the city of Amsterdam. In the RCL meeting of 4 February 1946, Amsterdam and Schiphol officials presented two expansion plans to the RCL commission: Plan 7 K/18 with a three-runway system and Plan 8A/19 with four-runway system. Both plans were based on the Montreal recommendations for the construction of class A airports. These two expansion plans were updated to Plan 5K/27 (four-runway system) and Plan 9A/25 (three-runway system), and presented to the commission during the following meeting of 13 February 1946. The uncertainty about the future development of airplane technology and the difficulty of forecasting the future developments in air traffic explain why airport planners updated the first two original expansion plans. However, the implementation of these two expansion plans needed much more land. Table 6.3 gives the estimated total surface of the four expansion plans.

During the 39th meeting of the Small Commission (7 October 1947), the managing director of Schiphol Jan Dellaert gave a detailed technical presentation about the advantages of implementing the tangential plan in terms of runway construction, terminal building and organisation of airport facilities.

Dellaert was against the parallel runway system (Plan 3T and the central Plan11B), which was widely applied during the early postwar period in most European countries (see Map 6.4). In his view, the parallel runway system is sensitive to safety issues because airplanes are allowed to cross the parallel runways in several directions. However, this problem was resolved by applying the PICAO requirements stating that in normal weather conditions the distance between runways should be at least 450 metres, in bad weather conditions (e.g. poor visibility) the distance between the start and landing runways should be 900 metres, and in the case of increasing numbers of airplanes landing, the distance should be extended to 1,800 metres.

Table 6.3 First postwar expansion plans of Schiphol airport (1946)

	Plan 7 K/18	*Plan 8 A/19*	*Plan 5 K/27*	*Plan 9 A/25*
Expansion (1946)	1,198,000 m²	1,034,500 m²	1,402,000 m²	1,419,000 m²
Paving platform	200,000 m²	200,000 m²	400,000 m²	400,000 m²
Parking, hangars, etc.	1,725,000 m²	1,631,000 m²	1,802,000 m²	1,819,000 m²
Total surface	*3,123,000 m²*	*2,865,500 m²*	*3,604,000 m²*	*3,238,000 m²*

Source: ACA, 1232 Amsterdam.

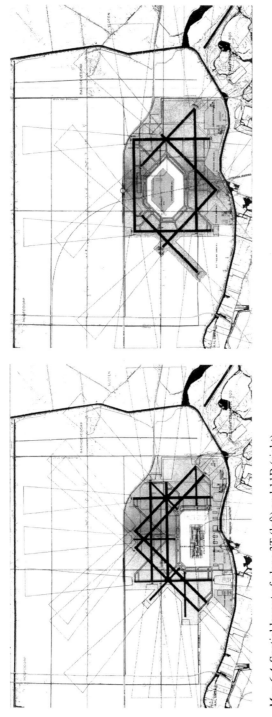

Map 6.4 Spatial layout of plans 3T (left) and 11B (right).
Source: Plan voor de Uitbreiding van de Luchthaven Schiphol. Scale 1:25000 (1948, pp. 5–6).

However, the main drawback of the parallel runway system for Schiphol was the limited possibility for the future spatial expansion of the airport. This was precisely what the designers of the Schiphol expansion plan had tried to avoid because they anticipated a continuing increase in airport capacity. Both Plans 3T and 11B were then rejected by the managing director of Schiphol airport in favour of the tangential plan (Plan 12A).

Dellaert was thoroughly convinced that the tangential plan was the best expansion plan for Schiphol airport, not only from a technical point of view but also in terms of cost-effectiveness and the possibility for future spatial expansion of airport activities.

Dellaert developed his ideas about the tangential plan during his numerous trips to visit US airports and his extensive discussions with experts in various commissions during the period of Occupation. Note, however, that the basic ideas for the future expansion plan for Schiphol were partly developed by Anthony Fokker during the 1930s (the so-called Fokker plan). At that time, Fokker was asked by his friend the mayor of the city of Amsterdam, Willem de Vlugt (1921–41), to design an expansion plan for Schiphol airport as an alternative to the KLM plan.

Although Dellaert considered the Fokker plan as 'revolutionary', he believed that it was more suited to very large airports and not to airports of moderate size like Schiphol. In his search for the ideal tangential plan, Dellaert had to look abroad for airports that were constructed following this plan, especially in the US. Dellaert had excellent contacts with airport authorities in the USA, and during his numerous trips to the USA, he spoke with many specialists and airport operators about the advantages and disadvantages of the tangential plan. The newly constructed Idlewild airport in New York, Pampa airport in Argentina, and O'Hare airport in Chicago served as successful examples of modern postwar airports. In his presentation to the Small Commission, Dellaert referred extensively to these examples and his discussions with various American specialists about the (dis)advantages of the tangential plan (NA 2.16.39, No. 25–32).

Two versions of the tangential runway system were developed by Dellaert: the first plan with eight runways that could be expanded to ten; and the second plan with six runways, which could be expanded to eight to ten (see Map 6.5). The total land needed to realise the tangential plan was estimated to be approximately 7 per cent (12.96 km^2) of the total surface of Haarlemmermeer (185.28 km^2).

According to Dellaert, the tangential plan (Plan 12A) was more reliable, healthier, more orderly and more efficient, and offered many possibilities for future spatial expansion. Concerning this last point, Dellaert was aware of the fact that the scarcity of land for future expansion of the airport could affect its position in the future. That is why he devoted much of his time to designing a tangential plan that offered great flexibility with regard to the future growth of passengers, freight and airport facilities, and that was easy to adapt to unexpected changes in air transport technologies and the air market.

Basically, the first version of the tangential plan was based on eight runways. However, discussions about the optimal number of runways resulted in an updated version of the tangential plan with six runways, from which two runways were already operational (runways 14-32 and 01-19). Note that in the first draft versions of the tangential plan, much attention focused on the layout of the runway system and practically no attention was given to the planning of the terminal building area. Therefore the terminal building area was consciously left empty on the maps because of the uncertainty about the future development of airplane technology and the unreliable forecasts about the future increase in air traffic. In addition, the connection of the airport to infrastructure networks was also left aside because of its dependence on the planning of the terminal area.

The tangential plan for Schiphol airport was projected at a distance of four kilometres to the northwest perimeter of the original location of Schiphol, and consisted of a six-runway system around a central terminal area and in close proximity to the national motorway A4. The total costs of the tangential plan were estimated to be f 117 million, almost four million cheaper than the parallel runway system.

The expansion plan of Schiphol (*Plan tot Uitbreiding van Schiphol*) was presented on 4 February 1949. Two months later (6 April 1949), the city council of Amsterdam voted almost unanimously in favour of the implementation of the expansion plan of Schiphol.

In contrast to Amsterdam and the RLD, the Ministry of Transport and Energy and KLM were both less enthusiastic about the expansion plan because of the financial participation of these two parties in the construction of the new airport. KLM was expected to invest f 5 million in the construction of buildings, hangars, technical facilities, etc. This financial sacrifice from KLM would put much pressure on its financial position, knowing that KLM had invested large amounts of money in renewing its airplane fleet. Furthermore, according to KLM, the construction of a six-runway system was not necessary because new big airplanes were less sensitive to crosswind on landing and take-off.

However, the Ministry of Transport and Energy was prepared to financially support the expansion of Schiphol in exchange for more control and decision-making power in managing and operating the national airport. The shift in government policy toward Schiphol and the city of Amsterdam opened the door for further negotiations about the organisational form and participation of the state in the management of the airport.

When Amsterdam agreed with the government proposal, the Ministry of Transport and Energy, in cooperation with the Dutch railway company, was then prepared to invest in improving the accessibility of the airport to road and rail connections between Amsterdam, The Hague and Rotterdam.

To accomplish the expansion plan, 700 ha of land around Schiphol, which were managed by the foundation of the Ministry of Agriculture (*Stichting Landelijke Bezittingsschade* (SLB)), were transferred to the airport authorities. The total costs of the transfer of land ownership to Schiphol was f 2,800,000 (f 4,000/per ha) (NA, No. 2.16.39, No. 25–32, and ACA No. 1232).

The municipality of Haarlemmermeer showed great flexibility in cooperating with Amsterdam to bring about the Schiphol expansion plan. Amsterdam and

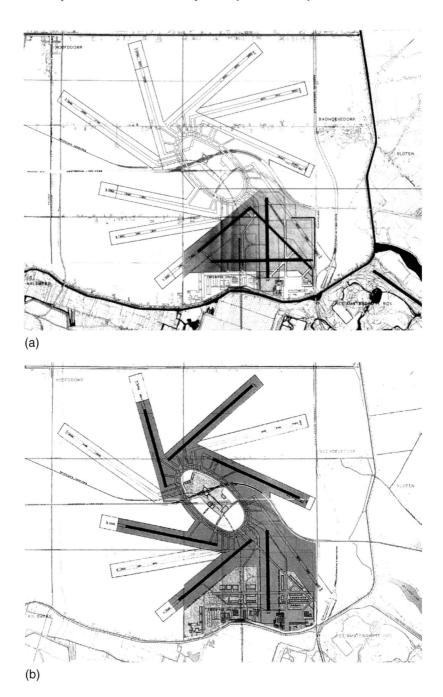

(a)

(b)

Map 6.5 Different layouts of the tangential plan of Schiphol airport (a and b).
Source: Plan voor de Uitbreiding van de Luchthaven Schiphol. Scale 1:25000
(1948, pp.10–13).

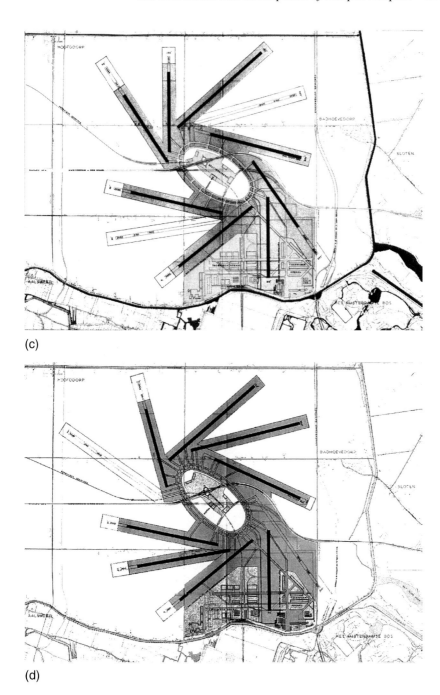

(c)

(d)

Map 6.5 Different layouts of the tangential plan of Schiphol airport (c and d).
Source: Plan voor de Uitbreiding van de Luchthaven Schiphol. Scale 1:25000
(1948, pp.10–13).

Haarlemmermeer agreed to integrate the plan into the urban expansion plan of Haarlemmermeer. Because of this, the plan was not greatly contested by the surrounding municipalities. In fact, most of these municipalities played only marginal roles in the discussions about the future development of Schiphol during the 1940s. In this sense, one may conclude that the relationship between Schiphol and its neighbouring municipalities and provincial authorities was more informative than cooperative. Schiphol took the initiative only to inform the surrounding areas about the possible effects of the future expansion plan of the airport on their urban expansion plans.

Nevertheless, there were also increasing voices from various local actors that contested the way in which the Schiphol authorities had gained support from local authorities for the execution of the Schiphol expansion plan. Among those actors were, for example, landowners and farmers that were directly affected by the restrictive measures for buildings and other requirements of zoning regulation. However, the reactions of Schiphol and Amsterdam were rather passive because of the weak and marginal position these actors enjoyed in influencing the decision-making process. This may be interpreted in light of the growing position of power of Schiphol as a dominant actor in the region, more particularly with regard to the economic and spatial development of Schiphol and its surroundings.

6.4.2 The updated expansion plan of 1956

During the summer of 1950, the Minister of Transport and Waterworks installed a temporary advisory board to supervise the airport management as the first step toward the official installation of the first board of commissioners. Three years later, with the fast increase in airplane technology, the Minister of Transport and Waterworks asked the temporary advisory board to review Schiphol's expansion plan. The tangential plan served as a basic framework, albeit with modifications and in somewhat reduced form, i.e. four rather than six runways with the (open) possibility of adding two additional runways.

The designers of the new expansion plan focused their attention on two main issues: the accessibility of the airport to public infrastructure networks, and the cost-effectiveness of the expansion plan, i.e. cost saving issues.

The expansion plan of 1956 was published on 20 November 1955 under the title: 'Fundamentals for the development of Schiphol Airport' (*Grondslagen voor de Ontwikkeling van de Luchthaven Schiphol*). At first instance, this plan was intended to serve as a master plan sketching the future expansion of Schiphol from the 1950s up to the 1970s. Two separate documents were published: the first document gives a general overview of the expansion plan, while the second document gives a detailed description of the nature and planning of the construction works.

The expansion plan was first approved by the Schiphol board of commissioners on 5 January 1956, and by the city council of Amsterdam in October 1956 and the state in December 1957.

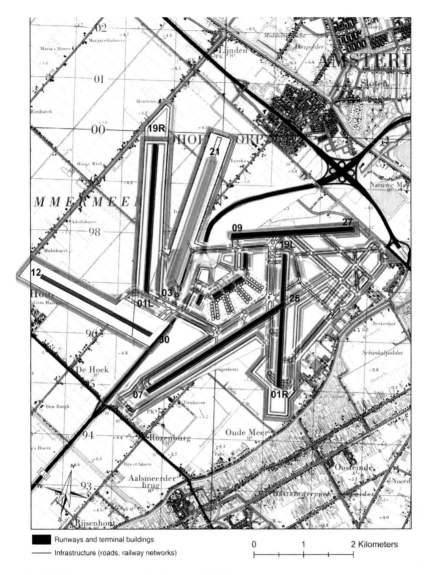

	0	1	2 Kilometers

■ Runways and terminal buildings
— Infrastructure (roads, railway networks)

Map 6.6 Expansion plan of Schiphol of 1956.
Source: based on Cadaster map of 1960 (scale 1:25000) and the original plan of 1956.

The expansion plan preserved the basic ideas of Dellaert's tangential plan, albeit with only four independent runways laid out around the central terminal to enable airplanes to land and take off in all wind directions (Map 6.6). Parallel to the existing North–South runway 01-09 (Aalsmeerbaan), two other runways were planned in the East–West direction (runway 07-25 (Kaagbaan) and runway 27-09

(Buitenvelderbaan)), and one additional runway in the western part of the central terminal area (runway 01L-19R (Zwanenburgbaan)) (see Map 6.6).

The runway system was based on the concept of the so-called 'sandwich system' – developed by the former Director of Public Works of the municipality of Amsterdam Mr J. W. Clerx – that might support three-wheeled airplanes with a total weight of 145,000 kg (45 to 65 tons on each wheel) and taxiing airplanes with double front wheels up to 185,000 kg. The capacity of each runway was estimated to be about 40 airplanes landing per hour, depending on the weather conditions. The costs of paving and asphalting runways, following the International Civil Aviation Organisation (ICAO) requirements, were estimated at f 240,000 per km (f 40 per m²).

The central terminal area, which was planned for construction during the second phase of the works, was projected close to the national Amsterdam–The Hague motorway. The connection of the airport to the infrastructure networks was planned to take place through a road tunnel under runway 09-27 and an underground rail service under runway 01-19. The terminal area was designed so as to minimise the taxiing distance of the aircrafts, and at the same time to preserve enough space for future expansion. Within the central terminal building, only the most essential airport facilities for passengers were planned and all other airport activities were removed to the technical area to the southern part of the airport.

The total surface of the airport terrain had been estimated at 150 ha, of which 100 ha were reserved for the expansion of the airport and 50 ha as a 'land bank' for future expansion. Note that the total surface of the airport was 700 ha in 1956, of which 300 ha were owned by Schiphol airport. However, with the accomplishment of the expansion plan, the total surface of the airport reached 1,350 ha. Note that by the end of 1956, only one (runway 01-09) of the four planned runways was completed by the Schiphol authorities. Map 6.7 gives an overview of land use and the spatial expansion of Schiphol between 1948 and ca. 1956.

The total construction costs of the new Schiphol airport were estimated at f 180 million, of which f 110 million were for the construction of three runways, taxiways, the platform, roads and the parking terrain, f 50 million for the construction of the central terminal area and f 20 million for the connection of Schiphol airport to the national motorway and the provincial 'Schipholweg' road. However, even before the beginning of the second phase of the construction works, the expansion plan became obsolete because of the rapid increase in airplane technology and the introduction of the jet airplane. This meant that the runways (in terms of length), taxiways, the terminal building area, etc., had to be reconstructed and/or extended following the new international standards to accommodate the new jet airliners. It was in this context that the whole village of Rijk was demolished in September 1957 in order to construct the new runway 06-24 (Kaagbaan, finished in 1960) (see Map 6.8). Six million guilders were spent by Schiphol as financial compensation for about 50 families that were living in this village. In addition, 295 land parcels making about 387.7 ha of additional land were expropriated from private owners, of which 11 were agriculture firms, to (re)construct the runway 07-25 (NA 2.16.39; No. 25–32).

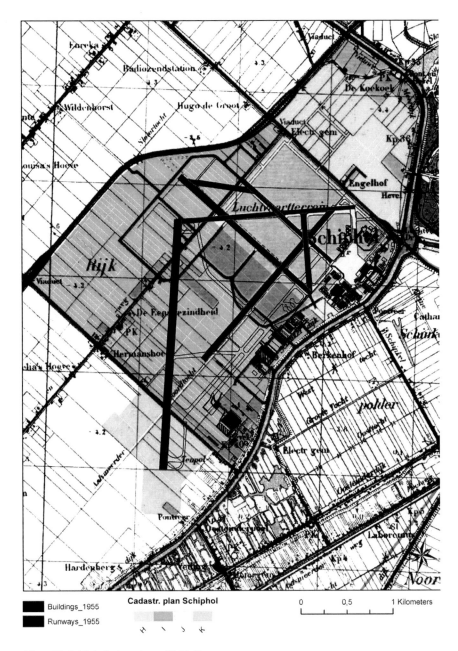

Buildings_1955	Cadastr. plan Schiphol	0 0,5 1 Kilometers
Runways_1955		

Map 6.7 Schiphol airport c.a. 1956–7.
Source: based on Cadaster map of 1960 (scale 1:25000) and various historical (Cadaster)
maps of Schiphol from the archives of Schiphol airport.

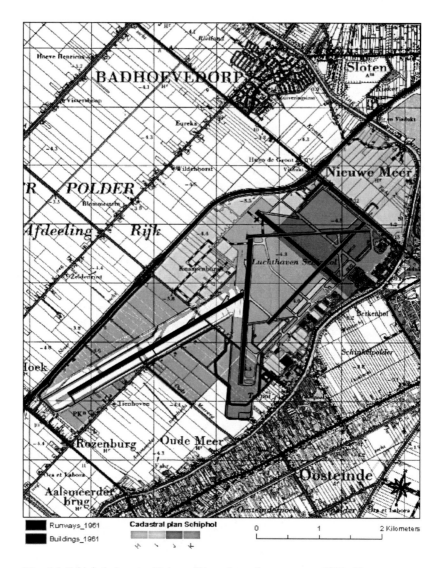

Map 6.8 Schiphol airport with two of four planned runways ca. 1957–62.
Source: based on Cadaster map of 1960 (scale 1:25000) and various historical (Cadaster) maps of Schiphol from the archives.

6.5 Towards a new collective arrangement: from municipal airport to Schiphol Airport Company

As mentioned before, the rapid advances in airplane technology and commercial aviation resulted in increasing complexity in the construction, management and operation of Schiphol airport. The growing operational and exploitation costs, combined with lack of revenues, demanded high financial sacrifices from the municipality in order to maintain and improve Schiphol's international position. From 1945 until 1957, the municipality of Amsterdam financially supported the Schiphol reconstruction and expansion works through municipal subsidies and other financial means (e.g. loans). The municipal financial support to Schiphol increased by 221 per cent from 1949 to 1952 (*f* 821,841 in 1949 to *f* 2,641,189 in 1952), and to *f* 2.9 million and *f* 3 million in 1956 and 1957. With the transfer of the ownership of Schiphol to the new Schiphol airport company in 1958, municipal financial support for Schiphol airport was officially ended.

The enormous financial costs of the reconstruction of Schiphol could only be realised with financial support from the state. This meant that full control over Schiphol would be difficult to maintain in the future.

When negotiations about the participation of the state in Schiphol airport were started, a provisional advisory board – formed by representatives from Amsterdam and the state – had been installed in 1950 to take over the management of Schiphol airport from Amsterdam.[4]

From the first collective arrangement of 1945, e.g. the designation of Schiphol as the world airport of the Netherlands, a new complementary collective arrangement emerged in 1957, the Schiphol Airport Company. This arrangement was formalised by the creation of a new jurisdictional status of Schiphol as a private organisation with three main shareholders: the state, Amsterdam and the municipality of Rotterdam. The State Commission on Airfields (RCL) played a crucial role in the emergence of both collective arrangements. The RCL saw the creation of a limited liability company as the best organisational form that could serve the interests of all participating parties.

However, negotiations between Amsterdam and the state took almost 12 years (from 1945 to 1957). This was due to the many problems that had to be resolved such as the status of the airport, the distribution of votes, the (use of the) veto right, the participation in the capital of the company, the control of the new organisation and the financial obligations of the shareholders.

Schiphol Airport Company was given full power to operate through an independent professional board of directors under the direct control of a supervisory board of shareholders. The creation of the management board was crucial to Amsterdam in order to break up the domination of the state within the board of shareholders (the state had two-thirds of the votes).

From 22 January 1958, when the final official document of the Schiphol Airport Company (*NV Luchthaven Schiphol*) was signed by the Minister of Transport and Energy and the two mayors of Amsterdam and Rotterdam, Schiphol was officially given the (financial and legal) instruments to spread its wings and realise its ambitious expansion plans (ACA 1323, Nr.1089–1242 (14); 1098–1109 LHD 1959; No. 1112–1138, LHD 1959).

More specifically, with the creation of the Schiphol Airport Company, a new powerful intermediate layer of governance was created between the municipality and the government. The board of shareholders operated as a 'hybrid' governance layer within the existing governance structure, which is quite unique in the administrative landscape of the Netherlands. In fact, this governance layer operated beyond existing administrative layers as Schiphol became a powerful actor and key player at the regional and national levels. The powerful position of Schiphol was strengthened further by the fact that it became a symbol of national pride and progress, and one of the most important economic engines in the country. Also, from an economic point of view, Schiphol represented an exceptional example of private organisation operating according to free market principles and at the same time strongly regulated by public authorities.

6.5.1 The new Schiphol airport

The construction of the central terminal was delayed because of technical and financial problems, e.g. the connection of Schiphol to the national highway and the increasing costs of construction. One of the most uncertain factors in the construction of the central terminal area was the connection of the terminal complex to the infrastructure networks.

The terminal complex was located at the intersection of the four runways, and was composed of four large piers accommodating 57 taxiing aircraft. The central terminal area is connected to the rail network through an underground tunnel passing under runway 09-27, where a railway station was built under the terminal building. The cargo area and the technical and maintenance facilities were located in the western and the northeastern parts of the terminal area (see Map 6.9).

The terminal complex area was designed by Van Wageningen (NACO), F. C. Weger (Rotterdam's Architects and Engineering bureau), Professor M. Duintjer (Professor of Architecture at the University of Amsterdam) and Kho Liang (an interior designer of station building complexes). However, for financial reasons, it took several years before the final version of the terminal building was accepted by the stakeholders of the Airport Company.[5]

The original expansion plan for the central terminal was replaced by a much more modest plan to save construction costs. Consequently, the final terminal building was much smaller than originally planned, and its location was a bit further to the southeast corner of the central area, now facing runway 01-19 instead of runway 07-25. Moreover, the terminal building had only three piers accommodating 25 taxiing aircraft. The main reason for moving the terminal building to the southeast corner was to create more space for hotels, office buildings and parking areas. The technical area was also shifted from its original location to where the original terminal building was first planned. In this location a cargo centre was constructed containing various buildings such as the RLD building and the KLM building.

Schiphol airport was designed according to the 'one concept terminal' where all airport facilities are brought under one roof (Bosma, 1998, 2004). The new central terminal area was based on the 'finger terminal system' (introduced first at Gatwick in 1958), providing various possibilities for the future expansion of

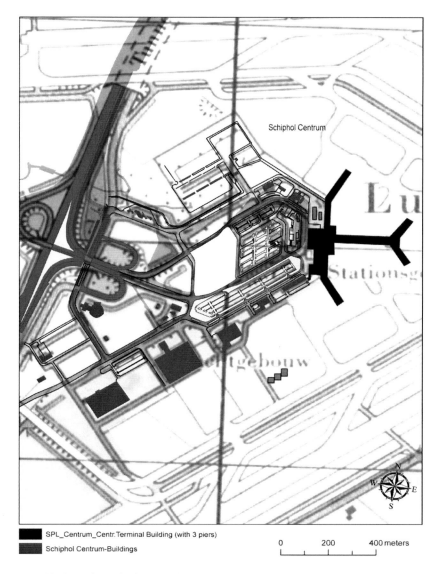

Schiphol Centrum

N
W   E
S

SPL_Centrum_Centr.Terminal Building (with 3 piers)
Schiphol Centrum-Buildings

0   200   400 meters

Map 6.9 Central terminal area and Schiphol centre ca.1969–70.
Source: based on various photos and maps from Schiphol's Archives.

existing terminal buildings, aprons, etc., and easy adjustments to different sizes
and door heights of different types of aircraft.

The central terminal building was divided into zones (vertically and
horizontally), with parking facilities in the basement and the arrival and departure
halls stacked above it. The top floor contained cafes for visitors, bars and

restaurants for 1,200 people, and a panoramic view to the airport terrain (Dosma, 2004: 59).

On Friday, 28 April 1967, the central terminal area was officially opened by Her Majesty Queen Juliana. The total construction cost for the central terminal area reached 95.8 million guilders.

After 20 years of preparations, discussions, studies and conflicts, the new international and world airport of the Netherlands was finally completed. However, expansion and construction works were definitely not finished … yet!

In contrast to the construction of the three first runways, the construction of the fourth runway 01L-19R (Zwanenburgbaan) and parts of the terminal complex area were delayed because of the uncertainty about the exact planning of infrastructures around the airport area and the adjustments that had to be made to road connections around and from/to the airport. Because infrastructure planning was the domain of the Ministry of Transport and Waterworks and the Dutch railway company (NS), a close coordination in the planning of airport expansion works with these two parties was crucial.

However, in 1970, Schiphol airport had only constructed two jet runways (Aalsmeerbaan and the Kaagbaan) out of the planned four. At the same time, the connection of Schiphol to the national infrastructure (motorway and rail networks) was lagging behind.

It took several decades (not before 1975) before the airport was finally connected to the national highway A4. The connection of Schiphol to the rail network was relatively less time-consuming in comparison to its connection by road. The railway line connecting Schiphol to Amsterdam–The Hague was completed in three phases: (1) the construction of the line between Amsterdam South and the airport, which was completed in December 1978; (2) the line connecting Schiphol to Leiden and The Hague, which was finished in 1980; and finally (3) the extension of the rail track from Amsterdam South to Central Station at the IJ-Over, which was finished in 1985.

Eighteen years after the opening of the terminal building complex in 1967, Schiphol airport was finally connected to the national railway network. The connection of Schiphol to public infrastructure in general and the development of a large transport network system linking Schiphol to Amsterdam and other cities of the region (by train, tram and metro) in particular during the earlier years of the 1960s may be considered a greatly missed opportunity for the airport authorities and the government. This is because during this period, the number of passengers reaching Schiphol by car increased more than was expected. The problem of the accessibility of the airport and increasing congestion were partly resolved by developing large parking facilities around the airport. However, because of the commercial policy applied, Schiphol authorities were in favour of connecting the airport by road because of increasing revenues from parking facilities.

Map 6.10 shows the definitive layout of the new Schiphol airport with four runways and central terminal complex at the heart of the airport area.

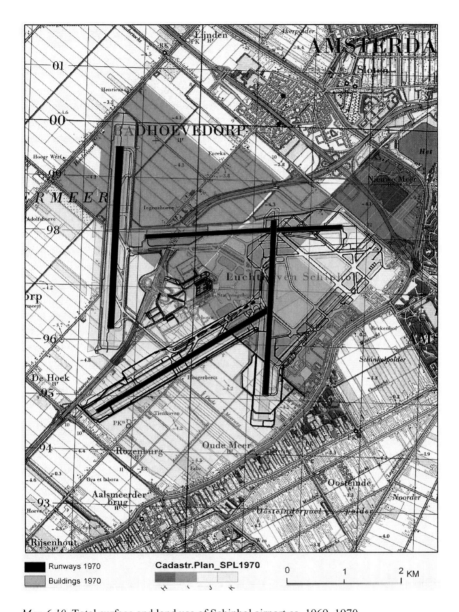

Runways 1970
Buildings 1970

Cadastr.Plan_SPL1970

0   1   2 KM

Map 6.10 Total surface and land use of Schiphol airport ca. 1969–1970.

6.6 Effects of external factors on the spatial expansion of Schiphol airport

The 1950s may be characterised as the era of high expectations concerning the technological advances in the air transport sector. Before the end of the 1950s, there was a great uncertainty about which aircraft technology would dominate the commercial air transport market in the near future. By the 1960s, when it became clear that aircraft technology would be decided by the jet airliners, airport authorities began to adapt existing airport buildings, runways, platforms, aprons, etc. to accommodate this new type of airplane.

The standardisation of airplane technology became clear when the British Overseas Airways Corporation (BOAC) introduced the first transatlantic jet services from Heathrow to New York's Idlewild on 4 October 1958. A few years later, Boeing responded by introducing the Boeing 707 jet airline, which was much larger, faster and with a much greater range.[6] As a reaction to the increased popularity of the American jet airliners, Russia and France introduced respectively the Tupolev Tu-104 and the Caravelle jets. However, the technological race between Europe and the US was almost lost in favour of the American jet airliners. Within a few years, the Boeing 707 jet airliners had crowded out all other propeller jet airliners from the air transport market.

In this perspective, preparations were then made by national airline companies and airport authorities to meet the technical and spatial requirements (i.e. ground services) of the jet airplanes. Just when airport architects and engineers had begun to understand the needs of the first generation of jets, they were required to accommodate new types of aircraft that were twice as big as the first jets. According to Bosma (2004), traditionally trained airport planners and designers were ill equipped to cope with the complexity of airport design in contrast to private specialised architects bureaus that were mostly well equipped to reassemble the technical and logistical knowledge concerning the construction and development of the new generation of airports.

In any case, the introduction of the Boeing 747 and similar jumbo jets changed the scale of everything on airport fields and in terminals. This resulted in a shift in the paradigm of airport planning, and more particularly with regard to air terminals. Airports were no longer seen as a single entity but as a complex of structures that have to be organised in relationship to each other as well as to existing runway patterns (Gordon, 2004: 166).

More generally, planning airports and their terminals became more complex. Designers and architects were pushed to think further about the ideal runway configuration, landing facilities, passenger and freight accommodation, the design of the building complex, and the relationship between the airport and its surrounding areas. The most complex issue for airport planners was the question of how to speed up the movement of large numbers of people from the terminal to the aircraft and vice versa. Passenger transfer speed became essential in maximising profits and in strengthening the competitive position of airports.

Different configurations of the airports were then proposed, such as: (1) the transporter configuration where aircraft and terminal buildings are physically separated from each other; (2) the finger satellite configuration, i.e. a terminal with 'fingers' (piers) and boarding satellites on the apron; (3) the centralised transfer machine configuration, which focuses on shortening the walking distance between the terminal and the aircraft and reducing the costs of taxiing; and

(4) the linear configuration, consisting of a spin with left and right exits that bring aircraft and passengers closer to each other (see Bosma, 1996).

In all these different types of airport configuration, the ultimate design of terminal building showed a strong emphasis on quick handling and short and direct routes for passengers and luggage from the car to the aircraft. All other buildings and constructions were subordinate to this main requirement (Altorfer, 1957).

However, with the extension of terminals, passengers became increasingly lost and disoriented. The specific design of air terminals that demanded symbolism and emotional streamlining of passengers was then needed. The solution was found by the designers in the elaboration of divided information systems to guide passengers from point to point through the volatile airport environment to their destinations. Moreover, the association of air travel (speed, light, sky and comfort) was met through the use of glass, colours, light, comfortable furniture and a smooth passenger processing system. To establish continuity in the terminal flow, the designers reduced objects to simplified icons and signs with particular colours (for example, a silhouette of a plane to designate a boarding gate, a suitcase for luggage claim, a coffee cup for restaurants/buffets, etc.). Symbols were also used when no icons and words could be assigned to particular objects (Gordon, 2004: 224).

In the Dutch case, with the standardisation of airplane technology, Schiphol and KLM started preparations to receive the new jet airliners. A few months after the opening of the new Schiphol, the airport management board started to improve the airport buildings, hangars, terminal complex and other airport facilities to receive the bigger DC-8 jet and the Boeing 747 engines. The most important expansion/construction works concerned: (1) the extension of the southern pier by 125 metres (1968), whereby four gates could then be used by the Boeing 747 or Douglas DC-10 wide-body aircraft; and (2) the expansion of the terminal building (the lower half of the landside facade of the building was moved), where a new section was opened in April 1975. Schiphol was then able to handle up to 16 million passengers per year.

At the same time, Schiphol airport started its commercial strategy oriented towards the diversification of activities, such as the leasing of land and buildings, concessions and the opening of tax-free shops.

The reconstruction and expansion works were financed through external loans and through the raising of airport fees, e.g. landing fees.[7]

At the spatial level, Schiphol airport needed more space for the implementation of its ambitious expansion projects. In terms of layout and airport facilities, Schiphol airport began to show new spatial and functional patterns which looked like a small downtown city centre, e.g. one or more islands containing offices, air traffic control towers, vast parking lots, low buildings containing gates to the aprons, etc. The economic and spatial position of the airport became dominant in the local and regional geographical and economic landscape. Besides its main function as a transfer machine and central node of connectivity in national and international air transport networks, Schiphol began to develop into a full economic centre generating its own economies of agglomeration.

6.7 Towards a market-oriented policy: the economic performance of Schiphol Airport Company

The introduction of bigger and faster airplanes in the 1950s opened new possibilities for further commercialisation in the air transport sector. Most airplane companies began to shift the focus of their commercial strategy from technology and luxury towards a strategy based on price competition, the quality of services and facilities offered to passengers (i.e. ground services in airports and service on board), diversification of destinations and the introduction of tourist class. Beside considerations such as the development of airplane technology and the increasing competition between airline companies, the increasing standard of living, incomes and free time throughout the population played an important role in accelerating the shift towards mass air transport for the ordinary people. In other words, due to continuing economic growth and increases in the disposable incomes of individuals, a large proportion of the population were now able to travel by air to distant destinations that were previously beyond their reach (Gordon, 2004: 176).

In addition, and under the Chicago agreement, the charter transport market was open to free competition, as charter airline companies were given dispensations from the requirements falling under existing bilateral agreements. In cooperation with low-cost airplane companies, travel agencies began to offer lower-priced tickets for clubs and organised travel packages.[8] As a consequence, the number of low-fare scheduled charter flights increased substantially, especially on the intercontinental services from the US to Europe and vice versa. These developments pushed the national carriers to sign agreements within the International Air Transport Association (IATA) in 1951, stressing the need to reduce the price of long-distance tickets through the introduction of tourist class, which was 32 per cent cheaper than existing (first class) standard class.[9] In 1958, in anticipation of the introduction of the jet airplane, IATA took the next step by introducing economy class, which was 20 per cent cheaper than tourist class. As a result, besides the opening of the protected air travel market, the number of scheduled services and the number of seats on the most profitable intercontinental services increased substantially.

More generally, airplane companies were fully aware of the potential economic importance of economy class and began to reorient their commercial strategy toward the leisure traveller. The democratisation of mass air travel began to emerge when increasing numbers of airline companies started to programme scheduled air services at reduced tariffs and/or low-priced tourist class fares (ACA 1323, Nr. 347; 8-1-1957). However, the increase in competition between the airline companies on intercontinental and intra-European services resulted in a significant decrease in their profits and in the average load per aircraft, i.e. total occupied seats per flight, especially between 1961 and 1964.

Taking KLM as an example, it was only after 1950 that KLM began to realise modest profits (an average of 14 million guilder between 1951 and 1960). In absolute figures, KLM's net result increased from 10.3 million guilders in 1954

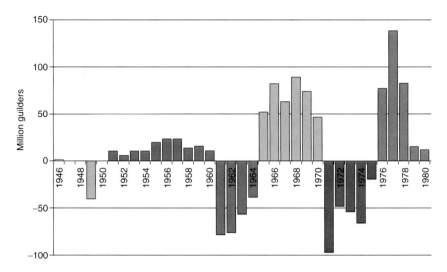

Figure 6.5 Annual net results of KLM between 1945 and 1980.
Source: Annual Reports of the KLM (1945–1980).

to, respectively, 23 and 22.9 million guilders in 1956 and 1957, before decreasing again to 10.3 million guilders in 1960 (Figure 6.5). This tendency towards nega-tive profitability continued from 1961 to 1964, and between 1971 and 1975 (i.e. the oil crisis).

From 1964 onward, however, the net results of airline companies recovered, partly because of the introduction by travel organisations of the concept of the 'inclusive tour' (i.e. the cheap fares for charter flights were combined with low-priced accommodation at the destination country in a single travel package). The market for charter travel offered a unique opportunity for airline companies to recoup part of their investments in jet propeller airliners that were not fully depreciated when the new jet airliners made their entrance in the air travel market.

Figure 6.6 shows the absolute figures for scheduled, charter and transit flights in total air transport from/to Schiphol between 1945 and 1980. From 1958 onward, charter flights through Schiphol airport increased from 3.6 per cent in 1958 to 27.5 per cent in 1971. In addition, the annual growth of transit/transfer through Schiphol was significantly higher between 1945 (4.7 per cent) and 1950 (25.5 per cent) than in 1969.

After 1960, the air transport market changed definitively into a mass transport market. The number of passengers increased spectacularly during the period 1960–79. In 1946, 297,550 passengers travelled through Schiphol airport. This number increased to 1.4 million passengers in 1960 and, respectively, to 5.1 and 9.7 million passengers in 1970 and 1980.

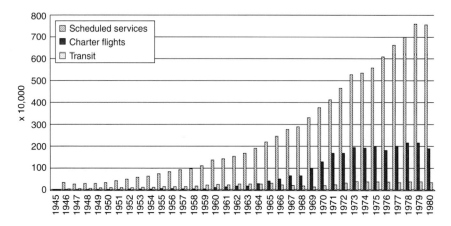

Figure 6.6 Growth of scheduled, charter and transit flights from/to Schiphol (1945–1980).
Source: Annual Reports Schiphol airport (1945–1980).

More generally, the increased number of passengers was largely due to the competition strategy of airline companies and the shift in commercial policy from a specialised market to more segmented markets, where the economy class and the charter flights formed an important share of the air travel market. However, the growing competition in the air transport market pushed the airline companies to seek cooperation in order to achieve economies of scale and preserve their market share. The first move in this direction was the creation of the Intergovernmental European Civil Aviation Conference (ECAC) in 1957, with the aim of exploring the possibilities of an air union between European countries. However, negotiations about the division of market shares between participating airlines within the air union framework collapsed in 1967 (Dierikx and Bouwens, 1997: 85).

In contrast to passenger air traffic, Schiphol was more successful in developing freight activities. Schiphol's share of intercontinental air cargo activities rose substantially, in contrast to the decreasing share of inter-European air cargo owing to the increased importance of container transportation by road. Especially during the 1960s and 1970s, cargo air traffic increased very rapidly, due to the geographical position of Schiphol airport as a distribution hub for cargo activities in Europe. Cargo air transport increased by 34 per cent between 1964 and 1965, 150 per cent between 1964 and 1970, and 84.5 per cent between 1970 and 1980 (see Figure 6.7).

As mentioned before, the increase in air traffic activities had a direct effect on airport planning and the spatial design of terminals and runways and airport facilities. The Schiphol Airport Company was supposed to take full advantage of its position as a private company to raise revenues and increase profits from airport activities. In this respect, the company took the first steps towards the diversification of its revenues by granting concessions to seven tax-free shops at the intercontinental departure hall (in 1957), and later in the European departure hall. Concessions for the selling of tobacco, liquor and chocolate, the restaurant

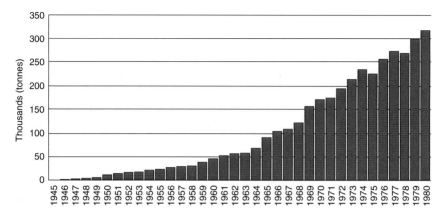

Figure 6.7 Annual growth of freight transport at Schiphol airport (1945–80).
Source: Annual Reports Schiphol Group (1945–1980).

and buffets, etc., went to KLM, while concessions for the selling of electronic products (cameras, watches, etc.) and perfumes went to specialised third parties from the city of Amsterdam (Dierikx and Bouwens, 1997: 139). This policy turned out to be successful as revenues from concessions increased by 60 per cent in 1957. Concessions to third parties became the fourth source of revenue for Schiphol airport.

Moreover, the increasing importance of landside activities was manifested by the supply of various services to passengers within the airport terminal such as catering, hotels, car rental services and the tax-free shopping malls. Many commercial facilities at the airport area were also opened to the public.

As Figure 6.8 shows, the main source of revenues for Schiphol between 1945 and 1980 were the airport fees charged to airline companies, followed by the

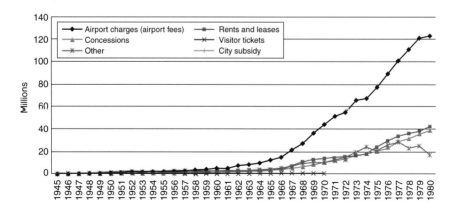

Figure 6.8 Sources of revenues of Schiphol airport (1945–80).
Source: Annual Reports Schiphol Airport (1945–1980).

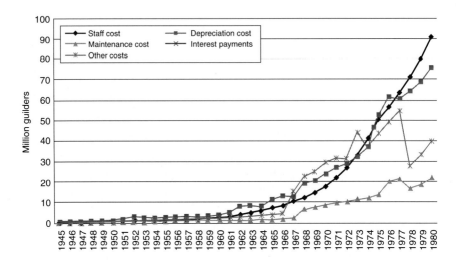

Figure 6.9 Total annual costs of Schiphol airport (1945–80).
Source: Annual Reports Schiphol Airport (note: data on interest payments are from 1945 until 1957).

rental and leasing of land, buildings and other facilities, and the concessions for shops, restaurants and buffets to third parties in the airport environs.

Despite the diversified sources of revenue, the Schiphol Airport Company realised moderate profits. This is because of the high costs of operation and maintenance of airport facilities, the high rent on financial loans and the rapid depreciation of airport buildings and facilities. For example, total personnel costs increased from 3.1 million guilders in 1960 to 9 million in 1980, suggesting that the number of employees at Schiphol airport increased substantially during this period. The depreciation costs (buildings, runways, etc.) grew very rapidly by the end of the 1950s and during the 1960s and 1970s: from 5 million guilders in 1961 to 23 million guilders in 1970 and 75 million guilders in 1980. This was mainly due to large construction works and enlargement of the terminal building, aprons, runways and airport infrastructure during the period 1945–80. Figure 6.9 gives detailed figures on the development of different categories of costs in this period.

When we compare the total costs and revenues (see Figure 6.10), it becomes clear that Schiphol was operating at loss during 1945–57. From 1957, however, the new Schiphol Airport Company became profitable, albeit with a very moderate positive net result, but it was not until 1969 that the company began to realise substantial profits. Nevertheless, the combination of the two oil crises and the increased safety issues during the 1970s (e.g. terrorist attacks) had strong negative effects on the airport's profitability, especially in 1975–7. However, Schiphol recovered rapidly as the net result increased to 6.7 million guilders in 1978 (from more than 14 million guilders in 1973).

Note that the commercial orientation of the airport was pushed further by the development of business parks and office buildings within the airport zone and

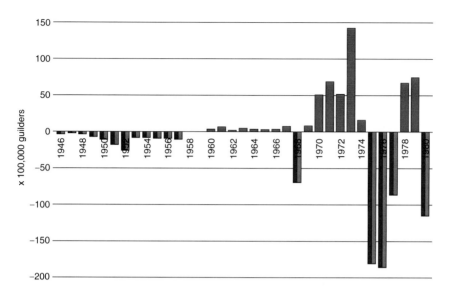

Figure 6.10 Annual net result of Schiphol airport: 1945–80.
Source: Annual Reports Schiphol Airport Company (1945–1980).

its environs. The development of landside activities was crucial in creating specific a local production milieu for activities that were directly (or indirectly) related to the airport's activities. As a result, the airport environment has gradually shifted to becoming a powerful economic centre creating its own agglomeration economies and exercising strong pull effects on workers, firms and service activities.

Schiphol became one of the fastest-growing economic centres of the region in terms of employment. The number of employees at Schiphol airport increased from 13,997 in 1953 to 17,993 in 1968 and 26,574 employees in 1979 (see Figure 6.11). Schiphol became the second largest employment centre in the Amsterdam-Schiphol region. Total employment in the Amsterdam region amounted to 686,000 in 1970 (out of 4,421,000 in the Netherlands), of which 404,000 were based in the city of Amsterdam and 282,000 in the suburban areas of Amsterdam (including the Schiphol region and the Haarlem-Ijmond areas). In 1979, total employment in the Amsterdam region was still 686,000 (out of 4,776,000 in the Netherlands as a whole), of which 377,000 were based in the city of Amsterdam and 309,000 in the suburban areas. Between 1980 and 1990, employment in Amsterdam registered a very modest growth rate of 0.26 per cent against 25.2 per cent in suburban areas (including the Schiphol region) and 12.46 per cent at the national level. Consequently, from an economic point of view, one may argue that 1979 marks a clear shift in the economic relationship between Amsterdam and Schiphol. The Schiphol region began to dominate the economic

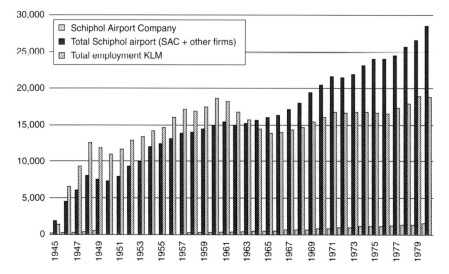

Figure 6.11 Employment growth at Schiphol between 1945 and 1980.
Source: Annual Reports (KLM and Schiphol Airport Company).

landscape of the whole region, not only in term of employment but also as one of the most attractive locations for firms and business services.

Within the airport area itself, before 1967, almost all employees of Schiphol were concentrated in the old airport area (i.e. Schiphol West). However, from 1972 onward, employment became more concentrated within and around the airport perimeter.

At the sectoral level, employment is highly concentrated in business activities such as the airline companies, retail activities, public services, air cargo, storage, distribution and expedition companies, travel agencies, restaurants, free tax shops, car rental, banks and money exchange offices, gas and oil companies, and operational services such as handling and supplying of airplanes, maintenance and reparation. Most of these companies have specific spatial and/or functional relationships with the airport, but the nature and the intensity of these relationships are diverse.

Analysis of the change in the total number of firms established in the Schiphol airport area during the 1960s and the 1970s shows an increase of 35 per cent (from 255 establishments to 345 in 1970) between 1967 and 1979. In the period 1970–5, a slight decrease of 8 per cent in the total number of establishments was registered (28 establishments) due to closure and/or delocalisation of firms to other locations within or outside the region.

Comparison between 1967 and 1979 shows an increase in the number of firms related to air cargo activities, airplane companies and related activities such as handling and maintenance of aircraft, travel agencies and retail companies (see Figure 6.12).

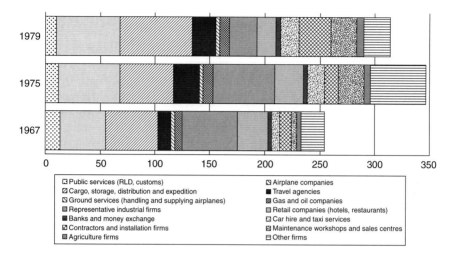

Figure 6.12 Total number of companies by sector at Schiphol airport area (1967–79).
Source: Annual Reports Schiphol Airport Company (1967–1979).

By the end of the 1970s, Schiphol had started in the direction of a new commercial strategy aimed at attracting more transfer passengers and strengthening the hub function of the airport in international air traffic networks. This strategy was based on the 'one terminal concept', where the focus was on promoting Schiphol as the best transfer airport in the world and as the 'Gateway to Europe' with regard to air cargo activities. This new commercial strategy was a prelude to the 'mainport strategy' of the 1980s.

6.8 Implications of airport spatial planning on the surrounding urban areas

During the 1960s, jet aircraft dominated commercial air traffic, and with the growing numbers of this type of airplane, the noise nuisance around airports increased substantially. Consequently, the effects of noise nuisance on the surroundings began to dominate public debates concerning the future expansion of Schiphol airport.

As noted before, with the publication of the expansion plan of 1956, the Schiphol Airport Company informed the neighbouring municipalities about the possible increase of noise nuisance for the surrounding areas. Unfortunately, most of the surrounding municipalities were more concerned with housing the increasing population and accommodating new activities and had planned new residential areas and business parks in locations that could be affected by noise nuisance from Schiphol. Examples of such urban expansion plans were the Kronenburg, Bancras and Kostverloren expansion plans developed by the municipality of Amstelveen in 1958.

To coordinate the urban expansion plans at the level of the Amsterdam agglomeration, the city of Amsterdam, in cooperation with the surrounding municipalities located in the south and southeast of the city, created the city-suburb commission (Stadsrandcommissie) in 1959. The province of North Holland was assigned the tasks of supervising this commission and coordinating the planning process at the regional level.

Note that during the 1950s, airport planning and urban planning were considered two separate fields because of the dominant idea that the airport expansion plans should be integrated into the general urban plans of the city and/ or region. However, by the end of the 1950s, the airport planning conflicted with the urban expansion planning of the surrounding municipalities. Besides the lack of information, consultation and coordination between Schiphol and its surrounding municipalities, the most important elements explaining the increased conflicts between the airport and its environs were the introduction of the jet airplane, the growing capacity of the airport's activities and, consequently, the increase in noise nuisance.

While the city planners were more concerned by the housing shortage and the increasing demand for industrial parks and office buildings, the planning for Schiphol airport was mostly dictated by the increased capacity in air traffic activities, and the complexity of airport design and construction of airport facilities.

In 1958, the need to coordinate airport planning with the urban expansion plans of Amsterdam and the surrounding municipalities became urgent. As a result, frequent consultation meetings took place between the planners of Schiphol airport and the members of the city-suburb commission, without reaching agreement about the noise nuisance issue. After the consultation with the Netherlands Air Traffic Office (RLD), the commission decided to maintain the general layout of the urban expansion plans of Amsterdam and Amstelveen.

A lack of understanding and trust, differences in their points of view, goals and perceptions and belief that only they were right pushed the parties further away from each other. Coordination of planning between the airport authorities and the surrounding municipalities was difficult to reach at this time. In fact, the parties pushed themselves into a situation of 'collective dissonance' in which each actor was defending its own interests and hoping that the other parties would be convinced to adjust their plans.

The explanation for this lies in the fact that the expansion plans of both parties were considered crucial for the future economic development of Schiphol and the surrounding areas. In addition, the greater scale of both projects and the appreciation of their own plans increased the likelihood of conflicting goals emerging. Another reason was the problem of administrative fragmentation, whereby the state, Schiphol, the local authorities and the regional authorities were not driven by the same motives to implement a common strategy aiming at reducing the noise nuisance of Schiphol to the surrounding areas. Finally, Schiphol, the state, and the surrounding municipalities were not equally informed, and lacked knowledge of each other's capabilities to deal with the problem of noise nuisance around the airport area and its implications for urban planning.

It was only in 1966, when the plans of both Schiphol and Amstelveen were realised, that coordination between the two planning fields came into discussion in the Council of Spatial Planning of the Council of Ministers.

When it became clear that the increasing conflicts between the airport and its surroundings concerning the noise nuisance were beyond the local and regional authorities, and because of the important economic position of the airport for the national economy, government intervention was concretised by integrating the Schiphol airport into the national planning scheme. The government was then able to control the effects of noise nuisance on the surrounding areas and at the same time opened the doors to Schiphol airport to expand further within specified limits. In this sense, the integration of Schiphol airport into the national planning policy may be considered to be another collective arrangement that created new opportunities for the future development of the airport.

But how did the increased noise nuisance of the airport result in serious conflicts with its surroundings? What effects has this change in the relationship between the airport and its surroundings had on the image and perceptions of the public vis-à-vis the airport and the air transport sector? The following sections provide answers to both these questions.

6.8.1 Environmental effects and changing perceptions about airports

The public enthusiasm about airports and airplane technology during the two decades after the Second World War was quickly dissipated with the introduction of jet airplanes and the increased level and scale of noise nuisance and pollution at airports and in their surrounding areas.

Back in 1956, Schiphol and Amsterdam contracted the Netherlands Organisation for Applied Scientific Research (hereafter TNO) to study the noise nuisance effects of jet aircraft on the surrounding areas, with regard to the planned construction of runway 09-27.

Although airport authorities recognised the increased noise nuisance of the jet aircraft, they claimed that the increase in the number of landings and take-offs could be maintained at acceptable levels by applying strictly the IATA procedures such as the change in landing approaches (e.g. landing angle and altitude) and take-off procedures. In addition, the construction of the new north runway 01L-19R was based on the recommendations of the US Civil Aviation Administration (FAA) stating that non-residential zones should be located at least 8 km by 2 km (length and width) from the end of the runway.

Instead of taking concrete steps to resolve the noise nuisance around the airport, Schiphol and KLM contracted external research institutes to measure the levels of noise nuisance within the airport perimeter and the surrounding areas. In the meantime, anti-airport sentiments increased with the growing concerns about the increasing noise nuisance to the surroundings. The first protest action against Schiphol airport took place in 1970, in which landing lights were destroyed and bundles of balloons were released in the vicinity of the runway 01L-19R. A new committee called 'Stop Schiphol' was then formed by the protesters and the residents of the surrounding areas, and a media offensive was started against the spatial expansion of Schiphol airport.

More generally, the increased sensitivity of the residents of the surrounding areas was also shared by the public in many other European countries. The whole industry then came under attack. In the popular imagination, air travel was equated with boredom and disaster. The media played a crucial role in changing the image and perceptions held by the public with regard to airports. In other words, the glamorised air travel of the earlier postwar period was swept away by a wave of new novels, movies and television documentaries exploring the dark side of the airport and airplane technology, e.g. airplane crashes, damage by pollution from airports, psychological and health problems among residents such as stress, sleep disturbance, cancer, etc.

With increasing public protests against the expansion of airport activities, residents of the surrounding areas, together with environmental and societal organisations, entered the public arena as new powerful actors that the airport authorities now had to deal with when planning airport expansion projects. Consequently, airport authorities and airline companies were forced to think seriously about the effects of noise nuisance on the surroundings, and to find suitable solutions to this problem (for example by developing new jet engines that produce less noise and pollution).

Most key actors involved in the discussions about the noise nuisance and the expansion plan for Schiphol agreed to investigate further the exact effects of noise nuisance on the surroundings. Therefore the Minister of Transport and Waterworks appointed the Advisory Committee on Noise Nuisance of Aircraft (ACNNA), known as the Kosten Commission, to study the issue of noise nuisance at the airport area and the surrounding urban areas. The Kosten Commission focused particular attention on the effects of noise nuisance from runway 09-27 on the residential areas of Buitenveldert (Nieuwer-Amstel) and part of the municipality of Aalsmeer, both among the most affected municpalities and with the greatest number of complaints in the surrounding urban areas.

At the same time, all over Europe, airport operators were confronted with the same problem. Most installed sound-monitoring systems to measure the spread of noise nuisance in order to map its intensity around the airport area (e.g. noise contours).[10] However, measurements of noise nuisance in decibels showed different figures over time (different years) and space, e.g. between different airports receiving the same jet airplanes.

In the case of Schiphol, the Kosten Commission proposed a prescribed minimum flight level for aircraft landing and taking off, a specified angle of descent and the preferential use of runways. In addition, the Commission suggested the creation of a specialised office to register and handle all complaints from residents suffering from the noise nuisance of aircraft landing in order to gain accurate information on the effects of airport activities on the surrounding areas. Unfortunately, the Schiphol authorities did not commit themselves to the Kosten propositions because of the absence of legal instruments to apply them in practice.

In the meantime, urban sprawl continued at the regional level due, among other things, to the increased demand for new residential areas, industrial parks and office buildings. The spatial expansion around the airport boundaries offered many opportunities to real estate developers to develop industrial and business parks for industry and service firms, especially to logistics and distribution firms, near the main transport networks (i.e. airport, railways and highways). One main feature of urban sprawl in the Amsterdam-Schiphol region is that it took place in different directions: from the city centre of Amsterdam agglomeration in the direction of Schiphol airport, but also from the Schiphol economic centre in the direction of the surrounding areas. As a result, new residential areas, industrial parks and prestigious office buildings gradually filled most of semi-urban areas located between these two urban centres.

In its final report of June 1966, the Kosten Commission advised the government to apply noise contours (in decibels and/or Kosten units) as an instrument to control the levels of noise nuisance around the airport and the surrounding areas. For example, the 62 decibel norm restricts the construction of housing and is equivalent to a noise contour of 65 Ke (e.g. Kosten units). The Ke units indicate the annual average noise nuisance (calculated by types of aircraft), the frequency of flights along specific routes and the timing (hour) of the noise nuisance. Based on the calculated annual average noise effects, various noise contours were drawn on the map, according to the intensity of noise nuisance and their effects on the surroundings. For example, in all areas falling within the zones between 65 and 45 Kosten units, about a quarter of the residential areas were identified as severely affected by noise nuisance. Although airport authorities were responsible for maintaining and respecting these zoning norms, the translation of the noise contours into an effective policy turned out to be difficult to realise in practice. Consequently, for various reasons, the power of the government to take concrete action to tackle this problem was very limited.

- First, the noise contours are not fixed in time and space, but depend on the rapidity by which land use is converted from open space to built-up area, and hence on urban sprawl and the spatial expansion of the airport itself. For example, an area of open space falling outside the noise contour in time t_0 could be built up as a residential area in time t_1, whereby large parts or the whole area may suffer from the effects of noise nuisance.
- Second, the use of measurement units, whether in decibels or Ke, has different implications on the definitive layout of noise contours.
- Third, developments in air technology (e.g. less noisy engines, new types of aircraft) and (international) regulations concerning landing and take-off procedures may result in a new layout of existing noise contours.
- Finally, the expansion of the airport, in terms of total number of runways, may lead to substantial changes in the boundaries of existing noise contours.

Because of this, noise contours show a dynamic character in the sense that they are subject to changes over time and space, as Map 6.11 of Schiphol airport shows.

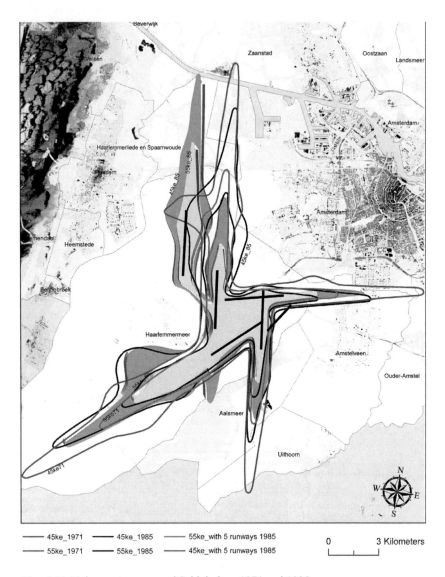

Map 6.11 Noise contours around Schiphol ca. 1971 and 1985.
Noise contours are based on four and five runways system.

It was only in 1 November 1972 that the Dutch government finally took concrete action to limit noise nuisance by allowing aircraft without a noise certificate to operate only from runway 06-24 between 24:00 and 6:00 hours. In case of bad weather conditions (e.g. strong wind), aircraft with fewer than four engines were strictly allowed to take off only from runway 01L-19R. These measures were largely based on the Chicago Convention on charting uniform noise emission standards issued by ICAO in 1971. Based on this agreement, the Netherlands government issued noise certificates to aircraft landing at Schiphol airport, and definitively banned all aircraft producing a high noise nuisance from using the (inter)national airport.

In 1978, the members of the European Civil Aviation Conference (ECAC) reached agreement about the final date (January 1987) on which all aircraft registered in ECAC countries would have to conform to the ICAO standards of 1971. After January 1987, aircraft that were not in possession of a noise certificate, following the ICAO standards, were not allowed to operate in Europe. Besides this international requirement aimed at limiting noise nuisance, the Dutch government has developed legal instruments for zoning regulation based on noise impact patterns. The National Aviation Law (hereafter NAL) provides tight government control on the growth of air traffic at the airport, and imposes building restrictions around the Schiphol area. However, despite these regulatory measures, the government was not able to stop the spatial expansion of the airport. The fifth runway was finally constructed, although with a delay of more than two decades, and Schiphol got its final shape as it was conceived by the first director of the Schiphol municipal airport and the designer of the tangential plan Jan Dellaert.

From its early years in the 1920s until today, Schiphol was and is the greatest and biggest infrastructural project in the Netherlands in the sense that the expansion and construction works at Schiphol never stopped during this long period. This is due, among other things, to the dynamic nature of the development in air transport technology and the civil aviation sector, and consequently the spatial expansion of the airport. However, since the 1970s, the rapid developments in aircraft technology and the commercialisation of civil aviation have determined largely the development path of Schiphol airport and the airport infrastructure. Dynamic changes in airside and landside activities went hand in hand. In the airside, faster and bigger aircraft made their appearance in the skies with the introduction of the supersonic airplanes and the jumbo jet aircraft. And with the introduction of the new generations of airplanes, the focus shifted from the size of aircraft to the fastest and, subsequently, to the improvement of aircraft technology such as new engines and the production of wide-body aircraft. The implications of these developments for the landside were manifested in the increasing size of airport facilities, the rapid spatial and economic development of airports and the shift in their functions and economic position at a local and regional level.

6.8.2 The safety issue

Because of the great attention that had been given by the media to safety issues, a latent feeling of fear among aircraft passengers increased after a series of airplane crashes during the 1970s, such as the crash of a Turkish Douglas DC-10 in the north of Paris in 1974, the crash at Chicago O'Hare in 1979 and the crash of a KLM Boeing 747 in Tenerife in 1977. These incidents changed the perceptions and image held by the public with regard to airplane technology and airports. A major element that played a key role in the changing of public perceptions was the sudden increase in hijacking incidents and attacks on airports during the 1970s.[11] International airports became the new front line of military and political struggles. The most dramatic hijacking took place in September 1970 when four hijacked planes (a Pan Am 747, a TWA707, a Swissair DC-8 and a BOAC VC-10) were destroyed in Jordan. A series of attacks on airports and airplanes followed this incident such as the attack on an El Al plane in Athens (1968), the PLO attack on an El-Al airplane in Zurich in 1968, the hijacking of a Sabena 707 at Lod Airport in Tel Aviv in 1972 and the attack inside the terminal of Da Vinci Airport in Rome in 1973. In response to the increasing numbers of attacks on airports, safety measures were strengthened after the ICAO passed the second anti-hijack treaty that was signed in The Hague in 1970.

The safety trend not only changed the mode of air travel but also had profound effects on airport design. In response to the airport and airplane assaults, airports adopted strict security measures such as the stationing of special armed forces inside high-risk terminals. Passengers were tightly controlled and questioned before boarding, and suspicious passengers on their own were directly singled out and interrogated in separate areas. Some airports, such as Heathrow, installed screening devices (electronic gallows) which passengers were required to walk through. The electromagnetic gateway made its entrance in airports and became the new point of transition. Departure was no longer determined by distance but rather by clearance, and security checkpoints replaced the boarding gate (Gordon, 2004: 232–4). In short, a new, more defensive style of architecture came along to match the new airport security requirements. Lobbies and concourses were closed and changed into segregated areas within the airport terminals. Passengers arriving from foreign destinations were not allowed into any other parts of the airport until they had cleared immigration control. New technology (video cameras, screening ports, electronic checkpoints, etc.) came to be widely and extensively used by airport authorities to monitor and control the movements of passengers and visitors in terminal buildings 24 hours a day. In fact, the whole airport area has become permanently observed by numbers of video cameras and other electronic detection devices. All these measures, which incidentally were further strengthened after 2001, raise several relevant questions about the meaning of airports as public spaces and urban centres.

One last important point to be stressed with regard to the implications of external factors on the air transport market in general and airport planning in particular is the implementation of deregulation policy in the USA and Europe.

With the signing of the Airline Deregulation Act in 24 October 1978 by US President Jimmy Carter, federal control over commercial fares and air routes was removed for ever (Gordon, 2004: 245). The Deregulation Act opened the doors for further liberalisation of the air transport market, and consequently more competition between scheduled airlines on lower-fare destinations, especially on transatlantic services. Airliners were then able to choose their own routes according to market conditions. As a result, airports offering high-quality services and airport facilities profited most from the deregulation in the air transport market, while less popular destinations languished. Nevertheless, deregulation also brought new uncertainty. Before deregulation, no major airline company had gone bankrupt, but in its aftermath, several leading companies in the US went out of business such as Eastern, Pan Am and Braniff.

Note that by the end of the 1970s, the USA and the Netherlands had signed a bilateral agreement that gave more landing rights to KLM in US airports in exchange for equivalent rights for scheduled and charter flights from the US to Amsterdam and other European destinations. This was the first bilateral agreement to open up completely the air transport market to airline companies from both countries. Germany and Belgium followed the Netherlands' example, and since then the deregulation of the air transport market at the international level became a fact with the application of the International Air Transport Competition Act in 1979 and the signing of a memorandum of understanding between the ECAC countries and the US concerning 'flexibility zones' for scheduled air fares on the North Atlantic route.

In Europe, the European Commission published a memorandum the main goal of which is to foster the deregulation and liberalisation of the inter-European air transport market. The Netherlands and Great Britain led the deregulation and liberalisation policy on air transport in Europe and agreed to fully liberalise air traffic between the two countries.

In this context of the deregulation and liberalisation of the air traffic market, airline companies started to concentrate their operations in a limited number of airports, and by doing this they inaugurated the concept of 'hubbing', which was seen as the most cost-effective way to link networks of remote destinations or 'spokes'. Since it was impossible to make every route profitable, flights would make (at least) one stop through a central point known as the 'hub'. For example, in the USA, Delta established its hub in Atlanta, American in Dallas and United in Chicago (Gordon, 2004: 246).

To maximise profits, hub airports adopted carefully coordinated patterns of flights arriving and departing at the peak hours. The problem for airport authorities was no longer how to move passengers from their cars to the planes, but rather how to move them from gate to gate. Hubbing demanded the friendly configuration of transfers in airports in terms of passengers and luggage.

6.9 Summary and conclusions

This chapter covers one of the most important periods in the history of airports in general, and of Schiphol airport in particular: the postwar reconstruction and development of the airport into one of the most important European transport nodes and economic centres at a regional and national level.

After the Second World War, Schiphol airport was almost completely reconstructed from scratch. Amsterdam and the government made the reconstruction of the old glorious Amsterdam-Schiphol one of their highest priorities. Despite the deplorable economic situation of the country, e.g. the severe shortage of goods, materials and equipment, and the bad financial position of Amsterdam, the city officials decided to finance the reconstruction works from its own means. With the help of the Royal Corps of Engineers and the US Air Transport Command, Amsterdam succeeded in completely rebuilding the runway system and making it operational for air traffic by the end of 1945. More attention was then given to the construction of the platform, aprons, station buildings and the technical area. By the end of 1948, Schiphol became operational and since then has developed into one of the most important junctions in transatlantic and inter-continental air traffic networks and a gateway to Central and Western Europe.

Thus Schiphol regained its position in international and European air traffic but this time in the light of two major shifts that determined largely its future growth and development. These two break moments can be considered as new collective arrangements: first the decision of the government to designate Schiphol as the country's world transatlantic and intercontinental airport in 1945; and second, the changing organisational form of Schiphol from a municipal airport into a private company with public shareholders. These two arrangements created the path through which Schiphol has been developed between 1945 and 1980. Our argument is that airport planning, the spatial expansion of the airport, the change in economic position of the airport, the rise of Schiphol as a powerful actor at the local, regional and national levels, etc., should be considered as directly and/or indirectly emanating from these two collective arrangements. Exogenous factors such changes in international regulations concerning the air transport market, changes in airplane technology and competition between national airplane companies also played a prominent role in determining the development path of airport. However, these exogenous factors have little or no impact on existing arrangements, e.g. the dynamic change of existing arrangements through the destruction and creation of new ones.

First, the rise of the first collective arrangement was the result of long discussions and debates involving various parties. The State Commission on Airfields played a key role in the decision-making process toward the designation of Schiphol by the state as the sole international airport in the Netherlands. Rotterdam and KLM were against the government decision. Rotterdam was disappointed because of the degradation of its own municipal airport, and KLM because of the desire of its director to concentrate all KLM activities in one central location, preferably in the southern part of Haarlemmermeer. Plesman started his offensive by producing a series of reports on the issue of the 'central location of the national airport', which he used to convince the government of Burgerveen it was the best location for the international airport of the Netherlands. After intense discussions, the government took the decision to close the Burgerveen dossier in 1948. The government decision opened the doors for the implementation of the ambitious expansion plan at Schiphol: the tangential plan. In itself, the tangential plan may be considered a collective arrangement in the sense that it has shaped the basic framework for the development of future expansion plans at the airport. In other words, the tangential plan is path-dependent because every expansion plan for the airport has been laid out according to this basic arrangement. The choice for the tangential plan had direct and/or indirect effects on various domains such as airport and urban planning, and on the economic, social and cultural fields (employment, noise nuisance, etc.). The revisited expansion plan of 1956 preserved the basic ideas expressed in the original plan of 1948 and brought only small changes to the tangential plan. However, regular changes to and revisions of airport planning were needed because of the fast increase in air traffic and airline technology. As aircraft became bigger and faster, airport authorities were obliged to reconsider their expansion plans with regard to the extension of runways, aprons, platforms, terminal buildings, etc.

Note, however, that during this period, the number of actors involved with the development of Schiphol was limited to a few key players (Amsterdam, the state, the RLD, KLM) sharing the same beliefs and ideas about the future development of Schiphol into an international airport. The case of Schiphol shows that the rise of a new collective arrangement was in the first place the result of long negotiations and consultations between actors with different interests and backgrounds and serving different agendas. During the long trajectory of the decision-making process, some privileged actors acquired stronger positions of power than others, some of them became weak and even disappeared from the playing field (as was the case of the Ministry of War for example), and other new actors took over their positions. In addition, some actors used their position of power to influence the decision-making process (such as KLM for example), while others were indirectly involved but have had considerable influence in changing the perception and vision of some of the actors involved and hence the decision-making process itself. This was the case, for example, with (contracted) external research institutes, which produced a number of important studies and reports supporting the point of view of some of the actors. In short, actors used research as weapons to influence the final decision about specific issues (see our discussion concerning the Burgerveen affair).

Perhaps the most important reason why collective arrangements were agreed in a relatively short time was the existence of a sense of urgency that was shared by the majority of actors about the need to rebuild Schiphol as an international airport. The general and dominant idea among people, business organisations and policy-makers at that time was that the reconstruction of the country and the recovery of the economy were among the country's highest priorities. To reach this goal, the recovery and improvement of the infrastructure was considered crucial.

Schiphol, which was fully dependent on Amsterdam, did not play any significant role as an independent actor. Schiphol was still functioning under the basic collective arrangement dating from the prewar period, namely the 'Schiphol municipal airport'. However, the rapid increase in air traffic and airline technologies during the first decades of the postwar period put much pressure on the financial capacity of the municipality of Amsterdam to meet the growing demands from the airport with regard to the construction and expansion projects that were needed. As a result, Amsterdam turned to the state and asked for financial support. This brings us to the birth and emergence of a second collective arrangement, which is complementary to the first: the rise of Schiphol as a private organisation serving public interests.

Second, the state was prepared to provide Amsterdam with the financial help it needed but under the condition that the ownership of Schiphol airport be shared. Long negotiations between Amsterdam and the state followed in the 1950s before a final agreement was reached in 1957. Amsterdam agreed to share the exploitation and ownership of Schiphol with the state. Under this agreement, Schiphol became officially an anonymous partnership company, with the state, Amsterdam and Rotterdam as the main shareholders. The formalisation of this agreement in 1958 constitutes the birth of a new collective arrangement and the death of the old one dating from 1926. Schiphol was then officially decoupled from Amsterdam and became an independent and powerful player whose main goal was to defend its own interests and realise its own objectives. This situation brought many changes to the relationship between Schiphol and the surrounding urban areas but also to Schiphol itself in terms of internal and external coordination and the economic position of Schiphol at the local, regional and national levels, e.g. commercialisation and a market-oriented strategy and the widespread economic effects on the region.

The implications of this collective arrangement touched many fields at the same time, among them being: (1) *the institutional field*, whereby the decision-making process for the expansion of Schiphol became complex due to the increased number of actors and the shifts in their positions and in the relationships between Schiphol and the surrounding areas; (2) *the urban planning field*, especially in terms of conflicts between the spatial expansion of the airport and the urban planning schemes of the surrounding municipalities; (3) *the economic field*, in terms of the shift in economic position of Schiphol at the regional and national level and the focus of Schiphol on market-oriented strategies (commercialisation and competitiveness). Let us recapitulate these three elements:

1. *The institutional field.* The number of actors increased substantially between 1960 and 1980. New actors entered the scene and with them, the roles and power positions of existing actors changed too. The following examples are worth mentioning in this respect:
    - The position of the state was strengthened through its direct involvement in the operation and development of Schiphol.
    - The position of Haarlemmermeer changed too as Schiphol became a private organisation. Haarlemmermeer was now able to negotiate directly with Schiphol about various issues related to airport expansion and land reservation for future expansion and the location of economic activities in the areas directly surrounding the airport.
    - Cooperation between Schiphol and the province of North Holland shifted too as the province became actively involved in indicating and controlling the localisation of firms around the airport. As a result, the

province integrated the future expansion plans of the airport into the provincial economic and spatial plans.

- With the increased negative effects of noise nuisance, the residents of the surrounding municipalities and environmental organisations became powerful actors that Schiphol had to deal with in order to realise its ambitious expansion projects.

2. *The urban planning field.* The increased capacity of the airport due to the introduction of jet airplanes and increased air traffic (passengers and freight) raised the issue of noise nuisance and the expansion of the airport. The airport expansion plan of 1956 and the urban expansion plans of the surrounding urban areas began to conflict with each other. While airport planning was mainly driven by the increased capacity and complexity of airport construction, urban planning was more driven by socio-demographic and economic changes. In other words, airport planning and urban planning were two separate worlds where coordination, exchange of information and consultation between the airport authorities and the surrounding areas were lacking.

With the introduction of bigger and faster airplanes, the spatial scale of the Schiphol airport area and the airport activities increased substantially. Airport planning became more and more complex because extensions to and/or construction of runways were determining factors for the construction of terminal buildings, platforms, aprons and so on. Schiphol airport was no longer a single entity but a complex structure formed by various integrated elements. The realisation of the expansion plans for Schiphol needed more space, and in terms of the layout and airport facilities, Schiphol began to show new spatial and functional patterns which looked very much like an existing small downtown city centre. The spatial and economic transformation of the airport was closely related to its transition from a pure provider of air services towards an integrated spatial node providing a wide range of functions related to airside as well as landside activities.

Note that with the spatial and economic development of Schiphol airport, the environmental costs increased substantially. Schiphol was confronted by increasing protests from the surrounding areas against the expansion plans due to the increase in noise nuisance. However, the noise nuisance would not be easy to solve by Schiphol alone. The intervention of the state and changes in international requirements to limit the noise nuisance at airport areas and their surroundings was necessary. After endless debates over noise contours and restriction zones around the airport, the government put into action new legal instruments for zoning regulation, based on noise impact patterns. The drawing of noise contours served as guidelines to control the future spatial growth of the airport. In addition, to avoid conflicts between airport planning and urban planning in the surrounding urban areas, the government integrated the spatial planning of the airport into the national planning scheme. The government was then able to control the environmental effects of the airport on the surrounding areas and, at the same time, give Schiphol the opportunity to expand further within specified limits.

3.   *The economic field*. From 1957, Schiphol had become a private organisation aiming to maximise profits. Due to the shift in the market structure of commercial aviation and the commercial policy of Schiphol, the airport grew substantially (albeit with relative stagnation during the oil crisis and the terrorist attacks of the 1970s) to become one of the most important hubs in Europe. The commercial policy of Schiphol shifted towards price competition, diversification of products and segmentation of the air market (i.e. by destinations, through leisure travel and through the introduction of the tourist class), and close cooperation with travel agencies. The marketing strategy shifted from the promotion of destinations to the promotion of high-quality services on board. However, the decreasing profits of airplane companies, due to increased competition and increasing costs, pushed the airport authorities to seek new ways to diversify their sources of revenue. The first steps taken in this direction were the granting of concessions for tax-free shops at the terminal building to third parties, and the rental of airport buildings, land and other airport facilities to external parties. This successful commercial strategy resulted in further improvements in commercial products in the airport area, e.g. hotels, restaurants, car rental, etc. The concept of the airport plaza turned out to be successful as the main driving source of additional revenue generated from landside activities.

The improvement of the economic position of Schiphol was manifested by the continuing growth of key economic variables such as employment, revenues and profits. As a result, Schiphol developed into one of the most successful growth centres of the Amsterdam-Schiphol region in terms of employment, productivity and economic growth.

The economic position of the Schiphol at the regional and national level was strengthened by two main factors:

- the development of Schiphol into one of the most important central transport nodes in European and international air transport networks, and the connectivity of Schiphol to different infrastructure networks (air, railroad, roads) at different scale levels (local, regional, national and international);

- the development of Schiphol into an economic centre generating important economies of agglomeration: Schiphol became a very attractive location with strong pull-effects on workers and firms, especially those who were related to airport activities such as the headquarters of multinational companies operating logistics and distribution activities, and in high-tech sectors and services (such as finance and banking).

From a spatial-economic perspective, the spatial structure and the economic functions of Schiphol airport show a strong similarity with the traditional urban centre of a large city. On the one hand, the morphological and economic transformation of the airport was closely related to the shift in urban systems, i.e. from a monocentric hierarchical system to a more polynuclear urban system (the rise of the city network system). Moreover, the spatial transformation of Schiphol airport was accompanied by the spatial expansion of the Schiphol region, due particularly to the growing demand for space for housing, business parks and office buildings in proximity to the airport areas and along transport corridors, e.g. highways and railway networks. From this perspective, urban sprawl took place in both directions: from the city of Amsterdam in the direction of the Schiphol region, and from Schiphol airport in the direction of the Amsterdam agglomeration.

On the other hand, the economic transformation of Schiphol was also affected by the shift in economic structure, i.e. from an industrial-based economy to a service-oriented economy, where connectivity, diversity, accessibility and proximity became the main driving forces of regional economic growth. Schiphol had all the necessary ingredients to play a prominent role in the service-oriented economy, especially from the 1980s onward.

Finally, it is worth mentioning that the changed market structure in the air transport market pushed Schiphol airport authorities to follow an aggressive market-oriented strategy at the end of the 1970s, which also played an important role in accelerating the spatial and economic transformation of Schiphol and the Schiphol region. For example, since the 1970s, Schiphol had started a new commercial strategy aimed at attracting more transfer passengers to strengthen the hub function of the airport in the international air transport market. This strategy was supported by the 'one terminal' concept as a marketing instrument in promoting Schiphol as the best transfer airport in the world and as the 'Gateway to Europe' (especially for cargo activities). Based on the successful 'one terminal' concept strategy, in the 1980s the Schiphol authorities introduced a new policy aimed at developing the position of Schiphol as a 'mainport'. But this time, Schiphol was supported by local, regional and national authorities alike.

7 Spatial-economic transformation of the Amsterdam-Schiphol region 1945–80

From monocentric to polynuclear
urban system

7.1 Introduction

The spatial and economic transformation of cities and the countryside is a long continuing process that goes back to the industrialisation of western countries during the nineteenth century. However, during the second half of the twentieth century, the processes of urbanisation and industrialisation drastically changed the spatial and functional structures of cities and regions. The radical shift in spatial patterns and economic structure of cities is the result of complex processes involving various incremental small changes at the spatial, technological, political, economic, socio-cultural and institutional levels.

Many traditional industrial cities have lost their dominance and economic position to new emerging cities and suburban towns. As a result, the economic position of traditional urban centres was challenged by the growth and development of suburban towns.

More generally, the spatial transformation of cities and their suburbs is strongly related to changes in land use patterns and activities, and the movements of people, goods, capital and information that, together, generate the structure, size and functions of urban areas. In this sense, the transformation of the topographic (or geographic) space represents the transformations occurring in the topological space (or economic space). In other words, there is not only a transition in terms of urban forms/patterns, but also a transition in the functional relationships within and between cities and their surrounding areas and the countryside. As a result, complex patterns of flows, which vary with the form, functions and structure of cities and regions, occur (Daniels, 1999). In this sense, one may argue that the transformation of urban patterns and the economic structure, functions and position of regions and cities can be traced back to global shifts, which took place in the economic space and the geographical space at different spatial scales (regions, cities, countryside, etc.) during different periods.

Globally, two different points of views may be distinguished. First, from an economic point of view, the sequence and rhythm of the urban transformation of cities and the countryside can be understood in terms of change in economic structure occurring in the economic space. That is, the sectoral shift from agriculture to industry and from industry to services, and the corresponding changes in the dominant modes of organisation and production, e.g. from Taylorism (management structure of firms (nineteenth century)) to Fordism or the mode of mass-production and finally to post-Fordism or the flexible production system.

The literature shows that the shift from industrial to post-industrial society was the result of the increased deindustrialisation, economic decline and decrease in economic growth which occurred during the 1970s in most industrialised countries. In turn, the increasing deconcentration of the population was concomitantly followed by an increasing spread of economic activities over larger geographical areas, together with the accompanying change in the organisational structure of firms from vertically integrated production units to more (vertically and horizontally) disintegrated industrial firms. In other words, firms became spatially more 'footloose', due to the increase in communication and information technologies and the decreasing importance of traditional locational factors such transport costs and accessibility to natural resources or suppliers of intermediate goods.

Another important shift in economic structure was the transition from an industry-based economy to a services-oriented economy in most industrialised countries. With this shift, (dynamic) external economies (diversity and knowledge spillovers) became crucial in determining the locational behaviour of workers and activities. The strong concentration of economic activities in large agglomerations resulted in an increase in the functional specialisation and diversity of large cities, and hence to more competition between cities and between cities and their surrounding areas.

Some authors (for example, Scott, 2001) suggest that the combination of both strong externalities and high transaction costs have triggered a shift towards more flexible modes of production and organisation, and hence to the formation of urban networks through the spatial clustering of firms and activities.

Second, and from the geographical point of view, the sequence and rhythm of urban transformation of cities and the countryside can be understood in the light of the shift from monocentric hierarchical urban structures towards polynuclear urban networks that are formed by multiple complementary urban sub-centres, which are referred to as a city region, urban network, urban field, urban nebula, metropolis, etc.

The growing mobility of the population (i.e. interregional and international migration) has put cities under considerable pressure, especially with regard to the increasing exodus of the middle-class from cities to suburban areas, which resulted in relatively weak social structure of cities, i.e. deteriorating living conditions and livability in city neighbourhoods. Moreover, the extensive and expansive land use, agglomeration and deconcentration of people and activities resulted in the emergence of the city region as the new geographical expression of more or less self-contained social, demographic, cultural and economic processes taking place in the housing and labour markets, transport, etc. (Musterd and Salet, 2003: 16).

Note, however, that the transformation of urban system from a monocentric to a polynuclear urban system and the rise of the regional city (as opposed to the central city) is a complex process involving various aspects such as the content of urban forms (patterns) and functions (structure). In this sense, the emergence of the city region or urban nebula reflects the physical, social and economic fragmentation or 'splintering' of economic space, resulting in unbalanced economic, political, environmental and spatial systems (Graham and Marvin, 2001).

Within the urban nebula, different spatial nodes of (new) economic development may show strong functional relationships through the integrating forces of infrastructure, communication, technologies, agglomeration economies and their linkages to the increasing scale of the labour and housing markets. In other words, there is not only a transition in terms of forms, e.g. expanding urban areas with the associated linkages and communications, but also in terms of functional relationships in the larger territorial space. Viewed from this perspective, transformations of urban space involve changes in the functional relationships between urban activities and changes in the spatial patterns of the territorial space. In turn, continuing changes in the production process produce new spaces of production in new urban configurations (Storper, 1993, 1995; Scott, 1988a, 1988b 1998; Amin, 1994).

Besides the fact that cities and towns are the product of economic and social forces, they are strongly dependent for their existence on processes of governance and government policy. In the collective life of the city, the government intervenes in the economic, social and political domains to balance many different interests and interactions between actors (local authorities, individual citizens, organisation groups, etc.) and provides suitable instruments and guidelines aimed at resolving regional and urban problems that could hamper the quality of life in cities. More specifically, government policies, especially the spatial and (regional) economic policies, try to influence the spatial and economic processes by applying spatial planning schemes based on simultaneous process of both centralisation/decentralisation and industrialisation policies in order to solve regional discrepancies with regard to economic growth and development. However, the realisation of prescribed policy objectives is difficult because of the nature of external factors that structurally alter the economic position of cities.

In order to identify and analyse the main urban development processes, we retrospectively focus on an examination of urbanisation processes and economic changes from a historical perspective, and at the same time identify the simultaneity of continuity and discontinuity of (historical) changes in the spatial patterns and economic structure of the Amsterdam and Schiphol regions between 1945 and the 1980s. This analytical approach provides a better understanding of how cities and regions function and transform over time.

This chapter is organised as follows. The first section (section 7.2) examines and describes the main aspects of the socio-cultural and demographic changes that took place in the Netherlands during the postwar period 1945–80s. Section 7.3 analyses the factors affecting the economic change at the national and regional levels, with special focus on the underlying factors explaining the shift from an industry-based economy to a services-based economy. In section 7.4, we extend our analysis to the Amsterdam region, with a special focus on the economic structure and the economic transformation of the Amsterdam economy. We turn then in section 7.5 to the analysis of the spatial structure and the spatial transformation of Amsterdam between 1945 and 1990. In this section, more attention is devoted to the relationships between the spatial transformation of Amsterdam and the Amsterdam-Schiphol region. Section 7.6 extends the analysis in sections 7.4 and 7.5 to the Schiphol – and more particularly to the Haarlemmermeer-Schiphol – regions. Section 7.7 concludes.

7.2 Socio-cultural and demographic changes in the Netherlands

7.2.1 Socio-cultural changes: 1960s–90s

Since 1900, the social, cultural and political construction of the Netherlands was based on the gradual 'pacification' of different social groups (Catholics, Protestants, Socialists and Liberals) along social, political and religious lines. This has been described as the 'pillarisation' of the Dutch society (Goudsblom, 1967). Within this typical Dutch corporatism, cities, regions and societal organisations were considered to be self-governing entities in the sense that they could perform some public responsibilities and provide goods and services to their citizens, such as, for example, housing, health care, sports, libraries and media (radio/television).

More generally, up until the 1950s, traditional family values and the pillarisation formed the basic structure of Dutch society. However, since the 1960s, structural societal transformations have taken place in the Netherlands. The most important societal transformation was the transition from a traditional family-based society to a more individualised society, as a result of the shift from a materialist to a post-materialist culture (Terhorst and Ven, 2003: 93). Under the influence of the secularisation process, the emergence of powerful urban social movements, the increase of mass-consumption, women's emancipation, youth culture, etc., the very conformist and traditional Dutch society evolved into a modern and open society. The diminishing influence of traditional moral values, the decreasing importance of societal norms and the increasing standard of living gave rise to new consumption patterns and lifestyles based on individual freedom (Pater *et al.*, 1989). In turn, the diversity in lifestyles of individuals and households resulted in different preferences and tastes with regard to the living environment and consumption patterns (Vijgen and Engelsdorp Gastelaars, 1992).

Furthermore, the democratisation of the automobile and the growth of mass motoring, which fuelled the processes of suburbanisation and urban sprawl, also played an important role in increasing the differences between social classes. While many of the new lifestyles and labour class thrived in the city, the more traditional and middle-class households started a massive migration to the suburban areas. In this context, the state initiated national physical planning around 1960 with the main goal to guide and control, as much as possible, the suburbanisation process and the deconcentration of the population and activities from larger cities to suburban areas and the countryside. To reach this goal, the state forced smaller municipalities to merge with their neighbours, and designated several middle-sized towns as growth centres (Terhorst and Ven, 1998: 472).

In the early 1980s, the Netherlands was badly hit by the economic crisis and rising unemployment. A growing consensus among social partners (e.g. employers' organisations and labour unions) and the state about the need to reform the social security and taxation systems in order to stimulate the Dutch economy became urgent. This resulted in the signature of the so-called 'Wassenaar Agreement' in 1982. Following this agreement, the labour unions accepted the freezing of wages and refrained from making wage demands. Additional policy measures were launched by the government aimed at reforming the welfare state, such as cuts in public spending and the salaries of state employees, the deregulation of markets and the privatisation of state-owned companies as well as further administrative decentralisation. By the end of the 1980s, these measures resulted in a lower budgetary deficit, lower social security contributions and taxes and a moderate rate of economic growth.

At the regional level, the government policy measures affected directly the economies of cities and regions, and indirectly the relationships between cities and the government, which was until then based on strong cooperation between the two parties. Large cities were directly affected by the reduction in public funds, especially the four big cities in the Randstad that were forced to shift their policy from a welfare-state city policy to a more urban pro-growth policy. The state and state agencies stimulated private initiatives and private-public cooperation in the development of common (urban) projects.

7.2.2 Demographic changes: 1960s–90s

The western regions of the Netherlands witnessed a high increase in the urban population during the first half of the twentieth century. However, this tendency was reversed during the second half of the twentieth century, as most of the densely populated central cities have lost population in favour of suburban areas and to the surrounding countryside. As a result, new settlement patterns have emerged that are determined by a variety of motives, e.g. living, commuting, recreation and retirement. Many suburb areas, such as Haarlemmermeer, once fully rural, have been absorbed into the thriving metropolitan region. Retail centres and office parks have followed the movement of the urban population to the suburbs. In turn, the spatial range and patterns of commuter movements have expanded further.

More generally, the demographic changes have had a direct influence on the spatial distribution of population within and between the cities and regions. This is because of existing differences in (housing) preferences, tastes, income, education, age, etc., and between different categories of population. Consequently, the growth in population and the accompanying change in the structure and composition of households are key determining elements of the urbanisation and suburbanisation processes that took place in the Netherlands during the 1950s to the 1970s.

First, the structure of the Dutch population between 1950 and 1970 was char-acterised by a continuing increase (in absolute terms), a low death rate and a high birth rate, an increase in the proportion of of elderly households (55 years and older) in the total population, and a relatively high increase in inter-regional and international immigrations flows.

Between 1950 and 1960, the population of the Netherlands increased by 13.8 per cent, from 10 million inhabitants to 11.4 million. This was the largest increase in the past 50 years. Over the whole period 1950–2000, the Dutch popu-lation doubled (from 8 million to 16 million). The share of women in the total population is slightly higher than men (especially since the 1980s), but the growth rates show almost the same levels. However, when looking at the growth rate of the population by age, a different picture emerges. The population cate-gory under 20 first increased by 35 per cent between 1945 and 1966 (from 3.4 million to 4.6 million in 1966), and then decreased below 4 million between 1967 and 2000. The 'baby boom' reached its highest level in 1966. The popula-tion category 20–45 increased progressively from 1945 to 1992, and relatively faster between 1960 and 1992 (from 3.7 million to 6.1 million), before declining to 5.6 million in 2007. Finally, the population categories of 45–65 years and above 65 show in general a continuing increase in the total population. This can be interpreted as evidence of the rapid increase in the proportion of the elderly category in the total population from the 1980s onward.

Other factors determining demographic change are the natural increase in the population, i.e. increasing births and decreasing deaths, and the internal and external migration flows.

As Figure 7.1 shows, the decline in natural growth and the growth of the popu-lation as a whole followed much the same pattern, while the decline in the natural growth of the population seems to be compensated by the growing excess of migration since the 1960s. In this sense, migration flows have become of equal importance to the natural growth of the population.

Two waves of emigration flows can be distinguished during the postwar period: the first wave took place between 1947 and 1949 in which some 53,000 Dutch people emigrated to Australia, Canada and the USA. The second wave of emigration followed in the 1950s (i.e. the period 1951–60), in which a total of 180,000 people moved to various foreign countries. However, from the beginning of the 1960s, international immigration has been continually rising, in both abso-lute and relative terms. Between 1960 and 1990, the numbers of foreigners increased by more than five times, due mainly to the increase in family reunions and the inflows of refugees. In 1960, fewer than 120,000 foreigners were living in the Netherlands. By 1990 the country had approximately 640,000 foreigners, representing about 4.3 per cent of the total population (Nijkamp and Goede, 2002: 10–11).

Another important demographic factor is the development of the potential labour force. In the Netherlands, the increase in labour supply has been estimated at approximately 60,000 man years annually in the period 1975–90, which is significantly higher than in any other period since the Second World War

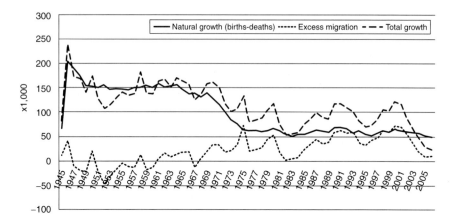

Figure 7.1 Growth of population and migration flows between 1945 and 2005.
Source: CBS, Historical Data (Historische Bevolking Nederland).

(De Beer and Veeneklaas, 1978). This high increase in the potential labour force was caused by a change in the structure of the population and the increased participation of women in the labour market. The share of women in total employment increased from about 26 per cent in 1969 to 31 per cent in 1976 and 40 per cent in 1993 (see Figure 7.2).

Note, however, that there exists a clear difference in the level of employment between men and women and the type of job exercised by each of these two categories in the labour force. While the majority of men have a full-time job, women are over-represented in the segments of the labour market offering part-time and flexible jobs. Between 1969 and 1983, the total number of women that have a part-time job doubled (from more than 400,000 to almost 800,000), while

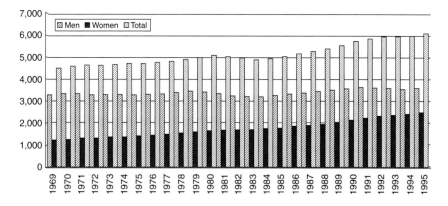

Figure 7.2 Labour participation in the Netherlands between 1960 and 1995.
Source: CBS (EBB, NR).

those working on a full-time basis increased slightly between 1969 and 1979 (from 700,000 to 800,000), and decreased in the period 1980–9.

Turning now to the changes in household formation and type of household, one may argue that the demographic, social-cultural tendencies and economic conditions have had (in)direct effects on household formation (marriages, divorces, moving out, etc.). In turn, the composition and size of household directly affect the housing market and the demand for public services.

In the Netherlands, the rate of household formation has been declining since 1947, as the average size of household has decreased from 3.7 in 1947 to less than 2.5 today. This means that the same number of people in 2007 require more housing than in the 1960s, for example (up to 30 per cent more housing). One explanation of the decreasing tendency in household formation is the changing lifestyle and the increase in wealth of households since the 1960s, which has resulted in a lower birth rate and the number of children per household, and an increase in the proportion of one- and two-person households in the total population, especially in larger cities (Jobse and Musterd, 1992). In addition, and as a result of the increase of female participation in the labour market, the number of two-earner households has been increasing in the Netherlands during the period 1970–2007.

Finally, a strong relationship exists between the change in household composition and land use. One of the main driving forces of suburbanisation is the change in the formation and size of households. For example, due to the effects of the economic crises of the 1970s, many small family households could not afford to move to suburban areas. In contrast, during the second half of the 1980s, the recovery of the Dutch economy resulted in an increase in the number of households that moved to suburban areas. However, due to the success of large-scale urban renewal projects in the traditional inner-city neighbourhoods of the big cities, especially in Amsterdam, Utrecht and Rotterdam, a significant number of high-income households (the so-called 'yuppies') began to move to these areas (i.e. the process of gentrification). This tendency for re-urbanisation has been explained by the increased importance of cultural and creative industries in big cities, and the shift from an industry-based to a more services-based economy.

Evidence supporting urbanisation, de-urbanisation and re-urbanisation tendencies can be demonstrated by analysing the changes in the housing market, more particularly the total production of and changes in the housing stock in the four big cities of the Randstad in 1970, 1980 and 1995, and by verifying whether these changes followed the same patterns in the urban population and household composition.

Because the majority of the population and households in the Netherlands live in the western part of the country, the largest amount of housing construction would be expected to take place in this region. Indeed, as Figure 7.3 shows, the highest levels of housing production, e.g. total number of new houses, took place in the four big cities of Amsterdam, Rotterdam, Utrecht and The Hague, where the highest concentrations of population and activities can also be found.

Further examination of the type of housing and the total number of rooms between 1947 and 1993 shows a spectacular increase in single-family housing, with four rooms or more, from the 1950s to the 1970s. This may be interpreted

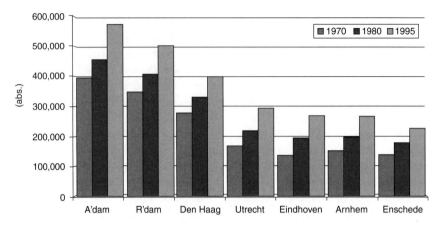

Figure 7.3 Housing production in larger Dutch cities (1970, 1980, 1990).
Source: CBS (REJ and NR).

as evidence supporting the fact that new housing outstripped basic household formation, particularly in the type of housing built in (sub)urban locations, e.g. single family houses with more than four rooms. Note that the majority of new housing units built during this period concern mainly the social housing sector and, to a less extent, privately owned dwellings. While this is true for the core urban areas in the Randstad-Holland, the suburban and peripheral areas, however, have generally more private homeowners than the urban areas. Amsterdam, for example, has less homeownership than its surrounding urban areas.

7.3 Economic transformations at the national and regional level: from an industry- to a services-based economy

During the Second World War, most big cities were severely damaged and suffered great shortages in almost everything after the war (goods, construction material, labour force, capital, etc.). Fortunately, Amsterdam, The Hague and Rotterdam recovered relatively quickly. By the end of the 1950s almost all functions of these urban agglomerations had been restored and further improved (Rooy *et al*., 2007: 338). The road to recovery for the Dutch economy was set up by generous external financial support (the Marshall Plan), massive investment (public and private), public financial support and other measures applied by the state to stimulate the economy. As a result, the production of goods increased significantly, as well as the levels of employment, value added and investments. More generally, the early years of the post-Second World War may be described as a period of relatively strong economic growth. The government was directly involved in setting up, managing and sustaining high-quality public infrastructure, including physical infrastructure and public services, and played an important role in stimulating economic growth through the implementation of successive industrialisation and regional policies. Note, however, that because of

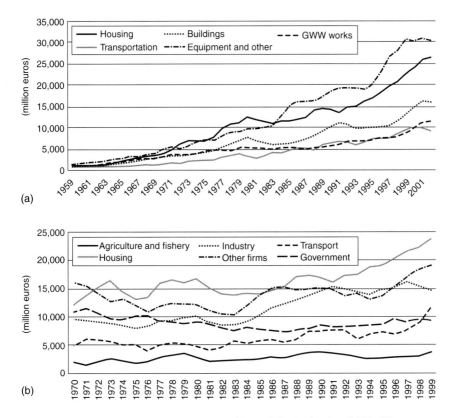

Figure 7.4 Investments by (a) type (1959–2002), and (b) destination (1970–99).
Source: CBS (NR/National Account and REJ/regional data).

the specific financial circumstances of the state, austerity and cost-effectiveness
were the key determining elements of public investments aimed at strengthening
the economic structure during the early years after the Second World War.

As Figure 7.4 shows, a large part of public investment concerned housing
construction, other buildings and equipment. By destination, investments were
more oriented towards industry, the construction sector and public services.
While the share of investment in the industry and construction sectors maintained
high levels following the 1970s, total investment in services increased rapidly
during the second half of the 1970s, before dropping to less than 8 million euros
in 1987. However, in relative terms, the share of public investment in total investment (public and private) decreased, respectively, from 20 per cent to 17 per cent,
14 per cent and 12 per cent in 1970, 1980, 1990 and 1999, while the share of
investment by private firms increased in the same years from, respectively, 80 per
cent to 83 per cent, 86 per cent and 88 per cent in 1999.

At the regional level, the highest levels of investment (private and public) were
registered in the two provinces of the Randstad-Holland, and more particularly in the

cities of Amsterdam and Rotterdam. Since the 1980s, North Brabant, with Eindhoven as an important urban centre, and Gelderland (the agglomeration of Arnhem and Nijmegen) were clearly in a race to catch up with the big cities of the Randstad.

Note that because of the limited size of the national market, the Dutch economy was greatly dependent on activities with either regional or international supply and demand markets. The Netherlands' position in international trade helped the Dutch economy to recover rapidly and to reach high levels of economic growth, and in particular the intra-European trade increased significantly from the 1950s. In this respect, the two cornerstones of the Dutch economy – the port of Rotterdam and the airport of Schiphol – played a major role in supporting the increase of intra-European trade.

In 1950, 72 per cent of the Netherland's total exports were destined for Europe. This percentage increased from 74 per cent in 1960 to 82.5 per cent in 1980 and to 85 per cent in 1990. Compared to intra-European trade, the Netherlands' exports to the USA formed a marginal (and decreasing) share of the total exports: about 1 per cent in 1950, 1.06 per cent in 1960, 0.8 per cent in 1970, 0.4 per cent in 1980 and 0.5 per cent in 1990.

In addition to investments and the gains from trade, economic growth in the Netherlands can be analysed by looking at other economic indicators such as the level and growth of GDP, employment, incomes, production and value added at the sectoral level.

The ratio of gross government spending to GDP rose from 45 per cent to 67 per cent in the period 1970–83, while the GDP per capita grew even faster, from 100 per cent in 1960–70 to 300 per cent by the end of 1996. Between 1960 and 1989, GDP per head of the population was 24,200 in 1960, 50,000 in 1973 and 60,600 in 1989 (values in price levels of 2007 Int$).

While the share of agriculture in GDP decreased between 1970 and 1980 to under 20 per cent, the share of business and commercial services increased spectacularly, as well as the share of the non-profit sector. Over the whole period 1970–2000, the proportion of industry in GDP was decreasing, while trade and retail industry, transport and communication, and business services increased their share of GDP from the 1980s.

At the regional level, the evolution of the GDP of the 40 Dutch urban agglomerations (e.g. Corop-regions) from 1970 to 2000 shows a clear domination of the four urban agglomerations of the Randstad-Holland, i.e. greater Amsterdam (growth rate of more than 5 per cent), greater Rijnmond (4 per cent), Utrecht (3.76 per cent) and The Hague (2.3 per cent).

While the regions of the Randstad show a sustained and increasing growth in GDP, peripheral regions by contrast show swings in the growth rate, e.g. a high growth rate during the period 1970–80 followed by a significant decrease in the period 1980–90, and in some cases even a negative growth rate, as in Groningen for example (9.5 per cent to –4 per cent).

More generally, and over the whole period 1970–2000, the growth rates for GDP realised in the northern part of the Randstad (northern wing) and the southern part (southern wing) were almost equal at, respectively, 15.95 per cent and 15.15 per cent (see Map 7.1).

From Map 7.1, three main observations can be made. First, the periphery and intermediate regions show the highest GDP levels in the agriculture and fishing sector. This is the case, for example, in North Friesland, the southern parts of South Holland (Zeeusch-Vlanderen and parts of Zeeland), the eastern regions of Veluwe and Achterhoek-Arnhem/Nijmegen and southeast Gelderland, and the southeastern region of North Brabant.

Second, the industry is more concentrated in the Randstad, especially within and around the agglomerations of Amsterdam and Rijnmond (Rotterdam and the surrounding areas) and in the northern part of Groningen (Delfzijl and surroundings). From 1980, however, the regions of Utrecht, Zeeusch-Vlanderen, the Brabant region (North Brabant), and Arnhem-Nijmegen registered high GDP growth. This increase can be explained by the delocalisation of industry from the central regions of the Randstad to the intermediate and peripheral zones, and more particularly in the proximity of and along the corridors (highways) linking the Randstad with the border regions (Germany and Belgium).

Third, business services, particularly in finance and banking, and transport and communication are highly concentrated in the Amsterdam region and in the cities of Utrecht and Rotterdam.

The growth in GDP is mirrored by the increase in employment, production and value added. With regard to employment, the labour force grew by 38,000 per year during the 1950s and by 52,000 per year during the 1960s. The total labour force doubled between 1960 and 1980: from approximately 4.2 million in 1960 to 4.7 million in 1970 and 8.9 million in 1980.

The distribution of the labour force by sector shows significant changes in employment levels. Between 1947 and 1971, the absolute number of jobs in agriculture declined from 747,000 to 291,000, and in the mining sector from 54,000 jobs to 20,000. By contrast, the total number of jobs in manufacturing industry increased from 1 million to 1.2 million. The most remarkable growth took place in the services sector: from 1.7 million jobs in 1947 to 2.6 million in 1971.

However, some 356,000 jobs in the private sector were lost in the period 1970 to 1980 as a result of decreasing employment in agriculture (51,000), manufacturing industry (252,000) and the construction sector (53,000). The sharp decline in employment in industry during 1974–83 pushed policy-makers to implement new policy instruments aimed at stimulating investment in innovative projects (Bartels and Duin, 1981: 11). In the tertiary sector, e.g. business and commercial services, the number of jobs increased by 142,000. Between 1970 and 1995, employment in financial and business services grew by 4 per cent, and in services related to real estate activities by 3.5 per cent. Figure 7.5 shows the growth of employment by sector in the Netherlands between 1970 and 1995.

At the regional level, the total number of jobs in all economic sectors was higher in the two provinces of North and South Holland, the province of North Brabant and Gelderland, and finally in the provinces of Utrecht and Limburg. Figure 7.6 shows the regional distribution of employment (absolute number of jobs) in agriculture, manufacturing industry and services (tertiary sector) in 1973, 1983 and 1993.

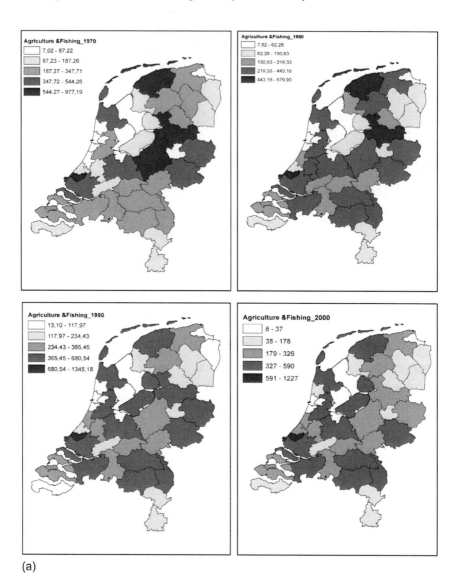

(a)

Map 7.1 Regional growth of GDP by sector (maps a, b, c, and d): 1970–2000.
Source: based on CBS data (REJ). Data based on 4 broad sectors at NUTS-3 level
e.g. Dutch 'Corop regions'.

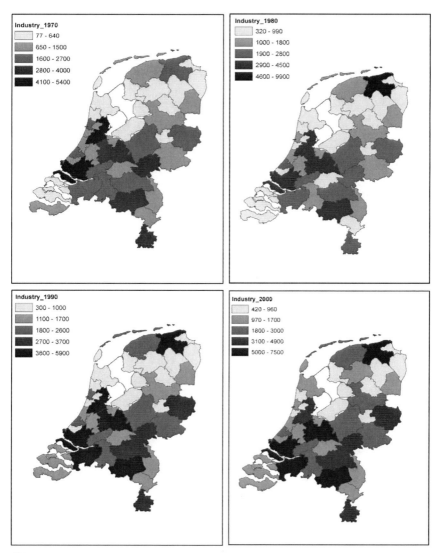

(b)

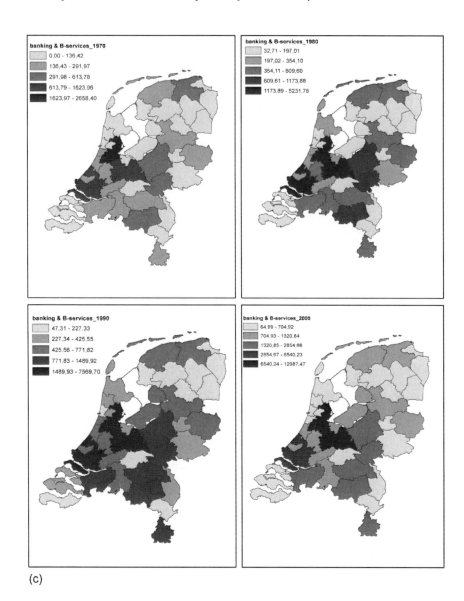

(c)

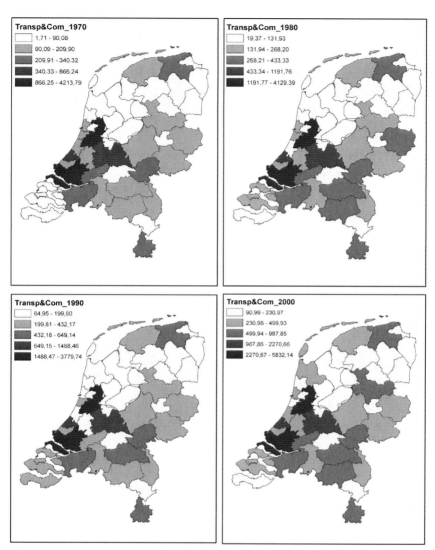

(d)

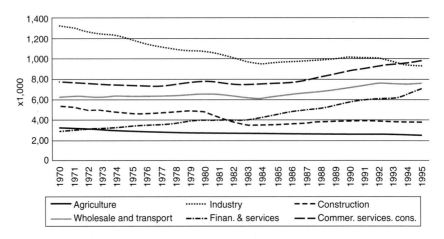

Figure 7.5 Employment by sector in the Netherlands: 1970–95.
Source: CBS (NR and REJ).

A remarkable increase in employment took place in the provinces of North Brabant (5,526 new jobs in 1973–83 and 207,973 jobs in 1983–93), Gelderland (7,626 and 142,783 new jobs), Utrecht (31,173 and 117,257 jobs) and Overijssel (lost 16,180 jobs in 1973–83 but created 83,394 new jobs in 1983–93). Most of new job creations in these provinces took place in the agriculture sector.

In manufacturing industry, the general tendency was a persistent decline in almost all Dutch regions during the 1970s and 1980s, with a structural decrease in the provinces of North and South Holland during the 1990s, and a slightly increase in the provinces of North Brabant, Gelderland, Limburg, Overijssel and Utrecht. The decrease in the number of jobs in the Randstad regions was largely made up for by the rapid increase of jobs in the services sector, in transport and communication, and in the wholesale and retail sectors. Utrecht and Gelderland followed this trend as well as the province of North Brabant during the period 1983–93.

To resume, there has been a continuing decrease in employment in agriculture since the 1970s, and to a lesser extent in industry, accompanied by the increasing importance of business services in the province of North Holland, especially in Amsterdam and Utrecht.

The increase in employment was also reflected in the growth in incomes. The total number of people with regular income grew from 4 million in 1948 to 6.1 million in 1969 and to 10.1 million in 1989. This corresponds to a growth rate of 55 per cent in 1950–70 and 30 per cent between 1970 and 1980. As a result of increasing incomes, the living standards of the working population have improved significantly since the 1960s which has caused radical changes in consumption patterns and the lifestyle and living conditions of the Dutch population. Furthermore, changes in household patterns from one breadwinner to two- (multiple-) income households raised the disposable income of households, which in turn stimulated the mass consumption of durable goods like cars, televisions, refrigerators,

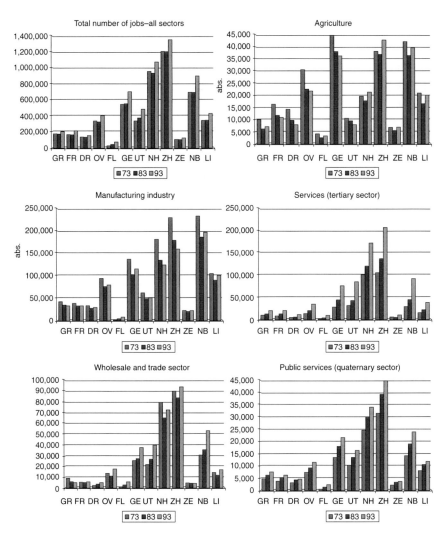

Figure 7.6 Employment by province and sectors in 1973, 1983 and 1993.
Source: CBS (REJ/Regional Economic Data, 1973–1993).
Note: GR (Groningen); FR (Friesland); DR (Drenth); OV (Overijssel); FL (Flevoland);
GE (Gelderland); UT (Utrecht); NH (Noord-Holland); ZH (Zuid-Holland); ZE (Zeeland);
NB (Noord-Brabant); LI (Limburg).

telephones, computers, etc., together with services (banking, insurance) and
housing. The generous tax incentives to homeowners and the relatively low mort-
gage rates gave a boost to the housing market. As a result, owner-occupied housing reached higher levels in the 1990s.

Note, however, that the Dutch economy could only sustain the rise in real
incomes as long as high levels of production and productivity went hand in hand

with low unemployment and high capital intensity, i.e. a high ratio of capital to labour. This was the case during the first three decades after the Second World War, except for the 1970s when the Dutch economy was hit by the two oil crises. Having said that, compared to other European countries, the Netherlands was generally less affected by the oil crises because the Dutch government was able to weather the storm through state royalties on the export of natural gas.

Examination of production levels during the period 1970–99 reveals a continuing increase from more than 2 per cent during the period 1970–83 to almost 4 per cent from 1996 to 1999. At the sectoral level, the highest growth in production was achieved in the real estate sector (5.5 per cent) and agriculture (4 per cent), followed by financial and business services (3.8 per cent), wholesale trade and transport (3 per cent), and finally by non-profit sector and industry, with respectively 2.9 per cent and 2.1 per cent during the first period 1970–80.

However, the period 1983–96 shows a completely different picture. It was mainly the financial and business services sector, and the wholesale and transport sector, that registered the highest growth rate, respectively 5.3 per cent and 4.3 per cent. Consumer services (retail, hotel and catering, etc.) and real estate grew faster than the construction and industry sectors (3.6 per cent against 2.9 per cent). The same tendency can be observed for the period 1996–9.

More generally, sectoral changes in production levels and growth can be interpreted as a result of the shift in the economic structure from an industry-based economy to more services-oriented economy (see Figure 7.7).

Further examination of productivity (value added) provides clear evidence supporting our observations concerning the structural shift of the Dutch economy from industry to services.

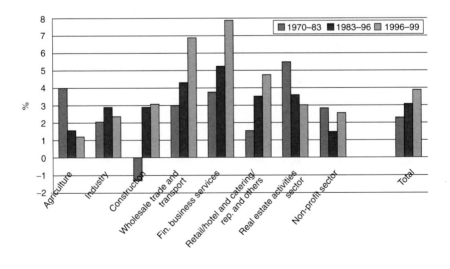

Figure 7.7 Growth rate of production by sector: 1970–2004.
Source: CBS (REJ/Annual Regional Economic Data).

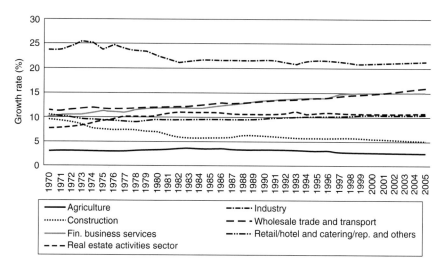

Figure 7.8 Growth rate of value-added by sector: 1970–2004.
Source: CBS (REJ/Annual Regional Economic Data).

As Figure 7.8 clearly shows, productivity in traditional sectors such as manufacturing industry, construction and agriculture was in decline from the 1970s, but on the increase in financial, business and commercial services (wholesale), and trade and transportation, between 1970 and 2004.

At the regional level, the total value added shows a gradual decline in the Randstad regions between 1970 and 1985 (from just above 50 per cent to approximately 46 per cent), and an increase of 49 per cent from 1985 up to the 1990s. The share of the Randstad in the total value added in business services was around 57 per cent.

While the Randstad is business-services oriented, it has apparently not strengthened significantly its position vis-à-vis the rest of the Dutch regions. Throughout the early 1970s, 90 per cent of the value added and jobs in the Randstad were created in the cities of Amsterdam, Rotterdam and Utrecht.

The growth rate in financial and business services over time, however, is very much the same as for the national economy. This was the result of the deconcentration of business services from the city centre to the emerging suburban areas. Note, however, that between 1997 and 2002, the share of business services in the Amsterdam agglomeration increased slightly from 25 to 26 per cent. This may be explained by, among other things, the increasing economic significance of Schiphol airport and the Schiphol region for business services and logistics activities.

7.4 Economic structure and economic transformation of the Amsterdam region

According to the literature on urbanisation and urban systems, the development of cities involves three phases: the pre-industrial city, the industrial city and the post-industrial city (Herbert and Thomas, 1991; Castells, 1992). Taking the case of Amsterdam, the industrialisation of the Netherlands had structural effects on the economic and spatial structure of Amsterdam. The restructuring of the manufacturing-based urban labour market resulted in the decentralisation of employment from the traditional city centre to the surrounding urban fringes and to other regional urban cores around the Amsterdam region.

The emergence of the post-industrial city during the second half of the twentieth century was manifested by an increase in services activities and the relative decline of industry, the increase in a highly qualified labour force in total employment, the increase in technological innovations and R&D activities and the growing dominance of the ICT sector. All these developments have resulted in the increasing concentration and centralisation of activities and population in a limited number of urban areas, often in the larger metropolitan urban centres. Furthermore, with the increased internationalisation of economic activities and the importance of communication networks since the 1980s, connectivity and the exchange of knowledge and information at the global scale have become important locational factors and key elements of the competitiveness of cities and regions (Musterd and Salet, 2003). Beside these locational factors, firms and residents are still attracted by specific local assets and the quality of specific cities and regions in terms of specific local institutional and cultural aspects (Storper, 1997).

Although the Randstad comprises four provinces and 165 municipalities, economic activities have gravitated around its four major big cities. Amsterdam and the adjacent localities have steadily shed many of their old manufacturing and commercial functions in favour of business services activities such as finance and banking services, consultancy, tourism, distribution and trade, etc.

However, the present economic position of the Amsterdam region in the national economy has gone through different and successive development phases that have affected its economic structure since the Second World War.

From an economic point of view, local authorities and policy-makers were deeply convinced of the important economic position of the port of Amsterdam for the local economy. This explains why local authorities gave much attention to the development of the port activities in Amsterdam, and subsequently why they underestimated the development of Schiphol airport and other economic sectors like, for example, the services sector (Rooy *et al.*, 2007). For a long time, the port of Amsterdam functioned as the main economic driving force of the Amsterdam economy.

Another reason why local authorities invested heavily in the port of Amsterdam has to do with the strong position of some influential local actors that were directly and/or indirectly related to the port activities, especially the chamber of commerce whose director was considered the shadow of the mayor of Amsterdam. However, the port of Amsterdam was severely hit by the sudden freezing of trade between the Netherlands and Indonesia in 1949, when several firms in the trade of goods and transportation of passengers to and from the former colonies and shipbuilding and maintenance and repair firms were severely hit and some had to close their doors.

One major factor explaining the decline of port activities in Amsterdam was the (low) level of water and the lack of appropriate infrastructure and equipment to accommodate the increasing scale in tonnage (containers) and size of new ships. Despite this, up until the 1960s, the economic policy of Amsterdam's authorities was still oriented towards the development of port activities and related sectors, especially trade and transport activities. The idea was to expand the port area by 40 km² in order to create a unique industrial growth pole for capital-intensive industries, especially the petrochemical industry and trans-shipment and storage companies. Unfortunately, because of low demand from industry-based activities, most of this area remained a vast wasteland in 1970 (Engelsdorp Gastelaars, 2003: 298).

More generally, between 1945 and the 1970s, the structure of Amsterdam's economy was dominated by industry, construction, transport and trade sectors that were sustained by well-developed service activities, especially in finance, insurance and banking. Employment grew rapidly during the first two decades after the Second World War due to government interventions through its indus-trialisation policy and the rising investment in capital-intensive industries.

In the period 1940–57, a clear shift in the local economic structure took place. While employment was growing in the metallurgy industry, construction, the graphic industry and the (petro) chemical industry, employment in traditional manufacturing industries was declining, especially in industries producing consumer goods like clothing (–4 per cent between 1950 and 1957) and food (–24 per cent). The number of firms by industry shows an almost similar tendency between 1950 and 1957.

The general tendency during the 1950s and 1960s was a general increase in employment in capital-intensive industries, and a decrease in employment in the labour-intensive traditional sectors like the clothing industry, the extraction and transformation of raw materials, the leather and rubber industry and the food industry. Note, however, that despite the decline in employment and the number of firms, the total turnover of industrial firms increased spectacularly, from 413,491guilders in 1952 to 756,038 in 1960 and to more than 1 million guilders in 1967.

In contrast to the 1950s and 1960s, Amsterdam's industry registered a sharp decline in employment between 1970 and 1990 (from 82,000 in 1970 to about 53,000 in 1980 and to 38,408 in 1990), which was caused by the negative effects of the oil crisis of 1973 and by the deindustrialisation and delocalisation of indus-trial firms from Amsterdam to other regions.

Like Amsterdam, other urban centres like Haarlem were also badly hit by the economic crisis. Note that there are differences in the growth in employment between different parts of Amsterdam as well as between Amsterdam and its surrounding urban areas. While the north of Amsterdam shows a clear decline in employment, the southeastern urban areas show a rapid increase in employment between 1960 and 1980.

More generally, the decrease in employment in industry was counterbalanced by the fast increase in employment in the financial sector and business services.

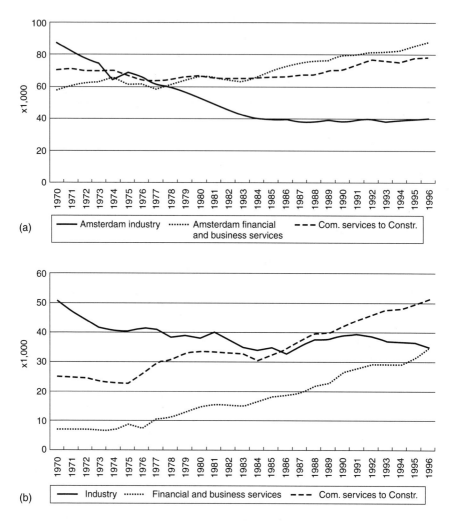

Figure 7.9 Employment in Amsterdam (a) and suburban areas (b) during 1970–96.
Source: CBS (REJ).

Figure 7.9 shows the existence of a close relationship between employment
growth in business services and the spatial organisation of economic activities in
Amsterdam and its suburban areas. While the share of industry shows a continuing decline in Amsterdam, the growth of employment in financial services, and
especially in commercial and business services, increased relatively more quickly
in suburban areas.

The financial and business services sector increased by more than 108 per cent
between 1970 and 1980 and by 125 per cent between 1981 and 1996. In absolute figures, employment grew from 7,018 employees in 1970 to 34,695 in 1996.

After a slightly decline between 1970 and 1975 (from 24,723 to 22,573), employment in the commercial services increased from 25,782 employees in 1976 to 51,183 in 1996. Based on these figures, one may conclude that the development of business services followed closely the suburbanisation process to suburban areas of the Amsterdam region.

More specifically, the figures above provide clear evidence in favour of a shift in the economic structure of the Amsterdam-Schiphol region, in the sense that the economy of this region became more oriented towards financial, business and commercial services.

Analysis of the levels of production by economic sector (see Figure 7.10) shows almost the same tendency, and confirms once again the idea of a local economic shift and the spatial distribution of activities between Amsterdam and its suburban areas. While the Ij area and the traditional industrial sites in the port area

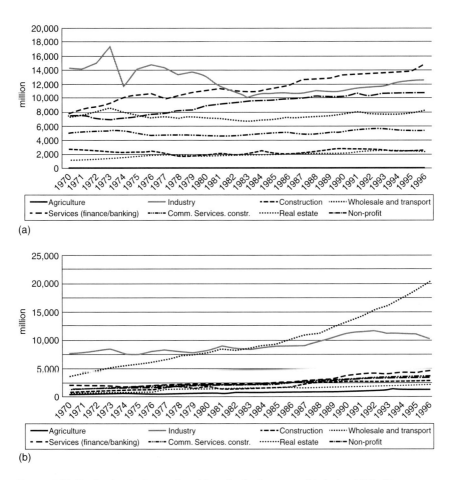

(a)

(b)

Figure 7.10 Production in Amsterdam (a), and suburban areas (b) during 1970–96.
Source: CBS (REJ; SBI'74). Note: calculations based on prices of 1987.

were losing firms (e.g. petrochemical, shipbuilding, automobiles, breweries, food, textiles and clothing, etc.) in 1970–96, a rapid increase in the number of firms and production in the services sector took place in the southern urban fringes, especially in the proximity of the ringroad from Amsterdam to Schiphol airport.

By the end of the 1980s and during the 1990s, the economy of Amsterdam recovered and performed above the national average. The economic upheaval of the 1990s was supported by the rise of large-scale suburban office complexes. Growth has been spurred on by the emergence of new leading sectors and locations such as business and financial services in the southern urban fringe, tourism, leisure and new media in the historic city centre, and logistics activities around the airport area. In addition, a new large retail centre was built in the Amsterdam South East district containing many leisure activities (the Amsterdam Arena near the relocated stadium of the Ajax soccer team). Note, however, that despite the fact that the inner city lost its position as the main centre for business services, the traditional city centre of Amsterdam is still very important to the region in terms of culture, shopping and leisure and as an incubator for specific high-tech business activities such as graphic design and multimedia.

The emergence of Schiphol as a new economic centre at the edge of Amsterdam has profited largely from the relocation of service firms (mainly business services) in the proximity of the national airport boundaries, more particularly in the southwest areas of Amsterdam. In this sense, the new growth pole is complementary to rather than competing with other locations in the Amsterdam agglomeration. The localisation advantages offered by the Amsterdam-Schiphol region in terms of knowledge spillovers, information, R&D, a highly skilled labour force, cultural amenities, etc., constitute important local assets in attracting international, knowledge-intensive and services-oriented firms to the region. In addition, the proximity and accessibility of work centres by train, air, public transport, highways, telecommunication, etc., are considered key locational advantages of the Schiphol-Amsterdam region. Together, these locational advantages are sustained by a wide and diversified labour market, where the best and most productive education institutions in the country are located (e.g. two international universities and many high schools and research institutes).

In this respect, the city of Amsterdam and its suburban areas show a significant increase in the share of highly educated people in the total labour force (from more than 300,000 in 1970 to more than 2,000,000 in 1980). When we compare these figures with the annual growth of financial and business services in Amsterdam, its suburban areas and the city region, a clear picture emerges: there exists a positive, high correlation between the increase in employment of highly educated people and the growth of finance and business services in suburban areas and at the level of the city region. This can be interpreted as evidence supporting the idea that Amsterdam's economy is becoming more knowledge-based. Within the business services sector, knowledge-based firms are now setting up at the edges of the city centre and more particularly at the level of the city region.

7.5 Spatial structure and spatial transformation of the Amsterdam-Schiphol region 1945–90

Based on the general guidelines outlined in the General Expansion Plan (AUP, 1935), Amsterdam has been developed according to the concentric urban form known as the lobe or finger model. The first large urban expansion plan implemented by Amsterdam was the construction of a large recreational area, known as the 'Boschplan' located between Nieuwer-Amstel (later Amstelveen) and Schiphol. The general widespread belief among the city department planners (Stedelijke Ontwikkeling) was that urban expansion plans and spatial development of the city should be realised through 'survey before planning'.

Note that, during the prewar period, the urban expansion of Amsterdam and the neighbouring municipalities was integrated into the regional plan (Streekplan) falling under control of the 'fast commission on expansion plans' of the province of North Holland. Through this commission, Amsterdam's department of public works was able to control the urban expansion planning of the neighbouring municipalities, and indirectly the urban expansion policies at the regional level.

The progressive spatial expansion of Amsterdam into the urban fringe and suburb areas continued after the Second World War with the construction of the garden city of Slotermeer in September 1953 and the neighbourhood of Geuzenveld in 1953. This spatial expansion progressed gradually with the construction of two additional large neighbourhoods to the east and southeast urban fringes: the neighbourhood of Slotervaart (1954) with a new large recreation park (the Sloterplas, opened in 1957), and the new neighbourhood of Buitenveldert (1959). At the same time, intense debates took place in Amsterdam concerning the reconstruction of the historical city centre and the north–south metro line. In his study concerning the construction plans for the Amsterdam 'North–South' metro line, Davids (2000) describes the influence of the Amsterdam's department of public works on the planning and development of this last urban project. Map 7.2 gives an overview of the spatial expansion of Amsterdam-Schiphol region until 1950.

In 1958, Amsterdam published the second urban expansion plan, entitled the 'Structure Plan of Amsterdam North', which focused on improvements to the accessibility of the port of Amsterdam (the projection of a new canal in the municipalities of Landsmeer and Oostzaan) and the construction of new settlements in Amsterdam North. The city council voted in 1959 in favour of the construction of two new tunnels (the Coentunnel and the IJtunnel) under the IJ river, that would connect the city centre to Amsterdam North and to other northern suburban areas. The IJtunnel was opened in October 1968, following the Coentunnel a few years earlier.

Furthermore, the structure plan for Amsterdam North formed the basis for the regional expansion plan of the North Sea Canal area (Noordzeekanaal), in which the province of North Holland was expected to take the lead in resolving the problems of infrastructure at the regional level, i.e. at the level of the greater agglomeration of Amsterdam.

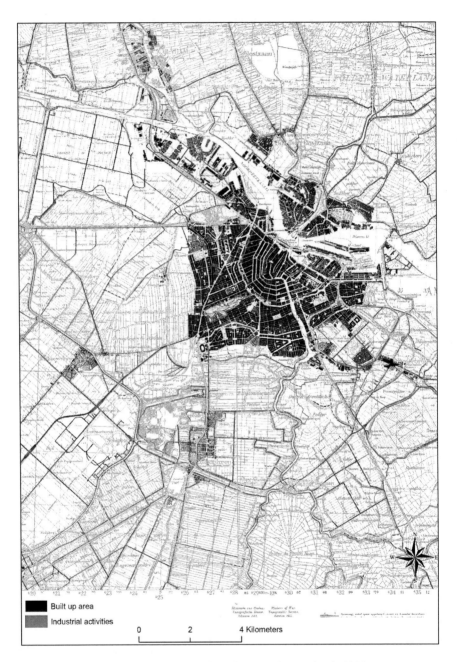

Map 7.2 Urbanisation and urban expansion of Amsterdam region in 1950.
Source: based on Cadastral maps and expansion plans of Amsterdam and Schiphol
(Scale 1:25000).

During this period, Amsterdam officials and city planners were conscious of the fact that most urban problems related to (sub)urbanisation and urban sprawl were now taking place at the agglomeration level and not only at the city level. Accordingly, urban spatial planning should take place at a much larger urban scale because of the rapid increase in the number of commuters as a result of the increasing mobility of individuals and the increasing attractiveness of suburban areas as living places for the middle class, especially for households with many children. In this perspective, close cooperation between Amsterdam and the surrounding municipalities around common issues related to urban expansion planning became necessary. The law of 'common regulation' (*wet gemeenschap-pelijk regeling* (WGR)) provided the needed policy instruments to reach this goal.

It was also in this context that the study commission under the chair of J. Donner-G. van den Bergh was set up in 1956 to study the problems related to urban governance at the level of the greater Amsterdam region. One year later (1957), the 'city-suburban' committee (*stadrand commissie*) was created to coordinate the urban expansion plans of Amsterdam and the surrounding municipalities. This resulted in the development of the general plan (*plan in hoofdzak*) for the southern and the eastern parts of the suburban areas of Amsterdam, and its integration with the structure plan of the greater agglomeration of Amsterdam in 1965. The general plan document formed the basis for the implementation of the urban expansion plans (e.g. structure plans) of the south and the southeast lobes.

Between 1955 and 1978, urban sprawl took unprecedented forms as the expansion of Amsterdam took place first within the growth centres in the eastern parts of the harbour area (*havengebied*) and to the east side of the city, along the (planned) metro line, and then further to the northern, southern and southeastern areas.

More generally, the 1950s may be considered a period of large-scale urban expansion, which was largely guided by infrastructure planning and urban sprawl to the north, east and southeast lobes. It was also a period where the formation of the greater Amsterdam agglomeration began to emerge as a result of spatial deconcentration and decentralisation of the population and activities (see Map 7.3).

It is worth mentioning that in 1953 Amsterdam had already started (legal) procedures to integrate the suburban Bijlmermeer polder, located in the southwest side of the city, into Amsterdam. The increased housing shortage in Amsterdam pushed local authorities to consider the annexation of this satellite settlement in order to construct a new neighbourhood comprising 1,128 new houses. As a result, the total surface of Amsterdam was extended by 2,547 ha.

However, because this new settlement area was relatively distant from the city centre, city officials had to develop infrastructure plans to connect Bijlmermeer by road and a metro line to the city centre.

At first instance, it was planned that the neighbourhood of Bijlmermeer would become the new residential area of the Amsterdam's working class. Unfortunately, things did not turn out as policy-makers and urban planners expected. Instead of a new settlement for native Amsterdam people, Bijlmermeer became the preferred settlement location for immigrants from Surinam and the Antilles.

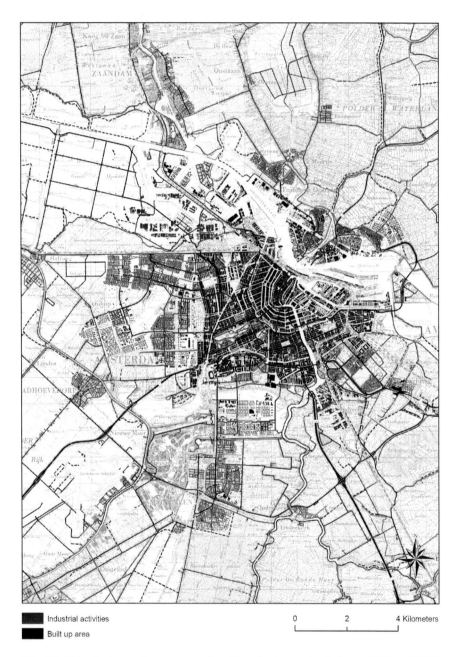

Industrial activities

Built up area

0   2   4 Kilometers

Map 7.3 Urbanisation and urban expansion of Amsterdam region between 1950 and 1960.
Source: based on Cadastral maps and expansion plans of Amsterdam and Schiphol
(Scale 1:25000).

In the 1980s and 1990s, another wave of non-western immigrants (from Morocco and Turkey) followed the first settlers to this suburban area. In this sense, the urban development of Bijlmermeer (1966–75) turned out to be a living example of the failure of urban planning doctrine from the senior officials of the department of public works (Rooy *et al.*, 2007: 46).

With regard to planning, a large infrastructure system connecting the radial road and railway networks was already in place in Amsterdam before the Second World War. Up to 1970, local authorities developed various plans indicating the location of the land needed that should be reserved for infrastructure development. Because of the deliberate policy of the city officials of Amsterdam to reserve land for future use and infrastructure expansion plans, a unique morphology of infrastructure networks has emerged within and around the city, combining radial and tangential nodes that intersect well inside and around Amsterdam (Bertolini, 2007) (see Map 7.4). The main idea was to facilitate and improve accessibility to the city centre by tram and bicycle (shopping and working), and by bicycle and pedestrians (for recreational activities). Additional open space was also reserved by Amsterdam for the future cargo railway line in the eastern area of the city centre, providing access to the port of Amsterdam.

It was believed that increasing mobility of people could be resolved by increasing the capacity of the road and rail networks. For example, the design of the A10 motorway takes into account the potential expansion of the city to the west and south. The planning of a new radial infrastructure network system (roads and metro lines) around the city was based on forecasts indicating an increase in the movements of residents of new neighbourhoods on the urban fringe, like Bijlmermeer and Buitenveldert, both to the city centre and to other surrounding areas, and in the direction of the newly reclaimed Flevopolder, which was, at that time, in construction. The outer-suburban areas of Weesp, Aatsveldsche and Bloemendalepolder were expected to grow into independent middle-size cities.

In addition, urban planners took into consideration the possibility of the expansion of Amsterdam following a lobed spatial structure whose main characteristics are determined by the concentrations of new office buildings, firms and urban services along the road traffic axis in the direction of Utrecht.

While intra-regional infrastructure linkages were given a high priority by local authorities, (sub)urbanisation processes resulted in an increase in demand for inter-regional infrastructure, especially between Amsterdam and the surroundings areas and between the cities of the Randstad.

Since the 1970s, the movements of people and households have taken place over a relatively short distance, usually at the level of the Amsterdam-Schiphol region and between cities of the northern wing of the Randstad. Even today, the majority of the commuter movements (about 85 per cent) still take place at this same geographical level. In this sense, most of the daily commuters crossing the regional borders are directed towards the suburban areas and the outer fringes falling within the metropolitan region, such as the case of commuter movements from the northern areas of North Holland and from Almere to Amsterdam.

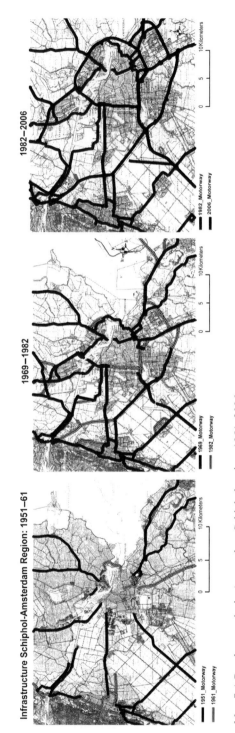

Map 7.4 Road networks in Amsterdam-Schiphol region: 1951–2006.
Source: based on various planning maps from archives and historical maps of transport networks from the Ministry of Transport and Waterworks (Geo-Info_AVV).

From 1956, the numbers of commuters living outside greater Amsterdam and working in the city and the Schiphol region increased substantially. The majority of commuters lived in the province of North Holland. Since 1970, the total number of people living and working in Amsterdam has been decreasing, while the share of commuters living in Amsterdam and working in the surrounding areas has increased considerably, especially in the Schiphol region. At the Randstad level, there exist intensive commuter relationships between Utrecht and Amsterdam and between The Hague and Rotterdam. The major motives for commuters travelling between regions are home-to-work trips, business trips and school trips.

Given the fact that daily urban mobility is hardly influenced by spatial planning policy, what has changed is the end destination of home-to-work trips, although the number of long-distance trips by private car and the total distance travelled has not changed significantly (Martens, 2000; Bontje, 2001).

A final remark that we want to stress in this respect is the fact that transport policy in Amsterdam has been closely related to the contested plans for a mass transit system (rail networks and the new metro lines). However, the rapid growth of the services sector and the increased demand for office locations (including universities, hospitals, RAI exhibition centre, etc.) have pushed local authorities to search for alternative locations at the intersection of the radial roads and the tangential highway. It was in this context that the development of the west side, the southeast and the southern side of Amsterdam took place. During the 1960s, the fashion sector had already moved to the western part of Amsterdam after the eviction of firms from the city centre to make room for the construction of the IJtunnel and the Coentunnel connecting Amsterdam to the northern areas of the city. The fashion centre was located at the junction of the radial tramline No.1 and the first part of the highway ring. New office buildings were constructed and soon other firms like Elsevier and the national labour union followed the example of the fashion sector and moved to this location. The emergence of this sub-centre was completed when the highway ring (A10) and the railway ring were finally realised. In addition to this sub-centre, three other sub-centres were established: (1) Amsterdam southeast in the proximity of the railway and the A2 highway connecting Amsterdam to Utrecht and Schiphol through the A9 ring road; (2) Amsterdam south in the proximity of the highways and the railway line to Schiphol (and The Hague); (3) the 'teleport centre' Sloterdijk near the western harbour, which is located along the railway line connecting Schiphol to Amsterdam central station. From these three sub-centres, the Amsterdam southeast area is the most developed with regard to the total number of office buildings, shopping malls and entertainment activities (a stadium, multiplex cinema, a musical hall, etc.). Amsterdam south has become a hub for public transportation and a magnet for major Dutch banks, international company headquarters and other high-end service firms.

After the 1960s Amsterdam was severely affected by a mass outflow of middle-class families with children to the suburbs. As a result, Amsterdam lost a substantial part of its population to the surrounding suburbs. This loss of urban population was counterbalanced by a larger inflow of immigrants from western

and non-western countries, which substantially changed the structure of the population of Amsterdam and presented new challenges to the local authorities (i.e.
unemployed inhabitants and an increase in poverty among the elderly and some
ethnic groups) (Jobse and Musterd, 1992; SCP, 2001). The policy-makers and
city planners then began to realise that these developments provide a clear indication that new social and cultural changes were at work, and that these changes
could be contained by rethinking the existing urban planning policy.

More generally, the 1960s and the 1970s may be characterised as a rather
turbulent period for Amsterdam, which has resulted in increasing residential
segregation and discrepancies in education and the housing and labour markets
(Dieleman and Musterd, 1992). It was also a period of large urban renewal
projects aimed at revitalising slum neighbourhoods in order to stimulate
economic activity, social stability and the economic viability of the city. The city
of Amsterdam shifted its urban policy from expansion of the urban fringe to
development of the city centre. Once again the city became central (see Map 7.5).

Within the context of the urban renewal policy of the 1960s, Amsterdam planners and city officials launched various plans to demolish existing old historical
buildings in the city centre to make room for the development of large office
buildings, e.g. to form the central business district (CBD). These plans were
supplemented by the construction of a mass transit system connecting the city
centre to suburban areas.

The city expansion plans were met with strong opposition from the residents'
social group movements, which were in favour of the renovation and restoration
of old buildings to their original state. Under increasing and strong protests from
the citizens of Amsterdam against the demolition of traditional buildings in the
historical city centre, the municipality was forced to shift its urban renewal policy
toward a policy of 'building for the neighbourhood'. The new urban expansion
policy now became focused on the renovation and preservation of the traditional
city centre.

Another example of unpopular urban renewal projects was the construction of
the underground metro line connecting the north and the south of the city.
In 1968, under continuing protests by the population of Amsterdam against
expansion plans for both the urban motorway and urban railway, the city council
decided to replace the original plan for the metro line with a reduced construction
plan under which only the western line (including supplementary lines) would be
realised. However, this decision had been taken after many years of disputes,
conflicts and confrontations between protester groups and city officials, especially from the Department of Public Works, who were also protagonists in other
large-scale urban renewal projects.

In the end, the local authorities were forced to shift their policy in favour of
'management of mobility' instead of direct interventions in urban infrastructure
planning. Furthermore, the realisation of the north–south metro line was technically
not possible due to high uncertainty about the financial feasibility of the project and
the high risks involved in its realisation, especially risks related to the demolition
of many historical buildings in the city centre or their collapse. In 1977, only the

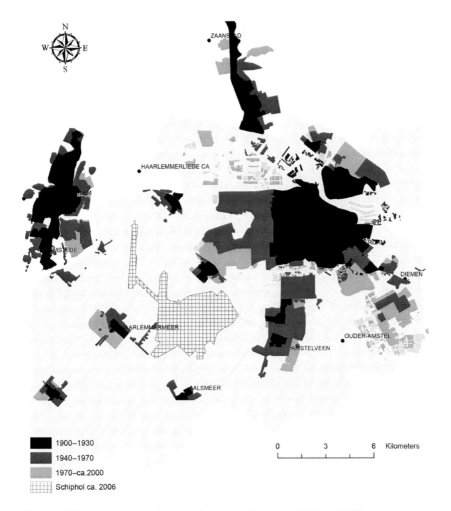

Map 7.5 Urban expansion of Amsterdam region between 1960 and 1980.
Source: based on Cadastral maps and expansion plans of Amsterdam and Schiphol
(Scale 1:25000).

metro lines between Weesperplein and Holedrecht/Gaasperplasm, Holendrecht and
Gain (finished in 1980) and the central station and Amstelveen (end of 1990) were
constructed. Map 7.6 illustrates the original map of the north–south metro line as
planned by city officials and what was in the end realised by Amsterdam.

In opposition to earlier urban expansion plans, the structure plan (parts A and
B) of 1974 focuses on just one sector of spatial planning: the preservation of the
quality of housing in the city centre.

The introduction of a new Dutch planning regime gave local authorities more
freedom to develop their own land use planning schemes and to focus on a planning policy based on preferred spatial development rather than on function.

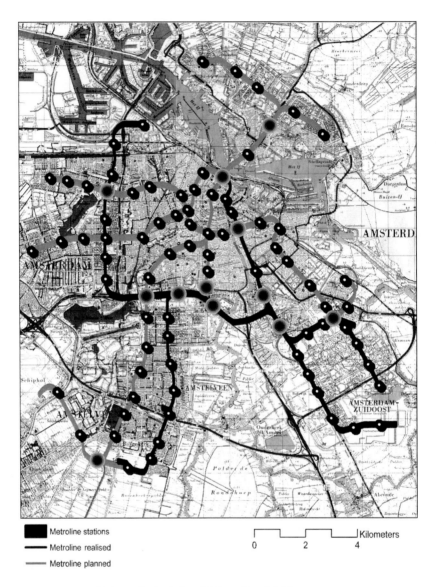

Metroline stations
Metroline realised
Metroline planned

Kilometers
0   2   4

Map 7.6 Map of (planned) North-South Metro line (1966).
Source: based on original planning map from Amsterdam City Archive (ACA) projected on Cadaster topographic map (Scale 1:25000).

However, because of the scarcity of land in the city centre to accommodate business and commercial services, new urban growth centres emerged along the city borders such as Sloterdijk and Riekerpolder, located in the south and south-east areas of the city. The deconcentration of firms and business service companies to these urban fringes stimulated the rise and formation of the city region

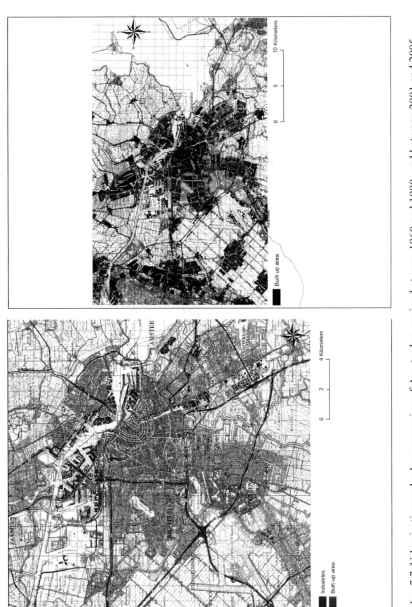

Map 7.7 Urbanisation and urban expansion of Amsterdam region between 1960 and 1990, and between 2001 and 2005.
Source: based on Cadastral maps and expansion plans of Amsterdam and Schiphol (Scale 1:25000).

(see Map 7.7). Jobs and residential areas became more and more spread over the whole Amsterdam agglomeration, and at the same time, the economic position of the city centre weakened in comparison to the rising suburban growth centres. Accordingly, the spatial and economic development of Schiphol and the Schiphol region increased substantially because of the deconcentration process of firms from the city centre to the city borders. Schiphol airport itself made tremendous progress and became one of the most important centres of the agglomeration in terms of employment and economic growth.

The spatial defragmentation and increasing urban sprawl of Amsterdam and the surrounding areas raised many questions about the optimal administrative structure and urban governance of the emerging city region. Discussions about these issues resulted in the application of the law on the formation of agglomerations in 1971. The main goals of this law were the creation of 44 urban agglomerations at the national level, and the restructuring of the Dutch governance system by eliminating the provinces as an intermediate governance layer. According to this law, the greater agglomeration of Amsterdam would be divided into 29 municipalities, together with elected regional councils.

In 1972, Amsterdam reached agreement with 25 surrounding municipalities to enhance voluntary cooperation within an informal representative organ (*Informeel Agglomeratie Overleg* (IAO)) instead of creating a new governance structure.

Since 1981, various administrative tasks have been decentralised to the municipalities of Amsterdam, and at the same time, the Amsterdam city council took over new tasks that were previously in hands of the province. As a result, Amsterdam's urban expansion plans acquired the character and status of regional plans.

7.5.1 Spatial transformation and urban governance in the Amsterdam region

As mentioned before, the issue of urban governance was raised for the first time when the spatial expansion of Amsterdam increased spectacularly through a series of much disputed annexations, and especially after the annexation of the Bijlmermeer polder in 1966. Further annexations since then were not possible simply because Dutch cities in general and Amsterdam in particular lacked significant region-wide political organisation that was capable of winning political support from parliament (spatial annexations required special legislation). The alternative solution in the absence of legitimate political organisation then was the formation of (political) coalitions between the municipalities within the metropolitan area. In this respect, Amsterdam entertained numerous proposals for creating a consolidated metropolitan government (Hendriks, 1997).

In 1986, a group of 23 municipalities in the Amsterdam region formed a new voluntary association of local governments – the *Regionaal Overleg Amsterdam* (ROA) – as the first step in the direction of creating a city province. This was the third major attempt made by Amsterdam to reorganise the administrative structure of local government during the twentieth century. The idea was to create a metropolitan government with two layers: the city province and the municipalities.

The new metropolitan government was meant to be more powerful than the existing province and to take over several strategic responsibilities from the municipalities such as, for example, the distribution of public funds, transportation policy, regional economic policy and environment and housing policies.

With the intention of establishing a city province, under the label of regional government (*Regiobestuur*) in July 1994 the city council of Amsterdam agreed to divide the city into 16 sub-municipalities (*stadsdelen*), each with its own elected government (the city centre was recently added as the seventeenth municipality). However, the divergence in points of view between the city and the surrounding municipalities was not easy to bridge, and in the end the whole project of metropolitan government was abandoned. The main reason for this failure was that most of the surrounding municipalities wanted to preserve their (administrative and economic) autonomy and to reduce as much as possible the authority of the city province.

In the meantime, the city of Amsterdam and the surrounding municipalities (including Almeer) continued to work together within the informal organ, the ROA, which from 1992 became the *Regionaal Orgaan Amsterdam* (ROA). The ROA acted as a joint forum between the city of Amsterdam and the surrounding municipalities with the main purpose of representing the metropolitan government in major national bureaucracies and acquiring grants from the government to finance common projects such as housing, transportation and public amenities (Veer, 1998: 37).

The efforts of Amsterdam to reform the political and administrative structure of the Amsterdam region by establishing a metropolitan government culminated in 1999, when Amsterdam's residents were given the opportunity to vote, through a general referendum, in favour or against the formation of a city province. An overwhelming majority of the citizens of Amsterdam (93 per cent) rejected this bill categorically. Since then, discussions about the establishment of a city province became taboo in Amsterdam's political circles. However, the ROA still exists as a regional informal body, albeit under a new name: *Regionale Samenwerking Amsterdam* (RSA). The province has resumed its former role as government intermediary within the tripartite Dutch governance structure.

The most important lessons that can be drawn from this experience are twofold: (1) guiding urban transformation is difficult to achieve by political and administrative reforms only; (2) factors influencing urbanisation and urban processes often change faster than the expected change in existing institutional structures. Furthermore, administrative reforms centred around intra-municipal cooperation and/or the creation of a regional administrative authority with regard to the redistribution of financial means are difficult to combine within the existing Dutch governance structure, e.g. municipalities and provinces. This is because cooperation entails voluntary vertical as well as horizontal linkages between local authorities and authority requires powerful regulatory hierarchical decision-making.

It seems that the urban governance problem lies more in the historically constructed and path-dependent Dutch governance system itself, which no longer fits within the new urban reality. For example, in the last decades of the twentieth century and the first years of the twenty-first, cooperation between local authorities (municipalities), national government bodies and non-governmental organisations (such as the Delta-metropolis initiative) have taken over many policy areas that were previously administered by local authorities. As a result, complex patterns of multi-level and multi-actor governance based on formal and informal relationships between different actors are now taking place at various levels and encompassing various aspects of the metropolitan region. Perhaps one of the most intriguing examples in this matter is the multi-actor and multi-governance structure involving the national airport at Schiphol.

7.6 Spatial-economic transformation of the Haarlemmermeer-Schiphol region

7.6.1 Economic transformation

The postwar period 1945–70 may be characterised as a period of rapid urbanisation and industrialisation in the Haarlemmermeer-Schiphol region. Urbanisation and industrialisation are key explanatory factors of the increase in employment, the diversification of economic structure and the spatial expansion of the Schiphol region, especially in the northern suburban core areas of Haarlmmermeer, i.e. Badhoevendorp and Zwanenburg.

Before the Second World War, the increase in population and employment was restricted to the small towns of Hoofddorp, Badhoevedorp and Nieuw-Vennep. Between 1945 and 1960, Haarlemmermeer preserved its countryside character dominated by agriculture, including horticultural activities in Aalsmeer. The spectacular growth of Schiphol airport attracted an increasing number of industrial firms. However, compared to Amsterdam or Haarlem, for example, the size and importance of industry was less significant in Haarlemmermeer. Only a couple of large industrial firms were active in this location such as the machine factory Spaans in Hoofddorp and the Vicon factory in Nieuwe Vennep producing agricultural equipment.

In 1954, the majority of firms located in Haarlemmermeer were small and medium-sized firms managed by a single person or a partnership. Of these firms 70.3 per cent started with capital of between 2,000 to 10,000 guilders, and about 20 per cent with less than 2,000 guilders. Only 1.2 per cent of the total firms were large firms with total capital between 100,000 and 750,000 guilders. Table 7.1 below gives detailed figures of the different types and sizes of firms in Haarlemmermeer that were officially registered with the chamber of commerce in 1954.

By the end of the 1960s and during the 1970s, employment in the Haarlemmermeer-Schiphol area increased substantially in the industry and construction sectors in 1969 and 1979, from 1,954 employees to 8,590 in industry and from 732 to 2,416 in construction respectively. This increase in employment was accompanied by a rapid increase in the number of firms from 93 in 1963 to 453 in 1977 (20 per cent).

Between 1970 and 1990, total employment (excluding Amstelveen) in this region increased from 38,398 in 1970 to 50,595 in 1980 and to more than 65,000 in 1990, while the number of establishments grew from 630 in 1970 to 954 in 1986.

Note that employment in the Schiphol region is more concentrated in the airport area and Amstelveen, while firms are more concentrated at the borders of the airport area, particularly in Aalsmeer, Amstelveen and other locations outside the core areas of Haarlemmermeer-Schiphol (see Figure 7.11).

Table 7.1 Categories and type of firms in Haarlemmermeer (1954)

Start-up capital (guilders,	One-person firm	Partnership	Limited partnership	Limited liability company	Coop. associate	Multinational affiliate	Total
Fewer than 2,000	182	29	2	9	6	1	**229**
2,000–10,000	461	96	6	7	4	1	**575**
10,000–25,000	194	66	5	8	–	–	**273**
25,000–50,000	57	47	6	5	3	–	**118**
50,000–100,000	12	20	2	4	–	–	**38**
100,000–500,000	3	4	2	4	1	–	**14**
500,000–1,000,000	–	–	–	1	–	–	**1**
5,000,000–7,500,000	–	–	–	1	–	–	**1**
Total establishment	5	5	–	4	1	–	**15**
Total (incl. all establishment)	**914**	**267**	**23**	**43**	**15**	**2**	**1,264**

Source: Schröder (1955, p. 182).

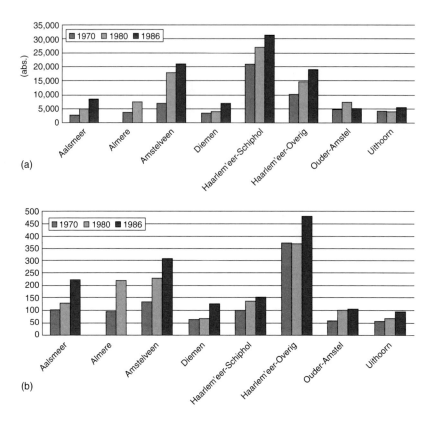

(a)

(b)

Figure 7.11 Employment (a) and number of establishments (b) in Schiphol region between 1970–86.
Source: Gemeentelijke bedrijvenenquête (O+S Amsterdam 1963–1979) and Annual Report Schiphol Airport (1970–1986).

Since the 1980s, a growing number of firms have delocalised their activities not only from the Amsterdam region but also from the Randstad to the Schiphol region because of the relatively low price of land and abundant space, the accessibility to the big cities of the Randstad and the proximity to the airport, e.g. connectedness to regional and European capital cities.

A direct result of the increasing employment in industry and services was the continuing decline of employment in the agriculture sector. During the 1950s, about 60 per cent of the active population of Haarlemmermeer was employed in agriculture. This percentage dropped to 40 per cent in 1962, of which only 18 per cent of the total in employment had a job in the agriculture sector and 22 per cent in other sectors related to horticulture and farming activities. By 1973, only 10 per cent of the active population (2,000 persons) were employed in the agriculture sector, 33 per cent in trade, transport and manufacturing industry and 57 per cent in the services sector.

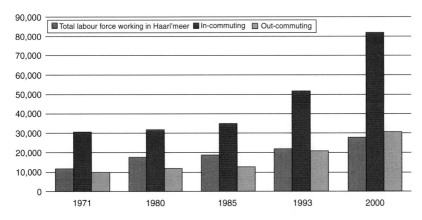

Figure 7.12 Commuting flows and labour force in Haarlemmermeer between 1971 and 2000.
Source: based on Boersma (2003, p. 62).

A close look at the commuter flows from other urban cores to the Schiphol region indicates a clear tendency towards the increasing economic importance of this region in general and Schiphol airport in particular. Of the 42–43,000 employees (including Schiphol) working in Haarlemmermeer in 1971, only a quarter were living in the municipality while three-quarters were commuters living in regional municipalities (e.g. in-commuting). In contrast, the total number of commuters living in Haarlemmermeer and working outside the municipality (e.g. out-commuting) was 10,000 (50 per cent of the total labour force of Haarlemmermeer) (see Figure 7.12).

Because of the rapid growth of Schiphol since the 1970s, Haarlemmermeer became one of the fastest growing working centres of the province of North Holland. This meant that the total number of in-commuters from the region was increasing, especially in the distribution, trade and transport sectors.

This tendency for employment and the number of firms to increase continued after 1985. Consequently, the number of in-commuters working in the Schiphol region but living outside has accelerated over the years. By the end of 1993, more than 55,000 workers in this region were in-commuters and less than half (almost 20,000) were out-commuters, while in 2000, the total out-commuters increased to 30,000 and in-commuters to 82,000.

7.6.2 *Spatial transformation of the Haarlemmermeer-Schiphol region*

Up until 1960, Haarlemmermeer had preserved its countryside character. Out of a total surface area of 18,500 ha, Schiphol airport occupied only 10 per cent (1,850 ha). In 1949, almost 80 per cent of employment was directly or indirectly related to agriculture. Outside the two core centres of Hoofddorp and Niewe Vennep, this rose to 86 per cent.

In 1960, Haarlemmermeer had 40,000 inhabitants, divided between Badhoevendorp (12,000 inhabitants), Zwanenburg (10,000 inhabitants) and 17 other small neighbourhoods (18,000 inhabitants) in the Haarlemmermeer polder. Between 1970 and 1990, the population of Haarlemmermeer increased from 58,966 to 95,782, before reaching 143,295 inhabitants in 2007. Today, almost 50 per cent of the inhabitants of Haarlemmermeer live in Hoofddorp and the rest of the population is spread between 16 villages and neighbourhoods, from which Nieuwe Vennep (23,000 inhabitants) is the largest town and Leimuiderbrug (50 inhabitants) the smallest village (Boersma, 2003: 3).

There are two main suburban core centres and two sub-centres in Haarlemmermeer, Hoofddorp and Nieuwe Vennep, and Badhoevendorp and Zwanenburg respectively. Besides these sub-centres, there exist three smaller sub-centres with total populations between 2,000 and 4,000 inhabitants. These are Rijsenhout (horticulture), Haarlem's Schalkwijk and Lisserbroek (bulb-culture). Of the 23 sub-centres in Haarlemmermeer, 17 are located along the borders of the municipality and only six municipalities are situated within the municipality of Haarlemmermeer itself.

One of the main factors driving the population growth in Haarlemmermeer is the continuing increase of inward migration from outside the polder, especially from the Amsterdam region and the Randstad. Over the whole period 1960–2006, Haarlemmermeer registered positive high levels of migratory movement, especially during the periods 1962–9, 1971–6 and 1998–2001.

A close look at the geographical patterns of migration in Haarlemmermeer, e.g. with regard to origin and destination, show that the majority of migration flows have their origin in various urban centres of the metropolitan region, e.g. Amsterdam, Haarlem, South Kennemerland, Amstelland-Meerlanden (Aalsmeer, Uithoorn, Amstelveen and Ouder-Amstel) and the Bollenstreek. At a higher spatial scale level, migration movements have their origin in one of the three Randstad provinces: North Holland, South Holland and Utrecht. Most settlers from these regions in Haarlemmermeer followed jobs instead of other considerations such as, for example, the choice of particular living conditions.

More generally, the majority of settlers in Haarlemmermeer have moved from the surrounding municipalities, particularly from Amsterdam and South Kennemerland. By contrast, people departing from Haarlemmermeer were equally divided between the three geographical areas of Amsterdam, South Kennemerland, and other surrounding areas, with a slightly higher number of people departing to greater Amsterdam. Finally, migration flows from the rest of the country to Haarlemmermeer were nearly constant and not significant (or negative) over the whole period 1964–2002.

The rapid increase in population, migration flows and the growth of Schiphol airport have radically changed the economic structure and the geographical patterns of Haarlemmermeer in general and the Schiphol region in particular. All these changes have put much pressure on local authorities with regard to spatial planning and economic development policies.

Local authorities were confronted by increasing demands for new housing, public amenities (schools, hospitals, public services, recreation parks, etc.), and industrial and office parks for businesses. This was not always an easy task because of conflicting objectives and ambitions between the main actors in the region, especially between the municipalities of Haarlemmermeer, and between Haarlemmermeer and the Schiphol Airport Company.

As argued before, the development of urban expansion plans for Haarlemmermeer was strongly dependent on the spatial planning strategies of Schiphol airport. The first general expansion plan for Haarlemmermeer was developed in 1941. This plan sketched the future urban expansion of Haarlemmermeer for a period of 50 years. Local authorities (and the national government) believed in the idea of selective and limited urbanisation of Haarlemmermeer, which guaranteed the preservation of the open space and the countryside character of the polder. Beside the preservation of the open 'Green Heart', the first national spatial planning document in 1958 was rather restrictive with regard to the development of Randstad into a metropolis. According to government policy, the urbanisation and urban sprawl should be contained and redirected towards the northern urban centres of Amsterdam, the Northern Wing of the Randstad, and the newly reclaimed polder in the northwest of Amsterdam (the Ijsselmeerlpolder). Haarlemmermeer and Sparenwoude were designated as buffer zones separating Haarlem from Amsterdam. It was in this context that permission was given to Haarlemmermeer to build only 60 houses per year. This was insufficient by far in response to the increasing housing shortage caused by, among other things, the depreciation and deterioration of the existing housing stock.

With the increased urbanisation and urban expansion of Amsterdam and Schiphol, the municipality of Haarlemmermeer commissioned the Geographic Institute of Utrecht University in 1951 (hereafter GIUU) to conduct a social-geographic study of the Haarlemmermeer polder. According to this study, urban expansion of Haarlemmermeer should be restricted to two core areas: Zwanenburg and Badhoevendorp. Zwanenburg would then develop into a working centre and Badhoevendorp into the core centre for the middle class to live.

Based on the results of the GIUU report, a new planning document sketching the future spatial expansion of the Haarlemmermeer municipalities was published in 1964. This planning document stressed once again the necessity of preserving the countryside character of the polder while at the same time stimulating the localisation of industry in Haarlemmermeer, which could compensate for the loss of employment in agriculture. Although the spatial structure plan noted the increase in the numbers of commuters and the number of Schiphol workers living in Haarlemmermeer, the regional effects of the future increase in employment in the Schiphol area and in the Fokker Company were ignored.

In addition, Hoofddorp would become a central urban core only on condition that the total population increased from 6,500 to 10–20,000 inhabitants. Forecasts of housing production showed the need to build 845 dwellings per year between 1964 and 1980, and a maximum of 1,480 additional dwellings should there be an unexpected increase in the demand of new housing by Schiphol workers. In this scenario, the total population was expected to increase to 50,000 in 1964 and 88,000 in 1985.

In the second national spatial plan of 1966, Haarlemmermeer was still considered an agrarian area with Hoofddorp and Nieuwe Vennep as the main living core areas (Ministry of VROM, 1966: 166).

In the orientation document of the third national spatial policy document, the government was explicitly in favour of the development of the core centres outside Haarlemmermeer (Ministry of VROM, 1976: 187). However, this policy was not realistic and difficult to maintain because of the growth in suburbanisation, the increased mobility of the population and the rapid spatial development and growth of Schiphol airport.

In 1972, the province of North Holland developed the regional plan for the Meerlanden,[1] by taking into account a strong increase in the population of Haarlemmermeer during the next 5–10 years (1970–80) and employment in the Schiphol airport area. According to this expansion plan, the population of Haarlemmermeer was expected to grow to 15,000 inhabitants, which meant that the municipality had to construct between 5,000 and 6,000 new houses annually, in addition to other public facilities and services in the two main core centres of Hoofddorp and Nieuwe Vennep. Haarlemmermeer got the green light from the province of North Holland (and the state) to build two new neighbourhoods: Graan voor Visch (2,000 dwellings) in Hoofddorp and Linquenda (16,000 dwellings) in Nieuwe Vennep. Shortly after the completion of these two new neighbourhoods, two more – Pax and Bornhom in Hoofddorp (respectively 2,100 and 3,300 new dwellings) – were realised.

Note that one of the main objectives of the spatial expansion of Haarlemmermeer was the creation of the necessary conditions for the implementation of the urban expansion plans without hampering the future economic development of the region, while at the same time preserving the open character of the suburban areas. To reach these goals, local authorities applied a restrictive policy aimed at controlling the growth of the population by restricting employment in the region. However, this policy could only succeed with the full cooperation of the province of North Holland in restricting the urban expansion of the so-called 'in between areas'. This meant that economic activities and new housing should instead be facilitated in the northern areas of the region (Purmerend, Hoorn and Alkmaar) and in Flevoland (Almere and Lelystad).

In 1978, the national spatial planning document designated the northern part of Haarlemmermeer as a new location for the construction of new housing. Haarlemmermeer was considered by the state as a growth centre, which meant that Haarlemmermeer was now able to get financial support from the state to realise its construction projects. However, this contrasted with the spatial planning of North Holland (known as 'NORON') – published one year earlier (1977) by the province of North Holland – where large areas in the western part of Hoofddorp were designated as new residential locations. The main reason behind this choice of location was the increasing shortage of land for housing construction in the southern part of the North Sea canal, the very low number of firms established in the northern parts of the province and, finally, the rapid increase in employment in the southern areas of Amsterdam.

It was expected that Haarlemmermeer would build 10,000 new dwellings. However, within ten years, the total number of new-build dwellings in Hoofddorp was more than 20,000 (see Figure 7.13).

The smaller town of Vijfhuizen was chosen by policy-makers as a potential location (a so-called NORON location) for the construction of 6,500 new dwellings.

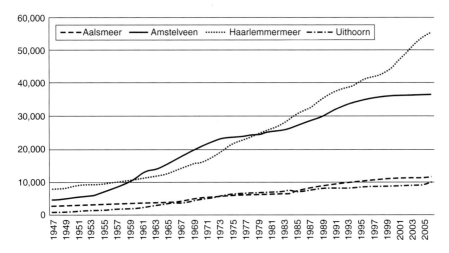

Figure 7.13 Housing production in Haarlemmermeer and Schiphol region: 1947–2006.
Source: CBS (WT, 1947–2006).

Because of the economic crisis of the 1980s, the state was unable to support financially the construction of Vijfhuizen and the whole project was abandoned. Consequently, similar numbers of new dwellings were built in Hoofddorp: the new neighbourhoods of Overbos in the south (4,800 new dwellings) and Toolenbrug in the southwest (5,800 new dwellings). Apart from these two locations, there were no other potential locations because of zoning restrictions implied by the noise contours of Schiphol airport. What was left as open space for housing construction amounted to only a few small scattered areas in the southern and western parts of Haarlemmermeer.

Finally, during the 1980s, the national spatial planning policy was fundamentally changed from the concentrated concentration to compact city policy. According to this policy, Haarlemmermeer was able to construct 10,000 to 15,000 new dwellings between Hoofddorp and Heemstede during the period 1995–2005. In close cooperation with the province of North Holland and the regional consultation forum of Amsterdam (ROA), two new locations (the so-called VINEX locations) were designated for housing construction: the locations of Floriande in West Hoofddorp and Getsewoud in West Nieuwe Vennep. Both were completed during the 1990s–2000s.

It is worth mentioning that a large discrepancy existed between the spatial planning and the infrastructure planning. The development of infrastructure networks, especially road and railway construction, lagged far behind the relatively fast spatial expansion of the Haarlemmermeer-Schiphol region. Ever since the 1960s, various attempts had been made by local authorities to connect Haarlemmermeer, by extending the existing railway and/or by constructing intermediate rail stations, to the railway network between Amsterdam and The Hague without much success. The same observation also applies to road construction.

For example, the planned A9 road in the 'Amsterdam–North Sea Canal' regional plan of 1978 was finally realised, but with a delay of 25 years.

7.7 Summary and conclusions

The postwar period may be considered an epoch of major radical and structural transformations that set up the fundamental structures of the present Dutch society. It was a period of outstanding changes in social-cultural, demographic, economic and institutional domains.

At the social and cultural level, the very conformist and traditional Dutch society, which was based on pillarisation and the dominance of traditional values, evolved into a modern and open society. In a short time, the depillarisation and secularisation of the Dutch society resulted in the emergence of powerful urban social movements, an increase in individualisation, mass-consumption, women's emancipation and the rise of a new (youth) culture and new lifestyles for individuals and households. In addition, the increase of wealth and the democratisation of the automobile and mass motoring fuelled the processes of suburbanisation and urban sprawl, and played an important role in decreasing the importance of the pillars and the differences between social classes.

At the socio-demographic level, the most important changes of the 1950s and 1970s were the increase in inter-regional and external migration flows, the rapid growth of population and the changes in the structure and composition of households. The tendency for the natural growth of the population to decrease was largely counterbalanced by a positive migration balance. In this sense, inward and outward migration movements became as important as natural growth in determining the growth of the population and labour force. The same tendency occurred at the regional level but with one small difference: within the two traditional core provinces of the Randstad (North Holland and South Holland), the four big cities began to lose population in favour of small and medium-sized cities. The explanation for this decline lies in the decreasing natural growth of the population combined with the increasing suburbanisation fuelled by the deconcentration of the middle classes from the big cities to suburban areas. By contrast, the labour supply increased substantially during this period because of the change in the age structure of the population and the increased participation of women in the labour market. Consequently, rising employment and growth in disposable incomes had a direct effect on the composition and size of households and on the housing demand (new type), and hence the demand for more land. As a result, the average size of household has been declining since 1947, while the share of one- and two-person households in the total population, especially in the largest cities, has increased rapidly from the 1960s onwards. These changes in the structure and composition of households have put pressures on the housing market, as a result of which the social housing sector grew significantly in the core urban areas and the private housing sector in suburban and peripheral areas.

With regard to the economic changes, Amsterdam, like other larger cities in the Randstad, recovered relatively more quickly from the disastrous effects of the

Second World War, and by the end of the 1950s almost all urban (economic) functions were restored and had been significantly improved. Investments aimed at increasing production capacity and strengthening the economic structure of cities have had a great impact on the development of economic activities such as the construction sector, equipment manufacturing, business and commercial services, public services and the manufacturing industry. The highest levels of investment (private and public) took place in the two provinces of the Randstad Holland, more particularly in the cities of Amsterdam and Rotterdam.

While the share of agriculture in the GDP at the national level fell to below 20 per cent between 1970 and 1980, the share of business and commercial services increased spectacularly as well as the non-profit sector. Over the whole period 1970–2000, the growth of industry, in terms of GDP, has decreased while the trade and retail industry, transport and communication and business services increased since the 1980s. In addition to investments and growth in GDP, the levels of employment, incomes, production and value added increased in almost all economic sectors.

With regard to employment, the distribution of the labour force shows significant differences in employment structure by sector. The main tendency between 1947 and 1971 was the decline in the number of jobs in agriculture and their increase in manufacturing industry and the tertiary sector.

Regionally, the total number of jobs in all economic sectors was increasing in the two provinces of North and South Holland and the province of North Brabant, Gelderland, Utrecht and Limburg. Between 1973 and 1983, the province of North Holland, and especially Amsterdam, lost thousands of jobs due to the successive economic crises of the 1970s and the 1980s. The first signs of economic recovery in Amsterdam became visible by the end of the 1980s.

More generally, since the 1970s, there has been a gradual decrease in employment in agriculture, the dispersion of employment from the central regions to the intermediate and peripheral regions along the corridors, and an increase in employment in business and commercial services in the Randstad and the province of North Holland.

Production and value added at the sectoral level followed a similar tendency, namely an increase in productivity in capital-intensive industries and the tertiary sector, especially in business and commercial services and the wholesale and transport sectors, and a decrease in traditional labour-intensive sectors. However, at the urban agglomeration level, the shares of production and value added declined in favour of emerging suburban areas, as in the case of Haarlemmermeer-Schiphol. This was caused by the deconcentration of industry and business services from big cities to suburban areas and the periphery regions.

From the analysis of various key indicators at the national and regional levels, the following conclusions may be drawn. First, the emergence of the post-industrial society since the 1970s was manifested by a shift in economic structure from an industry-based to a more service-oriented economy, accompanied by an increase in the highly qualified section of the total labour force in employment. Second, a simultaneous shift in the spatial organisation of economic activities (i.e. vertical and horizontal disintegration) took place with the shift in economic structure. Industry firms became more and more dispersed in space (at the regional as well as national level), and (some) business services firms started to delocalise their activities from the city centre to the suburban areas and urban fringes.

Economic growth and employment were, however, not uniform in all Dutch regions. Interregional disparities increased during the first three decades after the Second World War. The Dutch government applied successive regional economic policies and expansive industrial policies to help regions lagging behind to catch up with the central regions of the Randstad.

Regional policy focused on both the enhancement of economic efficiency and the reduction of interregional discrepancies through public investment in infrastructure and by subsidising firms and social organisations in regions lagging behind. The main guiding principle of the regional policy was the realisation of equality objectives, i.e. more balanced economic growth at the regional level. However, regional economic policies based on the principles of equality were less effective in decreasing regional disparities in terms of economic growth and employment. Thus policy interests have shifted since the 1980s towards a more innovation-oriented outlook (principle of efficiency), where regions are considered economic centres that should focus on technological innovations and existing local opportunities to resolve local economic problems. More recently, interest in infrastructure as the engine of economic development became central in the regional economic policy. In this respect, accessibility and connectivity are considered crucial factors in enhancing the competitiveness of city regions in the globalised world.

Beside the regional economic policy, the government applied successive spatial planning policies that reflected changes in theoretical ideas, ideologies and visions. The main challenges facing the government after the Second World War were the acute shortage in public (social) housing and improvements to the infrastructure and public services. Spatial planning was an important policy instrument to realise spatial-economic goals with regard to equity and efficiency in the distribution of wealth between regions, and in stimulating economic growth.

Since the early years of the 1950s, national planning policy has vigorously focused on constraining employment and housing construction in an effort to avoid urban sprawl (concentrated concentration and compact city policies) and preserve the open space. National authorities were merely concerned by the question of how to reach a more balanced distribution of population and economic activities between the central core and the peripheral regions.

Various national spatial planning documents were implemented since the 1950s. The spatial planning policy of concentrated deconcentration of the 1960s and the 1970s was abandoned in favour of the compact city policy during the 1980s, before switching to the city networks policy during the early years of the twenty-first century.

Based on extensive analysis of the economic and spatial transformations of the Amsterdam and Haarlemmermeer-Schiphol regions, we can classify the urbanisation and transformation of spatial structure of this region as a phased evolutionary process comprising four periods corresponding to different spatial urban models, as follows:

- *Period 1945–60*: city versus countryside in a hierarchical monocentric urban system model.
- *Period 1960–80*: the rise of the city region (centre-multi-core city) in a poly-nuclear urban system model.
- *Period 1980–99*: urban field/city networks in a defragmented polycentric urban system.
- *Period 1999–present*: urban nebula (glocal-urban networks).

Basically, the spatial transformation of urban spaces is caused by various factors interacting such as socio-demographic and cultural factors, economic factors and political and institutional factors (government policy, protection of ownership) affecting land use and the spatial organisation of people and activities. Having said that, the main findings of the development trajectory of spatial urban system at the level of the Amsterdam-Schiphol region since 1945 may be summarised as follows:

1. *The period 1945–60.* This period was dominated by the hierarchical monocentric urban system à la Christaller, in which the separation between city and country-side, in terms of socio-demographic, cultural, geographic and functional structure, largely determined the urban landscape of the Amsterdam-Schiphol region.

   In 1945, Amsterdam began its planning agenda of developing the city into a national centre of industrial and services activities with the execution of the General Expansion Plan (AUP). The effective execution of the AUP started with the extension of the city centre and the construction of new dwellings within the city borders. The progressive spatial expansion of Amsterdam at the western, northern and southern edges of the city resulted in the construction of the garden city of Slotermeer and the neighbourhood of Geuzenveld in the 1950s. From then on, the spatial expansion of Amsterdam progressed rapidly in the direction of the southeast and south of the city, with the construction of the urban area of Slotervaart (1954) and the new neighbourhood of Buitenveldert. To the southeast of Amsterdam, Haarlemmermeer managed to preserve its countryside character (low density of population and abundant land) dominated by agricultural activities. However, the spatial expansion of Haarlemmermeer followed the spectacular growth of Schiphol airport, which became a major growth centre attracting workers and industrial firms related to the airport's activities and transport. The increase in population of Haarlemmermeer resulted in an increase in the demand for housing and public amenities (schools, hospitals, public services, recreation parks, etc.), which was difficult to realise because of conflicting objectives between the municipalities of Haarlemmermeer and between Haarlemmermeer and Schiphol airport. Furthermore, the development of urban expansion plans (housing, amenities, business parks, etc.) of Haarlemmermeer was strongly dependent on the future spatial planning strategies of Schiphol airport.

Between 1945 and 1960, household composition and incomes between Amsterdam and the surrounding municipalities showed significant differences in favour of Amsterdam. This is because the majority of the urban population and jobs were still highly concentrated in and around the city centre.

The urban spatial structure of greater Amsterdam was dominated by radial patterns of transport infrastructure towards the centre of the city because of the spatial concentration of jobs and urban functions in the city centre, and the rather limited scale of spatial interactions, in terms of movements of individuals and households between regions (commuting flows). It is not surprising then that the dominant infrastructural means of transport were the train, tram and bicycle. Connections between the larger cities of the Randstad took place from city centre to other city centres. However, by the end of the 1950s and during the 1960s, the increase in motorised mobility and the use of the private car resulted in the separation of living places from working places, as the movements of individuals commuting from suburban areas and the countryside in the direction of the city centre or the municipal core centres increased significantly (see Brand, 2002: 65). At the same time, the increasing number of specialised suburban municipalities, predominantly rural areas, emerged as attractive living places. Gradually, a new urban hierarchy of cities and suburbs in the existing urban system emerged pointing in the direction of the formation of the city region (*stadgewest*).

The dominant position of Amsterdam weakened slightly as some of the surrounding municipalities developed into places of work, e.g. the municipality of Haarlemmermeer and Schiphol. The significant negative migration balance at the level of the city of Amsterdam and the positive migration balance at the level of suburban areas were clear manifestations of this gradual shift in the spatial organisation of population and activities in the Amsterdam and Schiphol region.

More generally, the change in the spatial functional structure of cities during the period 1945–60 was the result of population growth, interregional migration movements, the increasing mobility of individuals and households, and the growth of employment in the industry. Note that during this period, the spatial urban policy had little effect on the spatial organisation of population and economic activities between regions.

2.   *The period 1960–80*. This period saw the formation of the city region and the emergence of the polycentric urban system. During the 1960s, deconcentration became the dominant tendency in urban development in the Amsterdam-Schiphol region. The emphasis in urban development moved towards suburbanisation. Consequently, the traditional separation between city and countryside began to fade. Note that this period coincided with strong economic growth and increasing welfare in the Netherlands. The combination of high incomes and low transport costs stimulated the mobility of individuals and broadened the choice for households of more distant residential areas.

However, between 1970 and 1980, a sharp decline in employment was registered by Amsterdam's industry as a result of the oil crises of the 1970s and the deindustrialisation and delocalisation of industrial firms to other regions.

The sharp decrease in employment in industry was partly counterbalanced by the relatively rapid increase in employment in commercial and business services in the city as well as in the suburban areas of the greater Amsterdam region.

After 1970, the average disposable income in the Schiphol region was significantly higher than in Amsterdam. Beside the increased differences in incomes between social classes which resulted in the deconcentration of the middle class from the city to the suburban areas, the decentralisation of economic activities and the improvement of the infrastructure (road networks) also played an important role in increasing suburbanisation and urban sprawl. Jobs and housing became more spread over the Amsterdam agglomeration as some key sectors such as storage and distribution centres, wholesale and transport activities decentralised their activities to the proximity of the main motorway corridors. Accordingly, the economic position of the city centre weakened in comparison to the rising suburban growth centres. As a consequence, a clear spatial differentiation of urban functions and the specialisation of activities began to emerge at the level of the metropolitan region.

The dynamic spatial development of business services followed the suburbanisation process while at the same time a clear shift in the structure of the Amsterdam and Haarlemmermeer-Schiphol economies took place in this period. The Amsterdam economy became more oriented towards financial, business and commercial services, while Haarlemmermeer-Schiphol moved towards activities related to the airport such as logistics and distribution, commercial services, wholesale and retail activities, transport and tourism, etc.

Although the construction sector showed strong growth in suburban areas and the countryside, the city centre of Amsterdam was still dominant. The wholesale sector grew mainly at infrastructure corridors and in the countryside, while the retail sector was mainly concentrated in the city centre, albeit a gradual shift in the direction of suburban areas was registered. It seems that the retail sector followed the movements of population between the city of the city and the suburbs. The same tendency also took place in the transport sector, e.g. concentration in the city centre and a gradual shift to suburban areas and corridors.

In short, the increased suburbanisation and the emergence of specialised growth centres such as Schiphol and the Schiphol region resulted in a significant decrease in urban densities between the city centre and the surrounding urban areas, i.e. urban density decreased in the centre of the city and increased in the suburban areas. Consequently, the spatial structure of the Amsterdam-Schiphol region became more fragmented and much more complex than before.

Finally, the regional daily urban system of the 1970s and the 1980s was becoming more and more intertwined into a network of cities characterised by the spatial organisation of urban agglomerations organised around many nodes, centres and hubs, which were clearly larger in size than the traditional daily urban system of the 1960s. Indeed, the increased mobility of people resulted in substantial increases in the distance travelled between living and working places. As a consequence, the daily interactions now took place at a larger spatial scale where spatial patterns of urban areas shifted from radial to transversal transport systems. The private car became the dominant means of transportation and public transport (tram and train) began to lose its position to the private car.

3. *The period 1980–99.* This period was characterised by further defragmentation/splintering of the polynuclear urban system and the rise of the urban field. In the 1980s, the size of the municipalities of the Amsterdam-Schiphol region grew substantially, as a result of the continuing growth of population and population density. For example, the growth of the population of Haarlemmermeer was essentially determined by suburbanisation and urban sprawl occurring at the level of the greater Amsterdam region and the Randstad. However, since the second half of the 1980s, migration movements from the surrounding areas to Haarlemmermeer, like South Kennemerland, have been much higher than migration movements from Amsterdam.

Amsterdam itself was economically less successful than the Schiphol region during this period. The centre of the city was severely hit by the crisis. Unemployment rose to high levels, a number of important industrial firms were lost, and financial firms, banks and business services delocalised their activities from the city centre to the suburbs (Zuidas and the Schiphol region). However, the functional spatial structure at the level of the Amsterdam-Schiphol region showed a more structural character in the sense that the spatial hierarchical separation between the central city of Amsterdam and suburban areas has disappeared. In addition, the difference in the morphology of the greater Amsterdam and Schiphol region has faded, and consequently a clear delimitation of the geographical borders at the level of urban networks became difficult. A new spatial urban model emerged: the urban field or city networks. This urban spatial system is formed by several suburban core centres maintaining dense patterns of social and economic interactions with Amsterdam and other suburban areas, and is characterised by a high density of commuting movements between the city centre and suburban cores.

Travel time between living and working places has increased considerably, as well as the total number of displacements by motive, e.g. shopping, work, visits, recreation, etc. The daily urban mobility of individuals and households now take place at the level of the metropolitan region and between regions. In other words, the action radius of daily urban mobility has become larger with the increasing scale and density of commuting flows between regions.

Finally, the national authorities have launched several policy measures, through the spatial planning of the compact city policy, to stop urban expansion but without much success because of the continuing increase in mobility via the car, intra- and interregional mobility, and the changing preferences of households for specific living environments, e.g. the type of housing and urban amenities. These same factors still played an important role in the following transition phase of urban spatial system, namely the transition from urban field to urban nebula during the twenty-first century.

8   From mainport to airport city

The spatial-economic transformation of Schiphol since 1980

8.1 Introduction

Historically, the first three decades of the postwar period can be characterised as periods of increasing economic growth and wealth, increasing international trade, urbanisation and technological innovations. In contrast, during the last three decades of the twentieth century dramatic changes in the existing economic, political and social-cultural fields took place in western European countries. The most visible change in the economic field was the emergence of a new economic order characterised by the spread of neo-liberal ideas and a deep belief in the superiority of the 'market economy', which resulted in increasing deregulation, privatisation and globalisation of economies. At the political level, European integration and the enlargement of the European Union were a direct result of the integration of West and East Germany, and the disintegration of the Soviet bloc opened the doors to former socialist countries to join the EU.

Another important change was the gradual shift in economic and political powers from the western continent to the Asian continent with the resurgence of India, China and the former 'Asian tigers' (Malaysia, Indonesia, Hong Kong and Taiwan).

At the same time, the structure in most western European countries shifted from a manufacturing and industry-based economy to a knowledge and informational-based economy. This shift in economic structure resulted into deep social and cultural changes in which information technologies, knowledge and connectedness (social, cultural, economic and political) became the main elements structuring the functioning of the modern society.

As was the case with rail transport during the nineteenth century, the commercial aviation sector evolved into one of the most important economic sectors of central hub-cities, (air)ports and regions. The explanation for this lay in the democratisation of air travel that had been facilitated by the speed of changes in aviation technology and commercial aviation, especially with the introduction of bigger and faster new jet airplanes, and the fall in transport costs as reflected in the low air fares. As a result, the number of frequent passengers and air cargo transport increased significantly from the 1960s. Consequently, the changes in aviation technology and the democratisation of air travel had direct consequences on the construction, management and the operation of airports.

Since the 1970s, the structural changes in the aviation sector (i.e. the introduction of new jet and jumbo-jet airplanes, the deregulation and liberalisation of commercial aviation, and the continuing increasing demand for landside activities at the airport zones) resulted in a significant increase in the size of airport facilities (i.e. buildings, aprons, runways, etc.) and the diversification of airport activities (airside versus landside). In addition, the development of the air transport sector has accelerated the speed and scale of movements of people, capital and information between core cities and regions at the international level, and hence further economic and spatial disintegration of firms (material, production and distribution) across geographical locations.

A major implication of these changes was the lack of sufficient available space for airport expansion in the surrounding urban areas that were gradually being filled by housing, high-rise office buildings and industrial parks. Because of this, and the increase in the environmental effects of airports on their surroundings, the spatial expansion of airports became somewhat problematic and difficult to realise without the close cooperation of multiple (public and private) actors, each with their own agenda, objectives and ambitions. This multi-actor, multi-level governance field posed a great challenge to airport authorities in terms of reorganising existing and/ or developing new collective arrangements aimed at realising a balanced growth policy and safeguarding the implementation of ambitious airport spatial planning policy. Therefore, airport planning policy gradually shifted from traditional airport planning to a more flexible approach as the response to increased uncertainties in the air travel market and changes in EU and national regulations. Thus the Masterplan became the standard document for medium- and long-term airport planning.

The advantage of the flexible planning approach is that it offers the airport authorities the possibility to update the Masterplan during the planning process according to changes in market conditions, regulation and the coalitions of actors involved in the planning process.

During the 1990s, the traditional role and nature of Schiphol airport shifted from a provider of public services to a fully commercially oriented business company, whose main goals are to increase profitability and improve its competitive position in air traffic networks.

The commercial policy focused on the diversification of sources of revenue and more particularly on the development of landside activities aimed at attracting consumers (fast-food stands, retail stores and shopping malls, hotels and restaurants, and other concessions) and businesses to the airport zone and its surrounding areas (industrial parks and office business parks). During the twenty-first century, commercialisation activities within and around Schiphol airport zone have gone far beyond the development of consumer activities to include a large variety of commercial and real-estate activities such as business and industrial parks, international trade centres, conference and exhibition centres, five-star hotels, amusement and cultural meeting centres and modern working centres, all of which one could find in a typical downtown city centre.

The shift of Schiphol airport from a policy oriented towards the development of mainport functions to the airport city strategy confirms the ongoing process of evolution of the airport from a commercially oriented business organisation coordinated by hybrid market networks into a 'nebula city' generating strong agglomeration effects which spill over to the whole metropolitan region and the Randstad. In this sense, the direct and indirect economic effects of the airport city involve multiple spatial scale levels, i.e. local, regional and national levels.

The aims of this chapter are the identification, analysis and discussion of the key transformation processes and changes described above, and their implications for the spatial and economic development of Schiphol airport and the Schiphol region from 1980 until the present. In section 8.2, we discuss briefly the nature, causes and consequences of the restructuring processes that have taken place in the air transport sector in Europe since the 1980s and their implications for the development of Schiphol airport. In section 8.3, we present a quantitative assessment of the economic performance of Schiphol airport during the period 1980–2009.

In section 8.4, the focus will be on the underlying causes and factors that resulted in the adoption of the mainport strategy. The analysis takes into account the historical conditions of the decision-making processes and the resulting policies in order to understand the economic and spatial evolution of Schiphol airport into one of most important mainports and economic growth centres of the Netherlands. Based on policy documents and Schiphol reports and archives, we describe the spatial implications of airport planning measures for the airport zone and Schiphol region. Subsequently, in section 8.5, we focus attention on the role of actors in the decision-making process concerning the spatial-economic development of Schiphol airport. We adopt a multi-actor and multi-spatial scale level in identifying the key actors, their degree of involvement, decision-making powers and coordination mechanisms within a hybrid governance structure.

In section 8.6, we discuss the shift in the policy vision from mainport to Schiphol airport city and the underlying explanatory factors that could help us understand how this policy vision has been realised and developed in practice. Next, in section 8.7 we turn attention to an analysis of the economic effects of Schiphol on the local and regional economy, and the development of Schiphol into a strong cluster and top location for business services and activities in the metropolitan region. In addition, problems related to noise nuisance and environmental issues will be discussed. Section 8.8 concludes.

8.2 Restructuring the air transport sector: deregulation and liberalisation policies in Europe

There have been major regulatory and structural developments in both the air transport industry and airport activities since the 1970s. The deregulation of the air transport sector has resulted in the formation of alliances and cooperation between well-established national home carriers and the emergence of a small number of European airports in the international air-transport market. In this sense, the deregulation and liberalisation of the air market, the privatisation of airports, and globalisation had far-reaching consequences on the operation and management of airports, especially during the 1980s and the 1990s.

It was in this context that hub and spoke airports began to emerge as a strategic response aimed at internalising the effects of changes in the air transport environment. The main determinant factors of airport competitiveness were the increased capacity of airports, the extension of air connections through tight time planning of scheduled flights arriving and departing during peak intervals, the increasing load factor and consequently the increase in productivity levels (Courtwright, 2005: 159).

In Europe, the European Commission announced in 1985 new policy measures aimed at liberalising the air transport market. These measures followed the resolution of the European Council of Ministers of Transport in May 1984 stipulating the deregulation of air transport in Europe.

The Netherlands and Great Britain were among the first European countries to implement the EU liberalisation policy by signing a bilateral agreement based on a system of 50:50 share of their air traffic market. The choice of the European Commission for a phased liberalisation of air transport, through the introduction of three deregulation packages in 1987, 1990 and 1993, was intended to stimulate the creation of the internal European market (by the end of 1992) and to increase the flexibility of the European air transport sector, i.e. to stimulate competition between European airlines. In other words, according to the European Commission, the deregulation and liberalisation of the air transport market would allow more differentiation of fares on scheduled air services between European countries. Accordingly, one airline could then capture more than 75 per cent of air traffic in any given bilateral air route (Dierikx and Bouwens, 1997: 237).

The most important effect of the deregulation policy in Europe was the increased competition between the traditional large home carriers and the low-cost airline companies. As result, transnational airline companies shifted their strategy from traditional origin–destination (OD) or point-to-point flights to multiple air connections passing through hub-and-spoke airports. This meant that air traffic networks between origin and final destinations should be reorganised through intermediate hub airports serving as major collection and redistribution points for flights between origin and final destinations.

Consequently, major European airports like Frankfurt, Heathrow, Paris Charles de Gaulle and Amsterdam became the world's busiest airports in terms of capacity of air traffic, especially during peak hours. A slot allocation system between airports was then implemented to control the air traffic movements of airplanes during the peak hours. One important element of this system was the reorganisation of commercialisation of landing rights for European airlines that gave a clear advantage to airlines – usually the home carriers – possessing landing rights at certain airports (for example, KLM at Schiphol) (Dierikx and Bouwens, 1997: 239).

These structural changes in the air transport sector pushed airports to adopt new business management styles. This was achieved by the transfer of ownership from public to different forms of private ownership such as strategic partnerships, private management contracts, etc. (Graham, 2003: 6).

As a result, airports were once again confronted by new challenges concerning the organisation, operation and management of capacity in order to face the increase in air traffic movements and passengers.

8.2.1 Changing the traditional role and nature of airports: causes

Up to the 1990s, most airports were owned by public authorities or jointly with local governments (local-public ownership). However, albeit that airports were considered public utilities with public service obligations (Doganis, 1992), their management differed widely between countries. Some airports were strictly controlled by the government while others were given some degree of autonomy in operating and managing their facilities and services. However, from the 1980s, the majority of European airports shifted their commercial and operational management towards a more market-oriented management style in order to increase efficiency and integrate the airport activities within the local and regional economy. In this sense, the commercial aspects of managing an airport, such as financial management, non-aviation activities and marketing, became crucial in running airport activities in a context of increasing uncertainties in the air traffic sector (Graham, 2003: 10). Viewed from this perspective, airports became pure business organisations seeking to maximise profits from their aviation and non-aviation activities. For example, in 1984, for the first time in its history, Amsterdam Schiphol airport realised higher revenues from non-aviation (retail and other airport facilities) than from aviation activities.

More generally, the traditional role of airports as providers of public services shifted towards a more proactive role in the marketing and promoting of airports as businesses, i.e. the management and development of retail businesses and other commercial facilities, real-estate development, cost control and optimisation of internal organisation, increasing productivity and quality management, etc.

As mentioned above, the deregulation, liberalisation and reorganisation of airline networks in Europe have had direct effects on the management and operation of airports. Consequently, the planning and management of airports have become subject to high risks and uncertainty concerning the scale and direction of future spatial and economic growth. In addition, the emergence of hub-and-spoke networks has weakened the position of the main national airports in the sense that national home carriers could no longer be forced to choose their national airport as the main basis for their operational activities. In this context, in addition to the traditional advantages of geographical location and accessibility, other factors like cost-effectiveness (costs charged to airlines), the quality of the airport facilities and services offered to consumers, and the airport environmental quality became determining factors of competitiveness.

Moreover, the increase in consciousness of environmental issues has pushed airport authorities to think about alternative strategies that integrate more balanced environmental policies which could make airports environmentally friendly places.

The environmental programmes applied by most European airports were in line with EU guidelines aimed at limiting the noise nuisance of airports for the surrounding areas (the so-called Chapter 2 and 3), e.g. penalising most noisy and less clean aircraft and rewarding cleaner and less noisy aircraft. Simultaneously, airports began to apply several measures to limit the effects of noise nuisance on the surrounding urban areas like the enforcement of take-off and landing (approach) procedures, noise regulations and other measures (taxiing and handling procedures, instigating insulation programmes for neighbourhoods located in the vicinity of the airport, etc.).

8.2.2 The increasing importance of landside activities and long-term planning policy: the consequences

During the second half of the 1980s, most European airports followed the example of Roissy-Charles de Gaulle – the leader in the development of business and office parks in the airport area and its surroundings – and began to shift their commercial policies towards the optimisation of business activities through a gradual shift from airside activities to landside/non-aviation activities. Since then, airports have became strongly involved in developing wide and diverse landside activities, especially real estate, office buildings, industrial parks and logistics and distribution centres around their perimeters. Airports saw their economic position changing from traditional airport-based activities to more diversified activities and functions within the regional economy. Airport zones and the surrounding urban areas became highly attractive locations for businesses activities and the greatest concentration of work centres in their regions.

In the case of Schiphol airport, the commercialisation of airport activities was closely related to the development of the airport as a mainport and powerful economic centre in the region. This double strategy could only be achieved by offering high-quality services and facilities to airlines while at the same time improving the accessibility of the airport, especially to the high-speed train linking Amsterdam to Brussels, Paris and London. On the one hand, the interconnectivity of Schiphol airport terminals with the high-speed national railway network and the motorway system was considered of vital importance to achieving the hub position in European and international air traffic networks. On the other hand, the diversification of airport operations and activities by adding to existing airside activities the development of business parks, real estate and industry parks for light industry in the surrounding areas was seen as essential to strengthening that hub position.

The second stage in increasing the level and size of airport facilities and services offered to consumers was the development and management of dynamic 'airport cities'. The airport city provides various landside services for visitors and the inhabitants of the surrounding areas 24 hours a day. These services include shops, hotels and restaurants, information and communication facilities, business facilities, medical services, cultural facilities, and sport and recreation facilities. The concept of the airport city came from the development of real-estate activities to support and enhance the airport activities, intensify space usage within and around the airport zone and improve the quality of the location.

The 'airport city' formula was intensively commercialised by Schiphol as a marketing strategy and branding symbol to gain market share, by entering into alliances with other airports, local authorities and financial and commercial partners in the Netherlands and abroad.

Note that the shift in airport strategy towards a policy of the optimal use of airport services and business activities demands structural change in internal management and organisational structure of the airport. In this respect, Schiphol Airport Company was split up into four relatively independent business units in 1991, each with its own management. These are airside, landside, terminals and facility management (a special project bureau was added to this last business unit). It is important to note that this change in the internal organisation of Schiphol Airport Company was the result of two factors: (1) long discussions about the necessity to reconsider airport business practices in light of ongoing European liberalisation and deregulation; and (2) the involvement of Schiphol in managing airport activities at various other international airports.

With the increasing diversity of activities of Schiphol in the Netherlands and abroad, Schiphol implemented a new organisation structure in 1998, whereby the Schiphol Airport Company became the Schiphol Group. The name 'Schiphol' was consciously used as a brand name (e.g. image) that ranks among the top ten most trusted brands in the Netherlands, with a sound international reputation as the manager of high-quality airport services. The new organisational structure consisted of three business units: Amsterdam Airport Schiphol (divided into three supporting units: Consumer Services, Airline and Handling Services and Schiphol Support Services), Schiphol Real Estate and Schiphol Project Consultants, and four independent subsidiary units (Schiphol International, Information and Communication Technology, Regional Airports (Rotterdam airport, Eindhoven airport and Lelystad airport) and Schiphol Support Services).

Today, the internal organisation structure of the Schiphol Group is composed of the following five independent subsidiary units: participation, Schiphol Real Estate, Schiphol Project Management, Amsterdam Airport Schiphol and Schiphol International, and two supporting units: Schiphol support services and information and communication technology (see Figure 8.1).

8.3 Economic performance of Schiphol airport since the 1980s: implications

During the 1970s and 1980s, the dominant tendency in the air transport sector was the fast increase in airside activities. However, since the 1990s a clear shift in air transport activities towards the increase of non-aviation activities in the total revenues became apparent. Most of the revenues from aviation activities come from landing and passengers fees, while non-aviation revenues come from concessions, sales and rents. For example, the share of non-aviation in the total revenues of Schiphol reached 53 per cent in 2001, against 43 per cent of revenues generated by aviation activities. Other major European airports show the same tendency.[1] For example, 38 per cent of total revenues realised by Brussels airport came from non-aviation activities against 62 per cent of revenues realised by aviation activities. These percentages for other airports were respectively: 30 per cent against 70 per cent for Frankfurt, 28 per cent against 72 per cent for Milan, 60 per cent against 40 per cent and 59 per cent against 41 per cent for Heathrow

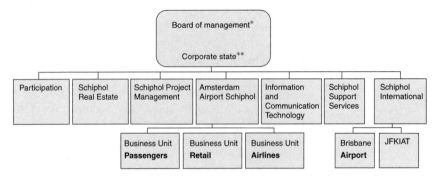

Figure 8.1 Internal organisational structure of the Schiphol Group (2002).

Source: Annual Report Schiphol Group (2002).

* The board of management is formed by the president and chief executive officer, the executive vice president and chief operational officer, and the executive vice president and chief financial officer.

** Corporate state is organized as follows: department of airport development; treasury and risk management; corporate communications; audit service; corporate control; corporate secretariat/legal services and business development.

and Gatwick, 56 per cent against 44 per cent for Paris CG airport, and 48 per cent against 52 per cent for Zurich (Graham, 2003: 58).

Note that most airports experience economies of scale. This means that the structure of costs and revenues depend on airport size and the volume and nature of traffic networks, which in turn have direct effects on the economic performance of the airport (Doganis, 1992; Pels, 2000).

The economic performance of airports can be analysed by looking at the relationship between labour and capital inputs (e.g. total number of employees, employees' wages and salaries, the production capability or capacity of the airport, depreciation, asset value) and outputs, either in financial or physical units (e.g. productivity, value-added, number of aircraft, passengers and cargo, and total revenues). Based on data on inputs and outputs, one may develop several indicators to measure the economic performance of airports such as cost-efficiency indicators, labour and capital productivity, revenues performance and profitability indicators, as well as indicators on the level and quality of airport services (see Graham, 2003: 64).

To clarify the economic performance of Schiphol airport during the period 1980–2007, we focus attention on both input and output figures, and more particularly on the total number of passengers, cargo transport, aircraft movements, the financial result and total costs and revenues.

8.3.1 Spectacular increase in airside activities

In terms of passengers and cargo transport, the growth of Amsterdam Airport Schiphol has been spectacular since 1980. The number of passengers increased on average by 5.6 per cent in the 1980s, 9 per cent in the 1990s and 3.37 per cent in the period 2000–7. The average increase in the number of transfer passengers was, respectively, 1.33 per cent and 1.76 per cent during the 1980s and the 1990s. By contrast, a sharp decrease of 20.27 per cent in transfer passengers was registered between 2000 and 2007.

In 1984, Schiphol airport was connected to 184 destinations (183 destinations in 1983) distributed over 89 countries (85 countries in 1983), and served by 64 airlines. Eleven years later, Schiphol was connected to 240 destinations, served by 88 airline companies, from which six airlines were operating in cargo air transport. A record number of passengers was registered in 1985 (11.7 million passengers), which corresponds to an increase of 7.8 per cent compared to 1984. The total number of passengers reached 13.6 million in 1987, and 15 million in 1988.

Two major tendencies were registered during the 1980s: first, an increase in intra-European air traffic services (7.3 per cent in 1985) as well as in intercontinental services, especially on the North Atlantic routes (USA and Canada); second, an increase in the number of transfer passengers since 1980 compared to

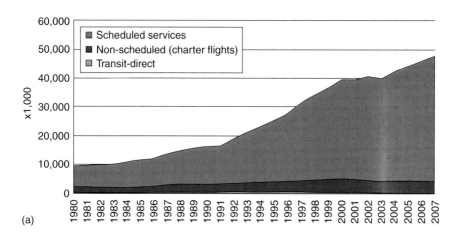

(a)

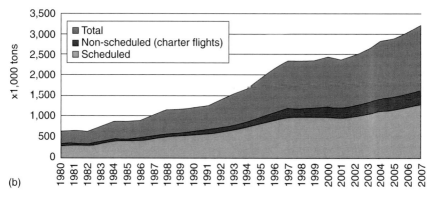

(b)

Figure 8.2 Passengers (a) and cargo (b) transport at Schiphol airport between 1980 and 2007.
Source: Annual Reports Schiphol Airport (1980–2007).

origin–destination (OD) transport as a result of the increase in the total number of connections to/from Schiphol airport.

Despite the severe effects of the first Gulf War of 1991 (i.e. increases in oil prices) and the international economic recession, Schiphol recovered relatively more quickly than other European airports. While the charter air travel market decreased significantly in 1991, scheduled traffic grew by 0.9 per cent. In total 16.5 million passengers (including transit passengers) passed through Schiphol airport during this year. The increased number of passengers was, partly, due to the remarkable growth in air traffic to/from Eastern European destinations and the conversion of the southern European charter services of Transavia and KLM-Cityhopper (KLM and Netherlines) into scheduled flight services. In addition, air traffic services to the Far East and the Caribbean regions increased significantly, with the increase in popularity of these two regions as holiday destinations.

As a result of the increased frequency and quality of air transport networks, KLM managed to increase its market share (70.8 per cent in passengers and 63.4 per cent in cargo transport in 1995), by signing partnership and strategic alliance agreements with KLM Cityhopper, Northwest Airlines, Air UK, Transavia, Martinair and Eurowings. As a result, the international position of Schiphol airport was considerably improved as it became the second largest European cargo airport (after Frankfurt) in 1996, and the fourth largest airport in Europe (27.97 million passengers).

Schiphol was developing into Europe's fourth 'mainport' with a strong position in transfer passengers (13.8 per cent) compared to (OD) transport (7.1 per cent). Of the total number of passengers travelling through Schiphol airport 40.2 per cent were transfer passengers (38.7 per cent in 1995). The increase in transfer passengers was stimulated further by the expansion of KLM's 'wave' system (i.e. KLM partners adapt their schedules to the three waves of arriving and departing KLM flights), and the extension of air networks and frequencies of regional and European flights by KLM and its partners.

During the first years of the twenty-first century, the low-fare air transport sector increased substantially with the entrance of low-budget airline companies to the air travel market. The low-fare market expanded by more than one million passengers to reach 3 million in 2002 and 4.5 million in 2005, thereby accounting on average for 8.8 per cent of the market share of European passenger transport at Schiphol between 2002 and 2005. The enlargement of the EU to 25 countries in 2004 has increased the number of intra-EU passengers by approximately 1.5 million on an annual basis at Schiphol. From 2005 to 2007, the airport retained its position as Europe's fourth-largest airport in terms of number of passenger (47.8 million in 2007) and third largest cargo airport in 2007 (1.61 million tons), recording an average growth rate of passengers of 3.8 per cent and 3.7 per cent in cargo transport during this period.

Finally, the growth in aircraft movements grew on average by 5.5 per cent during 1980–90 and 8.1 per cent in the period 1990–2001 (Figure 8.3). In 2002, for the first time since 1982, the number of aircraft movements decreased by 3.6 per cent (from 416,000 in 2001 to 401,385 in 2002).

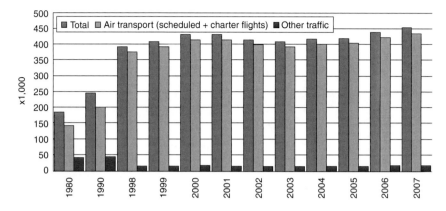

Figure 8.3 Total aircraft movements at Schiphol airport: 1980–2007.
Source: Annual Reports Schiphol Airport (1980–2007).

The decrease in the number of aircraft movements was caused essentially by the rise in insurance premiums for airline companies after the attacks of 11 September 2001 and the reduction in the frequency of flights. The 11 September 2001 attacks on the USA resulted in a worldwide sharp decrease in international passengers on scheduled air services (4 per cent) and international air cargo transport (8 per cent). Several European airline companies were severely affected, like the Belgian home carrier Sabena and Swissair. Schiphol was the only European airport that ended the year with an almost identical number of passengers (–0.2 per cent including transits) and aircraft movements (+0.4 per cent) as in 2000.

During the period 2005–7, the number of air transport movements at Amsterdam Airport Schiphol increased by 2.7 per cent (from 404,594 in 2005 to 435,973 in 2007). Note that a higher aircraft load factor (up to 76 per cent) and the use of larger aircraft explain why transport of passengers increased much more than the number of air transport movements. The average maximum take-off weight (MTOW) stabilised at an average of 98.7 tons between 2004 and 2007.

8.3.2 Significant improvements in financial conditions of Schiphol airport

As result of the economic crisis and the slow recovery of the air transport market during the early years of the 1980s, Schiphol registered successive negative financial results (losses) in 1981 and 1982 of, respectively, –11.15 million and –1.56 million guilders (see Figure 8.4). The next two years (1983, 1984), only moderate, albeit increasing, positive financial results were realised (3.63 million and 4.42 million guilders). The positive financial results were mainly due to the recovery of the Dutch economy in general and the air transport market in particular.

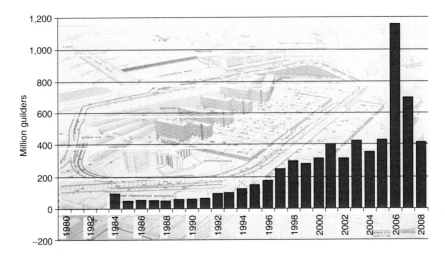

Figure 8.4 Financial results of Schiphol airport: 1980–2008.
Source: Annual Reports Schiphol Airport (1980–2009).

Note that the unexpected high increase in net financial result in 1984 (85 million guilders) was the direct result of the re-evaluation of Schiphol's existing assets by an additional 54 million guilders. Between 1985 and 1995, the financial results show a spectacular increase of 23.4 per cent (from 43.6 million guilders in 1985 to, respectively, 55 million and 145.7 million guilders in 1990 and 1995), corresponding to an annual average growth rate of 17.6 per cent in the period 1990–5.

In the period 1996–2007, Schiphol airport focused on the improvement of the quality of airport services and the active marketing of both passenger and cargo transport in order to strengthen its competitive position as a mainport. Stimulated by the growth in the air transport market, Schiphol's net results grew from 19.4 per cent in 1996 to 21 per cent in 1998, 35.4 per cent in 2002 and 19.8 per cent in 2005. However, the net result of 1999 was somewhat lower than 1998 (280.1 million guilders) because of the abolition of duty-free sales within the European Union (from 1 July 1999) and the adjustments applied in Schiphol's accounting system.[2] This last observation applies also to the year 2004 when Schiphol implemented new accounting practices based on the International Financial Reporting Standards (IFRS) of the International Accounting Standards Board (IASB). Since January 2005, the new EU regulation on the application of the IFRS to all airport companies registered on the stock market was enforced. The Schiphol Group possessed at that time important amounts of debts registered on the London stock market. Consequently, the unexpectedly high increase in net results in 2006 (1.16 billion guilders) is directly related to the application of this new EU regulation.

Furthermore, the improvement in the net financial results was also due, among other things, to the government decision of March 1998 to allow Schiphol airport to grow to 380,000 aircraft movements, with an additional 200,000 aircraft movements in the years after 1998. As result, the number of air transport movements increased to 460,000 in 2002.

Finally, from 1998, non-aviation revenues became a major contributor to the company's financial result. In 1998, the non-aviation revenues represented about 37.6 per cent of total revenues and 45.8 per cent of airport fees, i.e. landing fees, aircraft parking and charges to passengers. Airport fees represented 50 per cent of total revenues in 2000, while revenues from non-aviation activities increased to 50 per cent in the same year. Incomes from lease activities grew substantially because of the high occupancy rate of new office buildings.

Analysis of the balance sheet (assets, liabilities and ownership equity) gives valuable information on investments in fixed capital, either through borrowing money from third parties or by using the company's own financial resources (e.g. owners' or stockholders' equity). As Figure 8.5 shows, the fixed assets of Schiphol doubled between 1990 and 2000, from 1.7 billion to 3.4 billion guilders. This reflects at first instance the increase in investments aiming to improve the level and quality of airport facilities and services, such as extensions of terminal facilities, parking areas, cargo facilities, infrastructure, runways, aprons, etc.

A major increase in Schiphol's fixed assets took place between 2001 and 2009 – from 6.3 billion to 12 billion guilders – with the construction of the fifth runway, various extensions and construction works to improve the mainport functions of the airport and the implementation of the airport city concept, e.g. extensive investment in real-estate activities such as industrial parks and office buildings. Moreover, Schiphol invested a great amount of money in purchasing land and improving the accessibility of the airport area, i.e. the construction of roads within and around the airport zone (see Table 8.1).

Schiphol's balance sheet during 1980–2009 shows high levels of stockholders' equity compared to the share of third parties as the main source of investment. In 1980, stockholders' equity was 956 million against 417 million guilders from

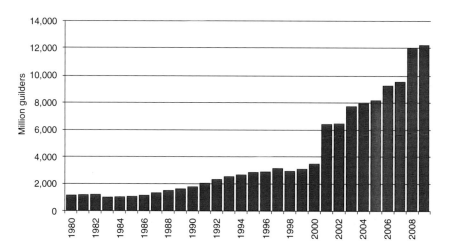

Figure 8.5 Growth of fixed assets of Schiphol (1980–2009).
Source: Annual Reports Schiphol Airport (1980–2009).

Table 8.1 Total investments in fixed assets between 1989 and 2009 (in million guilders)

	1989	1994	2000	2005	2009
Runways, taxiways and aprons	1.1	29.8	539.5	373.3	374.2
Land and roads	6.3	65	54.1	423.2	431.6
Buildings	18.6	145	−16.6	717.5	712.8
Installations	19.2	85.8	206.4	562.7	578.3
Other fixed assets	11.7	16	26.1	98.4	101.3
Asset under construction	170.1	22.5	−62.3	289.9*	548.2**
Total	227	319.1	263.2	2175.3	2198.5

Source: Annual Reports Schiphol Airport (1980–2009).
* Including 136.6 million guilders invested in real estate activities. ** Including 154.9 million guilders invested in real estate activities.

third parties, and in 2000, respectively, 3.4 billion and 1.9 billion guilders. Between 2001 and 2009, the growth rate of stockholders' equity increased by 58.5 per cent. Although the share of third parties was increasing, the share of investments financed by the company's own financial resources significantly improved during 2001–9. This meant that the financial position of Schiphol was strengthened as a result of the continuing increase in revenues earned from airside activities as well as from the landside activities. However, to provide supporting evidence to our suggestion, we should look closely at the changes in total income (revenues) and total costs of the airport during the same period (1980–2009) (see Figures 8.6 and 8.7).

Indeed, as mentioned before, a major part of the revenues earned by Schiphol still comes from airside activities. However, the increase in revenues from landside activities has two sources: first the increase in airport charges to airlines

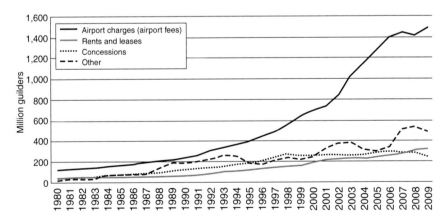

Figure 8.6 Total revenues of Schiphol airport (1980–2009).
Source: Annual Reports Schiphol Airport (1980–2009).

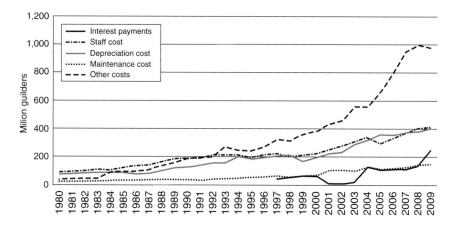

Figure 8.7 Total costs of Schiphol airport (1980–2009).
Source: Annual Reports Schiphol Airport (1980–2009).

and passengers; and second the increase in the number of airlines using Schiphol as origin and/or destination or hub to final destinations. Both sources of revenues from landside activities have been increasing since 1990: from 442.8 million guilders in 1990 to 689.2 million guilders in 2000 and 1.4 billion guilders in 2007. Other sources of revenue are rents and concessions of shops, restaurants, etc., at the airport terminal area and the airport zone. However, since 2007, revenues earned from leasing airport facilities and buildings at the airport and surrounding areas has increased considerably.

With regard to the total costs of Schiphol Airport Company, personnel costs, the payments of interest on loans and depreciation costs on fixed capital constitute the major components. Note, however, that personnel costs decreased slightly between 1992 and 2000 due to successive reorganisations implemented by the company.

Depreciation costs maintained a stable growth over the whole period 1987–2009: from 107 million guilders in 1987 to 206.4 million guilders in 1997 and 376 million guilders in 2007. The same observation also applies to the total maintenance costs for the airport equipment and facilities.

8.4 Strengthening the economic position of Schiphol under the free market regime: the mainport strategy as national policy

After the deregulation and liberalisation of the airline sector in Europe, a strong competitive struggle between the airline companies and national airports took place in the 1990s. The competition between the four major mainports of Europe – Schiphol, Frankfurt, Heathrow and Charles de Gaulle – focused on the attraction of passenger and cargo airlines. Most European airports were searching for new ways to expand further their spatial reach and increase the frequency of inter-European and long-distance flights and their landside activities.

More generally, since the 1980s, the following major trends had strong effects on the operation and functioning of airports around the world: (1) the high increase in international air transport in terms of passengers and cargo air transport; (2) the increase in competition between national airlines; and (3) the continuing decrease in profit margins and increase in operational costs caused by the high depreciation rates on aircraft and airport facilities. As a result, many airlines around the world entered into a wave of mergers and acquisitions and the formation of alliances which have resulted in the reorganisation of international air traffic networks and, hence, the restructuring of airport activities. At the same time, the growing importance of information and communication technologies has changed radically the organisation of commercial airline activities, e.g. worldwide marketing and sales of tickets. In turn, the Internet revolution has stimulated cooperation between airlines in sharing international air connections passing through hub airports. Connectivity, in terms of tight flight schedules and enlargement of air connections, became a determining factor in airport competitiveness.

In the Netherlands, the liberalisation of the air transport sector and the structuring effects of the air transport market pushed the airport authorities to adopt the mainport strategy. This strategy focuses on the development of Schiphol into an international mainport by improving and extending air traffic connections and increasing the frequency of air traffic through Schiphol. The mainport strategy was integrated into the national spatial policy aimed at promoting the Netherlands as the largest distribution and logistics centre of unified Europe. Schiphol and the port of Rotterdam got special attention from the state as the two main drivers of economic growth of the Dutch economy (Ministry of Spatial Planning and Ministry of Transport and Energy, 2005).

The Dutch government has implicitly supported the spatial expansion of Schiphol by making important concessions with regard to environmental requirements and subsidising, directly or indirectly, the growth of the airport (Bosma, 1998: 11). However, from the mid-1990s, because of the increasing awareness of the negative external effects of the mainports, the mainport policy received less attention, especially in the Fifth Spatial Planning Report (2001). More recent policy documents such as *Pieken in de Delta* (2004), *Nota Mobiliteit* (2004) and the *Nota Ruimte* (2004), mainports again received special attention from the government. The mainports are considered to be important to the improvement of the business environment and competitiveness of the Dutch economy as a whole.

8.4.1   The mainport strategy: developing the mainport functions in the era of globalisation

As a result of the liberalisation of European air transport, air traffic became concentrated in a limited number of mega-carriers operating worldwide. Few of the mainports succeeded in maintaining and/or strengthening their market position by securing the continuity of airport activities through land reservation for future spatial expansions. In the case of Schiphol, the spatial expansion of the airport was becoming problematic because the urbanisation of the Randstad region was reaching the maximum, which was making it very difficult to find new and suitable open space to realise large spatial expansion plans (Bosma, 1998: 14). Another major problem facing the government was the facilitation of the growth ambitions for the mainport Schiphol, while keeping the environmental effects within acceptable limits. However, under growing protests from citizens and environmental organisations, Schiphol took several measures aimed at reducing noise nuisance such as: the imposition of additional charges to noisy aircraft, restrictions of night flights, use of the runway 01L-19R in two directions during night flights, and the execution of a large programme of insulation in neighbourhoods falling within 40 Ke (Kosten units) noise contours.

Encouraged by the government support, Schiphol expressed its ambition to become a mainport by developing the 'Concept Masterplan Schiphol 2003' in 1989. In this Masterplan, Schiphol sketched the future spatial expansion of the airport and improvements to the airport capacity during the next 15 years (Map 8.1). The aim of the 2003 Masterplan was the development of 'gateway functions' through the improvement of the transfer functions of airport, e.g. the punctuality and the speed of passenger movement and baggage handling and freight transport. The implementation of the Masterplan was planned to take place in three phases (1989–93, 1994–8 and 1998–2003), and focused on the expansion of airport facilities such as the terminal buildings, aprons and piers, the handling capacity, the infrastructure (road networks, parking facilities), the construction of a new cargo area in the southern part of Schiphol and the construction of a fifth runway (see Map 8.1).

The airport authorities considered the role of the government in strengthening the economic position of Schiphol as crucial, especially with regard to improvements in accessibility to the airport and the region (i.e. the expansion of rail, roads and European HSL), and strengthening the position of Schiphol as an attractive location for living and working.

The Masterplan Schiphol 2003 was approved by the state, the province of North Holland, the municipalities of Amsterdam and Haarlemmermeer, the KLM airline company, the Dutch Civil Aviation Service (RLD) and Schiphol airport. Policy agreement involving these actors resulted in the publication of the 'Strategy Plan for Schiphol and the Surroundings' (*Plan van Aanpak Schiphol en Omgeving* (PASO)) in 1991.

The PASO was a major step forward in the development of the various legal procedures that have facilitated the implementation of the mainport strategy and the realisation of Schiphol's expansion plans. The PASO contained a number of environmental commitments while pushing forward the development of Schiphol as a European mainport and multimodal transport hub. However, the successful application of the PASO was challenged by the complexity of the decision-making process involving various instruments and procedures, which demand close coordination between the various actors. By this we mean essentially the coordination between the key planning decision on Schiphol (PKB),[3] which follows the directives of the fourth report on spatial planning, the Regional Development Plan for the North Sea Canal of the Province of North Holland and the Civil Aviation Act.

In accordance with the PKB regulations and the government policy plan for Schiphol, the regional plan for the Amsterdam North Sea Canal was partly

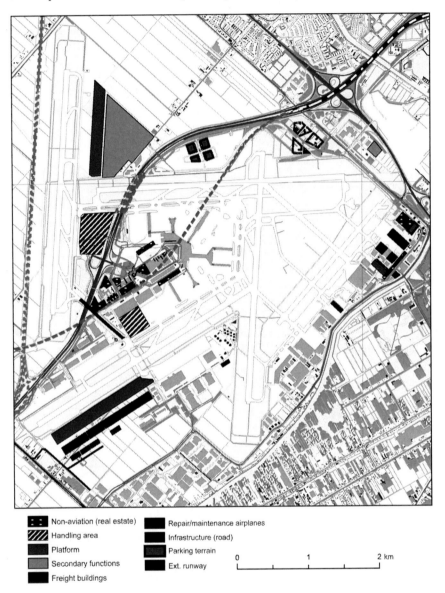

Map 8.1   Master plan Schiphol 2015.

Source: based on Schiphol Master plan (archives Schiphol), projected on Cadastre maps (Scale 1:10,000) .

revised to take into account the future development of Schiphol, more particularly with regard to the future construction of about 15,000 new houses in Haarlemmermeer. Note that the PKB could be reviewed only after the accomplishment of the Integral Environmental Impact Assessment (IMER) and the Integral Economic Effects (IEE) reports.

According to Bosma (1998: 140), the IMER procedures turned out to be time-consuming in examining and re-considering various subtle variants without reaching consensus about the exact environmental effects of the expansion of Schiphol. Initially, the minimum traffic level for a mainport was estimated to be 36.6 million passengers per annum, which corresponds to about 375,000 aircraft movements per year. However, the IMER assessment report (1993) has indicated that under existing airport capacity, e.g. the runway system, and because of safety and environmental reasons which limit the airport maximum capacity to 29.2 million passengers and 300,000 aircraft movements per year, Schiphol would not be able to attain the status of mainport. Against this background and the complexity of the decision-making process, Schiphol asked the government for permission to use the Zwanenburg runway 01L-19R in two directions (north and south) and to extend runway 06-24 in order to respond to the rapid increase in air traffic at Schiphol. The government rejected this proposal and, in doing so, the status quo of lengthy planning procedures was prolonged.

At the end of 1993, the government published the physical planning key decision (PKB, Part 1) for Schiphol and its environs. The mainport policy was set in stone by direct support to the airport authorities to expand the terminal facilities and the runway system and to improve the connectivity of the airport by starting construction of the high-speed train network. One year later (1994), the Aviation Act came into operation, which meant that the noise norms for night flights, noise surcharge and noise zones were now legally enforcible.[4]

It was in 1995, after 25 years of discussions and bargaining, that Schiphol finally got permission to develop into a mainport, and consequently to start the construction of the fifth runway. To that end, some 25 infrastructural projects were implemented to enable Schiphol to retain its position as the fourth European airport.

Note that the long-term growth strategy for Schiphol mainport was based on three core objectives: (1) strengthening the mainport position of Schiphol; (2) expansion of the non-aviation revenues; and (3) the diversification of risks to respond more adequately to market uncertainty (see also Figure 8.8).

The Dutch government allowed Schiphol to increase in size selectively by imposing limits to its growth as set out in the Key Planning Decision of 1995. In the long term, however, the Dutch government expressed its intention to reconsider the possibility of expanding air traffic capacity at Schiphol airport, and at the same time to investigate other alternatives in case Schiphol should reach its capacity. The engineering office DHV, in collaboration with Siemens and the Port Authority of Rotterdam, investigated three possible alternatives: (1) Schiphol plus a second airport on Maasvlakte in Rotterdam; (2) Schiphol and an island in Markermeer in the province of Flevoland; and (3) the construction of a new offshore location in the North Sea. The first two locations were rejected because of the strict framework of environmental and safety requirements. However, Schiphol was in favour of the third alternative because of its potential economic value for the airport and the region. The choice of the Schiphol authorities was surprising because the construction of a completely new airport in the North Sea would mean the closure or downgrading of Schiphol to a second airport (in case

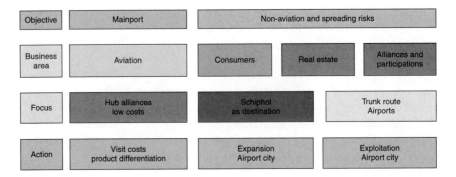

Figure 8.8 Long-term growth strategy of the mainport Schiphol.
Source: Annual Report Schiphol Airport Group (2004).

of dual hubs), and consequently the demise of the collective arrangements constructed in the past and their related accumulated advantages, not only for Schiphol itself but also for the region and the whole nation. Furthermore, there would be a good chance that intercontinental flights would be transferred to competing mainports and other regional airports.

The government position was rather vague. Although the government authorities were principally in favour of further growth of the Dutch aviation sector, they did not specify the precise location at which this additional growth should be accommodated. According to the government, further investigation of the effects of the growth of air traffic on the long-term development of Schiphol was needed. One of the major obstacles in the discussions was the overlap between the short- and medium-term and long-term airport planning, i.e. the perspective of expanding the airport facilities with a fifth runway and long-term growth prospects. In 2003 the government abandoned the idea of constructing a new offshore facility in the North Sea because of the high operational costs for airline companies and KLM, the negative forecasts on future traffic demand during the 2000s, the increasing volatility in the air transport sector and uncertainty about the future strategic position of Schiphol with regard to the KLM-Air France alliance (Burghouwt, 2005: 249). The government decision was positively received by Schiphol because it gave the airport authorities the opportunity to realise their short- and medium-term strategy aimed at creating the legal and regulatory basis for the construction of the fifth runway (Map 8.2).

In 2000, the Schiphol Group started the masterplan entitled 'Airport Development Plan 2020'. The most important strategic goals of the 2020 masterplan were:

- the development of Schiphol into one of the four major European transfer hubs while maintaining (and improving) its position in the origin–destination market;

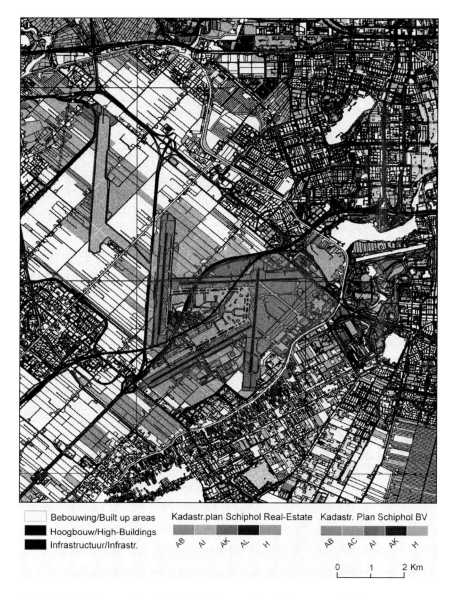

Bebouwing/Built up areas	Kadastr.plan Schiphol Real-Estate	Kadastr. Plan Schiphol BV
Hoogbouw/High-Buildings		
Infrastructuur/Infrastr.	AB AI AK AL H	AB AC AI AK H

0   1   2 Km

Map 8.2   Spatial expansion of Schiphol airport with a fifth runway (2008).
Source: based on Cadastral map 'TOP10NL' (scale 1:10,000).

- further development of the hub position by attracting alliances other than Sky-Team such as low-cost carriers;
- the development and marketing of the 'airport city' formula worldwide; and
- expansion of the capacity of Schiphol to accommodate 85 million passengers and 3 million tons of freight by 2020, of which 55 million passengers

would be transported by KLM and its partners and 40 million by other carriers.

This growth in airport capacity could be accommodated by constructing the fifth runway, the extension of the West terminal, the construction of the J- and H-piers and the optimisation of the runway system. Additional expansion of the runway system and the terminal capacity in 2020 might be needed to safeguard the future growth of Schiphol.

The Schiphol authorities opted for flexible strategic planning by applying a phased and modular planning process, e.g. construction/extensions could be reversed and/or transformed to meet the market demand and in order to respond effectively to future changes in the air transport market and/or changes in the strategies of the actors involved in the planning process. Four different runway configuration options were considered under different growth alternatives: the 5P, 6PK, 6P and 7P options. In the configuration options for six and seven runways, additional terminals, aprons and airport facilities would be required on top of the secondary terminal area in the northwestern part of the airport zone.

According to the Schiphol airport authorities, the best scenario for future growth would be the construction of a sixth runway between the Zwanenburg runway 01L-19R and the fifth runway (which was opened in 2003). In case of bad weather conditions, the construction of a seventh runway parallel to existing runway 06-24 (Buitenveldert runway) would compensate for the loss of capacity. However, the major disadvantage of the seventh runway is the increase in the number of flights (and hence the noise nuisance) above Amsterdam. In addition, various scenarios for the future position of Schiphol as an intercontinental hub were examined further, such as the establishment of KLM-Air France and Sky Team alliance partners at the central terminal area to speed up connection time, and the location of non-hub carriers (including origin-destination airlines such as alliances, low-cost and charter airlines) in the new decentralised area (G-, H- and J-piers) to increase the capacity of the central terminal area.

In order to develop the mainport functions, Schiphol started large-scale construction works in the airport zone during the 1980s and the 1990s, especially at the Schiphol Centre (Schiphol Centrum), Schiphol West (the cargo transport area) and Schiphol East areas. From an extensive and long list of large expansion and construction works since the 1980s, we mention only the most important projects such as the upgrading of the fourth runway 01L-19R and the renovation of both the Aalsmeer (01R-19L) and the Kaagbaan runways in 1982, 1983 and 1984, the construction/extension and/or renovation of A-, B-, C- and E-piers, extensions to the station building (post office, check-in desks, retail stores and shopping centre, etc.) and baggage handling system, and significant construction of and/or extensions to the cargo area (cargo stations II, III and V, cargo terminal 3 and terminals 6 and 7, hangars and office buildings, etc.) at Schiphol South.

In 1983, Schiphol started the development of real estate and commercial activities within and around the airport zone such as the development of the industrial site De Hoek, the opening of the World Trade Centre (WTC) and the Hilton, Ibis and Golden Tulip hotels, the development of the industrial park De

Beukenhorst in Hoofddorp and Amsterdam South East, and the construction of the third European Distribution Centre (EDC) for Mitsubishi Motors Europe at Schiphol Rijk, in addition to the existing distribution centres for Canon and Yamaha. All these expansion and construction works took place between 1981 and 1990.

In the period 1991–2000, Schiphol continued to develop mainport functions by improving the quality of airport services and the optimal use of the existing runway system during peak hours, reducing the time for taxiing and the boarding of passengers and freight transport. Major extension/construction works during this period were: the construction of the new office building (Triport), the construction of B-, E-, G- and D-piers, a new taxiway flyover above the A4 motorway, extensions to the cargo and technical area at Schiphol West, and the development of the new Schiphol South East cargo area. In addition, a new 22,000 m² shopping centre Schiphol Plaza was opened (in 1995), and the passenger bridges in C- and F-piers were renewed as well as the central departure hall and all the counters, baggage belts, floors and ceilings used by KLM and its partners in the central terminal building (see Map 8.3).

In the terminal building complex, the opening of the 12,000 m² Terminal West in May 1993 increased the total capacity of Schiphol from 18 million passengers to around 27 million per year. The new section of the terminal building offers new facilities to passengers such as a casino, a business centre, a tax-free shopping centre (15 new free-tax shops and 8 cafés), a hotel, a sauna, a fitness centre and an airline lounge. Beneath this terminal building, an advanced computerised baggage handling system was installed. The new west wing of the terminal building is connected to the existing terminal complex by an 80 metre wide and 18 metre long lounge which enables Schiphol to maintain the one-terminal concept, i.e. all airport facilities under one roof (see Map 8.4).

The construction of Terminal West marks the completion of the first-five year phase of Schiphol's masterplan, involving total investment of over 1.4 billion guilders.

In the period 2001–7, Schiphol realised various ambitious expansion projects such as the substantial expansion of the terminal building (i.e. the extension of Terminal West in 2001), the extension and renovation of the southern lounge and the baggage handling system, new J- and H-piers, the construction of the 3,800 m long by 60 m wide fifth runway 18R-36L (the Polder runway), the renovation and extension of lounges (1, 2 and 3) and the 'See Buy Fly' shopping centre, the extension of the WTC and the opening of the Tristar office building, the extension of parking area P1 and baggage handling area in Hall D, the construction of B and C aprons and the renovation of E, F, and C fingers, and the installation of 60 self-service automated check-in points in the departure hall (departure 2), etc.

In April 2006, the government published its position with regard to the future development of Schiphol. The government gave Schiphol the opportunity to grow from 500,000 to ca. 600,000 aircraft movements in 2020, but under specific conditions. One of these conditions was that Schiphol (civil aviation sector) and the state should sign a new agreement to reduce noise nuisance and improve livability in the Schiphol region. Another condition was that Schiphol airport and the Dutch air traffic service should investigate the short- and medium-term

Map 8.3 Spatial extensions in the central terminal area (1982–5 (left) and the 2000s (right)).

Map 8.4 Expansion of Schiphol central area with new terminal Station West.
Source: based on various archives (ACA, Avidrom, and NACO Archive Nr: NL-NED
Schiphol 14-5.re).

environmental effects and safety measures around the airport zone and its
surrounding areas.

To gain support for the future growth of the airport, the Schiphol Group
became involved in various consultation platforms. One example of such a
consultation body involving stockholders, the region and the government bodies
is the Alders platform chaired by the Commissioner of the Queen for the Province
of Groningen, Hans Alders.[5] This consultation body was created in December
2006 with the aim of examining short- (up to 2010) and medium-term effects
(until 2020) of the future growth of Schiphol, the noise nuisance and the environmental effects of the airport on the surroundings. The participation of Schiphol in
various regional and national platforms created a complex urban governance
structure in the sense that in order to reach agreement based on clearly defined
tasks, goals and resources to support the planning and growth of Schiphol airport
became very difficult.

8.5 Airport planning and development: the role of actors in the decision-making process

To understand the history of the spatial and economic development of Schiphol
airport and its impact on the surrounding areas, one should examine the role and

type of actors involved in the decision-making processes. This is critical when dealing with airport spatial development because it concerns a 'shared' space among different and heterogeneous parties with different powers in the decision-making process, different economic and financial resources, and different goals, ambitions, visions and agendas. For example, land reservation for airport spatial expansion may conflict with the urban spatial planning of the surrounding municipalities and other local actors. This could pose serious problems that could affect existing arrangements between the airport authorities and local and regional actors. Regulatory instruments, such as spatial planning schemes and/or the Aviation Act, may (partly) resolve these problems by imposing common regulation and specific procedures but are in general not sufficient.

As argued before, the main striking feature in the case of Schiphol airport is the substantial increase in the number of actors involved in the decision-making process since the 1960s. Thus the decision-making process itself takes much more time than in the case of other sectors of the economy, as Bosma has rightly noticed. According to Bosma: '... the assessment of the issues takes longer and the expected advantages of the undertaking require even more cogent proof' (Bosma, 1998: 9). This is because of the lengthy procedures concerning spatial planning in the Netherlands in general and airport spatial planning in particular. In addition, because of the unique position of Schiphol at local, regional and national levels, the spatial development of Schiphol airport touches a number of sectors, e.g. the economy, planning and environment, and actors (stockholders, local and regional bodies, designers, planners and architects, managers and researchers, etc.) at different spatial scale levels. It is for this reason that we argue that a multi-actor and multi-spatial scale approach that takes into account the combination of rule-making, funding support, knowledge sharing (consultation and research) and strategic thinking (visions, goals, strategic planning) of the actors involved in the airport decision-making process is crucial to an understanding of the spatial-economic evolution of Schiphol and the Schiphol region. Together, these actors add specific strategic options, visions and goals through a step-wise and path-dependent process, which affects the airport development process in the long term. For instance, the development of the Schiphol Masterplan 2020 is a result of the combination of the various visions of the strategic partners of Schiphol (airline companies, KLM, the National Air Traffic Control) and the national, local and regional authorities and other social and environmental bodies. Some of these actors have been closely involved with the development of the airport since its early years, e.g. KLM, the municipalities of Amsterdam and Haarlemmermeer, and the National Air Traffic Control. Other actors have joined the alliance of actors during the postwar periods, for example the national government authorities, the province of North Holland, social and environmental organisations, local business organisations and other local and regional actors (see Figure 8.9).

In addition to national and regional/local actors, the decision-making process may be indirectly affected by external actors. For example, several international organisations act in concert to affect the design, management and operation of

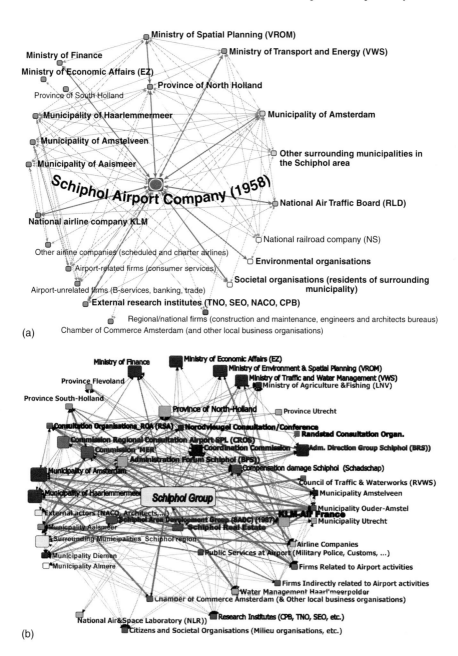

Figure 8.9 Typology of actors involved in the development of Schiphol airport (periods 1958–80 (a), and 2006–7 (b)).

airports such as the International Civil Aviation Organisation (ICAO), the International Air Transport Association (IATA), the Air Transport Action Group (ATAG) and the Airports Council International (ACI). Each of these international organisations strives to represent the needs of different airport stakeholders and to define airport best practice. Together, they promote the common goals of airport safety and security, efficiency and fair competition.

Another example is the direct involvement of the European Union through its agencies, departments and forums such as the European Aviation Safety Agency, the European Energy and Transport Forum, the Committee on Transport and Tourism, etc. The European Union sets policies for transportation – and therefore for airports –the main goals being to create an integrated transport system based on common rules and procedures and to deal with impending capacity problems.

8.5.1 Type of actors and their spatial scale

At the company level, e.g. the Schiphol Group, two important departments are involved in outlining the future strategic development of the airport. First, the airport planning department is responsible for the long- and medium-term strategic planning of the airport, i.e. the masterplan and development planning. The objective of this department is to match and adapt airport facilities to changes in the external business environment. One example of such activity is making flexible strategic decisions about land reservation for the future growth of Schiphol. Second, the management team of the Schiphol Group has the decision-making power concerning the final draft of the long- and medium-term airport plans.

The main users of the airport infrastructure, e.g. KLM and partners and other airline companies, have significant power to influence the decision-making process over the future development of Schiphol. The main requirement of KLM, for example, is the optimal accommodation of its hub operations at Schiphol, especially the peak-hours capacity and other airport facilities and services (e.g. terminal, baggage handling, landside accessibility, etc.).

At the local and regional levels, Schiphol is dependent on local and regional authorities with regard to the development of a strong origin–destination market, regional accessibility, a diversified labour market and land reservation for future growth. In this sense, Schiphol airport is strongly dependent on its main stakeholders and the regional authorities, e.g. the national government, the province of North Holland and the municipalities of Amsterdam and Haarlemmermeer, and to a lesser extent the municipalities of Amstelveen and Aalsmeer.

As one of the major stakeholders of Schiphol airport, the municipality of Amsterdam can influence the decision-making process about the future development of the airport through its active participation in various informal consultation groups such as the BFS consultation body (Bestuursforum Schiphol). The BFS is formed by the Schiphol Group, the municipality of Haarlemmermeer, the province of North Holland and the Schiphol Development Area Company (SDAC), and is chaired by the province of North Holland. The main focus of participating parties within this consultation body is the creation of common ground and regulatory measures concerning the optimisation of economic growth in the Schiphol airport zone and the surrounding areas, for example the designation and development of business locations and office buildings for selected firms whose activities are related to the airport. Other important consultation bodies involving the same actors are the small BRS and large BRS (Bestuurlijke Regiegroep Schiphol). Schiphol participates only in the large BRS in collaboration with the province of North Holland, the municipalities of Amsterdam and Haarlemmermeer and about 30 to 40 other municipalities surrounding the airport. The same participating parties in the BFS (e.g. Amsterdam, Haarlemmermeer, the North Holland province and the Schiphol Group), in cooperation with the Dutch National Investment bank (ING), play a prominent role within the real-estate development company SADC (Schiphol Area Development Company), which is responsible for land acquisition, development, management and (international) marketing of office buildings and business parks in the Schiphol-Amsterdam region.

The Schiphol Group is also involved in the Regional Consultation Committee for Schiphol (*Commissie Regionaal Overleg Luchthaven Schiphol* (CROS)), which is an independent consultation platform formed by the representatives of the provinces of North Holland, South Holland, Utrecht and almost 30 municipalities, the inhabitants of the surrounding urban areas, the Netherlands Air Traffic Control (*Luchtverkeersleiding*), Transavia, KLM and Martinair. CROS has no competency to take decisions but acts mainly as a forum and 'complaint centre' where citizens can submit their objections concerning environmental and safety issues related to airport activities. More generally, the actors in the different consultation bodies have different roles and positions, and serve different goals and agendas in relation to different issues. However, all these consultation platforms are linked to each other by Schiphol airport.

At the provincial level, the province, assisted by the Provincial Spatial Planning Commission (*Provinciale Planologische Commissie*), is responsible for the development and implementation of regional plans that can facilitate or limit the growth of the airport. For example, the extension and/or construction of runways requires building restrictions at the regional level because of noise and safety issues. Furthermore, restrictions on the zoning and land use plans of the surrounding municipalities may be enforced by the regional plan. Because Schiphol is one of the Haarlemmermeer municipalities, any airport development plan has to meet the municipal zoning and land use plan Also, there exist various cases of hybrid consultation bodies competing with the province where several municipalities cooperate together on a voluntary basis at the metropolitan level. These regional associations of cities focus their effort in stimulating cooperation between cities in specific fields, more particularly in urban public transport and the preparation of strategic regional spatial plans (*Regionale Structuurplannen*).

At the national level, the government makes a decision, through its ministries,[6] on any substantial reconfiguration, extension and reconstruction of airport infrastructure facilities through the Airport Planning Decree (Ministry of Transport and Waterworks (*Directoraat-Generaal Rijksluchtvaartdienst*)). This decree defines the airport area and its boundaries and designated areas where housing, office building and industrial park construction should take place and existing housing/buildings that should be banned from the airport area. Consequently, all regional and land use plans of the regional and local authorities surrounding the airport area should be assessed in light of the Airport Planning Decree. The Air Traffic Decree set the environmental and safety standards at the national level and define the limits for the use of runways, flight paths and traffic regulation. Both the Airport Planning Decree and the Air Traffic Decree must be backed by an environmental impact assessment (IMER).

Finally, other external parties such as consultation and engineering bureaus may influence the decision-making process in an indirect way, for example the engineering and consultancy bureau Bentham-Crouwler NACO (Netherlands Airport Consultants) which has been involved in numerous airport planning and development projects at Schiphol since the 1960s. In addition, the following external parties should be mentioned in this respect: local firms engaged in trade, logistics and transportation, Aalsmeer's flower auction, constructors, services firms (banking sector, hotel and catering industry, retail and wholesale trade, etc.), local organisations representing the inhabitants of the surrounding areas, external research institutes and consultation bureaus such as the Air and Space Laboratory (*Lucht- en Ruimtevaartlaboratorium* (NLR)), the Dutch Centraal Planbureau (CPB), the environmental assessment report committee (Commissie MER) and the Council for Traffic and Water Management (Raad voor Verkeer en Waterstaat), and other architects and planning bureaus.

8.5.2 Problem of administrative coordination and governance

The involvement of increasing numbers of actors in the decision-making process has had negative effects on airport development in terms of the coordination and governance of different administrative tiers in the Netherlands, e.g. Schiphol authorities, the municipalities, the province and the government authorities. For example, the administrative and political power is weak at the municipality level and strong at the level of the government ministries, e.g. public servants within the ministries. This is because the state lacks control over the different departments and local and regional actors that have conflicting objectives, visions and hence different policies concerning the growth of Schiphol airport.

Problems arising from the administrative coordination of actors at the regional and national level and related governance issues were examined by the mixed committee on 'governance coordination' in 2005 (*Gemengde Commissie Bestuurlijke Coördinatie*, 2005) and the Kok Committee in 2007, chaired by the former Dutch premier Wim Kok (*Advies Commissie Versterking Randstad*, 2007). Both commissions have referred to the main problems arising from the existing governance structure, and more specifically in relation to Schiphol. The first committee reported the following problems arising from the existing governance structure:

1. Lack of effective control by the state over the decision-making process due to the nature of the ownership structure of Schiphol airport. As an example,

in 2002, the negotiations between the two main stakeholders of Schiphol concerning the partial privatisation of the airport resulted in conflict between the municipality of Amsterdam (the Alderman of Economic Affairs Hordenijk Asscher) and the state (the former Minister of Finance Gerrit Zalm). Under great pressure from Amsterdam, the privatisation of Schiphol was abandoned by the state.

2. The dependence of Schiphol airport on various, and sometime conflicting, regulatory procedures and policy instruments (e.g. Aviation Act, PKB, spatial planning scheme, transport planning, economic policy, etc.) emanating from different state departments, each with its own instruments, objectives and policy goals. In addition, the implementation of different government policies toward Schiphol could also conflict in terms of objectives and policy instruments.

3. The 'Schiphol' dossier is dispersed between the various national and regional departments and networks of actors. The time needed to reach agreement between local and regional parties may be surpassed by the speed of economic changes creating new challenges and new realities so that existing arrangements become obsolete. Because of that and the limited power of the provincial authorities, reaching agreement between parties is very time-consuming and a successful result is not always certain.

4. Some actors are more focused on defending their own interests and imposing their visions on other coalition parties. This situation may be strengthened further by the absence of checks and balances concerning claims, transparency and the clear responsibilities of involved parties. Since the 1980s, the Schiphol Group invested heavily in highly profitable real-estate activities, especially the development of office parks instead of industrial parks for logistic activities. This strategy was tolerated (not to say stimulated!) by the municipality of Haarlemmermeer and the province because such activities generate additional financial resources for the municipality and the region than other urban projects.

In order to resolve the governance issues concerning Schiphol airport, the commission proposed the application of a more consistent and coherent approach integrating airport spatial planning with urban planning and economic, transport and environmental policies. According to the commission, this goal can be achieved through the application of the existing Common Regulation Law (*Wet Gemeenschappelijke Regeling*), which stimulates close cooperation between local and regional actors. Another possibility is the creation of a new governance structure such as, for example, a new independent department at the state level which can supervise, manage and monitor the Schiphol dossier. Alternatively, the creation of an intermediate governance tier between the municipality and the province may be conceived as a solution to the existing governance structure. In this respect, the airport authorities may get full administrative and regulatory powers to develop airport growth and planning policies by taking into account local and regional needs, resources and economic potentials of the metropolitan region and the national economy.

More generally, what is needed is a clear definition of the tasks and responsibilities of cooperating actors involved in the development of Schiphol and Schiphol region as well as the application of appropriate monitoring instruments, through legal and regulatory measures, of applied spatial, environmental and economic policies.

8.6   From mainport to airport city: the rising nebula city

Beside the application of the mainport strategy, in 1995 Schiphol launched two new concepts with the aim of developing Schiphol into a business and distribution centre for international companies: the 'Business City Schiphol' and the 'Cargo World Schiphol'. The concept of Business City Schiphol marks the first step towards the development of the airport city concept, which goes beyond the development of an efficient hub or mainport. Of great importance on the road towards the crystallisation of the airport city concept was the change of management towards more business-oriented approach in running and managing the airport. As a first step, in 1998 Amsterdam Schiphol Airport was changed into the Schiphol Group to stress the importance and priority that has been given to the development of non-aviation and commercial activities as major sources of revenue. The 'airport city' concept sketches a view of the airport as a form of urban environment as well as a gateway (Sudjic, 1992). Schiphol authorities describe the airport city as follows:

> Airport city offers its visitors – passengers, employees, meeters and greeters – but also the Schiphol-based companies – airlines, distribution companies, and logistics and business services providers – services 24 hours a day in the field of shops, hotels and catering, information and communication, corporate business conference facilities, and recreation and relaxation. (Schiphol Group, Annual Report, 1998, p. 5)

In fact, what the airport authorities were implicitly saying is that Schiphol airport is becoming a city. The airport city was presented as a fresh generation of post-industrial cities (Edwards, 1998) that show several similarities, in term of functions, with the typical downtown city. However, although the airport city shows several functions of a generic downtown city, it still lacks, as Edwards correctly suggests, the sense of geographical justification which is evident in most urban areas such as, for example, housing and democratic city government.

According to Schiphol, the most important characteristic of the airport city concept is the integration of various activities into a coherent and sustainable suburban entity that is closely related to its geographical surroundings and the metropolitan region. This is because in a fragmented city network system, the economic position of the metropolitan region depends on its size, market share and the number of its connections and position in international air transport networks (Schaafsma, 2003: 28).

Having said that, the Schiphol Group started a high-profile marketing campaign during the 1990s to promote internationally the airport city concept by emphasising the high quality of commercial facilities offered to transfer passengers and business firms. In order to meet the diversity in demand for airport facilities and services (consumers and firms), Schiphol airport focused its commercial strategy on a different type of consumer, e.g. leisure passengers, regular business travellers, transfer passengers and business companies, and started to develop business sites within the airport zone and the wider areas surrounding the airport zone.

The implementation of the airport city concept started in 1995 with the opening of the 5,400 m^2 shopping centre 'Schiphol Plaza'. In 2004, the total space of the shopping centre, including the shopping areas in different lounges, reached 14,500 m^2, in addition to 16,200 m^2 of shopping space occupied by 51 retail outlets (12 in Schiphol plaza and 39 in different lounges) (see Table 8.2).

With the increasing scale of Schiphol's landside activities, e.g. hotels, office buildings, industrial parks, freight warehousing and distribution centres, Schiphol has also expanded far beyond the airport zone. As Table 8.3 shows, the total surface of the Schiphol airport zone has increased substantially since the 1980s as a result of the expansion of the airport capacity and the fast increase in real-estate activities, especially the acquisition, development and management of office buildings and industrial parks. The highest increase occurred, however, between 1995 and 2004 with the construction of the fifth runway and the realisation of major expansion/construction works.

The World Trade Centre Schiphol (WTC) was opened in 1996, together with two five-star hotels (the Sheraton and the Hilton). In the same year, the location of Elzenhof in the north-eastern part of the airport zone was developed into a fully-fledged national office location with a four-star 200-room hotel, conference rooms and health club facilities for transfer passengers, hotel guests and the staff of the companies located in and around the airport.

From a wide regional perspective, the airport environment was becoming a unique suburban location for shopping and commercial facilities e.g. tax-free shops, catering facilities, banks, car hire, meeting rooms, congress facilities,

Table 8.2 Shopping centre and retail activities at Schiphol airport (2004)

	Number of shops	*Number of retail outlets*
Schiphol Plaza	30	12
Lounges	70	39
Total	100	51
Total area (in m^2)	14,500	16,200
Turnover (€)	€402.9 million	€89.1 million

Source: Annual Report Schiphol Group (2004).

Table 8.3 Total surface of Schiphol airport between 1920 and 2006 (in hectares)

1920	*1938*	*1957*	*1965*	*1968*	*1980*	*1990*	*1995*	*2000*	*2004*	*2005*	*2006*
76	210	700	1,250	1,480	1,700	2,000	2,400	2,678	2,787	2,787	2,787

Source: Annual Reports Schiphol Airport (1920–2007).

hotels, secretarial support, Internet access, fitness and health facilities, etc., and a top international business location like, for example, the South Axis (*Zuid As*). The South Axis is a brand new office area which runs from Hoofddorp-Beukenhorst through Amsterdam South to Amsterdam South East and has great potential to join the best European top business locations such as Canary Wharf in London and La Défense in Paris. This top location covers an area of 30 hectares, of which 45 per cent is reserved for office space, 45 per cent for housing and 10 for facilities (Salet and Majoor, 2005: 14). Total employment in the South Axis location was 24,000 in 2005 and is expected to grow to 53,000 by 2030.

Kasarda (2000) identifies the increasing diversity and concentration of activities and firms around and/or in close proximity to airports as an 'aerotropolis'. While the Schiphol Group authorities were not consciously involved in developing Schiphol into an 'aerotropolis', they were fully aware of the fact that the mainport strategy and the airport city concept should be integrated in order to achieve high growth levels.

The Schiphol real-estate company (SRE) played a major role in marketing the airport city concept at the regional and international levels. The main goal of SRE is the diversification of a mix of office buildings and other commercial real-estate activities in combination with the acquisition and sale of land within and around Schiphol and other regional airports such as Rotterdam, Eindhoven and Lelystad.

Between 2000 and 2001, SRE increased its property portfolio from 250,000 m^2 in and around Schiphol to 310,000 m^2, of which 147,000 m^2 were reserved for office buildings and 163,000 m^2 for industrial parks. In 2003, these figures were 291,086 m^2, of which 165,764 m^2 were reserved for office buildings and 125,322 m^2 for industrial parks. The market value of the SRE portfolio in 2003 reached €649 million against €477 million in 2002. Table 8.4 gives a detailed overview of SRE land acquisition and land transactions between 1997 and 2005.

Between 2006 and 2007, the total property portfolio of SRE increased by 16 per cent (from 427,297 m^2 to 495,513 m^2). Ninety per cent of the total portfolio

Table 8.4 Land transactions of SRE between 1997 and May 2005 (value in €)

Location	Type	Total surface (m^2)	Value (in Euro)	Average price/m^2
A4-zone	Farmland	1,792,194	70,370,390	38.7
SPL NV	Farmland	429,482	11,019,999	25.6
SPL-ZO	Farmland	614,980	17,180,000	27.9
Hoofddorp	Farmland	533,905	4,723,213	8.75
Lijnden	Farmland	351,146	4,564,898	13
Aalsmeerderburg	Farmland	6,200	806,000	130
Badoevendorp	Farmland	575,707	24,327,714	42.4
Rozenburg	Farmland	118,912	2,276,471	20.5
Rijsebhout	Farmland	705,967	9,883,538	14
Total		8,578,693	257,870,010	

Source: Duivestijn and Tellinga (2006, p. 22).

concerns real-estate activities at Schiphol airport, 4 per cent in the two regional airports of Rotterdam and Eindhoven and 6 per cent in Malpensa airport (Italy). The market value of the real-estate investments of SRE reached €888 million in 2007, against €660 million in 2006 (Schiphol Group, Annual Report, 2007).

Map 8.5 shows the total land parcels owned by the Schiphol Airport Group in the Schiphol region. The ownership of land is divided between the Schiphol Airport Company and the Real Estate Company. The map is based on most recent data published by the Dutch land registration office Kadaster. According to this data, the total surface of land parcels owned by the two companies is

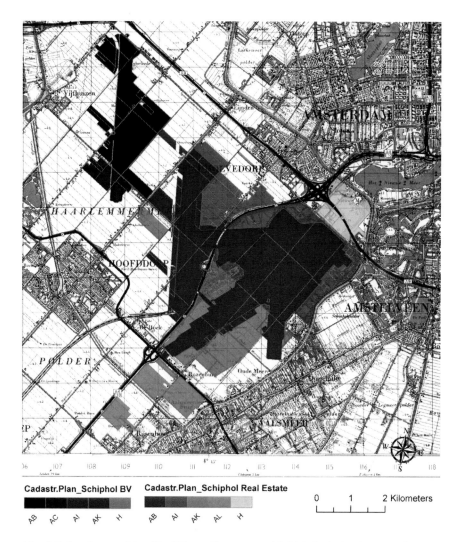

Map 8.5   Land ownership of Real Estate Company and Schiphol Airport Company in 2008.
Source: based on land parcels register of Cadaster (2008).

27,844,173 ha, of which 9,763,717 ha is owned by SRE and about 1,808 ha by the Schiphol Airport Company.

Beside the commercial real-estate activities of SRE, there is also the Schiphol Area Development Company (SADC was created in 1987), which is engaged in land development activities in and around the Schiphol airport zone and the attraction of business companies to these areas. The main shareholders of SADC are the Schiphol Airport Company (25 per cent of the capital shares), the province of North Holland (16.7 per cent), the municipalities of Amsterdam (16.7 per cent) and Haarlemmermeer (16.7 per cent) and the Dutch ING bank (25 per cent). SADC focuses on the acquisition of land, the development, marketing and management of office buildings and business parks in the airport zone and the surrounding areas, and the realisation of infrastructure projects to enhance the accessibility of business parks and Schiphol airport. The SADC operates under the umbrella of the governing body Schiphol (*Bestuursforum Schiphol* (BFS)), which is responsible for the outlining of the spatial-economic policy and attracting new firms to Schiphol and the Schiphol region.

By the end of the 1980s, SADC opened the first 100 ha industrial park 'Oude Meer' in the proximity of the Schiphol cargo area and the European Distribution Centre office cluster 'Sky Park' (8.05 ha), which provides office buildings and facilities to large and medium-size international companies. In the 1990s, the European distribution centre 'Schiphol Rijk'(24.23 ha), located south of the airport zone, was opened for large international companies such as Canon, Mitsubishi, Yamaha, Microsoft HQ Benelux, BMC Software, Unisys (EHQ), UPC, Eaton, Renault, BAT and KLM.

One of the most ambitious projects realised by SADC during the second half of the 1990s was the office business park 'Riekerpolder', which accommodates high-service activities. This business park makes up part of the prestigious top business location South axis (*Zuid As*).

In 2005, the total land property portfolio of SADC reached 2,131,500 m^2, distributed among various locations such as distribution centre Schiphol Rijk, the airport business park Lijnden, the logistic park Schiphol, Houtrakpolder, the RID area, the Riekerpolder, Oude Haagseweg, Elzenhof and Work City A4 (see Table 8.5).

However, SADC's most important development project in terms of its size and importance for the future development of Schiphol airport is the business park 'Schiphol Logistic Park'. With a total surface of 207 ha, this park is intended to accommodate large-scale (and high value-added) logistics and distribution activities, and makes up part of a much larger development project (about 300 ha of which 130 ha are reserved for business parks) known as 'Work City A4' (*Werkstad* A4). The first preparations for the construction of the A4 zone started in 2005, and the whole project is expected to be realised by the end of 2014. Map 8.6 shows the existing and planned industrial and business parks in the Schiphol area and region between 2005 and 2009.

The increased importance of real estate and commercial activities at Schiphol is reflected in the increasing tendency for revenues to come from real-estate consumer activities (see Figure 8.10). In 2003, total revenues from aviation and consumer activities represented 77 per cent of the total revenues of Schiphol.

Table 8.5 SADC property portfolio in 2001–10

	Locations	Surface (m²)	Planning 2001–5	Planning 2006–10
Location 2001	Park SPL Rijk (SADC)	242,300	32,000	132,000
	Airport business park Lijnden (SADC)	350,000	95,200	0
	Park SPL Rijk/Oude Meer (SADC)	1,000,000	0	0
	SPL Logistic Park (SADC)	2,070,000	33,000	300,000
	Total	3,662,300		
Location 2005	Houtrakpolder	180,000		
	RID area	50,000		
	Riekerpolder	113,000		
	Oude Haagseweg	36,500		
	Elzenhof (in development 2001)	200,000		
	Werkstad A4 zone	1,552,000		
	Total (m²)	2,131,500		

Source: Duivestijn and Tellinga (2006, p. 22) and Leeuwen (2001, Gemeente Haarlemmermeer, Sector Economische Zaken Hoofddorp).

In 2009, the total revenues earned from aviation activities decreased by 8 per cent, while revenues from consumer activities increased by 3 per cent. Revenues from real-estate activities increased from 18 per cent to 26 per cent between 2003 and 2009.

Note that the increased importance of commercial activities, especially consumer activities, is strongly related to the marketing strategy of Schiphol, which focuses on branded shops, catering outlets and sale of local products as well as of international products such as Dutch cheese and tulips, electronic equipment, clothing, cell phones, etc. In addition, the airport has chosen to enhance and promote the airport product 'See Buy Fly' worldwide. The name, logos, design, signing, merchandising and advertising of 'See Buy Fly' products strengthen Schiphol's own identity and specific products (e.g. the bright yellow branded shopping bags). Today the Schiphol 'See Buy Fly' logo is recognised all over the world as the branding identity of Schiphol airport.

More recently, Schiphol has made intensive use of new communication technologies like the Internet, SMS, social media and e-mail services in the marketing and promotion of Schiphol products (e-commerce), offering a wide range of travel- and non-travel-related products, e.g. virtual travel agency, online purchasing from the See Buy Fly shopping centre, Schiphol Travelport, advertising in the public squares, Schiphol real-estate properties, etc. In addition, Schiphol created the facility management Schiphol Inc. Company (EMS) in 1994, which offers more than 80 different services and products in the fields of office accommodation and housekeeping, data information, logistics, communication design and general

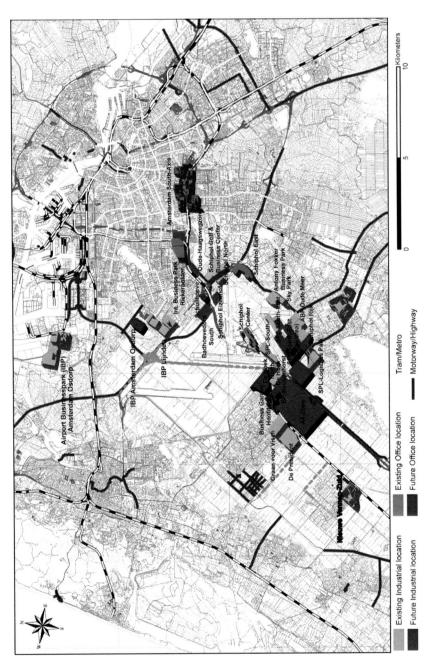

Map 8.6 Existing and future industrial and office business parks in Schiphol-Amsterdam region.

Source: based on SADC maps (2009).

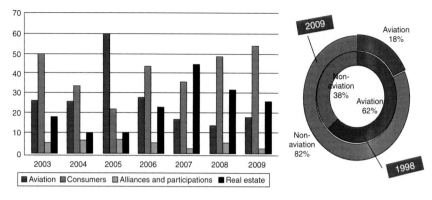

Figure 8.10 Net income from aviation and non-aviation activities (%): 2003–9.
Source: Annual Reports Schiphol Group (1997–2009).

services. In this respect, advertising and promoting the Schiphol airport image through both traditional and interactive forms generate significant amount of revenues.

A final remark worth mentioning is that since the 1990s, Schiphol started to develop new concepts for shopping sales, property development and services in the area of consultancy and airport management and operational services to other international airports. Moreover, the marketing of Schiphol's airport city formula became one of the most important international activities for the Schiphol Group during the 2000s. In 2004, for example, Schiphol signed a joint venture with Stockholm Arland Airport to operate and exploit the retail activities in its international terminal (north terminal) up to 2019. Similar airport-related investments have been made in Australia, Austria, Hong Kong, Indonesia and Italy.

8.7 Economic effects of Schiphol on the surroundings and the region

The size, capacity and quality of airport facilities contribute to regional economic growth and development, but the extent to which this potential enhancement to economic growth is realised is a function of several factors. In high-concentration urban areas with extensive systems of roads, highways and commuter rail facilities, improvements in airport capacity and the quality of airport facilities contribute to the attractiveness for the population and economic activities because of the potential market size, employment opportunities and agglomeration economies (i.e. pull-effects). Consequently, the growth in incomes and employment attracts new workers and households to these urban areas, and this increase in the urban population in turn generates demand for additional jobs, consumption, investment and production.

Empirical studies show that the economic benefits of airport development are much stronger at the local and regional levels than at the national level. This is because airports are vital components of local and regional economic growth, which strengthen the attractiveness of cities and regions and create strong agglomeration advantages. In turn, the development and growth of an airport is affected by the size and structure of the local and regional economy in terms of wealth, population size, spatial distribution and concentration of economic activities. Consequently, the ability of an airport to generate jobs and attract firms and businesses should be seen in a much broader context involving, among other things, direct, indirect and induced effects of agglomeration economies (positive and negative externalities), and the socio-economic and institutional contexts of cities and regions.

Today Schiphol airport contributes to the attraction of a broad range of economic activities to the Amsterdam-Schiphol region. Schiphol airport possesses most of the functions and physical infrastructure of a city centre and shares many of the social, economic and political relationships with the surrounding urban areas and the region. In terms of employment, Schiphol airport and the Schiphol region have evolved into important economic centres offering jobs to a great number of the active population of the region.

Indeed, since the 1970s, Schiphol has attracted an increasing number of employees to the region. Employment at Amsterdam Schiphol Airport increased on average by 4 per cent per year against 1 per cent at the national level, and represented 0.5 per cent of the total employment in the Netherlands. During this period, the employees of Schiphol airport earned 40 per cent more than the national average. The estimated direct employment at Schiphol increased from 27,448 to 37,000 jobs between 1983 and 2005. The indirect employment effect grew at an average rate of 4.7 per cent to 5 per cent and reached 57,573 jobs in 2005.

In terms of value added, the contribution of Schiphol to the Dutch economy has been estimated to be €8 billion in 2003 (Regioplan, 2004b: 4). The contribution of Schiphol airport in the total value added of the province of North Holland is estimated to be 11 per cent and 20 per cent of the total value added of the greater Amsterdam region.

During the 1990s, the direct value added increased at an annual rate of 5.7 per cent while the indirect value added registered an increase of 6.1 per cent (Priemus, 2001: 147). Figure 8.11 gives an overview of employment growth at Schiphol airport and KLM between 1980 and 2007.

Between 1980 and 1990, the total employment at Schiphol airport grew from 28,508 to 42,641 employees. During the following decades (1990 and 2000), employment increased by 28 per cent and by 13.8 per cent in the period 2000–7. Over the whole period 1980–2007, employment at Schiphol increased by 118 per cent. Note that this rapid increase in employment indicates the increased economic importance and attractiveness of Schiphol for economic activities. Schiphol become the most preferred location in the region for businesses and large international distribution companies in Europe.

As Figure 8.12 shows, growth in employment and the number of companies at Schiphol airport during the period 1980–2008 have followed the same tendency as described above.

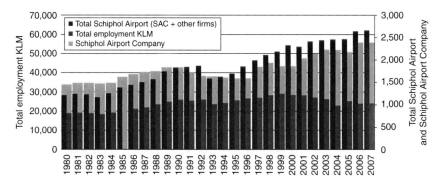

Figure 8.11 Employment growth of Schiphol airport and KLM between 1980 and 2007.
Source: Annual Reports Schiphol Airport (1980–2007).

Several empirical studies, using input-output methods or cost-benefit analysis (CBA), have been conducted to assess the total economic effects of Schiphol for the Schiphol region and the Amsterdam Schiphol region, in terms of employment, value added and economic growth. The research institute Nyfer (2000) estimated that 1 per cent growth at Schiphol, in terms of employment, results in an average growth of 0.18 per cent in the services sector (Nyfer, 2000: 125). In terms of growth, 1 per cent growth at Schiphol results in 0.17 per cent additional economic growth for the region. In contrast, 1 per cent additional economic growth in the region results in an average growth at Schiphol of 2.65 per cent (e.g. in terms of passengers). Furthermore, growth of the services sector at the national level has significant effects on Schiphol, e.g. 1 per cent growth of this sector results in an average of 0.52 per cent growth at Schiphol.

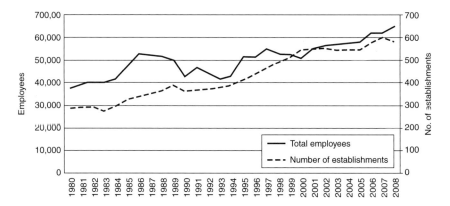

Figure 8.12 Employment and number of establishments at Schiphol airport area (1980–2007).
Source: Annual Reports Schiphol Airport (1980–2007).

Hakfoort *et al.* (2001) conducted a study on the economic impact of Schiphol Airport on the greater Amsterdam region between 1987 and 1989. Using an extended input-output model, this study indicates that the growth of Schiphol has resulted in an additional 42,000 jobs in the greater Amsterdam region in 1989. The results of this study are in line with existing studies that indicate combined indirect and induced multiplier effects of around 2 per cent.

In another study, Louter at al. (2005) assessed the full economic impact of Schiphol airport on the region from a wider perspective, e.g. direct and indirect effects on employment, value-added, the geographical spread of economic activities, accessibility and environmental effects. According to this study, the indirect number of jobs generated by Schiphol airport is estimated at 27,800 to 32,500 jobs (year 2001) and the value-added between 2,859 million and 3,418 million euro.

The estimated forward indirect effects of related activities lay between 14,900 and 19,700 jobs and the value-added between 750 and 1,006 million euro. The major part of these effects concerns activities related to travel agencies and tour operators. The estimated backward indirect effects of Schiphol-related activities represent 27,800 to 32,500 jobs and a value added of 1,522 to 1,793 million euro (Louter *et al.*, 2005). Backward indirect effects are spread between the transport and distribution sector, business services (security, cleaning, finance, ICT, etc.), and hotel and catering.

The geographical distribution of backward indirect effects shows that 50 per cent of these effects benefit the southern region of North Holland (Ijmond, agglomeration of Haarlem, Zaanstreek and greater Amsterdam region) and 8.8 per cent the rest of North Holland (Louter *et al.*, 2005: Table S.2, p. iv). From the total backward indirect effects, 78 per cent of jobs and 79 per cent of value-added are distributed between the Randstad provinces (North Holland, South Holland, Utrecht and Flevoland) where 90 per cent of the total direct and indirect effects of Schiphol are taking place.

However, the local effects of Schiphol, in terms of employment, are stronger in Haarlemmermeer (74,100 jobs in the Schiphol cluster) and to a lesser extent in Aalsmeer (10,400 jobs in the horticulture cluster) and Diemen (8,800 jobs in the services cluster, e.g. banks and insurance etc.). At the level of the Schiphol region and greater Amsterdam, these effects are even stronger, respectively 84,100 and 76,900 jobs. Without the existence of Schiphol, the total effects on these two regions have been estimated to be, respectively, 35,700 and 29,000 jobs.

To summarise, most empirical studies show the great economic importance of Schiphol airport for the local and regional economy. The total economic effects differ between sectors and regions but the common belief in those studies is that the direct and indirect effects are higher in the urban areas surrounding the airport and at the level of the metropolitan region. In most empirical studies, the economic effects on employment are based on an estimated multiplier coefficient of 0.63 to 0.66 in the case of indirect backward effects, and 0.34 in the case of indirect forward effects.

8.7.1 Schiphol as a cluster magnet and top business location

Schiphol airport and its surrounding areas act as a magnet attracting industries and business services. The spatial concentration and clustering of activities are relatively higher in these areas compared to other locations in the metropolitan region. More particularly, the Schiphol airport zone has developed into a large logistics and distribution centre and top location for business services. This is because of Schiphol's ability to attract transport and distribution activities, large international companies, leisure hotels, business and financial services, and telecommunications industries to the region (Priemus, 2001: 158).

During the last 30 years, the economic growth of Schiphol and Haarlemmermeer has been exceptionally higher than the national average. In the period 1973–2003, 48 per cent of the growth in employment in the greater Amsterdam region took place in Haarlemmermeer, especially in the logistics and distribution sector and business services. In a period of 20 years, total employment at Schiphol has doubled, from 28,500 in 1986 to 57,600 in 2004. During the same period, the regional income per inhabitant was 50 per cent above the national average (Louter *et al.*, 2005: i). Consequently, the Schiphol region has registered high economic growth since the 1990s. In this context, it is not surprising that large numbers of international companies in the Netherlands, especially the European distribution centres (EDC) and European headquarters (EHQ), are located around Schiphol airport and its surrounding area.

Since the opening of the Holland International Distribution Centre (HIDC) in 1984, the number of international firms attracted to the Schiphol region increased considerably: from more than 40 companies in 1986 to 550 in 1997 and 650 in 2002 (see Warffemius, 2007). Of all the foreign companies located in the Netherlands in 2004 (1,591 companies), 21 per cent were established in the Schiphol region (20 per cent in 2001), 10 per cent in Haarlemmermeer (500 companies in 2001) and 9 per cent in Amsterdam (463 companies in 2001). Only 2.6 per cent of all foreign companies in the Netherlands are located in the Schiphol airport zone (134 companies in 2001). In terms of national percentage, the following four sectors are strongly represented in the Schiphol region: business and financial services (50.5 per cent), logistics (38.6 per cent), European headquarters (38.1 per cent), and ICT, marketing and consultation services (22 per cent).

Because of the airport's excellent network of frequent connections, Schiphol is highly attractive for European distribution centres (EDCs) and European headquarters operating in the high tech and electronics sectors, life sciences (pharmaceuticals, biotech), consumer products (non-food), fashion and clothing, chemicals and machinery (NDL/BCI, 2001: 19).

The distribution of international companies by country of origin shows high representation of companies from Japan, the USA, South Asia, the UK and to a lesser extent Scandinavia and other West European countries. Of all the US companies established in the Netherlands, 26 per cent are located in the Schiphol region, 12.6 per cent in Amsterdam and 11.2 per cent in Haarlemmermeer. Japanese companies are strongly represented in the Schiphol region (45.7 per cent),

Haarlemmermeer (23.2 per cent) and to a lesser extent in Amsterdam (16.2 per cent). This observation also applies to other international companies from South Asian countries (24 per cent, 15.2 per cent and 7.6 per cent). Similarly, companies from the UK are mainly concentrated in the Schiphol region and Amsterdam (21.6 per cent and 10.7 per cent).

The case of Germany is somewhat surprising in that only a small fraction of the 978 companies established in the Netherlands is located in Amsterdam and Haarlemmermeer (about 4.7 per cent and 5.5 per cent). Figure 8.13 shows the geographical distribution by sector of international companies established in the Schiphol-Amsterdam region in 2004.

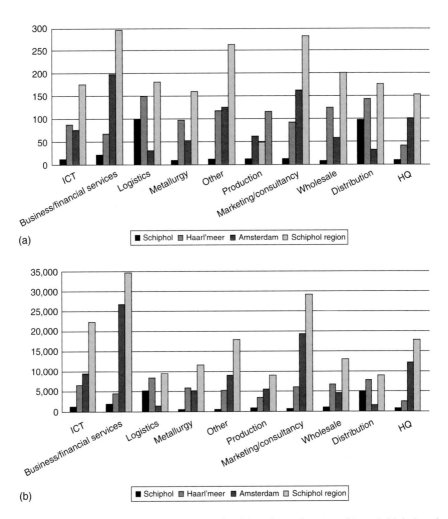

Figure 8.13 Number of foreign companies (a) and employment (b) at Schiphol and Schiphol region in 2004.
Source: Louter *et al.* (2005), based on CBIN/stec database.

Note that the demand for office buildings and industrial parks in the Schiphol region increased substantially from the second half of the 1980s, although the total open space available at Schiphol and in the region is limited. That is why the allocation of space for industry and business services took place mainly along the ring roads around Amsterdam, especially in the southern and southeastern parts of the city, and at Schiphol airport zone and its surrounding urban areas (Hoofddorp and Schiphol-Rijk).

It has been estimated that the total office building space generated by the operations of Schiphol airport for the region lies between 190,000 and 206,000 m^2 (gross floor space) (Louter *et al.*, 2005: iv). Forty-seven per cent of the total supply of office buildings is to be found in the southern areas of the North Holland region. With regard to industrial parks, estimates indicate a total supply of 202 to 225 ha (excluding Schiphol airport), with the southern areas of the North Holland region accounting for 56 per cent of the total supply.

Of the total open land around the airport, 60 ha were reserved for airport activities. In this respect, Schiphol Airport is one of Europe's few large airports that still have enough space to accommodate additional activities.

The attractiveness of Schiphol and the Schiphol region can be demonstrated by analysing the supply of industrial and business parks and the evolution of rental prices per floor space between 1982 and 2007. Figure 8.14 shows the supply of office buildings measuring 500 m^2 or more between 1982 and 2007.

More generally, while the supply of office buildings is higher in the greater Amsterdam region than in the Schiphol region, the annual rental price per m^2 is much higher in Schiphol than in Amsterdam. This suggests that, in terms of attractiveness and the valuation of economic potential for business firms, the Schiphol region scores much better than Amsterdam and its surroundings. Furthermore, while office vacancy rates increased to high levels in Amsterdam in 2003 and 2004, the business locations along the Schiphol south axis were only marginally hit, because these locations are more internationally oriented than other business locations in the greater Amsterdam region.

If we now look at the industrial parks, the supply of such parks in the Schiphol region and Amsterdam show little divergence in the period 1990–2005. However, the rental prices of industrial sites at Schiphol are much higher than in Amsterdam, Hoofddorp, Haarlem and Nieuwe Vennep (see Figure 8.15). Once again, the explanation for this is the scarcity of space at the Schiphol airport zone and the environmental and regulatory measures limiting the establishment of firms whose activities are not closely related to the airport's activities.

To summarise, economic growth takes place mainly at the levels of the Schiphol and Amsterdam-Schiphol regions. This is due, on the one hand, to the rapid growth of Schiphol airport itself and its strong agglomeration effects on economic activities and workers. On the other hand, the economic growth of the Schiphol-Amsterdam region is the result of the shift in the economic structure of this region toward a knowledge-intensive and service-oriented economy, and the increasing spatial spread of Schiphol's activities over much larger urban areas in the region. Consequently, the rise of Schiphol as a nebula city should be

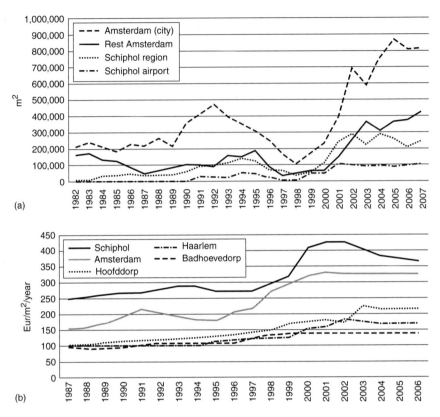

Figure 8.14 Supply (a) and rental price of office buildings (b) at Schiphol-Amsterdam region: 1982–2007.
Source: DTZ Zadelhoff Research (2008).

understood in relation to these developments and their role in improving the position of Schiphol as a top location for business services.

8.7.2 Noise nuisance and other environmental effects

The expansion of Schiphol airport has been subject to strict regulatory measures to limit the negative effects of noise nuisance, pollution, safety and other environmental effects on the surroundings. Noise nuisance has been identified as the main source of the environmental effect of Schiphol airport.

It was believed that the enforcement of a new law on noise nuisance and the application of zoning regulation laws, in combination with other measures such as the application of a large insulation programme, the use of Zwanenburg as a two-way runway, the construction of a fifth runway and the application of the new European regulations on noise nuisance (chapters 1, 2 and 3) would be sufficient to decrease the noise nuisance around the airport and its surroundings.

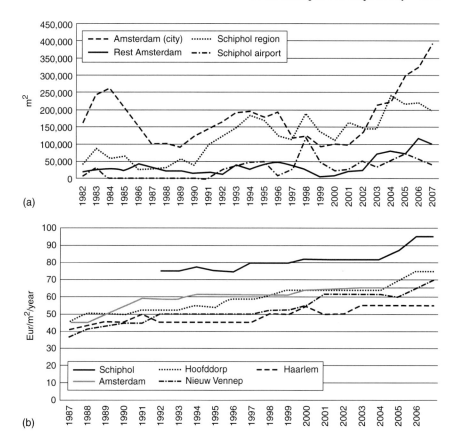

Figure 8.15 Supply (a) and rental price of industrial parks (b) at Schiphol-Amsterdam region: 1982–2007.
Source: DTZ Zadelhoff Research (2008).

Furthermore, under a new European Community directive, aircraft without a noise certificate have been banned from European air traffic since 1988, especially those aircraft falling under the so-called chapter 1 such as the Boeing 707, the Caravelle, the BAC-11, the Trident and the DC-8. Many airlines then started to replace aircraft falling under chapter 2, such as the DC-9 and the Boeing 747, 737-100 and 737-200.

In 1990, the existing noise contours were reconsidered and Schiphol airport, in cooperation with the Civil Aviation Authority, set up a new noise monitoring system (NOMOS) using 20 measuring points around the airport. The NOMOS measuring system is linked to the Civil Aviation Authority's FANOMOS system, which permanently registers the source of noise, e.g. aircraft flying over. The results are made available to the Schiphol Noise Nuisance Committee and the public.

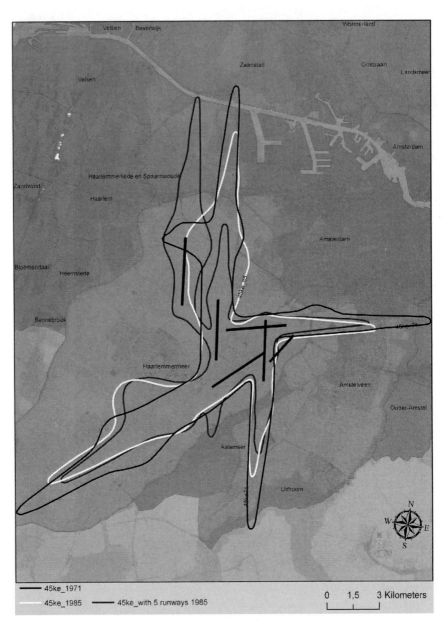

Map 8.7 The 45 Ke noise zone with four and five runways (1971 and 1985).

The inhabitants of the surrounding areas, especially Amstelveen, were complaining about the increase in air traffic at night. In 1992, the number of aircraft taking off and landing during the night (24:00–06:00 hours) grew by 17.6 per cent to 8,526 aircraft movements, of which 64.4 per cent were performed on the Kaag runway (76.8 per cent in 1991) and 25.2 per cent on the Zwanenburg runway (14.4 per cent in 1991). Schiphol responded by applying additional measures such as the extension of the night-time ban for landing and take-offs. In addition, Schiphol doubled the surcharges imposed on chapter 2 aircraft and raised the noise surcharge by 50 per cent (in 1997).

In 1993, a new standard on a noise level equivalent (LAeq) for night flights (23:00–06.00 hours) was introduced. Under this standard, only runway 06-24 and the fifth runway were used for night flights. The noise load limits (Lden in dB(A)) for a 24-hour period as well as the limits for cumulative noise from all the movements over a period of one year are monitored at 35 points distributed around the airport zone (see Map 8.8). There are an additional 25 points for the night-time period (Lnight) applicable from 23:00 to 07:00 hours. The aim of the system is to limit the number of homes affected by high noise levels (over 35 Ke) during the day to a maximum of 10,000, and the number of people that might be subject to more than 20 Ke to no more than 45,000. For night noise, the goal was set at maximum of 10,100 homes in the area falling under 26 dB(A) LAeq or more, and a maximum of 39,000 people subject to more than 20 dB(A) LAeq.

Between 1997 and 2000, the maximum noise loads were higher than the prescribed standard at 35 NOMOS points in 1997 and, respectively, 14 points, 11 points and 5 points in 1998, 1999 and 2000. As a result, the Ministry of Transport, Public Works and Water Management imposed a penalty of *f* 5 million on Schiphol airport (in 2000).

Today, Schiphol airport is regulated by the Aviation Act of 27 June 2002 (*Wet Luchtvaart*), which came into force on 20 February 2003. The Aviation Act was complemented by two Decrees amended in 2004 by the Council of Ministers and established detailed regulations for the protection of the environment. These are: the Air Traffic Decree Schiphol (*Luchthavenverkeerbesluit Schiphol* (LVB)) and the Airport Zoning Decree Schiphol (*Luchthavenindelingbesluit Schiphol* (LIB)). The first Decree (LVB) establishes the maximum limits for noise and air pollution, regulates third-party risk and provides detailed regulations for the operation of the runways and the use of airspace in and above Schiphol. The second Decree (LIB) regulates the use of land around the airport for environmental, safety and operational purposes. This Decree prohibits building in areas where it would be undesirable in terms of noise, air pollution or safety.

In 2000, the Dutch parliament agreed on new preliminary regulations for the environment and safety, which allowed Schiphol to increase the annual number of aircraft movements by 20,000. However, the increase in airport capacity and the direct impact on the environment and safety put great pressure on the surrounding urban areas concerning the implementation of urban expansion plans. In particular the construction of new housing became problematic, not only because of the scarcity of land but also because of the applied zoning regulations

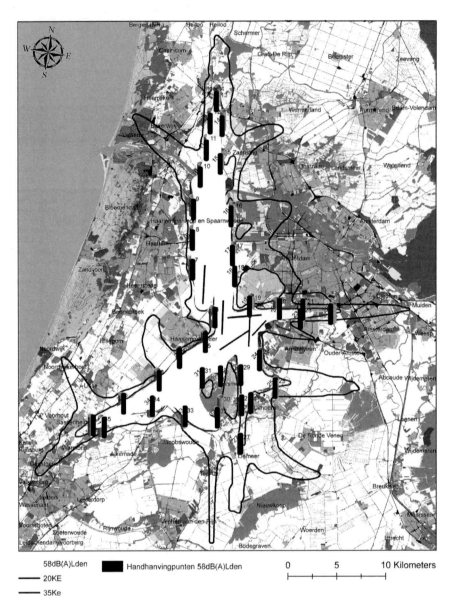

Map 8.8 The 35 NOMOS points around 58dB(A)Lden, 20Ke and 35 Ke zones.
Source: based on 'Schiphol en u: de regels' Ministerie van Verkeer en Waterstaat, map p. 5.

Map 8.9 Building restriction area in the Schiphol-Amsterdam region.
Source: based on the maps 'Schiphol en u: de regels' Ministerie van Verkeer en Waterstaat.

and the environmental restrictions imposed by the Schiphol noise contours. As Map 8.9 shows, there exist very few potential open spaces for (social) housing construction in the Amsterdam metropolitan region. As a result, the implementation of national and regional planning policies became difficult in a region characterised by the high density of the built-up area and the high concentration of population and economic activities.

8.8 Summary and conclusions

The liberalisation and deregulation of the 1980s accelerated the restructuring of the air travel market in terms of the reorganisation of air transport networks and the increased competition between a limited number of consolidated airline groups and hub airports. As is the case for most airports in Europe, Schiphol was affected by changes in air transport regulations, their impact on airline operations and the reorganisation of international air networks. These changes were first manifested on the ground by the increased competition between hub airports and the shift in the role of Schiphol as a provider of public services towards a more commercial business organisation operating in a highly uncertain market.

It was in this context that Schiphol airport, supported by the government and local and regional authorities, started the development of the mainport strategy aimed at improving Schiphol's mainport functions. The mainport strategy may be viewed as an extension of the existing collective arrangements regulating the functioning of Schiphol as the international airport of the Netherlands. In other words, the mainport strategy is determined by earlier decision-making processes involving various actors, e.g. the decisions made by the government to concentrate air traffic at the international Schiphol airport, and to integrate the growth policies for Schiphol with the national spatial and economic policies. A direct implication of this arrangement is a spectacular increase in airside activities between 1980 and 2009, especially the increase in transfer passengers in intra-European and intercontinental air services and cargo transport.

The economic performance of Schiphol airport had been impressive since the 1980s, with the exception of the Gulf War, the SARS epidemic and the attacks of 9/11 in 2001. Analysis of key input and output figures such as the net result, investments in fixed assets, the balance sheet, and the growth of passengers, cargo transport and airplane movements clearly confirms the tendency towards continuous growth of Schiphol airport.

Another implication of the mainport strategy concerns the increased spatial expansion of Schiphol airport and the optimisation of spatial conditions for further development of the mainport functions. However, the growing environmental effects of Schiphol and the increasing shortage of space in the region pushed local and national authorities to adopt a conservative balanced-growth policy aimed at the efficient use of existing open space within clear environmental limits. As a result, a fundamental change in the spatial morphology and the functional structure of Schiphol airport took place. As we have shown in this chapter, the impressively long list of expansion and construction projects realised by the Schiphol authorities since the 1980s such as runways, aprons, taxiways, platforms, terminal buildings, cargo facilities and commercial buildings, etc., resulted in the largest spatial expansion of Schiphol airport in its entire history.

Since the publication of the structure programme on civil airports (*Structuurschema Burgerluchtvaartterreinen*) in 1979, discussions about the future development of Schiphol airport were mainly guided by the fundamental questions concerning the noise nuisance and other environmental effects of the airport activities on the direct surrounding urban areas, landside accessibility and the economic position of Schiphol within the region. With the application of the Physical Planning Key Decision (PKB) in 1987, and the Strategy Plan for Schiphol and Surroundings (*Plan van Aanpak Schiphol en Omgeving*, known as PASO) in 1991, the future spatial expansion of Schiphol airport, including the construction of the fifth runway, was then regulated, and airport growth policy became strongly intertwined with national and regional spatial and economic policies.

In the Masterplan of 1989, the main objective of Schiphol was the mainport strategy. However, in the Masterplan of 1997, alongside further development of the mainport functions, the main goals of the Schiphol authorities were the development of the airport into a major European and intercontinental hub in international air traffic networks and the development of the airport city in which Schiphol would became a multi-functional growth centre with diversified economic functions and commercial activities for air travellers, the urban population and business firms.

Remarkably, analysis of the decision-making process shows two striking features. First, the number of actors involved in the discussions about the future growth of Schiphol increased substantially during the postwar period (especially since 1970). The number, role and position of the actors involved increased continuously over time and included not only the most closely related actors to Schiphol airport such as the national, regional and local authorities but also various other actors operating at various spatial scale levels. However, the airport authorities were generally supported by the government and the regional authorities in implementing the future growth strategies of Schiphol airport. In other words, in a multi-level and multi-scale complex governance structure, Schiphol has always managed to realise its ambitious expansion plans and was able to gain the support of the most powerful actors from the national and regional political field.

Second, reaching an agreement based on predetermined tasks, goals and resources in order to support the improvement of the competitive position of the airport became very difficult and time-consuming. By this we mean that the time lag following the decision-making process was considerably lengthened and the decision-making process itself became highly complex. One solution to resolve this issue was the creation of a national mainport administrative department/unit, in which the Schiphol and port of Rotterdam authorities were able to play a key role in the decision-making process, in cooperation with local and regional authorities whose main tasks were the development of a more consistent and coherent approach integrating airport spatial planning, urban planning and economic, transport and environmental policies.

Since the early 2000s, Schiphol's growth strategy and its underlying basic collective arrangements changed from being a mainport or hub airport into a more diversified strategy, e.g. an airport city.

The Masterplan 2020 initiated by Schiphol in 2001 confirmed once again the airport city strategy as core to the future development of Schiphol airport into what some authors call an 'aerotropolis' or 'airport corridor centre', which goes a step further in the development of the city port into a full nebula city.

The airport city is of great importance as a catalyst for generating growth and helping Schiphol to develop into a top location attracting a broad range of economic activities to the region, especially logistics and distribution activities, large international companies, leisure hotels, business and financial services and telecommunications industries. With the application of the airport city strategy, Schiphol airport was further stimulated to develop into one of the biggest growth poles and business centres of the region, possessing the various functions and physical infrastructure of a typical downtown city centre and sharing many social, economic and political relationships with the directly surrounding urban areas and the city region.

From this perspective, Schiphol airport and its direct surroundings act as a magnet for industries and business services. Most companies located at Schiphol tend to display a high degree of spatial concentration and clustering in order to benefit from agglomeration economies and gain competitive advantage.

The spatial concentration of industry and business services takes place alongside the ring roads around Amsterdam, especially in the southern and southeastern parts of the city, and in the proximity of the Schiphol airport zone and its surroundings, e.g. Hoofddorp and Schiphol-Rijk. However, because of the scarcity of land and the attractiveness of these areas, the price of land and the rental price of office buildings and industrial parks are among the highest in the Netherlands. This is due to the international orientation of Schiphol and the Schiphol region and their attractiveness to international companies and business services in the Netherlands.

Analysis of the economic impacts of Schiphol on the Schiphol-Amsterdam region shows the existence of strong direct and indirect effects of Schiphol in terms of employment, value added, investments, regional gross product and the high values of residential property and office buildings. The economic benefits of Schiphol airport are much stronger at the levels of the Schiphol and Amsterdam metropolitan regions than at the national level. However, the size, capacity and quality of the airport facilities and the landside activities in Schiphol's contribution to local and regional economic growth depend strongly on accessibility, potential market size, employment opportunities and the induced effects of agglomeration economies (positive and negative externalities).

Finally, it is worth mentioning that the growth of Schiphol generates serious negative externalities for its surroundings in term of safety, pollution and noise nuisance. Perhaps the most negative effect of Schiphol on the region is the environmental and noise nuisance regulations, which restrict housing construction around the airport zone. This has direct implications on local and regional spatial planning policies, especially for Amsterdam, Haarlemmermeer and other surrounding municipalities of the province, because of the lack of open space to realise urban expansion plans in this highly densely populated area of the Netherlands.

Another negative factor affecting Schiphol and the Amsterdam-Schiphol region is the worsening of accessibility and road congestion around Schiphol. One of the main causes of road congestion is the increased attractiveness of Schiphol as a working centre due to the increase in business parks and office location and hence the increase in the number of commuters to the Schiphol area from other regions. Moreover, despite the relatively important investments made by the state and Schiphol to improve the public infrastructure, the development of Schiphol into a multimodal infrastructure network is heavily affected by noise regulations and increasing congestion around the airport zone and throughout the region.

9 Conclusions

Studying the continuity and changes in the spatial and economic configurations of cities and regions is very difficult and challenging because of the complex structures that compose these configurations, which touch on a wide variety of heterogeneous aspects, e.g. the economic, spatial, political, demographic, socio-cultural and cognitive, actors and other factors. In order to understand the long-run spatial and economic metamorphosis of cities and regions, a multi-disciplinary approach, based on key innovative ideas developed by various theoretical strands in urban and regional economics, geography and planning, is needed. This poses great theoretical and empirical challenges because of the absence of synthesised work that links, for example, the extensive theoretical approaches and analytical tools developed in urban and regional economics to institutional theories.

The aim of this book is to fill this gap both theoretically and empirically. Our proposition is that continuity and change in the structure and patterns of urban space are caused by collective interventions and arrangements, whether planned or unplanned, that are reflected in policy and planning documents, the economic actions of agents, and agreements and covenants involving different actors and stakeholders. Our case study concerns the rise and development of Schiphol and the Schiphol region into a nebula city in the contemporary city network urban system. We show, throughout this book, that the spatial configuration and economic structure of Schiphol and the Schiphol region have been created by purposive interventions during different historical periods that can be described as collective arrangements (for detailed discussions, see Chapters 1 and 3).

At the theoretical level, this study is largely inspired by various theoretical strands treating the economic and institutional aspects of the formation and growth of cities and urban systems. Besides the fact that most of the existing theoretical approaches emphasise the spatial and economic impact of the continuous processes of specialisation, differentiation, complementarities and organisation of spatial and economic networks, special attention is given to specific theories developed in the fields of urban and regional economics and institutional economics that analyse the formation and growth of cities in general, and the restructuring effects of spatial, institutional and economic relationships in cities and regions in particular.

In this book, specific attention is given to both traditional monocentric city models and the polycentric city models describing the spatial (de)concentration of population and employment in cities, and hence the formation and change of urban forms, through the combined effects of transport costs, incomes, land and commuting costs, and the spatial distribution of economic activities and the variation in wages and (labour) productivity between cities. Additionally, other factors such as the shift in the industrial composition of production, technological changes, transport costs, changes in the spatial densities of households, employment and the dynamics of the migration of population and firms should be taken into consideration as explanatory factors for the formation and growth of cities and regions, e.g. increased urbanisation and urban sprawl.

My argument is that these two theoretical models can be easily related to the theory of agglomeration economies in explaining the transformation and continuity in the patterns of urban forms and the spatial organisation of economic activities within and between cities and regions. The economic and spatial dimensions of agglomerations involve not only concepts of specialisation and differentiation, clustering and spatial proximity but also socio-institutional dimensions that facilitate the economic growth of cities and regions. This is to say that the application of the theory of agglomeration economies has the advantage of offering elegant theoretical explanations and powerful empirical evidence concerning the formation and development of cities in terms of the spatial concentration of activities and workers, and the synergetic effects of localised networks for firms and individuals. Both localised and non-localised networks of firms contribute to the economic growth of cities and regions. Conceptually, the spatial linkages of firms in localised networks stimulate locational advantages of proximity that result in economies of scale, scope and learning, and the stimulation of non-market relations. Note that similar external benefits from agglomeration economies may be realised by localised and non-localised networks of firms.

This opens the possibility of integrating both theoretical approaches, by making a clear distinction between networks in the territorial space and in the economic space, e.g. physical networks in agglomerations and economic networks in agglomerations, in a unified framework that explains the spatial economic transformation of urban space. In addition, both theoretical approaches may be combined with the institutional aspects of agglomeration, urbanisation and urban sprawl by linking the concept of agglomeration economies to the various dimensions of proximity, e.g. spatial, economic and institutional proximity. In particular, the institutional proximity of non-market interactions at the level of cities is crucial in identifying the factors and actors that trigger the mechanisms of change and continuity in the spatial and economic configurations of cities and regions. This is because the creation and exploitation of local production resources in the context of institutional proximity is strongly dependent on the efficiency of existing institutions and institutional arrangements that may facilitate or constrain market and non-market relations, and ultimately stimulate growth.

In this perspective, we consider the configuration of cities and regions to be a mosaic of functions and arrangements that, together, shape their economic structure and urban forms. Therefore, any change or continuity in this configuration may result in an equivalent change in the urban patterns and economic position of cities. Based on this idea, we propose a conceptual framework to highlight changes in the spatial forms of cities, and their capacity to adjust to co-evolutionary outcomes resulting from the mutual reinforcement of interactions between the technological space, the organisational or economic space, the territorial space and the institutional space. Together, all these types of spaces act simultaneously to influence the behaviour of (economic) actors, the spatial distribution of firms and population, the forms and nature of interrelationships between actors and activities, and the physical structures of cities and regions.

Our argument is that this conceptual framework opens new possibilities for approaching the complexity and the multi-faceted nature of the evolutionary processes of spatial-economic transformation of urban space from a new spatial-institutional perspective. The main novelty of our theoretical approach is the extension of this conceptual framework by integrating institutions and institutional arrangements that structure people's expectations, behaviour and interactions between actors, and between actors and their environment, including the socio-cultural, political, economic and spatial environment.

Furthermore, we consider institutions, whether formal and/or informal, as economic and social organisations operating through rules, beliefs, traditions, customs, norms, strategies and regularities. These are the 'rules of the game' that define and limit the sets of choices for economic agents, determine the form of economic organisations and influence economic efficiency. Such a conception of spatially bounded institutional arrangements sheds more light on spatial and economic change as an ongoing multi-faceted process of spatial interactions and linkages relating economic agents and other actors to each other and to their local production milieu.

In addition, the institutional paradigm evokes different readings with regard to the nature and efficiency of institutions to the economic organisation of markets, firms and networks. However, to our knowledge, no unifying approach exists that explicitly relates institutional and collective arrangements to the long-term spatial-economic transformation of cities and regions. Most economic institutional approaches, partly inspired by the old American institutional economics, focus on economic transactions as the most elementary building blocks of economic institutions. In opposition, the undervalued theoretical contributions of the German Historical School provide convincing evidence of the existence of a strong relationship between the localisation of economic activities, territorial development and the role of institutions. My contention is that future research aimed at reviving the scientific legacy of this school of thought would certainly enrich our understanding concerning the formation, self-reinforcement and dynamic change of institutions and institutional arrangements in a spatial context.

Building on these ideas, we set up a conceptual theoretical approach centred on the concepts of institutional and collective arrangements in relation to institutions and territorial and economic space. Because we are interested in positioning the nature, role and importance of collective arrangements in a spatial context, we present a clear definition of this concept and its particular meaning by taking into account the nature, forms, criteria and various dimensions of collective arrangements. This is to say that we conceive of collective arrangements as the first building blocks of institutional arrangements and institutions. On the one hand, both concepts of institutional and collective arrangements are context-dependent and spatially bounded. On the other hand, they operate in a specific institutional regime and differ from each other according to their degree of institutionalisation through law, regulation and other formal arrangements. Viewed from this perspective, institutional arrangements are essentially rules and conventions operating within governance systems, and include formal institutions and regulations as well as informal arrangements, which include traditional law, values and norms, and customs.

In order to identify and describe the evolution of collective arrangements and their interventions in determining the spatial and economic transformation of cities and regions, we present a conceptual framework based on three determinant processes of accumulation, transformation and reconfiguration/recombination. These three processes describe the processes of creation, selection and change of basic and complementary (new) arrangements, and their transformation and reconfiguration in time within a specific local institutional configuration or institutional regime. This conceptual framework reveals the possibility of the existence of a variety of evolutionary institutional forms and arrangements according to the degree of coherence of spatial, economic and institutional configurations of cities and regions in the long run.

However, the complexity and dynamics of collective arrangements structuring the territorial and functional organisation of cities and economic activities may result in a complex urban governance structure, especially when a growing number of actors interacting with conflicting objectives and goals are involved in the decision-making process. This is because collective arrangements result in the first place from actors interacting, and therefore they provide a framework in which various actors and organisations may work together (in partnership or networks of relationships) in order to achieve common goals. In this sense, collective arrangements are relevant in examining market and non-market modes of coordination that govern interactions between actors and economic agents and their effects on the spatial configuration and transformation of urban areas and regions.

At the empirical level, we follow a chronology of successive historical periods of (dis)continuity and change in the configuration of spatial patterns and economic structure at the level of Schiphol, at the level of greater Amsterdam and at the level of the Schiphol-Amsterdam region during the twentieth century. Three historical periods are extensively examined: the period 1870–1940, the period 1945–80 and the period 1980–present.

9.1 The period 1870–1940

In this period we examine the main causes of industrialisation, urbanisation and economic growth in the Netherlands, in the Randstad-Holland and in the

Amsterdam-Schiphol region (see Chapter 4). On the one hand, the industrialisation of the country is attributed to the unprecedented high levels of public investment in transport networks (waterways, rail and road networks) and public services, and to the rapid advance in transport technology and technological innovations, e.g. steam machines and electricity-driven engines, and the structural shift of the Dutch economy towards an industry-based economy. The industrialisation had far-reaching consequences on the configuration and spatial organisation of the Dutch urban landscape. For example, because of the modernisation of the transport infrastructure, the accessibility of cities and regions for individuals, goods and information was significantly improved. People and activities were released from the tyranny of distance in the sense that the travel distance between cities and regions was reduced significantly, and this resulted in an increase in the mobility of people and the expansion of the daily urban system in urban areas. The other side of the coin, however, was the reverse negative side effects of industrialisation and urbanisation such as an increase in urban density and the overpopulation of larger cities, an increase in road congestion, housing shortages, an increase in health and safety problems and, more generally, the deterioration of living conditions among the urban population.

On the other hand, the industrialisation and modernisation of the Netherlands were also related to radical changes that occurred in the political, social and cultural domains. In the political domain, important institutional reforms were introduced such as the introduction of a new governance structure based on the strong financial and fiscal autonomy of local authorities, the municipality law of 1851 and the Thorbeck constitutional reforms of 1848, which limited the power of the monarchy and increased the participation of the citizens in the politic.

In the socio-cultural domain, Dutch society became strongly dominated by the 'pillars' that govern the political, social and economic life of social groups along cultural lines, and the rise of a culture of 'consensus', which became the symbol of the Dutch polder-culture across the world.

In the socio-demographic domain, the modernisation process was accompanied by structural demographic changes such as, for example, the changes in the structure and composition of households between cities and the countryside, the continuous decrease in the number of people and the number of children per household in big cities, and the increase in the number of single households in the total urban population.

In short, the rapid urbanisation and industrialisation of the Netherlands were directly related to changes in the economic structure, the development of new technologies, socio-demographic and institutional changes and the development of new infrastructure networks.

At the economic level, the revival of the Dutch economy from the late nineteenth century was stimulated by high levels of capital accumulation from (colonial) trade, the increase in investments in manufacturing industry and public services, and the relatively rapid technological changes. The increasing economic growth was sustained by the increasing size of the market, the increased specialisation and division of labour that allowed manufacturing firms to realise economies of scale, and subsequently the increase in production, productivity and incomes and wages in manufacturing industry and services.

Moreover, the industrialisation of the Netherlands was reflected in a shift from a high concentration of large-scale manufacturing industry dominated by a few family companies to a more diversified economy dominated by competitive small and medium-sized firms. The growth of manufacturing industry was further stimulated by the introduction of new technologies in production, and the use of new resources and materials (like oil, electricity and steel), the implementation of a market-oriented industrialisation policy, international specialisation and, finally, the improvement in infrastructure networks. As a result, the economic structure of the Dutch economy shifted from agriculture to manufacturing industry and services. However, the share of agriculture in the total economy was sustained by fundamental reforms aimed at modernising this sector through capital intensification, rationalisation and optimal use of resources, and the creation of new institutions and institutional arrangements such as the creation of cooperative organisations, learning and innovation centres, financial institutions and insurance companies.

At the regional level, industrialisation stimulated urbanisation because of the attractiveness of industrial cities to the ever-growing numbers of job-seekers released from agriculture in the countryside. As a result, urban population and urban density increased substantially and, subsequently, the demand for housing and urban services increased rapidly. The priorities for the larger Dutch cities, especially Amsterdam and Rotterdam, were the improvement of existing public facilities and infrastructure networks, and the acquisition of additional land to accommodate the fast-growing urban population and manufacturing firms in and around the city centre.

For the first time in the history of Dutch cities, medieval city walls were broken in order to create more space for the construction of new neighbourhoods, which were often built by private land developers and/or private initiatives. This was because the construction sector before 1901 was mainly driven by market mechanisms and speculative motives.

To bring an end to uncontrolled suburbanisation and speculation in the land and housing markets, the Dutch government introduced the Housing Act in 1901. This Act allowed municipalities to control land use and the housing market and to realise large urban expansion plans.

Following the implementation of the Housing Act, Dutch cities made considerable efforts to dictate housing planning, housing production/stock, the quality of urban amenities and the social composition of city districts. Furthermore, urban planning was brought under the full responsibility of the municipal and regional planning units. In the case of Amsterdam, for example, many city expansion plans were developed by some influential city planners, which have left their trace on the contemporary urban design of the city. Note that Amsterdam's local authorities were forced to apply successive and selective urban expansion projects because of structural municipal financial shortages and lack of space for the realisation of big urban expansion projects. Therefore, the annexations of several surrounding areas to Amsterdam offered new possibilities to local authorities to realise their ambitious large urban expansion plans such as that of Amsterdam South (Berlag), the eastern suburban parts of the city (Slotervaart and Slotermeer) and the southeast neighbourhood of Bijlmermeer.

With regard to the industrial structure of the Amsterdam region, industrialisation resulted in an increasing gap in economic growth between the city and the countryside, which reflected a much broader tendency of increasing discrepancies between the Dutch regions, especially between the four cities of the Randstad and other cities and regions. The economic revival of Amsterdam started with the opening of the North Sea Canal in 1876 and the increase in colonial trade. This increase gave a great boost to some industries and service activities like transport, banking and insurance, shipbuilding, food processing, the textile industry, and the equipment and machinery industry.

With the increase in employment, the number of in-commuters from the countryside to the city increased spectacularly, and from the 1920s, a gradual increase in out-commuters from Amsterdam to suburban areas took place as a result of the delocalisation of some manufacturing industries to these locations such as the tobacco industry and food processing industry in the Zaanstreek area.

As this study clearly shows, the economic structure of the Amsterdam-Schiphol region is clearly service-oriented, while the rest of the province shows a high proportion of manufacturing and agricultural activities. Empirical evidence shows a high level of diversity in the economic structure of the Amsterdam-Schiphol region, a high level of specialisation in commercial and business services and some specialised manufacturing industries, unlike other cities in the Randstad.

During the period 1870–1940, the countryside area of Haarlemmermeer was functionally and economically dependent on the central city of Amsterdam. The relatively young population of Haarlemmermeer, the diversity of agricultural activities and the modernisation of the agriculture sector played a decisive role in the development of Haarlemmermeer into one of the most productive agrarian regions of the Netherlands. By the end of the nineteenth century, Haarlemmermeer was one of the wealthiest areas of agrarian countryside in the Netherlands with strong economic linkages with the city of Amsterdam and the province. However, the emergence and development of airport activities during the 1930s changed radically the spatial and economic configuration of Haarlemmermeer.

The spatial and economic impact of Schiphol on the surrounding areas became apparent with the increase in activities related to the municipal airport such as trade and transport and commercial activities. In this sense, the development of Schiphol airport played, among other things, a key role in the shift in the economic structure of Haarlemmermeer from an agrarian to a more diversified economy.

In addition, the suburbanisation process that took place at the level of greater Amsterdam was accompanied by the subsequent urbanisation of Haarlemmermeer that was driven by the rapid growth of Schiphol and economic activities related to air transport. In this sense, the urbanisation and industrialisation of

Haarlemmermeer are closely related to the emergence and development of airport activities.

It bears emphasising that the rise and development of Schiphol airport is at first instance the result of a basic collective arrangement that gave shape to the military airfield at Schiphol between 1917 and 1925. The military authorities played a key role in the decision-making process concerning the choice of the location and the construction of a military airfield in the Haarlemmermeer polder.

In 1919, this basic arrangement was then transformed into a new arrangement when it was decided to concentrate the commercial operations of the newly created Dutch airline company KLM at the military airfield at Schiphol. As a result, Schiphol became a mixed airport where both military and commercial operations took place. A few years later (1926), Schiphol became officially the municipal airport of the city of Amsterdam.

Many reasons could be put forward to explain why the military authorities agreed to transfer the ownership of the military airfield to the city of Amsterdam. One reason is the increase in scope and size of airport services provided by the military to civil aviation, which, in the view of the military, was not the main priority of the military authorities. Second, neither the state nor the military authorities were prepared to cover the rising operational costs of the airfield or provide financial support to improve the airfield facilities and infrastructure. Thus Schiphol was, between 1919 and 1925, a very rudimentary airfield that lacked appropriate facilities, e.g. terminal buildings, hangars and passenger check-in desks, etc., and infrastructure linking the airport to Amsterdam and the surrounding areas.

From its early days as a municipal airport, the Amsterdam authorities made great financial sacrifices to improve the airport facilities and related equipment at Schiphol. Despite the fact that the municipality lacked the expertise, political power and financial means to effectively operate and manage the airport, at a time where almost none of the European and American airports and airlines were able to make a profit, Amsterdam was, nonetheless, keen to take over Schiphol and invest in its future development. It seems that the influence of a conglomerate of local lobbyists, civil aviation enthusiasts and local and national businessmen was decisive in pushing Amsterdam city council to take over Schiphol airport. They succeeded in turning civil aviation and airport development from an issue of military strategy or mere aviation enthusiasm into an economic issue using the rhetoric of progress and modernity, which fed into the self-perceived need of Amsterdam's governors to improve their city's economic position and competitiveness. This was the reason the municipal authorities considered Schiphol airport a potential contributor to the future economic development of the city, and in their view Schiphol ought to be managed and operated as a municipal project. In this sense, the development of Schiphol was primarily dictated by local motives to serve the interests of the city of Amsterdam. Improvements in the airfield infrastructure and airport facilities at Schiphol and road access to the airport were carried out shortly after Amsterdam had taken over the airport from the military authorities. Within the course of two decades, the rather primitive Schiphol airfield had developed into a modern European airport.

Note that the close cooperation and personal influence of some key actors seem to have been decisive for the development and growth of the airport in its early years. Each of these actors had their own vision, ambitions and objectives, but they all played an essential role in determining the future development of Schiphol. In fact, together, these actors formed a coalition which largely shaped the history of Schiphol during the interwar period. For example, The Hague lacked such a conglomerate of (powerful) local authorities, businessmen and aviation enthusiasts able to catalyse airport development in or near their city.

More generally, the early history of Schiphol shows how a basic collective arrangement can be transformed without losing its constituent components. The relatively simple character of the first basic arrangement evolved, as time passed and the number of involved actors increased, into a complex arrangement. The growing complexity mirrored the growing economic importance of Schiphol for the urban and regional economy. This can be understood in light of the strong efforts made by Amsterdam's local authorities to diversify the economic structure of the Amsterdam economy that was centred on the development of the port and port-related activities.

However, the rise and development of Schiphol airport, as well as the development of civil aviation during the 1920s and 1930s, did not play such an important role in the economic development of the region. This is because neither Schiphol and the national airline KLM would survive without financial support from the state and the municipality of Amsterdam, as economically they were very inefficient businesses. One may argue in this respect that the state and Amsterdam's local authorities, for many reasons other than purely economic motives, kept Schiphol and KLM alive.

The history of Schiphol shows that its early development was mainly guided by civic pride and local boosterism, urban competition between Amsterdam and Rotterdam, (local) political considerations and great enthusiasm for civil aviation technology, airport infrastructure and – let us not forget – the heroism and great danger which surrounded the early history of aviation.

From a spatial planning perspective, during the 1920s the design and planning of airports were not internationally standardised. A common basic framework for airport construction and design and the operation of airports at an international level was lacking. So, technical problems on the field were resolved by copying existing practices and experiences at other airports. Information about the requirements of airport construction and new technological developments in the aviation sector were diffused through formal and informal networks of airport operators and professionals in civil aviation, often through direct meetings (conferences, work visits) or indirect contacts (correspondence, professional magazines) between the airport authorities.

The circulation of information and knowledge spillovers were beneficial for Schiphol in resolving some difficult and specific technical issues like the construction of a drainage system and paved runways in swampy ground situated several metres below sea level. In this sense, the expansion of airport facilities and the improvements in technical standards at Schiphol airport were largely inspired by foreign experiences, especially in the US and some other European airports.

During this period, the departments overseeing urban planning and Schiphol airport in the city of Amsterdam were responsible for the planning and spatial development of Amsterdam Schiphol airport, often in cooperation with local and regional actors. For example, the airport expansion plan for Schiphol of 1935, developed by the urban planners of the city of Amsterdam, was the result of close cooperation between the airport authorities, the municipality of Haarlemmermeer and the province of North Holland.

From the early 1930s, spatial planning at Schiphol formed an integral part of the urban expansion plans of Amsterdam and Haarlemmermeer and represented a first attempt to coordinate the airport spatial planning and urban expansion planning of the surrounding areas. Contrary to existing views concerning the spatial planning at Schiphol, our analysis shows clearly that the Amsterdam authorities had a clear vision for the region concerning the long-term spatial development of Schiphol. However, because of a lack of sufficient financial means, spatial planning at Schiphol in terms of the size, scope and design of the airport equipment and facilities was less impressive than at other major European airports.

In this sense, wide differences existed across European airports in terms of their construction, design, management and exploitation, but most importantly because of the financial support that they got from their central governments. In the case of Schiphol, the continuous financial deficit of the airport and the increase in operational and investment costs pushed Amsterdam to seek additional funds from the financial market, which in turn resulted in high interest payments and hence higher costs. Things became worse during the 1930s with the increased complexity of airport construction, and consequently the increasing costs of airport extension and construction projects. Amsterdam's financial situation worsened, and the municipal authorities turned to the national government for financial support in order to secure the continuity of commercial operations at the airport. However, the financial assistance expected from the state could only take place after the final decision had been made regarding the definitive location of the Dutch international airport somewhere in the Randstad.

KLM and a number of other actors were in favour of the construction of a new central airport for the Netherlands at Leiderdorp near the cities of Leiden and The Hague. At first instance, the choice of this location was positively received by the national authorities. However, under fierce protests from Amsterdam, the national government was persuaded to designate Schiphol airport as the sole central airport of the country, although the final decision was not taken till after the Second World War.

In order to reach its desired status as the Dutch national airport, a new collective arrangement had to be established, which involved the national state as one of the key actors alongside the municipality of Amsterdam. Bringing the state back in, however, involved several risks for Amsterdam in terms not only of losing ownership of the airport, but also of losing control of the management and operation of the airport activities, with effects on the economic position of Amsterdam.

After long negotiations between Amsterdam and the central government, a new collective arrangement emerged, which would determine the postwar spatial and economic development of Schiphol and the surrounding areas.

9.2 The period 1945–80

During the Second World War, Schiphol was almost completely devastated during the German occupation. After the war, the airport had to be reconstructed from scratch. Amsterdam took the initiative and began immediately. By the end of 1945, the runway system was completely rebuilt, in close cooperation with the Allies. Two years later, the platform, aprons, station building and technical area were constructed, and by the end of 1948, all of Schiphol airport was fully reconstructed and made operational for air traffic.

In a relatively short time, Schiphol regained its prewar position in international and European air traffic networks. However, the decision of the government to designate Schiphol as the world transatlantic and intercontinental airport of the country in 1945, and the change of Schiphol from municipal airport into a private company controlled by public stockholders, i.e. Schiphol Airport Company, were determining factors in the future growth and spatial-economic development of Schiphol during the postwar period.

These two collective arrangements turned to be path-dependent in the sense that they both determined to a great extent the development path followed by Schiphol from 1945. As we have mentioned before, the first collective arrangement was the result of a long discussion and debates involving various parties. The State Commission on Airfields, which was set up by the government in 1945, played a key role in the decision-making process toward the designation of Schiphol as the sole international airport in the Netherlands. The most important reason why such a collective arrangement could take place in a relatively short period of time was the existence of a sense of urgency shared by all actors concerning the reconstruction of Schiphol as an international airport.

As our discussion of the Burgerveen affair shows, the desire of the KLM director to concentrate all airline activities in one central location, e.g. in the southern part of Haarlemmermeer, was met once again by strong resistance from Amsterdam and Rotterdam. Several attempts were made by the director of KLM Albert Plesman to convince the small commission on airfields and the government of the advantages of Burgerveen as the optimal location for the new central airport of the Netherlands. However, after long discussions between KLM and the State Commission on Airfields, the government followed the recommendation of the Commission to designate Schiphol as the sole international airport of the country. The Burgerveen affair was then closed definitively in 1948.

The government decision was formalised in a new collective arrangement that served as the basic framework for future spatial planning at Schiphol, and more particularly for the implementation of the ambitious tangential expansion plan for Schiphol that was developed by the managing director of Schiphol Jan Dellaert.

Nevertheless, it took three years (up to 1948) before Amsterdam and the government authorities accepted the final version of the airport expansion plan.

Seen from this perspective, the acceptance and implementation of the tangential plan became itself an arrangement in the sense that all future expansion plans developed by Schiphol airport were based on this basic arrangement, although regular changes and revisions of the plans were needed because of the growing air traffic activity and the rapid changes in airline technology. The choice for the tangential plan had direct and/or indirect effects on various fields/domains such as the airport spatial planning and urban expansion planning fields, and the economic, social and environmental fields, e.g. employment, noise nuisance, etc.

Second, the rapid development of commercial aviation and airline technologies during the first decades of the postwar period put much pressure on the municipality of Amsterdam to expand the airport infrastructure and enlarge the existing facilities. The state was prepared to provide Amsterdam and Schiphol with the needed financial help but on the condition it shared the ownership, management and control of the airport. The long negotiations between Amsterdam and the state, before a final agreement could be reached at the end of 1957, resulted into the formalisation of the second collective arrangement (1958), which put an end to the existing basic arrangement for 'Schiphol municipal airport' dating from 1926. According to this new arrangement, Schiphol became officially an anonymous partnership company in public hands. This arrangement brought radical changes to the relationship between Schiphol, which became a fully independent player serving its own agenda, and its surrounding urban areas, but also to Schiphol itself in terms of the internal management and the external coordination of airport activities at the local, regional and national levels. In other words, the implications of this collective arrangement touched the institutional field in the sense that the decision-making process concerning the spatial expansion and economic development of Schiphol became much more complex. This complexity came about on the one hand because more actors became involved and on the other because of those actors' continuous changes in their position on the playing field, their power to influence the decision-making process and their relationship with Schiphol. In addition, the urban planning field was also directly affected by this collective arrangement in the sense that the divergent goals, agendas and ambitions of Schiphol and the surrounding areas became apparent in the discussions about the development and implementation of airport expansion plans and their effects on the urban expansion plans of the surrounding municipalities, including Amsterdam. For example, the airport expansion plan of 1956 and the urban expansion plans of the surrounding urban areas were clearly in conflict.

While airport planning was mainly driven by the increased capacity of air traffic and the complexity of airport construction due to the developments in air transport technology, urban planning was more driven by socio-demographic and economic developments, e.g. an increase in population and structural shifts in economic activities. To avoid conflicts between airport planning and urban planning, the government integrated the spatial planning of Schiphol airport into the national planning scheme. In doing so, the government was then able to control the environmental effects of the airport's activities on the surrounding areas, and at the same time give room to Schiphol to expand under specified conditions and environmental limits.

The spatial scale of the Schiphol airport area increased substantially with the introduction of bigger and faster airplanes. Consequently, airport planning became more complex because the construction of terminal buildings, platforms, aprons and other airport facilities were largely dependent on the extension and/or construction of runways. Gradually, a complex structure formed by various elements of the tangential configuration began to emerge.

The realisation of the expansion plan at Schiphol demanded additional land around the airport perimeter. This did not pose any problems for the Schiphol authorities because of the existence of abundant land in the relatively empty Haarlemmermeer polder, and the willingness of the municipality of Haarlemmermeer to sustain the realisation of Schiphol's ambitious plans on its soil.

In terms of the layout and design of airport facilities, Schiphol shifted from being purely a large infrastructure project towards the creation of an integrated logistic node providing a wide range of functions related to airside and landside activities. Morphologically, Schiphol began to show new spatial and functional patterns resembling a small downtown city centre. However, with the spatial and economic development of the airport, the environmental effects increased substantially. After endless puzzling with noise contours and restriction zones around the airport, the government implemented legal instruments to bring in zoning regulations based on noise contours around the airport area.

Another major implication of the two collective arrangements is the shift in economic position of Schiphol at the regional and national level, caused by the commercial orientation policy of Schiphol and the change in the market structure of the commercial air transport sector.

From the 1970s, Schiphol started a new commercial strategy aimed at attracting transfer passengers and strengthening the hub functions of Schiphol airport in the international air transport market. The 'one-terminal' concept became the main focus of the commercial policy in promoting Schiphol as the best transfer airport in the world and as the 'Gateway to Europe' (for cargo activities). Furthermore, Schiphol followed a competitive strategy based on price competition, diversification of products, the segmentation of the air market, e.g. destinations, leisure travel and the introduction of the tourist class, and improving cooperation with travel organisations. Consequently, the marketing strategy also shifted from the promotion of destinations toward the supply of high-quality services on board.

It was also in this context of increasing competition and decreasing air travel costs that Schiphol began to search for new ways to diversify its sources of revenue. Landside activities became important sources of revenue, especially from concessions, offices and buildings rental, airport facilities and tax-free shops at the terminal building. Schiphol's successful commercialisation strategy resulted in an increasing supply of commercial products in the airport zone, e.g. hotels, restaurants, car rental, etc. The one-terminal concept and the airport plaza turned out to be successful as the total revenues generated by the exploitation of landside activities increased spectacularly.

The economic significance of Schiphol for the region became substantial. In terms of employment, Schiphol became the second economic centre in the region after Amsterdam, and in terms of productivity and growth, Schiphol surpassed by far Amsterdam and the rest of the region. Schiphol became a unique growth centre exercising strong pull-effects on workers and firms, especially companies related to airport activities, distribution centres and the headquarters of multinational businesses.

Besides the fact that Schiphol had developed into a multi-modal transport node connected to different infrastructure networks (air, railroad, roads) at different scale levels, the spatial structure and the economic functions of Schiphol show clear similarities with the traditional urban centre of a large city.

However, it is worth mentioning that the spatial transformation of Schiphol airport is closely related to the suburbanisation of Amsterdam and the spatial expansion of the Schiphol region, fuelled by the growing demand for space for housing, business parks and office buildings in the proximity of the airport areas and along transport corridors, e.g. the highway and railway networks.

Similarly, the change in the economic position of Schiphol was also stimulated by the shift in economic structure of the Amsterdam region from an industry- to a service-based economy, with connectivity, diversity, accessibility and proximity being the main driving forces of economic growth. Schiphol possessed the necessary ingredients to develop into one of the fastest growing economic centres of the region, especially from the 1980s onward. It was in this context that in the 1980s the Schiphol authorities started a new policy aimed at developing Schiphol into a 'mainport', with the close support of local, regional and national authorities.

Note, however, that the mainport policy coincided with a period of structural change, e.g. the liberalisation and deregulation of the air travel market and the aviation sector, that had direct effects on the spatial-economic transformation of Schiphol airport and the Schiphol region.

9.3 The period 1980–present

As we have mentioned earlier, the implementation of liberalisation and deregulation measures in the 1980s had deep restructuring effects on the air travel market (see Chapter 8). Schiphol was affected by air transport regulation measures and their impact on airline operations and the organisation of international air transport networks. Due to the increase in competition between hub airports in a highly uncertain market, Schiphol was forced to redefine its commercial and long-term business strategies. In this context, and with full support from the government and local and regional authorities, Schiphol airport started the development of the so-called 'mainport strategy' with the goal of developing and improving Schiphol mainport functions.

Having said that, the mainport strategy was largely determined by earlier decisions made by the state and Schiphol authorities to concentrate air traffic activities at the international Schiphol airport, and consequently to integrate the future growth policies of Schiphol into the national spatial and economic policies. A direct implication of the mainport strategy is the spectacular increase in the volume of air traffic networks as well as the increase in passengers, air cargo transport and airplane movements at Schiphol between 1980 and 2009. In particular, the growth of transfer passengers in intra-European and intercontinental air services and international freight transport registered remarkable growth in this period. A close look at the key inputs and output figures such as the net result, the investments in fixed assets, the balance sheet and the growth levels of passengers, cargo transport and airplane movements provide clear evidence confirming the impressive economic performance of Schiphol since the 1980s.

Another implication of the mainport strategy is the increase in spatial expansion of Schiphol airport and the optimisation of spatial conditions for further development of the mainport functions. The government backed up the spatial planning of Schiphol airport, including the construction of the fifth runway, and accordingly the future growth policies of Schiphol then became a matter of national interest.

However, because of the growing environmental concerns about Schiphol, the increasing shortage of space in the Schiphol region and the increasing awareness of landside accessibility to the airport and the region, local and national authorities followed a more conservative policy of balanced growth. Nevertheless, the impressive list of spatial expansions and construction projects realised at Schiphol since the 1980s changed fundamentally the morphology and the functional structure of the airport.

To achieve the goals of the mainport strategy, a more flexible approach to airport planning was needed. The Schiphol authorities abandoned the traditional airport planning model in favour of the development of the 'Masterplan', which offered more flexibility to the changing market circumstances. The masterplan of 1989 set out the goals and objectives of the mainport strategy while the Masterplan of 1997 extended the development of the mainport functions of Schiphol to the development of the airport city as a multi-functional growth centre with diversified economic functions and commercial activities for air travellers, the urban population and business firms.

Analysis of the decision-making process concerning the future development and growth of Schiphol shows a substantial increase in the number of actors involved since the 1980s. This concerns not only those actors that were identified in the postwar period 1945–80, but also a wide variety of other actors emanating from different fields, e.g. economic, societal, environmental and political organisations, ranging from the national to the local and regional levels. In this multilevel and multi-scale complex governance structure, Schiphol became a powerful actor that has always managed to realise its ambitious expansion plans. However, with the increasing number of actors involved in the discussions over the future growth of the airport, the decision-making process became very difficult, time-consuming and highly complex. This complexity is partly due to the position of Schiphol as dependent on various and conflicting regulatory procedures and policy instruments emanating from different state and regional departments, each with its own instruments, objectives and policy goals.

Since the early 2000s, the growth strategy of Schiphol has changed from being a mainport to becoming an airport city. The Masterplan of 2020 initiated by Schiphol in 2001 confirmed once again the airport city strategy as the core strategy for the future development of Schiphol, which goes a step further in the development of Schiphol into a full nebula city. Schiphol airport would then became a unique business centre, possessing various functions and a modern physical infrastructure and sharing many social, economic and political relationships with the direct surroundings and the city region.

The airport city of Schiphol is becoming one of the most important catalysts for growth and an international top location that attracts a broader range of economic activities to the region, especially logistics and distribution activities, large international companies, leisure hotels, business and financial services, and information and telecommunications companies. In this sense, Schiphol airport and its surrounding areas act as a magnet for industries and business services. Most companies located in the Amsterdam-Schiphol region tend to display a high degree of spatial concentration and clustering alongside the ring roads around Amsterdam, especially in the southern and southeastern parts of the city, and at the Schiphol airport zone and its surrounding urban areas (Hoofddorp and Schiphol-Rijk).

The attractiveness of the Schiphol region combined with the increasing scarcity of land are reflected in the higher prices of land and the rental charges for office buildings and industrial parks in the region. The existence of strong agglomeration effects and the international orientation of Schiphol and the Schiphol region explain why urban locations in this region are among the most attractive for national and international companies and, more particularly, business services in the Netherlands.

In terms of the economic effects Schiphol has on the region, our analysis reveals the existence of strong direct and indirect effects in terms of employment, value added, investments, regional gross product and property values. The economic benefits of Schiphol airport are much stronger at the level of the Schiphol region and the Amsterdam metropolitan region than at the Randstad and national level. However, the total economic effects of Schiphol for the surroundings and the region is conditioned by the size, the capacity and the quality of airport facilities and landside activities that are strongly dependent on accessibility, employment opportunities and market size. Similarly, the negative economic effects of Schiphol in terms of negative externalities (safety, pollution and noise nuisance) are considerable compared to other regions. The most important environmental effects Schiphol has on the region are the noise nuisance and existing zoning regulations that restrict housing construction around the airport zone. The zoning regulations have direct implications for local and regional spatial planning policies, especially in the case of Amsterdam, Haarlemmermeer, Amstelveen, Aalsmeer and other surrounding municipalities, because of the lack of potential open space to realise urban expansion plans.

Another important negative effect of the airport is the worsening of accessibility because of increasing road congestion around Schiphol and the Amsterdam-Schiphol region. The main causes of road congestion around Schiphol are the increase in car transport and commuting flows in the Randstad, and the attractiveness of Schiphol and its surroundings for business companies and industries. Thus the attractiveness of Schiphol as a business centre leads to an increase in the number of business parks and office buildings, and consequently an increase in employment within and around Schiphol airport and, hence, to the increase in commuters working in the Schiphol region and living in or outside the metropolitan region.

Having said that, it bears emphasising that the development of Schiphol cannot be fully understood without a comprehensive analysis of the spatial-economic transformations which occurred at the level of the Amsterdam-Schiphol region during the postwar period. This is because the spatial and economic transformation of Schiphol and the Schiphol region is inseparable from the spatial (e.g. suburbanisation and urban sprawl) and functional changes that took place at the level of the metropolitan region, including the greater Amsterdam-Schiphol region.

Indeed, the postwar period 1945–80 may be considered a period of major structural economic, demographic, socio-cultural and institutional changes that have set up the fundamental structures of the present Dutch society (see Chapter 7). At the socio-cultural level, the very conformist and traditional Dutch society evolved into a modern and open society, together with accompanying institutional changes. The depillarisation and the secularisation processes of Dutch society resulted in more freedom for individuals and the emergence of urban social movements, the individualisation of society, the rise of mass-consumption, female emancipation and the emergence of new (youth) cultural values and lifestyles. These socio-cultural changes were fuelled by the increase in wealth and incomes, which decreased the gap in disposable incomes between social groups and, as a consequence, increased the consumption of land and the mass consumption of durable goods such as cars, televisions, etc.

At the demographic level, the tendency for the natural growth of the population to decline was largely counterbalanced by a significant increase in inter-regional and external migration during this period. In this sense, migration flows became of equal importance to the natural growth of the population.

From a regional perspective, most of the larger cities in the Randstad lost population to small and medium-sized cities as a result of the declining rate of natural growth and the deconcentration of the middle class from big cities to suburban areas. However, while the urban population decreased in larger cities, labour supply increased during this period, due to the increasing share of the active population and the participation of women in the labour market. Furthermore, the average size of household has been declining since 1947, while the share of one- and two-person households in the total population in the larger cities increased from the 1960s onwards. These changes in the size and composition of households, in combination with the growth in employment and incomes, resulted in increasing demand for more space and new housing, so that the social housing sector grew significantly in the core urban areas and in the privately owned dwellings in suburban areas.

At the level of economic changes, the larger cities in the Randstad recovered relatively quickly during 1945–50 because of the increase in investment in manufacturing industry, the construction and equipment sectors and public services. An examination of the key economic indicators reveals some interesting findings. First, since the 1970s, there has been a gradual decrease of employment in agriculture, the dispersion of employment from central regions to intermediate and peripheral regions along the transport corridor and, finally, an increase in employment in business and commercial services in the Randstad and the province of North Holland.

Second, the disaggregation of production and value added by sector shows a similar tendency: an increase in production and productivity in the tertiary sectors, especially in business and commercial services and the wholesale and transport sector, and a decrease in the traditional labour-intensive sectors.

However, at the urban agglomeration level, the shares of production and value added in total production and value added declined in the larger cities and increased in the emerging suburban areas, as the case of Amsterdam and Haarlemmermeer-Schiphol clearly shows. This increase may be attributed to the deconcentration of some industries and business services firms from the city centre to the suburbs.

More particularly, empirical analysis shows a clear shift in the economic structure, both at regional and national levels, from an industry-based economy to a more service-oriented economy since the 1970s. This shift in economic structure was accompanied by a parallel shift in the spatial organisation of economic activities in the sense that manufacturing industry became more dispersed in space and business and commercial services more concentrated in the urban fringes and suburban areas of the larger cities.

Because economic growth, production, employment and incomes were not uniform across the Dutch regions, the intervention by the state through the application of regional economic policy and expansive industrial policy was necessary to achieve balanced regional growth. The focus of these policies was oriented towards the enhancement of economic efficiency and the reduction of inter-regional disparities in incomes and employment levels, and ultimately relatively equal growth rates in central and regions and those lagging behind. However, regional economic policies proved to be less effective in reducing regional disparities in terms of growth and employment. Therefore, since the 1980s, the government has applied innovation-oriented policies based on efficiency in order to reduce the gap in employment and economic growth between the regions. Today, infrastructure networks are considered the main engine of economic development and competitiveness, and as such they have become the focus of the new regional economic policy.

Complementary to regional economic policy, the national spatial planning policy was more concerned with the issues of a balanced spatial distribution of population and economic activities between the central and peripheral regions. Since the 1950s, national planning policy has vigorously focused on constraining employment and housing within cities and regions through the application of the concentrated concentration policy and later the compact city policy, in order to control suburbanisation and urban sprawl and to preserve the environment. More generally, one may argue that practically all spatial policies applied in the Netherlands were anti-urban sprawl.

Examination of the spatial metamorphosis of the Amsterdam-Schiphol region during the postwar period reveals the existence of three distinct periods of spatial transformation corresponding to the three development trajectories of the spatial urban models.

9.3.1 The period 1945–60

The period 1945–60 is the period in which the Amsterdam-Schiphol region was dominated by the hierarchical monocentric urban system à la Christaller. The main characteristics of this urban system are as follows. First, there is clear separation between the central city and the countryside, not only in terms of spatial and functional structure but also in terms of socio-demographic and cultural aspects. Second, there is a high spatial concentration of jobs and urban functions in the centre of the city, and a corresponding radial transport infrastructure network. Third, spatial interactions between regions, in terms of the mobility of individuals and households, are limited in scale, e.g. greater Amsterdam. Fourth, traffic is dominated by public transport such as the train and tram, and the use of the motorcycle and bicycle, while connections between Amsterdam and other larger cities of the Randstad took place from centre to centre. Finally, the share of households in the total population, employment and incomes between Amsterdam and the surrounding municipalities showed significant differences in favour of Amsterdam because of the high concentration of population and jobs in the centre of the city.

During this period, Amsterdam expanded progressively first in the western, northern and southern edges of the city and later to the southeast and to the south of the city. However, the spatial expansion of the city, in the spirit of the General Urban Expansion of Amsterdam (AUP), followed the finger city model. In contrast to the fast suburbanisation and urban sprawl of greater Amsterdam between 1945 and 1960, the Schiphol region and in particular Haarlemmermeer managed to preserve their countryside character during this period, even with the spectacular growth of Schiphol airport.

However, by the end of the 1950s and the 1960s, the growth of mobility by means of the car resulted in a large increase in commuting movements, and consequently in a clear separation of living places from working places. As a result, an increasing number of specialised suburban municipalities emerged in the urban scene as attractive living places, such as the municipalities of Haarlemmermeer. Gradually, a new urban hierarchy of cities and suburbs, e.g. the city region, began to emerge as a result of the shifts in the spatial organisation of population and activities in the Amsterdam-Schiphol region.

9.3.2 The period 1960–80

The period 1960–80 marks the formation of the city region and the shift from monocentric to polycentric urban system. The key determining forces of this urban transformation are the deconcentration and suburbanisation processes, which became the dominant tendency in urban development. The spatial manifestations of these processes are the gradual disappearance of the traditional separation between city and countryside as people, jobs and housing began to spread all over the region, and the decentralisation of some activities such as storage and distribution centres and wholesale and transport activities to the proximity of the main motorway corridors.

The dynamic development of business services followed the suburbanisation process and, at the same time, a clear shift in the economic structure of Amsterdam and the suburban areas took place. The Amsterdam economy became more oriented towards financial, business and commercial services, and Haarlemmermeer-Schiphol towards airport-related activities such as logistics and distribution, commercial services, wholesale and retail activities, transport and tourism, etc. In short, the increased variety of spatial-economic structure in the Amsterdam-Schiphol region resulted in the spatial specialisation of activities and the physical rearrangement of urban functions between suburban areas and the central city. Consequently, the spatial structure became more differentiated, fragmented and complex than ever before.

Finally, the mobility of people increased further in the 1970s and 1980s, which resulted in a substantial increase in the travel distance/km between living places and working places. Spatial patterns of infrastructure shifted from a radial to a transversal transport system. In addition, public transport lost its dominant position in favour of the private car as the main means of transportation in daily traffic activities. The daily urban system now takes place at the level of network of cities organised around many nodes, centres and hubs on a much larger geographical scale than was the case for the traditional daily urban system of the 1960s.

9.3.2 The period 1980–99

The period 1980–99 may be characterised as a period that saw the further splintering of the polynuclear urban system and the emergence of the urban field. The growth levels of the population and urban densities are nearly equal between the city centre and the suburban core areas. The growing size of suburban municipalities in the region, particularly the municipalities of the Schiphol region, was determined essentially by the suburbanisation and urban sprawl occurring at the level of the greater Amsterdam region. Furthermore, the hierarchical separation between the city centre of Amsterdam and suburban areas has faded away, and consequently a clear delimitation of the geographical borders at the level of urban networks has become difficult because almost the same dense patterns of spatial, social and economic interactions take place now at the higher geographical level.

The functional spatial structure of this emerging urban field shows a high specialisation of activities at the level of the Amsterdam-Schiphol region, and a rapid increase in commuting flows that show a criss-cross pattern. This pattern of commuting flows between the city centre and suburban cores and between suburban areas themselves are accompanied by an increase in travel time as well as the total number of displacements by motive, e.g. shopping, work, visits, recreation, etc. The daily mobility of individuals and households now takes place at the level of the metropolitan region and between regions. That is the reason why some authors have interpreted this new spatial urban model as an indication of the emergence of the urban field or city network.

Strictly speaking, it is perfectly possible to argue that the spatial and functional structure of cities and suburban cores in the Amsterdam-Schiphol region are more strongly intertwined with the metropolitan region and the Randstad than ever before. This suggests also that the new urban system is evolving into an urban field, where most of the urban functions and activities are now taking place on a much larger geographical scale than the city region.

Notes

1 Spatial-economic transformation of the Schiphol region

1. A mainport may be broadly defined as a central hub connecting different national, continental and intercontinental transport networks, that has good accessibility and high-quality infrastructure (including modern ICT infrastructure), and provides a highly attractive location for firms and businesses.

2 Spatial-economic transformation and the rise of the nebula city

1. Note that the assumption of a single centre of attraction is intended to escape the so-called Starret (1978) theorem. This theorem states that there is no competitive equilibrium with positive transport costs, in the absence of agglomeration economies. In the absence of transport costs, activities will be distributed uniformly through space, creating the so-called 'backyard capitalism', i.e. each individual produces what he/she consumes.
2. According to Glaeser and Kohlhase (2004: 199), the average cost of moving a ton per mile in 1890 was 18.5 cents and today only 2.3 cents (in 2001 dollars). At their height, transportation industries represented 9 per cent of GDP. Today, if we exclude air travel, they represent only 2 per cent of national product.
3. In the USA for example, the proportion of jobs located in central cities fell from about 75 per cent in 1950 to about 45 per cent in 1990 (Mieszkowski and Mills, 1993).
4. Networks may be physical, e.g. infrastructure, or non-physical, e.g. based on social, cultural and economical relations/links.
5. This is because space is directly influenced by production, transaction, transport and logistics costs and trust because recurrent market relationships need to be based on contracts and trust between parties.

3 Institutional foundations of spatial-economic changes

1. We make a distinction between the following different actors: *institutions* such as the state, provinces and local government bodies, private sectors/firms, social organisations, etc.; *communities of actors* such as lobby groups, professional advisers, research institutes, architects, planners, policy-makers, universities, etc.; *corpora* such as architecture, design, infrastructural and spatial planning concepts, visual images, photos, PR and marketing campaigns, etc.; and the *electorate*, especially citizens that are concerned by the development of the Schiphol region such as, for example, employees, investors, inhabitants of the surrounding areas, consumers and visitors.

2. The neoclassic institutionalists consider institutions in term of prevailing Nash equilibrium behaviour. They focus attention on the stability rising from preferences and optimising behaviour of interacting rational individuals and actors.

3. This conception of institutions consists of strategies of organisations and governance structures resulting from the protection and control of property rights (private or public), as analysed in transaction cost theory.

4. The theoretical arguments proposed by Acemoglu *et al.* (2001) are based on three assumptions: (a) different types of colonisation policy created diverse sets of institutions; (b) the colonisation strategy was influenced by the feasibility of settlements; and (c) the colonial state and the corresponding institutions persisted even after independence.

5. Note that Hume's idea of the importance of imagination is remarkably similar to Schelling's concept of prominence.

6. Roscher (1865) considered land use as dependent on the cultural, social and economic contexts of actors. He enlarged the idea of industrial localisation by introducing the division of labour, transport infrastructures, capital and resources as the main driving forces of the spatial localisation of firms. In addition, Roscher integrated into his study the qualitative advantages of cities such as the intellectual and cultural atmosphere, potentiality for innovations and the quality of the local labour force.

7. The localisation of activities may be explained by the degree of attractiveness of cities, e.g. agglomeration economies. Schaeffle stresses the existence of spatial inequalities related to the development in (transport) infrastructure, costs and returns on capital, the climate and the size of consumer centres. He focused on the importance of the qualitative locational advantages such as the presence of a highly qualified labour force and financing, that is the facility to acquire capital.

8. The idea of idle curiosity places emphasis on the human tendency towards experimentation, creative innovation, speculation and novelty.

9. Williamson (1975: 7) adds bounded rationality and opportunism to uncertainty in explaining market failure.

10. The first type of institutional structure manifests itself in exchange relationships based on direct reciprocity, that is a service must be immediately matched by a counter-service. This happens mostly in weak civil societies associated with patterns of cooperation that are largely limited to family relations, systems of patronage and clientelism. The second type of institutional structure is manifested by exchange relationships based on generalised reciprocity, that is it involves the confidence that a service will result in a future counter-service. This happens very often in dense and diversified networks of organisations.

11. Actors range from individuals or groups who are property right owners (residential groups, commercial tenants, firms, churches, socio-cultural, political and civic groups, etc.) to organisations with coordination and control power such as city government bodies (municipalities, provinces, inter-provincial entities, etc.) and the state with its different constituent bodies (parliament, ministries, public bodies, etc.).

12. Note that Ostrom (2005) focused on the institutions (not their components/forms, that is collective arrangements) and studied them from political theory in a policy analysis framework.

13. The notion of a common-property resource refers to economic goods with high exclusion costs, where one person's consumption subtracts from the total. Ostrom makes distinction between: (1) *operational rules* – that is day-to-day decisions made by actors (monitoring, information exchange, sanctions, etc.); (2) *collective choice rules* – that is rules that are used by area developers, planning authorities and land use owners in making policies about how a city or urban area should be managed; and (3) *constitutional choice rules* – that is determining the specific rules to be used in crafting the set of collective-choice rules that affect the set of operational rules.

14. The Dutch administrative-territorial structure, for example, consists of three government entities: the central government, the provinces with primarily administrative tasks and the municipalities enjoying a certain level of autonomy. Where changes have occurred within this model of territorial governance, it has mainly involved changes in size and numbers (e.g. newly reclaimed land resulted in an additional province (Flevoland) and the reduction of the number of municipalities from an initial 1,200 to 489 in 2003 because of a continuing process of annexation and amalgamation).

15. For example, the Dutch state structure is built on the Thorbecke constitution drawn up in 1848 which was inherited from the French Napoleonic system, settling the division of powers between the state, the provinces and the municipalities.

4 Urbanisation and industrialisation of Schiphol and the Amsterdam-Schiphol region 1900–45

1. According to Groote (1995: 179), during the early nineteenth century, about three-quarters of total capital formation in infrastructure was spent exclusively on realising the 'North Holland Canal' project, providing direct access for Amsterdam to the North Sea.

2. During the second half of the nineteenth century, urban activities become more dispersed in space, mainly because of increasing negative agglomeration economies (e.g. poor quality of life in cities, pollution, congestion, etc.), and substantial improvement in transportation networks.

3. During the first half of the twentieth century, Dutch society was segmented along divided cultural lines in the sense that each 'pillar' (Catholics, Protestant, Socialists and Liberals) had its own political, economic and cultural organisations.

4. This ratio is calculated as the proportion of the total labour force in sector s in municipality m divided by total area of the municipality (in km^2).

5. Unfortunately, such variables of interest do not exist at the municipality level for the period 1900–47.

6. The first sawmill was bought by an entrepreneur in Zaandam and it became the basis of a flourishing wood-processing industry. Initially, sawmills worked mostly for Amsterdam traders, but soon the Zaan region started to produce its own wooden products as well. The most successful offspring of those sawmills was shipbuilding. The Zaan region rose to international fame when the Russian Tsar Peter the Great travelled to Zaandam to study its shipbuilding industry.

7. In the case of the Plantage (Kerklaan, Middenlaan), the municipality sold land parcels to private developers (*f*1.50 per m^2 for a first-class location, with the remaining land parcels for *f*100 per m^2), with the result that large parcels of land came into the hands of land speculators (in 1878, land parcels were sold at *f* 45.10 per m^2). However, speculation in building new houses was limited in this neighbourhood – in comparison with other parts of the city – because of the high prices of land (Wagenaar, 1998: 157).

8. For further details, see the excellent study by N. H. ter Veen (1925) on the socio-economic situation of the first inhabitants of Haarlemmermeer.

9. Note that the Haarlemmermeer polder registered very high levels of child mortality. Between 1856 and 1860, one-third of total deaths concerned this category of the population. In 1861, 41 per cent of total deaths was attributed to child mortality, against 22 per cent at the national level.

5 The rise and development of Schiphol airport

1. These actors were: the Dutch Trade Company (*Nederlandsche Handelsmaatschappij*), the Rotterdam's and Tweent's Bank (*Rotterdamsche en Tweentsche Bank*), House of

Finance of Lippmann, Rosenthal and Co. from Amsterdam, the Batavia Oil Company (*Bataafsche Petroleum Maatschappij*) and some shipping companies.

2. Directly after 15 August 1920, Plesman came into conflict with Fokker because of deficiencies in the cooling system of the Fokker F-II.
3. Bednarek defines 'urban boosterism' as 'the effort to promote the growth and development of one's city, one that often included a sense of competition with rival cities' (Bednarek, 2001: 7).
4. See 'Demonstratie voor het behoud van Schiphol', *Het Vaderland*, 3 July 1938, morning edition.

6 Reconstruction and development of Schiphol airport 1945–80

1. Commercial aviation was fully restored by July 1945 (Swedish carrier ABA started a scheduled service to Schiphol on 18 July, and the KLM intercontinental services to Batavia started on 10 November).
2. These are: Swedish Airline (ABA), Air France, British European Airways (BEA), Czechoslovakian Airlines (CSA), Danish Airlines (DDL), Norwegian Airlines (DNL), Belgian Airlines (SABENA) and Swissair as well as new airlines such as Finnish Airlines and Aer Lingus (operating from Dublin and Manchester to Amsterdam in cooperation with KLM).
3. In a meeting of the RLC, Professor Zwiers said that the decision about this issue was already taken, and further discussions about this issue were irrelevant (13th meeting of 13 November 1945; NA 2.16.39, No. 25–32; correspondence of 24 October 1945).
4. In 1954, it was decided to include Rotterdam as third shareholder of the company. The government was then represented by five participants, Amsterdam by three participants and Rotterdam by one representative. In 1955 (one year before the signing of the final agreement) two additional participants were added to the board of commissioners – one representing the state and the other representing Amsterdam.
5. To save construction costs, space was downsized, the number of gates was reduced from 31 to 25 and less costly construction materials were used (e.g. glass instead of steel or concrete).
6. The non-stop flight of the Boeing 707 to Europe took more than seven hours. The jet airplane reduced the distance between countries by 40 per cent (see Gordon, 2004: 174).
7. Schiphol raised airport fees by almost 30 per cent upon the opening of the terminal, and 50 per cent again in 1968. During the first oil crisis, the Schiphol Company raised airport fees by 10 per cent in April 1976 and 5 per cent in January 1977. Rents were also raised by 23 per cent during the 1970s and concession fees by 15 per cent (in 1976).
8. During the 1950s, KLM, in cooperation with an American travel agency, started the organisation of tourist trips (*Vlieg-rij-ski vakantie*) from the USA to the Netherlands and/or Europe (ACA 1323; No. 347; 8-1-1957).
9. As result, the number of tourist class tickets sold in 1953 on the transatlantic and intercontinental services increased by 53 per cent in comparison to 1951 (Diericks and Bouwens, 1997: 81).
10. Some airports such as Nice banned completely night flights of Caravelle airplanes due to increasing protests from the public. In the case of Kloten Airport in Zurich, local authorities were put under pressure by citizens to vote against the airport expansion plan.
11. According to Gordon (2004: 231), there were 154 hijacking attempts in the US between 1969 and 1978.

7 Spatial-economic transformation of the Amsterdam-Schiphol region 1945–80

1. Meerlanden area is composed of the municipalities of Haarlemmermeer, Aalsmeer, Uithorn, Amstelveen and a (small) part of the municipality of Ouder-Amstel.

8 From mainport to airport city

1. According to an ICAO survey (2001), airports with more than 25 million passengers (on average) generated 58 per cent of their revenues from non-aviation activities (see Graham, 2003: 60).
2. From January 1999, the Schiphol Group changed its valuation policy for operating assets. These assets are no longer carried at replacement value, but at historical cost. Commercial property is carried at current value.
3. The structure programme for civil airports (*Structuurschema Burgerluchtvaartterreinen* (SBL)) of 1979 constitutes the basic document of the Physical Planning Key Decision plan for Schiphol, which sketches the long-term development policy of the airport. The most important issues raised in the structure programme were the close relationship between future developments in the air transport market and their effects on airport capacity, and hence on land use and spatial expansion of the airport.
4. The night-flight restriction period runs from 23:00 hours to 06:00 hours (local time). All aircraft certified to ICAO Annex 16 Chapter 2 are not allowed during night period. Aircraft certified to ICAO Annex 16 Chapter 3 for which the margin of the sum of the three certification noise limits is less than 5 EPNdB are allowed with restrictions depending on the bypass ratios.
5. The main actors in this consultation body are: the Ministries of Transport and Waterworks and the Ministry of Spatial Planning, Schiphol airport, KLM and the Dutch Air Traffic Service (LVNL), the province of North Holland, the municipalities of Amsterdam, Haarlemmermeer and Uitgeest, and the representatives of the inhabitants of the surrounding areas (*Commissie Regionaal Overleg Luchthaven Schiphol* (CROS)) and the VGN (*Vereniging Gezamenlijke Platforms*).
6. These are: the Ministry of Transport and Waterworks, the Ministry of Spatial Planning and Environment, the Ministry of Economic Affairs (EZ), the Ministry of Finance, and the Ministry of Agriculture and Fisheries.

List of archives consulted

Amsterdam City Archives (ACA)/Dienst Luchthaven Schiphol Archive

Note: The ACA archive 1323 for Schiphol is not inventoried yet and the numbers reported below are taken directly from the boxes and documents examined. This archive covers the period 1935–63 and is divided into two parts: from 1 to 238 (about 34 metres long), and from 1001 to 1133 (about 12.5 metres).

ACA, Gemeenteblad 1926-II. City council minutes; ACA, 1323, No. 1-238; No. 1001-1133; No. 932a-b-S49; No. 1334 DH 1947; No. 72/1027; No. 79/1066; No. 1089-1242 (14); No. 1098-1109 LHD 1959; No. 1112-1138, LHD 1959; No. 1141-1170; No. 1175-1197 S1957; No. 909-1197. S1957; No. 110-2; No. 1198-1229, No. 1217 (1957); No. 1230-1241 (1957); No. 69/12; No. 1010 S1935; No. 1471S1935; Nr. 531; No. 78; No. 1051-1200; LHD 1949 (box nr 11); No. 1179/ S1949; No. 1185/S1949; No 139, 139A, 139B; No. 5183; No. 5497 (0061-0117); No. 5370 (264, 267, 447-448); No. 5370 (179.8 C67; 179.9 C67a; 07-25); No. 4; LHD 1949 [132]. 1946; No. 9-16; No. 16-26; No. 35 (1945); No. 36 (1946); No. 12-13 LHD 1949 (163-164); No. 1542; LHD 288 (871-900); LHD 270 (1-5); LHD 271 (12-48); LHD 276 (609-653); LHD 277 (654-720); LHD 278 (721-814); LHD 279 (815-870); No. 5168; No. 1010; No. 1011 (1935); No. 1051-1200; LHD 1949 (box nr. 11); No. 1179/ S1949; No. 1185/S1949; No 139, 139A, 139B; No. 12; LHD 1949 [163] (Dienst PW; 1949); No. 13; LHD 1949 [164]; No. 4; LHD 1949 [132]; No. 9-16; No. 16-26; No. 35 (1945) and No. 36 (1946); No. 347; 8-1-1957; No. 79; No. 72; No. 1027; No. 31-543, 51II; No. 102S, 51III; No. 316S. 1942, No.51 and No. 51II; No. 823-DH1940, No. 51II and No. 252. S.1940; No. 17/135-S45; No.19/1011 S35 and 1471.S35; No 17/ 739; 777 S39; 717 S46; 27, 7; 73DH1938; 713DH1946.

ACA, 1323, 832a-z-DH1940/51; No. 252.S.1940; No. 531, 19-35; No. 309-S43, 51III; No. 305-S43, 51III; No. 138-S43, 51III; No. 316 S42, 51; No.3/35S, 51III; No. 262S, 51III; No. 311-543, 51 III; No. 102S, 51III; No. 832-DH1940, No 51II; No. 252.S.1940; ACA, Public Affairs Archive 5181, Nr. 4125; No. 1761. ACA, 5169, No. 216, No. 2/35; ACA, 5497, No. 112-113; ACA, 5183 No. 1482-1493; No. 1514-1548; No. 1482-1492; No. 2913; No. 2163, 2164, 2165; ACA, 5376.A, No. 12

National Archive (Rijksarchief, The Hague)

NA, 2.16.39, No. 10-14; No. 1; No. 2; NA 2.16.39, No. 25-32 (Archieven van de Noodcommissie Luchtvaartterrienen, 1945–1946), The Hague.

Aviodrom Archive (Lelystad)

Note: No inventory list for this archive exists, which is why only the numbered boxes which have been examined are reported, without giving a description of the contents of each box.

    Box 1: Dienst Handelsinrichtingen 1940–1945, Commissie van Advies Luchthavenvraagstuk. Box 2: Kadaster documents Schiphol area 1979–1982. Box 3 and Box 4: Luchtvracht (1) and (2) (Diverse brochures and documents). Box 4 and 5: maps and documents 'development of Schiphol from 1920–now. Box 6: public offers documents of B&W Amsterdam 17/2-1930, maps and documents from the department of 'Pers & Publiciteit (NVLS)'. Box 7 and 8: Maps of the new station building complex, Schiphol zone, expansion plans, divers maps of Schiphol from 1926–present. Box 9: divers maps of Schiphol terrain after May 1967. Box 10: construction projects Schiphol (Divers documents such as maps, public offer documents, photos, etc.). Box 10.1: Hangar 11/12, new Station building (1967). Box 10.2: expansion of C-pier (1971 and 1974), expansion plan of station building North and new D-pier (1975), C-pier with luggage room (end 1987), and diverse other construction projects. Box 10.3 and 10.4: expansion Terminal East en Div. Documents (photos). Box 10.5 and 10.6: documents of the working group air traffic tower (1958 and 1960). Box 10.7: construction documents of 'douane-entrepot (Gebouw 72) Schiphol Oost', 1978; runway 01L-19R (Zwanenburgbaan) and 06-24 (and v/h 23) (Schiphol Oostbaan), Hangar 9 (Kingsford Smith); Hangar 10 (Albert Plesman). Box 10.8: design and construction of 'Verkeersareaal (Schiphol Centrum)', maps new station building and station complex area. Box 11.1: Annual Reports Schiphol airport (NV Luchthaven Schiphol 1926–1949). Box 11.2: Annual reports/Jaarverslagen NV Luchthaven Schiphol 1950–2005 (12 boxes).

Archive of the Municipality of Haarlemmermeer (Hoofddorp)

Deel inventaris 1910–1945: Economische aangelegenheden; arbied en maatschappelijk zorg en verzekeringen: I. Economische aangelegenheden: B. No. 3-37; No. 38-40; No. 50

    II. Arbeid: No. A.205; B.206; C. 1. 208; No. I.G.2 (planning garden city 1927–1929); No. I.G.3 (154) (spatial expansion plan Hoofddorp, nieuwe Vennep); I.G.3 (155) (expansion Schiphol and surronding 1934–1940); I.G.3 (156-159); I.G.4 (161-167) (different expansion plans Haarlemmermeer). No. IV.D.3.509 (expropriation land parcels for expansion of Schiphol 1933–1935); No. IV.D.3.510 (land parcels in the vicinity of Schiphol areas, 1936).

Archive 1946–1979 (VNG. Code-1.7) No. 67 and No. 69; No. 3003-305; No. 338-354; No. 386-404; No. 478-496; No, 725-733; No. 1151; No. 1153; No. 1156.
Inventaris Archief 1946–1979 (V.N.G. Code-1.8), No. 10-12; No. 14; Nr. 375-377; No. 378; No. 379-381; No. 382-386; No. 402-410.
Deel Inventaris Archief 1947–1979 (VNG. Code-07/08), No. 8; No. 10; No. 20.

NACO Archive (The Hague)

NACO archives (Netherlands Airport Consultants BV) Archive NR: NL-NED Schiphol 14-5-re (Bentham-Crowler Architektenbureau, Amsterdam). Onderzoek Bouwkunde voorzieningen voor Decentrale Transferbagage Invoer (1990). 2889-NL-NED Schiphol A't-D9-7 (various reports, studies, books, etc., 1948–1986). 3787- NL-NED Schiphol 14-5-re (onderzoek bouwkundige voorzieningen voor decentrale transferbagage invoer, 8 februari 1990).

North-Holland Archive (NEHA), Haarlem

Kadastrale legger; Luchthaven Schiphol (Cadastral parcels register of Schiphol airport) 1925–1985.

Bibliography

Abdel-Rahman, H. M (1990) 'Agglomeration economies, types, and sizes of cities', *Journal of Urban Economics*, 27: 25–45.

Abdel-Rahman, H. M. and Fujita, M. (1990) 'Product variety, Marshallian externalities and city sizes', *Journal of Regional Science*, 30: 165–83.

Acemoglu, D., Johnson, S. and Robinson, J. A. (2001) 'The colonial origins of comparative development: an empirical investigation', *American Economic Review*, 91(5): 1369–401.

Advies Commissie Versterking Randstad (2007) Zoetermeer: FWA, January. Available online at: http://www.minbzk.nl/actueel?ActItmIdt=103987 (accessed 11 March 2008).

Alchian, A. A. and Demsetz, H. (1972) 'Production, information costs, and economic organization', *American Economic Review*, 62(5): 777–95.

Alchian, A. A. and Demsetz, H. (1973) 'The property right paradigm', *Journal of Economic History*, 33: 16–27.

Almeida, P. and Kogut, B. (1999) 'Localisation of knowledge and the mobility of engineers in regional networks', *Management Science*, 45: 905–17.

Alonso, W. (1964) *Location and Land Use*. Cambridge, MA: Harvard University Press.

Altorfer, E. (1957) *Planning the Terminal Building*. Paper presented at the 9th Western European Airport Conference, 24–28 May, Oslo (Amsterdam City Archive, inv. nr 1232. Doc. No. 903, S.1957).

Amin, A. (ed.) (1994) *Post-Fordism: A Reader*. Oxford: Blackwell.

Amin, A. (1999) 'An institutionalist perspective on regional economic development', *International Journal of Urban and Regional Research*, 23(1): 365–78.

Amin, A. and Thrift, N. (eds) (1995) *Globalization, Institutions, and Regional Development in Europe*. Oxford: Oxford University Press.

Amin, A. and Cohendet, P. (1999) 'Learning and adaptation in decentralised business networks', *Environment and Planning D: Society and Space*, 17(1): 87–104.

Anas, A., Arnott, R. and Small, K. A. (1998) 'Urban spatial structure', *Journal of Economic Literature*, 36: 1426–64.

Arthur, B. (1994) *Increasing Returns and Path Dependence in the Economy*. Ann Arbor, MI: University of Michigan Press.

Arts, B. and Leroy, P. (2003) *Verandering van politiek, vernieuwing van milieubeleid: klassieke en postmoderne arrangementen*. Nijmegen: Nijmegen University Press.

Arvanitidis, P. A. (2006) *A Framework of Socioeconomic Organization: Redefining Original Institutional Economics Along Critical Realist Philosophical Lines*. Paper presented at the 46th Congress of the European Regional Science Association (ERSA), Volos, Greece, 30 August – 3 September.

Ascher, F. (1995) *Métapolis ou l'Avenir des Villes*. Paris: Editions Odile Jacob.

Aydalot, P. (eds) (1986) *Milieux Innovateurs en Europe*. Paris: GREMI.

Ayres, C. E. (1962) *The Theory of Economic Progress: A Study of the Fundamental Economic Development and Cultural Change*, 2nd edn. New York: Schocken.

Bailly, A. and Huriot, J. M. (1999) *Villes et Croissance: Théories, Modèles, Perspectives*. Paris: Anthropos.

Bairoch, P. (1988) *Cities and Economic Development: From the Dawn of History to the Present*. Chicago: University of Chicago Press.

Baldwin, R. and Martin, P. (2003) 'Agglomeration and regional growth', in V. Henderson and J. F. Thisse (eds), *Handbook of Regional and Urban Economics: Cities and Geography*. Amsterdam: North-Holland.

Bartels, C. P. A. and Duin, J. J. van (1981) *Regional Economic Policy in a Changed Labor Market*. Paper presented at the European Regional Science Association Conference in Barcelona, Spain, 25–28 August 1981. Available online at: http://www.iiasa.ac.at/Admin/PUB/Documents/WP-81-064.pdf (accessed 25 May 2008).

Batten, D. F. (1995) 'Network cities: creative urban agglomerations for the 21st century', *Urban Studies*, 32(2): 313–27.

Batty, M. (2005) *Cities and Complexity*. Cambridge, MA: MIT Press.

BCI, TNO and SEO (2006) *Economische Effecten Schiphol*, SEO-report Nr. 885. University of Amsterdam, Amsterdam

Bednarek, J. R. D. (2001) *America's Airports: Airfield Development, 1918–1947*. College Station, TX: Texas A&M University Press.

Beeson, P. E. and Husted, S. (1989) 'Patterns and determinants of productive efficiency in state manufacturing', *Journal of Regional Science*, 29(1): 15–28.

Bertolini, L. (2001) *Evolutionary Urban Transportation Planning? An Exploration*. Amsterdam Institute for Metropolitan and International Development Studies (AMIDSt), University of Amsterdam.

Bertolini, L. (2007) 'Evolutionary urban transportation planning? An exploration', *Environment and Planning A*, 39(8): 1998–2019.

Black, D. and Henderson, J. V. (1999) 'A theory of urban growth', *Journal of Political Economy*, 107(2): 252–84.

Boersma, H. (2003) *Haarlemmermeer, Wonen tussen stad en platteland: De problematiek van verstedelijking van een agrarische gemeente*. Afstudeeronderzoek Sociale Geografie & Planologie (Stadsgeografie), Faculteit Ruimtelijke Wetenschappen, Universiteit Utrecht.

Boltanski, L. and Thévenot, L. (1991) *De la justification. Les économies de la grandeur*. Paris: Gallimard.

Bontje, M. (2001) *The Challenge of Unplanned Urbanization: Urbanization and National Urbanization Policy in the Netherlands in a Northwest-European Perspective*. PhD thesis, Department of Geography and Planning, University of Amsterdam.

Boschma, R. A. and Lambooy, J. G. (1999) 'Evolutionary economics and economic geography', *Journal of Evolutionary Economics*, 9: 411–29.

Bosma, K. (1996) 'European airports, 1945–1995: typology, psychology, and infrastructure', in J. Zukowsky (ed.), *Building for Air Travel. Architecture and Design for Commercial Aviation*. Munich and New York: Art Institute of Chicago and Prestel Verlag, pp. 51–65.

Bosma, K. (1998) 'The demise of the dinosaur? Reflections on the expansion of Schiphol', *Archis*, 2: 9–17.

Bosma, K. (2004) 'In search of the perfect airport', in A. von Vegesack and J. Eisenbrand (eds), *Airworld: Design and Architecture for Air Travel*. Wheil am Rhein: Vitra Design Stiftung, pp. 30–86.

Boyer, R. (1987) *Technical Change and the Theory of Regulation*. Paris: CEPREMAP.

Boyer, R. (1990) *The Regulation School: A Critical Introduction*. New York: Columbia University Press.

Boyer, R. (2004) *À quelles conditions les réformes institutionnelles réussissent-elles? Contribution au contrat finalisé*. Commissariat Général du Plan – CEPREMAP 2003–2004. Available online at: http://www.cepremap.ens.fr/ boyer/ (accessed 23 April 2008).

Boyer, R. and Orléan, A. (1992) 'How do conventions evolve?', *Journal of Evolutionary Economics*, 2: 165–77.

Boyer, R. and Saillard, Y. (eds) (2002) *Théorie de la Régulation: L'état des Savoirs*. Paris: La Découverte.

Brand, A. (2002) *Het stedelijk veld in opkomst: de transformatie van de stad in Nederland gedurende de tweede helft van de twintigste eeuw*. Proefschrift, Faculteit de maatschappij –en gedragswetenschappen, Universiteit van Amsterdam, Overveen.

Brenner, N. (1998) Global cities, glocal states: global city formation and state territorial restructuring in contemporary Europe, *Review of International Political Economy*, 5(1): 1–37.

Brenner, N., Jessop, B., Jones, M. and MacLeod, G. (eds) (2003) *State-space: A Reader Regulating Risk*. Oxford: Blackwell.

Breschi, S. and Lissoni, F. (2001) 'Localised knowledge spillovers vs. innovative milieu: knowledge "tacitness" reconsidered', *Papers in Regional Science*, 80(3): 255–73.

Brodherson, D. (1993) *What Can't Go Up Can't Come Down: The History of American Airport Policy, Planning and Design*. PhD dissertation, Cornell University.

Brueckner, J. K. (2001) *Urban Sprawl: Lessons from Urban Economics*, Brookings-Wharton Papers on Urban Affairs, pp. 65–97. Available online at: http://www.jstor.org/stable/25058783 (accessed 15 April 2008).

Bryant, C. R., Russwurm, L. J. and McLellan, A. G. (1982) *The City's Countryside: Land and Its Management in the Rural-Urban Fringe*. London: Longmans.

Buck Consultants International (BCI) (1990) *Centrale Europese Distributie bij Amerikaanse en Japanse bedrijven*. Nijmegen.

Buck Consultants International (BCI) (1999) *Ontwikkeling vestigingspatronen Amerikaanse en Japanse bedrijven in Europa*, Ministerie van Economische Zaken, Den Haag.

Burghouwt, G. (2005) *Airline Network Development in Europe and Its Implications for Airport Planning*. PhD thesis, SEO, University of Amsterdam.

Bush, P. D. (1987) 'The theory of institutional change', *Journal of Economic Issues*, 21(3): 1075–116.

Camagni, R. (eds) (1991) *Innovation Networks: Spatial Perspectives*. London and New York: Belhaven Press.

Camagni, R. (1993) 'Inter-firm, industrial networks: the costs and benefits of cooperative behaviour', *Journal of Industry Studies*, 1(1): 1–16.

Camagni, R. and Gibelli, M. C. (1994) 'Réseaux de villes et politiques urbaines', *Flows*, 16: 5–22; available online at: http://www.persee.fr (accessed 10 February 2008).

Cappellin, R. (1988) 'Transaction costs and urban agglomeration', *Revue d'économie régionale et urbaine (RERU)*, 2: 261–78.

Carlino, G. (1985) 'Declining city productivity and the growth of rural regions: a test of alternative explanations', *Journal of Urban Economics*, 18(1): 11–27.

Castells, M. (1992) *European Cities, the Transformation Society, and the Global Economy*. Amsterdam: Centrum voor Grootstedelijk Onderzoek UvA (Universiteit van Amsterdam).

Castells, M. (1995) *The Informational City: Networks and Society*. New York: Blackwell.

Chardonnet, J. (1953) *Les Grands Types de complexes industriels*. Paris: A. Colin.

Clawson, M. (1962) 'Urban sprawl and speculation in suburban land', *Land Economics*, 38(2): 94–111.

Coase, R. H. (1937) 'The nature of the firm', *Economica*, 4: 386–405.

Coase, R. H. (1960) 'The problem of social cost', *Journal of Law and Economics*, 3: 1–44.

Coleman, J. S. (1988) 'Social capital in the creation of human capital', *American Journal of Sociology*, 94: S95–S120.

Coleman, J. S. (1990) *Foundations of Social Theory*. Cambridge, MA: Harvard University Press.

Colletis, G. and Pecqueur, B. (1993) 'Intégration des espaces et quasi intégration des firmes: vers de nouvelles rencontres productives?', *RERU*, 3: 489–508.

Commons, J. R. (1924) *Legal Foundations of Capitalism*. New York: Macmillan.

Commons, J. R. (1934) *Institutional Economics: Its Place in Political Economy*. New York: Macmillan.

Cooke, P. and Morgan, K. (1998) *The Associational Economy: Firms, Regions, and Innovation*. Oxford: Oxford University Press.

Coriat, B. (1994) 'La Théorie de la régulation: origines, specificités, enjeux', in *Future Anterieur*, Special Issue of *Thérie de la Régulation et Critique de la Raison Economique*. Paris: L'Harmattan.

Courtwright, D. T. (2005) *Sky as Frontier: Adventure, Aviation, and Empire*, Centennial of Flight Series, No. 11.

Daniels, T. (1999) *When City and Countryside Collide: Managing Growth in the Metropolitan Fringe*. Washington, DC: Island Press.

Davids, K. (1997) 'Familiebedrijven, familisme en individualisering Nederland, ca. 1880–1990: een bijdrage aan de theorievorming', *Amsterdams sociologisch Tijdschrift*, 527–54.

Davids, K. (2000) 'Sporen in de Stad. De metro en de Strijd om ruimtelijke ordening in Amsterdam', *Historisch Tijdschrift Holland*, 32(3/4): 157–82.

Davis, L. E. and North, D. C. (1971) *Institutional Change and American Economic Growth*. Cambridge: Cambridge University Press.

De Beer, N. and Veeneklaas, F. R. (1978) 'Het arbeidsaanbod op lange termijn' ('Labor supply in the long run'), *Economisch Statistische Berichten (ESB)*, 63: 1160–3.

De Groene Amsterdammer, 8 October 1927, 6 March 1932, 6 August 1932.

De Vries, J. (1984) *European Urbanization, 1500–1800*. London: Methuen.

Dekker, K. and Kempen, R. van (2004) 'Urban governance within the big cities policy ideals and practice in Den Haag, the Netherlands', *International Journal of Urban Policy and Planning*, 21(2): 109–17.

Demsetz, H. (1967) 'Towards a theory of property rights', *American Economic Review*, 57(2): 347–59.

Demsetz, H. (1997) 'The firm in economic theory: a quiet revolution', *American Economic Review*, 87: 426–9.

Deurloo, M. C. and Hoekveld, G. A. (1980) *The Population Growth of the Urban Municipalities in the Netherlands between 1849 and 1970, with Particular Reference to the Period 1899–1930*. Free University Institute for Geographical Studies and Urban and Regional Planning, Amsterdam.

Dieleman, F. M. and Musterd, S. (eds) (1992) *The Randstad: A Research and Policy Laboratory*. Dordrecht: Kluwer Academic.

Dienst Ruimtelijke Ordening (DRO), Gemeente Amsterdam (2003) *Stadsplan Amsterdam: Toekomstvisies op de ruimtelijke ontwikkeling van de stad: 1928–2003*. Rotterdam: Nai Uitgevers.

Dierikx, M. L. J. (1991) 'Struggle for prominence: clashing Dutch and British interests on the colonial air routes, 1918–42', *Journal of Contemporary History*, 26(2): 333–51.

Dierikx, M. L. J. (1999) *Blauw in de lucht: Koninklijke Luchtvaart Maatschappij, 1919–1999*. The Hague: Sdu.

Dierikx, M. L. J. (2002) 'Wings of silver, wings of gold: money and technological change in the aircraft industry during the 1920s and 1930s', in C. Vermeeren (ed.), *Around Glare: A New Aircraft Material in Context*. Dordrecht: Kluwer Academic, pp. 81–97.

Dierikx, M. L. J. and Bouwens, B. (1997) *Building Castles of the Air: Schiphol Amsterdam and the Development of Airport Infrastructure in Europe, 1916–1996*. The Hague: Sdu.

Dijkink, G. and Mamdouh, V. (2003) 'Identity and legitimacy in the Amsterdam region', in S. Musterd and W. Salet (eds), *Amsterdam Human Capital*. Amsterdam: Amsterdam University Press, pp. 331–55.

DiMaggio, P. J. (1998) 'The new institutionalisms: avenues of collaboration', *Journal of Institutional and Theoretical Economics*, 154(4): 696–705.

DiMaggio, P. J. and Powell, W. W. (1983) 'The iron cage revisited: institutional isomorphism and collective rationality in organizational fields', *American Sociological Review*, 48(2): 147–60.

Djelic, M. L and Quack, S. (2007) 'Overcoming path dependency: path generation in open systems', *Theory and Society*, 36(2): 161–82.

Doganis, R. (1992) *The Airport Business*. London: Routledge.

Dolan, D. A. (1990) 'Local government fragmentation', *Urban Affairs Quarterly*, 26(1): 28–45.

Dosi, G. (1982) 'Technological paradigms and technological trajectories: a suggested interpretation of the determinants and directions of technical change', *Research Policy*, 11(3): 147–62.

Douglas, D. (1995) 'Airports as systems and systems of airports: airports and urban development in America before World War II', in William M. Leary (ed.), *From Airships to Airbus: The History of Civil and Commercial Aviation, Vol. 1: Infrastructure and Environment*. Washington, DC and London: Smithsonian Institute Press.

Draperi, J. F. (2003) 'L'entreprise sociale en France, entre économie sociale et action sociale', *Revue internationale de l'économie sociale*, 82(288): 48–66.

Dugger, W. M. (1979) 'Methodological differences between institutional and neoclassical economics', *Journal of Economic Issues*, 13: 899–909.

Duivestijn, A. and Tellinga, J. (2006) *De verkoop van een luchthaven: de privatisering van een werkstad. Initiatienota*. Tweede Kamer der Staten-Generaal, PVDA Fractie, The Hague, 15 March 2006.

Dupuy, C. and Torre, A. (2004) 'Confiance et proximité', in B. Pecqueur and J. B. Zimmermann (eds), *Economie de proximités*. Paris: Hermès Lavoisier, pp. 65–87.

Dupuy, J. P., Eymard-Duvernay, F., Favereau, O., Orléan, A., Salais, R. and Thevenot, L. (1989) 'Introduction', *Revue Économique*, Special Issue *Économie des Conventions*, 40(2): 141–5.

Duranton, G. and Puga, D. (2004) 'Micro-foundations of urban agglomeration economies', in J. V. Henderson and J. F. Thisse (eds), *Handbook of Regional and Urban Economics*, 4(48): 2063–117.

Edwards, B. (1998) *The Modern Terminal: New Approaches to Airport Architecture*. London and New York: Routledge.

Eggertsson, T. (1990) *Economic Behaviour and Institutions*. Cambridge: Cambridge University Press.

El Makhloufi, A. (2001) *Regroupement d'Industries et Dynamique Organisationnelle*. PhD thesis, Faculty of Economics and Econometrics, University of Amsterdam, Amsterdam.

Ellison, G. and Glaeser, E. (1997) 'Geographic concentration in US manufacturing industries: a dartboard approach', *Journal of Political Economy*, 105(5): 889–927.

Engelsdorp Gastelaars, R. (2003) 'Landscapes of power in Amsterdam?', in S. Musterd and W. Salet (eds), *Amsterdam Human Capital*. Amsterdam: Amsterdam University Press, pp. 289–309.

Enjolras, B. (2002) *L'économie solidaire et le marché*. Paris: L'Harmattan.

Enjolras, B. (2004) *Individual Action, Institutions, and Social Change: An Approach in Terms of Convention*. Series: Cahiers de la Maison des Sciences Economiques. Centre National de la Recherche Scientifique (CNRS), Université Paris. Available online at: ftp://mse.univ-paris1.fr/pub/mse/cahiers2004/R04052.pdf (accessed 11 August 2008).

Erickson, R.A. (1983) 'The evolution of the suburban space economy', *Urban Geography*, 4(4): 95–121.

Favereau, O. (2002) 'Conventions et régulation', in R. Boyer and Y. Saillard (eds), *Théorie de la Régulation: L'état des saviors*. Paris: La Découverte, pp. 511–20.

Foster, J. (1991) 'The institutionalist (evolutionary) school', in D. Mair and A. G. Miller (eds), *A Modern Guide to Economic Thought: An Introduction to Comparative Schools of Thought in Economics*. Aldershot: Edward Elgar.

Frey, B. S. (1990) 'The economic approach to institutions. Institutions matter: the comparative analysis of institutions', *European Economic Review*, 34: 443–9.

Friedman, J. (2001) 'Intercity networks in a globalizing era', in A. J. Scott (ed.), *Global City-Regions: Tendency, Theory, Policy*. Oxford: Oxford University Press, pp. 119–38.

Friedman, J. and Miller, J. (1965) 'The urban field as human habitat', *Journal of the American Institute of Planners*, 31(4): 312–20.

Fujita, M. and Krugman, P. (2004) 'The new economic geography: past, present and the future', *Papers in Regional Science*, 83: 139–64.

Fujita, M. and Ogawa, H. (1982) 'Multiple equilibria and structural transition of non-monocentric urban configurations', *Regional Science and Urban Economics*, 12: 161–96.

Fujita, M. and Thisse, J. F. (1997) 'Economie géographique, problèmes anciens et nouvelles perspectives', *Annales d'Economie et de Statistiques*, 45: 37–87.

Fukuyama, F. (1995) *Trust, Social Virtues and the Creation of Prosperity*. London: Hamish Hamilton.

Furubotn, E. and Richter, R. (2000) *Institutions and Economic Theory: The Contributions of the New Institutional Economics*. Ann Arbor, MI: University of Michigan Press.

Gambetta, B. (eds) (1988) *Trust: Making and Breaking Cooperative Relations*. Oxford: Basil Blackwell.

Garreau, J. (1991) *Edge Cities: Life on the New Frontier*. New York: Doubleday.

Gemengde Commissie Bestuurlijke Coördinatie (Commissie De Grave) (2005) *Je gaat er over of niet. Rijksbrede takenanalyse*. June. Available online at: http://www.andereove rheid.nl/AndereOverheid/Web/Publicaties (accessed 11 March 2008).

Genosko, J. (1997) 'Innovative milieux and globalization', *European Planning Studies*, 5(3): 283–97.

Giddens, A. (1984) *The Constitution of Society: Outline of the Theory of Structuration*. Cambridge: Polity Press.

Glaeser, E. L and Kohlhase, J. E. (2004) 'Cities, regions and the decline of transport costs', *Papers in Regional Science*, 83(1): 197–228.

Glaeser, E. L. and Kahn, M. E. (2003) *Sprawl and Urban Growth*, Harvard Institute of Economic Research Discussion Paper No. 2004.

Glaeser, E., Kallal, H., Scheinkman, J.A. and Schleifer, A. (1992) 'Growth in cities', *Journal of Political Economy*, 100(6): 1126–52.

Goffette-Nagot, F. (2000) 'Urban spread beyond the city edge', in J.-M. Huriot and J.-F. Thisse (eds), *Economics of Cities: Theoretical Perspectives*. Cambridge: Cambridge University Press, pp. 318–40.

Gordon, A. (2004) *Naked Airport: A Cultural History of the World's Most Revolutionary Structure*. Chicago: University of Chicago Press.

Gordon, P. and Richardson, H. W. (1996) 'Employment decentralization in US metropolitan areas: is Los Angeles an outlier or the norm?', *Environment & Planning* A, 28(10): 1727–43.

Gottmann, J. (1961) *Megalopolis*. Cambridge, MA: MIT Press.

Goudsblom, J. (1967) *The Dutch Society*. New York: Random House (Studies in Modern Societies No. 31 / A Random House Study in Sociology).

Grabher, G. (1993) 'The weakness of strong ties: the lock-in of regional development in the Ruhr area', in G. Grabher (eds), *The Embedded Firm*. London: Routledge, pp. 255–77.

Graham, A. (2003) *Managing Airports: An International Perspective*, 2nd edn. Oxford: Elsevier Butterworth-Heinemann.

Graham, S. and Marvin, S. (2001) *Splintering Urbanism: Networked Infrastructures, Technological Mobilities and the Urban Condition*. London and New York: Routledge.

Granovetter, M. (1985) 'Economic action and social structure: the problem of embeddedness', *American Journal of Sociology*, 91(3): 481–510.

Greenwood, M. and Stock, R. (1990) 'Patterns of change in the intrametropolitan location of population, jobs, and housing: 1950–1980', *Journal of Urban Economics*, 28: 243–76.

Gregory, I. N. (2000) 'Longitudinal analysis of age- and gender-specific migration patterns in England and Wales: a GIS-based approach', *Social Science History*, 24: 471–503.

Greif, A. (1994) 'Cultural beliefs and the organization of society: a historical and theoretical reaction on collectivist and individualist societies', *Journal of Political Economy*, 102(5): 912–50.

Greif, A. (1998) 'Historical and comparative institutional analysis', *American Economic Review*, 88: 80–4.

Greif, A. (2002a) *The Game-Theoretic Revolution in Comparative and Historical Institutional Analysis*. Available online at: http://bbs.cenet.org.cn/UploadImages/200641023463128028.pdf (accessed 20 June 2008).

Greif, A. (2002a2b) 'Institutions and impersonal exchange: from communal to individual responsibility', *Journal of Institutional and Theoretical Economics*, 158(1): 168–204.

Greif, A. (2006) *Institutions and the Path to the Modern Economy: Lessons from Medieval Trade*. Cambridge: Cambridge University Press.

Greup, G. M. (1936) *Gedenkboek samengesteld ter gelegenheid van het 125-jarig bestaan [van de] Kamer van Koophandel en Fabrieken voor Amsterdam Deel II, Het tijdvak 1922–1936*. Amsterdam: Kamer van koophandel en fabrieken voor, 165–6, 172–4.

Groote, P. D. (1995) *Kapitaalvorming in Infrastructuur in Nederland 1800–1913*. Capelle aan den IJssel: Labyrint.

Grossetti, M. and Bès, M. P. (2003) 'Dynamiques des réseaux et des cercles. Encastrements et découplages', *Revue d'économie industrielle*, 130: 43–58.

Grossman, G. M. and Helpman, E. (1991) *Innovation and Growth in the Global Economy*. Cambridge, MA: MIT Press.

Hakfoort, J., Poot, T. and Rietveld, P. (2001) 'The regional economic impact of an airport: the case of Amsterdam Schiphol airport', *Regional Studies*, 35(7): 595–604.

Hall, P. (1984) *The World Cities*, 3rd edn. London: Weidenfeld & Nicolson.

Hall, P. (2001) 'Global city-regions in the twenty- first century', in A. J. Scott (ed.), *Global City-Regions: Tendency, Theory, Policy*. Oxford: Oxford University Press, pp. 59–77.

Hall, P. A. and Soskice, D. (eds) (2001) *Varieties of Capitalism: The Institutional Foundations of Comparative Advantage*. Oxford: Oxford University Press.

Hall, P. A. and Taylor, R. C. R. (1996) 'Political science and the three new institutionalisms', *Political Studies*, 44: 936–57.

Hall, R. E. and Jones, C. I. (1999) 'Why do some countries produce so much more output per worker than others?', *Quarterly Journal of Economics*, 114(1): 83–116.

Hamilton, W. H. (1932) 'Institutions', in E. R. A. Seligman and A. Johnson (eds), *Encyclopaedia of the Social Science*. New York: Macmillan, vol. 8, pp. 84–9.

Harkes, N., Nieuwenhuizen, S., van der Krabben, E. and van der Lande, P. (2006) *Verkoop van een Luchthaven*, Analyse en oordeel Nota 30 494, Nr. 2 (Concept). Rotterdam: Ecorys Nederland BV.

Hayek, F. A. (1960) *The Constitution of Liberty*. Chicago: University of Chicago Press.

Healey, P. (1998) 'Building institutional capacity through collaborative approaches to urban planning', *Environment & Planning A*, 30: 1531–46.

Healey, R. G. and Stamp, T. R. (2000) 'Historical GIS as a foundation for the analysis of regional economic growth: theoretical, methodological, and practical issues', *Social Science History*, 24: 575–612.

Henderson, J. V. (1974) 'The sizes and types of cities', *American Economic Review*, 64(4): 640–56.

Henderson, J. V. (1986) 'Urbanization in a developing country: city size and population composition', *Journal of Development Economics*, 22(2): 269–93.

Henderson, J. V. (1997) 'Externalities and industrial development', *Journal of Urban Economics*, 42: 449–70.

Henderson, J.V. and Mitra, A. (1996) 'The new urban landscape: developers and edge cities', *Regional Science and Urban Economics*, 26: 613–43.

Henderson, J. V., Kuncoro, A. and Turner, M. (1995) 'Industrial development in cities', *Journal of Political Economy*, 103(5): 1067–90.

Hendriks, F. (1997) *Politics, Culture and the Post-Industrialising City*. Enschede: Netherlands Institute of Government.

Herbert, D. and Thomas, C. (1991) *Cities in Space: City as Place*. London: David Fullow.

Hildenbrand, W. (1997) 'On the empirical evidence of microeconomic demand theory', in Antoine d'Autume and Jean Cartelier (eds), *Is Economics Becoming a Hard Science?* Cheltenham : Edward Elgar, pp. 154–64.

Hodgson, G. M. (1988) *Economics and Institutions*. Cambridge: Polity Press.

Hodgson, G. M. (1998) 'The approach of institutional economics', *Journal of Economic Literature*, 361: 66–192.

Hodgson, G. M. (1999) *Evolution and Institutions: On Evolutionary Economics and the Evolution of Economics*. Cheltenham: Edward Elgar.

Hodgson, G. M. (2000) 'What is the essence of institutional economics?', *Journal of Economic Issues*, 34: 317–29.

Hodgson, G. M. (2006) 'What are institutions?', *Journal of Economic Issues*, 40(1): 1–25.

Hoover, E. M. (1937) *Location Theory and the Shoe and Leather Industries*. Cambridge, MA: Harvard University Press.

Hume, D. (1740) *A Treatise of Human Nature*. London: Valpy (original); republished by Clarendon Press, London, in 1888, and reproduced by Dover Publications, New York in 2003).

Huriot, J.-M. and Thisse, J.-F. (eds) (2000) *Economics of Cities: Theoretical Perspectives*. Cambridge: Cambridge University Press.

Isard, W. (1956) *Location and Space-economy*. Cambridge, MA: MIT Press.

Jackson, S. (2008) 'The city from thirty thousand feet: embodiment, creativity, and the use of geographic information systems as urban planning tools', *Technology and Culture*, 49: 325–46.

Jacobs, J. (1969) *The Economy of Cities*. New York: Random House.

Jaffe, A. B., Trajtenberg, M. and Henderson, R. (1993) 'Geographic localization of knowledge spillovers as evidenced by patent citations', *Quarterly Journal of Economics*, 108: 577–98.

Jansen, A. C. M. and de Smidt, M. (1974) *Industrie en Ruimte*. Assen: Van Gorcum.

Jessop, B. (1990) *State Theory: Putting Capitalist States in Their Place*. Cambridge: Polity.

Jessop, B. (1995) 'Regional economic blocs, cross-border cooperation, and local economic strategies in post-socialism: policies and prospects', *American Behavioral Scientist*, 38(5): 674–715.

Jessop, B. (1999) 'The dynamics of partnership and governance failure', in G. Stoker (eds), *The New Politics of Local Governance in Britain*. Oxford; Oxford University Press. Available online at: http://www.comp.lancs.ac.uk/sociology/papers/Jessop-Dynamics-of-Partnership.pdf (accessed 22 November 2008).

Jessop, B. (2000) 'Institutional (re)turns and the strategic-relational approach', *Environment & Planning A*, 33(7): 1213–37.

Jessop, B. (2002) 'Liberalism, neoliberalism and urban governance: a state-theoretical perspective', *Antipode*, 34(3): 452–72.

Jobse, R. and Musterd, S. (1992) 'Change in the residential function of the big cities', in F. M. Dieleman and S. Musterd (eds), *The Randstad: A Research and Policy Laboratory*. Dordrecht: Kluwer Academic, pp. 39–64.

Johansson, B. and Quigley, J. M. (2004) 'Agglomeration and networks in spatial economies', *Papers in Regional Science*, 83(1): 165–76.

Kaal, H. (2008) *Het hoofd van de stad; Amsterdam en zijn burgemeester tijdens het interbellum*. Amsterdam: Aksant.

Kasarda, J. (2000) *Aerotropolis: Airport-driven Urban Development*, ULI on the Future: Cities in the 21st Century. Washington, DC: Urban Land Institute.

Keefer, P. and Shirley, M. M. (2000) 'Formal versus informal institutions in economic development', in C. Ménard (ed.), *Institutions, Contracts, and Organizations: Perspectives from New Institutional Economics*. Cheltenham: Edward Elgar, pp. 88–107.

Klerk, L. de (2008) *De Modernisering van de Stad: 1850–1914*, De opkomst van planmatige Stadsontwikkeling in Nederland. Rotterdam: NAi Uitgevers.

Knaap, G. A. van der (2002) *Stedelijke Bewegingsruimte: Over Veranderingen in Stad en Land*. The Hague: Wetenschappelijke Raad voor het Regeringsbeleid.

Knack, S. and Keefer, P. (1995) 'Institutions and economic performance: cross country tests using alternative institutional measures', *Economics and Politics*, 7(3): 207–28.

Knippenberg, K. and de Pater, B. (1988) *De eenwording van Nederland. Schaalvergroting en integratie sinds 1800*. Nijmegen: Sun.

Knowles, A. K. (ed.) (2002) *Past Time, Past Place: GIS for Historians*. Redlands, CA: ESRI Press.

Koopmans, T. C. and Beckmann, M. (1957) 'Assignment problems and the location of economic activities', *Econometrica*, 25(1): 53–67.

Krabben, E. van der and Lambooy, J. G. (1993) 'A theoretical framework for the functioning of the Dutch property market', *Urban Studies*, 30(8): 1381–97.

Kreps, D. M. (1990) 'Corporate culture and economic theory', in J. E. Alt and K. A. Shepsle (eds), *Perspectives on Positive Political Economy*. New York: Cambridge University Press, pp. 90–143.

Krugman, P. (1991a) 'Increasing returns and economic geography', *Journal of Political Economy*, 99: 483–99.

Krugman, P. (1991b) *Geography and Trade*. Cambridge, MA: MIT Press.

Krugman, P. (1995) *Development, Geography, and Economic Theory*. Cambridge, MA: MIT Press.

Lambooy, J. G. (1993) 'European cities: from Carrefour to organisational nexus', *Journal of Economic and Social Geography (TESG)*, 84(4): 258–68.

Lambooy, J. G. (1998) 'Polynucleation and economic development: the Randstad', *European Planning Studies*, 6(4): 457–67.

Lambooy, J. G. (2002) *Ruimte voor Complexiteit; over veranderende structuren, zelforganisatie en netwerken in de Economische geografie*. Utrecht: Afscheidsrede Universiteit Utrecht.

Lambooy, J. G. (2004) *Geschakelde Metropolen en de tussengebieden. Essay voor de VROM-Raad*. The Hague: Ministerie van VROM.

Lambooy, J. G. (2005) *Essay Ruimtelijke kwaliteit*. The Hague: VROM-Raad.

Lambooy, J. G. and Moulaert, F. (1996) 'The economic organization of cities: an institutional perspective', *International Journal of Urban and Regional Research*, 20(2): 217–37.

Lambooy, J. G. and Oort, F. G van (2003) *Agglomeratie(s) in evenwicht?* Amsterdam: Koninklijke Vereniging voor de Staathuishoudkunde (KvS), pp. 67–94.

Langlois, R. N. (1986) 'Rationality, institutions, and explanation', in R. N. Langlois (ed.), *Economics as a Process: Essays in the New Institutional Economics*. Cambridge, MA: Cambridge University Press.

Lee, C. K. and Saxenian, A. (2008) 'Coevolution and coordination: a systemic analysis of the Taiwanese information technology industry', *Journal of Economic Geography*, 8: 157–80.

Leeuw, R. (1989) *Albert Plesman; Luchtvaartpionier en visionair*. Uitgeverij van de VNG, 's-Gravenhage.

Lewis, P. G. (1996) *Shaping Suburbia: How Political Institutions Organize Urban Development*. Pittsburgh, PA: University of Pittsburgh Press.

Linders, G.-J. M., Henri, L. F. de Groot and Nijkamp, P. (2004) *Economic Development, Institutions and Trust*. Department of Spatial Economics, VU University Amsterdam, Amsterdam.

Longley, P. A. and Batty, M. (eds) (2003) *Advanced Spatial Analysis*. Redlands, CA: ESRI Press.

Lösch, A. (1940) *Die Räumliche Ordnung derWirtschaft*. Jena: Gustav Fischer (1954); English translation: *The Economics of Location*. New Haven, CT: Yale University Press.

Louter, P. J *et al.* (2005) *Maatschappelijke waarde analyse Mainport Schiphol*, Bureau Louter Report Nr. 04026. Delft.

Lucas, R. E. (1988) 'On the mechanics of economic development', *Journal of Monetary Economics*, 22: 3–22.

McGuirk, P. M. (2003) 'Producing the capacity to govern in global Sydney: a multiscaled account', *Journal of Urban Affairs*, 25(2): 201–23.

Mak, G. (2003) 'Amsterdam as the "Compleat Citie": a city plan road in five episodes', in S. Musterd and W. Salet (eds), *Amsterdam Human Capital*. Amsterdam: Amsterdam University Press, pp. 31–48.

Mak, G. (2005) *Een kleine geschiedenis van Amsterdam*. Uitgeverij Atlas.

Malmberg, A. and Maskell, P. (1997) 'Towards an explanation of regional specialization and industry agglomeration', *European Planning Studies*, 5: 25–41.

Manshanden, W. and Knol, H. (1990) *Functionele samenhang in de noordvleugel van de randstad*. Amsterdam: Koninklijk Nederlands Aardrijkskundig Genootschap.

March, J. G. and Olsen, J. P. (1996) 'Institutional perspectives on political institutions', *Governance*, 9(3): 247–64.

Margo, R. (1992) 'Explaining the postwar suburbanization of population in the United States: the role of income', *Journal of Urban Economics*, 31: 301–10.

Marshall, A. (1920) *Principles of Economics*, 8th edn. London: Macmillan Press (first published in 1890).

Martens, C. J. C. M. (2000) *Debatteren over mobiliteit: over de rationaliteit van het ruimtelijk mobiliteitsbeleid*. PhD Thesis, University of Nijmegen/Thela Thesis Publishers, Nijmegen/Amsterdam.

Martin, R. (2000) 'Institutional approaches in economic geography', in E. Sheppard and T. J. Barnes (eds), *A Companion to Economic Geography*. Oxford and Malden, MA: Blackwell, pp. 77–94.

Martin, R. and Sunley, P. (2006) 'Path dependence and regional economic evolution', *Journal of Economic Geography*, 6: 395–437.

Matthews, R. C. O. (1986) 'The economics of institutions and the sources of growth', *Economic Journal*, 96: 903–18.

Mauro, P. (1995) 'Corruption and growth', *Quarterly Journal of Economics*, 110: 681–712.

Medema, S. G. *et al.* (eds) (1998) *Coase Economics: Law and Economics and the New Institutional Economics*. Dordrecht: Kluwer Academic.

Ménard, C. (1995) 'Markets as institutions versus organizations as markets? Disentangling some fundamental concepts', *Journal of Economic Behavior and Organization*, 28(2): 161–82.

Menger, C. (1871) *Principles of Economics*, eds James Dingwall and Bert F. Hoselitz. New York: New York University Press, 1981.

Mieszkowski, P. and Mills, E. S. (1993) 'The causes of metropolitan suburbanization', *Journal of Economic Perspectives*, 7(3): 135–47.

Miller, E. S. (1978) Institutional Economics: Philosophy, Methodology and Theory. *The Social Science Journal*, 15 (1978), pp. 13–25.

Mills, E. S. (1967) 'An aggregative model of resource allocation in a metropolitan area', *American Economic Review*, 57: 197–210.

Mills, E. S. (1999) 'The brawl over so-called sprawl', *Illinois Real Estate Letter*, pp. 1–7.

Ministry of Economic Affairs (Ministerie van Economische Zaken) (1999) *Mainports: Schakels tussen Nederlandse clusters en internationale netwerken*. The Hague: Ministerie van Economische Zaken.

Ministry of Economic Affairs (Ministerie van Economische Zaken) (2004) *Pieken in de Delta: Gebiedsgerichte Economische Perspectieven*. The Hague. Available online at: http://www.ez.nl (accessed 5 February 2008).

Ministry of Housing, Spatial Planning, and Environment (VROM) (1966) *Tweede Nota over de Ruimtelijke Ordening in Nederland*. Staatsuitgeverij Den Haag.

Ministry of Housing, Spatial Planning, and Environment (VROM) (1976) *Derde Nota over de Ruimtelijke Ordening*, Deel 2: Verstedelijkingsnota, Staatsuitgeverij Den Haag.

Ministry of Spatial Planning (2004) *Nota Ruimte (Spatial Strategy)*. The Hague. Available online at: http://www.vrom.nl/notaruimte (accessed 21 June 2009).

Ministry of Spatial Planning and Ministry of Transport and Energy (2005) Mainport Schiphol, policy information (*beleidsinformatie*), December.

Ministry of Transport and Waterworks (VWS) (2004) *Nota Mobiliteit*. The Hague. Available at: http://www.verkeerenwaterstaat.nl/kennisplein/2/5/254511/ (accessed 20 June 2009).

Mirowski, P. (1987) 'The philosophical bases of institutionalist economics', *Journal of Economic Issues*, 21(3): 1001–38.

Molenaar, F. G. (1968) *Het ontstaan van het militaire vliegterrein Schiphol in 1916*. Unknown publisher/edition.

Moomaw, R. L. (1981) 'Productivity and city size: a critique of the evidence', *Quarterly Journal of Economics*, 96(4): 675–88.

Moomaw, R. L. (1988) 'Agglomeration economies: are they exaggerated by industrial aggregation?', *Regional Science and Urban Economics*, 28(2): 199–211.

Moulaert, F. and Djellal, F. (1995) 'Information technology consultancy firms: economies of agglomeration from a wide-area perspective', *Urban Studies*, 32(1): 105–22.

Musterd, S. and Pater, B. de (1994) *Randstad-Holland: Internationaal, Regionaal, Lokaal*. Assen: Van Gorcum.

Musterd, S. and Salet, W. (2003) 'The emergence of the regional city: spatial configuration and institutional dynamics', in S. Musterd and W. Salet (eds), *Amsterdam Human Capital*. Amsterdam: Amsterdam University Press, pp. 13–27.

Muth, R. (1968) *Cities and Housing*. Chicago: University of Chicago Press.

Myerscough, J. (1985) 'Airport provision in the inter-war years', *Journal of Contemporary History*, 20: 41–70.

Myrdal, G. (1957) *Economic Theory and Underdeveloped Regions*. New York: Harper & Row.

NDL/BCI (2001) *Van EDC naar ELC*. Den Haag.

Nelson, R. R. and Winter, S. G. (1982) *An Evolutionary Theory of Economic Change*. Cambridge, MA: Belknap Press of Harvard University Press.

Nelson, R. R., Bhaven, N. and Sampat, B. N. (2001) 'Making sense of institutions as a factor shaping economic performance', *Journal of Economic Behavior and Organization*, 44: 31–54.

Netherlands Scientific Council for Government Policy (WRR) (1990) *Institutions and Cities: The Dutch Experience*. Report No. 37.

Nijkamp, P. and Goede, E. (2002) *Urban Development in the Netherlands: New Perspectives*, VU Research Memorandum 2002-1A, Department of Economics, Free University, Amsterdam.

North, D. C. (1981) *Structure and Change in Economic History*. New York: W. W. Norton.

North, D. C. (1990) *Institutions, Institutional Change and Economic Performance*. Cambridge: Cambridge University Press.

North, D. C. (2005) *Understanding the Process of Economic Change*. Princeton, NJ: Princeton University Press.

Nussbaumer, J. (2002) *Le rôle de la culture et des institutions dans les débats sur le développement local: la contribution de l'Ecole Historique Allemande*. PhD thesis, University of Lille I, Faculty of Social Science, Lille, France.

Nussbaumer, J. (2005) *Le rôle des débats méthodologiques dans la constitution de l'économie spatiale: La contribution de l'Ecole Historique Allemande à une approche institutionnaliste du développement local*, Séminaire du Matisse, 11 February.

Nyfer (2000) *Hub, of Spokestad? Regionaal-economische effecten van luchthavens*. Nyfer report available online at: http://www.nyfer.nl (accessed 16 April 2008).

Oort, F. van, Burger, M. and Raspe, O. (2006) *Economische netwerken in de regio*. Rotterdam: NAi Uitgevers.

Orléan, A. (ed.) (2004) *Analyse Économique de Conventions*. Paris: PUF, collection Quadrige.

Ostrom, E. (1986) 'An agenda for the study of institutions', *Public Choice*, 48: 3–25.

Ostrom, E. (1990) *Governing the Commons: The Evolution of Institutions for Collective Action*. New York: Cambridge University Press.

Ostrom, E. (1998) 'A behavioral approach to rational choice theory of collective action', *American Political Science Review*, 92: 1–22.

Ostrom, E. (2000) 'Private and common property rights', *Encyclopedia of Law and Economics*. Indiana University, pp. 332–48. Available online at: http://encyclo.findlaw. com/2000book.pdf (accessed 15 June 2008).

Ostrom, E. (2005) *Understanding Institutional Diversity*. Princeton, NJ: Princeton University Press.

Overman, H. G. (2006) *Geographical Information Systems (GIS) and Economics*, London School of Economics (LSE) Working Paper No. 5. Available at: http://personal.lse.ac. uk/OVERMAN/research/GIS_and_economics_web.pdf (accessed 17 June 2008).

Paasi, A. (2001) 'Europe as social process and discourse: considerations of place, boundaries and identity', *European Urban and Regional Studies*, 8: 7–28.

Painter, J. (1997) 'Regulation, regime, and practice in urban politics', in M. Lauria (ed.), *Reconstructing Urban Regime Theory*. Thousand Oaks, CA: Sage, pp. 122–43.

Pater, B. van, Ginkel, J. A. and Hoekveld, G. A. (1989) *Nederland in delen*. Houten: Unieboek.

Pecqueur, B. and Zimmermann, J. B. (eds) (2004) *Economie de proximités*. Paris: Hermès Lavoisier.

Pels, E. (2000) *Airport Economics and Policy: Efficiency, Competition, and Interaction with Airlines*. PhD thesis, Nr.222, Tinbergen Institute, Vrije Universiteit van Amsterdam, Amsterdam.

Perrin, J. C. (1991) 'Réseaux d'innovation, milieux innovateurs, développement territorial', *Revue d'Économie Régionale et Urbaine*, 3(4): 343–74.

Perroux, F. (1955) 'Note sur la notion de pôle de croissance', *Economique appliquée*, 7: 307–20.

Piore, M. J. and Sabel, C. F. (1984) *The Second Industrial Divide*. New York: Basic Books.

Pompili, T. (2006) *Networks Within Cities and Among Cities: A Paradigm for Urban Development and Governance*. Paper presented at the 46th Congress of the European Regional Science Association (ERSA), Volos, Greece, 30 August – 3 September.

Porter, M. E. (1998) *On Competition*, A Harvard Business Review Book. Cambridge MA: Harvard University Press.

Powell, W. W. (1996) 'Inter-organizational collaboration in the biotechnology industry', *Journal of Institutional and Theoretical Economics*, 152(1): 197–215.

Powell, W. W. and DiMaggio, P. J. (1991) *The New Institutionalism in Organizational Analysis*. Chicago: University of Chicago Press.

Praag, B. M. S. van and Baarsma, B. E. (2000) *The Shadow Price of Aircraft Noise Nuisance: A New Approach to the Internalization of Externalities*, Discussion Paper TI-2001-010/3. Amsterdam: Tinbergen Institute.

Priemus, H. (2001) 'Mainports as integrators of passenger, freight and information networks. From transport nodes to business generators: the Dutch case', *EJTIR*, 1(2): 143–67.

Puga, D., Burchfield, M., Overman, H. G. and Turner, M. A. (2005) *Causes of Sprawl: A Portrait from Space*. Available online at: http://diegopuga.org (accessed 25 June 2008).

Pumain, D. (2003) 'Urban sprawl: is there a French case?', in H. W. Richardson (ed.), *Urban Sprawl in Western Europe and the United States*. Aldershot: Ashgate, 137–57.

Putnam, R. D. (1993) 'The prosperous community: social capital and public life', *American Prospect*, 13: 35–42.

Raco, M. (1999) 'Competition, collaboration and the new industrial districts: examining the institutional turn in local economic development', *Urban Studies*, 36: 951–68.

Rauch, J. E. (1993) 'Productivity gains from geographic concentration of human capital: evidence from the cities', *Journal of Urban Economics*, 34(3): 380–400.

Regioplan (2000) *Overzicht van de werkgelegenheid op de luchthaven Schiphol*. Amsterdam.

Regioplan (2004a) *Overzicht van de werkgelegenheid op de luchthaven Schiphol*. Amsterdam.

Regioplan (2004b) *De Economische betekenis van Schiphol*. Amsterdam.

Regioplan (2005) *Overzicht van de werkgelegenheid op de luchthaven Schiphol*. Amsterdam.

Reynaud, B. (2002) *Operating Rules in Organizations: Macroeconomic and Microeconomic Analysis*. Basingstoke: Palgrave-Macmillan.

Richardson, H. W. (1988) 'Monocentric vs. polycentric models: the future of urban economics in regional science', *Annals of Regional Science*, 32: 1–12.

Richardson, H. W. and Kumar, G. (1989) 'The influence of metropolitan structure on commuting time', *Journal of Urban Economics*, 27(3): 217–33.

Roback, J. (1982) 'Wages, rents, and the quality of life', *Journal of Political Economy*, 90(6): 1257–78.

Rodrik, D., Arvind, S. and Trebbi, F. (2002) *Institutions Rule: The Primacy of Institutions over Geography and Integration in Economic Development*, NBER Working Paper No. 9305.

Romer, P. M. (1986) 'Increasing returns and long run growth', *Journal of Political Economy*, 94: 1002–37.

Romer, P. M. (1990) 'Endogenous technical change', *Journal of Political Economy*, 98(5): S71–S102.

Rooy, P. de *et al.* (2007) *Geschiedenis van Amsterdam 1900–2000*. Amsterdam: Tweestrijd om de stad. Sun.

Roscher, W. (1906) *Grundlagen der Nationalökonomie*. Stuttgart: Cotta; originally published in 1854.

Rosenthal, S. S. and Strange, W. C. (2003) 'Geography, industrial organization and agglomeration', *Review of Economics and Statistics*, 85(2): 377–93.

Rosenthal, S. S. and Strange, W. C. (2004) 'Evidence on the nature and sources of agglomeration economies', in J. V. Henderson and J.-F. Thisse (eds), *Handbook of Regional and Urban Economics: Cities and Geography*, Vol. 4. Amsterdam: North Holland, pp. 2119–79.

Rosenthal, S. S. and Strange, W. C. (2005) 'The micro-empirics of agglomeration economies', in R. Arnott and D. McMillen (eds), *Companion to Urban Economics*. Malden, MA: Blackwell.

Rutherford, M. C. (1994) *Institutions in Economics: The Old and the New Institutionalism*. Cambridge: Cambridge University Press.

Salais, R. and Storper, M. (1993) *Les mondes de production: Enquête sur l'identité économique de la France*. Paris: Édition de l'école des hautes études en sciences économiques.

Salet, W. (2003) 'Amsterdam and the north wing of the Randstad', in W. Salet, A. Thornley and A. Kreukels (eds), *Metropolitan Governance and Spatial Planning: Comparative Case Studies of European City-regions*. London: Routledge and Spon, pp. 175–88.

Salet, W. and Majoor, S. (eds) (2005) *Amsterdam Zuidas European Space*. Rotterdam: 010 Publishers.

Salet, W., Thornley, A. and Kreukels, A. (2003) *Metropolitan Governance and Spatial Planning: Comparative Case Studies of European City-regions*. London: Routledge and Spon.

Sassen, S. (2001) 'Impacts of information technologies on urban economies and politics', *International Journal of Urban and Regional Research*, 25(2): 411–18.

Schaafsma, M. (2003) 'Airports and cities in networks', *disP – The Planning Review*, 154(3): 28–36.

Schaeffle, A. E. F. (1873) *Das gesellschaftliche System der menschlichen Wirtschaft: ein Lehr- und Handbuch der ganzen politischen Oekonomie*, 3rd edn. Tübingen, vol. 2, ch. 4, pp. 275–302.

Scharpf, F. W. (1997) *Games Real Actors Play: Actor-Centered Institutionalism in Policy Research*. Boulder, CO: Westview Press.

Schmal, H. (2003) 'The historical roots of the daily urban system', in S. Musterd and W. Salet (eds), *Amsterdam Human Capital*. Amsterdam: Amsterdam University Press, pp. 67–83.

Schmoller, G. (1897/1905) *Principes d'Economie Politique*, trans. into French in 1905 by G. Platon, Partie I, Tome II, éd. V. Giard et E. Brière, Paris.

Schotter, A. (1981) *The Economic Theory of Social Institutions*. Cambridge: Cambridge University Press.

Scitovsky, T. (1954) 'Two concepts of external economies', *Journal of Political Economy*, 62: 143–51.

Scott, A. J. (1988a) *Metropolis: From the Division of Labor to Urban Form*. Berkeley, CA and Los Angeles: University of California Press.

Scott, A. J. (1988b) *New Industrial Spaces*. London: Pion.

Scott, A. J. (1998) *Regions and the World Economy: The Coming Shape of Global Production, Competition, and Political Order*. Oxford: Oxford: University Press.

Scott, A. J. (ed.) (2001) *Global City Regions: Tendency, Theory, Policy*. New York: Oxford University Press.

Scott, W. R. (1991) 'Unpacking institutional arguments', in W. Powell and P. DiMaggio (eds), *The New Institutionalism in Organizational Analysis*. Chicago: University of Chicago Press, pp. 164–82.

Scott, W. R. (1995) *Institutions and Organizations*. Thousand Oaks, CA: Sage.

SCP (Sociaal Cultureel Planbureau) (2001) *Ruime kavel of compacte stad?*, Werkdocument 77. The Hague: SCP.

SEO, TNO, BCI (2006) *Economische Effecten Schiphol*, SEO Report No. 885. Amsterdam.

SGM Group (2004) *Economic Impacts of Airports – A Review of the Literature*, February. Available at: http://www.the-sgm-group.com. Last (accessed 7 June 2008).

Siebert, L. (2000) 'Using GIS to document, visualize, and interpret Tokyo's spatial history', *Social Science History*, 24(3): 537–74.

Sieverts, T. (2003) *Cities Without Cities: Between Place and World, Space and Time, Town and Country*. London: Routledge.

Sivitanidou, R. and Wheaton, W.C. (1992) 'Wage and rent capitalization in the commercial real estate market', *Journal of Urban Economics*, 31: 206–29.

Smajgl, A., Vella, K. and Greiner, R. (2003) *Frameworks and Models for Analysis and Design of Institutional Arrangements in Outback Regions.* Available online at: http//purl.org/dc/elements/1.1 (accessed 6 September 2008).

Stone, C. N. (1993) 'Urban regimes and the capacity to govern: a political economy approach', *Journal of Urban Affairs*, 15: 1–28.

Storper, M. (1993) 'Regional worlds of production: learning and innovation in the technology districts of France, Italy and the USA', *Regional Studies*, 27(5): 433–55.

Storper, M. (1995) 'The resurgence of regional economies, ten years later: the region as a nexus of untraded interdependencies', *European Urban and Regional Studies*, 2(3): 191–221.

Storper, M. (1997) *The Regional World: Territorial Development in a Global Economy.* New York and London: Guilford Press.

Storper, M. and Scott, A. J. (1989) 'The geographical foundations and social regulation of flexible production complexes', in J. Welch and M. Dear (eds), *The Power of Geography.* Boston: Unwin Hyman, pp. 21–40.

Sudjic, D. (1992) *The 100 Mile City.* New York: Harcourt Brace & Co.

Sugden, R. (1989) 'Spontaneous order', *Journal of Economic Perspectives*, 13(4): 85–97.

Sveikauskas, L. (1975) 'The productivity of cities', *Quarterly Journal of Economics*, 89(3): 393–413.

Sykuta, M. E. and Chaddad, F. R. (1999) 'Putting theories of firm in their place: a supplemental digest of the new institutional economics', *Journal of Cooperatives*, 14: 68–76.

Taverne, E. (1978) *In 't land van belofte: in de nieuwe stad. Ideaal en werkelijkheid van de stadsuitleg in de Republiek 1580–1680.* Maarssen: Guy Schwartz.

Taylor, P. J. (2003) *World City Network: A Global Urban Analysis.* London: Routledge.

Terhorst, P. and Ven, J. C. L. van de (1998) 'Urban policies and the polder model: two sides of the same coin', *Tijdschrift voor Economische en Sociale Geografie (TESG)*, 89(4): 467–73.

Terhorst, P. and Ven, J. C. L. van de (2003) 'The economic restructuring of the historic city center', in S. Musterd and W. Salet (eds), *Amsterdam Human Capital.* Amsterdam: University of Amsterdam Press, pp. 85–105.

Thelen, K. (1999) 'Historical institutionalism in comparative politics', *Annual Review of Political Science*, 2: 369–404.

Thelen, K. (2003) 'Comment les institutions évoluent: Les enseignements d'une analyse historique comparative', *L'année de la régulation No. 7 (2003–2004).* Paris: Presses de Sciences Politiques, pp. 13–43.

Thelen, K. and Steinmo, S. (1992) 'Historical institutionalism in comparative politics', in S. Steinmo, K. Thelen and F. Longstreth (eds), *Structuring Politics: Historical Institutionalism in Comparative Analysis.* New York: Cambridge University Press.

Tiebout, C. (1956) 'A pure theory of local expenditure', *Journal of Political Economy*, 64: 416–24.

Toffler, A. (1980) *The Third Wave.* New York: Morrow.

Ullmann-Margalit, E. (1977) *The Emergence of Norms.* Oxford: Clarendon.

Veblen, T. (1899/1919) *The Theory of the Leisure Class: An Economic Study of Institutions.* New York: Macmillan (reprinted in 1994 by Dover Publications, New York).

Veen, N. H. ter (1925) *De Haarlemmermeer als Kolonisatiegebied.* PhD thesis, University of Amsterdam.

Veer, J. van der (1998) 'Metropolitan government in Amsterdam and Eindhoven: a tale of two cities', *Environment & Planning C*, 16: 25–50.

Veltz, P. (1996) *Mondialisation, villes et territoires: l'économie d'archipel*. Paris: Presses Universitaires de France.

Vijgen, J. and Engelsdorp Gastelaars, R. Van (1992) *Centrum, stadsrand, groeikern – bewonersprofielen en leefpatronen in drie woonmilieus binnen het gewest Amsterdam*. Amsterdam: Centrum voor Grootstedelijk Onderzoek, Universiteit van Amsterdam.

Von Thünen, J. H. (1875) *Der isolierte Staat in Beziehung auf landwirtschaft und Nationalökonomie* (*The Isolated State*). Berlin: Weigandt, Hempel & Parey; English trans. Oxford: Pergamon, 1966.

Vromen, J. J. (1995) *Economic Evolution: An Enquiry into the Foundations of New Institutional Economics*. New York: Routledge.

Wagenaar, M. (1990) *Amsterdam 1876–1914: Economische herstel, ruimtelijke expansie en de veranderende ordening van het stedelijk grondgebruik*. Historisch Seminarium, Universiteit van Amsterdam, Amsterdam.

Wagenaar, M. (1998) *Stedenbouw en Burgerlijke Vrijheid: De Contrasterende carrière van zes Europese Hoofdsteden*. Uitgeverij THOTH Bussum, Nederland.

Warffemius, P. M. J. (2007) *Modeling the Clustering of Distribution Centers around Amsterdam Airport Schiphol: Location Endowments, Economies of Agglomeration, Locked-in Logistics and Policy Implications*, TRAIL Thesis Series T2007/9, The Netherlands.

Weber, A. (1909) *The Theory of the Location of Industries*, trans. Carl Friedrich. Chicago: Chicago University Press, 1929.

Weimer, D. L. (eds) (1995) *Institutional Design: Overview*. Boston: Kluwer Academic.

Wijk, M. van (2007) *Airports as Cityports in the City-region, Spatial-economic and Institutional Positions and Institutional Learning in Randstad-Schiphol (AMS), Frankfurt Rhein-Main (FRA), Tokyo Haneda (HND) and Narita (NRT)*. PhD thesis, Utrecht University, Utrecht: KNAG/NGS.

Williamson, O. E. (1975) *Markets and Hierarchies.* New York: Free Press.

Williamson, O. E. (1979) 'Transaction-cost economics: the governance of contractual relations', *Journal of Law and Economics*, 22(2): 233–61.

Williamson, O. E. (1985) *The Economic Institutions of Capitalism*. New York: Free Press.

Williamson, O. E. (1993) 'Transaction cost economics and organization theory', *Industrial and Corporate Change*, 2: 107–56.

Williamson, O. E. (1998) 'Transaction cost economics, how it works, where it is headed', *De Economist*, 146(1): 23–58.

Wisman, J. D. and Rozansky, J. (1991) 'The methodology of institutionalism revisited', *Journal of Economic Issues*, 25: 709–37.

WRR (Netherlands Scientific Council for Government Policy) (1999) *Spatial Development Policy: Summary of the 53rd Report*. The Hague: Sdu.

Yin, R. K. (2002) *Case Study Research, Design and Methods*, 3rd edn. Newbury Park, CA: Sage.

Zanden, J. L. van (2002) *Agricultural Productivity in the Low Countries ca. 1800*. Paper presented at the XIIIth World Economic History Congress, Buenos Aires, 22–26 July.

Zanden, J. L. van and Riel, A. van (2000) *Nederland 1780–1914: Staat, Instituties en Economische Ontwikkeling*. Amsterdam: Edition Balans.

Zingler, E. K. (1974) Veblen vs. Commons: a comparative evaluation', *Kyklos*, 27: 322–44.

Index